HORACE ON POETRY

★   ★

HORACE

ON

POETRY

★ ★

THE 'ARS POETICA'

BY

C. O. BRINK

Kennedy Professor of Latin in the University of Cambridge and
Fellow of Gonville and Caius College

CAMBRIDGE

AT THE UNIVERSITY PRESS

1971

Published by the Syndics of the Cambridge University Press
Bentley House, 220 Euston Road, London N.W.1
American Branch: 32 East 57th Street, New York, N.Y.10022

Cambridge University Press 1971

Library of Congress Catalogue Card Number: 79–116746

Standard Book Number: 521 07784 2

Printed in Great Britain
at the University Printing House, Cambridge
(Brooke Crutchley, University Printer)

CONTENTS

PREFACE

In this book I have brought together some of the varying modes of criticism which we associate with the verbal arts. The *Ars Poetica* is not really so elusive as we are told it is, but it demands more approaches than one, and above all an understanding that these approaches are not mutually exclusive, let alone contradictory. Those readers who wish to see from the outset where I am tending are asked to start by reading the section entitled 'The Poem'. But the solution which I propose in that section is only one part of the subject of this book.

A sound text has yet to be established on the foundation of a sound selection of manuscripts; that calls for one kind of criticism. Vocabulary and metre, style and tone, play all-important parts in the poem and demand their own kinds of criticism, not indeed divorced from the first but having a different scope. Moreover, nothing that concerns the literary theory of the poem, and hence its order and arrangement, is agreed. Some scholars talk as if all that is needed is agreement on that literary theory. In fact such disagreements conceal a literary problem, and that calls for another kind of criticism still.

Scholars like E. Norden and A. Rostagni have tried to make sense of the *Ars* as literary theory. For that exercise a criticism of sources and content suffices. Yet the *Ars* will not make sense in purely conceptual terms; its poetry rebuffs the conceptualist. Others like F. Klingner, and more recently G. Williams (*Tradition and Originality in Roman Poetry*, 1968), have thought that its poetry could be read, as it were, straight off; they have ignored the literary theory which it proclaims as its subject and primary concern. To that kind of approach the *Ars* will not yield either; its subject, the literary theory, resists and will not let itself be pushed out of the way by references to 'the imaginative play of ideas in a world of fantasy' (*ibid.* p. 357), however compelling the poet's imagination. We are faced with a work of the imagination that makes a poetic symbol out of a literary theory. Hence we need to determine the literary theory as well as what the poet made of it—the two are interdependent. They call for a criticism of sources that does not lose sight of literary criticism; we need to remember that we are dealing with a poem. It seems to me imperative, therefore, if we want to rise to the level of a major work by a major poet that we should go all the way from establishing a reliable text to a reliable commentary on subject-matter, style and tone, to an attempt to ascertain how that subject-matter, a conceptual theory, becomes poetry. I have found this an engrossing but very hard thing to undertake, because bridges from one of these areas to another have still to be constructed.

My procedure is, I fear, bound to involve a certain amount of repetition, if the reader is to see at every stage of the argument why and how I draw the conclusions which I do draw. I began with source-criticism in my *Prolegomena*. In this volume an assessment of the manuscripts and a critical edition lead off; then, in the commentary, there follow assessments of the vocabulary and style as well as a first attempt to disengage Horace from the tradition determined in the *Prolegomena*; next I suggest a mode of reading the poem on the basis of the commentary and, finally, I make value-judgement explicit by asking whether we are right in thinking of the *Ars* as lowly as many of our contemporaries say we should, or as highly as readers in earlier centuries did. All these are forms of criticism, and all are needed to make the poem readable.

The textual introduction offers no new manuscript material. It seeks to establish a selection of indispensable codices that satisfies a century's experience of dealing with these sources of the text. Fewer rather than more codices than are used in recent editions will, I hope, improve the critical apparatus. Secondly the introduction offers what I regard as strong arguments against the varying classifications of manuscripts proposed by Keller, Vollmer, and Klingner. I abandon the class-sigla that have been proposed. The critical apparatus is designed to present variant readings as clearly as possible, while not obliterating what traces of original class-divisions survive. This is a practical problem, and little else besides. The critical aspect here is largely negative—to ascertain, in the face of persistent editorial overstatement, what in fact we do not know.

In orthography I have adopted standard forms throughout, abandoning what might be described as Lachmann's doctrine, which Housman propagated in his editions. I find it hard to describe the avoidance of *summa constantia* as illiberal (Lachmann on Lucr. I. 125, cf. Housman's Juvenal, p. xxi); what in fact should be avoided is the inconsistency that arises when an occasional old form appears in the text *vis-à-vis* dozens of instances of ordinary spelling. Perhaps there is a case for summarizing the orthography of important codices, as Housman did in the case of Manilius. But since anything like an author's practice is hard or impossible to establish, I have long since canvassed the view recently expressed by G. P. Goold in *Harvard Studies*, LXIX (1965), 11, that these rarities should not be offered in the text of a critical edition. This remains convincing even though in B and C we have corruptions that clearly arise from old spellings, and in the *Vaticanus Reginae* we have an outstanding orthographer at work. I have however changed the practice of *Prolegomena*, retaining *u* for *v* in Latin texts.

The framing of a trustworthy text is hard, not least because this and other Horatian poems are now set in the form of a vulgate handed from one recent editor to the next with much assurance and little reliability. I have printed only what I think I can understand and translate (having made a translation for my own use), but have indicated what I cannot, and put cruces whenever the reason for that seems to me to lie in the inadequacy of the transmission and not of myself. This procedure would not call for notice in certain other authors;

in the editing of Horace it does. That is my reason for erring (if I do) rather on the side of scepticism in obelizing when there remains an area of doubt concerning an emendation, for example at lines 60 and 65. As far as conjecture in Horace is concerned it is hard, at this stage, to put forward something that is (as Housman would have said) both new and true; I have had to restore to older scholars a number of emendations which I had found independently. But it is not always conjectural emendation that demonstrates a critical view of the text.

There are commentators in plenty who expound what is plain and who happily hold their farthing candle to the sun. Such commentaries are not required after centuries of good or at any rate competent work. We need, and need badly, commentaries that tackle the great difficulties abounding in the *Ars*, and apply the same critical mind that can shed light on textual problems to other verbal aspects of a text, whether they are labelled 'style' or 'subject-matter'.

The aspect of style in Horace's poems needs to be opened up afresh, from vocabulary to the structure of sentence and paragraph. With consummate irony Horace called the poetry of his *sermones* 'prose'. What he meant by that must be gauged not only from the Callimachean and Lucilian background, and the differing settings of his literary *Satires*, but from his own practice. A few 'unpoetische Wörter' apart, Latin prose would have demanded a very different vocabulary from that which he employs. Throughout I have not grudged space for determining the penumbra and source of Horatian words, and I hope that readers will not grudge it either. Similarly we must reassess the delicately judged middle level of poetic style, and its variability in these *sermones*, particularly in the *Ars*.

Such are the elements into which we can dissect the limbs of a poem's unity—its sections and paragraphs in humdrum language. The flow of thought, sentiment, expression seems as continuous in this poem as anywhere in ancient poetry, Greek or Latin. In spite of that I have used paragraphs, thus deviating from many editors of Horace, and making the job more difficult for myself but, I hope, easier for others. Indentation, E. Fraenkel dryly reminded editors (*Horace*, p. 139 n. 3), was invented for the purpose of assisting readers in the business of reading. Scholars will wish to be told what an editor thinks the 'parts' of this poem are. Recent discussions on the layout of the *Ars* show only too clearly that opinions on this matter are by no means undivided.

The most controversial aspect of the *Ars* is its content, so called. If we are right in thinking, paradoxically, that the content of a true poem is indistinguishable from its wording and pattern, then here lies the crux of the matter. We cannot even begin to sense what the poet did with the materials he had at hand unless we have a clear view of these materials, that is, the literary theory he was writing about. It was this state of affairs that caused me to publish a volume of prolegomena. There I have stated as clearly as I can what I think was the literary theory that provided these materials.

Apart from Aristotle's *Poetics* Horace's work is the only comprehensive *Ars Poetica* that has come down to us from antiquity. 'Longinus' offers only one primary aspect—the Sublime—which for him fills the whole horizon; Demetrius restricts himself to ἑρμηνεία, style; Cicero or Quintilian or Dionysius offers rhetorical theory, which, however alike, is not identical with poetic theory; and the late sketches of the *Grammatici Graeci* or *Latini* are too desiccated to be representative. A historical accident (that the *Ars* was by Horace, and thus preserved) has lent it the virtue of not only being a poem by one of the great Roman poets but of representing a lost ancient genre—as far as a poem can represent an essentially conceptual mode of writing. If the *Ars* has this additional role to play, a commentator must place it within the tradition which it represents. This is my reason for citing relevant material so fully. The *Ars* recalls literary theory in almost every word. We must remind ourselves of what it recalls.

Even a sketchy acquaintance with ancient literary theory

suggests that a conventional tripartite or quadripartite structure is, in some way or other, part of the *Ars Poetica*. This could have been, indeed was, noticed before Neoptolemus of Parium, Horace's reputed authority, had reappeared from the shades. What could have enabled anyone to sense this feature was the submergence of the conventional pattern, and the multiplicity of less conventional patterns that overlie it. Here for all to see was Horace at work.

Once the Neoptolemic material (such as it is) had reappeared, the way was open for making into a hypothesis what was earlier a mere guess prompted by the feature of Horace's style which has just been mentioned. Such a hypothesis is put forward in my *Prolegomena*. It rests on a comparison of the *Ars* with the fragments of Neoptolemus and those treatises of Aristotle that are relevant to both Neoptolemus and Horace, chiefly the *Poetics* and *Rhetoric*. My hypothesis was simple in conception though complex in execution. The technical substratum, I suggested, and many of the technical details of the *Ars* were certainly traditional, and probably derived by Horace from Neoptolemus' work on literary theory. Horace, if this view prevails, cannot be regarded as the originator of such features as the basic tripartite (or quadripartite) layout. On the contrary, such features were among the characteristic data of the didactic and critical genre, around which the poet—to the dismay of romantic readers—wove his poetic patterns.

I can see two ways in which this hypothesis may be verified, both severely limited by the nature of our evidence, and neither providing anything like a complete proof of my contention.

The first is a full statement of the evidence concerning Neoptolemus. This I have offered in *Prolegomena*. It amounts to a discussion of the remains of Neoptolemus' critical work, a comparison with Aristotle's *Poetics* and *Rhetoric*, on which, directly or indirectly, the Hellenistic critic seems to have drawn, and finally a comparison of Neoptolemus and Aristotle with similar portions of the *Ars*. Clearly it must be remembered that the Neoptolemic material is scanty, and although something can be known about his teachings, anything like a 'reconstruction' cannot be attempted. Moreover, not even the Aristotelian side of the picture is complete. That is why some features of the putative Greek theorizing can be demonstrated with greater assurance than others and, in each case, the varying degree of probability has to be borne in mind. But as long as allowance for that difference is made, comparison reveals a fairly consistent brand of Hellenistic Aristotelianism.

The second way in which my hypothesis may be verified is to ascertain what Horatian creativeness has made of that traditional poetic theory. Suppose Horace's poem makes consistent and unforced sense on the assumption that its author did not himself 'make up' the technicalities of an *ars poetica* but reflected and re-created such an *ars* in the patterns and spirit of his own poetry. This would be a kind of proof of the initial hypothesis. A *kind* of proof only, for the Hellenistic, and especially the Neoptolemic, provenance of a given detail cannot be demonstrated in that way, even if one of the poem's several patterns—the basic pattern of literary theory—is shown to be a coherent entity. But it would be a step forward to show the coherence of that (pre-Horatian) entity, and more than a step, if we are aiming (as indeed we are) at Horace, and not primarily at his predecessors.

Such, with the limitations inherent in the evidence, are the proofs that can be advanced. How strong is the force of any rebuttal that has been put forward? My volume of prolegomena has provoked a gratifyingly diverse and protracted discussion. Out of more than thirty reviews I select three that seek to disprove one or other of my basic contentions. Some of their disagreements may serve further to clarify the position.

Professor G. M. A. Grube (*Phoenix*, xix (1965), 79) denies that over such matters as appropriateness (*decorum*), unity, and the nature of poetic vocabulary, it was necessary to bring in Aristotle via Neoptolemus. These ideas were discussed by

Cicero, by Dionysius of Halicarnassus, Horace's contemporary in Rome, and many others; they were in fact common currency. I agree, they were discussed by many, but it does not follow that, for this reason, we should not bring in Aristotle and Neoptolemus. Professor Grube's reaction would have been natural and salutary in the face of the more rigid kinds of nineteenth-century 'source-criticism'. The objections resemble those kinds of source-criticism which they oppose in mistaking for mechanical commonplaces the traditions of thought built up over some centuries. Because the ancient literary critics share certain assumptions that are not ours they seem to us to purvey common and indistinguishable currency. We have to distinguish between tradition and individual expression. Having learned to understand the community of thought and feeling in an ancient civilization, we have to school ourselves to discern the fine and subtle differences between fine and subtle minds within this community. I am concerned with these differences as well as with the community of thought.

Professor Brooks Otis (*Gnomon*, xxxv (1964), 265) thinks that the *Prolegomena* have 'added a new dimension of thought to a familiar scene', and considers the juxtaposition of Horace, Neoptolemus, and Aristotle, to which Professor Grube objects, the most original and significant part of the book. His own complaints are different. Porphyrion, he suggests (pp. 226–7), should be used more extensively for the reconstruction of Neoptolemus than I have done. Nothing would suit my case better than if he could. But I am less sanguine for reasons set out in my textual introduction (pp. 40–1).

Professor Otis' second suggestion cuts rather more deeply, and requires consideration. While accepting my contention that in the *Ars* we find combined 'specific bits (in some cases consecutive sections) of Aristotle's *Poetics* and *Rhetoric*', he doubts whether this combination is likely to be pre-Horatian. The poet, he urges (pp. 270 ff.), did not simply follow the order of Neoptolemus or some other Aristotelian critic but freely restructured materials from the *Poetics*, *Rhetoric*, Neoptolemus, and perhaps others such as Cicero. The point about Horace's freedom of combination is well taken, but it is in fact what I myself believe. Where we differ is in the judgement of how this freedom was exercised. No new evidence or argument has appeared since to persuade me that Horace had nothing better to do than apply his formative skill to a conflation of Aristotle's *Poetics* and *Rhetoric* with Neoptolemus and perhaps others. The basic trichotomy which Professor Otis mentions (p. 267), and its consequences for matters of poetic theory, are precisely the kinds of things the literary scholars and critics concerned themselves with; and, in spite of many similarities, the arrangement, purpose, and ethos of Cicero's *Orator* (Otis, *loc. cit.*) are quite alien to Horace's known preoccupations. I return to this matter at a later place in my commentary (p. 132).

According to a long review by Professor Gordon Williams (in *JRS*, LIV (1964), 186–96, especially 194–5) my book is open to a major logical objection—its argument is circular. It would indeed be circular if I concluded that *because* Horace is said to have brought together the most outstanding precepts of Neoptolemus we can reconstruct Neoptolemus from Horace, and then use that reconstruction to explain the *Ars*. But that is not at all how I argued. The tripartite (or quadripartite) order of Horace's basic scheme was asserted long before Neoptolemus' adherence to the triad *poema–poesis–poeta* had become known. Nothing was wrong with that assertion except its rigidity, which neglected all the other principles of ordering in the *Ars*. It was again without recourse to Neoptolemus that my re-examination of the poem's layout endorsed these earlier findings, however limited their importance in view of Horace's complex patterning. Moreover Philodemus' reports on Neoptolemus do not, for elucidation, require this analysis of the *Ars*, nor in elucidating them did I require it (Williams, *op. cit.* p. 194). Rather, in ch. 2 of *Prolegomena*, I unravelled Philodemus' reports without these adventitious aids, being particularly concerned at this stage of my argument not to conflate Neoptolemic and Horatian evidence. I made a case on inherent grounds that Neoptolemus had not only referred to the literary triad (as Philodemus says he did) but laid out his work in accordance with it (*Prol.* 72–3). It was only in ch. 3 of my study that I widened the factual basis, and made the assumption that much more of the literary theory of the *Ars* than is commonly assumed may have come from Neoptolemus. This was a hypothesis which should chiefly be judged by the number of puzzles it solves if it were correct. The greatest puzzle it would solve is this: where in the Aristotelian material of the *Ars* does the persistent note originate which is neither Aristotelian nor Horatian nor even Roman? The answer would then be that it originates from the poet's Hellenistic material rendered Horatian, Augustan, and Roman by him.

Finally Neoptolemus' putative position between Aristotle and Horace is allegedly required, after having been inferred from the *Ars*, to 'disentangle the structure and composition of the *Ars*' (Williams, *loc. cit.*). But is it? On the contrary, it happens to be one of the virtues of the Neoptolemic hypothesis that it allows us to make two related observations, once the triad has been safely lodged with Neoptolemus. (1) Horace seems to have attached scant importance to the tripartite scheme of the literary experts; it appears that he took it over from them in order to put it in its place as only he could, by making it part of a larger and more complex order; (2) if allowance is made for that, 'the structure and composition of the Ars' are characteristically Horatian, and require no Neoptolemus to be 'disentangled'.

I would say therefore that the boot is on the other foot; it is Professor Williams who mistakes the logic of my procedure. He has tried (unsuccessfully in my view) to push the debate back to an earlier stage when critics still argued that the *Ars* was either a treatise based on a rigid conceptual triad of *poema–poesis–poeta*, or else a loosely organized poetic *sermo*. We are again supposed to get impaled on one of two available horns of a false dilemma. It is true, instead of 'loosely organized poetic *sermo*' we are asked to say 'imaginative play of ideas in a world of fantasy' (Williams, cited above pp. vii–viii); that sounds more contemporary but otherwise makes no odds.

Professor Williams' brief sketch of the *Ars* at the end of his review, and his longer sketch in *Tradition and Originality in Roman Poetry* (1968, pp. 329–57), have put on record that their author thought he could ignore a century's critical work on these problems. Yet he claimed that he was examining the *Ars* 'as a work of poetic imagination in which Horace modified the sort of material provided by Aristotle's *Poetics* (together with much else) in accordance with artistic principles of his own' (*Tradition* etc. p. 355). But it is precisely 'the sort of material' provided by earlier literary theory that critical scholarship in this field has subjected to intense scrutiny. To do otherwise is to involve the practitioner in a most damaging *non sequitur*; he must by his definition pronounce on Horace's modification of material which he yet declines to determine. No wonder the ground on which he stands is infirm.

Since this procedure is now on record there is perhaps here no need for further argument. Readers will doubtless make their own choice. I have however referred to Professor Williams' thesis in my commentary whenever specific issues made clarification desirable. The instance cited in Appendix 2 is striking; if he had been more willing to take note of previous critical work, he might have avoided traps repeatedly signposted in the long history of Horatian scholarship.

So much for proof or rebuttal of the Neoptolemic hypothesis. These discussions have suggested to me the following arrangement of the commentary. As I said earlier, I have paragraphed the poem, although very much aware that the paragraphs and sections are valid as divisions of literary theory rather than in the final poetic analysis. I have prefaced nearly all of these paragraphs by two separate introductory notes, headed 'The Tradition' and 'Horace' respectively. In the former I have set down what relevant information on the traditional bases of Horace's literary doctrine has come to my notice; a wider and not strictly relevant purview would have brought in many more parallels. In the latter I have indicated briefly what I think Horace has done to that traditional scheme of things to make it amenable to his own purposes. In a few places I have specified that 'The Tradition' is in fact 'Neoptolemus'. I have felt free to do that only when extraneous evidence for Neoptolemic origin comes to hand, especially in the basic tripartite (or quadripartite) layout. In the places where a concurrence of Horace and a modified Aristotelianism suggests (to me) Neoptolemus, I have been content to affix the label 'The Tradition', and to refer the reader to my discussion in *Prolegomena*, unless additional evidence or argument has made renewed discussion desirable. In the places where there is no concurrence of Horace and Aristotle I have indicated what traditional affiliations I could discover, which then may or may not be Neoptolemic.

This procedure may seem unduly cautious. I have adopted it for a reason. It will, I hope, make the commentary usable also for those who are not persuaded that behind the *Ars Poetica* there lies a consistent literary theory which Horace has broken up, and used for his poetic purposes. Such readers will at any rate agree that what I call tradition contains important 'parallels'. They will also be willing to regard as Horatian any devices that are alien to the aims of a literary theorist but demonstrably relevant to those of a poet.

Such remarks hint broadly that, in spite of Horace's reliance on it, the work of Neoptolemus or any other literary critic can have been the model for the *Ars* in some senses of that word but not in others. It would be folly to impute to a poet of Horace's stature simply the versifying of one or more Greek 'sources'. Neoptolemus, I suggest, was Horace's source in that the poet picked up the technical structure of an *ars poetica* from him. If so, that structure, in the didactic genre of literary theory, fulfilled the same function as the form of any lyric genre in the *Epodes* or *Odes*; it stimulated the poet's formative imagination, moving him to overlay (and thereby qualify) this simple and humdrum order of things with other kinds of arrangement less simple and humdrum. In another sense Neoptolemus was Horace's source for an indeterminate number of technical matters, Porphyrion's *praecepta Neoptolemi ...de arte poetica, non quidem omnia sed eminentissima*; these the poet clearly viewed with the same ironic detachment of the amateur which he applied to the *praecepta* forming the structure of literary theory. Finally Neoptolemus may have stimulated Horace's mind by his combining, as he seems to have done, a Callimachean enthusiasm for artistic elaboration with an Aristotelian belief in the viability of the large poetic genres and the seriousness of poetry. That is much, yet far from all there is in the *Ars*. The poet, a reader with wide sympathies and great erudition, must have had a hundred-and-one other 'sources' in different senses of this word. To say that Horace 'was certainly not deriving his material simply and *seriatim* from one Greek handbook', or to call 'inconceivable that Horace based himself on a single treatise' (G. Williams, *Tradition* etc. pp. 336, 355), is to deny what I do not maintain.

When Horace remembers the most recent scholarly research on the *initia* of the Greek elegiac metre, he lets his learning enable him to give a neat turn to what I take to be his Hellenistic authorities—*A.P.* 77–8 *quis tamen exiguos elegos emiserit auctor,* | *grammatici certant et adhuc sub iudice lis est*; here he is manifestly using a different 'source' from Neoptolemus. The criticisms of contemporary *descriptiones* at *A.P.* 16–18 must surely have been suggested by 'contemporary sources'. So must have been the implied condemnation of 'neoteric' aesthetics or its counterpart, the opposition to the archaism of Varro's poetic theory, although this formidable if superannuated adversary is never mentioned. It needs no saying that Latin literature is ever-present in allusion, approval, or rejection; the Lucretian colouring of a verse like 49; Caecilius and Plautus, Cato and Ennius, Virgil and Varius (53–8); or the strictures on scenic metre (270) and the critique of Roman drama (285); or the sidelong glances at Cicero's and others' writings on friendship (419 ff.), or such covert quotations of Lucilius as 431–3 and doubtless many others which we cannot now specify; or the influence of Virgil that permeates the whole *Ars*. At any time Roman can coalesce with Greek and with the theory of the literary critics, over music (202) or Satyric plays (*satyros* 221 et al., but *Fauni* in Rome (244)) or Greek and Roman drama (275, 285). 'On the face of it, virtually everything in the *Ars* is Horatian and Roman. Yet matters demonstrably Horatian and Roman may be no more than a Horatian construction placed on Neoptolemus' teachings' (*Prol.* 135). Clearly we must beware of working with an unrealistic and mechanical notion of what we call a 'poetic source'. Pindar's *Second Olympian Ode* is preserved and thus we can see for ourselves how similar, and yet how utterly different is *Odes* I. 12. I suspect that we would find the same if Neoptolemus' *Ars* could be read in its entirety; but that seems harder to accept because Neoptolemus was primarily a critic, and Horace was a poet.

Thus we are carried from content, text, style, and tone to Horace's architectonic skill and the pattern of the poem as a whole. It is only in the complexity of this pattern that the apparent contradictions of the 'problem of the *Ars*' can be resolved. The structural imagination at work, in spite of the disparateness of genre, is no different in type in the small and tightly controlled lyrics and the largest of the hexameter poems, the *Ars*. In order to find the terms needed for a description of the whole poem I have recalled some structural features which the *Ars* shares with the *Odes*.

I have resisted the temptation of drawing descriptive literary criticism into the commentary; the step from textual and stylistic criticism to literary would not otherwise be clearly made, and it should be so seen to be made. Although my description of the poem is based on the line-to-line commentary, it is set apart from it. I have adopted a method of narration but not of continuous narration. Instead I have retained the division into sections, although the final impression of the poem is one of continuity and not division. My aim has been to show how the poet made the basic pattern of the literary critics find its place in a larger and more comprehensive framework, thus overcoming the inherent contradictions of the rigid conceptual scheme (style versus content and arrangement, 'poem' versus 'poet', etc.), while yet displaying poetry as a kind of philosophy, *sapientia*. The criss-cross of the patterns is so complex that a charting of the ground such as I have attempted cannot do it justice. Further reading will bring out further links and connexions. All I can do is to show a new mode of reading which is not constrained to neglect one essential aspect of the poem for another.

Such reading finally involves making value-judgements explicit, and not leaving them unexpressed. I have ventured to do this because I suspect my view of the poem depends ultimately on a value-judgement. Most classical scholars think meanly of the *Ars Poetica*. I believe that it is a great work and that it needs to be brought back to the centre of the stage, at any rate of Latin scholarship. What that involves cannot here be said, though it it will be sensed from the terms in which in this book I speak of the poem. But I have no doubt that the centre of the stage is its rightful place—the place to which the Italians and French of the sixteenth and seventeenth centuries assigned it. There it remained, exercising a decisive influence in the eighteenth century, until the Romantics of the nineteenth removed it, at the very moment when it had ceased to be a major cultural concern. Its cultural concern is beyond our reach though not beyond our purview; its scholarly concern is within our reach. If in these two books I have made some steps in the right direction I shall feel richly rewarded for work that has already taken ten years and, to be extended to *Epistles* ii, will take yet a few more.

This volume has been long in the making and the obligations that I have incurred during that time have been considerable. Once again my wife has assisted me over the bibliography and many details of the book. Mrs A. Johnson, research typist of Gonville and Caius College, has helped me in drafting the indexes, Mrs L. Hatfield in checking references. I have received many compliments on the design and appearance of the first volume, which I now wish to pass on to their proper recipients, the staff of the Cambridge University Press: they have also spent much time and thought on the complicated layout of the present volume. Many librarians have readily assisted my searches for *Horatiana*; I wish to thank especially Mr J. C. T. Oates and Mr R. V. Kerr, of the Cambridge University Library, and Dr W. Hörmann, formerly Director of the Department of Manuscripts at the Bayerische Staatsbibliothek, Munich. The Institute for Advanced Study at Princeton again granted me the advantages of membership; this enabled me to complete the first draft of the commentary in 1966, and raise a number of Aristotelian questions with Professor Harold Cherniss. I have made use of some of Professor F. Solmsen's notes on the first volume, and in general have attempted to bear in mind what reviewers of that book have said. Dr W. Ehlers of the *Thesaurus Linguae Latinae* has kindly made the materials of that great storehouse of Latinity available to me on several occasions. The authorities of the Warburg Institute gave me advance notice of a book that has since appeared in their *Studies*. So many friends and colleagues in Cambridge and elsewhere have answered my importunate questions that I cannot here mention them all. I am particularly grateful to Professor U. Limentani for help with matters Italian. I am greatly obliged to Mr E. J. Kenney for the rigour with which he has brought my proofs closer to consistency of presentation; even at that late stage he most helpfully queried some of my suggestions, and contributed others. Mr R. E. H. Cotterill gave me welcome further assistance with the proofs. Miss J. M. Reynolds remembered an inscription which has enabled me to clarify the old problem of *urceus* and *amphora*; on this problem I also had the benefit of advice from Professor S. S. Frere, Dr M. H. Callender, and Mr J. J. Patterson. I have consulted Professor E. W. Handley on the Menandrean topics raised at pp. 249–50, and Dr D. O'Brien on the Empedoclean evidence mentioned at pp. 427–8. Dr J. G. Landels of Reading drew my attention to the *aulos* recently acquired by his university, and considered with me the bearing of this instrument on the interpretation of a well-known but badly understood section of the *Ars Poetica*. Professor L. Golden of Florida State University did much to confirm my feeling that a chapter on the *Ars* as a Horatian poem should be part of this book. My largest debt is to Professor F. R. D. Goodyear, who made many acute and perceptive observations on an earlier draft, and suggested numerous improvements. All these are more favours than I can easily repay. But, at any rate, *qui grate beneficium accipit, primam eius pensionem soluit.*

C.O.B.

ABBREVIATIONS

AAM	*Abhandlungen der Akademie . . . in Mainz*
ABAW	*Abhandlungen der Bayerischen Akademie der Wissenschaften*
AGG	*Abhandlungen der Gelehrten Gesellschaft zu Göttingen*
AJP	*American Journal of Philology*
APA	*Abhandlungen der Preussischen Akademie*
BVSA	*Berichte über die Verhandlungen der Sächsischen Akademie*
CIL	*Corpus Inscriptionum Latinarum*
CP	*Classical Philology*
CPG	*Corpus Paroemiographorum Graecorum* ed. E. L. von Leutsch and F. G. Schneidewin
CQ	*Classical Quarterly*
CR	*Classical Review*
*CRF*³	*Comicorum Romanorum Fragmenta* ed.³ O. Ribbeck
CW	*Classical Weekly*
EC	*Les Études Classiques*
FPL	*Fragmenta Poetarum Latinorum* ed. W. Morel
GG	*Grammatici Graeci*
GL	*Grammatici Latini* ed. H. Keil
GR	*Greece and Rome*
H	*Hermes*
HS	*Harvard Studies in Classical Philology*
*HV*²	*Herculanensia Volumina, Collectio Altera*, Naples, 1862–76
IG	*Inscriptiones Graecae*
JB	*Jahrbuch, Jahrbücher*
JP	*Journal of Philology*
K.–H.	A. Kiessling's commentary on Horace, re-edited by R. Heinze, see 'Select List of Editions and Commentaries'
L.–S.–J.	H. Stuart Jones' New Edition of Liddell and Scott's *Greek–English Lexicon*
MH	*Museum Helveticum*
Mnem.	*Mnemosyne*
N.F.	Neue Folge
NGG	*Nachrichten der Gelehrten Gesellschaft zu Göttingen*
n.s.	New series, nouvelle série, nuova serie
P	*Philologus*
PIR	*Prosopographia Imperii Romani*
PW	*Philologische Wochenschrift*

R-E	Paulys *Real-Encyclopädie d. classischen Altertumswissenschaft:* Neue Bearbeitung
REA	*Revue des Études Anciennes*
REL	*Revue des Études Latines*
RFIC	*Rivista di filologia e di istruzione classica*
RM	*Rheinisches Museum*
RP	*Revue de Philologie*
SBAW	*Sitzungsberichte der Akademie, Wien*
SBBA	*Sitzungsberichte der Bayerischen Akademie der Wissenschaften*
SBHA	*Sitzungsberichte der Heidelberger Akademie der Wissenschaften*
SBPA	*Sitzungsberichte der Preussischen Akademie der Wissenschaften, Berlin*
SI	*Studi Italiani di filologia classica*
SVF	J. von Arnim's *Stoicorum Veterum Fragmenta*
TAPA	*Transactions . . . of the American Philological Association*
TLL	*Thesaurus Linguae Latinae*
TRF³	*Tragicorum Romanorum Fragmenta* ed.³ O. Ribbeck
WS	*Wiener Studien*
YCS	*Yale Classical Studies*

The Grammars of Kühner–Stegmann, Hofmann–Szantyr, and Neue–Wagener have been cited by authors' names, volumes and pages, J. Wackernagel, *Vorlesungen über Syntax* etc., Erste Reihe², zweite Reihe² as Wackernagel, *Vorl.* I². I ff., II². I ff., and E. Löfstedt, *Syntactica* as Löfstedt, *Syn.* I². I ff., II. I ff. A. Otto, *Die Sprichwörter &c. der Römer* (1890, repr. 1962) has been cited as Otto, *Sprichwörter* and page-number, O. Immisch's commentary on the *A.P.* as Immisch, pp. I ff., my *Prolegomena* (1963) as *Prol.* I ff.

INTRODUCTION TO MANUSCRIPTS
AND EDITIONS

1. The Selection of Manuscripts

Contemporary editions of the *Ars Poetica* and other Horatian poems are open to two objections. First, and most importantly, they tend to fall below the critical level long since attained, being either complacently conservative, or else, like A. Y. Campbell's editions of the *Odes*, wildly audacious in conjecture. To these procedures P. Maas's concise paper on the text of the *Odes*[1] offers a welcome antidote. The objection I am here concerned with is less important—the manner in which manuscript evidence is offered. Editors, without exception, either group the selected codices in classes, as though all could be classed, or else they offer a string of symbols, as though no codex was related to any other. A valid case cannot be made for either procedure.

Nobody has seen all the manuscripts of H. Nobody knows even their number. A palaeographer has tabulated about 300, and estimates that approximately 250 of these were copied before 1300.[2] If the next two centuries were included, the estimated number would be 'many times 250', indeed the *paene infinitus numerus* of an eighteenth-century editor.

Of this unknown total more than 60 manuscripts including nearly all the early ones—none written before the ninth century—were collated by O. Keller and his colleagues. A paper by W. von Christ[3] and later work on the text has reduced the unmanageable number to a few (12–15) manuscripts, which are indispensable for a sound text. No one can deny the possibility that there is textual gold hidden in the uncollated codices; there is at any rate some silver in cod. K, unknown

---

[1] *SI*, xxvii–xxviii (1956), 227–8.
[2] Hilda Buttenwieser, *Speculum*, xvii (1942), 54.
[3] *SBBA* (1893), 83-116.

until F. Vollmer chanced upon it; cf. his 2nd ed. p. viii, *casu contigit ut adinvenirem codicem K Kellero Holderoque non notum.* But there is scarcely much of it and while *Textgeschichte* is likely to profit from a much more extended study, the text of H. is not likely to profit.

As for collation, I doubt if anyone can seriously fault Keller's and Holder's painstaking and meticulous work. I have tried to do so, collating codd. CK and δ, and working continuously with microfilms of K and R, and the Leiden facsimile of B. Except for the details of K, the harvest has been minute. Improvement of text and app. crit. is not to be hoped for from recollation.

For the *Ars* none of the following manuscripts can be entirely dispensed with; they are set out in alphabetical order: aBC (E in the last 36 verses where C fails us) KRV and the pairs δπ λl φψ. I describe them in the sequel; for more detailed descriptions Keller's edition may be consulted. I have jettisoned the readings of other codices which may be seen in the editions of Keller, Klingner, and Lenchantin–Bo. Cod. L in particular[1] does not in the *Ars* seem to me to deserve the attention paid to it by D. Bo.[2]

a = Ambrosianus O 136 sup. (formerly Avennionensis), s. ix–x. Contains all the poems, *S.* ii. 7. 28–8 fin. in a different hand. For specimens of writing, see E. Chatelain, *Paléographie des classiques latins*, i, pl. 81. Introduced by Keller and Holder in 1869 (vol. ii[1]), but later and especially in the *Ars* unduly neglected by Keller. The codex contains ancient material, e.g. *C.* i. 12. 15, iv. 14. 28, *S.* i. 4. 110, *Ep.* ii. 1. 27; for the *Ars* see below, pp. 31–2; I do not share Klingner's opinion of its character. Its affinity with any of the best codices—not codices of the second rank such as M and γ in Klingner's group Q—can be defined only where the Parisinus A happens to be preserved; in those poems—not the *Ars*—codd. a and A are often closely akin.

---

[1] Laurentianus 34. 1, s. x–xi.   [2] Paravia edition, ii[2] (1959), ix.

B = Bernensis 363, s. ix, a major source of the text of H.; earlier owned by a well-known collector of manuscripts, Jacobus Bongarsius (d. 1612 at Paris).[1] A complete facsimile appeared in S. de Vries's *Codd. Gr. et Lat.* ii (Leiden, 1897), with a full description by H. Hagen. First used by Orelli, 1837 (1st ed.). A codex of excerpts from various authors including contemporary or near-contemporary poems; Hagen, Introd. p. ii n. 3, gives a full list of its contents. The Horatian excerpts were perhaps selected to display a large variety of metres. Apart from one of the ps.-Acronian Lives, B contains selected odes and epodes, many complete, some fragmentary, some repeated; also the *C.S.* and *A.P.* 1–440, *S.* i. 1–3. 134. Neither the date nor the provenance of cod. B is agreed. The script is Irish and the codex contains Irish glosses. The marginal scribbles are of considerable historical interest; they refer *inter alia* to life and politics in the ninth century. Keller and others point out that the reference on fol. 186^r to queen Angelberga, wife of King Hludovic II of the Langobardi, applies to the years 856–90; she married in 856 and died in 890; the *carmen ad Tadonem*, archbishop of Milan (fol. 194^v), points to the years of his episcopate, 861–9. There are other references to slightly earlier events. At one time the codex was believed to be the oldest surviving manuscript of H. Subsequently dates after the middle of the ninth century were canvassed; Keller, on the basis of the above dates, suggested 850–70. On the other hand, expert palaeographers have dated B later, E. Maunde Thompson to the tenth century,[2] L. Traube to the late ninth: '*vor dem Ausgang des 9. Jahrhunderts ist er nicht geschrieben*'.[3] The marginalia might then, as Traube thought, be copied from the source. As place of origin Fleury on the Loire used to be suggested (Keller and Holder, 1st ed. p. xi, Chatelain, *Paléog.* i, 23.) But for this origin there is no valid evidence.[4] The marginal allusions and

[1] Cf. H. Hagen, *Jacobus Bongarsius, &c.* (Bern, 1874).
[2] Cit. T. Gottlieb, *WS*, ix (1887), 151.
[3] 'O Roma Nobilis', *ABAW*, xix (1892), 349.
[4] Keller, 2nd ed. p. xix.

1-2

other features rather point to northern Italy, though the Bobbio catalogue, s. x, records no Horace. A competent study of all the contemporary material in B is desirable. Until this is undertaken, chronological conclusions concerning the survival of Horatian copies on the European continent and in Ireland are precarious; cf. P. von Winterfeld,[1] A. Bernardini, *Appunti cronologici intorno al 'cod. bernensis' 363* (Sinigaglia, 1911) cited by Pasquali, *Storia della tradizione*, 2nd ed. (1952), p. 385 n. 3, and Pasquali's own remarks *ibid.* and pp. 374 f.; see also below p. 30. Medieval Italy was not so well provided with copies of H. as were France and Germany.[2] The comparatively uncontaminated text of B could then be due to geographical rather than chronological causes. The scribe's writing is careless and sparsely corrected; many slips and false word-divisions survive. But the superficially disordered and unsophisticated codex preserves much ancient and good material and, with its younger relatives C and probably K, represents a distinct form of the Horatian text. Examples will be given below.

C/E = Monacensis lat. 14685, s. xi,[3] earlier owned by, and perhaps written at, one of the major Benedictine monasteries in south Germany, St Emmeram (Regensburg). The monastery, founded in the eighth century, was for a long time rich in Carolingian manuscripts; B. Bischoff, whose knowledge of the Regensburg MSS is unrivalled, has written about St Emmeram in 'Die südostdeutschen Schreibschulen...in der Karolingerzeit',[4] I (1940), 171 ff. C/E was first used by Keller and Holder in their ed. min. of 1878; the editors thought that the codex consisted of two codices bound together—C, s. xi, and E, s. xii. But the evidence does not favour such a simple hypothesis. Prolonged work on the C/E readings, and a week, scrutinizing the manuscript in the library at Munich, have

---

[1] *RM*, LX (1905), 32 ff.
[2] Buttenwieser, *Speculum*, XVII (1942), 54.
[3] *S.* II. 5. 83–6. 33 probably s. xii, see below.
[4] *Sammlung Bibliothekswiss. Arbeiten*, p. 49.

convinced me that, in principle, Klingner was right when he based the distinction between C and E on the use of two different sources rather than on the putative difference of scripts, inks, and dates; see F. Klingner, *H*, LXX (1935), 379–81.

I would describe the position as follows. Unlike B, cod. C is something like an 'edition' of Horace. Fulness was aimed at; and, having more than one source to draw on, the scribe largely succeeded, the exception being *C.* IV 7. 21–*Epod.* 1. 23, which are missing completely. Three times an incomplete portion was supplemented by a text apparently taken from a different source. In each case the former of the two texts shows marked similarities with B and K where each is extant. These texts are best described by their old siglum 'C' in order to distinguish them from the additional portions, Keller and Holder's 'E'. The priority of the incomplete portions is rendered probable by the larger amounts available for supplementation. In one case, that of the *Satires*, the C text[1] could have been dispensed with altogether, since the E portion that follows offers the whole of the *Satires*, and thus duplicates the C portion, though the readings differ in a number of places. In another case, the lyric poems, C offered no more, and perhaps had no more to offer, than *C.* III. 27. 1–IV. 7. 20, *Epod.* 1. 24–17 fin. and *C.S.* The rest was drawn from E, I mean I. 1. 1–III. 26 fin., accommodated on the two quaternions before *C.* III. 27; *C.* IV. 7. 21–*Epod.* 1. 23 have already been seen to be missing. In the remaining case, C, unlike its older relative B, took the *Ars* only up to l. 440. While B explicitly declared that poem to be 'finished', C filled the page with two ornamental drawings and a bit of exposition. The missing 36 verses of the *Ars* were taken from E, and fill one column of the next page; some scholia occupy one half of the second column, the rest is left blank. The readings, with one possible exception, are poor. Between the two groups of *Satires* come the *Epistles*, with no difference in externals that I can find. They

[1] *S.* I. 4. 122–6. 40, II. 7. 118, II. 8.

may therefore belong to either C or E, and require more argument than is apposite here since the codices closest to C are not extant in the *Epistles*. I have not therefore attempted to adjudicate between Keller and Holder, who call this portion E, and Klingner and Lenchantin, who call it C, though Klingner has left an awkward trace of the earlier nomenclature at *Ep*. I. I. 72.

By way of summing up I list the C and E texts in their distribution over the codex: fols. 56–70 *C*. I. I. I–III. 26 fin. (E); fols. 71–81ʳ *C*. III. 27. I–IV. 7. 20, *Epod*. I. 24–17 fin., *C.S.*, *A.P.* I–440 (C); fol. 81ᵛ *A.P.* 441–76 (E); fols. 82–83ᵛ *S*. I. 4. 122–6. 40, II. 7. 118, II. 8 (C); fols. 83ᵛ–92ᵛ *Ep*. I–II (?C, ?E); fols. 92ᵛ–102ᵛ *S*. I. I. I–II. 5. 82, and fols. 104–5 *S*. II. 6. 34–8 fin. (E). The remaining portion of the *Satires* (II. 5. 83–6. 33) is added on fol. 103, written in a single column over the width of the page, not in two columns as in the rest of the codex. The script differs; B. Bischoff[1] assigns it to the twelfth century. Thus *S*. I. 4. 122–6. 40, II. 7. 118, and II. 8, are duplicated.

K = codex St Claude, Dép. Jura (Bibl. Municipale), no. 2, s. xi; received from the local Benedictine abbey of St Oyan (*S. Eugendus*) to which the name of St Claude was later applied. The codex was listed in 1492 in the catalogue of the abbey but does not appear in the surviving fragment of the eleventh-century catalogue. Introduced by F. Vollmer, *Horace*[2] (1912).[2] A collection of pieces from various authors; the Horatian poems were probably part of a different codex, a palimpsest; now they amount only to *A.P.* and *S*. I. I. I–II. 2. 24. K contains good and clearly ancient material. The manuscript is not so closely related to B or C as Vollmer and Klingner have confidently asserted, although for better or worse BCK often agree. It is also true that some of K's best readings are shared with B or C or both, but other good readings are not. For

[1] *Ap*. Klingner, *H*, LXX (1935), 380 n. 4.
[2] Cf. praef. p. viii, *SBAW* (1913), pt. III, 'Zum Homerus Latinus', pp. 5–7.

example contrast *A.P.* 237, 289, 393, 400 with 5, 7, 230, 305, 339, 371, 378, 420, 430, 458. The correct wording *quiduis* (23), which appears only in K and, as a correction, in ψ, is possibly but not certainly due to conjecture in both cases.

R = Vaticanus Reginae 1703, dated by Keller to the eighth century, but palaeographers now assign it to the middle of the ninth. Even so it is probably a little older than B, and hence may be the oldest known manuscript of H. Though recorded much earlier, the codex was fully used first in Keller and Holder's ed. min. of 1878. It is one of a large number of manuscripts (several Horatian among them) and books that came to the Vatican by the bequest of Queen Christina of Sweden (d. 1689 at Rome); earlier it belonged to the Monastery of St Peter and St Paul at Wissembourg, Alsace. This is one of the finest specimens of Carolingian script, carefully, though not always felicitously, corrected. For a photograph, see Chatelain, *Paléog.* I, pl. 87; I have recollated the codex from a microfilm. Housman thought that it is 'probably the best MS (of H.) on the whole, and certainly much the best in orthography'.[1] For the preservation of old forms in its spelling, see Keller, ed.[2] praef. p. lxiii. But R cannot be called the best manuscript of the *Ars*. This is not to deny the all-round excellence of the codex in this poem. In many passages good evidence is preserved, often against the BC tradition (e.g. 226, 230, 234, 235, 237, 373, 461). There are not a few places where the codex propagates a poor paradosis, e.g. 62, 72, 94, 100, 133, 187, 237, 261. There are however no places in the *Ars* where R alone preserves the correct wording as it does for example at *C.* II. 7. 5 *Pompei* (*pompi, pompili* cett.; *pompi* even in A a B though the correct name is in the title), III. 5. 2 *derepta* R *di-* cett., III. 20. 15 *nireus*;[2] at *C.* I. 18. 5 R and the corrupt text of Nonius suggest the probability of the acc. *militiem*[3] and at III. 25. 12 R with δπ and φψ preserves the

---

[1] *CQ*, XXII (1928), 7.   [2] Cf. *nirea, Epod.* 15. 22 a R.
[3] Cf. *TLL*, VIII. 957. 23–4.

correct *naiadum*, while the other codices have the unmetrical *naidum*. Moreover since many editors have tended to succumb to the lure of class-division, it is worth noting that what may be our oldest manuscript offers a text that cannot be assigned to any one distinct group of readings. As early as the ninth century, and probably earlier, classes of readings must already have been conflated to produce the evidence presented by R.

V = Blandinius Vetustissimus, now lost, apparently the oldest of four codices from the Benedictine monastery of St Blanchin (Blankenberg) in Ghent, and used by the Flemish humanist Jacobus Cruquius in his editions of H. from 1565 onwards. The manuscript cannot be dated. A case has been made by P. von Winterfeld[1] for the assumption that like B it was written in Irish script. The monastery was burnt down in 1566 by the 'iconoclasts' (Cruquius on *S.* I. I. I) and the codices were destroyed. The readings of V and the other Blandinii are known therefore only from Cruquius' very selective collations, and may be inferred in some cases for the poems—not the *Ars*—contained in the codex Gothanus B 61, which seems to have been copied from V in the fifteenth century. Much has been written about V and assessments of its value have oscillated between wholesale acceptance and wholesale condemnation. For a balanced judgement, see M. Lenchantin di Gubernatis in the introduction to his Paravia edition of H.[2] and G. Pasquali, *Storia della trad.*, 2nd ed. pp. 381–5. Also F. Leo's remarks[3] are well worth pondering still. But a judicious opinion could have been had from Bentley. 'Few' (Housman remarked)[4] 'know what Bentley's opinion was: it is to be discovered, not by pouncing on one or two loose expressions and running away with them, but by observing his practice.' In any case the V readings were the best available to Bentley, since of the codices now recognized as indispensable only δ was known to him. As is the case with

---

[1] *RM*, LX (1905), 32.
[3] *Ausgew. Kl. Schr.* II, 164.
[2] 2nd ed. by D. Bo (1957), pp. xvi–xviii.
[4] *CR*, XXII (1908), 89.

other manuscripts, V's contributions differ in value in the different parts of the Horatian *œuvre*, though there are poor readings in all parts. V contributes most in the *Satires*, and next perhaps in the *Ars*. Out of twenty-three genuine variants, one only is likely to be in error: 49 *rerum et*. Three are doubtful: 92 *decenter*, 154 *plosoris*, 345 *sosis*. Nineteen of them (excepting the ancient spelling at 426), none only in V, are certainly or probably right: 7 *aegri*, 53 *cadent*, 72 *ius*, not *uis*, 161 *imberbus*, 196 *amice*, 201 *uincta*, 237 *et* as in BC, 249 *fricti* against BC, 294 *praesectum* as in BC, 319 *locis* as in aBC, 328 *eu* as in BC al., 330 *an* as in B, 360 *operi*, 371 *nec scit* as only in BK and one other Bland., 378 *decessit*, 385 *ue*, 393 *rabidos* as only in BK and Cruquius' other manuscripts, 394 *urbis*, 426 *quoi* for the vulgate *cui*, *qui* B.

Finally I list three pairs of codices, all but one denoted by Greek letters.

δ = Harleianus 2725, s. ix. Facsimiles in Chatelain, *Paléog.* I, pl. 83, *Cat. of Ancient MSS in the Brit. Mus.* pt. II (1884), pl. 60. δ contains parts of all Horatian poems but the *Ars* is complete. It is now in the Harleian collection of the British Museum. The codex was bought for Edward Harley, second Earl of Oxford, by his librarian Humfrey Wanley, on 20 October 1725 (not in 1703 as the Paravia editors say, I², p. xiv). It had belonged earlier to J. G. Graevius (d. 1703). The tricky negotiations that led to the purchase of the Graevius MSS were traced by A. C. Clark.[1] The reader can now follow them up in a meticulous edition of *The Diary of Humfrey Wanley*.[2] The catalogue of Graevius' collection, compiled after his death, does not contain cod. δ because it had been borrowed by Bentley. Nothing is known of its earlier history. Graevius had bought it from a bookseller in Cologne, and lent it to Bentley in 1702: *mitto tibi meum codicem, quem olim*

---

[1] *CR*, v (1891), 365–72.

[2] C. E. and R. C. Wright, 2 vols, Bibliog. Soc. London, 1966, cf. the index in vol. II under cod. 2725, and under Graevius and Zamboni; Mr R. V. Kerr of the University Library Cambridge has kindly drawn my attention to this publication.

mihi paravi Coloniae Agrippinae taberna ubi veteres membranae vendebantur, ut Blandinius ille, quem quaeris, esse non possit.[1] This is Bentley's 'Graevianus'—the only one of the important manuscripts known to him. No wonder he held on to it as long as he could. A German man of letters and bibliophile, devoted to travelling and learned gossip, heard scandalous reports when he was shown the Graevianus, in 1711, in the library of the Elector Palatine at Düsseldorf:[2] 'welchen (Codex) Grävius Herrn Bentley gelehnt, der ihn auch lange nicht restituieren wollen, bis man ihm gedrohet der Churfürst würde desfalls an die Königin schreiben'. Uffenbach had visited Cambridge two years before, and had called on Bentley.[3]

π = Parisinus 10310, s. ix–x, formerly Augustodunensis (in the Cathedral library of Autun). Facsimile in Chatelain.[4] Contains all the poems, but the *Satires*, which come last in the series, break off at 1. 2. 70.

δ and π are closely though not invariably akin in their readings; in a sizeable number of cases π and R go together.

λ = Parisinus 7972, s. ix–x, which came to the royal library in 1670 from the library of J. J. Mentelius (Jean-Jacques Mentel), a Parisian physician. Written probably in the monastery of St Ambrose at Milan.[5] Contains the whole of H., the Mavortian subscript,[6] and some contemporary Latin verse relevant to the date of the codex.

l = Leidensis lat. 28, s. ix, complete except for *C.* II. 16. 1– 19. 4, *S.* II. 8. 59–95, was owned in the thirteenth century by the cathedral of St Peter in Beauvais (*Beluacum*). Keller, 2nd

[1] *Richardi Bentleii...Epistolae*, ed. F. T. Friedemann (Lipsiae, 1825), ep. 42, p. 115.
[2] Z. C. von Uffenbach, *Gelehrte Reisen*, III, 740, cit. Clark, *CR*, v (1891), 365–72.
[3] J. E. B. Mayor, *Cambridge under Queen Anne* (1911), pp. 135 ff., 421.
[4] *Paléog.* I, pl. 86.
[5] Cf. L. Traube, *Poetae Carol.* III, 754 f.
[6] After the *Epodes*, shown in Chatelain's facsimile, *Paléog.* I, pl. 79.

ed., praef. p. xxix, points out that Beauvais belonged to the diocese of Rheims, from which codd. φ and ψ originated. The codex is written in a handsome and careful script; for a facsimile, see Chatelain, *Paléog.* 1, pl. 78. Selected readings were known to Bentley from Burman's report of N. Heinsius' excerpts from the codex.

The similarity of the λ and l texts is close; both agree also in offering the Mavortian subscript.

φ = Parisinus 7974, s. x. Originally belonged to and perhaps was written at the monastery of St Remy at Rheims, cf. fol. 1ᵛ *Liber Sancti Remigii Rhemensis*. In the sixteenth and seventeenth centuries it belonged successively to D. Gothofredus, the brothers Puteani and C. Fauchetius. For a facsimile of the elegant script, see Chatelain, *Paléog.* 1, pl. 84. Offers a complete text of H.

ψ = Parisinus 7971, s. x. Like φ originated from Rheims but, as fol. 3 shows, was presented to the Benedictine Abbey of Fleury by Herbert (d. 992), Gerbert's former pupil at Rheims. The codex came later to Fontainebleau and from there to the Bibliothèque Nationale. A facsimile in Chatelain, *Paléog.* 1, pl. 83. A complete text of the poem is followed by a tract on the metres of H.[1] and the Suetonian Life.

The texts of φ and ψ are closely akin, probably copies of the same original. Although in quality, like the preceding two pairs, below that of other codices, they occasionally preserve ancient and good material, e.g. *procne* at *A.P.* 187, where all other manuscripts offer the vulgate *progn(a)e*. The codices, occasionally referred to earlier, were systematically used in Keller and Holder's 1st ed., where their source is labelled F (Remensis), as it is later in the editions of Vollmer and Klingner.

[1] *GL*, IV. 468–72.

2. Can the Horatian Manuscripts be Classified?

I think the Horatian manuscripts cannot be classified, for the only valid criterion for classification, a statistically significant number of textual agreements between the manuscripts, cannot be established. This is not to say, however, that editors have refrained from classification. Much scholarly work in the nineteenth century was devoted to the tracing of relationships between manuscripts and, in an ideal case, say Catullus, or Lucretius, where Lachmann demonstrated affiliation, a stemma can do a useful job. But, having brought ideal cases into a system of archetypes, hyparchetypes, and the rest, Paul Maas said wisely, 'Gegen die Kontamination ist noch kein Kraut gewachsen'.[1] There are comparatively few ideal cases among Latin verse authors, who were much read in late antiquity and the Middle Ages. The texts of such authors do not tend to stay in the watertight compartments of a 'closed transmission'. The text of H. certainly did not.

It is instructive to scan the major attempts that have been made to force the Horatian manuscripts into the straight-jacket of 'classes'. In his second edition[2] O. Keller divides them into three groups, from which I select mainly those that are relevant to the *Ars*:

(1) aM et al., in the *Odes*, *Satires*, *Ars*, also C/E, and in the *Epistles* A and R. But large portions of aC/E are said to belong to Class II, and *inter alios* R to Class III.

(2) BCV and, largely, aC/E.

(3) δπ λl φψ, partly also R et al. But in the lyrics λl frequently belong to class II.

These exceptions largely invalidate the rule. Moreover Keller's long and impressive lists of readings,[3] though arranged in three columns, have a knack of dividing into two. Thus the first ten out of his thirty-four from the *Ars*:

[1] *Textkritik*[2], 31.
[2] Pp. xviii, lxxx, cf. *Epil.* 793.
[3] 2nd ed. pp. lxxxiii ff.; *Epil.* 813 ff.

A.P.			
18	*pluuius* aM, etc.	*pluuius* B, etc.	*fluuius* F, etc.
20	*expes*	*expes*	*expers*
35	*ego me*	*ego me*	{ *egomet* { *ego me*
43	*ut*	*ut*	*aut*
53	*cadant*	*cadent*	*cadent*
76	*inclusa est*	*inclusa est*	{ *iunctis* { *iunctus*
92	*decenter*	*decentem* *decenter*	*decenter*
111	*effert*	*effert*	*et certi*
120	*achillem*	*achillem*	{ *achillen* { *achillem*
145	*cum*	*cum*	{ *omittunt* δ *ct al.* { *cum*

It appears that only one out of ten instances is a possible (not certain) case for tripartition. The same judgement would be passed on the other two dozen; tripartition is rare, see below pp. 21–2. Keller (*Epil.* 833) expressed the sanguine hope 'that in future no one will deny the existence of these classes'. The opposite has been the case; few if any competent judges have accepted them. One assessment may stand for most. J. Gow,[1] reviewing Keller and Holder's first edition, ends his neat rebuttal by saying, 'the advantage of...making three Classes...is obvious. It saves an editor from the appearance of merely counting his MSS, and it deceives the unwary into laying odds of two to one on his readings.'

But old habits die hard. Seeing that manuscript readings tend to fall into two rather than three groups (though there are such cases as well), F. Vollmer, the next Teubner editor, attempted to base his text on the twofold classification. He prepared the ground in a long paper, *Die Überlieferungs-geschichte des Horaz* (*P*, Supplement x), which appeared in the same year, 1907, as the first edition of his text. Vollmer's selection of codices agrees largely with W. von Christ's, mentioned at the beginning of this introduction: Vollmer

---

[1] *CR*, iv (1890), 340.

I = A B C/E D (the readings of the lost Argentoratensis C vii. 7, s. x) to which, in his 2nd ed., he added K, cod. S. Eugendi; Vollmer ii = δπ λl φψ R V. Thus the bulk of Keller i and ii became Vollmer i, and the bulk of Keller iii became Vollmer ii.

Like von Christ and indeed F. Leo[1] Vollmer persuaded himself that the arrangement of H.'s poems in the different codices provided an external and convincing criterion. His diagram[2] leaves no doubt of his criterion; it is the position of the *Ars* (apart from the brief *Carm. Saec.* and the two neighbours *Ep.* and *Serm.*) that differs in the two classes.

Class i

	C/E	B	A	D
1	Carm.	Carm.	Carm.	Carm.
2	Epod.	Epod.	Epod.	—
3	Carm. Saec.	Carm. Saec.	Carm. Saec.	—
4	Ars	Ars	—	—
5	Serm.	—	Ep.	Ep.
6	Ep./Serm.	Serm.	—	Serm.

Class ii

R δπ λl φψ		V (?)		Porph.	
1	Carm.	1	Carm.	1	Carm.
4	Ars	4	Ars	4	Ars
2	Epod.	2	Epod.	3	Carm. Saec.
3	Carm. Saec.	3	Carm. Saec.	2	Carm. lib. V (= Epod.)
5	Ep.	6	Serm. (?)	5	Serm.
6	Serm.	5	Ep. (?)	6	Ep.

The *Ars* comes fourth in Class i, and second in Class ii. (Whether Class ii aimed at an alphabetical order of initial letters, as has been suggested, I do not know. The sequence *Carmina, De arte poetica, Epodi, Epistulae, Sermones* may give rise to this assumption, but *Carmen Saeculare* coming as it does after the *Epodes* requires special pleading, and the sequence *Ep.–Serm.* is dubious throughout.) Now Vollmer argued that the

[1] *AGG*, 1904, 851, repr. *Ausgew. Kl. Schr.* ii (1960), 161.
[2] *Op. cit.* p. 290.

distribution of readings agreed with the classification suggested by the arrangement of poems. This however is not the case.

In the first place, cod. a, which was jettisoned by Vollmer, cuts across his neat division; it exhibits the order of Class II but in its readings it is often akin to cod. A, which belongs to Vollmer's Class I. Moreover the readings of individual manuscripts do not regularly follow the lines demarcated by the classes.

In his first edition he defined, in the *Ars*, I by aBC and II by RΦ (= φψ λl δπ). Yet the reader scanning the apparatus criticus will be disappointed by continuous disagreements with the proud initial declaration, let alone the scheme of his article. Thus 18 reads *pluuius* I/II *fluuius* Φ, but the true distribution is *pluuius* aBCR *fluuius* cett.; here a and R, which are Class II in his article, go in fact with Class I, cod. a against the article, cod. R against both the article and the initial declaration II = RΦ. Again, 49 reads *rerum* I *rerum et* II; the true distribution is *rerum* BCR *rerum et* aV δπ λl φψ; here R and a have changed places, and V is on the 'right side' (Class II) whereas in other places it is attached to I—against the principle provided by the order of poems. Nor do the Greek-letter manuscripts always reside where one would expect them to; λl is often detached from the rest and even δ and π, φ and ψ, are occasionally separated. It would appear therefore that the varying sequence of the poems in different manuscripts is an insufficient criterion for classifying the textual diversity of the same manuscripts.

The last attempt to impose order on the disorderly scatter of variant readings is that of Klingner in the current Teubner text (1959, earlier 1939 and 1950). It was again an external criterion that was thought to provide illumination—the difference between the titles prefixed in the manuscripts to the lyric poems. This criterion had been suggested by W. von Christ (*op. cit.* p. 83) and by others before him. Klingner worked it out to his own satisfaction in *H*, LXX (1939). His paper falls into two parts. The first (pp. 249–68) deals with the titles of *Epodes* and *Odes* and seeks to establish two classes of manuscripts on this basis. The second (pp. 361–403) seeks to show by a comparison of variant readings that the class-division based on the titles is valid also for variant readings. I believe that this demonstration has miscarried. This is not the place to discuss details. Since it was Klingner's purpose 'to lay the foundation for a simple and unprejudiced apparatus criticus' (p. 403, last sentence, cf. p. 255, para. 3), it must be sufficient to show that it is not wholly unprejudiced.

The titles of the *Epodes* and *Odes* suggested to Klingner (pp. 256 f.) a division of the best manuscripts that reduced Keller's three classes to two—the codd. ABC of Keller Class II are denoted by Ƶ, and the codd. R δπ φψ of Keller Class III by Ψ. In addition he assumes the existence of a subarchetype, Q, to account for the mixed titles of cod. a (in Keller's nomenclature part of Class I) and, additionally, of M and γ. But a glance at the same editor's text shows that, in the app. crit. of the *Epodes*, Ƶ is said to stand for ΛaBC, to which at times λl is added. This procedure makes good editorial sense quite often, since cod. a tends to attach itself frequently to A in its readings. Unfortunately however this fact invalidates the derivation from the titles. But nevertheless, let the classification be based on the titles, as Klingner proposed, and let it be extended from the titles of the *Epodes* (where it has some justification) to the *Odes* (where it has much less), and finally to the hexameter poems (where it has none). Even then the distribution of variant readings makes against this division.

Contrast for example the textual variants in *Epod.* 6, where Klingner saw a clear case for division by titles.

Epod. 6. 2. *aduersus* C φψ *aduersos* B *aduersum* AaR γ δπ λl. This cuts across the simple division ABC *vs.* R φψ, etc.; the text pulls in a different direction from the titles. *Ibid.* 3 *uertis* AaBCR pr. γ λl π *uerte* δ φψ. Here the codexes do divide according to the simple prescription ABC *vs.* φψ but R goes with ABC.

Likewise doubts are raised by such places in the *Epodes* as

2. 29   *aut* BC *at* AaR δπ λl φψ

4. 15   *eques* BCR δπ φψ *et eques* Aa λl

5. 11   *haec trem.* AaBC λl *haec et trem.* δ¹π φψ *haec et rem.* R
 71   *a(h)a(h)* uel sim. Aa δπ l φψ om. BCR λ
8. 20   *quid* AaR¹ δ¹π λl φψ *quod* BCM γ.

The falsity of Klingner's classification is clearly seen when the manuscripts in his app. crit. are checked against the family label. They sometimes square, at other times they do not. In the *Odes*, B not infrequently stands apart from the rest of '℥', although a promising assurance '℥ = ABQ (= ABDEM *acc. interd.* R) *acc. interd.* λl' heads the app. crit. Thus (I omit references to cod. M)

C. 1. 12. 32 (dividing into three, not the usual two, groups)
            qui B *quod* D pr. R pr. (?) *quia* AaER corr. δπ λl φψ
  1. 13. 6   *manet* B *manent* cett.
  1. 17. 9   *(h)aedili(a)e* BR δπ λl φψ *(h)aedilia* AaDE
      19   *disces* B *dices* cett.
  1. 21. 14 *in* preserved and correctly placed B
            om. AaD¹ER¹ transferred to l. 15 δ¹π λl φψ
  1. 27. 16 *ingenuo* AaDER λ *genuo* l
            ingenio B δ pr. π *genio* φψ
  1. 28. 15 *nox* ABE δπ λl φψ *mors* aDE uar. R
  1. 30. 1   *cnidi* BR δπ φψ *gnidi* AaE λl
  1. 31. 10 *ut* BR¹ δ¹π λl φψ *et* AaET
  1. 35. 39 *diffingas* AaDER δ φ *diffindas* π
            deffingas λl *defingas* R ψ

Similar difficulties arise, though less frequently, over Klingner's other blanket siglum, Ψ, the supposed archetype of R (except when R goes with ℥!) δπ λl (except when λl go with ℥!) φψ. '*crepat* ℥ (acc. λl R)', we are told at 1. 18. 5; and yet φψ, that mainstay of this class of readings, offer *increpat* along with δ and E (and π²). *attinent* at 1. 19. 12 is said to be in ℥Ψ; and yet *attinet* (the more likely reading) is in φψ and R¹. All these are instances from Book 1 only; many others could be adduced from other parts of the *Odes*.

In the hexameter poems the job of classifying is trickier still; the evidence that Klingner claims for 'Class ℥' is even more scanty. BK offer some portions of the *Satires* and K only some others, C only offers part of the *Epistles*, and there is no evidence at all in the large area where B and C as well as K fail us, for '*deest* K, *S*. ii. 2. 25–Ep. ii. 2. 116'. Cod. g, which is claimed as an occasional auxiliary ('*acc. interdum* g') is best left out of account altogether since its well-known adherence to the readings of the *Blandinius Vetustissimus* implies the possibility, if not more, of a third line of transmission apart from Ƶ and Ψ. When all fails we are told soothingly (*S*. ii. 2. 25 ff.) 'Q *modo ad rec.* Ƶ, *modo ad* Ψ *pertinent. uestigia rec.* Ƶ *praeterea in* g m σ x u λ'. But uncertain 'vestiges' cannot supply a badly needed criterion for distinguishing one of two undefined ingredients of a 'mixture'.

In the *Ars*, at any rate up to 440, 'Class Ƶ' is said to be represented by BCK, apart from that dubious ally called Q by Klingner ('= a γ M *acc. interd.* R'), part of Keller's Class i; λl, which in other poems not infrequently adhere to BC, are in the *Ars* usually on the side of the Greek-letter codices. Yet K, apparently also C, had access to more than one source. In any case BC stand by themselves so frequently that no evidential value can be said to accrue from a position where K and B, or K and BC, disagree. Let us therefore allow for the shifting allegiances of cod. a (the other two members of the 'Q class', γ and M, can be disregarded for textual purposes) and R, and ask ourselves how often Ƶ really = BCK and, at the same time, Ψ = δπ λl φψ. The answer is, sometimes but by no means invariably or even in a majority of cases.

37	*ue*	BCK (?)	*que*	(aR)	δπ λl φψ
49	*rerum*	(R) BCK	*rerum et*	(aV)	δπ λl φψ
100	*uolent*	(a) BCK	*uolunt*	(R corr.)	δπ λl φψ
103	*tum*	BCK	*tunc*	(aR)	δπ λl φψ
117	*uirentis*	(aR²) BCK	*uigentis*	(R¹)	δπ λl φψ
212		(a) BCK	om., add. sec. man.	(R)	δπ λl φψ
226	*auertere*	BCK	*ita uertere*	(aR)	δπ λl φψ
259	*enni*	(aR) BCK	*ennii*		δπ λl φψ
289	*que*	BCK	*ue*	(aR)	δπ λl φψ
311	*sequuntur*	BC(-quon-)K	*sequentur*	(aR)	δπ λl φψ
327	*albani*	(a) BC(*alba ni-*)K	*albini*	(R², *bini* R¹π pr.)	δπ λl φψ
345	*sosis*	(a¹V) BCK	*sosiis*	(a²R², *sociis* R¹)	δπ λl φψ

Can the Horatian Manuscripts be Classified?

This is clear evidence but beyond it the ground is less firm. In such places as 234, 237, 276, 288, 294, and 421, the sequence BCK is broken, in the first four C² and K (or K²) show themselves aware of the opposite reading, and in the fifth the K¹ reading is not known—but, nevertheless, let them be counted for argument's sake.

234 *nomine*	BC¹(?)	*nomina*	(aR)	δπ λl φψ C²K
237 *el*	(V) BC	*an*	(aR)	δπ λl φψ K post ras.
276 *plausis*	BC¹K¹	*plaustris*	(aR)	δπ λl φψ C²K²
288 *togatis*	BCK¹	*togatas*	(aR)	δπ λl φψ K²
294 *pr(a)esectum*	(V) BC(K¹ n.l.)	*perfectum*	(aR)	δπ¹ λl φψ K²
		perspectum		π² (?)

A few more dubious cases of this kind may be adduced and beyond them there stretches the large and murky area where it is the scribes of δπ or λl or φψ that do the 'contaminating'. That area will be surveyed below (pp. 24 ff.).

There are then in the 476 verses of the *Ars* about twenty variants and a few instances of spellings to which the equations Ƶ = BCK, Ψ = δπ λl φψ apply, though not always fully. There are many more, up to three times that number, where the distribution of readings in 'Class Ƶ' alone invalidates that simple division, and by the same token renders its use inadvisable anywhere. Of this fact Klingner must have been uneasily aware, for his procedure is by no means consistent. I append six passages in which K stands apart from B and C or from B or C singly. In three of these Klingner uses the class label Ƶ (= BCK), in the other three he does not, although they are identical in character. It is noted that at 222 and 371 a reading (*iocum, aulus*) is labelled ƵΨ and yet, in one case, BK¹ δπ and, in the other, BC¹ differ.

Klingner (Bl = Bland. Vet.)			MSS (cett. denotes the remainder of the MSS selected in this edition)	
locum B(?)K¹R² δπ	*iocum* ƵΨ	222	*locum* BK¹R² δπ φ pr. ψ	*iocum* C cett.
an B Bl	*ad* CKΨ *at* π²	330	*an* BV pr. *ad* (*at* V corr. π²)	K cett.
nec BC Seru.	*ne* KΨ	339	*nec* BC Seru.	*ne* K cett.
ue BK	*que* CΨ	358	*ue* BK	*que* C cett.
nec scit Ƶ Bl	*nescit* CΨ	371	*nec scit* BKV	*nescit* C cett.
ausus BC¹(?)	*aulus* ƵΨ	371	*ausus* BC¹(?)	*aulus* K cett.

19

The same criticism is prompted by any other passages where the triad BCK is broken—5, 54, 92, 134, 178, 190, 202, 230, 249, 276 (*uexisse*), 277, 298, 305, 319, 360, 393, 420, 421, 424–5, 434, 441–76, which K took from a source not available to BC; and the instances in which the Greek-letter codices are separated give rise to even greater difficulties. For here in particular Klingner duplicates the class label so that the same siglum comes to denote different groups of manuscripts. Thus

ue Ψ (δπ Raγ)	*que* ΞΨ (Fλ′R¹(?))	65	*ue* δπ aR	*que* BCK λl φψ
aera ΞΨ	*aere* CF λ′δ	345	(*a*)*era* δ²πa(?)BC²KRλ²l²	(*a*)*ere* C¹δ¹λ¹l¹ φψ
fallant F δπ corr. R²	*fallent* ΞΨ	437	*fallant* δπ corr. φψ R²	*fallent* cett.

I conclude that there is no health in Klingner's classification. The distinction by titles of epodes is not sufficiently borne out by the shifting allegiances of manuscripts. Variants fall into classes but manuscripts do not. Class labels therefore are unsound. Nor can Klingner's attempt to combine class labels with manuscripts' sigla be upheld. This compromise is impracticable as long as all the indispensable manuscripts are used and their variations specified. The reason for that is not far to seek. Our oldest manuscripts of H. are already cross-fertilized in various degrees; they do not preserve unmixed traditions. M. Lenchantin therefore was justified in rebutting the new doctrine; his argument deserved more attention than it received when he published it in *Athenaeum*, n.s. xv (1937), 129 ff. and *RFIC*, n.s. xviii (1941), 34 ff. F. Villeneuve's introduction to his Budé edition of the *Odes* (1927) also may be consulted.

It should be added that in such a type of transmission a stemma is no use. For a stemma can illustrate only established classes of a given manuscript tradition. A glance at the stemmas offered in Klingner's *Praefatio* will show what I mean. There, in the words of the archaic Greek philosopher, everything was together, πάντα ἦν ὁμοῦ. But it is the purpose of a stemma to depict lines of tradition that can be separated from other lines of tradition.

I can see only three methods whereby the major differences of the Horatian paradosis are presented in a reasonable app. crit. One procedure is A. Meineke's in his important edition of 1834—a listing by readings and a total omission of all references to manuscripts. This method has the virtue of a masterly brevity; it draws attention away from the symbols for manuscripts, and directs it where it belongs, to the variety of readings. I have been tempted to apply it, and have abandoned it chiefly because it loses the one solid advantage that has accrued in the study of H.'s text over a century— the assessment of the major codices. Another viable procedure is that adopted by Lenchantin in the Paravia series[1] and by Villeneuve in the Budé series. The result is an unbiased if indistinct survey of the provenance of readings. The weakness of this procedure cannot however be concealed. Some manuscripts are more closely related than others and this relation remains unnoticed when codices are arranged according to their putative dates. The third procedure seeks to bring out these similarities, while allowing for the variability of some of the surviving sources. This is the procedure I have adopted. It has no especial virtue, apart perhaps from disclosing more evidence than the two others. This evidence is known and has already been adverted to; but it does not happen to have been presented clearly. A somewhat fuller account now follows, which leads on to a brief discussion of the archetype, or archetypes, of our manuscripts.

3. Classes of Readings

Trying to ascertain the number of variants in any passage in H., we find that there are some where three variants have been transmitted. But the number of clear instances is small— in the *Ars* no more than perhaps four of them.

154 *plusoris* (*plus oris*) R² δ¹π λl¹ φ¹ψ *plosoris* aBCKR¹V δ² *plausoris*
    l²λ uar. φ², Pseudacro: '*plosoris*' et '*plausoris*' *legitur*
190 *spectanda* aCRπ² φψ post ras. *exspectanda* BKψ in ras. *spectata* δπ¹ λl

---

[1] 2nd edition by D. Bo.

196 *amice* aBCK $\delta^2\phi^2\psi^2$ *amici* $\delta^1(?)\pi\phi^1\psi^1$ *amicis* R λl
360 *operi* BCRV λl π φψ Hier. Ep. 84. 8. codd. uett. necnon cod.
Cantab. s. xii. (Coll. Emman.)   *opere* K δ pr.   *opere in* a δ corr.
Hier. codd. recc.

Other cases, e.g. 168, 305, 327, 328, 402, etc., may not be transmitted readings but the quirks of individual scribes. Even the genuine cases are small beer, none of them equal in importance to such a passage as *C.* ii. 13. 23 *descriptas/ discriptas/discretas*, where each reading yields some sense, and the third, recommended by Bentley, tends to be unjustly neglected by editors. The remaining variants, seventy or more in number, are bipartite.

It has already been demonstrated that comparatively few of them fall into the simple patterns assumed by Klingner. But overstatement must not be allowed to obscure what affiliations have been known for some time.

The similarity between B and C was observed by Keller and Holder, and has been noted above. Most important of all is the omission, in B and C, of verses 441–76. Some conclusive instances of common faults are listed by Keller ed.², pp. xx f., lxxxiii ff., 5 *-um missi* for *-um am(ad)missi*, 234 *nomine*:*nomina*, 288 *togatis*:*togatas*, 420 *ad lucrum iubet* unmetrical for *iubet ad lucrum*, etc. Such instances may be multiplied, e.g. at 54, 225, 230, 277, 307, 339, 396, 416.

C, however, as Keller recognized, is not a copy of B. Rather it seems to have been derived, after two centuries or so, from the same exemplar as B itself, or from an intervening copy. Moreover the scribe of C was able to supply additional material, either from evidence in the same exemplar not taken up by B, or from other sources; thus verses 2 and 283 are in C, but not in B, 7 *aegri* in C but the faulty *aegris* B, 63, 67 *iniquom* C om. B, 371 *ausus* BC¹ (?) but *aulus* C corr., 378 *pergit* BC *uergit* C uar. cett. Sometimes C divides words wrongly where B has correct divisions, as 327 *alba nisi* C pr. *albani si* BC corr. But very many of the faulty word-divisions of B—a sure sign that *scriptio continua* was not far away—are eliminated in

C, because its scribe was either better able to spell out the common exemplar, or again had access to other sources. Thus 1 *pectore quinam* B but *pictor equinam* correctly C cett.; 38 *Iā m̄r* (? *iam mater*, ? *iam matrem*) B but *materiam* C[1] cett. in reverse order, 119 *si quere* B *sequere* C cett., 137, 166, 252 *iri metris* B but *trimetris* C cett., 298 *barbas secreta* B for *barbā secreta* C cett., 334 *iucundę tidonea* B but *iucunda et idonea* C cett., 337 *omnes super-* B but *omne super-* C cett., 342 *praeter cunctaūra* B but *praetereunt austera* C cett., 430 *rore mallet* B[1] but *rorem saliet* C cett., etc. Likewise instances in B of apocope (usually corrupted), which may preserve an ancient spelling, are eliminated by correction; thus 264 *uenia est*] *uenias* B, 304 *tanti est ergo*] *tantis tergo* B, 353 *ergost* B, 386 *iudicium est, ea*] *iudicium stea* B, 409 *quaesitum est. ego*] *quaesitum stego* B. Yet there are enough passages where the C reading, even when it differs from B, points to a common source. Thus 134 *dissilies* C *disilies* B *desilies* cett.; 154 *aulaea* (the correct word and spelling) of C stands between *aulae* B and *aulea* cett.; 202 *non corichalco* C[1] resolves *scriptio continua* in one way, *nunc corichalco* B in another, *nunc orichalco* C[2] cett. being the true reading; 279 *pulputat ignis* is one of the few instances where C misman-ages word-division, whereas B, unusually, gets the division right: *pulputa tignis*, cf. *pulpita tignis* cett.; 311 *sequontur* C (with the scribe's favourite vocalization), *sequuntur* B, *sequentur* cett.

Cod. K has already been shown to be related to the BC tradition (above pp. 6, 18). The relation however is not so close as that between B and C. I have already given examples of another textual tradition intervening (above pp. 19 f.).

All these facts impose a restraint on an editor who is unwilling to go against the evidence. BC, and less definitely K, represent a well-marked paradosis. No harm is done if this is signified by a class symbol in those cases where BCK agree. But when B and C, and even more B, C, and K, disagree, this tradition cannot be recovered with any certainty and a general symbol lacks justification. Since this happens more often than not, it is perhaps preferable, in this tradition, to eliminate the general symbol altogether.

The same preference applies to the other class of readings that was distinguished above. This is often represented by the Greek-letter manuscripts, conveniently so called although cod. l figures among them. Of the pairing of δπ, λl, and φψ there can be no doubt, although occasionally each codex indulges its own individual vagaries. Thus, apart from the dozens of instances where a pair joins one or two of the others, a few passages may be cited where each appears more or less isolated from its cousins.

65	*ue* δπ aR	*que* cett.
203	*pauco* δ²π¹ aBCK	*paruo* δ¹π² cett.
207	*coibat* δ corr. π BC al.	*cohibat* λl pr. φψ
393	*rapides* δ *rapidis* π pr.	*rapidos* uel *rabidos* cett.
428	*pulchrae* δ pr. π R pr.	*pulc(h)re* cett.
439	*aiebat* δπ KR²	*ag(i)ebat* cett.

λl (labelled λ′ by Keller) adhere in the *Ars* usually to the group δπ φψ. But λl in separation are shown for example at

79	om. λ¹l¹ add. λ²l²	habent cett.
196	*amicis* λl R	*amice* uel *amici* cett.
222	*iocum* λl φ corr. etc.	*locum* δπ φ pr. ψ R²
349	*remuttit* λl	*remutit* uel *remittit* cett.
402	*tyrceus* (-*eus*) λl	alii alia
461	*demittere* λl π² R	*dimittere* cett.

φψ (labelled F by Keller)

79	*archilochum* φψ aR	*archilocum* cett.
96	*thelephus* φψ	*telephus* sim. cett.
187	*procne* (recte) φψ tantum	*progn(a)e* cett.
207	*catus* φψ¹ (*cautus* ψ²)	*castus* cett.
233	*propteruis* φψ	*proteruis* cett.
339	*posset* φ pr. ψ pr. δ¹(?)	*poscat* cett.

δπ λl and φψ coincide in a sizeable number of cases (above p. 18), and in those cases represent a distinct class of the paradosis. The most convincing instance is the omission of a whole verse (212) in δπ λl φψ and R, repaired by second hands in all of them. The omission was caused by homoeoteleuton, produced in turn by a faulty ending of the final word in the preceding line; this clearly must have occurred in the common ancestor of the whole group—the confusion obligingly preserved by R and π, two manuscripts that show some affinity:

211 accessit numerisque modisque licentia maior (malorum R^1)
212 indoctus quid enim saperet liberque laborum (malorum π^2)

These cases are instructive but not large in number. For again and again either one or more of the three pairs, or even one of the partners, detach themselves from their family, betraying a knowledge of the neighbour's property on the other side of the fence, and sometimes resisting but often succumbing to the lure. Thus the omission of l. 211 was made good. Thus, misguidedly or not, readings were changed in numerous cases.

18 *fluuius* δ^{1}π λ^{1}l^1 φ^{1}ψ^1 R^2 *pluuius* (recte) δ^2 λ^{2}l^2 φ^{2}ψ^2 aB, etc.

56 (*h*)*ennii* δπ^2 λl φψ   *enni* (recte) π^1 cett.

76 *iunctis* δ^{1}π corr. λl φ^{1}ψ^1 *iunctus* π pr. R^1 *inclusa est* (recte) δ^2 φ^{2}ψ^2 R^2, etc.

111 *et certi* π λl φψ R^1(?)   *effert* (recte)δ φ^2 uar. ψ^2 uar. aB (*efferet*), R^2, etc.

154 *plusoris* (*plus oris*) δ^{1}π λl^1 φ^{1}ψR^2 *plosoris* δ^2 aBCKR^{1}V   *plausoris* λ uar. l^{2}φ^2 (*plausori* B superscr.)

196 *amici* δ^1 (?) π φ^{1}ψ^1 *amicis* λl R   *amice* (recte) δ^2 (?)φ^{2}ψ^2 aB, etc.

203 *paruo* δ^{1}π^2 λl φψ R   *pauco* δ^{2}π^1 cett.

223 *incelebris erat* δ^{1}π^{2}l pr. φψ R   *inerat* (*illecebris* superscr.) λ *erat* om. φ pr. ψ pr.   *il*(*in-*)*lecebris erat* π^1 aBC corr. K.

Many other passages may be compared, e.g. 235, 258, 319, 328, 417.

Nor is it a matter of 'early second hands' only. The scribes show by their own corrections that they are aware of the variant readings which constitute the specific differences between the groups:

55 *uaro* δ π post ras. λl φψ   *uario* (recte) π ante ras. a ante ras. B, etc.

168 *permutare* δπ corr. λ pr. l φψ (*mutare* π pr.)   *mox mutare* λ (?) corr. aB, etc.

249 *fricti* (recte) δ corr. π² λ¹l¹ φψ aKV   *fracti* δ pr. π¹ λ²l² BC²K

279 *aeschynus* (-*inus* π φ pr.) δ pr. λ pr. l φ corr. ψ -*yuus* R   *aeschylus* (recte) δ corr. λ corr. aBC (*hae*-) K

305 *ex*(*s*)*ors ipsa* (recte) δπ² λl corr. φψ KR²   *ex*(*s*)*ortita* δ²uar. π¹(?), λ uar. aBCR¹(?)

Again there are many other instances, e.g. 145, 331, 339, 434, 435, 462.

It follows that, with the exception of B, all manuscripts so far surveyed are, in various degrees, 'mixed' or 'contaminated'—C and K are, and so are δπ, λl, and φψ. I regard it as misleading therefore to contrast the unmixed or pure codices BCK and the Greek-letter codices with others that are mixed. The lines of transmission are separated only where BCK *together* preserve a different text from δπ, λl (in this poem), and φψ *together*. But those places are comparatively few in number.

Yet the degrees of contamination are of some importance. Other manuscripts of the same age conflate readings much more freely, because they do not take the basic selection of either BCK or δπ λl φψ for granted. Thus codd. a and R each follows its own lines of conflation. The two lines differ, although since as a rule there are only two sets of readings to choose from they frequently converge.

R in particular offers its own mixture of the (at least) two traditions. In many places the codex adheres to the Greek-letter tradition, and the conjunction Rπ to which Keller, and later Klingner,[1] have drawn attention is one aspect of this adherence. Nevertheless there are many passages in this poem and others in which R selects the text that is now represented by the BCK tradition, or a mixture of the two traditions.

If this state of affairs is to be gathered from the layout of the critical apparatus, an attempt should be made to set the

[1] *H*, LXX (1935), 384 ff.

two basic groups apart, without however subsuming them under such group labels as I, II or Ƶ, Ψ. This is the layout of the present apparatus, in which the sigla are arranged alphabetically within each group, keeping together the pairs of Greek-letter codices δπ, λl, φψ over against aBCKRV. For that reason I have abandoned Lenchantin's roughly chronological arrangement within the groups since no precise chronology of the manuscripts can be established. So I print, for example, 53 *cadent* BC¹KRV δ¹π λl φψ *cadant* a C² δ², rather than, with Lenchantin, *cadent* VBC¹M²LRφψδ¹π *cadant* C²aUM¹δ². The gain in clarity will be obvious since I operate at the same time with fewer manuscripts. On the other hand I refrain from unwarranted classification such as Vollmer's *cadent* I, II, Bland. *cadant* a ς, or Klingner's *cadent* Ƶ Ψ Bl. *cadant* Q. In this as in certain other transmissions of Latin classical texts it is expedient to distinguish between classes of variants, which can be established, and classes of manuscripts, which cannot be established.

4. The Archetype or Archetypes

The cardinal fact in the paradosis of H.'s poems, as far as we know it, has emerged in the preceding discussion. No manuscript is older than the ninth century, and probably not the early ninth century either. If it happened that R was the oldest surviving codex, it would happen too that our transmission would begin with a fully contaminated text. Whether this contamination was the work of the scribe of R, or whether he derived the text as it stands from his exemplar, we have no means of knowing. The codex is carefully written and remarkable for its many traces of an older type of spelling. It may well be that text and spelling alike represent an earlier copy. If on the other hand one or two of the other ninth-century manuscripts, for example δ, antedate R, then a different conglomerate begins the known history of the Horatian text in the Carolingian age and R comes soon after. In either case, when our manuscripts begin, contamination is already established. It is worth pondering the lesson inherent in the date of B. This codex, which offers a less 'mixed' text than say δ or R, is in fact likely to be later than they are.

H.'s text at the earliest stage known to us—the ninth century—does not then allow of a convincing division into families. We are dealing with an 'open tradition' and variant readings spread, horizontally as it were, from manuscript to manuscript. This is of course no new doctrine. It is *doctrina Housmanniana* and I do not here enlarge on it, but refer to Housman's Lucan, pp. vi f. and his Juvenal, p. xxiv.[1] There would have been no need to labour the point if the Teubner edition (the Oxford Classical Text of H. does not seem to have been revised since 1912) did not continue on the old road, undisturbed by Lenchantin's justified strictures concerning (as he reminded Klingner)[2] 'il fluttuare delle varianti trasmesse tanto verticalmente quanto orizzontalmente'.

In the majority of instances the variant readings fall into two groups—a state of affairs not unusual in the transmission of ancient Latin texts. A. Dain's remarks[3] on *les stemmas... bifides* of Latin texts should be carefully pondered, although clearly they do not offer the only explanation of this phenomenon.[4] B, C and K, where they agree, often have a better and less vulgarized text than the other extant manuscripts. But for all that, δπ and the other Greek-letter codices remain indispensable; Vollmer's list[5] is too haphazard to carry conviction, rather consider *Ars* 37, 226, 230, 234, 288, 305, 311, 378. The same holds good for single manuscripts or pairs of them. Third independent readings cannot however be ruled out, as I have suggested above (pp. 21 f.). Moreover G. Pasquali[6] was right to argue in his very instructive survey of the Horatian paradosis that V, the Oldest Blandinian, probably respresents a separate line of transmission.

---

[1] Cf. E. Fraenkel, *Gnomon*, ii (1926), 499 f.
[2] *Athenaeum* n.s. xv (1937), 173.   [3] *Les Manuscrits*, nouvelle éd. p. 134.
[4] See S. Timpanaro, *La genesi del metodo del Lachmann* (1963), 112 ff.
[5] *Die Überlieferungsgeschichte des Horaz*, p. 296.   [6] *Storia della tradizione*[2], p. 385.

Over the whole work the variant readings are too numerous and too consistently separated to render at all likely the assumption of a single immediate exemplar. The only plausible explanation of this state of affairs at the very beginning of our manuscript tradition is the survival to the ninth century of at least two ancient copies which represented the two divergent classes of readings. The Blandinian may represent a third tradition.

The age of these copies or sub-archetypes (*hyparchetypi* in P. Maas's terminology) can only be guessed at. It may have been as early as the late fourth or the fifth century. To mention a well-known example, the Puteaneus of Livy's third decade is dated to the fifth; it was copied four centuries later by monks of St Martin's of Tours, who must have borrowed the codex from Corbie. The abundance of falsely divided words in B and such errors in various manuscripts as *celo* C. i. 12. 2 for *clio, uelorum* C. i. 2. 18 for *ultorem, forem Ep.* ii. 1. 226 for *eo rem, iri metris A.P.* 252 for *trimetris,* may apply to any source in *scriptio continua* and capital writing. Yet a later date is more likely than an earlier. The fifth century and the early part of the sixth are the time to which the 'subscripts' in the codices of a number of Latin authors are to be traced; so O. Jahn showed in a celebrated paper, 'Über die Subscriptionen in den Handschriften römischer Classiker',[1] cf. Dain, *Les Manuscrits,* p. 120. These may be the putative latest dates for the sub-archetypes of a number of classical Latin texts.

H. in particular was widely read, quoted and imitated, up to the early sixth century. After that time the traces are, to put it cautiously, infrequent and indefinite. I am not however asserting the wholesale disappearance of Horatian texts during the three centuries *c.* 550–850, as Vollmer[2] was prepared to do on the basis of the evidence collected by M. Hertz[3] and M. Manitius.[4] The citations of Venantius Fortunatus

[1] *BVSA,* iii (1851), 327–72.
[2] *Op. cit.* pp. 32 ff.   [3] *Analecta carm. Hor. hist.* 1876–82.
[4] *Analekten zur Gesch. des H. im Mittelalter,* 1893.

alone should give us pause. Nor do the likely date of cod. B and the unknown date of the lost Oldest Blandinian provide a secure base for the conclusion that in the second half of the ninth century H. was brought back from Ireland to a continent of Europe that could no longer draw on any copies of the poems (cf. above p. 4). Nor are we reduced to guessing, at any rate so far as the *Ars* is concerned. The famous booklist, or 'catalogue', in cod. Berol. Diez B 66 is now securely dated to the late eighth century by E. A. Lowe;[1] and that list contains a copy of the *Ars*. Less extravagant views have prevailed, as the summaries of Pasquali[2] and J. Perret show.[3] But even so the traces of H.'s *Nachleben* from the middle of the sixth to the middle of the ninth centuries are infrequent and weak.

The early sixth century is therefore the latest date to which these sub-archetypes of H. may be conjecturally ascribed. And that of course is the time of *subscriptio Mauortiana*; Mavortius was consul in 527. The subscript has frequently provoked large overstatements. They begin with Bentley's remark in his preface (where he published his important discovery)—*Flaccum ex Mavorti recensione hodie habemus*. This is not at all likely, if H.'s text was transmitted by more than one sub-archetype. Mavortius' pronouncement as it appears in various codices was meticulously reprinted by Keller in its proper place at the end of the *Epodes*. Keller too has listed the codices in which it appears, A λl and half a dozen others, clearly not a homogeneous group. '*Ma la subscriptio è in pochissimi codici*', said Pasquali,[4] wisely, '*per vero non strettamente collegati tra loro.*' The subscript must have travelled, like textual variants, *orizzontalmente* as Pasquali also remarked, from one codex to others that are different in character, quality, and affiliation. Mavortius' words, *legi et ut potui emendaui* still require elucidation in comparison with other subscripts.[5] What-

---

[1] *Codd. Lat. Antiq.* VIII (1959), no. 1044.   [2] *Op. cit.* pp. 374–5, 385.
[3] *Horace* (1959), pp. 224–5, 251–2.   [4] *Op. cit.* p. 377.
[5] Cf. Jahn, 'Über die Subscriptionen...', pp. 364 ff., and Leo, *AGG* (1899), p. 174 n. and (1904), p. 855 (repr. *Ausgew. Kl. Schr.* II, 166).

ever their precise meaning, there is no information that Mavortius concerned himself with any poems apart from the lyrics, and strictly, apart from the *Epodes*,[1] although the brevity of *Epodon liber* renders that restriction less likely.

The conclusion is that we cannot identify such a thing as the 'Mavortian tradition'. But a Mavortian copy of unknown extent (beyond the *Epodes*) *must* have been part of our paradosis—for that alone explains the appearance of the subscript in manuscripts as different in character as A and λl. A Mavortian copy *may* have been one of the sub-archetypes of our extant manuscripts.

5. Ancient Variants

Anyone wanting to penetrate beyond the sub-archetypes postulated in the last section needs to ponder the age of the variant readings that occur in the manuscripts. That kind of textual study is clearly beyond the scope of this textual introduction. An editor however should attempt to decide whether he is dealing with truly ancient material or with the conjectures of medieval scribes. According to Vollmer the variants in R δπ λl φψ are Carolingian. This assessment has been rejected, notably by P. Lejay (in an article to be mentioned presently) and Housman.[2] But Klingner, who also rejected it, regarded in turn as medieval the readings of cod. a—the only codex of his class Q (aγM) used in this edition. Even Lenchantin, who usually kept his head and rejected Klingner's classifications, accepted the medieval provenance of the 'Q readings'.[3]

Yet a scrutiny of the alleged medieval recension raises serious doubts. One of the four 'Sonderfehler' of cod. a in the *Ars*, cited by Klingner,[4] 53 *cadant* for *cadent*, occurs also in Servius' citation of the passage, *Aen.* vi. 34. Another, 360

[1] So for example says Dain, *op. cit.* p. 119.
[2] Review of Vollmer's 2nd ed., *CR*, xxii (1908), 89.
[3] *RIFC*, n.s. xviii (1941), 38.
[4] *H*, lxx (1935), 389 n. 2; Lenchantin reasonably omits 178.

opere in for *operi* (*opere*), may possibly be alluded to as early as Porphyrion's paraphrase *in tanto opere*. A third, 178 *morabimur*, an open choice for *morabitur*, occurs not only in K but in ps.-Acro's commentary, contrary to his lemma, which is *morabitur*; the pl. therefore may be an ancient variant. This leaves only one passage that cannot be paralleled in extraneous and apparently ancient material.

The case is clearer still when one comes to consider the main divisions in our manuscripts. In a perceptive paper, significantly entitled 'Les recensions antiques d'Horace',[1] P. Lejay rejected Vollmer's submissions. He pointed out that certain variants, in proper names as well as in other instances, cannot be understood except by the assumption that they are in fact ancient. For such a demonstration the testimony of the scholia and the indirect transmission in ancient citations is of considerable value.

C. I. 8. 2 is perhaps the most telling instance. For here, after l. 1 *Lydia, dic, per omnes*, the manuscripts divide into three groups:

(1) *hoc deos uere* AaBDER
(2) *hoc deos oro* δπ
(3) *te deos oro* λl φψ.

There is no doubt that the third reading alone conforms to Horatian usage;[2] the first does not, and the second offers a simple compromise between (1) and (3). The true reading however is preserved only in the weaker codices, λl and φψ, and not even in all of them, since δπ offer the compromise text (2) and, moreover, scribes then attempted to conform to each other, φ² going with δπ, and π² going with λl φψ. Porphyrion has the right text in his lemma, but the ps.-Acronian comments (Γ'cp) presuppose the faulty reading (1). On the other hand the best codices unanimously offer reading (1), which is false. It is even more remarkable that as early as the Neronian age, two generations after H.'s death, a scholar of standing, the metrist Caesius Bassus, operated

[1] *Mélanges Chatelain* (1910), pp. 59–74.
[2] L. Mueller *ad l.*, Vahlen, *H*, xlv (1910), 308.

with the same false text (1); so did other ancient experts after him. The precise relations between the metrists' and the manuscripts' texts are not at all clear.[1] What is clear is that these differences between our manuscripts go back all the way to the first century; Caesius Bassus was a contemporary of Probus, the critic of the text of H. and other classical poets.

A threefold division also occurs at *C.* II. 13. 23. The *sedes piorum* in the Lower World are called:

(1) *descriptas* in DERπ (most of the poem is missing in δ)
(2) *discriptas* in AaB
(3) *discretas* in λl φψ (and A²π²).

(1) is certainly erroneous. (2) might possibly stand, yet, as Kiessling said, and Heinze repeats with unusual decisiveness, the point is not that they have a place to go to but that they have an especial place apart from the others; hence, with Bentley, *discretas*, coll. Virg. *A.* VIII. 666–70, *Culex* 375, Lact. *Inst.* VII. 7. 13. Again therefore the λl φψ text is justified. The division is ancient, for Porphyrion, whose lemma is *descriptas*, in fact comments on the right reading, *separatos...a ceteris locis*, and so do the λφψ scholia, whose lemma is *discriptas*. At *C.* IV. 14. 28 the manuscripts divide into two—*meditatur* aR, *minitatur* (wrongly) A δπ λl φψ, further corrupted to *minatur* in the codices of Nonius, p. 203—Servius (*Aen.* IV. 171) like Porphyrion citing the true text. Servius (*A.* XII. 83) also shows the false BC reading *nec* at *A.P.* 339 to be ancient.

In several other places Porphyrion, whose best manuscripts[2] are as old as the oldest of H., notices divergent readings, which commonly reappear, four or more centuries later, in our manuscripts; rarely is the variant lost from sight altogether, as is the vulgarized ending of *C.* II. 6 *uatis Horati* in place of the genuine *uatis amici*, which takes up the motif of friendship from the beginning of the poem. Thus *C.* III. 6. 22 *fingitur artibus* but *artubus* (wrongly) δπ l φψ and Porphyrion, '*artubus*' *legendum quia non uenit a nominatiuo* '*artes*' *sed* '*artus*',

---

[1] Cf. Lejay, *op. cit.* pp. 70 f., Pasquali, *op. cit.* pp. 380 f.
[2] Vat. 3314 ninth century, Monac. 181 tenth century.

significat per molliores saltatus puellas discere turpes...motus rerum ueneriarum. Thus Priscian a century or so later citing *C.* III. 17. 4 *per memores...fastos,* and adding (*GL,* II. 256) *apud Horatium duplicem inuenio scripturam...fastos, et fastus in aliis codicibus.*

Even the thin trickle of the ps.-Acronian scholia occasionally carries textual information. The note on *Epod.* 5. 28 *currens aper* reads *furens, ut 'inhorruit armos'* (Virg. *A.* x. 711)—'*quod varia potius lectio, quam interpretatio videatur...Sane, quid currens aper hic faciat, nullus video'*, etc. (Bentley). At *C.* III. 3. 34 the manuscripts divide between *discere* and *ducere*; also, one of ps.-Acro's notes deals, like Porphyrion, with *discere*, the other with *ducere*; this does not rule out either word but renders it likely that the division is ancient. This lesson may be borne in mind for such passages in the *Ars* as 4, 32, 154 '*plosoris*' *et* '*plausoris*' *legitur*, etc., 305, 345.

Finally it is worth recalling that ancient citations—the 'indirect transmission'—may preserve some valuable material in a few instances.[1] This is not likely to be so in the case of our oldest witness—Seneca[2] citing *S.* 1. 2. 27 with the name Buccillus rather than the Rufillus of H.'s manuscripts. Lejay[3] has shown that either name is possible; Rufillus' reappearance in *S.* 1. 4. 92 may help to defend the Horatian paradosis. Nor is Quintilian's *intonsis*[4] likely to supplant *incomptis*, codd. Hor.; and the other two or three divergences from our MSS, out of two dozen literal quotations, are certainly erroneous, see M. H. Morgan, *HS*, XII (1901), 234–6. But a case may be made for the *lactea* of Flavius Caper[5] citing *C.* I. 13. 2. against the unanimous approval not only of the manuscripts of H. but also Porphyrion and ps.-Acro. There is a good case for Servius' citation of *C.* II. 18. 30 with *sede* instead of the manuscripts' *fine* (whether or not H.'s manuscripts are influenced by the grammarian) and for Priscian's of *C.* III. 6. 11 with *nostris*, not the manuscripts' *nostros.* Finally at *C.* III. 14. 19 Charisius'

---

[1] Keller, *Epil.* 799, Vollmer, *op. cit.* p. 277. [2] *Ep.* 86. 13.
[3] *Les recensions antiques d'Horace,* p. 73.
[4] *I.O.* IX. 3. 18 citing *C.* I. 12. 40–1. [5] *GL,* VII. 98.

uagacem may well be right against *uagantem*, MSS, even though the word does not seem to be attested elsewhere. This is not a large bag and I have not found anything in the numerous quotations of the *Ars* for which I could make a like case.

6. Ancient Variants and the Edition of Probus

In the last section I considered several ancient variants in the text of H. Some conclusions have to be drawn from these examples.

There is a sufficient body of evidence invalidating any attempt, such as Vollmer's, to deprive the Greek-letter manuscripts—all or some of them—of ancient authority, if authority is the word. It is surprising that an editor of H. should ever have conceived of such a notion. δπ and their congeners clearly offer a vulgarized and often impossible text. But their genuine variants are ancient, and some of them can claim to be superior to the better tradition. The same applies to codd. a and R, on whose status Klingner has attempted to throw doubt, and perhaps most of all, for good and ill, to the preserved readings of the Oldest Blandinian. All readings of the *codices selecti* and the scholiasts may have ancient warrant; they need to be considered on their merits.

Nor is this all. Since F. Leo's thesis of the 'unified character' of the Horatian paradosis still survives, though in a shadowy and uneasy existence, Eduard Fraenkel was right to reprint the few pages on which it was based in his selection of the author's *Kleine Schriften* (II, 159–67), originally *AGG* (1904), a review of Keller and Holder's edition. The essay is well written and closely argued. It still deserves consideration, although more in the spirit of contradiction than of assent.

It was one of Leo's great merits to introduce into Latin studies Wilamowitz's notion of Greek *Textgeschichte*. The history of a transmitted text is part of the editor's evidence and should not therefore be ignored. It is largely because Leo raised these problems so effectively that it has now

3-2

become clear that he overstated the similarity, here and in analysing the history of the texts of the archaic Roman playwrights.[1] The transmission of Latin texts differs in certain fundamentals from that of Greek. This point is well made in books as diverse as Pasquali's *Storia della tradizione* and Dain's *Les Manuscrits*.

Leo was more successful in raising than in solving these problems. His thesis was misleadingly simple. He regarded the Horatian text as essentially unified, *einheitlich*, and marred by comparatively few mistakes and variants. 'There could be no doubt', in his opinion, that the transmission was so consistent because Probus' edition of the first century A.D. had given it a consistent shape (p. 165). But when a man starts an argument with the words, 'Es kann kein Zweifel sein', it is as well to make sure that the evidence really is indubitable. I doubt if it is. For I have never been able to discover the meaning of Leo's pronouncement (pp. 165–6) that 'we cannot be sure in all cases that we have the text of Probus. But it is the aim of *recensio* to recover it.' Leo himself admitted that we know not a single detail of Probus' text. We know only about the procedure he employed.

M. Valerius Probus appears to have been the outstanding textual critic of his time.[2] His activities are dated to the second half of the first century.[3] He was born and brought up at Beirut, then in a Roman province, and it was *in prouincia* that he studied with his master *quosdam ueteres libellos, durante adhuc ibi antiquorum memoria necdum omnino abolita sicut Romae.* Thus Suetonius,[4] in an account which is, unfortunately, far from clear. After further biographical detail, Suetonius continues, *multaque exemplaria contracta emendare et distinguere et annotare curauit, soli huic nec ulli praeterea grammatices parti deditus.* The celebrated if regrettably brief remarks on his criticism may

---

[1] *Plautinische Forschungen*, ch. 1.

[2] See Gell. I. 15. 8 *grammaticum illustrem*, IX. 9. 12 *docti hominis et in legendis pensitandisque ueteribus scriptis bene callidi*, et al., Hier. *Ol.* 208. 4 *eruditissimus grammaticorum.*

[3] Cf. R. Hanslik, *RE*, VIII A, 197.   [4] *De Grammaticis*, 24.

derive also from Suetonius: *postremo Probus qui illas* (sc. *notas*, the critical signs of the Alexandrian school) *in Virgilio et Horatio et Lucretio apposuit, ut ⟨in⟩ Homero Aristarchus*.[1]

That is all we know, and whereas some evidence survives for Probus' Virgil, none does for H. The Horatian scholia contain no reference to the critic. Suetonius says nothing about a Probian commentary and perhaps by implication excludes one. I believe that the words *emendare et distinguere et annotare* refer to texts with critical signs[2] and probably critical notes such as Serv. Dan. *Aen.* XII. 605 implies.[3]

Leo based his ascription not on any specific evidence but on general considerations and the features shared by all manuscripts. Thus the titles of the books, *carmina, epodon liber, sermones*, not *odae, iambi, saturae*; also the main stock of the titles of the lyrics, and the order of the books (apart from *A.P.* and *C.S.*) in the Horatian corpus. Yet it is as hard to ascribe to Probus the false title *Ars Poetica* as the specific titles of the lyric poems. Moreover, while the survival of the spurious verses introducing *S.* 1. 10 could be accounted for by the (hypothetical) omission of a Probian obelus in parts of our paradosis, the sizeable number of *cruces* in all our manuscripts can surely not. Since some of these faults do not appear in citations by ancient grammarians and others, it seems that the Probian hypothesis does not explain what it was designed to explain—the state of the text in the manuscripts we possess. The evidence therefore seems to me to invite us to admit that we know too little to fit Probus into the picture of our paradosis.

Leo's Probian hypothesis is rejected by Pasquali[4] for H. and Plautus as much as by G. Jachmann for Terence.[5] Pasquali accepts that some of the pervasive features of the text, such as the type of title, *carmina*, etc., are Probian. But in order to

---

[1] Frag. Paris. de notis, *GL*, VII. 534, Reifferscheid, *Suet. Rel.* p. 136, Funaioli, *Gram. Rom. Fr.* pp. 54 ff.

[2] Probian editions have been doubted, on (I think) insufficient grounds, by N. Scivoletto, *Giorn. It. Fil.* XI (1958), 97–124 = *Studi di lett. lat. imp.* (1963), 155–221, and K. Büchner in *Gesch. der Textüberlieferung der antiken und mittelalt. Lit.*, Zürich, I (1961), 329 f., 335–9.   [3] Pasquali, *op. cit.* p. 347.

[4] *Op. cit.* p. 379.   [5] *Geschichte des Terenztextes im Altertum*, 1924; *RE*, V A, 647–9.

account for the features just mentioned he postulates for H., as well as for Plautus and Terence, a single post-Probian edition which already contained many of the flaws marring the whole tradition, and itself preceded the (at least) two copies from which the two types of the lyric titles and variants are derived.

This picture has at least the merit of explaining some features of our tradition. It is however complicated and wholly hypothetical. A full case cannot be made even for the titles since all manuscripts offer the nickname *Ars Poetica* for *Epistula ad Pisones*.[1] I prefer therefore to adhere to the results of our earlier discussion. The (at least) two lines of transmission into which the medieval manuscripts divide are traceable to a certain degree also in antiquity; in some cases they go back a very long way. The ancient copies thus presupposed may have been the ultimate ancestors of our tradition. They may already have been subjected to conflation in antiquity. A painstaking comparison between manuscripts' variants and ancient commentaries and citations may serve to substantiate this picture. But I doubt if it will change it. For the early evidence fails us. A most damaging gap in our knowledge is the relationship between those putative copies and the putative text of Probus. This gap is likely to remain until new evidence accrues.

Opinions diverge also on the impact that the ancient commentaries have made. I briefly mark my own position as far as it relates to the present edition. H. is a hard poet and must have seemed hard to his own countrymen. The amount of scholarly interest appears to have been considerable during the first three centuries A.D., although smaller than in the case of Virgil. The anonymous writers *De personis Horatianis*,[2] Modestus, and Claranus may belong to the first century, the two names are however not definitely identified;[3] Helenius

---

[1] *Prol.* 233, 243 n. 4.
[2] Leo, *Ausgew. Kl. Schr.* II, 392 n. 2, Teuffel, *Gesch. der röm. Lit.* III⁶, 98.
[3] Teuffel, *op. cit.* pp. 206, 339, Schanz–Hosius *Gesch.*⁴, p. 155.

Acro of the early second century made the largest impact. It is a sign of his standing that his name got attached to the later scholia, although they may contain some of his contributions.[1] Terentius Scaurus apparently wrote a large work on the *Ars* in the time of Hadrian; *Q. Terentius Scaurus in commentariis in artem poeticam libro x* can hardly refer to the tenth book of a commentary on the whole of H.[2] But if it does not, the amount of literary material so injected into the tradition concerning the *Ars* should not be underestimated. Porphyrion[3] is the last commentator whose name is known to us. He became 'the commentator' to later scholiasts; the ps.-Acronian scholia introduce a long quotation from him, not by his name but by *commentator* (*A.P.* 120). He compiled his commentary in the third or fourth century, using much old material including probably the genuine Acro. This commentary was excerpted in the work now surviving under Porphyrion's name. These were the excerpts used along with other material in the various forms of the 'Acronian' scholia from the fifth century onwards; the strands are cleanly separated in Keller's edition of *Pseudacronis in Horatium Scholia Vetustiora* and H. J. Botschuyver's editions of the not very useful λφψ scholia and other still later notes. The *Tractatus Vindobonensis* is a Carolingian rehash of one set of ps.-Acronian scholia.[4] 'Commentator Cruquianus' is Cruquius' title for a hotch-potch of comments collected by him largely from the various Blandinian codices. The commentary, unduly neglected by Keller, contains material also from the Oldest Blandinian, which occasionally deserves especial attention, just as Blandinian readings do.[5]

If I have set down the evidence correctly, two conclusions may be allowed. One concerns the material on which the ancient commentators have drawn. The amount of available comment must have been large, its scholarly quality high, if

---

[1] Wessner, *RE*, vii, 2840 ff.   [2] Teuffel, *op. cit.* p. 68.

[3] *Pomponius Porfyrio*, MSS.

[4] Ed. J. Zechmeister, cf. Keller ed. Hor. I[2], lxxix f.

[5] Cf. Leo, *Ausgew. Kl. Schr.* ii, 163.

one may judge from the quality of some extant scholia. On the other hand the amount of comment derived from named older sources is very small. The Porphyrian excerpts name Claranus, Helenius Acro, and Scaurus, once each, all in the *Satires*.[1] And there are two references, again in the *Satires*, to *qui de personis Horatianis scripserunt*.[2] But *alii*, *ueteres*, *antiqui*, etc. appear many times. The ps.-Acronian scholia name Porphyrion (apart from the *commentator* mentioned above), Modestus, and Helenius Acro at the end of the second Life of H., with a special mention of the last named: *Acro omnibus melius*; Acro also at *C*. IV. 9. 37 (Schol. Γ b). The rest of the material is anonymous.

Frequently the scholiasts (as scholiasts will) mix up incompatible versions, suppress badly needed information or argument, and in its place offer facile and insupportable guesses. N. Rudd[3] offers some examples; many more could be adduced. But these drawbacks need not move us to write off Porphyrion and other scholiasts, except 'where they provide corroborative evidence'. Rather the Horatian scholia need to be interpreted in the light of external evidence. At times, when such evidence is available, it shows that the scholiasts had better information than we give them credit for. At other times, therefore, when it is not available, we ought to suspend judgement, and not jump to condemnatory conclusions. H.'s portrait of Canidia may only have overtones hinting at a real person, whether Canidia or no.[4] Yet the Campanian affiliations of Canidia, Pactumeius, and Cupiennius, of which Porphyrion informs us, appear to be more than inferences from H.[5]

The likely competence of the sources and the utilitarian activities of the excerptors pull in different directions. Readers must be prepared to find excellent material—information concerning Neoptolemus of Parium,[6] or Choerilus (357), or

---

[1] I. 8. 25, II. 3. 83, II. 5. 92. [2] *S*. I. 3. 21, 90.
[3] *The Satires of Horace* (1966), 132. [4] Rudd, *op. cit.* 148.
[5] J. H. D'Arms, 'Canidia and Campania', *P*, CXI (1967), 141–5.
[6] Porph. on *A.P.* 1.

Alexandrian θρηνῳδοί (431), who were far removed from the horizon of the excerptors and pretty far from that of Porphyrion himself—cheek by jowl with elementary or nugatory teaching. Information comes in little dollops. Continuity of comment has been eliminated by ruthless excerpting. Any hopes of finding something like the continuity of layout deriving from Neoptolemus' critical *opus*[1] must remain unsatisfied. Life, or at any rate the life of scholiasts, is not like that. The rough and ready cutting up of the *Ars* into commonplaces—*praecepta*, καθολικά, παραγγέλματα[2]—smacks more of contemporary rhetorical teaching than of Hellenistic literary theory. It is most unlikely that even Porphyrion had at hand a copy of a minor Hellenistic treatise. But suppose Porphyrion's commonplaces were in fact Neoptolemus' *praecepta—non quidem omnia sed eminentissima*—even then they tell us very little, because they lack connexion and a viable context. The excerptors had done their job too well. Moreover important information comes from outside the Horatian literature; thus we know of Scaurus' obviously fundamental work not from Porphyrion or the other scholia but from a chance remark of Charisius.[3] The scholia tell us something, but not often what we would like them to tell us.

The other conclusion concerns the Horatian text. Vollmer assumed that the original 'Porphyrion' was a text with a line-by-line commentary. He assumed further that this text was derived, directly or indirectly, from Probus and that in turn Mavortius used *Porphyrionem cum commento*, and so passed him to the Carolingians. This is idle talk; not even the original connexion between an edition and commentary can be proved.[4] The possible ways in which texts of H. and Porphyrion's commentary became associated present difficult and still unsolved problems. Porphyrion cannot be attached to one 'class' of manuscripts. That is shown even by the

[1] B. Otis, *Gnomon*, xxxvi (1964), 266 f.
[2] Porph. on 1, 9, 14, 24, 29, 38, 42, 47, 73, 83, 99, 119, 128, 179.
[3] *GL*, i. 202.   [4] Teuffel, *op. cit.* p. 149.

discussion of Keller,[1] who after all wished to provide mechanical criteria for setting up classes. The textual value of Porphyrion, and to a less degree the ps.-Acronian scholia, lies precisely in the fact that they do not offer the same scatter of readings as our manuscripts.

The early history of the text or scholia, therefore, as far as it is at present known, gives little encouragement to confident assertions about a unified and outstandingly good paradosis. Rather it reinforces earlier arguments against a mechanical division of manuscripts and scholia into classes. Although clearly the quality of the manuscripts differs, the truth may lie, or be hinted at, in the reading of any one of the selected codices or scholia. An editor must present these readings in an unbiased fashion, as Lenchantin and Bo have done and as I attempt to do in a slightly different manner. The opinion that 'the text of H. is one in which, if some points must always remain in uncertainty, the uncertainty is of a very bearable kind'[2] is a myth introduced into Horatian studies by Keller and his successors. It has encouraged a complacent attitude towards the text and none of the recent editions is entirely free from that attitude. In this respect Vollmer's text was superior to that of his successor as Teubner editor; the editorial merits of the text of 1907 have been fairly assessed by Housman.[3]

Keller knew well enough that Bentley was a star of the first order among classical scholars,[4] and his *Horace* incomparable though not exemplary. Yet he thought that by *centum codices* and a mechanical system of classification *ratio et res ipsa* could be put out of business. The same editor complained that the critical work of Greek scholars like Meineke was inapplicable to the soundness of the Horatian paradosis.[5] Peerlkamp (a French editor of the *Ars* complained in 1886) was *un hollandais terrible, qui corrige tout, sabre tout, bouleverse tout* and it is true that his rearrangements of the *A.P.* need not claim any attention today. What must claim attention is that Bentley and,

[1] In 2nd ed. lxxxviii f. and again *Epil.* 796 f. [2] Wickham, 1³, p. 1.
[3] *CR*, xxII (1908), 88–9. [4] *Epil.* 804. [5] *Epil.* 807.

after him, Peerlkamp, Meineke, and Lucian Mueller, have shown the right, the sceptical, attitude towards the short-comings of the manuscripts of Horace. The comparative paucity of textual variants does not invalidate this attitude. On the contrary, the fewer the textual variants, the greater the need for editorial vigilance.

For stylistic and explanatory comment, though rarely for literary assessment, we are better off, as is shown by the long and distinguished line of commentaries from Parrhasius' to Kiessling–Heinze's, and beyond. The commentaries of the Italian Renaissance have been listed below; they have the added advantage of a literary tradition and theory that is close to H.'s own.

7. A Select List of Editions and Commentaries

A full and instructive list to the end of the eighteenth century is found on pp. xlii–cliv of C. W. Mitscherlich's very useful edition of the *Odes* (Leipzig, 1800), thereafter in the biblio-graphies. The following list is arranged chronologically. It is strictly selective, containing only editions, with or without commentary, either of all the poems or the *Epistles* or the *Ars* that, for better or worse, I have found especially relevant to textual criticism or exposition; commentaries on the *Ars* without the text have also been listed.

Texts of the Poems, Commentaries

c. 1470   Editio Princeps, '*nullam editoris, loci, temporis nota-tionem habet*' (Mitscherlich, p. lii). Description *ibid.* Copy in Brit. Mus. I have not listed other early editions from the famous presses, such as the Zarottina, Gryphiana, Aldina, Iuntina, and Stephaniana, all between 1474 and 1513, and later often repeated.

(1476)   I. Aloysius Tuscanus. First edition of *Odes*, *Epodes*, and *Ars Poetica* containing Porphyrion and the ps.-Acronian Scholia; *sine temporis et loci notatione* (Rome).

1482   Christophorus Landinus. Often repeated, Florence, Venice *et al*.

1492   A. Mancinellus. 'Horatius cum quattuor commentariis' [Mancinellus, Acro, Porphyrion, Landinus]. Often repeated, Venice *et al*.

1503   Iodocus Badius Ascensius with commentary: 'Ascensiana'. Often repeated, Paris *et al*.

1561   Dionysius Lambinus. The best text and commentary before Bentley, and still worth consulting. Often repeated, Lyon, Paris *et al*.

1578   Jacobus Cruquius. Complete text and commentary, with 'Commentator Cruquianus' and Blandinian readings; preceded by special editions of *Odes* book IV, *Epodes*, and *Satires*. Several times repeated, Antwerp, Leiden *et al*.

1606   Daniel Heinsius, Antwerp *et al*. Several times repeated, also without commentary.

1608   Laeuinus Torrentius, with commentary and P. Nannius' notes on *Ars Poetica*, Antwerp.

1671   Tanaquil Faber, with brief notes on the *Odes*, Paris.

1681   A. Dacier, text (largely based on T. Faber), French tr. and commentary, from 1733 with N. E. Sanadon's notes, often repeated, Paris.

1691   L. Desprez, *in usum Delphini*, Paris.

1699   P. Burmannus, with I. Rutgersius' *Lectiones Venusinae*, second edition 1713, Utrecht.

1711   R. Bentley, Cambridge, also 1713 and 1728 Amsterdam, etc. *Curae novissimae* in C. Zangemeister's revised reprint, Berlin 1869, II, 170–3.

1721   Alexander Cuningamius (Cunningham); also his *Animadversiones in Rich. Bentleii notas et emendationes*, etc., The Hague.

1752   W. Baxter's text and commentary (first 1701), re-edited by J. M. Gesner, second edition 1772, Leipzig.

1794   G. Wakefield, 2 vols, London.

1803   F. G. Doering, revised 1838, Oxford.

1811   C. Fea, Rome. Second edition by F. H. Bothe, 2 vols, Heidelberg 1827.

1834   (text) A. Meineke, second edition 1854, Berlin.

1837–8   I. G. Orelli, 2 vols, third edition by J. G. Baiter, 1850–2, Zürich; I⁴ ed. G. Hirschfelder, 1886; II⁴ ed. W. Mewes, 1892, Berlin.

1843   G. Dillenburger, several times repeated, seventh edition 1881, Bonn.

1853   A. J. Macleane, London.

1856–7   F. Ritter, 2 vols, Leipzig.

1864–9   (text) O. Keller and A. Holder, 2 vols, Leipzig; ed. min. 1888; I² ed. O. Keller, Leipzig 1909, II⁴ ed. O. Keller et amici, Jena 1925; O. Keller, *Epilegomena*, Leipzig, 1879–80.

1874, 1891   E. C. Wickham, 2 vols (I³ 1891), Oxford.

1880–3   H. Schütz, 3 vols (I² 1880), Berlin.

1884–9   A. Kiessling, 3 vols, Berlin; re-edited by R. Heinze (I⁶ 1916, I⁷ cur. A. Mauersberger, 1930, II⁵ 1921, III⁴ 1914); reprinted with R. Burck's *Nachwort und bibliog. Nachträge*.

1894 (text) J. Gow, in Postgate's *Corpus Poetarum Latinorum*, I, London.

1900 (text)   E. C. Wickham in *Script. Class. Bibl. Oxon.*, second edition by H. W. Garrod, 1912, Oxford.

1907 (text)   F. Vollmer, second edition 1912, Teubner, Leipzig.

1927–34   F. Villeneuve, Assoc. G. Budé, 3 vols with French tr.; reprinted, Paris.

1939, also 1950, 1959 (text) F. Klingner, Teubner, Leipzig.

1945 (text)   M. Lenchantin de Gubernatis, 2 vols, Paravia, Turin.

1957–9   *id.*, I² curante D. Bo, II ed. D. Bo, *ibid.*

Special Commentaries on the 'Ars Poetica'

I begin with the group of commentaries published during the Italian Renaissance, cf. *Prol.* p. 79 n. 1. Lambinus acknowledged Grifolus, Achilles Statius, and Luisinus. Collected editions appeared in 1555 and later; reprints also were

published. I omit several earlier commentaries (among them
Ars Poetica cum notis Fr. Petrarchae, sine loco, 1494), which I have
not seen. I omit also some of the works published after 1590.

1531   A. Ianus Parrhasius, Naples.

1539   Iodocus Willichius, Strasbourg.

1546   F. Philippus Pedimontius, Venice.

F. Robortellus, *Paraphrasis,* with Paccius' text and
Latin tr. of Aristotle's *Poetics,* and his own commentary on
the *Poetics,* Florence.

1550   V. Madius, with Paccius (see preceding entry), and
Madius' own commentary on Aristotle's *Poetics,* Venice.

I. Grifolus, Florence.

1553   J. de Nores, Venice.

Achilles Statius, Antwerp.

1554   F. Luisinus, Venice.

1555   G. Fabricius. Cologne.

1564   J. Sambucus, Antwerp.

1576   Aldus Manutius, Paulli f., Venice.

1757   (R. Hurd) *Epistolae ad Pisones et Augustum:* With an
English Commentary, etc. 2 vols, third edition, Cambridge.

1771   C. Batteux, *Les quatre Poétiques d'Aristote, d'Horace, de
Vida, de Despréaux,* with French tr., 2 vols.

1782   C. M. Wieland, *Hor. Briefe,* with Ger. tr., Dessau,
repeated.

1841   B. Gonod, Clermont-Ferrand.

1845   P. Hofman Peerlkamp, Leiden.

1856   L. Doederlein, *Episteln,* 2 vols with Ger. tr., Leipzig.

1869   O. Ribbeck, *Episteln,* etc., Berlin.

1885   A. S. Wilkins, *Epistles,* London, often reprinted.

1886   M. Albert, Paris.

1891, 1893   L. Mueller, *Sat., Ep.,* 2 vols, Vienna.

1911, 1912   P. Lejay, *Sat.* ed. maior; *Sat., Ep.* and *A.P.,*
ed. min. in Horace, *Œuvres,* ed. F. Plessis and P. Lejay, Paris.

1930   A. Rostagni, Turin, reprinted.

1932   O. Immisch, commentary without Latin text (*P,*
Supp. xxiv, 3), Leipzig, reprinted.

1939 W. Steidle, commentary on *A.P.* 1–294, in *Studien zur Ars Poetica des H.*, Würzburg, reprinted.

1941 F. Cupaiuolo, Naples.

1951 L. Herrmann, ed. and French tr., Coll. Latomus, vii, Brussels.

1958 W. Stegen, *Les Ép. littéraires*, Namur.

1964 E. Pasoli, with *Ep.* book ii, Bologna.

8. Excerpta ex codicibus Blandiniis Cruquiana
Ed. Hor. 1597

[Bland. = Blandinius, Busl. = cod. Buslidianus e bibliotheca Collegii Trilinguis Louaniensis a J. Buslidio conditi, Diu. uel Carr. = codex Diuaei uel Carrionis, Bentlei Zulichemianus, nunc Leidensis 127 A, Mart. = cod. Matthaei Martinii, Sil. = cod. Gualteri Siluii, Tons. = cod. e bibliotheca Tonsana.]

A.P. 7, p. 639[b] Cru. *aegri.* vnus cod. Bland. habet *aegris*, sed arbitror s litteram ei adrepsisse à τῷ somnia proxime sequenti, non enim videtur ei aptanda. reliqui lib. scripti sequuntur lectionem vulgatam.

49, p. 640[a] *rerum &.* sic habēt omnes scripti cod.

53, *ibid. Graeco fonte cadent*...Omnes Bland. cum Busl. & Sil. habent, cadent, sed Tons. & Mart. cadūt. Diu. cadant.

54, *ibid. dabit.* sic omnes lib. scripti. sed Bland. habent dabit, pro dedit, adnotatū.

59, *ibid. producere.* sic est in omnibus script. non etiā procudere, ut aliqui se inuenisse aiunt.

72, p. 640[b] *& ius.* sic omnes scrip. lib. non autem vis, vt vulgati aliqui.

92, *ibid. sortita decenter.* Blād. antiquiss. cum alio habet decentem.

114, *ibid. diuósne loquatur, an heros.* hic versiculus variè legitur, vt videre est apud Glareanum, & Lambinum, & alios: mihi certè probātur codices Bland. ex quibus duo habent, (p. 641[a]) diuósne (o pro u, vt saepius in scriptis antiquis) loquatur an heros, tertius, diuúsne loquatur an heros. Sed non

47

celabo lectorem, me ante annos non paucos, in bibliotheca Tonsana offendisse codicem scriptū, cui titulus erat Alphabetatum ex scriptis Horatij, Catonis & Theodoli, praeter alias nugas; qui satis videbatur antiquus, ubi legi hunc de quo agimus versum sic scriptū apertè: Intererit multum Dauúsne loquatur an haeres. Dispiciat lector, haeres ne pro herili filio positus credi possit, cui seruus erat Dauus.

117, p. 641ᵃ *virentis agelli.* vnus Bland. habet vigentis.

154, p. 641ᵇ *si plausoris.* Blād. uetust. habet plosoris.

161, *ibid. imberbus iuuenis.* sic habet cod. Blād. antiq. quem secutus sum ex auctoritate Sosipat. Carisij lib. 1. instit. Gramm. Imberbi autem dicuntur, inquit, non imberbes: sic enim & Varro De actionibus scenicis 5. Imberbi iuuenes. sic & Cicero imberbum protulit, nō imberbē. Ex Kalendis Ianuariis de lege agraria, imberba iuuentute. Titus historiarum 18 imberbes vulgariter. haec Caris.

193, p. 642ᵃ. Omnes quos vidi codices scriptos habēt, actoris parteis: à quibus nō discessi, certò persuasus de lectionis veritate, &c.

196, p. 642ᵇ *consilietur amicè.* sic legitur per s litteram in omnibus scriptis, quę secutus sum.

197, *ibid. peccare timent.* codex Busl. habet, pacare. quae genuina mihi videtur lectio, vt ei respondeat, & regat iratos. pro eo quod est, studeat dolenteis perturbatosq. placare, solari.

202, *ibid. vincta.* variant hic cod. scripti: duo Blād. habent cū Diu. & Tons. iuncta. Bland. antiq. cum aliis omnibus, legūt, vincta. quibus assentior...

203, *ibid. pauco.* Bland. duo habent paruo.

214, p. 643ᵃ *sic.* vnus cod. Bland. in hoc & sequēti versu, pro sic, habet, hic.

237, p. 643ᵇ *Dauusne loquat. & audax Py.* sic legitur in cod. Bland. antiq. & altero, vbi manifeste τὸ &, erasum est supraq́. positum, an.

249, p. 644ᵃ *fricti ciceris.* sic in omnibus scriptis, nō autē fracti, ut habēt vulgata. vide adagium, Ciceris emtor.

266–7, *ibid. tutus & intra spē veniae cautus.* miror Lambinum contra omnium scriptorum atq. adeò vulgatorum codicum cōsensum legere, extra spem veniae: cùm nihil velit Horatius aliud quam non ita se scripturum insipienter, ut erroris veniam poscat, sed tutiùs scribat, artisq́. praecepta seruet diligenti studio: nam intra spem veniae esse, est ad spem veniae non peruenire, nec quicquā velle scribere venia dignū: quod faciunt indocti stultiq́. poëtae, qui potius quàm non scribant, venia dignos se haberi malunt. hoc autem est quod notat Horatius, artis quidem peritiam hoc praestare solùm posse, vt venia non sit opus, sed eam per se non mereri laudem, quam natura maior, mentisq́. diuinior quidā instinctus parit perficitq́ue, teste Platone. De hoc autē loquendi genere, intra spem veniae cautus, lege Agelliū lib. 12, cap. 13.

270, *ibid. at vestri proaui.* sic habent scripta quae legi omnia, non etiam nostri, vt est in vulgatis olim.

294, p. 644^b *praesectum.* sic legūt duo cod. Bland. vnus cum antiq.

302, p. 645^a *purgor bili.* hanc lectionem reposui ex tribus Commentariis scriptis Bland. in quibus expressè legitur, purgor bilem: aliter, purgor bilibus, τò bilibus vertendo, bili.

318, *ibid. viuas hinc ducere.* desumere orationem. viuas legitur in omnibus scriptis, non veras: quae secutus sum.

319, *ibid. speciosa locis.* sic 4. Bland. sed Busl. speciosa iocis memorataq́ue rectè. reliqui speciosa iocis.

328, *ibid. eu.* sic Busl. & Blād. 4, non hem uel heus.

330, *ibid. an haec aerugo.* sic Blād. vetust. cum duobus aliis in quib. n littera erasa, & t posita.

336, p. 645^b *percipiant animi dociles.* Bland. vnus habet, percipiant animo dociles.

345, *ibid. liber Sosis.* sic 4 Bland. per syncopen pro Sosiis.

349, *ibid. persaepe remutit acutum.* sic scriptū est in vno Bland. Tonsa. Siluioq́. codicibus, quam vt genuinam dictionem reposui, pro eo quod Graecè dicitur ἀνατρίʒειν, pipire voce à pullis ficta, stridere.

350, *ibid. quodcumque minab.* Tons. lib. habet quocumque.

353, *ibid.*   *quid ergo est.* sic est in omnibus scriptis; iccirco τὸ est, omittere nolui.

360, *ibid.*   *verùm operi longo.* sic scripta omnia. non damno tamen vulgarem lectionem.

362, *ibid.*   *te capiat.* sic Bland. codices.

371, *ibid.*   *nec scit.* sic Bland. antiq. cum alio, sed reliqui cum duobus aliis Bland. habent, nescit. deligat lector.

378, *ibid.*   *summo decessit.* sic Bland. decedere à summo & ad imum vergere, est uix vllo esse numero.

385, *ibid.*   *dices faciésue.* sic scripta omnia: non etiam faciesque, vt vulgata quaedam.

393, p. 646ª   *rabidosq́; leon.* sic habent omnes lib. scripti, non rapidos, vt vulgati.

394, *ibid.*   *conditor vrbis.* sic habent omnia scripta, à quibus dissentire nolui, tametsi non improbem lectionem vulgatam.

422, p. 646ᵇ   *rectè qui.* sic cod. Busl.

426, *ibid.*   *voles cui.* Bland. antiq. habet quoi, antiquo more.

457, *ibid.*   *hic dum sublimis.* sic legitur in scriptis nostris omnibus, non autem sublimeis, ut in vulgatis.

'DE ARTE POETICA'

CONSPECTUS SIGLORUM

a   = Ambrosianus O 136, s. ix–x, u. supra p. 2.
B   = Bernensis 363, s. ix, u. supra pp. 3–4.
C/E   = Monacensis Latinus 14685, s. xi, u. supra pp. 4–6.
K   = St Claude 2 (cod. S. Eugendi), s. xi, u. supra pp. 6–7.
R   = Vaticanus Reginae 1703, s. ix, u. supra pp. 7–8.
V   = Lectiones Blandinii Vetustissimi, u. supra pp. 8–9
        atque Excerpta Cruquiana supra pp. 47–50.

δ   = Harleianus 2725, s. ix, u. supra pp. 9–10.
π   = Parisinus 10310, s. ix–x, u. supra p. 10.

λ   = Parisinus 7972, s. ix–x, u. supra p. 10.
l   = Leidensis Latinus 28, s. ix, u. supra pp. 10–11.

φ   = Parisinus 7974, s. x, u. supra p. 11.
ψ   = Parisinus 7971, s. x, u. supra p. 11.

Raro adhibentur
Bland.   = Lectiones Blandiniorum praeter V.
Flor. Nostr. = Florilegium Nostradamense, s. xiii, u. Hor.
               ed.[1] Keller–Holder, vol. ii, p. xiii.
M   = Mellicensis 177, s. xi.
u   = Parisiensis 7973, s. ix–x.
               Parisiensis 8212, s. xii.
ς   = codices recentiores.

Pap. Haw. 24 = Papyrus Flinders Petrie, Hawara 24, textus
               tertius; ad *A.P.* 78 referre uoluit J. Mallon;
               S. Dow, *JRS*, lviii (1968), 62, papyrum s. i
               scriptum esse putat.

Porph.   = Porphyrio, i.e. siue lectiones siue exposi-
              tiones codicis V = Vat. lat. 3314, olim
              Ursini, s. ix, uel codd. M = Monacensis
              lat. 181, s. x, P = Parisinus 7988, s. xv. al.;
              ed. A. Holder, 1894.
Schol.   = Scholiorum quae uocantur Pseudacronis
              siue lectiones siue expositiones; ed. O. Keller,
              II, 1904.
Comm. Cruq. = Commentator Cruquianus, u. supra p. 39.
Tract. Vind. = Tractatus Vindobonensis, s. xi, u. supra
              p. 39.

cett.   = ceteri codices selecti
codd.   = codices selecti et supra citati
codd. uett. = codices ueteres selecti
corr.   = correctum uel sim.
n.l.   = non liquet
pr.   = prius
uar., uar.l. = uaria lectio

Q. HORATI FLACCI
QVI VVLGO VOCATVR LIBER
DE ARTE POETICA

Humano capiti ceruicem pictor equinam
iungere si uelit, et uarias inducere plumas
undique collatis membris, ut turpiter atrum
desinat in piscem mulier formosa superne,
spectatum admissi risum teneatis, amici?   5
credite, Pisones, isti tabulae fore librum
persimilem cuius, uelut aegri somnia, uanae
fingentur species, ut nec pes nec caput uni
reddatur formae. 'pictoribus atque poetis
quidlibet audendi semper fuit aequa potestas.'   10
scimus, et hanc ueniam petimusque damusque uicissim;
sed non ut placidis coeant immitia, non ut
serpentes auibus geminentur, tigribus agni.
     inceptis grauibus plerumque et magna professis
purpureus, late qui splendeat, unus et alter   15
adsuitur pannus, cum lucus et ara Dianae
et properantis aquae per amoenos ambitus agros,

Poetica Oratii incipit *B* (*praecedit Carmen Saeculare*)
·L· Flacci Horatii liber carminum IIII explicit. Incipit de arte poetica *C* (*reuera
Carmen Saeculare praecedit, cf. supra p.* 14)
     Quinti (Q. *aφ, om.* δ) (H)oratii Flacci carminum liber IIII explicit. Incipit de
arte poetica *a R* δ φ
     Explicit Flacci Horatii quartus liber carminum. Incipit quintus de arte poetriae π
     Quinti Horatii Flacci carminum liber IIII explicit. Incipit eiusdem de arte poetica
liber *l ψ sim.* λ
     cf. Feliciter Porfyrionis commentum in Horati Flacci librum IIII explicit. Incipit
eiusdem carmen de arte poetica *Porph.*
     De ordine poematum u. supra p. 14; *post epistulas artem poeticam H. Stephanus posuit.*

     2 *om. B*   inducere] induere *R*[1]   **4** piscem] pistrim (*uel* pristim) ς
J. F. Gronouius   **5** admissi (amm-)] admisi (amm-) *KR*[1]   missi *BC*   **5–6** *de
distinct. u. comm.*   **6** pisones] -is δπ λ*l* φψ   **7** aegri *a post ras. CKR post ras.*
V δπ λ*l* φψ   aegris *a pr. BR pr*(?)' *Schol.*   **8** fingentur] finguntur ψ *corr. Tract.
Vind.* fingenter δ *pr.* finguentur *K* funguntur *B*   **10** quidlibet] quodlibet
π *pr. lemma Porph.* quilibet *K*(?)   quaelibet *Ven. Fort. C.* v. 6 *praef.* 7   **17** et]

aut flumen Rhenum aut pluuius describitur arcus.
sed nunc non erat his locus. et fortasse cupressum
scis simulare. quid hoc, si fractis enatat exspes   20
nauibus aere dato qui pingitur? amphora coepit
institui; currente rota cur urceus exit?
denique sit quiduis, simplex dumtaxat et unum.

   maxima pars uatum, pater et iuuenes patre digni,
decipimur specie recti. breuis esse laboro,   25
obscurus fio; sectantem leuia nerui
deficiunt animique; professus grandia turget;
serpit humi tutus nimium timidusque procellae;
qui uariare cupit rem prodigialiter unam,
delphinum siluis appingit, fluctibus aprum: 30
in uitium ducit culpae fuga, si caret arte.

   Aemilium circa ludum faber unus et ungues
exprimet et molles imitabitur aere capillos,
infelix operis summa, quia ponere totum
nesciet. hunc ego me, si quid componere curem,   35
non magis esse uelim quam naso uiuere prauo,
spectandum nigris oculis nigroque capillo.

   sumite materiam uestris, qui scribitis, aequam
uiribus, et uersate diu, quid ferre recusent,
quid ualeant umeri. cui lecta potenter erit res,   40
nec facundia deseret hunc nec lucidus ordo.

   ordinis haec uirtus erit et uenus, aut ego fallor,
ut iam nunc dicat iam nunc debentia dici,
pleraque differat et praesens in tempus omittat.

   in uerbis etiam tenuis cautusque serendis   46

aut ⌐   **18** aut] et R^1 pluuius $aBCKR^1$ δ^2 $\lambda^2 l^2$ $\varphi^2 \psi^2$ fluuius $\delta^1 \pi$ $\lambda^1 l^1$ $\varphi^1 \psi^1$ *Porph. C.* iv. 4. 38   **19** nunc non] non nunc *B*   nec non *Flor. Nostr.* **20** ex(s)pes] expers λ *uar. l* π φψ   **23** sit *om. B*   quiduis $K \psi^2$ quoduis *uel* quod uis *cett.*   **26** leuia] lenia ⌐   **32** unus ⌐ *Schol. Ioann. Saresber. Pol.* vi *Prologus* imus *codd. uett. Porph.*   **35** ego me] egomet δ^1 φ *ante ras.* ψ *ante ras.* **36** naso uiuere prauo (paruo)] prauo (paruo) uiuere naso ⌐ *edd. plur. ante Bentleium*   prauo] praue R^2 paruo δ *pr.* π *pr.* λ *pr.*   torto ⌐   **37** spectandum] spectatum ⌐   -que] -ue *BCK*(?)   **38** materiam] Iā m̄r̄ *B* (*supra p.* 23) materiem *edd. aliquot*   **40** potenter] pudenter ⌐   **42** aut *aC post ras. R* $\delta^2 \pi$ ψ^2 *Porph. Schol.* (*aud* $\lambda^2 l^2$)   haut *uel* haud *cett.*   **43** ut] aut $\delta^1 \pi^1$ λ^1 $\varphi^1 \psi^1$ **46–5** *sic transpos. Bentley*

hoc amet, hoc spernat promissi carminis auctor.   45
dixeris egregie notum si callida uerbum
reddiderit iunctura nouum. si forte necesse est
indiciis monstrare recentibus abdita rerum,
fingere cinctutis non exaudita Cethegis   50
continget, dabiturque licentia sumpta pudenter;
et noua fictaque nuper habebunt uerba fidem, si
Graeco fonte cadent parce detorta. quid autem
Caecilio Plautoque dabit Romanus ademptum
Vergilio Varioque? ego cur, acquirere pauca   55
si possum, inuideor, cum lingua Catonis et Enni
sermonem patrium ditauerit et noua rerum
nomina protulerit? licuit semperque licebit
signatum praesente nota producere nomen.

    ut siluae foliis †pronos† mutantur in annos,   60
prima cadunt   61*a*
                ita uerborum uetus interit aetas,   61*b*
et iuuenum ritu florent modo nata uigentque.
debemur morti nos nostraque; siue receptus
terra Neptunus classes aquilonibus arcet,
†regis† opus, sterilisue †diu palus† aptaque remis   65
uicinas urbes alit et graue sentit aratrum,
seu cursum mutauit iniquum frugibus amnis
doctus iter melius, mortalia facta peribunt,

---

45 spernat] spernet *BC*   **47** dixeris] dixerit *B*   **47–53** *de distinct. u. comm.*
48 est *om. a*[1]   **49** rerum *BCKR*   rerum et *aV* δπ λ*l* φψ   **52** si] et si *Madvig*
seu *L. Mueller*   **53** cadent *BC*[1]*KRV* δ[1]π λ*l* φψ   cadant *aC*[2] δ[2] ς *Seru. Aen.*
vi. 34   cadunt *Bland. excepto V*   parce] arte (*super* t *scr.* c) *B*   **54** ademptum] adeptum *BC*   **55** uario] uaro *a post ras.* δπ *post ras.* λ*l* φψ   **56** possum]
possim ς   **59** producere] procudere *Ald.* 1501 *alii*   nomen] nummum
Luisinus alii   **60** siluae foliis] foliis silue *Flor. Nostr.*   folia in siluis *Diom. GL,*
I. 400. 11   siluae flores *Valerius in Excerptis cod. Lauant. GL,* v. 326. 4   pronos
codd., Diom. Excerpta cod. Lauant.   priuos *Bentley fort. recte*   **61** lacunam *indic.*
Ribbeck alii   ita *codd., excerpta cod. Lauant. GL, loc. cit.*   ita et *Diom. GL, loc. cit.*
62 uigent] iungent *R*   uirent ς   **63** debemur *aCKR* δπ λ*l* φψ *Porph. Schol.*
Prisc. GL, II. 268. 1 *pars codd., Seru. Aen.* IX. 95   debemus *B Prisc. GL, ibid.*
pars codd.   **65** regis opus *codd. Prisc. GL,* vi. 268. 3   regium opus *Peerlkamp*
dubitanter, Meineke, fort. recte   sterilisue *aR* δπ   sterilisque *BCK* λ*l* φψ *Porph.*
Prisc. Seru. Aen. II. 69, vi. 107 *Seru. Hon. GL,* IV. 452. 32 *Beda GL,* vii. 238. 1   diu
palus] palus prius *Bentley*   palus diu *J. M. Gesner*   palus dudum *Sanadon, alii aliter*
68 facta] cuncta ς   saecla *Peerlkamp*

nedum sermonum stet honos et gratia uiuax.
multa renascentur quae iam cecidere, cadentque   70
quae nunc sunt in honore uocabula, si uolet usus,
quem penes arbitrium est et ius et norma loquendi.

  res gestae regumque ducumque et tristia bella
quo scribi possent numero, monstrauit Homerus.
uersibus impariter iunctis querimonia primum,   75
post etiam inclusa est uoti sententia compos;
quis tamen exiguos elegos emiserit auctor,
grammatici certant et adhuc sub iudice lis est.
Archilochum proprio rabies armauit iambo;
hunc socci cepere pedem grandesque coturni   80
alternis aptum sermonibus et populares
uincentem strepitus et natum rebus agendis.
Musa dedit fidibus diuos puerosque deorum
et pugilem uictorem et equum certamine primum
et iuuenum curas et libera uina referre.   85
descriptas seruare uices operumque colores
cur ego si nequeo ignoroque poeta salutor?
cur nescire pudens praue quam discere malo?

  uersibus exponi tragicis res comica non uult;
indignatur item priuatis ac prope socco   90
dignis carminibus narrari cena Thyestae.
singula quaeque locum teneant sortita decentem.
interdum tamen et uocem comoedia tollit,
iratusque Chremes tumido delitigat ore
et tragicus plerumque dolet sermone pedestri,   95
Telephus et Peleus cum, pauper et exsul, uterque
proicit ampullas et sesquipedalia uerba,
si curat cor spectantis tetigisse querella.

69 nedum sermonum] sermonum haud *Ald.* 1501   **75** primum] prima *Sacerd.*
GL, VI. 510. 3   **76** inclusa est *a*(?)*BCKR*² δ² φ²ψ² *Sacerd. GL*, VI. 510. 4 iunctis
(*ex* 75 *repet.*) λl π² φ¹(?) ψ¹ (?)   iunctus *R*¹π¹   iuncta est ς   **78** grammatici]
gramma[tici] *Pap. Haw.* 24 *si quidem recte ad hunc locum refertur*   **86** descriptas]
di- *Lambinus in comm., alii*   **92** del. *Lehrs Ribbeck, fort. recte*   decentem *BKR*¹(?)*V*
ducem *C*¹(?) ducent̆ *C*² decenter *cett.*   **94** delitigat] desaeuiet *Hier. Ep.* 54. 2. 1
96 *commate ante* pauper *et post* exsul *distinxi, Marcilium Peerlkampium alios secutus*
98 curat] curas ς

non satis est pulchra esse poemata; dulcia sunto,
et quocumque uolent animum auditoris agunto.　　　100
ut ridentibus arrident, ita flentibus adflent
humani uultus. si uis me flere, dolendum est
primum ipsi tibi; tum tua me infortunia laedent,
Telephe uel Peleu; male si mandata loqueris
aut dormitabo aut ridebo. tristia maestum　　　105
uultum uerba decent, iratum plena minarum,
ludentem lasciua, seuerum seria dictu.
format enim natura prius nos intus ad omnem
fortunarum habitum; iuuat aut impellit ad iram
aut ad humum maerore graui deducit et angit;　　　110
post effert animi motus interprete lingua.
si dicentis erunt fortunis absona dicta,
Romani tollent equites peditesque cachinnum.

　　intererit multum diuusne loquatur an heros,
maturusne senex an adhuc florente iuuenta　　　115
feruidus, et matrona potens an sedula nutrix,
mercatorne uagus cultorne uirentis agelli,
Colchus an Assyrius, Thebis nutritus an Argis.

　　aut famam sequere aut sibi conuenientia finge,
scriptor. †honoratum† si forte reponis Achillem,　　　120
impiger, iracundus, inexorabilis, acer,
iura neget sibi nata, nihil non arroget armis.
sit Medea ferox inuictaque, flebilis Ino,
perfidus Ixion, Io uaga, tristis Orestes.
si quid inexpertum scaenae committis et audes　　　125
personam formare nouam, seruetur ad imum
qualis ab incepto processerit, et sibi constet.

100 uolent *aBCK Schol. Seru. Aen.* IV. 415　　uolunt *R in ras.* δπ λ*l* φψ
101 adflent *a grammatico quodam anonymo bibl. Vigorniensis obiter citatum, Piccartus Marcilius Faber Bentley alii*　　adflant ς *teste Marcilio*　　adsunt (ass-) *codd. uett.*　　adsint (ass-) ς　　　　**103** tum *BCK*　　tunc *aR* δπ λ*l* φψ *Porph. lemm.*　　　**111** effert (exf-) (-ret *B*) *aCKR*² φ²ψ² *Schol.* (efferre *Flor. Nostr.*)　et certi *R*¹(?) λ*l* π φ¹ψ¹
114 diuus *a K*² δπ λ*l* φ¹ψ¹ *Porph.*　diuos *BCR*¹　da(u)us *K*¹ *R*⁹ φ²uar.ψ² *Seru. interpol. Aen.* XII. 18　dauos *R*²　　**116** et] an ς　aut *Ald.* 1501 *Iunt.* 1503　　**117** uirentis] uigentis *R*¹ δπ λ*l* φψ　　　　**119–20** finge, | scriptor] *de distinct. u. comm.*
120 honoratum] Homereum *uel* Homeriacum *Bentley, alii alia*

difficile est proprie communia dicere; tuque
rectius Iliacum carmen deducis in actus
quam si proferres ignota indictaque primus.   130
    publica materies priuati iuris erit, si
non circa uilem patulumque moraberis orbem,
nec uerbo uerbum curabis reddere fidus
interpres, nec desilies imitator in artum,
unde pedem proferre pudor uetet aut operis lex,   135
nec sic incipies ut scriptor cyclicus olim:
'fortunam Priami cantabo et nobile bellum.'
quid dignum tanto feret hic promissor hiatu?
parturient montes, nascetur ridiculus mus.
quanto rectius hic qui nil molitur inepte: 140
'dic mihi, Musa, uirum, captae post tempora Troiae
qui mores hominum multorum uidit et urbes.'
non fumum ex fulgore, sed ex fumo dare lucem
cogitat, ut speciosa dehinc miracula promat,
Antiphaten Scyllamque et cum Cyclope Charybdin.   145
nec reditum Diomedis ab interitu Meleagri,
nec gemino bellum Troianum orditur ab ouo;
semper ad euentum festinat et in medias res
non secus ac notas auditorem rapit, et quae
desperat tractata nitescere posse, relinquit,   150
atque ita mentitur, sic ueris falsa remiscet,
primo ne medium, medio ne discrepet imum.
    tu quid ego et populus mecum desideret audi.
si plosoris eges aulaea manentis et usque

129 deducis] diducis *uel* producis 𝔰   **132–7** *ex parte euanuerunt in* C,
135–7 *in initio tantum uersuum*   **133** uerbo uerbum] -um -o *CR Schol.*
Hier. Ep. 57. 5. 5 *pars codicum Seru. Aen.* I. 223, XI. I   **134** desilies] disilies *B*
dissilies *C*   **136** cyclicus (cic-)] ciclius *uel* cilicus codd. dett. 𝔰   **137** cantabo et]
cantarat *B*   nobile bellum] nobile regnum *Flor. Nostr. uar.*   **139** parturi-
ent] -iunt 𝔰 *Hier. Adu. Iouin.* I. I   **141** captae post] p. c. *C*   post *in*
ras. R   tempora] m(o)enia 𝔰 *Auson. Periocha Odyss.* I (p. 392. 2 *Peiper*) funera 𝔰
147 nec] et *Hier. Ep.* 10. 2. I   **152** imum] unum *B*   **153–5** *de distinct. u.*
comm.   **154** plosoris *aBCKR¹V* δ² *Porph.* plusoris (*uel* plus oris) δ¹ *R²* π
λ*l*¹ φ¹ψ   plausoris λ *uar. l.²* φ² 𝔰 *cf. Schol.* 'plosoris et plausoris legitur'   plausori

sessuri donec cantor 'uos plaudite' dicat,   155
aetatis cuiusque notandi sunt tibi mores,
mobilibusque decor naturis dandus et annis.
reddere qui uoces iam scit puer et pede certo
signat humum, gestit paribus colludere, et iram
concipit ac ponit temere et mutatur in horas.   160
imberbis iuuenis, tandem custode remoto,
gaudet equis canibusque et aprici gramine campi,
cereus in uitium flecti, monitoribus asper,
utilium tardus prouisor, prodigus aeris,
sublimis cupidusque et amata relinquere pernix.   165
conuersis studiis aetas animusque uirilis
quaerit opes et amicitias, inseruit honori,
commisisse cauet quod mox mutare laboret.
multa senem circumueniunt incommoda, uel quod
quaerit et inuentis miser abstinet ac timet uti   170
uel quod res omnes timide gelideque ministrat,
dilator, †spe longus†, iners, ⟨p⟩auidusque futuri,
difficilis, querulus, laudator temporis acti
se puero, castigator censorque minorum.
multa ferunt anni uenientes commoda secum,   175
multa recedentes adimunt. ne forte seniles
mandentur iuueni partes pueroque uiriles:
semper in adiunctis aeuoque morabimur aptis.
    aut agitur res in scaenis aut acta refertur.
segnius irritant animos demissa per aurem,   180
quam quae sunt oculis subiecta fidelibus et quae
ipse sibi tradit spectator. non tamen intus
digna geri promes in scaenam, multaque tolles

B^2 *superscr.*   **157** mobilibusque] nob- *B*   naturis] mat- ς   **158** certo] *n.l.*
C   **160** concipit *ed. Zarottina* (1474)   colligit (con-) *codd. Schol.*   **161** imberbis (in-) *aBKR* δπ λl φψ   imberbus (in-) *C in ras. V, cf. Schol.* 'inberbus
et inberbis sicut inermus et inermis'   **168–70** *om. et in marg. add.* δ
168 mox mutare] permutare δπ² φψ   mutare π¹   post mutare ς   mox mutare
uel mox munire ς   **170** ac timet *om.* C^1 et timet C^2 *Schol. S.* I. I. 42   **171** timide gelideque] gelide timideque *Flor. Nostr.*   **172** spe longus] spe tardus
Bentley, alii alia   pauidusque *Bentley*   auidusque *codd.*   **175–7** *del. Lehrs*   **178** *del.*
Ribbeck fort. recte   morabimur *aK* λ *corr.* ς   *Schol. in textu*   morabitur *BR* δπ λl φψ

61

ex oculis quae mox narret facundia praesens:
ne pueros coram populo Medea trucidet,   185
aut humana palam coquat exta nefarius Atreus,
aut in auem Procne uertatur, Cadmus in anguem.

Kent

quodcumque ostendis mihi sic, incredulus odi.

neue minor neu sit quinto productior actu
fabula, quae posci uult et spectanda reposci.   190
nec deus intersit, nisi dignus uindice nodus
inciderit; nec quarta loqui persona laboret.

actoris partes chorus officiumque uirile
defendat, neu quid medios intercinat actus
quod non proposito conducat et haereat apte.   195
ille bonis faueatque et consilietur amice,
et regat iratos et amet †peccare timentes†;
ille dapes laudet mensae breuis, ille salubrem
iustitiam legesque et apertis otia portis;
ille tegat commissa, deosque precctur et oret,   200
ut redeat miseris, abeat fortuna superbis.

tibia non ut nunc orichalco uincta tubaeque
aemula, sed tenuis simplexque foramine pauco
adspirare et adesse choris erat utilis atque
nondum spissa nimis complere sedilia flatu;   205
quo sane populus numerabilis, utpote paruus,
et frugi castusque uerecundusque coibat.

postquam coepit agros extendere uictor et urbem
latior amplecti murus uinoque diurno
placari Genius festis impune diebus,   210

(*scriptura euanuit in C*) Schol. *in lemm.* **184** *de distinct. u. comm.* **185** ne] nec
Schol. ς neu ς **190** uult (uolt)] uolet *Porph.* spectanda *aCR* π² φψ *post ras.*
Porph. exspectanda *BK* ψ *in ras.* spectata δπ¹ λl ς reposci *anonymi ap. Lambinum,*
alii reponi *codd. Porph. Schol.* **192** nec] ne φ *Diom. codd. pl. GL,* 1. 491. 1
196 amice] amici π φ¹ψ¹ amicis *R* λl *Schol.* **197** peccare timentes *corruptum*
uidetur peccare *aBCKR* δ²π λ φψ *Schol.* pecare δ¹ς paccare *l*¹ pacare ς ti-
mentes(-is)] tumentes ς **202** non ut *om. B* nunc orichalco] non o. *C*¹
Porph. codd. praeter P nunc oric(h)alc(h)o *aC²KR* δπ λl φψ *Porph. cod. P* nunc
cori- *B* (auri *super* ori *scr.*) *C*¹ uincta *aBRV* δ λl φψ ς *Porph.* iuncta *C(?)K* π ς
Schol. cincta *Reinach* **203** pauco *aBCK* δ²π¹ *Porph. Schol.* paruo *R* δ¹π² λl φψ
parco *Richards; an raro?* **206** quo] quod *B* **207** castus] catus φψ¹ cautus ψ²
208 urbem ς urbes *codd. uett.*

accessit numerisque modisque licentia maior.
indoctus quid enim saperet liberque laborum
rusticus urbano confusus, turpis honesto?
sic priscae motumque et luxuriem addidit arti
tibicen traxitque uagus per pulpita uestem;   215
sic etiam fidibus uoces creuere seueris,
et tulit eloquium insolitum facundia praeceps,
utiliumque sagax rerum et diuina futuri
sortilegis non discrepuit sententia Delphis.

   carmine qui tragico uilem certauit ob hircum,   220
mox etiam agrestes Satyros nudauit, et asper
incolumi grauitate iocum temptauit, eo quod
illecebris erat et grata nouitate morandus
spectator, functusque sacris et potus et exlex.
uerum ita risores, ita commendare dicaces   225
conueniet Satyros, ita uertere seria ludo,
ne quicumque deus, quicumque adhibebitur heros,
regali conspectus in auro nuper et ostro,
migret in obscuras humili sermone tabernas,
aut, dum uitat humum, nubes et inania captet.   230
effutire leues indigna Tragoedia uersus,
ut festis matrona moueri iussa diebus,
intercrit Satyris paulum pudibunda proteruis.
non ego inornata et dominantia nomina solum
uerbaque, Pisones, Satyrorum scriptor amabo;   235
nec sic enitar tragico differre colori,
ut nihil intersit Dauusne loquatur et audax
Pythias emuncto lucrata Simone talentum,

211 maior] malorum R^1 *per homoeoteleuton* 212 laborum *u. infra*   **212** *om.* R^1
$\delta^1\pi^1$ $\lambda^1 l^1$ $\varphi^1\psi^1$, *uersus sec. manu additus, cf.* 211   **214** luxuriem *aR* δ λl $\varphi\psi$
luxuriam *BCK* π *Porph.*   **215–18** *paene euanuerunt in C*   **221** nudauit
codd. necnon Porph. Schol. Mar. Vict. GL, VI. 82. 6, *uix recte* induxit *Peerlkamp*
nouauit *Diom. GL,* I. 487. 18, 491. 9   **222** iocum] locum $B(?)K^1R^2$ $\delta\pi$ φ *ante*
ras. ψ *Diom. GL,* I. 491. 10   **223** illecebris (inl-)] encelebris *C pr.* incelebris
R $\delta^1\pi^2$ *l pr.* $\varphi\psi$ illecerebris *Mar. Vict. GL,* VI. 82. 8   illecebris erat] inerat λ (illec.
superscr.) erat *om.* π φ *pr.* ψ *pr.*   et *om.* δ **224** spectator] spectatus *C*
226 ita uertere] auertere *BCK*   **230** dum] num *BC* uitat] -et ς
233 proteruis] propteruis $\varphi\psi$ **234** nomina] nomine $BC^1(?)$ **235** pisones
aBCKR δ^2 pisonis $\delta^1\pi$ λl $\varphi\psi$ **237** et *BCV an aK post ras. R* $\delta\pi$ λl $\varphi\psi$

an custos famulusque dei Silenus alumni.
ex noto fictum carmen sequar, ut sibi quiuis   240
speret idem, sudet multum frustraque laboret
ausus idem: tantum series iuncturaque pollet,
tantum de medio sumptis accedit honoris.
siluis deducti caueant, me iudice, Fauni
ne uelut innati triuiis ac paene forenses   245
aut nimium teneris iuuenentur uersibus umquam,
aut immunda crepent ignominiosaque dicta.
offenduntur enim quibus est equus et pater et res,
nec, si quid fricti ciceris probat et nucis emptor,
aequis accipiunt animis donantue corona.   250
   syllaba longa breui subiecta uocatur iambus,
pes citus; unde etiam trimetris accrescere iussit
nomen iambeis, cum senos redderet ictus
primus ad extremum similis sibi †non ita pridem†.
tardior ut paulo grauiorque ueniret ad aures,   255
spondeos stabiles in iura paterna recepit
commodus et patiens, non ut de sede secunda
cederet aut quarta socialiter. hic et in Acci
nobilibus trimetris apparet rarus, et Enni
in scaenam missos cum magno pondere uersus   260
aut operae celeris nimium curaque carentis
aut ignoratae premit artis crimine turpi.
   non quiuis uidet immodulata poemata iudex,
et data Romanis uenia est indigna poetis.
idcircone uager scribamque licenter? an omnes   265
uisuros peccata putem mea, tutus et intra
spem ueniae cautus? uitaui denique culpam,

---

249 fricti *aRV* δ *corr.*π² λ¹*l*¹ φψ   stricti *C*¹   fracti *BC*²*K post ras.* δ*pr.*π¹ λ²*l*²
250 ue *om. B*   que π   **252** trimetris] iri metris *B*   accrescere] accedere
lemma Porph. accersere *edd. uett.*   **253** *dist. post* iambeis *O. Jahn H. Weil,*
post ictus *Lejay*   iambeis] iambis *B, lemma Porph. in codd. plur.*   cum senos]
senos cum *Cunningham*   **254** *distinctio post* pridem *incerta, u. comm.*   non
ita pridem *corruptum uidetur;* iamque ita pridem *H. Schütz*   *post* 254 *lacunam*
statuit Ribbeck   **255** paulo] paulum π   **260** magno cum pondere ς
261 nimium celeris *a*ς   **265** an] ut *u* ς, *def. Bentley* et ς *Fea Peerlkamp*
266 intra] extra *Lambinus*

non laudem merui. uos exemplaria Graeca
nocturna uersate manu, uersate diurna.
at uestri proaui Plautinos et numeros et   270
laudauere sales:nimium patienter utrumque,
ne dicam stulte, mirati, si modo ego et uos
scimus inurbanum lepido seponere dicto
legitimumque sonum digitis callemus et aure.

    ignotum tragicae genus inuenisse camenae   275
dicitur et plaustris uexisse poemata Thespis,
quae canerent agerentque peruncti faecibus ora.
post hunc personae pallaeque repertor honestae
Aeschylus et modicis instrauit pulpita tignis
et docuit magnumque loqui nitique coturno.   280
successit uetus his comoedia, non sine multa
laude. sed in uitium libertas excidit et uim
dignam lege regi; lex est accepta chorusque
turpiter obticuit sublato iure nocendi.

    nil intemptatum nostri liquere poetae,   285
nec minimum meruere decus uestigia Graeca
ausi deserere et celebrare domestica facta,
uel qui practextas uel qui docuere togatas.
nec uirtute foret clarisque potentius armis
quam lingua Latium, si non offenderet unum   290
quemque poetarum limae labor et mora. uos, o
Pompilius sanguis, carmen reprehendite quod non
multa dies et multa litura coercuit atque
praesectum deciens non castigauit ad unguem.

    ingenium misera quia fortunatius arte   295
credit et excludit sanos Helicone poetas

---

270 uestri] nostri ς *edd. uett.*   **276** plaustris] plausis *BC*[1]*K*[1] plautus *uel* plauctus *Diom. GL*, I. 487. 28   uexisse] uixisse *a pr. BK*[1]*R* uexasse *l* uectasse *Cunningham*   **277** quae] qui ς *Don. Excerp. de com.* v. 9 (*p.* 25. 5 *W.*) *pars codd., sicut coniecerat Bentley*   peruncti] infecti *Diom. loc. cit.* 29   ora] atris *BC* **283** *om. B*   **284** obticuit] obmutuit ς   nocendi] loquendi *Don. pars codd.* (*p.* 25. 12)   **288** uel] ut φ *uar.*   togatas] togatis *BCK*[1]   **289** que *BCK* ue *cett.*   **293** *de distinct. u. comm.*   **294** pra(e)sectum *BC*(*K*[1]*n.l.*)*V* perfectum *aK*[2]*R* δπ[1] λ*l* φψ *Schol.* perpectum (s *super* r *scr.*) π[2]   deciens *B* decies *cett.*   **296–9** *paene euanuerunt in C*

Democritus, bona pars non ungues ponere curat,
non barbam, secreta petit loca, balnea uitat.
nanciscetur enim pretium nomenque poeta[e],
si tribus Anticyris caput insanabile numquam   300
tonsori Licino commiserit. o ego laeuus,
qui purgor bilem sub uerni temporis horam;
non alius faceret meliora poemata. uerum
nil tanti est. ergo fungar uice cotis, acutum
reddere quae ferrum ualet exsors ipsa secandi.   305
munus et officium nil scribens ipse docebo,
unde parentur opes, quid alat formetque poetam,
quid deceat, quid non, quo uirtus, quo ferat error.
    scribendi recte sapere est et principium et fons.
rem tibi Socraticae poterunt ostendere chartae,   310
uerbaque prouisam rem non inuita sequentur.
qui didicit patriae quid debeat et quid amicis,
quo sit amore parens, quo frater amandus et hospes,
quod sit conscripti, quod iudicis officium, quae
partes in bellum missi ducis, ille profecto   315
reddere personae scit conuenientia cuique.
respicere exemplar uitae morumque iubebo
doctum imitatorem et uiuas hinc ducere uoces.
interdum speciosa locis morataque recte
fabula nullius ueneris, sine pondere et arte,   320
ualdius oblectat populum meliusque moratur
quam uersus inopes rerum nugaeque canorae.
Grais ingenium, Grais dedit ore rotundo
Musa loqui, praeter laudem nullius auaris.
Romani pueri longis rationibus assem   325
discunt in partes centum diducere. 'dicat

---

298 barbam] barbas *B*   petit] fugit *Pompeius, GL,* v. 162. 31   **299** poeta *Peerlkamp*   poetae *codd.*   **300** si] qui *Ribbeck*   **302** purgor] purger ς *Peerlkamp*   **305** ex(s)ors ipsa *K* (*om.* ipsa) *R*² *Schol. in textu*   *Fr. Bob. GL,* VII. 542. 26   ex(s)ortita *aBCR*¹ δ²*uar.* π¹ *Schol. in lemm.*   **308** deceat] doceat *a*¹*R*¹ δ *pr.*   **311** sequentur *aR* δπ λ*l* φψ *Porph. Quint. I.O.* I. 5. 2 sequuntur *BK* -ontur *C*   **318** uiuas] ueras ς *edd. plur. uett.*   uoces] uoltus *Peerlkamp* **319** locis *aBCV* δ² *Porph. Schol.*   iocis *KR* δ¹π λ*l* φψ   morataque] memorataque ς **326** diducere] deducere ς *edd. uett.*   dicat] dicas ς

filius Albini: si de quincunce remota est
uncia, quid superat? poteras dixisse.' 'triens.' 'eu.
rem poteris seruare tuam. redit uncia, quid fit?'
'semis.' an haec animos aerugo et cura peculi   330
cum semel imbuerit, speremus carmina fingi
posse linenda cedro et leui seruanda cupresso?
   aut prodesse uolunt aut delectare poetae
aut simul et iucunda et idonea dicere uitae.
quidquid praecipies esto breuis, ut cito dicta   335
percipiant animi dociles teneantque fideles;
omne superuacuum pleno de pectore manat.
ficta uoluptatis causa sint proxima ueris:
ne quodcumque uelit poscat sibi fabula credi,
neu pransae Lamiae uiuum puerum extrahat aluo.   340
centuriae seniorum agitant expertia frugis,
celsi praetereunt austera poemata Ramnes;
omne tulit punctum qui miscuit utile dulci,
lectorem delectando pariterque monendo.
hic meret aera liber Sosiis, hic et mare transit   345
et longum noto scriptori prorogat aeuum.
   sunt delicta tamen quibus ignouisse uelimus.
nam neque chorda sonum reddit quem uult manus
                                                    et mens
[poscentique grauem persaepe remittit acutum]
nec semper feriet quodcumque minabitur arcus.   350
uerum ubi plura nitent in carmine, non ego paucis

327 albini si R^2 δπ *corr.* (bini si R^1 π *pr.*) λ*l* φψ *Schol.*   albani si *aBC corr. K*
alba nisi *C pr.*   **328** superat] superet ς   superest ς *uar.*   poteras] *om.* K^1
poterat *a* δ²π¹   triens eu] triens heu *K* ς   triens heus *uel* hem ς   triens est δ¹π²(?)
λ*l* φψ trienem *R*   **330** an *BV pr.* at *V corr.* π² ad *aCKR* δπ¹ λ*l* φψ et
Cunningham Peerlkamp   **331** speremus *R* δπ λ *pr. l* φψ *pr.* speramus *aBCK* ψ
corr.   **334** aut] et *Seru. Aen.* vi. 660   **337** *del. Guietus Bentley, uix recte*
339 ne *aKR* δπ λ*l* φψ nec *BC Seru. Aen.* xii. 83   uolet R^1 δ *pr.* (?) π λ*l* φψ uelit
a^1BC(?)KR^2 δ *corr. Schol.* uelis *a²* ς   poscat] posset δ¹ φ *pr.* ψ *pr.* (exposcat *superscr.*) poscet ς   **340** *om.* K^1 ncu] ₦ *B* ne ς   extrahet ς *Porph. codd. praeter P*
345 (a)era *a*(?)BC^2KR δ²π λ²*l²*   (a)ere C^1 δ¹ λ¹*l¹* φψ   (a)er(a)e *uel* (a)ereae *codd.
aliquot Horatii necnon codd. Porph. praeter P*   sosiis a^2R^2 (sociis R^1) δπ λ*l* φψ
Porph. Schol. uar. sosis a^1BCKV *Schol.*   **349** *del. A. Platt*   remittit] remutit
δ¹(?) φ *pr.* ψ ς   remuttit λ*l*   remugit *uel* reddit ς   **350** quodcumque] quocumque ς   quoicumque *Madvig*

offendar maculis, quas aut incuria fudit
aut humana parum cauit natura. quid ergo est?
ut scriptor si peccat idem librarius usque,
quamuis est monitus, uenia caret, et citharoedus   355
ridetur chorda qui semper oberrat eadem;
sic mihi qui multum cessat fit Choerilus ille,
quem bis terue bonum cum risu miror, et idem
indignor quandoque bonus dormitat Homerus;
uerum operi longo fas est obrepere somnum.   360

   ut pictura, poesis: erit, quae, si propius stes,
te capiat magis, et quaedam, si longius abstes;
haec amat obscurum, uolet haec sub luce uideri,
iudicis argutum quae non formidat acumen;
haec placuit semel, haec deciens repetita placebit.   365

   o maior iuuenum, quamuis et uoce paterna
fingeris ad rectum et per te sapis, hoc tibi dictum
tolle memor, certis medium et tolerabile rebus
recte concedi. consultus iuris et actor
causarum mediocris abest uirtute diserti   370
Messallae nec scit quantum Cascellius Aulus,
sed tamen in pretio est: mediocribus esse poetis
non homines, non di, non concessere columnae.
ut gratas inter mensas symphonia discors
et crassum unguentum et Sardo cum melle papauer   375
offendunt, poterat duci quia cena sine istis,
sic animis natum inuentumque poema iuuandis,
si paulum summo decessit, uergit ad imum.

   ludere qui nescit, campestribus abstinet armis,
indoctusque pilae disciue trochiue quiescit,   380

353 ergo est] ergost *B*   ergo ς *edd. nonnulli*   **355** et] ut *K*[2] *uar.* ς *Bentley, fort. recte*   **356** oberrat] oberret *a* δ *corr.*   **357** sic multum mi qui cessat *B*   **358** terue *BK* ς terque *cett.*   **359** bonus] magnus *Hier. Ep.* 84. 8. 2   **360** *del. C. Hammerstein L. Mueller, perperam* operi (*u. supra p.* 22)] opere *K* δ *pr.* opere in *a* δ *corr. Hier. Ep. loc. cit.* (*codd. recc.*) obrepere] ignoscere ς *Hier.* (*codd. uett.*)   **361** *de distinct. u. comm.*   **362** *om. K*[1] abstes (aptes *B*) *codd.* adstes ς absis *Postgate*   **371** nec scit *BKV* nescit *cett.* aulus] ausus *BC*[1]   **376** duci *om. B* dici *R*[1]   **378** uergit] pergit *BC* (uergit *C uar.*)

ne spissae risum tollant impune coronae:
qui nescit uersus tamen audet fingere. quidni?
liber et ingenuus, praesertim census equestrem
summam nummorum, uitioque remotus ab omni.

tu nihil inuita dices faciesue Minerua: 385
id tibi iudicium est, ea mens. si quid tamen olim
scripseris, in Maeci descendat iudicis aures
et patris et nostras, nonumque prematur in annum,
membranis intus positis; delere licebit
quod non edideris, nescit uox missa reuerti.   390

siluestres homines sacer interpresque deorum
caedibus et uictu foedo deterruit Orpheus,
dictus ob hoc lenire tigris rabidosque leones;
dictus et Amphion, Thebanae conditor urbis,
saxa mouere sono testudinis et prece blanda   395
ducere quo uellet. fuit haec sapientia quondam,
publica priuatis secernere, sacra profanis,
concubitu prohibere uago, dare iura maritis,
oppida moliri, leges incidere ligno.
sic honor et nomen diuinis uatibus atque   400
carminibus uenit. post hos insignis Homerus
Tyrtaeusque mares animos in Martia bella
uersibus exacuit. dictae per carmina sortes,
et uitae monstrata uia est, et gratia regum
Pieriis temptata modis, ludusque repertus   405
et longorum operum finis: ne forte pudori
sit tibi Musa lyrae sollers et cantor Apollo.

natura fieret laudabile carmen an arte
quaesitum est. ego nec studium sine diuite uena
nec rude quid possit uideo ingenium; alterius sic   410
altera poscit opem res et coniurat amice.

385 ue] que *a* δ *pr.* ϛ   **388–9** *de distinct. u. comm.*   **393** rabidos *BKV Seru. Dan. Aen.* VI. 645 rapidos *aCR* δ(-es)π (-is, -os *uar.*) λ*l* φψ   **394** urbis *a uar. BCKV* δπ λ*l* φψ   arcis *aR* δ *uar.*   **402** tyrt(a)eus] *aBCK*[1] *Schol.* dyrt(a)eus (div-, -c(a)eus) *uel* pyrt(a)eus (-ceus, -r(a)eus) *uel sim. cett. Porph.* **408** natura] ingenio *Ioann. Saresber. Met.* I. 8   **410** possit ϛ (*Ioann. Saresber. loc. cit.,* Luisinus '*in cod. illustrissimi Federici Cornelij*', Lambinus '*aliquot libri ueteres*') prosit *codd. uett.*   sic] sed *Peerlkamp*

qui studet optatam cursu contingere metam
multa tulit fecitque puer, sudauit et alsit,
abstinuit uenere et uino; qui Pythia cantat
tibicen, didicit prius extimuitque magistrum.   415
nec satis est dixisse 'ego mira poemata pango,
occupet extremum scabies; mihi turpe relinqui est,
et quod non didici sane nescire fateri.'
    ut praeco, ad merces turbam qui cogit emendas,
adsentatores iubet ad lucrum ire poeta   420
diues agris, diues positis in faenore nummis.
si uero est unctum qui recte ponere possit
et spondere leui pro paupere et eripere artis
litibus implicitum, mirabor si sciet inter-
noscere mendacem uerumque beatus amicum.   425
tu seu donaris seu quid donare uoles cui,
nolito ad uersus tibi factos ducere plenum
laetitiae; clamabit enim 'pulchre, bene, recte',
pallescet super his, etiam stillabit amicis
ex oculis rorem, saliet, tundet pede terram.   430
ut qui conducti plorant in funere dicunt
et faciunt prope plura dolentibus ex animo, sic
derisor uero plus laudatore mouetur.
reges dicuntur multis urgere culillis
et torquere mero quem perspexisse laborent,   435
an sit amicitia dignus; si carmina condes,
numquam te fallent animi sub uulpe latentes.

414 cantat *codd., malim* certat, *u. comm.*   **416** nec *Paris.* 7973 *pr.* (*s.* ix–x) ς
non *uel* num ς   nunc *codd. potiores Schol.*   **417** relinqui est *aC²R* δ²π λ*l* φψ
relinqui δ¹(?)   reliqui *BC*¹(?)*K*   **418** *de distinct. u. comm.; del. Peerlkamp
perperam*   **420** iubet ad lucrum] ad lucrum iubet *BC*   **421** = *S.* 1. 2. 13,
del. H. Schütz alii   agris] agri *BC*   **422** si] sin π *l*   unctum] iunctum
BC ante ras. punctum π *ante. ras. Porph. codd. praeter P*   **423** leui] uelit *J.*
Geel   artis ς   atris *codd. potiores.* a̲ t̲ ris *R post ras.* at,is (.r *super* t *scr.*) *l*
424–5 *conuerso ordine Bς*   **426** cui] quoi *V* qui *B*   **429** *de distinct. u.*
comm.   **431** qui conducti] quae conducti *M ante ras.* (?)   quae conductae
Kirchmann alii, perperam   **434** culillis π *ante ras.* cui. illis *B* cũ illis *K*¹(?)
culullis *aC* δ² *Schol.* cululis *K*² δ¹π λ*l* φψ cucullis *R*² (*R*¹ *n.l.*)   **435** per-
spexisse] prospexisse ς   laborent *aBCK* δ *corr.* ψ *pr.* laborant *R* δ *pr.*π λ*l* φψ
437 fal(l)ent *aBCKR*¹ δ *uar.*π *pr.* λ*l*   fal(l)ant *R*² δπ *corr.* φψ *Schol.*   animi sub

Quintilio si quid recitares, 'corrige sodes
hoc' aiebat 'et hoc'; melius te posse negares,
bis terque expertum frustra, delere iubebat   440
et male tornatos incudi reddere uersus.
si defendere delictum quam uertere malles,
nullum ultra uerbum aut operam insumebat inanem,
quin sine riuali teque et tua solus amares.
uir bonus et prudens uersus reprehendet inertes,   445
culpabit duros, incomptis allinet atrum
transuerso calamo signum, ambitiosa recidet
ornamenta, parum claris lucem dare coget,
arguet ambigue dictum, mutanda notabit;
fiet Aristarchus, nec dicet 'cur ego amicum   450
offendam in nugis?' hae nugae seria ducent
in mala derisum semel exceptumque sinistre.

ut mala quem scabies aut morbus regius urget
aut fanaticus error et iracunda Diana,
uesanum tetigisse timent fugiuntque poetam   455
qui sapiunt; agitant pueri incautique sequuntur.
hic, dum sublimis uersus ructatur et errat,
si ueluti merulis intentus decidit auceps
in puteum foueamue, licet 'succurrite' longum
clamet 'io ciues', non sit qui tollere curet.   460
si curet quis opem ferre et demittere funem,
'qui scis an prudens huc se proiecerit atque
seruari nolit?' dicam, Siculique poetae
narrabo interitum: deus immortalis haberi
dum cupit Empedocles, ardentem frigidus Aetnam   465

uulpe latentes *uix recte, u. comm.*   **439** aiebat *KR*² δπ λ*l* agebat *aBCR*¹(?) φψ
441–76 *deficiunt BC; subscr.* finit poetica. sermonum lib. I incipit *B; codicis C
reliquam partem littera E significauit Keller, cf. supra pp.* 4–6   **441** tornatos (torquatos
E)] formatos *Guyet* ternatos *M pr.* ter natos *Bentley*   **442** uertere] cedere ς
443 insumebat] sumebat πς *edd. uett.*   **445** reprehendet *aEK* δπ *uar.* repre-
hendit π *post ras.* λ*l* φψ   reprendit *R*   **450** nec *aEKR* δ²*uar.*   non
δπ λ*l* φψ   **455** fugiunt] fugient *aER* δ *corr.*   **458** si *K* δπ² *l corr.*   sic *cett.*
461 si quis curet *edd. plur. ante Bentleium*   demittere *R* λ*l* π² dimittere π¹ *cett.*
summittere ς   **462** proiecerit δ *pr.* λ*l* φψ deiecerit *cett.*

insiluit. sit ius liceatque perire poetis;
inuitum qui seruat idem facit occidenti.
nec semel hoc fecit, nec si retractus erit iam
fiet homo et ponet famosae mortis amorem.
nec satis apparet cur uersus factitet, utrum   470
minxerit in patrios cineres, an triste bidental
mouerit, incestus: certe furit, ac uelut ursus,
obiectos caueae ualuit si frangere clatros,
indoctum doctumque fugat recitator acerbus;
quem uero arripuit, tenet occiditque legendo,   475
non missura cutem nisi plena cruoris hirudo.

467 *del. Ribbeck L. Mueller, haud recte*   **473** obiectos] obiectas *E l pr.*

Subscriptione carent CE¹K, de subscript. codicis B u. supra ad 441
   Q. Oratii Flacci de arte poetica explicit. Incipit epodon ad Mecenatem *a*
   Q. Oratii Flacci de arte poetica explicit. Incipit epodon *R*
   Q. (*om.* δ) (H)oratii Flacci (-ii λ Flacti *l*) de arte poetica explicit. Incipit
eiusdem epodon δ λ*l* ψ
   F. Horatii de arte poetica liber explicit. Incipit epodon φ
   Dc arte poetica explicit π
   cf. Pomponi Porfyrionis commentum in Horatium de arte poetica explicit.
Incipit carmen saeculare feliciter *Porph.*
   Sequuntur Sermones in codd. BCK, cf. supra pp. 6, 14.

COMMENTARY

Ita enim multi in Artem poeticam scripsere, merito ut dubitari possit pluresne versus sint an interpretes.

1576

ALDVS MANVTIVS PAVLLI F.

How commentators each dark passage shun
And hold their farthing candle to the sun.

EDWARD YOUNG

How on earth does A— think he can understand Blake?
Why, he doesn't even understand philosophy!

WITTGENSTEIN (*attrib.*)

I. Poetic unity and *ars*.
Unity unattainable without 'art'; diction and
subject-matter; *ars* and *ingenium*, 1–41.

The initial and final parts of the poem are often said to be
personal to H. They are thought to be independent of a
critical tradition.[1] This judgement is attractive but, I think,
false. The final part will later be seen to be as traditional and
as personal as the rest of the *Ars*; it contains after all one of the
few certain links with Neoptolemus of Parium. The first
forty-one verses introduce the reader to two major concepts
of the poem, both highly traditional and highly personal—
unity, and that amalgam of rationality and skill, theory and
practice, called τέχνη or *ars* by the ancients. H. has however
entwined them so closely that only careful analysis can take
them apart to show their provenance.

The critical tradition and H. on *ars*

The *Ars Poetica* poetically reflects the ancient *ars*.[2] Recourse
to the introductory portion of these *artes* shows that H. has
in fact picked up one or two of the guiding ideas and made
them subservient to his own purposes. Books II–III of Quintilian's *I.O.* acknowledge the rhetorician's debt to this initial
part of the *artes*, although allowance must be made for his
independent judgement and for his own additions to the
standard scheme at the beginning of book II; cf. II. 11. 1 *iam
hinc ergo nobis incohanda est ea pars artis ex qua capere initium solent
qui priora omiserunt*. Hence the necessity there claimed for *ars*
and teaching (chs. 11–13), and the main topics (chs. 15 ff.):

[1] C. Becker in particular has made an impressive case for this proposition, *Das
Spätwerk des Horaz* (1963), pp. 67 ff., 78 ff., 101.

[2] Much relevant material is found in the works of Norden, Börner, and Dahlmann, cited *Prol.* ch. 2. E. Norden had directed attention to this curious kind of
ancient text-books, which he erroneously conflated with a similar though separate
genre, called εἰσαγωγαί, Introductions. R. Börner and H. Dahlmann have directed
attention to the introductory portions of these *Artes*, which they related to H.'s
Ars in what I have argued is a misleading manner.

the definition of rhetoric, its aim, its uses, its moral character, its material; in the third chapter of book III the division of the field of rhetoric is set out. In the language of Cicero's *De Inv.* (I. 4) this would be *de genere ipsius artis, de officio, de fine, de materia, de partibus*. The Greek terminology underlying the Latin can still be seen in some late examples that survive.[1] The necessity for trained craftsmanship is the demand which holds together all these preliminaries to the *Artes*: such a training enables the practitioner to make right choices and avoid wrong. This comes out very clearly in the incomplete introduction of the *De Sublimitate* where the faults incidental to sublimity are explicitly discussed (chs. 3–5). H. has very firmly grasped this principle. It is a salient point in his introduction as it is in those of the *scriptores artium*. *A.P.* 31 *in uitium ducit culpae fuga, si caret arte* may be compared with Quint. *I.O.* II. 12. 4 *est praeterea quaedam uirtutum uitiorumque uicinia, qua maledicus pro libero, temerarius pro forti, effusus pro copioso accipitur.* But there is no straightforward, unilinear, and literal-minded lecturing on precepts. We hear nothing of *ars*, and much of unity, until suddenly *ars* appears as a condition for the attainment of unity. When the principle of *ars* reappears, it is tied to the ability to create an artistic whole, and *ars* involves its logical opposite *natura*, talent (*A.P.* 38–40, 40–1). This pair of opposites—*doctrina* and *natura*—also has its place in the prefaces of the *artes* to ensure the status of the art and the quality of the student, e.g. Quint. *I.O.* II. 19 and 8, ps.-Long. *Subl.* ch. 2, Vitr. *Arch.* I. 1. 3. Again note the subtlety of the poet's treatment of the commonplace. Even the work of an intelligent but unsubtle mind like Quintilian's is miles away; so is the work of a distinguished but heated mind like ps.-Longinus'.

The introduction commonly closes with a *partitio*, cf. Cic. *Inv.* I. 9, Quint. *I.O.* III. 3, ps.-Long. *Subl.* ch. 8.

[1] Especially the Scholia to Dionysius Thrax.

ars and *unum*

H. links 'art' and 'unity'—a remarkable feat of imaginative organization; thus the dry bones of 'technography' come to life. The poet succeeds in letting the demands of *ars*–τέχνη grow out of the demand for unity of conception: only he who has mastered the art can produce a work that is all of a piece, a varied and articulate unity. Perhaps II. was not the first so to link art and unity in a preliminary plea for training. The celebrated 'purple patch' is set in precisely this traditional context by Quint. *I.O.* II. 11. 5–7, notably 7, *unde fit ut dissoluta et ex diuersis congesta oratio cohaerere non possit...; magnas tamen sententias et res bonas (ita enim gloriari solent) elidunt; nam et barbari et serui; et si hoc sat est, nulla est ratio dicendi*. It is not impossible that Neoptolemus of Parium, the poet's chief authority for the technicalities of literary criticism, had begun with a demand for *ars*, which alone could give a unity of conception—but evidence is sadly wanting. Whether he did or not, it is one thing to link two abstract concepts and another to show poetic pictures and let it slowly dawn on the reader that (as one might paraphrase) *unum atque totum non datur nisi arte*. H. does not begin with a solemn demand for *ars*–τέχνη, with reflections on unity attached. Instead it is the wholeness of a poetic conception which is made to impose itself on the reader (1–30). Then it is added—almost like an afterthought—that such a thing is not possible without the strenuous training of the craftsman. Yet the craftsman's training is not enough; it only leads to partial success. Wholeness belongs to a different order of things. Poetic intuition, or insight, is a matter of talent—*ingenium* (31, 32–7, 38–40). Such is the poet's advocacy of *ars*; it ends paradoxically with an appeal to *ingenium*.

The doctrine of unity in the critical tradition

Unity is among the leading literary concepts the West has inherited from the Greeks. The Sophists have been credited with its inception; see, for example, M. Pohlenz, *NGG* (1920), p. 171, and (1933), p. 54. It is true, Gorgias appears to have paid attention to the 'right moment', καιρός, and 'suitability', τὸ πρέπον, as principles of rhetorical order and perhaps style. The fifth-century teachers of rhetoric appear to have used the sections of a forensic speech as clues for the selection and arrangement of subject-matter and differentiation of style. These are rules of thumb, precisely what Plato's criticism in the *Phaedrus* alleges. Whatever Isocrates' share in this matter, it seems to have been left to Attic philosophy to establish 'unity' as a general principle.

Plato employs the idea of 'wholeness' in polemical contexts of two dialogues, *Gorgias* 503 e–4 a and, more specifically, *Phaedrus* 263–4. In both cases the 'arts'—painting, architecture, shipbuilding, etc.—are used as models for such wholeness. 'Cogent composition', ἀνάγκη λογογραφική (264 b), requires his dialectic method. It is likened to organisms: every discourse must fit together like the body of a living creature (*Phaedrus* 264 c). 'The fitting relation of every part to every other and the whole' (264 c) is the criterion demanded.

In spite of a glance at the tragedians, poetry is not primarily in view at *Phaedrus* 269 a. A serious application to tragedy and epic is not on record before Aristotle's *Poetics*. Unity is one of the fundamental postulates. Tragedy must be perfect and whole, 7, 1450 b 23; a whole, ὅλον, is that which has a beginning, middle, and end (7, 1450 b 26). The metaphor again is that of an organism, 7, 1450 b 34, or of any art that produces things made up of parts. The relation of the parts must be 'according to necessity or probability' (7, 1451 a 12, and 9, 1451 a 38). The inherent logic here demanded is not that of Plato's dialectic but of Aristotle's logic. The universality, καθόλου, of poetic statement, its philosophic element (9, 1451 b 7), resides precisely in this inherent logic. The necessity or probability by which a certain kind of person will act or speak in a certain manner has over-all validity, καθόλου. When necessary it recalls Aristotle's logic, which operates with attributes that belong to all instances of a given subject, and καθόλου is his term for it (*Post. Anal.* 1. 4–6); but when probable it merely resembles necessary connexions—it is only quasi-logical. Aristotle cannot have been unaware that poetry deals in contingent matters. But for all that, it is its approximation to καθόλου which to him renders it at any rate 'more universal', and hence 'more philosophic', than the mere factuality of history (*Poet.* 9, 1451 b 7 and 5).

This clearly is the home of H.'s *simplex. . . et unum.* Aristotle's postulate has been moved out of its restricted place within the context of tragedy, however great the importance there attached to it. Prefixed to the whole *Ars*, it is proclaimed as the grand law of all poetry, the reward to the poet who has acquired his τέχνη. I take the Aristotelian origin of these ideas to be established; it was rightly so conceived in the centuries following the Italian Renaissance. Neither of two alternative solutions that have been offered can stand up to examination. Why not, ask some, turn to Cicero, who was just round the corner, rather than to Aristotle, perhaps by way of Neoptolemus or some other shadowy figure? The answer is simple. However well H. knew his Cicero—I am quite willing to believe that he knew him very well—his knowledge is irrelevant because Cicero does not offer what H. clearly requires—a theory of poetic unity. 'For passages in the Ciceronian rhetorical *corpus* showing this [i.e. the Horatian] interrelation between variety and unity compare *De Oratore* 2. 41. 177; *Orator* 102, 109; *De Partitione Oratoria* 47; *De Inventione* I'; thus Grant and Fiske, *HS*, xxxv (1924), 18 n. 1. An impressive string of references but not *ad rem*. For *De Or.* ii, *De Part. Or.*, and *De Inv.* 1. 98–9 (if this is hidden under the reference '*De Inventione* I') inculcate variety of treatment by the well-worn rule of 'art concealing art' and 'avoid monotony'; no trace of unity here. *Or.* 102 and 109 advise the student to use, like the great poets, various styles, not only one; hardly H.'s idea of unity. And while I would not deny that the 'analogy. . .for Horace's ideal poet is Phidias, who is an artifex, not an opifex' (Grant and Fiske, *HS*, xxv (1924), 19, cf. Hack, *HS*, xxvii (1916), 40), this sentiment can hardly be built up into the theory of unity which the *Ars* professes; the Platonic motifs in Cicero's *Orator* (7–10) certainly do not assist this operation. The same applies to the splendid passage in the *Orator* (71–4) in which the Stoic theory of *decorum* is set out. B. Otis (*Gnomon*, xxxvi (1964), 269) juxtaposes it with Ar. *Poet.* chs. 7–8, and the beginning of the *A.P.* The Aristotelian chapters give us largely what we find in the *A.P.*, but Panaetius–Cicero's doctrine of τὸ πρέπον—*decorum*, is a different thing altogether, and emphatically fails to link Aristotle with H.

Nor should some stray resemblances to the *De Sublimitate* mislead the reader. For 'Longinus' any poetry or prose that conveys the thrill of greatness is sublime—the Old Testament or Sappho. For H. greatness resides in the great poetic genres. In this regard he is an Aristotelian. Like Aristotle, H. exemplifies unity from tragic drama and epic poetry. Parallels with Longinus require and readily find other explanations. O. Immisch's attempt (*Horazens Epistel über die Dichtkunst*, pp. 26 ff.) to explain them by attaching Horace to Antiochus of Ascalon and an alleged *Erhabenheitslehre* of the 'middle Academy' fails utterly.

Horace and Aristotle on unity

H. employed, for his own purposes, Aristotle's doctrine of unity. But this does not make the first forty-one lines of the *Ars* a transcript of Aristotle. It is hard to conceive of minds more different than those of the two men. The philosopher seeks to find a rationale for the tight unity of (certain specimens of) Attic tragedy—and he finds it in the teleology of the dramatic plot. Tragic diction becomes a poet's afterthought. Epic is devalued on this basis because its unity is less tight than that of tragedy. How iambics and comedy fared on this assessment we do not know. Other genres do not seem to enter the ring.

H. too talks largely of tragedy and epic. Aristotle's confron-

tation of the whole and its parts appeals to him. But the unity
that these forms evince to him is not simply unity of plot. It is
the unity of a work of poetry seen by a poet. It lacks Aristotle's
clarity of concept and coherence of argument. It cannot ultimately be resolved into a series of propositions. H. makes use
of Aristotle's propositions. They stimulate him to creativity in
a different medium. He takes some of the ideas of the *Poetics*
(though hardly from the *Poetics*), and submits them to the poetic
processes of his *sermo*. These processes are what he contributes.
They put a new complexion on the philosopher's thought.

One of the open secrets of Horatian poetic technique, in
lyric as much as *sermo*, is the variety of subject and sentiment
balanced so precariously by a largely concealed unity that his
admirers as much as his detractors happen to be divided—
some are conscious of the variety, and others are quite sure
that *series iuncturaque pollet*, not only in his theory but in his
practice. In the initial forty-one lines of the *Ars*, H. tells us
about these matters what he can tell. His theory mirrors his
practice. In argument and poetic performance alike unity is
to inform a manifold variety. These verses concentrate on
some features of the Aristotelian argument—a poem likened
to the works of art with their beginning, middle and end; the
'organic' metaphor; uniformity versus unity, the postulates
of *unum* (ἕν) and *totum* (ὅλον). Other features have been held
over or jettisoned. But comparison with works of art is turned
into description. A painting, a *grotesque*, all variety and no
unity, faces the reader like a symbol in the very first lines of
the poem (1–5). This may be a case for uniformity, and there
is a hint at the organic metaphor (6–9). But in the rapid
dialogue that ensues, though limitless daring is demanded,
only daring governed by the natural compatibility of subjects
is granted (9–13). Thus without a set argument a dialectic
position is indicated at the end of this brief section—neither
uniformity nor unrestricted variety is acceptable.

Now a fresh beginning, without any apparent transition;
but the first words show that talk is still of unity. Three tales

are told—that of an epic poet (14–19), of a votive painter (19–21), and of a potter (21–3). H. again gives a practical demonstration of variety; the three tales differ in detail. By adding inconsequential descriptive topics a poet loses the epic tone of his narrative; by adding a (?funereal) cypress to a seascape, a votive painter loses the point of the tablet, which is to commemorate an escape from danger at sea; by letting an amphora turn into a pitcher, a potter makes what he was not intending to make. The third case does not contain a gratuitous addition to the artist's topic but seems to comment on the other two: 'this tale resembles the case of the potter who was trying to make an amphora but—'. No external connexion follows: instead the three tales are seen, inductively, to lead to *one* conclusion (23): whatever the subject, it must be of 'one kind', *simplex...et unum*.

Now another new beginning, marked by an address (24). H. suddenly seems to talk of diction; moreover, for the first time in this poem, literary theory is before the reader. The literary theory is Peripatetic, though not apparently Aristotelian in origin (see 31 n.). Rising above the black and white of fault versus achievement, it looks at faults as virtues gone wrong. Diction is considered for four lines (25–8). In the fifth (29) the reader is given the help he requires. Diction was an example. The laws governing it also govern subject-matter. Lack of unity is a desirable thing gone wrong, and what is desired is variability of matter. Again a general axiom comes at the end: a virtue desired will turn into its adjacent fault unless 'art' keeps the practitioner straight (31). This goes beyond Aristotle in several ways: (1) variety is clearly seen as a desirable goal; and by that token, the unity achieved, if it is achieved, is stronger and less like sameness and uniformity; (2) success and fault are more clearly related; (3) diction is not as artificially separated from subject-matter as it is in Aristotle; (4) the great regulator, τέχνη, is taken for granted in Aristotle, it is not so in H.

Si caret arte: thus the last verse ended. 'What kind of *ars*?' is the question unasked that links the motif of unity pursued up to this line with that of 'wholeness' (32–7), which again begins without an external link. H. now talks of *operis summa* and *totum* (34); in Greek this is ὅλον, ultimately from Aristotle, *Poet.* ch. 7, the chapter that is governed by the organic metaphor and the order of 'every whole made up of parts'. H. deploys these ideas with a vast foreshortening. Having said *arte* (31), he starts talking of the craftsmanship of a bronze-founder. The reader may well jump to the conclusion that this is the *ars* now required. Craftsmanship is indeed required. Yet the bronze-founder is but an artisan; *ars* must be more than artisanship. The mere craftsman cannot *ponere totum*—that quality which the initial *grotesque* lacked and which distinguishes the artist (and poet) from the artisan.

Without any attempt at further qualification of *ars* there is another jump. The future practitioner is advised to select only a task he can master. Instead of a definition of *ars*, the advocate of craftsmanship demands talent (38–40). The poet who can master his subject will find at his call the right words and the right order (40–1). With *res–facundia–ordo* the critic arrives at the common terminology of ancient literary criticism. Although its abstract separation of matter–wording–arrangement is implicitly denied by the very sentence in which it is put, the poet must have found it enlightening enough to use it.

No conclusions can be drawn from H.'s poem as they can from Aristotle's argument. His 'argument' can only be perceived *in situ* and no summary can do it justice. But as an aid to reading I offer the following:

1. A *grotesque*: no part of a painting fits any other, 1–5.

2. A conversation on incoherence: not all variety in painting and poetry can be justified by a plea for creative freedom, 6–13.

3. Three instances exemplifying incoherence; unity demanded, 14–23.

4. A literary argument: faulty variety, like certain kinds of

faulty style, is a virtue misunderstood; uniformity and unity. 'Art' as regulator, 24–31.

5. A cautionary tale: the bronze-founder. Mastery of parts does not guarantee mastery of whole, 32–7.

6. Advice: choose a poetic task adapted to your talent, 38–40.

7. A promise: if you can master your *subject*, you will be able to *express* and *arrange* it, 40–1. The technical topics of an *ars poetica* are thereby implied: a *partitio* (above p. 76) into subject, diction, arrangement, which now follow in reverse order.

A number of observations may be made.

(*a*) This piece on poetic variety and unity is itself a remarkable poetic demonstration of variety and unity. H. practises what he preaches.

(*b*) I have noted after each heading the different styles and subjects.

(*c*) I have also noted variety of argument. A deft use of paradox adds to this variety. I set out four of these paradoxes in the shape of antitheses, which H. does not employ.

Unity and wholeness must be aimed at.
Variety must be aimed at.

Variety without unity is a fault.
Variety without unity is a virtue (misunderstood).

Craftsmanship is the key in poetry and the other arts.
Craftsmanship (alone) is not the key.

Craftsmanship is needed.
Talent is needed.

(*d*) But, perhaps surprisingly in this display of dialectical fireworks, unity emerges. For the progress from items (1) to (4) in my list above is also a progress from grotesque variety to variety mastered by unity. And the means of attaining unity in variety is *ars*. Heading (5) next distinguishes artisanship—a mere mastery of parts—from true artistry—mastery of a whole. Heading (6) ties that *ars* to talent, thereby setting aside the unreal antithesis between *ars* and *ingenium*. The final heading, (7), ties *ars*, based on *ingenium*, to the right choice of a 'task'. This task, the writing of poetry, is now, with a swift change, turned into the triad *res facundia ordo*. Thus the final surprise—we are at the beginning of a technical treatise on poetry, for *res facundia ordo* indicate the layout of such a treatise. The progress which I have described argues a high degree of poetic virtuosity and poetic depth.

(1) A grotesque: no part of a painting fits any other, 1–5

There are no preliminaries. The poem, as it were, jumps into a subject—the criticism of a painting. But this subject is deceptive. Its true identity is not recognized until 6. In the first four verses we are offered a *descriptio*, a fashionable device, presently derided by H. (14 ff.; 18 *describitur*). A painting is described that caricatures variety; no part fits any other. The wider context was discerned by Quint. *I.O.* VIII. 3. 60 *cui* (i.e. Σαρδισμῷ) *simile uitium est apud nos, si quis sublimia humilibus, uetera nouis, poetica uulgaribus misceat; id enim tale monstrum quale Horatius in prima parte libri de arte poetica fingit, 'humano capiti'*, etc. Inevitably the painting resembles the hybrid monsters of Classical art, cf. Plato, *Rep.* VI. 488a—scyllas, sirens, centaurs, goat-stags, etc. This monster recalls Virgil's Scylla, *A.* III. 426–8, *prima hominis facies et pulchro pectore uirgo | pube tenus, postrema immani corpore pistrix | delphinum caudas utero commissa luporum*, and his Triton, *A.* x. 210–11 *cui laterum tenus hispida nanti | frons hominem praefert, in pristim desinit aluus*. The point seems not to be that the image is untrue, as Lucretius maintained in discussing scyllas, centaurs and other monsters, IV. 739–40 *ex uiuo Centauri non fit imago, | nulla fuit quoniam talis natura animantis*; cf. Vitr. VII. 5. 3–4, on pictorial arabesques, *monstra potius quam ex rebus finitis imagines certae…haec autem nec sunt nec fieri possunt nec fuerunt*. Rather the gratuitous collection of limbs lacks verisimilitude; it is merely grotesque. Lucil. fr. 587 (Marx) *nisi portenta anguisque uolucris ac pinnatos scribitis* may or may not have occurred in a like context; G. C. Fiske,

Wisconsin St. VII (1920), 450, argues as if the likeness were certain. But see below 13 n.

1-2 As many as six words are placed before *si* in its own clause. Thus the reader is faced at once with the substance of the *si* clause—the violation of the law of unity. Instances of more than one or two words thus dislocated before *si* are not, to my knowledge, found in *C.* I–III (*pace* A. Y. Campbell (ed.) Hor. *Carm.*², *C.* III. 5. 17–18 n.), and once only in *C.* IV (12. 15). More extreme cases occur in the hexameter poems, though not frequently. For another instance of six words, see *Ep.* I. 12. 1, for more extreme cases *S.* I. 4. 56–7, II. 3. 247–9. Cf. below 87, 473.

1 *humano capiti:* adj., noun, contrasted with *ceruicem...equinam*, noun, adj., an emphatic incongruity. *humano capiti* is explained by 4 *mulier.*

2 *plumas* 'feathers', alleged Bentley, should at least be *pennas*, feathered wings; but the difference, even if it were invariable, is not here in point: *plumas* may apply to the feathers on the creature's body as well as on its wings; cf. Peerlkamp's and H. Schütz's notes. Nor does Bentley's vigorous advocacy of *formas* (again instead of *plumas*) convince; this too is shown by Peerlkamp. *una forma*, 8–9, is the shape of the entity as a whole, the parts being *membra*, l. 3, cf. Ov. *Met.* VII. 642 *humanam membris inducere formam*; at l. 2 the pl. *formae* would be more likely to denote different entities, the shapes of different creatures. Prud. *C. Symm.* II. 57 ff. may recall this passage and, at 59, he has *plumis*, but I doubt if H. recalls Virg. *A.* IV. 181.

uarias 'of different colours', i.e. from birds differently coloured, rather than 'mottled', cf. *Ep.* I. 10. 22 *inter uarias...columnas*, Ter. *Eun.* 683 *uaria ueste exornatus fuit*, Varro, *R.R.* II. 2. 4 *lingua (arietis) ne nigra aut uaria sit.*

inducere (not *induere*, R) is the *uox propria* for spreading colour or other materials over something, used either with an oblique case understood, as Plin. *N.H.* XXXV. 45 *purpurissum...inducunt*, or explicitly with such a case, especially dat., *ibid.* XXXV. 102 *huic picturae quater colorem induxit.* Hence *corpori* or the like need not be understood with *inducere plumas* (cf. K.–H. *ad l.*, *TLL*, VII. 1235. 5); *undique collatis membris* may be either a dat. dependent on *inducere plumas*, or an abl. abs. The dat. yields a clearer picture: to place feathers on the limbs joined to the neck.

3 *undique collatis membris, ut* etc.: according to Lucian Mueller and others, part of the *ut* clause. This it is not likely to be, since the words are required to complete the sketch of the imaginary figure, ll. 1–2.

What appears to be a dat. rather than an abl. (see prec. n.) is then further qualified by *ut = ita quidem ut*, 'not of result but of added qualification' (Wickham)—a concise phrasing often employed by H. Thus at *S.* II. 6. 82 *ut tamen* qualifies two preceding adjs., at *Ep.* II. 2. 87 *ut* qualifies a preceding clause, cf. J. Vahlen, *Ges. Phil. Schr.* I. 513.

undique 'from all animals', as *C.* I. 16. 13–15 *fertur Prometheus addere principi | limo coactus particulam undique | desectam.*

turpiter may possibly be joined ἀπὸ κοινοῦ with both *atrum* and *desinat.* K.–H. however assert that *turpiter atrum*, construed like *turpiter hirtum* (*Ep.* I. 3. 22), is contrasted with *formosa superne.* If a contrast with *superne* is intended, as I think it is, then *turpiter* is more likely to qualify *desinat* only.

atrum looks straightforward, but is not easily explained. It is not a general epithet. 'Black fish', this passage apart, seem to appear only at Pl. *Rud.* 998, a pun like 'black and blue'; Man. IV. 800 owes its appearance in *TLL* II. 1018. 67 to a false reading. The notion is probably 'black' = 'unsightly, repulsive' and thus like *turpiter* contrasted with *formosa.* Cf. perhaps *C.* III. 4. 17 *atris... uiperis* although there the connotation may be rather 'dangerous, sinister'. The evidence is too thin to counsel emendation; *turpiter hirtum*, from *Ep.* I. 3. 22, though advanced at various times (cf. Orelli *ad l.*, A. Y. Campbell, Hor. *Carm.* 1st ed. (1946), 'Horatiana Alia' *in calce libri*) is implausible.

4 '*in piscem. idest in beluam marinam, hoc est in pistricem*', ps.-Acro. J. F. Gronovius (*Obser.*, ed. Frotscher (1831), pp. 77–9) and N. Heinsius (*in marg. codicis sui*) were tempted by the Virgilian passages on Scylla and Triton (above 1–5 n.) to emend *atrum...piscem* to *atram...pristim* (*pistrim* in their spelling). They did not convince Bentley. But Peerlkamp attempted to judge the passage on its own merits, arguing (1) that the Acro gloss points to a reading *pristim*, (2) that the specific word *mulier*—not a generic word like *humano*, l. 1—favours the specific *pristim*, not the generic *piscem.* Now naturalists distinguished between fish and sea-monster; and in astronomy and mythology the two were quite distinct: Cic. *Arat.* 140–1 (384–5) *Andromedam...fera quaerere Pistrix | pergit* (Aratus 354 μέγα κῆτος), 171–2 (415–16) *inter Pistricem et Piscem... | stellas* (Aratus 390 κήτεος αἰθερίοιο καὶ ἰχθύος). The words are similar enough to be confused by scribes and at Man. I. 356, Germ. 725, and *Ciris* 451 the MSS falsely put the common word for the rarer, see Gronovius, *loc. cit.*, Housman, Man. I. 356 n., but contrast Man. IV 257 b where Housman rightly had second thoughts. The criterion from astronomy and mythology, which helps to correct some of these faults, is wanting in the Horatian passage and others. The Virgilian verses are likely to have been in H.'s mind, but whether he wanted to generalize (and therefore wrote *piscem*), or rather be specific (and therefore wrote the Virgilian *pristim*), is hard to tell, cf. passages like Ovid's on Glaucus, *Met.* XIII. 915 *ultimaque excipiat quod tortilis inguina piscis*, 963 *cruraque pinnigero curuata nouissima pisce.* T. Sinko, *Comment. Horatianae* (Cracoviae, 1935), p. 20 thought that H. wanted to contrast *animalia aquatilia* with *terrestria* (horse) and *aeria* (bird), and hence pleaded for the generic *piscem*—a poor argument in view of *equinam* and *humanum*. The Virgilian *pristim* would give more point to H.'s caricature, but no certainty can be attained and I therefore leave the MS reading in the text.

   5 *amici* may be voc. (so the scholia), or nom. with *admissi* and *teneatis*; A. Y. Campbell's *amice* (adv., cf. Hor. *Carm.*, 1st ed. (1946), 'Horatiana Alia' *in calce libri*) is off the mark. Bentley printed the verse without a comma before *amici* but also without an explanation; the nom. = *admissi utpote...pictoris amici* was rejected by Orelli, even though he quoted Virg. *A.* VIII. 127 *quando huc uenistis amici*. Kiessling, followed by Heinze and others, paraphrased 'however close friends'. This is not impossible but unlikely; the Virgilian case is clear in comparison. If on the other hand *amici* is voc., it should end the sentence. The interwoven order across the line-ending in Markland's punctuation is unparalleled in the addresses of H.'s hexameter poems: *teneatis? amici,* | *credite, Pisones.* (Orelli said aptly, *languidiuscule nonnulli distinguunt.*) What seems required is that the concealed address in *teneatis* should be completed by the voc. *amici.* Such an arrangement is not unparalleled in the hexameter poems. It distributes over two clauses or sentences two addresses, one more general and another more specific—*Ep.* I. I. 1 *prima dicte mihi...Camena* and 3 *Maecenas*, in two clauses; *Ep.* I. 7. 1 *tibi* and 5 *Maecenas*, in two full sentences, with *dulcis amice* following thereafter (12). Addresses in the different lyric medium may be compared, e.g. *C.* II. 14. 1 *eheu fugaces, Postume Postume* and 5–6 *non si...* | *amice*, in two clauses of the same sentence; *Epod.* I. 2 *amice* and 4 *Maecenas*, in two clauses; cf. E. Fraenkel's illuminating remarks, 'Kolon und Satz', I, *NGG* (1932), 209 (repr. *Kl. Beitr.* I. 87).

(2) Conversation on incongruity: not all variety in painting and poetry can be justified by a plea for creative freedom, 6–13

6–9 *formae:* having exploited the effect of the opening leap into art-criticism, H. now undeceives the reader. He is not talking about painting for its own sake but about poetry. His subject will be poetic unity in relation to *ars poetica*. These verses apply the judgement inherent in 1–5 to works of literature, and *librum* presently turns out to be a poem. If a poem is all variety it resembles the monster in the painting: the parts of neither make a whole. Such a work resembles a feverish dream. The point where literature is reached is marked by the mention of the Pisos; H. uses his addresses often for a poetic purpose.

The details of these verses must satisfy this twofold comparison: poem–painting, poem–dream. First then a close comparison between painting and poem. Lines 1–4 and 6–8 are related in thought and grammar: 3 (sc. *ita*) *undique collatis membris, ut...* resembles 7–8 (sc. *ita*) *uanae | fingentur species, ut.. ;* compare 12 and, for the construction, Kühner–Stegmann, II. 248 f. In both cases assumptions are reported: *iungere si uelit* above, the 'potential' future *fore–fingentur* here. Finally the results are alike: *ut–destinat* above, *ut–reddatur* here.

Secondly, the meaning of *species* (pl.) must satisfy the twofold comparison; to fit the description of the painting, it must be 'constituent parts' or 'shapes'; to fit the allusion to the feverish dreamer, it must be 'images' in the mind: both concur in the notion of 'figure' or 'shape'. The latter meaning has always been confidently asserted, and appears in such paraphrases as ἰδέαι, φαντασίαι, images, *idées*, *Vorstellungen*. The former, though necessary in the context, has not been championed. O. Immisch (p. 36) however was on the right track in asserting that *species* here represents Greek ἐμφερόμενα or λήμματα, the 'features' which the poet 'takes', and embodies in his poem. Yet Immisch was put off the scent by his tendency to look for resemblances between the *Ars* and the *De Sublimitate*. His reference to ps.-Longinus, ch. 10, is nugatory; the *De Sublimitate* studies vivid, poignant, and realistic features; the *Ars* studies variety and unity. Aristotelian usage furnishes one of the meanings required. The Greek word that appears in the guise of *species* is εἶδος, the qualitative or formative elements of tragedy in *Poetics*, ch. 6, and its quantitative parts in ch. 12; epic too has its 'parts', ch. 26. The several *species* then are the parts that make up a poem.

For 'subdivisions' of this kind the Latin language offers *formae*, *species*, *partes*, and the like. Their counterparts in dialectic and logic are noted by Sandys on Cicero, *Or.* 116 *quae sint eius generis siue formae siue partes*, cf. *Top.* 31 *in diuisione formae sunt quas Graeci* εἴδη *uocant; nostri si qui haec forte tractant species appellant.* For *species* subdividing *partes* or *genera* of grammar, see Varro, *L.L.* x. 18 and 31. In H.'s context *forma* is already pre-empted, denoting the poetic or artistic entity as a whole. Besides, *species* has the advantage of hinting not only at the shapes of the work of art but at the images of a feverish dream.

Unrelated forms call to mind feverish dreams in which images are in fact unrelated. Hence *aegri somnia* (*aegri* is shown by its counterpart *cuius* to be the true reading; the variant *aegris* simply repeats the initial letter of the following word). Dreams having been mentioned, *species* cannot remain unaffected. For *species* also denotes images conceived by the mind, cf. *S.* II. 3. 208–9 *qui species alias ueris scelerisque tumultu | permixtas capiet*; Cicero calls them visions, *uisa*, *Div.* II. 122 *insanorum uisis. . . somniantium uisis*, cf. Seneca cited 7 n. Commentators fastened on to this meaning, taking one of H.'s hints but not the other. The poet is concerned to make poetry out of literary concepts; he blends two notions. Read along with *librum. . . cuius*, the *uanae species* are the unrelated elements of a poem; but with *uelut aegri somnia* they are the imaginings of a feverish dream.

fingentur is taken from the shaping of forms by the artist. It oscillates between the shaping of the poetic elements—*carmina fingo C.* IV. 2. 32, cf. *Ep.* II. 1. 227, *A.P.* 240, 331—and the fashioning of ideas in the mind—Sen. *Ep.* 13. 12 *animus sibi falsas imagines fingit.*

This is a poetic ambiguity. H.'s poetry is full of them. Translators and commentators alike will be wise to choose a rendering which is flexible enough to allow for the ambiguity.

6 *Pisones:* so here and at 235; *o Pompilius sanguis* at 291–2. At 24 we learn that they are *pater et iuuenes patre digni*, the *iuuenes* being two, the elder addressed, 366–7 *o maior iuuenum, quamuis et uoce paterna | fingeris ad rectum et per te sapis*, cf. 385 ff. This does not dispose of addresses in the *Ars*. The fashion of pinning on the Pisos every address in the poem is open to objection: see my notes and J. Vahlen, *Ges. Phil. Schr.* II, 752–6, F. Klingner, *BVSA*, LXXXVIII, 3 (1937), 14. For the identity of the Pisos, see *Prol.* 239 f.

isti, cf. 376 n.

7 *uanae* qualifies the various *species* that will not add up to a whole; thus used the word means 'incomplete, indeterminate, ineffectual', cf. *C.* III. 24. 35–6 *leges sine moribus | uanae*, Liv. XXX. 10. 13 *uana pleraque, utpote supino iactu, tela in locum superiorem mittebant*; it is also related to the false dream-images to which the *uanae species* are compared, as *C.* III. 27. 38–42, *uigilansne ploro | . . . an. . . ludit imago | uana, quae porta fugiens eburna | somnium ducit?* Cf. Sen. *Const.* 11. 1 *uanas species somniorum uisusque nocturnos nihil habentes solidi atque ueri.*

8 *nec pes nec caput:* the metaphor proverbially applied to incoherence or inconsistency: A. Otto, *Sprichwörter*, p. 74. In talking of pictures, figures and shapes, H. brings the abstract speech of traditional theory back to concrete description, and thus makes it fit for poetic use: cf. Plato and Aristotle, cited above p. 78.

8–9 *uni reddatur formae:* this is the 'unity' of the literary theorists, Plato's and Aristotle's ἕν, cf. above.

uni: not 'assigned to one form instead of to several' but 'so assigned to a form that it becomes *one*': *uni* therefore seems 'proleptic', cf. Kühner–Stegmann, I. 239 f., Hofmann–Szantyr, 414.

reddatur 'give its due, render' as in *poenas reddo* and the like. Sometimes the debt or obligation is expressed, *C.* II. 7. 17 *obligatum redde Ioui dapem*, sometimes it is not, as here and *Ep.* II. 1. 214–16 *et his... curam redde.*

formae: '*hoc uerbum complectitur et... exemplar quod artificis menti obuersatur, et exteriorem (formam) quam nobis proponit artifex uel poeta*' (Orelli).

9–13 A rapid debate: incongruity in a work of painting or poetry is excused as an artistic prerogative. H. however limits creativity, insisting on natural compatibility of the parts created: a work of art or poetry must not only be striking (to use modern parlance) but also come out 'right'.

9–10 An objection by an interlocutor unnamed—the Pisos or anyone—without an indication like *ait*. This adds to liveliness, but is rarely employed, cf. *S.* I. 2. 92 '*o crus, o bracchia*', curtly rejected by *uerum*. Objections with *at* are of course normal in the style of *sermo*, e.g. *S.* I. 4. 48, 10. 20, 23.

For the content see Diphilus *ap.* Ath. VI. 223 b (Kock, *Com. Att. Fr.* II. 549) where tragedians alone are said to be able to risk whatever they like: ὡς οἱ τραγῳδοί φασιν, οἷς ἐξουσία | ἐστὶν λέγειν ἅπαντα καὶ ποιεῖν μόνοις. Dreams, poetry, and painting are so described by Lucian, *Hermot.* 72 ὅ... ἐπενόεις οὐδὲν τῶν ἱπποκενταύρων καὶ χιμαιρῶν καὶ γοργόνων διαφέρει, καὶ ὅσα ἄλλα ὄνειροι καὶ ποιηταὶ καὶ γραφεῖς ἐλεύθεροι ὄντες ἀναπλάττουσιν οὔτε γενόμενα πώποτε οὔτε γενέσθαι δυνάμενα, κτλ., *Pro Imag.* 18 παλαιὸς οὗτος ὁ λόγος ἀνευθύνους εἶναι καὶ ποιητὰς καὶ γραφέας. Lucian's terms sound reminiscent of H. but it is more likely that both hark back to current or earlier discussions. A different aspect is that noticed frequently by the rhetoricians and grammarians, e.g. Varro, *L.L.* IX. 5 *cum poeta[e] transilire lineas impune possit*, Himerius, *Or.* (1) IX Προθεωρία, 1 ποιητικῆς αὐτονομίας ἄδεια. *Licentia poetica* had hardened to a 'technical term' in literary theory, cf. J. E. B. Mayor, *JP*, VIII (1879), 260–2. Untrammelled poetic licence is the butt of Greek philosophers and ancient literary critics, even ps.-Longinus, *Subl.* 2. 2 ὡς ἐπικινδυνότερα αὐτὰ ἐφ' αὐτῶν δίχα ἐπιστήμης... ἐπὶ μόνῃ τῇ φορᾷ καὶ ἀμαθεῖ τόλμῃ λειπόμενα. If limitless daring is untutored daring it would, paradoxically, imply that talent without *ars*–τέχνη suffices, cf. *ibid.* 2. 1 εἰ ἔστιν ὕψους... τέχνη... καὶ μία τέχνη πρὸς αὐτά, τὸ πεφυκέναι. In the *Ars*, in spite of all the emphasis on unity, the problem of training according to principles arises at this point. The problem is soon to come to the fore as one of the motifs of the poem.

9 *pictoribus atque poetis:* the two arts brought together as 7 ff., below 21, 361 n.

10 *quidlibet:* for the variant readings *quod-*, *quae-*, see below 23 n. Simple relative pronouns are not in point here, e.g. *Ad Her.* IV. 34 *quod possunt audent, et quod audent faciunt.*

audendi: a term often denoting ventures of style, in Greek τόλμα, τολμᾶν *et sim.*; thus ps.-Long. *Subl.* 2. 2 ἀμαθεῖ τόλμῃ (cit. 9–10 n.), 38. 5 παντὸς τολμήματος, Aristid. *Rhet.* I. 142 (ed. Schmidt) πάσας μίξεις μῖξαι περὶ τοὺς λόγους... οὗ δ' εὕρεσις ἐνταῦθα ἡ διαχείρισις, οὗ δὲ τολμήματα ἐνταῦθα ἀσφάλεια. In Latin *audacia* and like words occur in various literary contexts, cf. *audacia TLL*, II. 1243. 8 ff., *audax ibid.* 1248. 2 ff., *audeo* 1256. 22 ff.; often in H., e.g. below 125, 242, 287 n. *audendi* here is absol. as at Quint. *I.O.* 1. 5. 72 *audendum tamen*, VIII. 3. 35 *audendum itaque*, and elsewhere.

fuit: for the tense, see 373 n.

aequa potestas: the fairness, not the likeness, seems to be stressed, as (with a different nuance) in Prudent. *C. Symm.* II. 415 *regnandi... aequa potestas.* At 5 artistic licence was denied to painters, at any rate by implication: that does not encourage the meaning 'equal' (thus H. Schütz, *ad l.*).

11 (*scimus...*) *petimus...damus:* ps.-Acro explains, '*petimus*' *quasi poetae*, '*damus*' *quasi critici*. H. changes roles not infrequently in the course of his work. At 25 he identifies himself with 'the poets', the Pisos included, and the pl. is genuine. Here the pl. differs from the sing. only by an authoritative note. For the 1st pers. sing. see 25–6 n.

-que...-que: an archaic idiom prevalent in epic poetry and metrically adapted to hexameter verse like its predecessor τε... τε, perhaps introduced by Ennius, cf. E. Fraenkel, *Plautinisches im Pl.* p. 211, *Elementi Plaut. in Pl.* p. 427. The locution probably had an epic flavour. In the *Ars* it appears also at 73, 207, 211, 280; but the ethos differs in the various places. Fraenkel observes that double *-que* (in *one* phrase) occurs as often as seven times in *S.* I, is avoided in *S.* II, and reappears once in *Ep.* I and once, or possible twice, in *Ep.* II. He concludes that after *S.* I it was no longer favoured by H. because

he had come to regard it as unsuitable for the style of his *sermo*. The observation of different frequencies is just, but the explanation dubious in view of the evidence in this poem.

ueniam is qualified in the next verse by *sed non ut*, etc; *uenia* unqualified is suspect, cf. 267.

12–13 These lines do not so much assert, *sunt certi denique fines*, as say where the *fines* lie. Variety is to be rejected when it produces the impossible (ἀδύνατον), runs counter to 'nature'. These words must however be read in conjunction with the preceding, 8 f., *ut nec pes nec caput uni | reddatur formae*. Aristotle had argued that, for poets, a convincing impossibility is better than an unconvincing possibility, *Poet.* ch. 25. H. is not propounding a theory of poetical or rhetorical 'impossibilities', but censuring those of a certain quality, monstrosities; one is reminded of the giraffe, *Ep.* II. 1. 195, *diuersum confusa genus panthera camelo*. Thus of the series of ἀδύνατα in *Epod.* 16. 25 ff. one group only is relevant—16. 30–2 *nouaque monstra iunxerit libidine | mirus amor, iuuet ut tigris subsidere ceruis, | adulteretur et columba miluo*, cf. *coeant, geminentur* here, and *iungentur*, *C.* I. 33. 8, Virg. *E.* 8. 27; πρίν κεν λύκος οἶν ὑμεναιοῖ, Aristoph. *Pax* 1076 a. For 13 *serpentes auibus geminentur*, see the remark on Lucil. fr. 587, above 1–5 n.

placidis, immitia: neut. pl., to express generality; but the words, though not *uoces propriae* for the purpose, denote the classes of tame and wild animals to which they are now applied. H. cleverly juxtaposes adjectives with different stylistic nuances. *placidus*, properly 'gentle, docile', is shown by a verse of Terence to have been early in current use, *Ad.* 534 *quom feruit maxume, tam placidum quasi ouem reddo*. But *immitis*, 'ungentle, cruel', belongs largely to poetry and Silver Latin, cf. *TLL*, VII. 1, 467; it is not known to have been applied to animals before Virg. *G.* IV. 17 *i. nidis*, where the transference of meaning is palpable.

(3) **Three instances exemplifying incoherence; unity demanded, 14–23**

There is still no straightforward literary argument. H. begins abruptly, and after a number of false starts a general law of unity is formulated, l. 23. 'False starts' because the outcome is negative in each case, showing what unity is *not*. Externally each case is unconnected with the preceding. In fact the passages fit together when the hint at l. 23 is taken. They offer examples illustrating the need for a law of unity: three cases from three diverse arts where lack of unity causes failure for diverse reasons. (1) A poet begins but fails to continue a poem in the grand manner. His descriptions invalidate the 'tone' of his poem, 14–19. (2) A painter of votive tablets disturbs the tenor of his work. Commissioned to produce a picture of survival from shipwreck, he fails his patron by introducing a cypress, which 'belongs' to a different kind of picture, 19–21. (3) A potter starts off on an amphora but he ends up with a pitcher; that is a plan gone wrong, 21–2. Nothing is amiss with these attempts *per se*—descriptions in poetry, a cypress in a painting, a pitcher. But in each case a plan has miscarried. Hence (23) unity of plan and execution are required in any art.

No distinction has as yet been made between subject-matter, arrangement, execution. It is a fair inference therefore, borne out by 23, that H. is dealing with unity of design, which contains the aspects of subject-matter, arrangement, and execution. It stands to reason that it is hard, even in a poetics that separates subject-matter and form, to divorce the wording of an irrelevant poetic description—the purple patch—from its subject and placing; Cicero and Quintilian class *descriptio* as a 'figure of thought', not of 'speech' (14–19 n.). H. cuts through that schematism.

14–19 *Case 1, the purple patch.* H. is still being negative and satiric. But by implication he is now hinting at a specific demand of poetic technique. The first two words show what he is hinting at, I mean 14 *inceptis grauibus*; and so do similar passages: 127 *ab incepto*, 136 *nec sic incipies*, 138 *promissor*, 139 *parturient montes*, 140 ff.; 1 *humano capiti*, 8 *capiti* may also be compared. Once the 'tone' of a poem is set by its first words the rest must be attuned to it. This is not an implied demand for sameness but the old Aristotelian demand for consistency of composition (cf. above 1–41 n., pp. 78–9). Aristotle's remarks about 'episodes' in Homer are related to this demand (*Poet.* chs. 8, 23). Polemic against digressive style has its parallel in Aristotle's condemnation of 'episodic plots' (*Poet.* 9, 1451 b 33).

Commentary

In the Hellenistic age when the classical concept of poetic form had become suspect, a premium was put on variety, ποικιλία, for its own sake. As an instance I mention Philod. *Poem.* v. 17. 18–22, in his critique of Ariston, πόλε[ων] αὐτ[οῖς] (i.e. the poems of Antimachus) καὶ τόπων οὕτως εὐαρμόστως ἐ[νόντων] σὺν τῷ καὶ τὴν τάξι[ν] διαφυλάττειν—clearly a discussion of descriptive passages and their placing in the whole of a poem. It is most likely that Neoptolemus talked about this topic, but Rostagni's reconstruction has miscarried (Immisch, p. 37).

H. is concerned with the age-old epic device of ὑποτύπωσις, *descriptio*, see below 18 n. *describitur*. He is reflecting on problems of contemporary poetic workmanship—the tendency to descriptive writing that is irrelevant to the unity of a large composition. The criterion, one feels tempted to guess, is in the Homeric epic and, in H.'s contemporary terms, the Virgilian unity of descriptive writing and poetic-narrative structure. More than half a century later *descriptio* is still a convention, Sen. *Ep.* 79. 5, 122. 11–13; and so it remained.

14 *inceptis:* see 14–19 n.

grauibus: for the context, see Quint. *I.O.* VIII. 3. 60 *si quis sublimia humilibus...misceat*, etc. (cit. above 1–5 n.). The adj. is used for the great poetic genres, *C.* IV. 9. 8 *Stesichorique graues camenae*, Cic. *Planc.* 59 *quae scripsit grauis et ingeniosus poeta* (i.e. Accius), *T.D.* I. 64 *ut...poetam graue plerumque carmen sine caelesti...instinctu putem fundere*, *Culex* 8–9 *grauiore sono tibi musa loquetur* | *nostra*, Prop. I. 9. 9 *graue dicere carmen*, Ov. *Am.* I. I. 1–2 *arma graui numero...parabam* | *edere*, III. I. 35–6 *quid grauibus uerbis, animosa Tragoedia,...* | *me premis? an numquam non grauis esse potes?*, *Met.* X. 150, *Tr.* II. 554 *grauis...coturnus*, Quint. *I.O.* X. I. 66 *(Aeschylus) sublimis et grauis et grandiloquus saepe usque ad uitium*, et al. The 'elevated genre' of the orators too is denoted by this word, *TLL*, VI. 2. 2287. 6 ff.

plerumque: as usually in H. in its poetic and Silver use = 'often, occasionally'. At 95 it takes up *interdum* (93) without change of meaning, see 93 n. At *C.* I. 34. 7 however it = 'as a rule'; cf. *plerique* 'most', *S.* I. 6. 5. Vahlen, *H*, XII (1877), 190, compares *plerumque...cum* 14–16 and 95–6.

15–16 *purpureus...pannus:* wide spacing, over two lines, of adjective

95

and noun, thus giving prominence to the two words to be emphasized. Cf. *S.* II. 1. 32–4 *omnis...uita senis*, and Fraenkel, *Hor.* 151 n. 1, on 'emphatic hyperbaton'.

The fame of the 'purple patch' must not make the reader forget that the expression is still unexplained. Comparisons of style with sewing and weaving are familiar from rhetorical and literary theory alike; so Quint. *I.O.* XII. 9. 17 and the Greek passages below. The best guides that I can find are Petronius and Quintilian on *sententiae*. Petron. 118. 5 writes, *praeterea curandum est ne sententiae emineant extra corpus orationis expressae, sed* intexto uestibus (intecto uersibus *uar.*) colore *niteant.* Homer and the lyric poets, Roman Virgil and *Horatii curiosa felicitas* are the true models. Quint. *I.O.* VIII. 5. 25 ff. is more long-winded but, at 28, uses a like comparison with clothing, *ut afferunt lumen clauus et purpurae loco insertae, ita certe neminem deceat intertexta pluribus notis uestis* (cit. H. Schütz). Quintilian may have in mind Horace's verses, although his wording may be influenced by such phrases as *chlamydemque auro...intertextam*, Virg. *A.* VIII. 167, describing the process of interweaving, not of sewing. *pannus* therefore has no business with *clauus*. 'The *panni* are not attached to the body of the work, but incorporated here and there in it' (Wilkins). Hence there is no thought of the *latus clauus* of toga or tunic, and Kiessling's reference to Demetr. *Interpr.* 108 τοῖς τῶν πλουσίων ἔοικεν ἐπιδείγμασιν, γείσοις λέγω καὶ τριγλύφοις καὶ πορφύραις πλατείαις is nugatory; for a possible explanation of the Demetrian passage, see G. M. A. Grube, *A Greek Critic: Demetrius on Style* (1961), p. 45. Nor does H.'s *late* allude to the *latus clauus* (Heinze). Metaphors based on *clauus* or its Greek counterparts do occur: thus εὐπάρυφος, 'with a (purple) border sewn on', describes the swaggering style ridiculed by Plutarch as εὐπάρυφα καὶ σοβαρὰ διηγήματα (*De se ipsum...laud.*, ch. 22). But this is not H.'s metaphor. Using as a clue H.'s *unus et alter | adsuitur pannus* we should be looking for 'one or two purple adornments sewn on' a piece of clothing. This description recalls the *segmenta*, trimmings of purple or gold, of Ov. *A.A.* III. 169, *quid de ueste loquar? nec nunc segmenta requiro*, Juv. 2. 124, et al. J. Marquardt and A. Mau, *Privatleben der Römer*², p. 548 n. 2, have plausibly identified H.'s purple patch with these *segmenta*. The conceit of the *pannus* is not used at *Ep.* II. 1. 73–5 *inter quae uerbum emicuit si forte decorum...iniuste totum ducit uenditque poema.*

16–18 There follow examples which are presumably designed to recall descriptions disturbing the narrative flow and stylistic unity in long epic poems of the time. Short narrative poems such as Catullus' *Peleus et Thetis* are digressive, and many may have contained long descriptions; but H.'s wording l. 14 shows they are not here in question.

16 *lucus et ara Dianae:* groves were a major topic of τοπογραφίαι, cf. Pers. 1. 70–1 *nec ponere lucum | artifices nec rus saturum laudare,* cf. Juv. 1. 7. The mention of Diana serves to particularize H.'s general point; she above all is the goddess of groves and mountains: Cat. 34. 9 ff. *montium domina... | siluarumque uirentium | saltuumque reconditorum,* Virg. *A.* iii. 681 *silua alta Iouis lucusue Dianae,* Hor. *C.* i. 21. 5, *C. Saec.* 69; cf. Wissowa, *Röm. Rel.*² 247 n. 4. This applies *a fortiori* to the most notable (for a Roman) of all these groves, that at Aricia, where Diana was worshipped as *Nemorensis* (Wissowa, *Röm. Rel.*² 247 nn. 6–7). But there is no indication that the Schol. Cruq. *ad l.* is right in naming exclusively the grove of Aricia. If H. had wanted to be more specific, he would not have found it hard to be so.

17 A mock *descriptio,* maliciously exaggerating features that can be discerned in such verses as Enn. *Ann.* 173 (V.²) *quod per amoenam urbem leni fluit agmine flumen,* cited by Macr. *Sat.* vi. 4. 4, who adduces some other instances. Cf. E. Norden on Virg. *A.* vi. 659 *plurimus Eridani per siluam uoluitur amnis.* The caricature resides in the combined rhythmic and alliterative schemes, although the sound-effects are mild. A hexameter line containing four pure dactyls, although not infrequent in the *Ars* (cf. D. Bo, *Hor. Op.* iii, 59), is made conspicuous by the repeated *a* sounds; without such alliteration, e.g. above in 2, the effect differs. For *ambitus* (wrongly derived by Roman scholars from *amnis*) in similar contexts, see *TLL,* i. 1859. 11 ff., G. B. A. Fletcher *Annot. on Tac.* (1964), p. 47, on Tac. *Ann.* xv. 4. 1. The idyllic character of the small stream is perhaps contrasted with the large river (Rhine) in the following verse. For different variations of a similar contrast cf. Callim. *Hymn* 2. 108 Ἀσσυρίου ποταμοῖο μέγας ῥόος–112 ὀλίγη λιβὰς ἄκρον ἄωτον, Hor. *Ep.* ii. 2. 120 (and my remarks *Prol.* 159 n. 3, 188 n. 4), ps.-Long. *Subl.* 35. 4 οὐ τὰ μικρὰ ῥεῖθρα θαυμάζομεν, εἰ καὶ διαυγῆ καὶ χρήσιμα, ἀλλὰ τὸν Νεῖλον καὶ Ἴστρον ἢ Ῥῆνον, πολὺ δ᾽ ἔτι μᾶλλον τὸν Ὠκεανόν.

18 *flumen Rhenum:* that the name of the river is here adjectival is noted by Porph., also ps.-Acro *ad l.* and on *C.* iv. 4. 38. This usage is found in poetry, as *C. loc. cit. Metaurum flumen,* and archaizing or poetic prose, although the older commentators tend to confuse it with such appositions as *mare Oceanus,* Tac. *H.* iv. 12. 2. Priscian, *Inst.* v. 43 (*GL,* ii, pp. 169–70), is probably mistaken in saying that *uetustissimi...dicebant...Histrum pro Hister, et Rhenum, Tanagrum, Metaurum...Oceanum; hoc tamen quotiens flumen sequebatur solebant facere.* For the adjectival use of names which provides the only known analogy in archaic Latin is almost entirely restricted to Roman names in -*ius*, of the type *aqua Appia, uia Appia, circus Flaminius, porticus Pompeia, basilica Iulia*, cf. W. Schulze, *Röm. Eigennamen*, pp. 510 ff., K. Meister, *Eigenn.* 1. 81 ff., E. Löfstedt, *Syn.* 1². 113 f.

From descriptions of the Rhine burlesqued at *S.* 1. 10. 37 many have concluded that the same poet is attacked in both places and that the poet is Furius Bibaculus. For this identification there is no clear evidence, and it would not be very relevant to the *A.P.* if there were. It would be more relevant if one could conclude from the mention of this river and the present context that H. has in mind an epic narrative of a recent war in Gaul.

pluuius...arcus: H.'s polemic suggests that contemporary verse narrative contained such descriptions of the rainbow as Lucan, IV. 79–82 *hinc imperfecto complectitur aera gyro | arcus, uix ulla uariatus luce colorem, | Oceanumque bibit raptosque ad nubila fluctus | pertulit et caelo defusum reddidit aequor.* The *tristicha de arcu caeli* (Riese, *Anth. Lat.* 1. 2², 69–72) could be compared if they were set loosely in a narrative context.

describitur: at the end of the *descriptiones* H. names the procedure, as often pulling together representative detail and variety by a conceptual term, a *sententia*, an occasional proposition. *descriptio*, ὑποτύπωσις, had long been claimed by the rhetoricians as a useful if poetic device, cf. *TLL*, v. 1. 665 ff., Steidle, *Studien*, p. 21 n. 27. Cic. *De Or.* III. 205 and Quint. *I.O.* IX. 2. 40 ff. mention it among the 'figures of thought', *lumina sententiarum*. Its attractions as much as its dangers to the orators lay in its poetic character. Sen. *Contr.* II, praef. 1 *in descriptionibus extra legem omnibus uerbis, dummodo niterent, permissa libertas.* Quint. *I.O.* II. 4. 3 (on elementary rhetorical exercises in narrative) *ut sit ea (narrandi ratio) neque arida...neque rursus sinuosa et arcessitis descriptionibus, in quas plerique imitatione poeticae licentiae ducuntur, lasciuiat,* Plin. *Ep.* VII. 9. 8 *saepe in oratione quoque non historica modo sed prope poetica descriptionum necessitas incidit.* The rhetorical device then was borrowed from the poets, and as a poetic device it is censured by H. Later critics noted *descriptiones* in Virgil and other poets (*TLL*, v. 1. 666. 23 ff., cf. Sen. *Ep.* noted above 14–19 n.). Evidence from contemporary verse apart from Virgil is lacking but so is narrative verse of the time. It follows from H.'s way of talking that he is concerned with contemporary writing: virtuoso pieces unrelated to the larger poetic aim. With customary fastidiousness he is content merely to hint at the technical term, *describitur* (noted by Steidle, *loc. cit.*). The particular form that H. picks out is description of landscape. Cf. Quint. *I.O.* IX. 2. 44 *locorum quoque dilucida et significans descriptio eidem uirtuti adsignatur a quibusdam, alii* τοπογραφίαν *dicunt*. For ethnographical τοπογραφία in lyric verse, see Fraenkel, *Hor.* 428 ff.

19 *nunc* 'at that time' or 'place', not '*nunc logicum*'. Since *descriptio* was a common feature of all epic poetry, H. can only mean to exclude it when it is so little integrated as to disturb poetic unity. The brief sentence in which *nunc* occurs is transitional, leading on to the second case in which the incriminated feature is to be wholly removed.

non erat is not a reference to a past time when the descriptions were penned. The present time is referred to, as in ll. 16 and 18. Some commentators have compared the poetic idiom *tempus erat*, which conveys a similar notion. Cf. *C.* 1. 37. 1–4 nunc est *bibendum*...nunc ...*ornare tempus erat*, etc., Ov. *Am.* 11. 9. 23–4 me quoque... | *defunctum placide uiuere tempus erat* (i.e. 'now'), 111. 1. 23–4 tempus erat thyrso pulsum grauiore moueri; | *cessatum satis est: incipe maius opus, Tr.* IV. 8. 24–5 me quoque donari iam rude tempus erat. | tempus erat, etc. (cf. *Am.* 11. 9 above), Mart. IV. 33. 4 tempus erat iam te...legi. Hor. *Ep.* 1. 4. 6 *non tu corpus eras sine pectore* has also been adduced, for example by L. Mueller *ad l.* This passage is not so close to *non erat locus* as *tempus erat*, but a similar time-scale is involved. E. Fraenkel, *Hor.* 324 n. 3, comparing the idiom ἦσθ' ἄρα, regards *Ep.* 1. 4. 6 (and Prop. 1. 13. 34) as Grecisms. The 'grammar books', as he says, are silent. (Or virtually so: H. Blase in Landgraf's *Hist. Gram. d. lat. Spr.* III (1903), 148 cited and disagreed with a note by N. Wecklein (*P*, XLIV (1885), 400) in which *non tu corpus eras* is said to correspond to Greek ἦσθ' ἄρα.) But this use of the imperf. in Latin verse needs to be surveyed in greater detail.

locus probably = Greek καιρός, as Steidle, *Studien*, p. 22 has noted. Ps.-Acro paraphrases *non erat locus ut haec describeres, sed quoniam bene describis ideo introduxisti*. The word does not here involve the chapter of the *Ars* known as *dispositio, ordo*, τάξις, which follows below, 41. *locus* here only hints at the placing of what amounts to a digression and thus disturbs unity, is not καίριον, cf. ps.-Long. *Subl.* 10. 1. In a similar way Quintilian adds a chapter *de egressione* when dealing with the sections of a speech, although such topics as *de partitione* and *de ordine* are not yet in view. Cf. Quint. *I.O.* IV. 3. 3, a good commentary on this passage: *in quo uitium illud est quod sine discrimine...utilitatis hoc, tamquam semper expediat aut etiam necesse sit, faciunt, eoque sumptas ex iis partibus* quarum alius erat locus *sententias in hanc congerunt, ut...quia alieno loco dicta sunt dici* suo *non possint.*

19 (*et*)-**21** (*pingitur*). *Case 2, the votive painting.* Porph. *ad l.: hoc prouerbium est in malum pictorem qui nesciebat aliud bene* *pingere quam cupressum. ab hoc naufragus quidam petiit ut casum suum exprimeret. ille interrogauit* num ex cupresso uellet aliquid adici. *quod prouerbium Graecis in usu est,* μή τι καὶ κυ⟨πά⟩ρισσον (the wording is uncertain) θέλεις; Whether this is an anecdote rather than a proverb is not known. Some commentators (e.g. H. Schütz) allege that the funerary associations of the cypress make the story more pointed, cf. *C.* II. 14. 23 *inuisas cupressos, Epod.* 5. 18 *cupressos* (-*us* uar.) *funebris;* Olck, *R-E,* IV. 1932 ff. R. Strömberg, 'Greek Proverbs' (*Göteborgs Kungl. Vetensk....Handl.* Ser. A, IV. 8, 1954), p. 74, says, 'the amusing point of the phrase is that the painter, by asking the shipwrecked man whether he wishes to have a cypress painted, uses this tree, which was symbolic of death and funerals, in an inappropriate macabre connexion'.

19 *et fortasse:* ironical and conversational transition, cf. Pl. *Bacch.* 220–1 '*nam istoc* fortasse *aurost opus*'.–'*Philippeo quidem.*'–'*atque eo* fortasse *iam opust.*' For the colloquial colour of *fortasse,* see Cledonius, *Ars* (*GL,* v. 66. 30), *forte, forsan et forsitan poeticum est, fortasse prosae,* B. Axelson, 'Unpoet. Wörter' (*Skr....Lund* 29, 1945), p. 32.

20 *simulare* 'represent', as *Ep.* II. 1. 241 *Alexandri uultum simulantia* (*aera*), Sil. xv. 427 *antrum...quod acus simulauit in ostro,* Stat. *Theb.* IV. 161–2 *foribus simulata salignis* | *hospitis arma dei,* Calp. *Decl.* xxi *simuletur hoc factum non tantum colore sed aere.*

quid hoc, si...? The context requires a colloquial locution meaning *quid ad rem?* or *quid refert?* A verb is easily supplied but the wording is not easily paralleled. For such phrases as Plaut. *Poen.* 1021 *quid istuc ad me?* are more explicit, and Plautus' *quid hoc?* or *quid si...?* differ in sense; so does Ter. *Phor.* 330 *qui istuc...?* As for Cicero, editors, probably rightly, now tend to repunctuate, *quid? hoc...,* e.g. *Sex. Rosc.* 42, *T.D.* I. 25; for *Att.* I. 16. 10 see D. R. Shackleton Bailey, *Towards a text of Cic. Ad Att.* 3. *quid est hoc?, Clu.* 127, is 'what does that amount to?', not the meaning required in H. While no strict parallel to the Horatian locution is known to me, I can see no reason why it should not stand. To say that *quid hoc?* is not Latin for 'what of that?' (Shackleton Bailey, *Towards a text, ibid.*) is something of an overstatement. *quid hoc?* seems to me acceptable Latin, though it is not, to my knowledge, *attested.* But not all acceptable Latin is attested.

20–1 *si fractis...qui pingitur?* Escape from peril at sea was

often acknowledged and depicted on Greek votive tablets, cf.
W. H. D. Rouse, *Greek Votive Offerings* (1902), pp. 228 ff. So too in
Rome. Cic. *N.D.* III. 89 *nonne animaduertis ex tot tabulis pictis, quam
multi uotis uim tempestatis effugerint in portumque salui peruenerint?*, Hor. *C.* I.
5. 13–16 *me tabula sacer | uotiua paries indicat uuida | suspendisse potenti |
uestimenta maris deo*, Comm. Cruq. on *S.* II. 1. 33 *uotiua tabula est quae
ex uoto posita est in templo aut aliquo loco publico, in qua descripta, hoc est
depicta, est fortuna alicuius; ita solent naufragi suum naufragium in tabella
depictum circumferre et in templis alicui deo consecratum suspendere* (Mayor on
Juv. 12. 27). Tablet painters must have been kept in business, at any
rate partly, by impecunious patrons; even professional beggars displayed such tablets (Mayor on Juv. 14. 301 f.), although that is not
the implication here.

The two verses are graphically foreshortened: *si...enatat...qui
pingitur* for prosaic *si pingitur qui enatat* (Kiessling); *aere dato* jostling
with the picture of the desperate swimmer; *exspes* (an expressive and
rare word, archaic and poetic, *TLL*, v. 2. 1902. 13 ff.) first explained
by *fractis...nauibus*, 'no hope left, his ship wrecked', next modified by
enatat 'desperately swimming to safety'. The pl. *nauibus* is unexplained, for one would expect one ship only, as at Pers. 1. 89–90
cum fracta te in trabe pictum | ex umero portes, Juv. 14. 301–2 (mentioned
above) *mersa rate naufragus assem | dum rogat et picta se tempestate tuetur*.
Thus, unless *naues* (like *classes* on occasion) is employed as a 'poetic
plural', a plural notion would be required. Is it a rich merchant's
fleet?

21–2. *Case 3, the potter's débâcle.* A craftsman's plan miscarries: an amphora is intended, a pitcher results. The potter
is an important type of craftsman in archaic technology,
notably Middle Eastern and Mediterranean; he is one of
those ἐξ ὧν πόλις γίγνεται (Plato, *Rep.* IV. 421 a). Hence the
references to him when *techne* is under discussion, in ancient
philosophy, theology, and literary theory. My wife reminds
me of Jeremiah, xvii. 1–4; verse 4 in particular is relevant:
'the vessel he was making of clay was spoilt in the potter's
hand and he reworked it into another vessel as it seemed good
to the potter to do' (*R.S.V.*). It should not be concluded (with
K.–H.) that the absence of a connective word makes this
anecdote not a third independent example but an elaboration
of the second. Nothing of the sort can be concluded from a

Horatian asyndeton; in any case, *denique* (23) sums up this case as well as the two preceding. The present example puts a new construction on the digressive style of narrative verse as it does on the painter's unsuitable addition to the votive picture: what poet and painter added to their work disturbed its plan, but in the present case the plan as a whole miscarries. Unsuitable variety therefore, however effective in itself, *resembles* the potter's botching; it is no better than the pitcher in the place of the amphora that was intended.

amphora, urceus: how do they differ? Commentators are divided. A majority of them think that a comment on size is intended (thus many Renaissance editors, later for example Dacier, Sanadon, H. Schütz, K.–H., Rostagni, Immisch); others on shape and kind (Orelli, Wickham, Lejay, E. Vandvik, *Symb. Osl.* xix (1939), 112); a third party on size as well as shape (thus Lambinus, Baxter, L. Mueller, Wilkins). Ancient or medieval commentators and writers seem to have been divided between the first two propositions. Ps.-Acro, Comm. Cruq. and Tract. Vind. talk of size. But Porphyrion and such an intelligent reader as St Jerome (*Ep.* 27. 3. 1, 103. 3. 1) apply the comparison to literary subject-matter, *materia*, implying a difference in kind or shape; Sid. Apoll. *Ep.* ix. 16. 4, where the change from prose to verse is in mind, can scarcely have any other significance. Now a comment on size could be intended only if *urcei* were commonly smaller than *amphorae* so that readers could at once see the point of the comparison. But this does not seem to be the case. When it rains *urceatim* (Petron. 44. 18), it hardly does so 'in jugfuls'. The *urceus nouus fictilis* which is recommended by Columella (xii. 46. 6) for storing pomegranates layer by layer, with sawdust trodden in between, must have been a large container; the same may apply to Cato, *Agr.* 13. 1, but the text is uncertain. Plautus' *urceus* at *Mil.* 831 could not have been quite so large, but must have been large enough to contain eight *heminae*, something like half a gallon. I conclude that size is not alluded to; hence there is no reason why H. should not be commenting on the shape. The *urceus* then is here likely to be a 'pitcher' rather than a jug; but this does not prevent Martial (xi. 56. 3) and others from using, in an appropriate context, the same word for a jug (doubtless with a single handle and lip for pouring), and when the size is very small *urceus* becomes *urceolus*.

That containers, smaller or larger, of the shape of a storage-jar were called *urcei* is shown also by an inscription. My colleague,

Miss J. M. Reynolds of Newnham College, draws my attention to *CIL*, XIII. 3. 1, no. 10008. 44, where a vessel for storing honey is inscribed *urceus*, in cursive writing. The type is described and illustrated on p. 86 of the same volume. There are no handles. Its shape will suggest why the potter could have started to make an amphora, and ended up with that kind of jar or pitcher.

coepit | institui: unlike *Ep.* II. 1. 149 *coepit uerti iocus*, which is likely to have middle connotation, this is a genuine pass. inf. This use of *coepit*, instead of *coeptus est*, is in verse first known from Lucr. (with inanimate grammatical subj.), in prose about the same time; with personal subj. in prose from *Rhet. Her.* and Sall., in verse from Hor. *Ep.* 1. 15. 27 *urbanus coepit haberi*, cf. *TLL*, III. 1425. 28 ff., 1424. 66 ff.; Hofmann–Szantyr, 288, G. B. A. Fletcher, *Annot. on Tac.* (1964), p. 58.

currente rota cur urceus: for the *u* and *r* sounds see Fraenkel, *Hor.* 25, 81 n.; for *curro*, τρέχω and the like, applied to rapid rotation, see A. Y. Campbell, *CQ*, n.s. VI (1956), 66.

rota is sufficiently defined by *amphora* as *figularis*, potter's wheel.

exit may be construed in two ways. Either *urceus* is grammatical subj.; then *exit = prodit*—off the lathe, from a workshop (Cic. *Parad.* 5), etc., even though the provenance may be expressed in other ways, e.g. *currente rota* above. If this is the notion, the passage is a little oddly placed at *TLL*, V. 2. 1364. 10. Or *amphora* persists as subj., *urceus* is pred., then *exit* = 'comes out as a pitcher'; cf. Pers. 5. 78–9 *uerterit hunc dominus: momento turbinis exit | Marcus Dama*—a passage perhaps influenced by the Horatian verse (F. Villeneuve, *Essai sur Perse* (1918), p. 472). But in spite of what may be an imitation of this line, I doubt if the abortive amphora could be called 'an amphora' in the same way as Marcus Dama was Dama before the *momentum*. The same reason is likely to disqualify the notion (also pred.) 'the amphora tails off into a pitcher'. This has been proposed by E. Vandvik, *Symb. Osl.* XIX (1939), 112, who compares the hybrid monster of 1 ff.

23 *Summary and Precept.* Lines 14–22 were superficially unconnected, varied, and deliberately puzzling; cf. P. Cauer, *RM*, LXI (1906), 238. The present verse offers the key. The unity of the whole passage is impressed on the reader in one brief and memorable phrase, a precept. (Brevity of precept H. himself advocates, 335 *quidquid praecipies esto breuis*, etc.) The precept hints at the Platonic–Aristotelian doctrine of artistic unity: Ar. *Poet.* chs. 7–8, cf. above pp. 78–9.

denique 'in short' as *S.* 1. 1. 92 *denique sit finis quaerendi*, 3. 34 *denique te ipsum | concute*, et al.

sit quiduis: quiduis K ψ² ς, *quoduis* or *quod uis* cett., cf. Keller, *Epil.* 735; the two pronouns are frequently confused in MSS, e.g. above 10, Juv. 8. 183, 223. Bentley made a strong, and in my opinion convincing, plea for *quiduis*; yet all recent editors ignore it—I do not know why. It is generally agreed that a grammatical obj. *quod (uis)* = *quod (instituis)* would be miserably weak, lacking the generalizing force of *quiduis*, cf. *S.* II. 3. 126–8 *quare, | si quiduis satis est, periuras* ... | *undique?* and also *quidlibet*, above 10 *quidlibet audendi...potestas (quod-, quae-* uar. ll.), Cic. *Att.* III. 23. 4 *id caput sane nolim nouos tribunos pl. ferre; sed perferant modo quidlibet.* On the other hand an adj. *quoduis* is highly suspect if the best that K.–H. can do to defend it is to make it pred. to something like the word *opus*, which moreover has to be understood from the context. *quoduis* may be used as an attrib. It is for the defenders of this reading to show that it is used in the relevant authors as a pred. and, what is more, as a pred. to a noun understood.

dumtaxat: for discussion of the derivation, see M. Leumann, *MH*, xxv (1968), 243–7. The word is a limiting particle, as Madvig, Cic. *Fin.*[3] p. 177 showed, not, as some commentators still think, a conjunction. The evidence may be seen in *TLL*, s.v. The word is prosaic, and very rare in classical verse. Of the six instances noted by B. Axelson, *Unpoet. Wörter*, p. 96, two occur in H.'s hexameter poems, cf. *S.* II. 6. 42. The word qualifies nouns, adj., or phrases. Its intermediate placing here resembles e.g. Cic. *Att.* II. 18. 2 *in circulis d. et in conuiuiis.*

simplex...et unum: unum corresponds to ἕν in the Aristotelian formula ἕν καὶ ὅλον or the like; but *simplex* does not quite correspond to ὅλον, which is later (34) expressed by *totum.* Rather *simplex* makes *unum* more concrete. H. avoids abstract terminology; *unum*, 'one', is insufficiently explained by the preceding verses, hence he adds *simplex* 'of one kind', a thing which is not *uarium.* Its Greek counterpart is ἁπλοῦς, with its opposite ποικίλος. In different connotations ἁπλοῦς occurs in the *Poetics;* it does not occur in chs. 7–8. But the terminology antedates Aristotle. The concept of ποικιλία is probably at home in rhetorical practice (Steidle, *Studien*, pp. 28 ff.) and is opposed on Platonic principles, e.g. *Rep.* x. 604 e 1 πολλὴν μίμησιν καὶ ποικίλην ἔχει, contrasted at e 3 by παραπλήσιον ὂν ἀεὶ αὐτὸ αὑτῷ. For applications to historiography, see Steidle, *op. cit.* p. 28 n. 46, F. W. Walbank, *A hist. comm. on Polybius*, 1. 43; cf. Diod. xx. 1. 5 τὸ γὰρ τῆς ἱστορίας γένος ἁπλοῦν ἐστι καὶ συμφυὲς αὑτῷ καὶ τὸ σύνολον ἐμψύχῳ σώματι παραπλήσιον κτλ.

(4) A literary argument: incoherent variety, like certain kinds of faulty style, is a virtue misunderstood; uniformity and unity; 'art' as regulator, 24–31

The poet has moved on, it seems, to matters wholly at variance with the preceding 'section'. Some would call it a digression. The two sections are overtly brought together only in the last few lines, 29–31: foolish variation derives from a desirable motive, avoidance of uniformity; but without 'art' avoidance of faulty uniformity produces faulty variety—a lack of unity. (H.'s own procedure thus mirrors his subject; being himself suspect of *uariare...prodigialiter*, he shows variety controlled by unity.) Nor is the intervening section only superficially related to his main theme. For while the preceding section largely dealt with 'subject-matter', the present deals with its companion, 'style'. In the end a new proposition is made (31), but it applies to poetry as a whole and art as a whole: the distinction between 'what' (subject) and 'how' (style) is no longer relevant.

Like much of H.'s poetry, this section is best read twice over in quick succession: in its natural order, and from the final point backwards. The retrograde procedure takes the reader from the final proposition that lack of art causes the artist to jump from the frying pan into the fire (31) to its application to variety of matter in a painting (29–30), thence to stylistic faults which are virtues unattained, to the initial proposition that the poetic faults are poetic virtues misunderstood. The natural order takes the reader after an abrupt start (24) into a theory of style with a strong Peripatetic flavour (25–8), on to the recognition that the inorganic variety of the arts with which poetry has been compared is a virtue gone wrong from lack of artistry.

(a) 24–8

The stylistic theories glanced at seem to be the 'virtues of style', *uirtutes dicendi*: ἀρεταὶ λέξεως, in 25–6, and the 'types of style',

Commentary

genera dicendi: χαρακτῆρες τῆς λέξεως, in 26–8. These are much-vented topics and I refer to the judicious survey by George Kennedy, *The Art of Persuasion* (1963), 273ff. and his bibliography in nn. 16 and 25. Although the evidence for the 'virtues' is less ambiguous than that for the 'types', I regard it as a mistake to underestimate the effect of both. Their relevance to the *Ars* was at issue between L. Spengel, *P*, ix (1854), 573ff. and J. Vahlen, *Ges. Phil. Schr.* i, 445 ff.; neither discussion is fully conclusive.

24 *maxima pars uatum: uates* occurs only twice in the *Ars*. Here, except by metre, it is indistinguishable from *poeta*, and used with a decidedly ironic nuance; contrast 400 n.

pater et iuuenes patre digni: for the address, see above 5 n. *Pisones*.

25 *decipimur specie recti:* not only an urbane extension of these strictures to H. (in spite of the fact that he later declines poetic status, 306) but also an indication that these are dangers every poet has to face.

For deception by 'semblance of right', see *Ad Her.* iv. 15, specie *grauitatis* falluntur *nec perspicere possunt orationis tumorem*, Quint. *I.O.* viii. 3. 56 *cacozelon uocatur quidquid est ultra uirtutem quotiens* ingenium iudicio caret et specie boni fallitur, *omnium in eloquentia uitiorum pessimum; nam cetera parum uitantur, hoc petitur*, Gell. vi. 14. 4 (cit. below), Aug. *Conf.* 11. 12–13 *quaedam defectiua species et umbratica, uitiis fallentibus, nam et superbia celsitudinem imitatur*, etc. (Origen's *Hom. in Exod.* viii. 158 [cit. Keller and Holder, *A.P.* 1–4 n.; Migne, *P.G.* xii. 353 f., Berlin Corpus, Orig. vi (1920), 221 f.], is no more than superficially alike: Platonizing ontology is something H. avoided.)

A technical fault therefore emerges as excellence attempted but unattained: ps.-Long. *Subl.* 5. 1 ἀφ' ὧν γὰρ ἡμῖν τἀγαθά, σχεδὸν ἀπ' αὐτῶν τούτων καὶ τὰ κακὰ γεννᾶσθαι φιλεῖ (adapted from Democr. в 172, Diels–Kranz, *Fr. d. Vorsokr.*). ὅθεν...ἀρχαὶ...καὶ τῶν ἐναντίων καθίστανται. Thus faults are considered 'deviations', παρεκβάσεις, from the right road, ὀρθόν, *rectum*, that was aimed at; the worst faults are neighbours of their respective virtues. This assessment had become something of a commonplace in ancient writing on literature and rhetoric. The term παρέκβασις is Aristotelian although Aristotle applied it to moral and political subjects, not to rhetorical and literary. For types of style vitiated by neighbouring faults, see Demetr. *Interpr.* 114, 186, 236, 302, ps.-Long. *Subl.* 3. 3,

Commentary

Ad Her. IV. 15 *est autem cauendum ne, dum haec genera consectemur,* in finituma et propinqua uitia *ueniamus,* etc. *in hoc genus plerique cum declinantur et ab eo quo profecti sunt* aberrarunt, etc. (cf. above para. 2 of this note), Quint. *I.O.* VIII. 3. 7 *uicina uirtutibus uitia,* X. 2. 16, XII. 10. 73 (cit. 27 n.), Plin. *Ep.* IX. 26. 2 (*de oratore*) *altis et excelsis adiacent abrupta,* Gell. VI. 14. 4 *his singulis orationis uirtutibus uitia agnata sunt pari numero quae earum modum...simulacris falsis ementiuntur* (followed by a cit. from Varro on *uera...et propria huiuscemodi formarum exempla*).

25–6 *laboro,* | *...fio:* H.'s astonishing practice of partly displaying and partly concealing his personality is at the root of his poetry both in the lyric and the hexameter poems; no brief note can do justice to it. In the *Ars* I observe the following rough divisions in the use of the first person sing. (1) At 55–6 we find the one poignantly personal passage in the *Ars*; here H. calls himself a creator of language, as in *Ep.* 1. 19 and elsewhere he calls himself a creator of Roman lyric. (2) In the final part of the poem he speaks of himself as a teacher (or critic) engaged in addressing this *ars poetica* to the Pisos while, to use the language of his self-imposed convention, 'not himself writing poetry': 301–6, 317, 351–60, 388, 409 f., 463 f. (3) 42 *aut ego fallor* and 272 *ne dicam* qualify affirmations in a quasi-personal manner. (4) Occasionally when H. censures amateurism or lays down the law he identifies himself with the poets censured, or he so legislates as though he were writing in the relevant genres. The former sweetens the medicine; so here *laboro...fio,* cf. 25 *decipimur,* 87–8, 265–74 (for 272, see (3)). The latter seems to involve him as a participant: 234–44. The palpable fiction is that H. is proposing to write Satyric drama (though it does not follow that he regarded Satyric drama in Rome as a fiction); 244 *me iudice* is part of this pretence; it does not differ from, say, 240 *sequar.* (5) In the section on drama H. occasionally identifies himself with other theatre-goers, 102–5, 153, 188. The motive is the same as under (4) above.

From what I have said it will be clear why I regard as inadequate the discussion of this problem by G. Williams, *JRS,* LIV (1964), 195.

esse: laboro with inf. occurs frequently in H., not only in the hexameter poems but also *C.* II. 3. 11. It is first known from Lucil. fr. 349–50 (Marx), occurs in Cicero but always negatively = 'not trouble to', perhaps originally colloquial. As an affirmation it is still poetic in H. and later appears in Silver prose: Kühner–Stegmann, I. 667, Hofmann–Szantyr, 346.

breuis... | *obscurus:* the *uirtutes orationis* so-called were often freely conflated with the *genera* and it is not impossible that H. found them so conflated in the tradition to which he adhered. Nevertheless the wording in *breuis–obscurus* hints at the former whereas the wording in 26–8 hints at the latter.

For the concept of brevity in ancient rhetoric see the basic study by J. Stroux, *De Theophrasti Virtutibus Dicendi* (1912). Isocrates seems to have demanded brevity (συντομία) in the narrative of speeches, but neither Aristotle nor Theophrastus in analysing diction considered brevity a virtue *per se*, *Prol.* 95 n. 1, 262. The Stoics characteristically did, since they considered talk 'good' when it expressed what was necessary, αὐτὰ τὰ ἀναγκαῖα (Diog. Laert. VII. 59); no need for them to trouble about obscurity (Stroux, *op. cit.* p. 39). The Peripatetics on the other hand made clarity a criterion of good style and this is the teaching which H. accepts. The guess may therefore be made that H.'s tradition in this matter ultimately derives from the post-Theophrastean Peripatos, when the school, while adhering to Aristotle's criterion of clarity, σαφήνεια, yet admitted brevity as a 'virtue of style'. In later works on rhetoric it may, in the manner of Isocrates, remain attached to the qualities of narrative (e.g. Cic. *De Or.* III. 202, Quint. *I.O.* IV. 2. 64), which are not here relevant. In the wider setting of stylistic criticism it is often attached to vividness of style—*euidentia, repraesentatio*—as at Quint. *I.O.* VIII. 3. 82 (brevity desirable but obscurity a bad imitation of brevity) or among the 'figures of speech', *I.O.* IX. 3. 58. 'Longinus' sets it in his section on composition, rhythm, etc., *Subl.* ch. 42.

This is the background which one needs to know if one wants to judge what H. has been trying to do. He avoids undue technicality. He hints at literary theory—*specie recti*; but such words as *uirtutes* and *genera* will be looked for in vain. In his own poetry he was a lover of conciseness—*raro et perpauca loquentis*, *S.* i. 4. 18—and one may well believe that this meant a fight against obscurity. *est breuitate opus*, he says of his genre of *sermo*, *S.* i. 10. 9–10, *ut currat sententia neu se | impediat uerbis lassas onerantibus auris* (cf. *Prol.* 261 ff.). In the *Ars breuitas* is related to clarity only by implication; conciseness mishandled loses clarity, becomes obscurity—a fault for a virtue. But this presupposes the Aristotelian criterion of σαφήνεια. If H. had defined his terms and included the other limb of the dilemma, he might have said, prosaically, '*obscurum autem aut longitudine aut contractione orationis*' (Cic. *Part. Or.* 19), or he might have latinized ἄν τε γὰρ ἀδολεσχῇ οὐ σαφής, οὐδὲ ἂν σύντομος (Ar. *Rhet.* III. 12, 1414 a 25). Thus Dion. Hal. *Demosth.* ch. 18 (Usener–Radermacher, I. 166. 8–9) equates τὸ σαφές with τὸ μέτριον in censuring the opposite fault of prolixity. Isocrates' style, he says, lacks συντομία: στοχαζομένη γὰρ τοῦ σαφοῦς ὀλιγωρεῖ πολλάκις τοῦ μετρίου. As it is H. excludes the second

limb. Moreover he talks in commonsense terms, jumping from *breuis*
to *obscurus* and omitting the intervening *contractus* or the like, of which
obscuritas is a consequence (H. Schütz *ad l.*). 'Longinus' makes the
painstaking distinction between 'brief' and 'constricted' which H.
avoids: *Subl.* 42 ἡ ἄγαν τῆς φράσεως συγκοπὴ . . . · συγκοπὴ . . .
κολούει τὸν νοῦν, συντομία δὲ κτλ.

26–8 The three standard types of style, *genera dicendi*, are handled
similarly, with a studied disregard of the niceties of theory but with
attention to its essentials. Such works as Demetrius' *De Interpr.*, the
Ad Her., and Cicero's *Orator* teach that each genus had its characteristic style, and to each style characteristic faults are attached. These
were pedagogic distinctions and Cicero (in the *Orator*) and Quintilian (*I.O.* XII. 10. 66 ff.) show themselves well aware of these limitations, cf. D. A. Russell, 'Longinus' *On the Sublime*, pp. xxxiv–xxxvi.
Doubtless H. was even more aware of them. But to him the *genera*
have their value as characteristic types of style. The types, hinted
at by key-words but not laboriously defined, are the High, 27,
Polished, 26–7, and Plain, 28. The *uicina uitia* of the schools are not
stated unambiguously. Just as *breuis* in the preceding verse is not
contrasted with *contractus* but with the consequence of undue brevity,
so these verses condemn the consequences of a mistaken choice, not
the faults themselves. Nor does H. observe the conventional order of
the types; he begins, in the middle as it were, with the intermediate
or 'smooth' style.

26 *leuia:* Bentley and Peerlkamp strongly but implausibly supported *lenia*, a conjecture in a late MS (cod. Ach. Stat.). The word
lenis is employed, in approval or dispraise, to suggest an absence of
forcefulness and vigour; its synonyms are *sedatus, placidus, summissus*
and so on. Thus it suggests a plain and sedate style more readily than
any other, although occasionally it may describe an 'intermediate'
position, as at Quint. *I.O.* XII. 10. 67, *ut illud* lene aut ascendit *ad
fortiora* aut *ad tenuiora* summittitur; cf. *ibid.* 60. Plainness of style
however is pre-empted for l. 28. The word *leuis* on the other hand is
the counterpart of Greek λεῖος, the key-term for 'smooth' or
'polished', an intermediate style. Bentley himself must have been
disposed to second thoughts, for he cites one of the Greek passages
containing λεῖος in his *Curae Novissimae*.

λεῖον–*leue* applies in particular to periodic composition, avoidance
of hiatus, choice of 'euphonic' words—features of the polished style,
in Demetrius' *De Interpretatione*, and of the 'intermediate' style in
some of the Latin rhetoricians. Isocrates is the prototype of this style
in oratory, but Dion. Hal. occasionally applies the term also to the

'plain' Lysias, cf. P. Geigenmüller, *Quaest. Dionys. de uoc. artis crit.* (Thesis Leipzig 1908), pp. 82 f. Cf. Demetr. *Interpr.* 48 (λειότης γὰρ καὶ τὸ εὐήκοον οὐ πάνυ ἐν μεγαλοπρεπείᾳ χώραν ἔχουσιν εἰ μή που ἐν ὀλίγοις, 176, 178; 258 ὅλως γὰρ ἡ λειότης καὶ τὸ εὐήκοον γλαφυρότητος ἴδια, οὐ δεινότητός ἐστιν, 299 smoothness of composition, practised by the Isocrateans, 300, Dion. Hal. *Isocr.* 18, *Din.* 6, *Lys.* 24, *Comp.* 22 (Usener–Radermacher, II. 108. 1), al., *Imit.* 2. 2 (*ibid.* II. 204. 13) and its counterpart Quint. *I.O.* x. 1. 52 *leuitasque* (*len-* uar. l.), (*Hesiodi*) *uerborum et compositionis probabilis, daturque ei palma in illo mediocri genere dicendi; contra in Antimacho,* etc.; *Ad Her.* IV. 11, and particularly 16 *qui in* mediocre genus orationis *profecti sunt, si peruenire eo non potuerunt, errantes perueniunt ad* confine genus *eius generis quod appellamus* dissolutum, quod est sine neruis et articulis; Cic. *De Or.* III. 171 f., 201, *Or.* 20 f. (unlike H. divides the grand style into rough and smoothly periodic), 110, and *Opt. gen. or.* 5 (two other passages in which Bentley erroneously preferred *lenitas* to *leuitas*), Quint. *I.O.* VIII. 3. 6 *ornatus...uirilis et fortis et sanctus sit nec* effeminatam leui-tatem...*amet: sanguine et* uiribus *niteat,* cf. Fortunat. *Ars Rhet.* III. 9 (cit. foll. n.).

nerui: in Greek a distinction between νεῦρα, 'sinews, tendons', and πόροι, 'nerves', was established and νεῦρα is not used exclusively for 'nerves' until Galen. In Latin *nerui* denotes 'sinews, tendons' but need not in its physiological sense exclude 'nerves' (A. S. Pease, Cic. *N.D.* II. 136 n.). The word is frequent in literary contexts and then always = 'sinews, vigour', e.g. Cic. *De Or.* II. 91 *neruos in dicendo,* *Brut.* 121, Quint. *I.O.* x. 1. 76. So too negatively, *S.* II. 1. 2–3 *sine neruis...quidquid | composui* (opp. *nimis acer*), *Ad Her.* IV. 16 (cit. prec. n.), Cic. *De Or.* III. 80, *Or.* 62. Tac. *Dial.* 18. *Ciceronem a Caluo quidem male audisse tamquam solutum et eneruem, a Bruto autem, ut ipsius uerbis utar, tamquam fractum atque elumbem,* Fortunat. *Ars Rhet.* III. 9 (Halm, *Rhet. L. Min.* p. 126) μέσῳ *quod est contrarium? tepidum ac dissolutum, id est uelut enerue.* The collocation with *animique* recalls *robur* combined with *nerui* at Cic. *Fam.* VI. 1. 3 *quantum in cuiusque animo roboris est atque neruorum;* contrast *Ciris* 43 *firmamus robore neruos,* Lucan III. 625 with Housman's note.

27 (*sectantem leuia nerui*) *deficiunt:* cf. *S.* II. 1. 12–13 *cupidum...uires | deficiunt.*

animique 'spirit, vigour', the pl. with reference to one person. Words denoting emotions or states of mind are frequently so used, cf. Kühner–Stegmann, 1. 80, Draeger, *Hist. Syn.*[2] 1. 19, Krebs–Schmalz, *Antibarbarus*[7], 1. 168. *animi* in particular is used in various connota-tions ranging from 'spirit, courage' (Cic. *Att.* VII. 2. 4) to 'arrogance'

Commentary

(Cic. *Clu.* 109) or 'anger' (Virg. *A.* VIII. 228). Hence *animi* often takes its colour from the context and the nuance is not always easily determined. Thus *Ep.* I. 19. 24–5 *numeros animosque secutus* | *Archilochi* may well denote 'his general disposition' as well as 'his characteristic θυμός, his angry temperament' (Fraenkel, *Hor.* 342). But Quint. *I.O.* x. 1. 60 (a sketch of Archilochus) *breues uibrantesque sententiae, plurimum sanguinis atque neruorum* suggests simply 'vigour, spirit' and *animi* does not occur. In the present passage it does, but the nuance of *nerui...animique* resembles Quintilian's *sanguinis atque neruorum*.

professus grandia: this recalls 14 *inceptis gravibus...et magna professis,* the context of great poetry; the reference there is to the beginning of an epic. Grandeur of style is frequently discussed by the rhetoricians and literary critics as the quality of a *genus dicendi,* Quint. *I.O.* XII. 10. 58 *alterum (genus) grande atque robustum, quod* ἁδρόν *dicunt, constituunt. Ad Her.* IV. 11–12 exemplifies how the rhetorical schools dealt with the concept, Cic. *Or.* 20 or 97 ff. and Quint. XII. 10. 58, how a great orator and a very intelligent teacher respectively did. It is the attraction of the *De Sublimitate* that to its author ὕψος is not a type of style but the expression of a certain kind of mind and character in any style (cf. D. A. Russell, *op. cit.* pp. xxxvii ff.). H. here is clearly using the established analysis of the elevated *genus dicendi.*

turget: grandeur aberrant, as in H.'s *turgidus Alpinus* (*S.* I. 10. 36). The medical metaphor is familiar in this connexion: *Ad Her.* IV. 15 *graui figurae quae laudanda est propinqua est ea quae fugienda; quae recte uidebitur appellari si sufflata nominabitur. nam ita ut corporis bonam habitudinem tumor imitatur saepe, item grauis oratio saepe* imperitis uidetur ea quae turget et inflata est, etc.; Quint. *I.O.* XII. 10. 73 (cf. x. 2. 16) *uitiosum et corruptum dicendi genus quod...aut* immodico tumore turgescit...*aut praecipitia pro sublimibus habet; ibid.* 80 *sic erunt magna non nimia, sublimia non abrupta...*grandia non tumida; Plin. *Ep.* IX. 26. 5 tumida *quae ego* sublimia...*arbitrabar,* et al. The metaphor is derived from Greek literature, where its application to speech occurs as early as the fifth century: Aristoph. *Ran.* 939 ff. ἀλλ' ὡς παρέλαβον τὴν τέχνην παρὰ σοῦ τὸ πρῶτον εὐθύς | οἰδοῦσαν ὑπὸ κομπασμάτων καὶ ῥημάτων ἐπαχθῶν, | ἴσχνανα...αὐτὴν κτλ. It is a standard feature of later Greek criticism, e.g. Demetr. *Interpr.* 221, ps.-Long. *Subl.* 3· 3–4, 28. 1, Philo, *De Plant. Noe* 157, Philostr. *V.A.* I. 17.

28 The next mishap relates to the Plain Style, above 25–6 n. (fin.). As before H. takes from the professional critics what suits his imagery. He does not call the plain style a *genus.* Nor does he call it fine or thin, *subtile (genus) quod* ἰσχνὸν *uocant* (Quint. *I.O.* XII. 10. 58), and its corresponding fault dry or bloodless or meagre: *qui non possunt in. . .attenuatione commode uersari ueniunt ad* aridum *et* exsangue *genus orationis, quod non alienum est* exile *nominari* (*Ad Her.* IV. 16). The plain style is seen as 'level' or 'lying in a low position'—a natural antithesis to loftiness, ὑψηλόν–*sublime*, which had become the characteristic feature of grandeur for the critics and rhetoricians from the first century B.C. (cf. F. Quadlbauer, *WS*, LXXI (1958), 89 ff., D. A. Russell, 'Longinus', Introd. ch. III). Thus *Ad Her.* IV. 14 *in attenuata figurae genere, id quod ad* infumum *et cottidianum sermonem* demissum *est*, Cic. *Or.* 76 summissus *est et* humilis, consuetudinem imitans. Height, said the theorists, involved risk, whereas security and safety were found in the valley; and the 'valley' may be a level type of style—as it is in this verse of the *Ars*—or, for a different kind of critic, it may be absence of high-mindedness, cf. Russell, Introd. *ibid.* Dionysius well represents the former type, 'Longinus' the latter: Dion. Hal. *Demosth.* 2 (ed. Usener–Radermacher, I. 130. 21 ff.), contrasting Lysias' caution with Thucydides' daring; ps.-Long. *Subl.* chs. 32–3, especially 33. 2. So too in Roman criticism: Quint. *I.O.* VIII. 5. 32 *qui fugiunt. . .omnem hanc in dicendo uoluptatem, nihil probantes nisi planum et humile et sine conatu; ita dum timent ne aliquando cadant semper iacent,* Plin. *Ep.* IX. 26. 1–2 *nihil peccat nisi quod nihil peccat. . .debet enim orator. . . saepe accedere ad praeceps, nam plerumque altis et excelsis adiacent abrupta. tutius per plana sed humilius et depressius iter; frequentior currentibus quam reptantibus lapsus, sed his non labentibus nulla, illis non nulla laus etiamsi labantur,* etc. For more references see Ernesti, *Lex. Tech. Lat. Rhet., periculum.*

humi: resemblances in phrasing indicate that H. again may be referring to rhetorical as well as poetic style: the plain style of the rhetoricians and the 'pedestrian' genres of poetry, that is, comedy, iambus, and satire. Cf. Callim. *Aet.* IV, fr. 112. 9 αὐτὰρ ἐγὼ Μουσέων πεζὸν ἔπειμι νομόν (and the passages there cited in Pfeiffer's edition); and H. himself, *S.* II. 6. 17 *quid prius illustrem saturis musaque pedestri?*, *Ep.* II. 1. 251 (*sermones*) *repentis per humum* (as opposed to 'high' epic), *A.P.* 95 *et tragicus plerumque dolet sermone pedestri, A.P.* 227–30 *ne quicumque deus. . . | migret in obscuras humili sermone tabernas | aut, dum uitat humum, nubes et inania captet.*

tutus, 'cautious, on his guard'. Peerlkamp's proposal, *cautus*, rides roughshod over an idiomatic usage. Of course, H. could have used *cautus* as he does *C.* II. 10. 2–3 *procellas | cautus horrescis*; but comparison with *S.* II. 1. 20 *recalcitrat undique tutus* shows that this word is equally established. *tutus* oscillates between 'safe', 'apparently safe', and 'on one's guard', cf. Forcellini s.v., D. R. Shackleton Bailey, *Propertiana*, pp. 86 f. The two words can even be combined to express prudent caution: *Ad Her.* III. 13 *quam...tute cauteque egerit.* H. below 266–7 combines them more pointedly: *tutus et intra | spem ueniae cautus,* 'on my guard, to stay carefully within the limits of pardonable offence'.

timidusque procellae: the gen. with adjectives is an area of innovation in Augustan verse. For the gen. of reference with *timidus*, Kühner–Stegmann, I. 445 cite, after this passage, Ov. *Met.* v. 100 *deorum*, Sen. *Dial.* VII. 20. 6 *lucis*, Lact. *Inst.* III. 26. 6 *doloris ac mortis*.

Spectacular natural phenomena have their place in discussions of the high style, as at Cic. *Or.* 29 (*Pericles*) *si tenui genere uteretur, numquam ab Aristophane poeta* (*Ach.* 530 f.) *fulgere tonare permiscere Graeciam dictus esset*, Quint. *I.O.* XII. 10. 64–5 *summam expressurus... facundiam et magnitudinem illi* (*Vlixi*) *uocis et uim orationis niuibus copia uerborum atque impetu parem tribuit* (*Homerus*, cf. *Od.* VIII. 173), etc., ps.-Long. *Subl.* 1. 4, 12. 4. In the style of the *Odes*, II. 10. 1–4 may be compared: *neque altum | semper urgendo neque dum procellas | cautus horrescis, nimium premendo | litus iniquum.*

(b) 29–31

This is the key to the section 24 ff. H. has not forgotten that his subject (up to 23) was 'unity in variety', cf. above 24–31 n. This subject he apparently abandoned at 24, but appearance is deceptive. In a prosaic argument his proposition would be something like this. Limitless variety resembles the stylistic faults of which the literary critics tell us so much. It is a (laudable) attempt to avoid mere uniformity—the virtue of variety gone wrong; just as obscurity often results from a (laudable) attempt to avoid prolixity—the virtue of brevity gone wrong, etc. The craftsman sees a fault and seeks to escape it. But his technique is insufficient, and escaping in the opposite direction he arrives at the opposite fault. Unity of subject and 'tone' then present problems to the artist that have to be solved by the same means as problems of diction. The road from fault to fault can only be blocked by *ars*. This language of argument is not H.'s language. Instead he juxtaposes a series of concrete cases which put the reader in the place of the artist, struggling five times over to find the right road, and missing it—*si caret arte*. The last line provides the point of vantage from which the whole of this little section has to be judged, see 31 n.

29 I find nothing amiss with either the text or the punctuation of this much-tried verse—if it is allowed to follow on naturally after the preceding four. Like them it needs to express an excellence sought: *breuis esse laboro*; *sectantem leuia*; *professus grandia*; *tutus*; and like them it needs to lead on to an adjoining fault. Variety—*uariare...rem... unam*—is a virtue; but it leads this practitioner to the grotesque error caricatured in the next verse. Hence *uariare* should not be separated from its object, *rem unam*, by punctuation after *cupit* (L. Jeep) nor should *rem* be deprived of its essential epithet *unam* (cf. 23) by change to *una* in addition to punctuation after *cupit* (J. C. G. Praedikow, ed. 1806); cf. Keller, *Epileg.* 736.

prodigialiter: adv. on record only here and Columella III. 3. 3; perhaps coined by H. for the occasion. The meaning could be 'monstrously'; but it could also be 'marvellously', like *prodigiosus*, for example at Ov. *Am.* III. 6. 17–18 *prodigiosa loquor, ueterum mendacia uatum;* | *nec tulit haec umquam nec feret ulla dies.* For the former (*tutus*) *nimium* may be called in evidence: *uariare nimium*, so to speak, would produce a monstrous variety. Yet the 'marvel' is preferable since it allows *cupit* full play. The ps.-Acro gloss, *admirabiliter*, is therefore likely to be right, and so is Lambinus' note *supra omnium hominum fidem*. Cf. Homer's *speciosa...miracula* at 144. The interweaving of *rem prodigialiter unam*, and the widish spacing *uariare— — prodigialiter*, presumably give prominence to the marvel.

30 Here is the débâcle, enunciated in the factual and devastating manner of the last few lines, *fio, deficiunt, turget, serpit.* Now however the attempt and the performance are each assigned a whole verse; H. has again reached his subject, 'unity'. Lack of unity has now turned into a laudable desire for variety, which however miscarries because it is uncontrolled. It has resulted in the same kind of carica-ture with which H. has disconcerted, or amused, his readers at 13 (and indeed at 1). The dolphin and the boar change places—the forest becomes the sea-animal's habitat, and the sea that of the land-animal. The antithesis is emphasized by the same order of words as at 13. Similar reversals of the natural order of things are found in the lyric language of *C.* 1. 2. 5–12. The dolphins exchange places with the θῆρες as early as Archilochus' celebrated χρημάτων ἄελπτον οὐδέν.

delphinum: the latinized acc. The original Greek acc., *-na*, offered a convenient choice of prosody and formation, of which the poets availed themselves on occasion, cf. Neue–Wagener, I. 461, 493, *TLL*, v. 1. 469 f. This occasion did not arise here; in view of the strict layout of the line, the similarity of endings, *delphinum–aprum*, was obviously convenient. Contrast Ov. *Met.* 1. 302 *siluasque tenent delphines*, Claud. XVIII. 355 *adsuetum siluis delphina*.

31 *in uitium...culpae fuga: uitium* 'fault', ἁμάρτημα, a term in literary theory and rhetoric contrasted with *rectum* or *uirtus: S.* 1. 4. 8–9 (*Lucilius*) *durus componere versus.* | *nam fuit hoc uitiosus*, etc. *Ep.* 1. 19. 17 *decipit exemplar uitiis imitabile.* Cf. Ter. *Heaut.* prol. 29–30 *nouarum (fabularum)...sine uitiis, Ad Her.* IV. 15 *ne, dum haec genera consectemur, in finituma et propinqua uitia ueniamus*, Cic. *De Or.* I. 116 *adest...nemo, quin acutius...uitia in dicente quam recta uideat*, Quint. *I.O.* 1. 5. 3 *uni uerbo uitium saepius quam uirtus inest*, X. 1. 25 *si uitia magnorum consequantur*, et al. *culpa*, 'blame', is combined, in a moral sense, with *uitium* at *S.* II. 6. 7, and is sometimes interchangeable with that word in literary contexts, *C.* 1. 6. 11–12, *laudes...Caesaris et tuas* | *culpa deterere ingeni*, below 267–8 *uitaui denique culpam*, opp. *laudem*, 446 *culpabit duros (uersus)*; cf. Varro, *L.L.* VIII. 8 *cur haec* (e.g. *uocabula*)... *sint in culpa*. Hence the variation in this verse.

H. takes up the 'deception' of 25, *decipimur specie recti*, and traces it to a lack of craftsmanship, *si caret arte* (the grammatical subject here is not a person but *culpae fuga*, a practice; for this transference *TLL*, III. 451. 32 aptly compares Cic. *Div.* I. 34 *alterum (genus diuinationis) quod arte careret*). Quintilian (more fully cited 25 n.) may have H. in mind, *I.O.* VIII. 3. 56 *quidquid est ultra uirtutem, quotiens ingenium iudicio caret et specie boni fallitur*. Judgement depends on training in an art. Again Quintilian remarks in the introduction to his *Ars, I.O.* II. 12. 4, *est...quaedam uirtutum uitiorumque uicinia, qua maledicus pro libero, temerarius pro forti, effusus pro copioso, accipitur; maledicit autem* ineruditus *apertius*, etc. The need for a particular *ars* or τέχνη was a commonplace in introductions to professional manuals (above pp. 75–6). But H.'s way of handling it is not at all commonplace. The demand is made in a manner which is itself a remarkable piece of artistry.

(1) This verse provides the key to the cases of misjudged diction that are castigated in 25–8. H. uses the lightest of touches. With the possible exception of 28, *timidus*, as Heinze points out, the *culpae fuga* is never stated but always implied. It is only by taking H.'s hint in this verse that his context is fully apprehended. The context is the Aristotelian Mean transferred from morals to poetry. In the moral field H. had early satirized its lack, *dum uitant stulti uitia in contraria currunt* (*S.* 1. 2. 24); *nil medium est* (*S.* 1. 2. 28). If allowance for *culpae fuga* is here made, an Aristotelian Mean between two Excesses

arises where, as the Master had said, the Excesses are opposed not only to each other but to the Mean (*Eth. Nic.* II. 8, 1108 b 13, *Eth. Eud.* II. 3, 1220 b 31). Here is the application to 25–8:

Excess, *culpae fuga*	Mean	Excess, opposite fault
[25–6, prolix]	brief, clear	too brief, obscure
[26–7, rough]	smooth	flabby
[27, low]	elevated	turgid
28, high, unsafe	plain	low

More than dislike of theory and schematism must have caused H. to avoid spelling out the *culpae fuga*. The 'opposite fault' seemed a greater danger to him than the fault from which the practitioner was anyway trying to escape. *ars* is needed to avoid the 'opposite fault' and find the Mean. Aristotle based right judgement in matters moral on perception, αἴσθησις (*Eth. Nic.* II. 9, 1109 b 23). In matters aesthetic H. bases it on *ars*.

(2) This verse too helps to explain 29–30 and widens the compass of the whole initial context, 1–23. Subject-matter and 'tone' are open to the same deceptions as diction, which is brought in chiefly as a criterion because here *species recti* is both manifest and established teaching.

Excess, *culpae fuga*	Mean	Excess, opposite fault
[29–30 uniformity]	varied unity	variety without unity

Once again one of the faults has to be elicited from *culpae fuga*. It makes a difference to the poet's purpose if it is not so elicited. For then the danger of uniformity is overlooked. Yet as under (1) deception by the *species recti* is what H. is attempting to cure; his prescription offers the severe discipline of the art.

(3) Finally it is noted that this verse ties together in a manner unique in extant classical literature the topics of unity and *ars*–τέχνη. The fact that the combination is unique must not deter us from marking its components, as it has deterred Steidle, *Studien*, pp. 44–5. Whether unity, τὸ ἕν, was in later teaching generalized and moved to a commanding position from its important but secondary place in Aristotle's *Poetics*, is a matter for conjecture; cf. *Prol.* 137. But there is no doubt that the *res una* has that place in the *Ars*. Largely by adroit placing H. has here brought the two motifs together. It is the craft of the poetic *ars*, on which alone the overall unity of a poem can be based.

(5) A cautionary tale: the bronze-founder; mastery of parts does not guarantee mastery of whole, 32–7

To unity, *unum* (14–31), is now joined wholeness, *totum*. The absence of these two qualities made the painting described at the beginning of the poem into a caricature (1–13). Aristotle too considered unity and wholeness fundamental. But in the *Poetics* the contrary sequence obtains: ch. 7 deals with *totum*, τὸ ὅλον, and ch. 8 with *unum*, τὸ ἕν; at the end of ch. 8 (1451 a 32) they are brought into the same locution, μιᾶς... καὶ...ὅλης (πράξεως). H.'s procedure however is different in three ways. (1) He speaks as a poet and critic. His concern is the wholeness of a poem—words, order, subject—not only the logic of a 'plot'. (2) He is realistic and particular, dealing with the instance of a smith working in bronze, not primarily with abstractions. (3) At this stage of the *Ars* he views wholeness only as a potential—the *capability* of producing a coherent work of art. An artist must be able to envisage the totality of a work. Mere dexterity in dealing with parts is not enough. The smith fails because he cannot bring the parts into the relationship which Aristotle (ch. 9) defined as 'necessary or probable'. The ability to set down *totum* (*A.P.* 34) distinguishes the true artist or poet from an artisan, *faber* (32).

32 *Aemilium circa ludum:* the proper name a quasi-adjective as in the archaic nomenclature discussed 18 n. (ad fin.), a usage metrically convenient and much extended in verse. H. has *Stertinium... acumen, Ep.* I. 12. 20; *uenena Colcha* (*Colchica* faulty variant), *C.* II. 13. 8; *Romulae | ...gentis,* IV. 5. 1–2; *Sulpiciis...horreis, C.* IV. 12. 18.

For the place, cf. Porphyrion's n., *Aemilii Lepidi ludus gladiatorius fuit quod nunc Polycleti balineum est.* The training school is said to have been *non procul a Circo* by the Comm. Cruq. Its location is discussed in H. Jordan's paper *H*, IX (1875), 416. The identity of this Lepidus has not been established; according to ps.-Acro and Comm. Cruq. Aemilius was the trainer's name. In any case it is implied that this neighbourhood contained workshops of bronze-founders.

As regards *faber imus* ps.-Acro offers three rival explanations. The first two are certainly false; *Imus* is not the man's name nor is his small stature in question. The third is taken from Porphyrion: *imus = in extrema parte ludi positum*; see below.

The grammar of the sentence is relevant to the meaning. That this is not a plain statement of fact is shown by (*a*) the 'potential' future tenses in 33 and 35 (for instances see Kühner–Stegmann, I. 142–3) and (*b*) the hypothetical note in *infelix...quia...nesciet*. Both features are found for example at 6–8 *fore librum | persimilem, cuius...uanae | fingentur species, S.* II. 4. 22–3 *peraget qui... | finiet*. When he speaks like that, I suspect, H.'s preference for particular cases is checked by his preference for generalizing—'a certain kind of person or thing' rather than 'this or that person or thing'. *faber imus* is then unlikely to be Porphyrion's 'smith in the shop at the corner'. Rather what seems to be intended is 'the *kind of* smith who will (successfully) represent in bronze nails and flowing hair, but will be unsuccessful in carrying out a whole design, because...'.

If then Porphyrion's corner-shop cannot be located, we are left with either *imus* = 'lowest in rank' or, instead, *unus*, strongly supported by Bentley; for any other guesses no longer deserve recording. Now assume that *imus* has the meaning which is certainly on record in *insignes et imos* (*C.* III. 1. 15), but is here uncertain beside the indication of a locality, *Aemilium circa ludum*. Even so it would detract from H.'s point. Indeed Lucian Mueller (32 n.) and Immisch, p. 40, argue convincingly that H. is at pains to commend, not decry, excellence of detail in order to condemn presently the statue's nullity as a whole.

All honour to Bentley, then, for sponsoring the reading (*correction intentionelle*, according to Lejay, Hor. *Sat.* p. cxxi) *unus* which he found in one of his late MSS and inferred from erasures in two more, and further from a citation in John of Salisbury; *unus* is also in ps.-Acro *ad l.*, codd. c 3 (s. xv). Even if *S.* II. 3. 24–5 *hortos...mercarier unus | cum lucro noram* = 'only', and is meant to be shameless braggadocio, *Epod.* 12. 4 *sagacius unus odoror*, and *S.* II. 6. 57–8 *unum | scilicet egregii mortalem altique silenti*, certainly confirm the equation *unus* = *praecipuus*, or rather *praecipue*. The idiom is established in verse as well as prose, cf. Bentley, Seyffert–Müller, Cic. *Lael.* pp. 9–11, H. Blase, *Comm. Woelfflin* (1891), pp. 87 ff., G. Landgraf, Cic. *Rosc. Am.*², p. 20, D. R. Shackleton Bailey, *Propertiana*, 171–2, a note on Prop. III. 11. 40 *una Philippeo sanguine adusta nota*, with the reminder that Cleopatra 'was not the only disreputable Lagid'.

imus–unus is not the sort of palaeographical problem that requires comment, but in a note on H. the variants at 152 and *S.* I. 4. 87 may be mentioned. Bentley's *unus* is rejected on irrelevant palaeographical grounds by H. R. Joliffe, *The critical methods...of Bentley's Horace* (1939), p. 112.

33 *exprimet...imitabitur aera:* the former = 'squeezing', hence it is applied to raised work in metal, carving, sculpting, etc., and finally it denotes 'representing' or 'expressing', which puts the word close to *imitari* 'represent'; cf. *TLL*, v. 2. 1787 ff., vii. 1. 435. 10 ff. For *exprimo* in the context of bronze statuary, see *Ep.* ii. 1. 248 *expressi uoltus per aenea signa*, Plin. *N.H.* xxxiv. 59 (*Pythagoras Reginus*) *primus neruos et uenas expressit capillumque diligentius, ibid.* 65 (*Lysippus*) *statuariae arti plurimum traditur contulisse, capillum exprimendo*, etc.

molles...capillos: naturalistic representation of flowing hair was achieved in Hellenistic and later statuary. This feature was much admired (cf. Pliny cit. prec. n.); Callistratus recurs to it in most of his descriptions of bronze or marble statues, as at *Descr.* 11. 3 ὡς δὲ...ἐξητάζομεν τὴν τέχνην..., ἀφασίᾳ πληγέντες εἱστήκειμεν· ὅ τε γὰρ χαλκὸς...πρὸς τὴν τριχὸς κίνησιν μεθηρμόζετο, ὁτὲ μὲν βοστρύχων οὔλων πλοκαῖς συνεξελιττόμενος, ὁτὲ δ' ἐθελούσῃ τῇ τριχὶ ἐκτάδην κατὰ νώτου χυθῆναι συναπλούμενος. *mollis* is an epithet for flowing hair, cf. Virg. *A.* ii. 683–4 *molles | lambere flamma comas*, Tib. i. 8. 9 *molles...coluisse capillos* (omitted in the list *TLL*, iii. 318. 22, cf. 1749. 35), etc. It also describes the art that makes bronze or marble supple and lifelike, Virg. *A.* vi. 847 *excudent alii spirantia mollius aera*.

34 *infelix operis summa:* Bentley probably remembered *infelix studiorum*, Virg. *G.* iii. 498 and the like, for he separated *summa* from the rest of the phrase: *infelix operis, summa: quia*, etc., 'failing in his work as a whole'. Nothing could be better—if *summa* were used like *ad summam* or *in summa*. Since apparently it is not, the grammatical problem of the abl. was forgotten along with Bentley's punctuation; Orelli's (3rd ed. 1852) is the last reference to it that I have seen. No other instance of the abl. in place of the gen. after *infelix* is mentioned in *TLL*, vii. 1. 1365. 8 to indicate *modum infelicitatis*. But half a dozen instances of the abl. are cited under *causa infelicitatis*, as Cic. *Fin.* v. 92 *infelix una molestia, felix rursus cum*, etc., Sil. vi. 404 *infelix nimia magni uirtute mariti*, Tac. *H.* iii. 34. 1 (*Cremona*) *bellis externis intacta, ciuilibus infelix.* This then is what the grammar of the phrase must be if *summa* is kept in the text; the artisan fails through, i.e. in, the sum total of the work. The abl. = 'by virtue of', not 'with regard to'; it is not an isolated case. The word *summa* used with the gen. is popular with the historians, e.g. Liv. iii. 61. 12 *paruaque certamina in summam totius profecerant spei*, xxxi. 37. 5 *non in praesentis modo certaminis gloriam sed in summam etiam belli profectum foret*, Tac. *Ann.* ii. 45. 4

Commentary

satis probatum penes utros summa belli fuerit, XIII. 38. 1 *nihil in summa⟨m⟩ pacis proficiebatur.*

ponere: cf. *exprimere* and *imitari*, 33. Like τίθημι, *ponere* may mean not only 'place' a figure in a work of art but 'make' a work of art: the former as at Virg. *E.* 3. 46 *Orpheaque in medio (poculi) posuit*, the latter as at Hor. *C.* IV. 8. 7–8 (Parrhasius, Scopas) *hic saxo, liquidis ille coloribus | sollers nunc hominem ponere, nunc deum*, Prop. II. 3. 41–2 *si quis uult fama tabulas anteire uetustas, | hic dominam exemplo ponat in arte meam*, Ov. *A.A.* III. 401 *si Venerem Cous nusquam posuisset Apelles*, etc. For representation in verse, cf. Pers. I. 70–1 *nec ponere lucum | artifices nec rus . . . laudare*, Juv. I. 155 *pone Tigellinum.*

totum hints at the ὅλον of Aristotle and the Greek literary critics, cf. above 32–7 n. But often when H. alludes to technical terminology the simple sense of the words satisfies a simple understanding. So *ponere totum* has a satisfactory meaning but its understanding is enhanced by Heinze's remark that the locution ushers in *componere* (35); for a simple verb followed by a compound of the same derivation, see some of Housman's instances at Man. I. 271, III. 122 nn. The converse idiom, simple verb preceded by compound, has been discussed more frequently, see Calvert Watkins' summary of the evidence, *HS*, LXXI (1966), 115–19.

35–6 For the indir. stat. after *uolo*, see Kühner–Stegmann, I. 714 f.

35 *ego . . . si . . . curem:* for the 1st pers. sing. see 25–6, 55 nn., Steidle, *Studien*, pp. 32 f.

36 *non magis . . . quam*, here and elsewhere in H., is discussed by L. Fritzsche, *P*, XXXIII (1874), 718–22.

naso uiuere prauo appears as *prauo uiuere naso* in some poor MSS and in early editions of H. Bentley rejected the latter reading partly because of an alleged cacophony of three *u* sounds, *-uo uiuere*. But neither Virgil nor H. eschews even a sequence of identical consonants with the same vowel: Virg. *A.* IV. 350 *quaerere regna*, cited by a less squeamish Bentley Hor. *C.* III. 24. 44 n.; Hor. *Ep.* I. 1. 95 *occurri rides*, Housman, *CQ*, XXII (1928), 4 n. 3, on *S.* II. 1. 2 *sine neruis* and on Man. II. 242 *aequantem tempora*, vol. V, *Addenda*, p. 140, G. P. Goold, 'Amatoria Critica', *HS*, LXIX (1965), 86; hence the matter would arise still less when the vowels differ. Roman poets do not seem to have paid much attention to the Isocrateans and later rhetoricians, who legislated against combinations like εἰποῦσα σαφῆ; nor do they appear to have objected to the allegedly obscene variety of the type *Dorica castra*, cf. Serv. on Virg. *A.* II. 27, Cic. *Or.* 154 (with Sandys's n.), Quint. *I.O.* VIII. 3. 44–7, *TLL*, III. 5. 79 ff. (*cacemphaton*). For instances from Latin verse see above and Pease on Virg. *A.* IV. 461, 662; Norden, Virg. *A.* VI. 88, R. G. Austin, Virg. *A.* II. 27 nn. on *Dorica castra*, with G. Luck's remarks, *Gnomon*, XXXVII (1965), 53, on the nomenclature. There is no reason therefore why *prauo uiuere* could not be right. But in this kind of case decision may rest with the better MSS.

paruo for *prauo* should not be entertained; *male paruus* of a puny boy at *S.* I. 3. 45 is another matter. Cat. 43. 1 *nec minimo puella naso* shows that a large nose could hardly help in a beauty contest; *naso...prauo* is rather to be compared with what Catullus in the language of his *hendecasyllabi* calls *turpiculo...naso* (41. 3). Cic. *Fin.* V. 46 *si quae in membris praua aut debilitata aut imminuta sint* relates in its latter part to the stunting or maiming of limbs. The same passage also shows *prauus* in the sense of 'crooked, deformed'; cf. *S.* I. 3. 47–8 *distortis cruribus...* | *...prauis...talis*, Cic. *T.D.* IV. 29 *uitium (appellant) cum partes corporis inter se dissident, ex quo prauitas membrorum, distortio, deformitas. prauum* in the moral sphere is 'crooked', deviating from the straight path, *rectum*, as at *S.* II. 7. 7–8.

37 *(me) spectandum:* the pregnant attributive use of the gerundive expressing fitness for the action expressed by the verb, 'worthy to be looked at', *spectabilem*, as at *C.* IV. 14. 17 *spectandus in certamine Martio*, Virg. *G.* IV. 469 *manesque adiit regemque tremendum*, et al. Cf. Kühner–Stegmann, I. 732–3.

nigris oculis nigroque capillo, not *nigroue*. Cf. *C.* I. 32. 11–12 *Lycum nigris oculis nigroque* | *crine decorum* (with a metrical variation *nigris–nĭgroque*, not employed here), Cat. 43. 2 *nec bello pede nec nigris ocellis* (for l. 1, see above 36 n.), Prop. II. 12. 23–4 *qui caput et digitos et lumina nigra puellae* | *... canat*, Ov. *Am.* II. 4. 41–3 *seu pendent niuea pulli ceruice capilli,* | *Leda fuit nigra conspicienda coma;* | *seu flauent, placuit croceis Aurora capillis.*

(6) The poet's advice, an apparent truism: choose a poetic task adapted to your talent, 38–40

'The poets', *qui scribitis*, are unexpectedly addressed. What they are told does not sum up 'wholeness' (*totum*, 32–7) in the same way as 23 and 31 summed up two different strands of 'unity' (*unum*, 14–22, 24–30). Rather they are left to draw the conclusion from the bronze-founder's tale: artisan, a maker of parts; artist, a maker of a whole. Nor is the application to poetry explicitly stated. The need for artistic understanding (*ars*–τέχνη) is not reiterated after *si caret arte* (in the context of unity, 31) and *ponere totum nesciet* (in the context of 'wholeness', 34–5). Instead of the need for artistry which enables the poet to create a whole, attention is concentrated on the condition that makes such artistry possible. The condition lies in the right choice of his task: he will fail to organize a whole unless such organizing lies in his power. The success of *ars* depends on the right choice of aim, and right choice depends on the degree of native talent. The untiring advocate of craftsmanship ends with a studied paradox by inculcating the need for talent, just as he reflected on the ideal of unity in terms of variety.

Among the abstract topics on which the writers of *artes* liked to advise in introducing their textbooks were *de materia*, and *de natura et doctrina*, for example Quint. *I.O.* II, chs. 19 and 21, cf. II. 8. These are the abstract and rigid precepts which H. has drawn into the particularizing process of his poetry. The *materia* here (38) is that of the individual poet and not of 'the poet' in the abstract. In relating *ars* and *materia* to talent (*natura*) he breaks down the artificial distinctions of the writers of textbooks. The ultimate achievement of poetic art—a poem in which words and thought have an indissoluble organic unity—justifies the poet's choice of his task. But, paradoxically, the choice of task can be justified only by the native talent of the chooser.

38 *materiam:* the word -*a* or -*es* occurs three times in H., twice in the fifth declension; *A.P.* 131 *publica materies* metrically excludes the -*a* form, but *C.* III. 24. 49 *materiem* (-*am* uar.) *mali* and this passage do not. Possible differences of stylistic flavour (cf. N. Eriksson, *Studien zu den Annalen des Tacitus* (1934), p. 8) are insufficient grounds for bringing this passage into line with the two others.

The word does not here denote subject-matter as opposed to diction—a division to be made presently—but the subject chosen by the writer, the task he is undertaking. Cf. *Prol.* 11–13, and for the literary connotations of the word, *TLL*, VIII. 459–61. A like though not identical distinction is made in such textbooks as Cic. *Inv.* I. 7 *materiam artis eam dicimus in qua omnis ars et ea facultas quae conficitur ex arte uersatur. ut si medicinae materiam dicamus morbos ac uulnera, quod in his omnis medicina uersetur, item quibus in rebus uersatur ars et facultas oratoria, eas res materiam artis rhetoricae nominamus, ibid.* 9 *quare* materia *quidem nobis rhetoricae uidetur artis ea quam Aristoteli uisam esse diximus;* partes *autem eae quas plerique dixerunt,* inuentio dispositio elocutio, etc.

qui scribitis: frequently writers of verse (the 'writers' here have been so identified: *poetis,* 9; *uatum,* 24), cf. 73–4 *res gestae. . . | quo scribi possent numero,* 119–20 *aut famam sequere aut. . .finge | scriptor,* 306–7 *munus et officium, nil scribens ipse, docebo, | . . .quid alat. . .poetam,* 309 *scribendi recte, C.* I. 6. 1–2, *S.* I. 4. 41–2, *Ep.* I. 2. 1 *Troiani belli scriptorem,* et al.

aequam with dat. expressing 'equal to' (here, slightly strained, 'not more than') is familiar from verse but not found in prose until Livy, cf. *TLL,* I. 1030. 59.

39 *uersate diu, quid,* etc.: the verb is from early times frequently used with pronoun, *secum,* or with such nouns as *(in) corde, pectore, animo* = 'turn over in one's mind, ponder'. But it appears less often without such a support, and not to my knowledge before this passage and Prop. II. 4. 16 (for III. 14. 32, see D. R. Shackleton Bailey, *Prop.* 185); later, for example, Val. Fl. I. 32, 725, Sil. XV. 541, XVII. 569, Sen. *Dial.* III. 17. 5, Quint. *I.O.* X. 3. 5. For the indirect question, cf. Virg. *A.* V. 701–3 *nunc huc. . .nunc illuc pectore curas | mutabat uersans, Siculisne resideret aruis,* etc., *ibid.* X. 285–6, Stat. *Theb.* V. 242–4, *Ach.* I. 713–16. Both idioms together I have noticed only here.

ferre recusent (umeri): for the wording cf. *S.* II. 7. 108–9 *pedes. . .ferre recusant | corpus;* for the thought and wording *Ep.* II. 1. 259 *quam (rem) uires ferre recusent.* The metaphor is listed by A. Otto, *Sprichwörter,* p. 355, *umeri.* Cf. Epict. *Diss.* III. 15. 9 ἄνθρωπε, σκέψαι πρῶτον τί ἐστι τὸ πρᾶγμα (i.e. φιλοσοφία), εἶτα καὶ τὴν σαυτοῦ φύσιν, τί δύνασαι βαστάσαι κτλ. (which, Rostagni believes, derives from H.).

(7) A promise: if you can master your subject, you will be able to express and arrange it, 40 (cui–41) (The technical topics of an 'ars poetica' are thereby implied—subject, diction, arrangement, which now follow in reverse order)

The sentence forms an important link in the structure of the *Ars.* It has three different but by no means incompatible aspects.

(1) It may be read as a *partitio* setting out the *partes* of a

literary discussion on arrangement (42 ff.), style (45, 47 ff.) and perhaps subject-matter (119 ff.), the discussion proceeding in reverse order to that of the *partitio* which goes from *res* (40) to *facundia* (41) to *ordo* (41). The topics may be paralleled from rhetorical theory, e.g. Cic. *Inv.* 1. 9 cited above 38 n. I regard the topics of *ordo* and *facundia* as certain, cf. 42 n., 46–5 n. *res* however is no more than possible, not because *res* here can only denote the task selected by the poet (Vahlen, cf. *Prol.* 12, followed by Heinze and others), for the word is sufficiently flexible to be taken as the task selected, as well as the topic of *inuentio* contrasted with style and arrangement. Doubt, though not insurmountable doubt, is caused simply by the stress placed on *lecta*, the act of selection.

(2) The sentence may be read too as a 'link passage' or 'gliding transition' smoothing the path between two 'sections' of the poem. Its beginning, *cui lecta potenter erit res*, links the sentence with *sumite materiam*, which itself followed on from the necessity of an *ars* that promises poetic unity. Its second part (41) links the contexts of *ars* and selection of a task with the specific problems of the *ars poetica*.

(3) The sentence finally expresses a conviction—the different aspects of a poem, its subject, arrangement, and style, will become *one* if certain conditions are fulfilled. The conditions are *natura* and *ars*, the former expressed by *aequam uiribus* and *lecta potenter*, the latter by the techniques which are here introduced. It is instructive to see the initial axiom of all modern criticism—the unity of style and content—expressed as a final act of grace which is granted, in spite of the dissociation of *res*, *facundia*, and *ordo*, when the necessary conditions have been fulfilled.

40 *lecta* for (*d*)*electa* as *Ep.* 1. 9. 4 *legentis honesta Neronis*, not for *collecta*, the parts of a composition (Doederlein). Cf. D. Bo, *Hor. Op.* III (1960), 388, for instances of simple verbs used by H. for compounds.

potenter: the word needs explanation, not emendation (*tot inter*, A. Y. Campbell, *CQ*, XXXIX (1945) 18). (i) Various attempts have been made to explain the adverb as though it described the execution of the act of choosing: (*a*) 'according to one's ability or powers' (Lewis and Short). This is the standard explanation, which goes back to the scholiasts: Porph. *qui legerit id quod praestare possit; potenter figurauit* ὡσεὶ δυνατῶς (ὡς εἶ δυνατός codd.), Ps.-Acro *secundum quod potest*, etc., Comm. Cruq. *pro sua potentia, quantum possit ferre*. Dictionaries do not however record this meaning, apart from the present passage. The materials of the *TLL* contain many instances, all denoting, as one would expect in the adverb of *potens*, 'powerfully, effectually': *C*. III. 16. 10–11 *perrumpere...saxa potentius* | *ictu fulmineo*, Sen. *Suas*. II. 18 *multo potentius dixit*, Val. Max. I. I ext. I (*Proserpina*) *se ipsa potenter atque efficaciter defendit*, III. 3 ext. I, Quint. *I.O.* V. 7. 37, VI. 4. 18, XII. 10. 72 *ad efficiendum quod intendit (orator) potenter*, ps.-Quint. *Decl.* 274 (p. 123. 13 R.), 276 (p. 127. 6 R.), al. The alleged meaning, then, is isolated; which perhaps could be borne if it arose clearly from the context. (*b*) 'with self-restraint', as opposed to *impotenter*, 'intemperately' (Wilkins). This meaning too is not on record elsewhere; Markland tried to introduce it by emending *potenter* to *pudenter*. (*c*) 'who spends all his powers on the choice, i.e. who makes every effort to choose aright' (Reid *ap*. Wilkins). This indeed is the usual meaning of *potenter*, though the drift of the whole sentence is dubious. But (*a*) and (*b*) produce a sense which is not only dubious lexicographically but ruled out by the context. For why should diction and lucid order (41) grace a subject chosen according to ability, if that ability is middling or low? Or why should they grace it if the choice is made with self-restraint? The context calls for mastery of a subject.

(ii) No attempt has been made to explain the adverb as commenting on the choice made, not on the manner of choosing. This, a well-worn Latin idiom, is sometimes overlooked; grammarians call it 'adverb of judgement', i.e. on the whole of a sentence, cf. Kühner–Stegmann, I. 795, Hofmann–Szantyr, 827. *male reprehendunt* need not mean 'they criticize badly' but can mean (as it does at Cic. *T.D.* III. 34) 'they are mistaken in criticizing'. H. has the same usage at 129 *rectius*, *S*. I. 10. 34 *insanius*, *C*. II. 12. 11 *melius*. Cf. Madvig on Cic. *Fin*. IV. 63, *Advers. crit*. II. 507, C. F. W. Müller on Cic. *Off*. I. 128, Löfstedt, *Syn*. II. 384 n. I. Thus understood the grammar of the sentence makes the attested meaning of the word (above under (*a*)) applicable. The meaning, I think, is 'he who is effective in his choice' or 'he whose choice has made him master of his subject'.

res 'subject', is opposed to diction or arrangement or both as at 311 and in earlier writings of H., cf. *Prol*. 181–2.

Commentary

41 *facundia* = (fluent) diction; contrast at 311 and often elsewhere *uerba*. The word was suitable for H.'s purpose since it must still have had an archaic or poetic tinge in his time. Cicero and Caesar avoid *facundia*, but the historians use it. It is unsuitable too as a rhetorical term; in the nomenclature of Cicero and the *Ad Her. elocutio* or *uerba* are used to express the Greek term λέξις. I can find no vagueness in the term (G. Williams, *JRS*, LIV (1964), 194); it is more expressive than *uerba*, and fits the hexameter, which *elocutio* does not.

deseret: H. stresses the unity of thought and expression in poetry while yet speaking of 'subject' and 'diction'. If the poet is master of his subject, diction and arrangement will not forsake him. The implication is not that *facundia* and *ordo* are easy, but that the poet, trained in the use of language, does not divorce the act of giving ordered expression to thought from the thought itself. Modern critics will say that in poetry the words *are* the thought; H. says that the right subject will elicit the right words (from the man who has been trained to use them). Cf. 311 *uerbaque prouisam rem non inuita sequentur.* A glance at an ancient textbook of rhetoric will show up the difference. So the definition *Ad Her.* I. 3 *elocutio est idoneorum uerborum et sententiarum ad inuentionem accommodatio,* Cic. *Inv.* I. 9. There wording is inorganically 'fitted to' subject-matter.

lucidus ordo: for *ordo* juxtaposed with *res* see *Ep.* I. 19. 29 *rebus et ordine dispar, Prol.* 181–2. The word is used by the rhetoricians but is less heavily technical than *dispositio.* Cf. *Ad Her.* I. 3 *dispositio est ordo et distributio rerum, quae demonstrat quid quibus locis sit collocandum,* Cic. *Inv.* I. 9 *dispositio est rerum inuentarum in ordinem distributio, De Or.* II. 179 *qui ordo...et quae dispositio argumentorum,* et al. *lucidus* recalls the *dilucidum* (*lucidum* specially in Quintilian)–*planum–apertum–perspicuum* of the rhetoricians. This is the σαφές of Theophrastus, a virtue of diction. The Isocrateans however declared clarity also to be a virtue ἐν τοῖς πράγμασιν, the facts of a narrative. This influenced later rhetorical theory, as J. Stroux has demonstrated, *De Theophr. Virt. Dic.* ch. 4. Cf. for example *Ad Her.* I. 15 *rem dilucide narrabimus si ut quicquid primum gestum erit ita primum exponemus, et* rerum ac temporum ordinem conseruabimus *ut gestae res erunt aut ut potuisse geri uidebuntur; hic erit considerandum ne quid perturbate...dicamus, ne quam in aliam rem transeamus, ne ab ultimo repetamus, ne longe persequamur, ne quid quod ad rem pertineat praetereamus.* For H.'s own view on *ordo* see below 42–4 n.

Commentary

II. The Arts of Arrangement and Diction in Poetry, 42–118

(1) Arrangement, 42–4

The first of the three 'technical' divisions now follows, closely tied to the second, Diction; about the place of 'Arrangement' in the economy of the poem I write below.

'Arrangement', τάξις, in Latin *dispositio* or *ordo*, is altogether a rhetorical term. It probably points to one of the oldest but also most enduring functions of Greek rhetorical teaching—to tell the learner how to deal with the set parts of a forensic speech, μόρια τοῦ λόγου, cf. F. Solmsen, *AJP*, LXII (1941), 35 ff., H. Caplan, [Cicero] *Ad Herennium*, p. 6 note (*a*). Treatment of *ordo*, as Quintilian noted (*I.O.* III. 3. 1–10), could vary considerably, and this also applied to the place of *ordo* in the rhetorical syllabus. Often, and perhaps most naturally, 'arrangement' followed 'subject-matter'. But Aristotle placed it after 'diction', at the end of his *Rhetoric* (III. 13–19). Arrangement and expression are hard to divorce and certain manuals made allowance for that in their placing of the topic; so one gathers from Quintilian's report (*loc. cit.* 8–9). He himself was carried from 'arrangement' to 'diction' at the end of book VII although he had adopted the traditional sequence of topics, with 'subject-matter' first, and 'arrangement' and 'diction' to follow. This flexibility needs to be remembered for the poet's own placing. He makes *ordo* precede *facundia*, and follow his introductory section on unity, in which content and form had already been closely joined.

Rhetoricians had worked up a complicated set of rules for *dispositio*. But they were well aware that the most effective arrangement must take account of the prejudices and weaknesses of an audience and the contingencies of individual cases. All students of the subject said so: philosophers, orators, and rhetoricians, e.g. Ar. *Rhet.* III. 16, Theophrastus (*ap.* Demetr. *Interpr.* 222), *Ad Her.* III. 16–18, Cic. *De Or.* II. 307 ff. (and, almost as briefly as in the *A.P.*, Cic. *Or.* 50), Quint. *I.O.* VII.

10. 11 ff.; and naturally, for undue completeness or false placing may kill a speech—and the case. *ubi adsumendum prooemium, ubi omittendum*; so Quintilian begins rehearsing the knotty problems that face the orator. To deal with them calls for consummate ability: *maxime proprium oratoris prudentiae*, says Cicero (*De Or.* II. 308); *imperatoria uirtus*, Quintilian (*I.O.* VII. 10. 13).

In literary criticism the role of *ordo* is much less clear than in rhetoric; yet evidence is not entirely wanting. Aristotle had linked his concept of unity with the Homeric technique of concentration on one main event of the great war; this involved postponement to 'episodes' of other events (*Poet.* 23, 1459 a 35). The Alexandrians paid attention to the *oeconomia* of the *Iliad* and *Odyssey*, but their notions were largely rhetorical, cf. 42, 43, 140–52, 148 nn. H. is not restricting his remarks to epic narrative; he may be thinking of any kind of poetic ordering, his own included. The exemplary status of Homeric *oeconomia* was not even restricted to poetry, cf. 148 n. on *in medias res*.

Other evidence is hypothetical. It rests on inference from the layout of the *Ars* in comparison with the *Poetics* and *Rhetoric*. The Greek term for arrangement, τάξις, 'is not found in the *Poetics* where the structure of the plot provides all that is required on that score' (*Prol.* p. 99 n. 2). The triad arrangement–diction–content is indeed Aristotelian, but it comes from the *Rhetoric*, not the *Poetics*, and I have argued that it was transferred to the literary field from the *Rhetoric*. I have conjectured (*ibid.* 93, 141 ff.) that this transference took place in the early Hellenistic age, and may precede Neoptolemus of Parium. (A further guess may here be added: Horace pronounces on *ordinis...uirtus*, that is ἀρετή τάξεως. Such an ἀρετή may have been formulated on the model of 'the virtue of diction', ἀρετή λέξεως, already established by Aristotle and analysed further by Theophrastus.) But whatever the date, the appearance of *ordo*, the label of the rhetoricians, marks an important change in literary criticism. A theory based on the consistency of the tragic plot now gives way to a rhetorical and literary order of things; the claims of 'arrangement' and 'style' now balance those of 'subject-matter'.

42 *ordinis* takes up *ordo* (41). Not infrequently in H. the last word of a line is repeated at the beginning of the next, cf. D. Bo, *Hor. Op.* III. 402. But this passage differs from the others there cited in its function: it ushers in the topics of the (concealed) *partitio* of 40–1, though in reverse order.

uirtus: the common meaning 'worth, excellence' is applied to speech by Cicero and others, cf. *De Or.* II. 241 *est autem haec huius generis (facetiarum) uirtus ut,* etc., *Brut.* 65 *omnes oratoriae uirtutes in eis (orationibus) reperientur.* But Cicero employs *laus* to render Greek ἀρετή (λέξεως) in its technical connotation as 'virtue of diction', whereas Quintilian also uses *uirtus* in the more technical meaning, *I.O.* 1. 5. 1 *oratio tris habeat uirtutes.* Even if there was an ἀρετή τάξεως modelled in Greek theory on ἀρετή λέξεως (above 42–4 n.) *uirtus* still seems to have a metaphorical tinge since it implies *uir,* 'manliness'. This connotation (as in *ui...corporis...uirtute animi,* Sall. *Cat.* 1. 5), rather austere for poetry, perhaps suggested the complementary word *uenus,* 'charm', and the pair *uirtus...et uenus* (alliterative like 414 *uenere et uino*); cf. Quint. *I.O.* IX. 3. 28 *ipsis sensibus cum gratiam tum etiam uires accommodat,* 4. 43 *cum uirtutes et ipsae taedium parant nisi gratia uarietatis adiutae;* Cic. *Part. Or.* 31 *nam ut dilucide probabiliterque narremus necessarium est, sed assumimus etiam suauitatem.*

uenus 'charm' as 320 *fabula nullius ueneris, sine pondere et arte,* Quint. *I.O.* X. 1. 79 *omnes ueneres,* 1.100 *sermo ipse Romanus non recipere uideatur illam solis concessam Atticis uenerem;* IV. 2. 116, VI. 3. 18 combine *uenus* and *gratia.* Since *uenus* (like *uenustas,* ps.-Acro's paraphrase of H.'s *uenus*) may render Greek χάρις, it is pertinent to recall such passages as Demetr. *Interpr.* 137 πρώτη ἐστὶ χάρις ἡ ἐκ συντομίας, or 139 δεύτερος δὲ τόπος ἐστὶν ἀπὸ τῆς τάξεως. τὸ γὰρ αὐτὸ πρῶτον μὲν τεθὲν ἢ μέσον ἄχαρι γίνεται, ἐπὶ δὲ τέλους χαρίεν.

This is not much to go by, but perhaps sufficient to allow of the following suggestions:

(1) What H. has described in terms of (Aristotelian) 'unity' before, he now describes in terms of (rhetorical) 'arrangement'; compare particularly *sed nunc non erat his locus* (19) with the present passage, and the '*partitio*', 40–1. The 'gliding transition' from the preceding portion to this is not

superficial; it reveals that H. is talking about different aspects of the same thing. In his tradition 'literary' and 'rhetorical' aspects were combined.

(2) The same polemical overtones are heard in both sections. Lack of unity and lack of arrangement are complementary.

(3) As before H. chiefly talks of poetic forms large enough to call for 'placing'. This does not mean that his words could not be applied to other genres than epic and drama.

(4) H.'s practice mirrors his own teaching; he concentrates on the *one* thing needful at this place. It is the charm (*uenus*, 42) of his procedure that this demand acquires a different complexion elsewhere in the poem, specially 149–50, Homer leaving aside *quae | desperat tractata nitescere posse*, and the qualification immediately following.

42 *aut ego fallor:* the variant reading *haud* (*haut*) *ego f.* being an obvious mistake. Not a polite disclaimer, as is sometimes thought, but a fairly outspoken and perhaps humorous insistence on the (apparent) truism; cf. P. Cauer, *RM*, LXI (1906), 236–7, '*Der Grundsatz ist einfach genug, aber die Anwendung gelingt so wenigen*'. That *aut fallor* is a way of insisting on the truth of what is said is shown by *Ciris* 227–8 *nec leuis hoc faceret…cura subegit, | aut fallor: quod ut o potius…fallar* the only other passage I know that lacks a second *aut* clause. The same insistence is shown by the full locution with double *aut*, as *aut ego fallor | aut ego laedor* (Ov. *Met.* 1. 607–8), 'I am surely wronged' and the other examples cited *TLL*, VI. 184. 16–18. Comparison is made with *ni fallor*, but that is less strong in emphasis.

43 Bentley's repointing of this verse is superficially attractive: a comma after *dicat* and the twofold *iam nunc* explained as *interdum*, meaning, 'that he should sometimes say all, at other times postpone much that needs to be said to another occasion'. But the attraction is superficial; the proposal could have been made only by a critic who took little interest in the subject-matter of this poem. To advise the poet 'to postpone what needs now to be said', *iam nunc debentia dici*, pulls the foundation of his creed from under H.'s feet. What needs to be said now must be said now, and only that—*ut iam nunc dicat iam nunc debentia dici*.

Ps.-Acro's paraphrase must rest on an excellent tradition. After giving the explanation for which I have just been contending, he continues, *ut Virgilius VIIII libro narrat in Italia iam posito Aenea, quo-modo fabricatae sint naues, quibus de Ilio nauigauit, cum in tertio non dicit.* This refers to the startling addition, in IX. 83 ff. of the *Aeneid,* to our information on the shipbuilding before the hero's emigration in book III. W. Kroll (*Studien z. Verst. d. röm. Lit.* (1924), p. 136) has observed that the same opinion is offered more fully by Servius Dan. on IX. 83: *sane haec narratio tunc iii (ii* codd.) *libri erat, sed dilata est ut hic opportunius redderetur, aut ne bis idem diceretur; potest ergo aut* κατὰ τὸ σιωπώμενον *uideri uut hysteroproteron.* This rhetorical way of accounting for what might well be an editorial lack of agreement between two books of the poem adds to the understanding of the *Ars*; for this is the Homeric–Virgilian context of H.'s precept on *ordo*, on which I have remarked in the introduction to this section (p. 128 above). For other points of contact between the *Ars* and the literary criticism underlying Homeric, Virgilian and other scholia, see below 126, 148 nn.

dicat: the lack of a grammatical subject, if 45 is transposed, causes no difficulty. The poet in question is still *cui lecta potenter erit res,* 40.

44 *pleraque:* cf. 14 n.

praesens in tempus: the Latin idiom in the acc. denoting, like Greek εἰς τὸ παρόν, 'for the time being' rather than 'at the moment', *in praesenti(a)*; cf. *C.* II. 16. 25–6 *laetus in praesens animus quod ultra est | oderit curare.* The opposite, *in futurum* or the like, may be implied and is actually put in such passages as Cic. *Cat.* I. 22, Liv. XXX. 17. I.

(2) Diction in poetry, 46/45–118: (a) Vocabulary, 46–72, (b) Norms of diction in poetic genres, 73–85 (88), (c) Styles of diction exemplified from drama, 89–118

In the initial portion of the poem H. has, by a poetic process, established the validity of certain principles. The 'table of contents', 40–1, is part of this poetic process. But at 42–4 he has glanced at a topic which to contemporary readers was familiar from literary criticism and rhetoric. Now he moves to a second and larger topic: poetry is made of words. The same poetic principles also inform this subject. Yet H. does not let the reader float freely; by the placing of his topics he reminds him of one of the basic divisions which were shared by literary and rhetorical theory: after *ordo* there follows *facundia.* [*facundia* (41), thus related to a section which is wholly concerned with diction, is indeed unobtrusive but not, what G. Williams calls it, *JRS*, LIV (1964), 194, 'vague'. For the word *facundia*, see above 41 n. That 46 ff. do take up the *facundia* of 41 was seen by an early commentator, who was still in touch with H.'s literary tradition, the Carolingian compiler of the *Tractatus Vindobonensis* (on 46, p. 5. 24 of J. Zech- meister's edition), *hactenus de ordine. nunc de facundia dicit, et continuatur ita: facundia non deseret hunc; et ut te non deserat facundia, tenuis,* etc. In the nineteenth century L. Spengel had to make the case afresh, *P*, XVIII (1862), 96; it is still clearly stated by Steidle, *Studien*, p. 36. But *JRS*, LIV (1964), shows that this lore is again lost.]

The Peripatetic–Aristotelian character of this section has been fully discussed in my *Prolegomena*. Similar theories are of course found in rhetoric, notably in Cicero, *De Or.* III. 149 ff., *Or.* 80 ff., 149 ff., cf. Fiske, *Lucil. and Hor.* 453 ff., Grant and Fiske, *Cic. 'Or.' and Hor. 'A.P.'*, 23 ff., *Cic. 'De Or.' and Hor. 'A.P.'*, 107 ff. 'Similar' however is not 'same'. The two tradi- tions although they sometimes converged had developed differently within their own spheres; and, even more impor- tant, Cicero's and H.'s aims are at variance. To link H. closely with Cicero is to link him with something alien to his inten- tion, ethos, and subject. Unlike Fiske, therefore, and unlike B. Otis (*Gnomon*, XXXVI (1964), 269), I do not regard the Ciceronian parallels as directly relevant to H., although I have no doubt about their value as illustrative material. Even less can I be persuaded that H. himself had levered these theories out of their divergent contexts in Cicero in order to reassemble them in an *ars poetica*. For relevance to the *Ars*, Ar. *Rhet.* III. 2–8 (applied to poetry by the literary critics), cannot be matched by these Ciceronian chapters.

(a) Vocabulary, 46/45–72

Again H. employs traditional material in order to express contemporary and personal views. The traditional material derives from Aristotle and his school, cf. *Prol.* 94, Ar. *Rhet.* III, chs. 2–6, *Poet.* chs. 21–2. The distinction between Choice of words, ἐκλογὴ ὀνομάτων—*delectus uerborum*, and Composition, σύνθεσις ὀνομάτων—*uerba continuata* or *coniuncta*, is potentially present in Aristotle and becomes fully operative with his successors: Ar. *Rhet.* III, chs. 2–6 and 8–9; Theophr. (probably from the περὶ λέξεως) *ap.* Dion. Hal. *Isocr.* 3 (U.–R. I. 58), καθόλου δὲ τριῶν ὄντων, ὥς φησι Θεόφραστος, ἐξ ὧν γίνεται τὸ μέγα καὶ σεμνὸν καὶ περιττὸν ἐν λέξει, τῆς τε ἐκλογῆς τῶν ὀνομάτων καὶ τῆς ἐκ τούτων ἁρμονίας καὶ τῶν περιλαμβανόντων αὐτὰ σχημάτων. Dionysius recurs to it frequently, for example *De Comp.* 1 (U.–R. II. 5. 5). ἐκλογῇ τε χρήσεσθαι...ὀνομάτων καὶ συνθέσει ταῦτα κοσμήσειν. The rhetoricians take it altogether for granted; it is the common mode of discussion for Cicero and Quintilian. Equally the classification of *delectus uerborum* is Aristotelian only by implication; cf. *Poet.* 22, 1458 a 21 (λέξις) ἐξαλλάττουσα τὸ ἰδιωτικὸν ἢ τοῖς ξενικοῖς κεχρημένη. ξενικὸν δὲ λέγω γλῶτταν καὶ μεταφορὰν καὶ ἐπέκτασιν καὶ πᾶν τὸ παρὰ τὸ κύριον. The rhetorical mode is yet more cut-and-dried, as in Cic. *De Or.* III. 152 ff., *Or.* 79–80, where common words, *usitata*, are contrasted with (1) *inusitata*, archaisms, (2) *nouata*, neologisms, either compounds or new coinages altogether, and (3) *translata*, metaphors. The tradition on which H. has drawn seems to have been that of poetic criticism rather than of rhetorical theory. The grammatical procedure in Varro's *L.L.* book IX differs again, in spite of some resemblances which are over-emphasized, for example, by R. Reitzenstein, *M. Varro und Johannes Mauropus von Euchaita* (1901), p. 64.

H.'s own concern comes out clearly both in the letter to Florus and its companion piece, the present passage. The former asks how to avoid flat writing: *Ep.* II. 2. 106 *mala carmina*, 111 *parum splendoris*, 112 *sine pondere, honore indigna*, in contrast to 116 *speciosa uocabula rerum*. Metaphors, surprisingly, enter neither here nor in the *Ars* (cf. below 47–8 n.). Choice of words is in question, largely old words brought back into currency, *Ep.* II. 2. 111–18; but there is a single verse on new coinages, 119. The *Ars* is more complicated. It enjoins attention to ordinary usage finding distinction in *callida iunctura* of current words, 46/45–8; but at some length new coinages are advocated for the expression of new ideas, 48–59, language being prone to change like any natural phenomenon or human creation, 60–9; current words die and old words are reborn, 70–2. Literary theory then is more strongly stressed in the *A.P.* Three ideas stand out: (1) the value attached to usage as a setting for the poet's creativeness; (2) the stress on language as changing; (3) the need for new words to express remote ideas.

These injunctions imply literary polemic in more than one direction; and tendencies rather than adversaries are attacked. Anxious purism is opposed by implication, for H. invites archaisms as well as neologisms, though he restricts both. Thus neither the purists nor the archaists nor the modernists could have taken much comfort from his words; he is seeking to demonstrate what (to him) is best in the verbal art of Augustan verse. The contemporary note is stronger in the *Florus*, where the theoretical note is weak. The *Ars*, on the other hand, brings doctrine to life by a touch of literary actuality; what at first sight gives the impression of traditional teaching turns out to be new practice justified by critical theory.

46–5 were transposed by Bentley. The sequence needs to be thus reversed if *facundia* as well as *ordo* are to bear out the promise of 40–1 *cui lecta potenter erit res, | nec facundia deseret hunc nec lucidus ordo.* So Vahlen argued (*Ges. Phil. Schr.* I. 452–5), but voices dissenting from Bentley have never been silent. Editors however must, among other difficulties, meet Vahlen's point as regards *etiam*, 46. '*etiam* shifts the argument from thematic to verbal ordering', says N. E. Collinge, in defending the transmitted sequence (*The Structure of H.'s Odes* (1961), p. 20 n. 2) but not finally rejecting the transposition; similarly J. H. Waszink, *Mnem.* Ser. IV, XXI (1968), 401, although he regards the transposition as unacceptable. Yet H.'s main subject is not verbal ordering but verbal choice, just as it was choice of a topic for a given place, in 42–3. The transmitted sequence

46 in uerbis *etiam* tenuis cautusque serendis
47 dixeris egregie, notum si callida uerbum
48 reddiderit iunctura nouum

does not express this notion of choice (least of all with a full stop after *serendis*, 46, in Immisch's pointing of these verses). For *tenuis cautusque* merely describes the poet as sparing in *uerbis...serendis*; yet *notum...uerbum*, 47, assumes that a comment on selection (and rejection) of words has been made. This however is the case only if 45 is transposed to the context beginning at 46. It is true that we find a 'gliding transition' from *ordo* to *facundia* (Waszink, *ibid.*). But that we find, whether 45 be transposed or not. It is the precise nature of that transition which may be questioned.

hoc amet, hoc spernat promissi carminis auctor (45) provides the notion of choice, which is otiose and stylistically disturbing in its transmitted place. The verse should not therefore be deleted (as proposed by C. Hammerstein, *Quaest. Hor. crit.*, Coloniae (1846), 1–15, and some nineteenth-century editors): it is needed between 46 and 47, where Bentley placed it. The lacuna after 45, proposed instead by G. Ramain (*RP*, 3me Sér. 1 (1927), 241), is a gratuitous assumption, which evades the problem posed by *etiam*, 46.

46 *in uerbis...serendis:* in the endless debates on the meaning of this locution, no basis for argument has been agreed. An explanation needs to satisfy two requirements. It must link *in uerbis...serendis* with the relevant Latin idiom and it must link the present passage with a later one in the poem that clearly refers back to it; I mean 242 *tantum series iuncturaque pollet.*

(1) As for the meaning, a search in the materials of the Latin *Thesaurus* has yielded an unexpected result. The prevalent Latin idiom is not, as one might expect, 'to join words together' but either 'to join speech with a person' or else 'to interchange a subject in speech'. For the former I cite Pl. *Curc.* 193 *mihi...seruos sermonem serat?*, *Mil.* 700 *mihi...sermones sera[n]t*. When the indirect object is omitted the direct one is still 'speech', not single words, but *cum* or *inter* or *per* usually take the place of the dative, thus: Caec. *CRF*³, 151–2 *inter suas | aequales...sermonem serit*, Liv. III. 17. 10 *sermones tempori aptos serere*, x. 19. 8 *populares orationes serere*, xxiv. 31. 3 *licentia ...colloquia serendi cum hoste*, 32. 4 *serebanturque colloquia per propinquos popularium*, xxviii. 24. 7 *sermones...occulti serebantur*, 25. 5 *sermones inter se serentium circulos*, xxxiv. 61. 7 *certos homines...cum eo secreta colloquia serere.* The second meaning, 'to interchange a subject (in speech)', I have not met before Virgil; E. Norden (Comm. on *A.* vi.

373) would like to date it back to Ennius: *A.* VI. 160 *multa inter sese uario sermone serebant,* Liv. III. 43. 2 *mentiones ad uolgus militum sermonibus occultis serentem,* VII. 39. 6 *haec . . . occultis sermonibus serunt,* Sil. XV. 283 *haec . . . alterno sermone serebant* (Heinsius, *fer-* codd.), cf. Stat. *Th.* VI. 942 *multa duces errore serunt,* and without an abl. Stat. *Th.* II. 150 *serere arcanas . . . atque euoluere curas.* The consistency of these idioms is recognized by Varro, *L.L.* VI. 64 *sermo . . . a serie . . .; sermo enim non potest in uno homine esse solo sed ubi ⟨o⟩ratio cum altero coniuncta,* Serv. on Virg. *A.* VI. 160 *hinc proprie dictus est sermo qui⟨a⟩ (scripsi,* cf. next passage) *inter utrumque seritur,* whence Isid. *Et.* VI. 8. 3 *sermo autem dictus quia inter utrumque seritur* (seq. Virg. *A.* VI. 160). It appears that none of these passages will bear out *uerba serere* = 'join words together'. Nor will Liv. VII. 2. 8 *argumento fabulam serere,* XXXVIII. 56. 8 *alia tota serenda fabula est,* Stat. *Th.* IV. 549 *carmenque serit,* because the result (*fabula, carmen*) *seritur,* not its parts, *uerba. uerba,* says Quintilian, are *omnia per quae sermo nectitur (I.O.* I. 5. 2).

I conclude that H.'s *in uerbis . . . serendis* and the only other comparable passage known to me (Sen. *Med.* 26 *querelas uerbaque in cassum sero*) stand apart from the rest. Does this result encourage a derivation not from *sero* 'to join, weave, compose' but *sero* 'to sow, place, set out, put forth'? Ps.-Acro seems to think so; ⟨*serendis:*⟩ (he says in his note on the present passage) *ordinandis, ponendis* (cf. *Tract. Vind.* p. 5. 29 Zechmeister). Does the notion of 'setting out words' fit the context and does it meet the second requirement—correspondence with what appears to be a later reference to this passage, at 242?

(2) In the larger setting, the notion of 'planting words' strikes me as just possible, although 'joining words' would be preferable in view of the *iunctura* that follows two verses later. This impression is greatly strengthened by the later reference which I have mentioned: in a similar argument—ordinary material placed in a pointed context—H. says *tantum series iuncturaque pollet* (242). Clearly the two nouns are used as near-synonyms for 'close weave' and 'context', 'texture' and 'combination'. I do not think that *series* there can be divorced from *in uerbis . . . serendis* here, nor *iunctura* in one place from *iunctura* in the other. Hence the notion of 'joining words', i.e. 'composition', must be preferred (cf. L. P. Wilkinson, *CQ,* n.s. IX (1959), 186 n. 3, Waszink, *Mnem.* Ser. IV, XXI (1968), 402).

I am led to assume therefore that H. has chosen an unusual and more direct way to express the idea of 'composition'—not *sermonem sero* but *uerba sero.* If this observation is just, certain applications of *sero* 'to sow' will have to be jettisoned in consequence; thus Dacier's 'creation of new words' (recently argued by G. Stegen, *Les Épîtres*

Commentary

Litt. d'Horace, pp. 28–9) or the *inuentio uerborum* asserted in Rostagni's note *ad l.*

These two introductory sentences then (*A.P.* 46/5–48) tie together σύνθεσις and ἐκλογὴ ὀνομάτων, composition and vocabulary. Words are used not in a vacuum but in contextual situations. This is H.'s system of reference, unlike the rhetorical mode which separates ἐκλογή and σύνθεσις. H. makes little of this technical distinction. I doubt if it is expedient to follow Vahlen in urging the difference between *uerba serere* as a rhetorical term (= σύνθεσις, *iunctura*) and as a simple notion for speech. The poet is largely concerned with the choice of words, but *iunctura* is glanced at, in the famous aside near the beginning (47–8), closely entwined with its counterpart, *delectus uerborum*. Thus *iunctura* continues, by implication, throughout the section. But what matters most is the searching and curiously moving appraisal of words as living things.

tenuis cautusque 'discriminately, and therefore proceeding with circumspection'. *tenuis* like Greek λεπτός rarely lacks the notion of thinness, small size or quantity; but, as in the word 'fine', finesse is not far away: 'discriminating, nice' in perception, taste, understanding. Note the various implications in *S.* II. 4. 36 *tenui ratione saporum*, Cic. *Ac. Pr.* II. 43 *similitudines dissimilitudinesque et earum tenuis et acuta distinctio*, 66 *rationes...non ad tenue elimatas*, Lucr. IV. 912 *tu mihi da tenues* (not *uacuas*) *aures animumque sagacem*, Pers. 5. 93 *dare tenuia rerum officia*, Mart. VI. 64. 17 *tenues finxerunt pectus Athenae*. The plain style of the rhetoricians, *tenue genus*, is discriminating as well as plain but H.'s poet is not restricted to plainness. References in H. to poetic λεπτότης are a different and more tricky matter.

45 For the transposition of this verse, see above. The Horatian texts of ps.-Acro and of Servius, like the rest of the known ancient tradition, had 45 in the wrong place preceding 46. It was therefore taken by them to concern 'subject-matter', not 'diction'. But unlike ps.-Acro, Servius believes 45 to be about the epic poet's personal involvement, his *amare* and *spernere*, as regards the topics of his narrative. This strange misunderstanding is shown in three citations, on Virg. *G.* II. 475, and *A.* IV. 412, 415.

hoc...hoc need not, *pace* J. H. Waszink (*Mnem.* Ser. IV, XXI (1968), 400), apply to subject-matter, but are likely to be part of the 'gliding transition', and refer to words, *uerba*.

amet (opp. *spernat*) has an emotional nuance: not simply 'accept, choose' but 'delight in or be partial to' as 234–5 *nomina... | uerbaque...Satyrorum scriptor amabo*, cf. *Ep.* II. 2. 58 *non omnes eadem mirantur amantque*.

promissi carminis auctor: L. Mueller's obelus against *promissi* and P. H. Damsté's conjecture *promus sit* (*Mnem.* n.s. xxxiv (1906), 363–4) perhaps derive from a misreading of the context. *promissi carminis* may recall *Epod.* 14. 7 *inceptos, olim promissum carmen, iambos* and *auctor* may be 'author', though there is no clear instance of this meaning in H.; *C.* I. 28. 14 should not be claimed as one. But the sentence also may imply a deliberate ambiguity; for, as Kiessling acutely observed, *auctor* next to *promissi* (*carminis*) suggests 'surety' or 'guarantor', cf. the legal and quasi-legal notions of *auctor* in *TLL*, II. 1194. 62 ff. The sense would then be, 'he who stands surety for the promised poem' or 'he who causes the promise to be fulfilled', that is the author *cui lecta potenter erit res,* 40, cf. *promissor,* 138.

47 *dixeris* (*dixerit* is erroneously adapted to similar forms in the vicinity), the second person, a stock device in the *sermo* as in the Greek diatribe, a sudden address to an imaginary listener or disciple as at 19–20 *et fortasse cupressum* | *scis simulare;* more explicit, 119–20.

egregie: excellence in the use of words as *Ep.* II. 2. 111 *parum splendoris,* 116 *speciosa uocabula rerum,* etc.; Cic. *De Or.* III. 150 (*ut orator*) *lectis atque illustribus utatur.* But against expectation H. is not commending unusual words.

notum...uerbum: a 'familiar word', an 'established expression', distinct from *uerbum notum alicui,* distinct too from *propria uerba,* κύρια ὀνόματα, rendered by *dominantia,* 234; cf. 47–8 n. *notum* (like 240 *ex noto*) resembles 234 *de medio sumptis* and *uerba togae* in the parallel passage of Pers. 5. 14; the common term for it is *usitatum,* the εἰωθός of Aristotle's *Poetics,* cf. his ἰδιωτικόν. Although people can be 'well known', *homines noti* (Cic. *Brut.* 85), not *noui,* and so can things and names be, the expression here may have arisen from the conjunction with *nouum*—perhaps a *callida iunctura.* The same inference may apply to the only other technical use of 'known words' I have come across, Cic. *Or.* 211 *neque enim esse possunt rebus ignotis nota nomina* (although *nota* here has been excised, wrongly, I think); contrast Cic. *Fin.* III. 4 *uocabulis...nobis incognitis, usitatis sibi.*

47–8 *notum...nouum:* the words in interwoven order a–b–a–b–a: *notum* (*si*) *callida uerbum* | (*reddiderit*) *iunctura nouum,* giving prominence to what is perhaps *callida iunctura, notum...nouum* (cf. preceding n.). Some kind of interwoven order is often found in connexion with this topic, see below 58 n.—Ciceronian rhetoric?

callida, like 'cunning', at one time, without pejorative notion, 'skilful, knowledgeable' as *S.* I. 5. 90, II. 7. 101, etc. (*TLL,* III. 171. 22 ff.). The word may be applied to the skill or as here to its product, cf. Cic. *T.D.* I. 47 *artificio,* Nep. *Eum.* 5. 4 *inuentum.*

(*callida...*) *iunctura:* the noun is not definitely attested before this passage and *A.P.* 242. M. Ruch, *REL*, XLI (1963), 254 f., suggests that *iunctura* is probably a Horatian coinage, adapted to hexameter verse and avoiding the implication of such rhetorical notions as *uerba iuncta* or *continuata, iunctio* or *coniunctio*, rendering σύνθεσις ὀνομάτων. He may be right. Yet *iunctura* in this rhetorical sense occurs frequently after H., thus at Pers. 1. 65 and 92, Sen. *Ep.* 114. 15, in Quintilian and the later grammarians. It is unlikely that the rhetoricians and grammarians would have borrowed a Horatian word in order to apply it to a different notion that is at home in rhetoric. A pre-Horatian origin for the rhetorical term must, at the very least, be considered possible. Dr W. Ehlers of the *TLL* reminds me that it is more than a possibility. For Mar. Vict. *GL*, VI. 55. 11 says *uersus est, ut Varroni placet, uerborum iunctura*. This does not ensure literal quotation but, in view of the later instances, renders it likely. In that case H. has attached a different notion to an existing word. For in the present passage no teaching concerning *uerba continuata*, σύνθεσις ὀνομάτων, follows *more rhetorico*. In spite of contrary assertions (e.g. Immisch's *ad l.* and F. Cupaiuolo's *A proposito della callida iunctura oraziana* (1942), 14 ff.) I can discover no rules on euphony, hiatus, rhythm—the rhetorical stock-in-trade; cf. Steidle, *Studien*, p. 38.

H. is concerned with semantic collocation, as is Persius in a passage patently derived from this: 5. 14 *uerba togae sequeris iunctura callidus acri*. Although I would not deny that metaphorical expression may be included (as Heinze and L. P. Wilkinson, *Horace*[2], 126, *CQ*, n.s. IX (1959), 186, say), this is not to the fore. For *uerba propria* need not be current words, nor need current words have literal meanings; so Ar. *Poet.* 22, 1458 b 21 (κυρίου εἰωθότος) shows himself well aware. A sufficient distinction is made between them at *Ad Her.* IV. 17 (*explanatio* 'clarity') *comparatur duabus rebus, usitatis uerbis et propriis. usitata sunt ea quae uersantur in* [*sermone*] *consuetudine cotidiana, propria quae eius rei uerba sunt aut esse possunt qua de loquemur*, and Cic. *Or.* 80 *sed etiam inusitata ac prisca sunt in propriis, nisi quod raro utimur*. H. is talking about the 'refreshment', which may or may not be metaphorical, of ordinary words in a pointed context, such as perhaps his use of *notum...uerbum* in conjunction with *nouum*, 47 n. This conveys admirably one aspect of the practice of the Augustan New Poets. It does not recall the ἐξαλλάττειν τὸ ἰδιωτικόν of Ar. *Poet.* ch. 22, but rather Ar. *Rhet.* III. 2, 1404 b 24–5 κλέπτεται δ' εὖ ἐάν τις ἐκ τῆς εἰωθυίας διαλέκτου ἐκλέγων συντιθῇ· ὅπερ Εὐριπίδης ποιεῖ καὶ ὑπέδειξε πρῶτος, a remark often restated and here put to new use. The remark occurs again, in the more traditional manner of art concealing art, at 242 *tantum series iuncturaque pollet*, cf. the passages there cited.

48–53 The problems of the next sentence, or sentences, are interdependent and I discuss them together. This is the text unpointed:

> si forte necesse est
> indiciis monstrare recentibus abdita rerum (et)
> fingere cinctutis non exaudita Cethegis   50
> continget dabiturque licentia sumpta pudenter
> et noua fictaque nuper habebunt uerba fidem si
> Graeco fonte cadent parce detorta.

How is it to be divided? Is *et* (transmitted only in some MSS) correct at the end of 49, and *si* at the end of 52? Many editors still believe these verses to form one lengthy sentence. Thus *et fingere...continget ... and et ficta...habebunt...fidem* correspond according to Kiessling and Heinze, Rostagni, and several others. Yet the two *et* clauses are logically and grammatically in imbalance; moreover the two *si* clauses (48, 52) serve to pull the asserted period to pieces. Lambinus hesitated between two possibilities, and doubtfully put a comma after *Cethegis* (50), to mark the end of the protasis, using *et* (49) to connect the two parts of the first *si* clause: *si...necesse est...monstrare ...et fingere...exaudita Cethegis*. Although Klingner's Teubner edition has sought to restore this punctuation (compare his discussion, *H*, LXXV (1940), 326–9, repr. in his *Studien z. gr. und röm. Lit.* (1954), pp. 405–9), it is rendered unlikely by the doublet *continget dabiturque licentia sumpta pudenter*. I regard it as preferable therefore to put a comma after *continget* (51) and a strong incision after *pudenter* at the end of the same verse. This counsels the omission of *et* (49), perhaps a falsely repeated *est* from the end of the previous verse. As for the incision after 51, the early editors but also Bentley and others preferred a full stop; Orelli, Schütz, Wilkins, Wickham, a semicolon.

This arrangement makes it possible to attach a more plausible sense to 52–3. For unless these verses are removed sufficiently from the preceding context, H. would be committed to the absurdity of allowing new words only after a Greek model. That restriction is unlikely in theory, and is ignored in *Ep.* II. 2. 119 *adsciscet noua quae genitor produxerit usus*. It is contradicted by Virgil's practice, to which H. makes reference at 55, and by the poet's own (cf. 55, 58). For with that restriction such neologisms as *ampullatur* (*Ep.* I. 3. 14) and *dominantia nomina* (*A.P.* 234) would be acceptable on the showing of ληκυθίζειν and κύρια ὀνόματα; but, say, *cinctutis* (*A.P.* 50) would not, because of the lack or apparent lack of a Greek model. Porphyrion

is misled and misleading when he instances Greek 'loan-words' such
as *triclinium*, but he is right in attributing no more than especial
authority to Grecizing: *magis, inquit, auctoritatem mereri possunt.*

How then can 52–3 be rescued from absurdity? By replacing *si* (52)
by either *et si* (Madvig, *Adv. Crit.* II. 62) or *seu* meaning *uel si*
(Mueller)? Scarcely, since this form of sentence would be intolerably
clumsy: 'and new coinages will (thus) gain credit, or (*sc.* will gain
credit) if they fall sparsely from a Greek mint'. Or by assuming a
lacuna of one verse, ending *aut si* (Lehrs)? Even less so, since there is
no gap in the sense, H. having already indicated what forms a legitimate basis for new coinages without a Greek precedent.

I doubt if any change of text is required, as long as *et* (52) is
allowed the emphatic sense of 'and indeed' which lies in the context
just discussed. Cf. *et*, Liv. I. 6. 3 *Romulum...cupido cepit...urbis con-
dendae. et supererat multitudo Albanorum Latinorumque*; *ac*, Liv. XXI. 40. 10
*reliquias extremas hostium, non hostem, habetis. ac nihil magis uereor quam
ne, cum nos pugnaueritis, Alpes uicisse Hannibalem uideantur.*

48 *si forte:* the demand for new words starts tentatively, with a
deprecating 'if by chance', and the reason why the demand is made.
'*Erst im Laufe der Erörterung wird der Ton sicher und sogar aggressiv*',
Steidle, *Studien*, 38.

necesse est: diction depends on content. New words are to express
'obscure' subject-matter, which has not yet been 'named'. Cf. Cic.
Or. 211 *in omnibus hoc fit artibus ut, cum id appellandum sit quod propter
rerum ignorationem ipsarum nullum habuerit ante nomen, necessitas cogat aut
nouum facere uerbum aut a simili mutuari.* The Epicurean χρεία may be
compared, though it is by no means identical, e.g. Lucr. v. 1028–9.

49 *indiciis...recentibus:* new signs or symbols, Greek σημεῖα or
σύμβολα. Aristotle, *Soph. El.* 1, 165 a 7, describes names (nouns,
ὀνόματα) as signs for things, τοῖς ὀνόμασιν ἀντὶ τῶν πραγμάτων
χρώμεθα ὡς συμβόλοις, but warns against taking the two as identical.
Hence the difficulty over their 'semantic' status, of which Hellenistic
philosophers make so much. Cf. Porph. *ad l.: indicia uerba appellauit;
philosophi enim dicunt indicandarum rerum causa inuentas esse uoces*, ps.-
Acro ...*quia indicia rerum uerba sunt secundum philosophos, qui aiunt*
ἔλεγχον τῶν πραγμάτων εἶναι τὸν λόγον. In Latin a complication
was added because new thinking often amounted to Latinizing
Graiorum obscura reperta (Lucr. 1. 136). Hence Lucretius' difficulty, 1.
138–9 *multa nouis uerbis...agendum | propter egestatem linguae et* rerum
nouitatem, cf. C. Bailey, *Lucretius*, 1, 51–2. The problem is familiar
from the proems of some of Cicero's philosophical writings (e.g.
below 58 n.), and from Varro. Sen. *Ep.* 58 may be compared. H. talks

in a Lucretian poetic vein. For him new words are a means of 'revealing', *monstrare* (cf. 74 n.), intellectual territory unperceived, although his topic is not philosophy; these two aspects have been unduly separated by M. Ruch, *REL*, XLI (1963), 253 f. To express word-symbols Varro uses *significare* (e.g. *L.L.* VIII. 27, 40; IX. 37, 73) or *designare* (*L.L.* IX. 37); Cicero *quasi rerum notis* (*Ac.* I. 32) or *res... notare*; both *uerba imponere rebus*. H.'s *indiciis*, being nowhere else so used in extant classical Latin (*TLL*, VII. 1. 1150. 34), may well be a Horatian coinage; *monstrare* continues the metaphor.

abdita rerum: the genitive after substantival neut. pl. adj. as *S.* II. 2. 25 *uanis rerum*, 8. 83 *fictis rerum*. Apart from certain comparatives and superlatives, this is a poetic usage, inherited by Sallust and Silver prose writers. Lucretius was fond of this idiom, e.g. VI. 809 *terrai... abdita*. H., using the idiom, thus adds to the overtones of such a phrase as Lucretius' *obscura reperta* (cit. in preceding n.). For the subject-matter, cf. Cic. *Fin.* III. 5 *de rebus non peruagatis inusitatis uerbis* (*uti*).

rerum [et]: MSS are divided between *rerum* and *rerum et*, on which editors differ as they do on the punctuation. See 48–53 n.

50 *cinctutis...Cethegis:* the old patrician family of the Cethegi prided itself on the retention of the *cinctus*, a broad waistband, as underwear in the place of a tunic so that the shoulders were left bare, *exerti*. Cf. Münzer, *RE*, IV. 1276–7, and Porph. *ad l.*, Schol. Bern. on Lucan, II. 543; Lucan, *Ibid. exertique...Cethegi*, VI. 794 *nudique Cethegi*, Sil. VIII. 585 (*Cethegus*) *umero exertus gentili more parentum*. In the present passage new words are said to be unknown to the Cethegi and conversely archaisms are described, at *Ep.* II. 2. 117, as *priscis memorata Catonibus atque Cethegis*. The conjunction with the elder Cato, and the literary context, may hint at M. Cornelius Cethegus, *suauiloquenti ore* and *flos delibatus populi suadaeque medulla*, Enn. *Ann.* 303–4, 308. *cinctutus* occurs in classical Latin only here and Ov. *Fast.* V. 101 *cinctutis... Lupercis*; probably a Horatian coinage, humorously apt in the context.

51 (*fingere*) *continget:* without a personal dative as Virg. *A.* VI. 108–9 *ire...contingat*, Ov. *A.A.* II. 638 *quod non contigit esse*.

sumpta pudenter 'in moderation': *Ep.* I. 17. 44–5 *distat sumasne pudenter | an rapias*, cf. Cic. *Fin.* II. 113 *inest moderator cupiditatis pudor*. At 53 H. has *parce* and Cic. *Or.* 81 combines (*in transferendis uerbis*) *uerecundus et parcus*. The social metaphor shields the reader from the full impact of literary theorizing. For moderation in the use of unfamiliar words and ornaments is enjoined by the critics, notably Aristotle, e.g. Ar. *Poet.* 22, 1458 b 12 τὸ δὲ μέτρ⟨ι⟩ον κοινὸν ἁπάντων ἐστὶ τῶν μερῶν, 15 ἁρμόττον, *Rhet.* III. 3, 1406 a 16 ἀλλὰ δεῖ στοχάζεσθαι τοῦ μετρίου.

52 *noua fictaque nuper,* to which *factaque,* the reading of some dett., should not have been preferred by Bentley. It is true *fingere* occurs two verses previously, but *fictaque* seems to pick up *fingere.* Bentley's examples are in the main Ciceronian, and Cicero does employ *facio* in most cases; *fingo* however at *Leg.* II. 28, *Fin.* IV. 7, v. 89. Yet in spite of Greek πεποιημένα, *fingo* is largely used to describe the coining of new words, note particularly Quint. *I.O.* VIII. 6. 32 *cum multa cotidie ab antiquis ficta moriantur. uix illa quae* πεποιημένα *uocant...nobis permittimus,* Fronto cit. below. So it is used by the experts, Varro, Festus, Quintilian (refs. are listed *TLL,* VI. 774. 14 ff.), but also in poetic language, Virg. *A.* III. 18 *Aeneadasque meo nomen de nomine fingo.* For *fingo* combined with *nouum,* see Cic. *Fin.* IV. 7 *noua uerba fingunt* (but *Or.* 211 *nouum facere uerbum*), Varro *ap.* Gell. XII. 10. 4 *recenti nouitate fictum,* Fronto, *Ep.* III. 13. 1 (p. 50 Naber) *uerba noua fingere,* Gell. IV. 15. 1 *uerborum...fingendi et nouandi studium,* Serv. Dan. Virg. *A.* III. 384 *noue uerbum fictum.*

habebunt...fidem 'acceptance, authority', *TLL,* VI. 683. 9 ff.

53 *Graeco fonte cadunt:* Greek derivatives according to Porph. *si a Graeco fuerint in Latinum deriuata, ut transtulimus triclinium; antea cenaculum illud uocabamus quia ibi cenabatur.* Or else Latin words formed on the analogy of Greek, as *dominantia nomina* (234) = κύρια ὀνόματα, and such compounds as *centimanus* = ἑκατόγχειρος (*C.* II. 17. 14, III. 4. 69)? The former view is commended by the metaphor of 'derivation' *Graeco fonte,* but rendered doubtful by the paucity of such newly borrowed Grecizing words as *diota* (*C.* I. 9. 8) in Horatian or contemporary verse. The latter is commended by Augustan neologisms, H.'s not apart; cf. A. Rothmaler, *De Horatio verborum inventore,* Thesis, Berlin 1862, K. Zangemeister, *De Horatii vocibus singularibus,* Thesis, Berlin 1862. H. may not here have distinguished between these two types of 'Greek derivations'. Does the latter stretch the words *Graeco fonte* unduly? Scarcely, since the '*dominantia*' type too comes *Graeco fonte*—in a sense. The sense is that expressed by Quint. *I.O.* II. 14. 1, where he objects to *oratoria* and *oratrix* as renderings of ῥητορική, and adds, *sed non omnia nos ducentes ex Graeco sequuntur, sicut ne illos quidem quotiens utique suis uerbis signare nostra uoluerunt;* cf. VIII. 3. 33 *multa ex Graeco formata noua ac plurima...quorum dura quaedam admodum uidentur ut 'queens' et 'essentia'.* Thus too Apul. *Apol.* 38 *uiuiparos...et ouiparos: ita enim Latine appello quae Graeci* ζῳοτόκα *et* ᾠοτόκα*...; ...nomina etiam Romanis inusitata...labore meo...ita de Graecis prouenire ut tamen Latina moneta percussa sint.*

143

cadunt: poetic and Silver prose for rivers springing from their sources, *TLL*, III. 30. 56 ff.—with *fonte* offers a consistent image of a stream; it counteracts the 'frozen' metaphor *fons* = origin, as 309 *scribendi recte sapere est et principium et fons.* For more elaborate imagery of poetic language quickening Latium, see *Ep.* II. 2. 120–1, *Prol.* 188 n. 4.

parce detorta continues the image of the stream; the lock is not opened fully as it were. *parce* recalls the moderation enjoined by *pudenter*, 51. *detorqueo* is applied to derivation of words as early as Cato (*Origines* II, fr. 53, H. Peter, *Hist. Rom. Rel.* I², 70, *Marrucini...de Marso detorsum nomen*) and, like *declino*, found in the grammatical terminology of H.'s time (Fest. p. 269) and earlier. But the vivid imagery of the verse counteracts the technical usage.

53–9 So far the theory. Now two vigorous rhetorical questions and a large assertion, tying (contemporary) poetic practice—the chief concern of *Ep.* book II—to poetic theory.

53 *quid autem:* R. Kassel, *RM*, CIX (1966), 5 commends F. Villeneuve's rendering '*Eh quoi!*', and punctuates *quid autem?*—implausibly, I think. In brief argumentative transitions with *quid, autem* seems to be unusual enough to make actually against repunctuation; contrast *quid? quid ita? quid enim? quid ergo? quid tum?*, etc. Moreover the similar content of the two questions, 53 *quid autem...* and 55 *ego cur...*, suggests similarity of wording: *quid* and *cur* agree in meaning. *quid* = *cur* has a colloquial nuance, cf. Hofmann–Szantyr, 458; *autem*, a prosaic word, occurs only three times in H. (here and *Ep.* II. 1. 199, 260), B. Axelson, *Unpoet. Wörter*, 85–6.

54–5 *Caecilio...Varioque:* for the wording, see Cic. *Fin.* III. 15 (about the younger Cato) *si enim Zenoni licuit, cum rem aliquam inuenisset inusitatam, inauditum quoque ei rei nomen imponere, cur non liceat Catoni?* The Roman reader, timelessly as it were, grants the old comic poets the privilege of new coinages, which he has just 'taken away from' Virgil and Varius. At *Ep.* II. 1. 247 too, *Vergilius Variusque poetae* are paired, but here *Vergilio Varioque* seem to echo mockingly *Caecilio Plautoque* in the same place of the line. Virgil was dead when *Ep.* II. 1 was written, and any of the probable datings of the *Ars* would necessitate the same conclusion for the present verse. Whether the death of Varius should be inferred from the juxtaposition in either passage seems to me uncertain. For Varius, see *R-E*, VIII A. 410–13, W. Morel, *FPL*, pp. 100–1; for the variant *Varo*, Housman, *CQ*, XI (1917), 44. H.'s views on Plautus are apparent from 270 ff., *Ep.* II. 1. 170 ff.; for Caecilius, see *Ep.* II. 1. 59 in the context indicated *ibid.* 60–1.

55 *ego* so shortly after Virgil and Varius makes against an

indefinite meaning ('poets'), and for personal emphasis as at *Ep.* II. I.
247 *Vergilius Variusque poetae*, 250 *ego*; cf. J. Vahlen, *Ges. Phil. Schr.* II.
748, G. Williams, *JRS*, LIV (1964), 195. The poet who *adsciscet noua*,
at *Ep.* II. 2. 119, is described as *qui legitimum cupiet fecisse poema* (*ibid.*
109).

pauca in comparison with the 'enrichment' (*ditauerit*) through
Cato's and Ennius' language and perhaps, by implication, through
that of Virgil and Varius. This is a case of H.'s self-belittling; the
contexts of such other cases as *Ep.* II. I. 257–8 *paruum | carmen, C.*
IV. 2. 31 *paruos*, differ.

56 *inuideor* like Greek φθονοῦμαι, apparently, a grammatical coinage translating his theory into practice. Porph. (on 55) *inuideor posuit
pro inuidetur mihi*, ps.-Acro *mire, dum de fingendis uerbis loquitur, secundum
Graecos ipse finxit 'inuideor'*, etc., Aug. *Regulae, GL*, v. 512. 17–18
quamquam Horatius poeta 'inuideor' dixit, sed hoc noua usurpatione, Prisc.
Inst. XVIII. 138 (*GL*, III. 271) *Horatius in arte poetica.* Cf. Kühner–
Stegmann, I. 102–3, *TLL*, VII. 2. 191. 68 ff.

lingua Catonis et Enni: cf. *Ep.* II. 2. 117 *priscis memorata Catonibus atque
Cethegis*, where however archaisms, not neologisms, are the subject.
Ennius is not here criticized by implication as at 259 and *Ep.* II. I. 50.
He is the great poet of the past, who has added much to the store of
the Latin language; H. in comparison little. The various assessments
of Lucilius in the literary satires may be compared, see *Prol.* 159,
165–6, 171–4.

57 *sermonem patrium ditauerit*: cf. *Ep.* II. 2. 121 *Latiumque beabit diuite
lingua. ditare* is an expressive word, frequent in Latin verse; it carries
in this passage some of the emotion of *beabit diuite* (*lingua*) in the other.
The first appearance of *ditare* in *Rhet. Her.* and Lucr. suggests an
archaism; in prose from *Rhet. Her.* and Livy, not in Cicero and Caesar, popular in Christian Latinity, *TLL*, v. 1555. 28 ff. Contrast the
sentiments at Lucr. I. 139 *propter egestatem linguae et rerum nouitatem*,
831–2 *quam Grai memorant nec nostra dicere lingua | concedit nobis patrii
sermonis egestas*, III. 260, Cic. *Ac.* I. 25, *Fin.* III. 3; and differently again
Fin. I. 10 *Latinam linguam non modo non inopem, ut uulgo putarent, sed
locupletiorem esse quam Graecam.*

58 (*noua rerum*) *nomina*: as Lucr. I. 139 (cit. 57 n.), Cic. *Ac.* I. 25
noua sunt rerum nouarum facienda nomina, 41 *plurimisque idem nouis uerbis
(noua enim dicebat) usus est, Fin.* III. 3 *imponendaque noua rebus nouis
nomina*, 4, 5, 15, *De Or.* III. 149, *Or.* 211 *cum id appellandum sit quod
propter rerum ignorationem ipsarum nullum habuerit ante nomen, necessitas
cogat…nouum facere uerbum*, Varro, *L.L.* v. 1 *quemadmodum uocabula
essent imposita rebus in lingua Latina, et al.*

protulerit: as Lucr. II. 656–7 *Bacchi nomine abuti | mauult quam laticis proprium proferre uocamen,* and *Ep.* II. 2. 116 *proferet in lucem speciosa uocabula rerum.*

licuit semperque licebit: for the polyptoton, see 70 n. The verb takes up *licentia* (51), the key-word in such discussions, e.g. Cicero cit. above 54–5 n., *De Or.* III. 153 *licentia,* et al. Varro, in the terms of his theory, *L.L.* IX. 20, says *uerbum quod nouum et ratione introductum quominus recipiamus uitare non debemus.* For Cicero's position see, for example, the passages cited 58 n. Similar considerations must have been well represented also in poetic theory. But the surviving evidence is scanty and we need to take into account the poetic practice of H. and his contemporaries.

59 *signatum praesente nota:* ps.-Acro *hoc a nummis tractum est,* etc. Thus Pliny, *N.H.* XXXIII. 43 *Seruius rex primus signauit aes...; signatum est nota pecudum, unde et pecunia appellata. praesente nota = nota praesentis temporis* (ps.-Acro *notamine ipsius temporis*), a concentrated phrase such as *Ep.* II. 2. 171 *uicina...iurgia = uicinorum iurgia.* In view of the frequent changes of the coin-face by the *tresuiri monetales* the metaphor is in point. The image is applied to coinage of words as at Quint. *I.O.* I. 6. 3 *utendumque plane sermone ut nummo, cui publica forma est,* Fortunat. *Ars Rhet.* III. 3 (*Rhet. Lat. Min.* ed. Halm, p. 122. 9–10) *uir perfectissimus dixit, uerbis utendum est publica moneta signatis.*

producere nomen as *Ep.* II. 2. 119 *adsciscet noua quae genitor produxerit usus. procudere* is likely to be a slip, reported with approval from their MSS by Renaissance scholars: de Nores, Lambinus, Luisinus. The last-named editor also changed *nomen* to *nummum*—and convinced Bentley. But in spite of *signatum...nota,* and such passages as Juv. 7. 55 (*qui*) *communi feriat carmen triuiale moneta,* the numismatic metaphor is not wanted here. For neither is *procudere* the *uox propria* for coining, nor can *nummum* plausibly replace *nomen.* For without *nomen* in this verse the subsequent simile lacks its natural base, and *uerborum* (61) would lack the connexion provided by *nomen* (59); also *producere* aptly anticipates the imagery of 60 ff.

60–72 There follows what poetically is perhaps the most remarkable piece of the *Ars.* A simile—words impermanent like leaves on a tree (60–2)—and another—words impermanent like the works of men (63–9)—open up a very different view of language: (1) old words die and new are born (61–2), (2) old words are reborn as current ones die off (70–2). Language here is not the poet's creation, but the common language which the poets share—Usage (71 n.) presiding over the change of words, as Nature presides over natural change. The similes lift the topic of 'words' out of its literary context; language is related to the unalterable conditions of life: the recurrence of the seasons and the impermanence of the human lot. Hence the sudden rise of poetic tone, to something like the lyric intensity of the Odes (say, *C*. I. 4 or IV. 7). *Ep*. II. 2. 111–19 lack this dimension.

Language in motion was a concept familiar to ancient writers on grammar: Varro, *L.L.* IX. 17, says *consuetudo loquendi est in motu*. So was the comparison of language with human generations, *ibid*. v. 3 . . . *neque omnis impositio uerborum extat quod uetustas quasdam deleuit*. (5) *uetustas pauca non deprauat, multa tollit; quem puerum uidisti formosum, hunc uides deformem in senecta. tertium saeculum non uidet eum hominem quem uidit primum.*

60 2, inspired by Homer, *Il*. VI. 146–9 οἵη περ φύλλων γενεή, τοίη δὲ καὶ ἀνδρῶν. | φύλλα τὰ μέν τ' ἄνεμος χαμάδις χέει, ἄλλα δέ θ' ὕλη | τηλεθόωσα φύει, ἔαρος δ' ἐπιγίγνεται ὥρη. | ὡς ἀνδρῶν γενεὴ ἡ μὲν φύει, ἡ δ' ἀπολήγει. Mimnermus' ἡμεῖς δ' οἷά τε φύλλα heads the long line of extant adaptations; cf. Sim. fr. 85 B.[4]; for a probable Pindaric trace, see E. Lobel on Pap. Oxy. 2622, XXXII (1967), 65, and H. Lloyd-Jones, *Maia*, n.s. III, XIX (1967), 215; for Bacchylides (5. 63–7) and Virgil (*A*. VI. 309–10), as well as for a postulated epic *Descent of Heracles*, see Norden on the passage of Virgil (pp. 223–4), Lloyd-Jones, *loc. cit*. The simile is not unknown to Christian writers, notably Hier. *Comm. in Osee*, lib. II, praef. 54 (*Patr. Lat.* XXV. 61) *postquam* . . . *alia uenerit generatio primisque cadentibus foliis uirens silua succreuerit*, Aug. *Civ. D.* XXII. 1.

The Horatian simile is (to my knowledge) unique in that it transfers from humanity to speech the comparison with leaves falling and growing, without abandoning the human aspect. Thus the comparison becomes threefold—leaves, words, humans—whereas the Homeric simile is two-sided, as indeed are the famous Virgilian verses *A*. VI. 309–10 (which in certain other respects seem close to H.'s) *quam multa in siluis autumni frigore primo* | *lapsa cadunt folia*.

Orelli and others have noted that the comparison is not completed: *prima cadunt* (61) is not, as at 62, followed by something like *florent modo nata*. They compare Lucr. IV. 375–6 *semper enim noua se radiorum lumina fundunt* | *primaque dispereunt*; but this passage illustrates only the sense required for *prima*, 'earlier', not the incompleteness of the comparison. Nor does it illustrate the lack of a connective particle in *prima cadunt*, a phrase, as Plessis–Lejay say, that sounds like the beginning of a prolonged Homeric simile, but is not so continued.

Recent editors tend to be silent about the text but I do not believe that it can stand. Let them bring forward valid examples of this kind of simile. Until that is done the text should be considered unsound.

Two ways have been adopted to correct it. Housman vigorously argued (in *JP*, xvIII (1890), 28) that (*a*) *prima cadunt* was incomplete, and (*b*) that not even Mevius, let alone Horace, would have employed the human simile at the same time as the simile of the leaves. He so changed the stops therefore as to remove both objections simultaneously—taking *prima cadunt* out of its isolation, and beginning a fresh image with *uetus interit aetas*, which easily accommodates the human simile: *ut siluae foliis…mutantur in annos,* | *prima cadunt ita uerborum. uetus interit aetas* | *et iuuenum ritu florent modo nata uigentque*. This is elegant but not wholly convincing. There is no objection to the human simile in the manner of the transmitted text, once the word *aetas* has been introduced: thereafter comparison is between generations of words and human generations; leaves are no more than hinted at by the verb *florent*. Nor is the position of *ita* entirely unobjectionable, for, in *ut–ita* (*sic*) clauses of H., *ita* (*sic*) seems to retain its first place. Finally I doubt the meaning imputed to *foliis mutantur* 'parted from their leaves' (J. S. Reid *ap.* Wilkins, p. 60 n.). For *mutari*, however construed, = 'to be changed', and the 'change of leaves' consists of new growth as well as of decay. Hence *mutantur…in annos* cannot be taken up by *prima cadunt* in the same sense and Housman's paraphrase (p. 29) is misleading: 'as each year's leaves are shed from the trees, so perish the earliest words'.

The expected subdivision of *mutantur* suggests a different way of correcting the text: the shedding and the growing of leaves, τὰ μὲν…χέει, ἄλλα δὲ…φύει. Whatever one may think of *succreuerit* in Jerome (cited above) and of *nam prima scilicet folia cadunt, noua succrescunt* in the *Tractatus Vindobonensis* on the *A.P.* (Zechmeister, p. 7), a word like *succrescunt* is likely to have been in the text: as to this I agree with Ribbeck (*ad l.*), Lehrs (edition, p. ccxix), and Nettleship (*JP*, xII (1883), 51 = *Lectures and Essays*, I, 177). The identity of the endings in *cadunt* and *succrescunt* will then have caused the omission of one line. I doubt the details of Nettleship's restoration, and adhere to Ribbeck's and Lehrs's lacuna, without attempting to assess the merits of such supplements as *prima cadunt.* ⟨*porroque cadentibus altera primis* | *succrescunt* ⟩, or ⟨*ut noua succrescunt nouus et decor enitet illi* ⟩ | *prima cadunt: ita,* etc.

60 *siluae foliis…mutantur:* the ablative is called instrumental by some, limitative by others; more convincingly abl. of respect. J. S. Reid, *ap.* Wilkins *ad l.*, illustrates it by *mutari ciuitate, Lex Salp.* xxII, Cic. *Balb.* 31; *finibus*, Liv. v. 46. 11; *uoluntate*, Cic. *Fam.* v. 21. 1; the meaning is clearly not 'parted from' but 'changed with regard to', though, as he says, the notion of severance comes in. *foliis mutantur* cannot however be paralleled. Ablatives with verbs in similar contexts are found at Sen. *Phae.* 768–9 *languescunt folio ut lilia pallido,* | *et gratae capiti deficiunt comae, Oed.* 452–3 *uerno platanus folio uiret,* Val. Fl. vi. 167 *quot foliis, quot floribus incipit annus.* Variant readings in ancient quotations—*siluae flores* and *folia in siluis*—may owe their existence to a wish to normalize idiomatic grammar, as do Bentley's conjectures *siluis folia* (introducing a metrical anomaly in its place), *siluae foliis...nudantur* or *uiduantur.* The grammatical subject, *siluae,* rather than *folia,* is illustrated by Housman (*loc. cit.*) from *Epod.* 15. 5 *hedera* (abl.), Ov. *Met.* iii. 729 *frondes* (acc.), rather than *hedera, frondes* (nom.).

†*pronos*†...*in annos:* obelized because I see no chance of defending the MS reading *pronos* and yet wish to indicate a slight doubt as to Bentley's outstanding emendation *priuos.* Bentley observed that such phrases as *in annos* (*dies, horas*), 'year by year', etc., either exclude an epithet, or else admit a numerical one, such as *singulos.* He therefore emended *pronos* to *priuos,* the archaic synonym for *singulos,* known from older Latin and particularly Lucr. v. 273–4 (*aer*) *corpore toto* | *innumerabiliter priuas mutatur in horas,* 733 *inque dies priuos aborisci quaeque creata* (*luna*), and at least five times elsewhere in the poem. H. might well have employed a Lucretian reminiscence in a passage containing other echoes of that poet. What gives me pause is the two occurrences where *priuus* is in the MSS of H. (*S.* ii. 5. 11, *Ep.* i. 1. 93). These can only be rendered by 'own'—a meaning that survives, it appears, in the colloquial language of the phrase, *aliquid* (*alicui*) *priuum dare* (not only Pl. *Ps.* 865 and Lucil. fr. 49–50 but Juv. 8. 68 *priuum aliquid da*). So a doubt remains whether H. employed the obsolete *priui* = *singuli,* although its probable occurrence at Liv. vii. 37. 2 *milites...* [*singulis*] (?)*priuis bubus binisque tunicis donati,* encourages that assumption. As for the MS reading, words for the rapidity of passing years naturally abound, in H. and elsewhere; but H.'s use of *pronus* cannot justify its conjunction with *in annos,* cf. *C.* iv. 6. 39–40 *celeremque* (*lunam*) *pronos* | *uoluere menses,* or *C.* iii. 27. 18 *pronus Orion.* Ps.-Acro's note, *decliues et cito labentes, instabiles, uolubiles,* should then be dismissed. Nor is G. Stegen's citation (*ad l.*) in point: ps.-Quint. *Decl.* xiii. 2 (ed. Lehnert, p. 248. 14) *cito labitur dies, et procliuis in pronum fertur aetas.*

61 *prima:* cf. Lucr. iv. 375–6, cited above 60–72 n. *prima* denotes the leaves before the change (*mutantur*), just as *prima* is opposed to *noua* in the passage of Lucretius; cf. Varro, *L.L.* ix. 73 *in tempore uere magis et minus non esse potest; ante et post potest. itaque prior est hora prima quam secunda, non magis hora.* In the same verse of H. *prima* is taken up by *uetus aetas. prisca* (Prädikow) is no improvement.

Commentary

uerborum uetus... aetas: Homer has φύλλων and ἀνδρῶν γενεή. *aetas* often = generation, a metonymy for the people concerned, as *Epod.* 16. 1 *altera, C.* I. 35. 35, IV. 15. 4, *Ep.* II. 1. 42; with gen. *Epod.* 16. 9 *deuoti sanguinis, C.* III. 6. 46 *parentum,* cf. *TLL,* I. 1137. 3 ff. H. does not bring in *aetas* until the incisive phrase 'generation of words' appears; for the punctuation, see above 60–2 n. Vocabulary had been talked about in historical terms before H., cf. Varro above 60–72 n. H.'s simile animates words: they live and die as do the people who make and use them.

interit: for the dying and thriving of words, see Varro, above 60–72 n.; Quint. *I.O.* x. 2. 13 *cum et uerba intercidant inualescantque temporibus* may be influenced by H.'s wording.

62 *iuuenum ritu:* as *C.* III. 14. 1 *Herculis r.,* III. 29. 33–4 *fluminis | r.* and often elsewhere in verse and prose. *iuuenes* 'the young', not, I believe, one of the 'four ages of man', 156 ff.; it is closer to 115–16 *adhuc florente iuuenta | feruidus.* The human comparison, one of the twin pillars of the twofold Homeric simile, has been shifted to the close of H.'s more sophisticated simile. *aetas, nata, florent...uigentque* (not *uirentque,* cod. Bentleii, Bentley, Meineke) apply to words as well as humans, *iuuenum ritu* to humans, thus providing a link with *nos,* in the next verse.

63 *debemur morti nos nostraque* appears to render θανάτῳ πάντες ὀφειλόμεθα from a sepulchral epigram, *Anth. Pal.* x. 105. 2 (Diehl, *Anth. Lyr. Gr.* II, Simonides, fr. 139), there ascribed to Simonides, but called ἄδηλον in the Planudean collection. H. has chosen, not the simple form of a commonplace, as Soph. *El.* 1173 πᾶσιν γὰρ ἡμῖν τοῦτ᾽ ὀφείλεται παθεῖν, Eur. *Alc.* 419, and the like, but the poignant Simonidean 'we'—*debemur,* ὀφειλόμεθα. (This is not noted by W. J. Oates, *The influence of Sim. of Ceos upon H.* (Princeton, 1932), p. 104, who is yet certain that H. corresponds most closely to Simonides.) And nothing in the Greek epigram answers to *nostraque* which, through an adroit 'zeugma', extends the comparison from man to his works; cf. *Ep.* II. 1. 89 *nos nostraque, A.P.* 444 *teque et tua.*

debemus is a decidedly weaker variant which however appears not only in one of the oldest Horatian MSS (cod. B), but in a number of ninth- and tenth-century MSS of Priscian. The reading lacks the force of ὀφειλόμεθα–*debemur:* ourselves debtors as well as a debt. It also lacks the idiomatic ambiguity of the passive, 'owed to' as well as 'destined for'; thus Virg. *A.* XI. 759 *fatis* (dat.) *debitus Arruns,* XII. 794–5 *indigetem Aenean... | deberi caelo,* also VI. 713–14 *animae, quibus altera fato* (abl.) *| corpora debentur,* and such formulae on tombstones as *mea debita fatis reddere, debitum persoluit,* cf. *TLL,* V. 1. 106.

Commentary

30 ff. The same variant, *debemur–debemus* (along with *debentur*), occurs in a similar phrase, probably an imitation, Ov. *Met.* x. 32 *omnia debemur uobis* (*fatis*). The choice between *poscimur* and *poscimus*, Hor. *C.* I. 32. I, should, I believe, be the opposite: *poscimus*.

63–9 One long and elaborate period marked by *siue...-ue...seu* (for -*ue*, see 65 n.). Such periods are sometimes found in the hexameter poems, see *S.* II. 2. 82–8 *siue–seu*, 118–22 *seu–siue*. The present passage recalls, both in its lyric note and its layout, such periods of the *Odes* as I. 2. 33–44 and IV. 2. 10–24, although its compass is more restricted and the description illustrates a maxim, *debemur morti nos nostraque*.

The subject is the impermanence of great human enterprises; *nostraque* (63) links this 'excursus' with what precedes it, the impermanence of words; *mortalia facta peribunt* (68) ends it, and *sermonum...honos* (69) brings it back to the subject of language. Three enterprises are set down, a harbour built, a marsh drained, and a river regulated. H. is not celebrating man the civilizer as is Cicero at *Off.* II. 14 *adde ductus aquarum, deriuationes fluminum, agrorum irrigationes, moles oppositas fluctibus, portus manu factos*, and *N.D.* II. 152. Nor is he celebrating the power of poetry to survive human material creations, as he did *C.* III. 30 *exegi monumentum aere perennius*; or similarly the power of philosophy, as Seneca did, *Brev. Vit.* 15. 4 (cit. Stegen). His point seems to be simply to give poetic 'body' to the idea that language is as prone to change as other creations of man. For this purpose he could be concrete and descriptive but none too specific; he could remind contemporaries of similar, not necessarily identical, enterprises. Virg. *G.* II. 161–4 shows how H. might have spoken, had he wished to identify these works.

Yet commentators persist in relating this passage to Roman engineering feats. Caesar indeed had plans of this kind (Plut. *Caes.* 58, etc.). If Porphyrion is right, H. was alluding to them; L. Preller, *Ausgewählte Aufsätze* (1864), pp. 515–22, A. Michaelis, *Commentationes ...in hon. Theadori Mommseni* (1877), pp. 425–7, and others, argued that he was. But then H. would be talking pointlessly since Caesar never got beyond preparing his plans—καὶ ταῦτα μὲν ἐν παρασκευαῖς ἦν, remarks Plutarch; no reader will be impressed by the impermanence of undertakings never undertaken. If on the other hand ps.-Acro has valid information and H. was alluding to Augustus or Agrippa (as Immisch *ad l.* and J. Carcopino, *Virgile et les origines d'Ostie*, 731 ff., maintain), then the verses would not only be pointless but in bad taste. For apparently these plans had not prospered under Augustus, and if they had, H.'s tact would doubtless have prevented him from crying woe over their success. I conclude then that P. Lejay,

Revue...de Belgique, XLV (1902), 376 ff., and others rightly rejected these identifications. They detract from H.'s poetic purpose. [Disregarding that purpose, J. Schwartz, *RP*, XXI (1947), 49–54, considers 63 *siue receptus*–68 *mortalia* an interpolation of the time of Claudius.]

63–4 *receptus | terra Neptunus* perhaps recalls Virg. *G.* II. 164 (*Tyrrhenusque*) *fretis immittitur aestus* (*Auernis*). The nuance of the sea 'received' on land is sensed by comparison with simpler usage, as Enn. *Ann.* 34 *quos homines quondam Laurentis terra recepit*, Pl. *Rud.* 276 *ut tuo recipias tecto...nos*, Caes. *B.C.* III. 102. 7 *qui...oppido ac portu recepti non erant*. The familiar metonymy, Neptune–sea (Quint. *I.O.* VIII. 6. 23, citing 63 *receptus*–64 *arcet*), is adroitly managed to convey the active force of *arcet*; cf. *Ep.* I. 11. 10 *Neptunum procul e terra spectare furentem*, rather than *Epod.* 7. 3–4 *campis atque Neptuno super | fusum est.* Vell. II. 33. 4 may be compared for subject and wording although the grammar differs: (*Lucullus*) *quem ob iniectas moles mari et* receptum *subfossis montibus* in terras mare...*Pompeius Xerxen togatum uocare adsueuerat.*

64 *classes aquilonibus arcet:* the rare construction of the object (acc.) defended against encroachment (abl.), as Virg. *Catal.* (*Priap.*) 2. 5, Avien. *Ar.* 1386–7 *te...procellis | arcebis rapidis*, and *Cod. Iust.* VI. 30. 10 (*TLL*, II. 446. 41). *aquilonibus* particularizes the idea of 'storm', as at *C.* III. 30. 3 *non imber edax, non aquilo impotens*, cf. Virg. *A.* I. 383 *undis Euroque.*

The harbour is Ostia, according to Porphyrion, which (he adds) *diuus Caesar...instituerat...facere*; but projects are not here in point (see above 63–9 n.) and the reference to Ostia is not safeguarded by applying it to Augustus instead, as Carcopino attempted (cit. above 63–9 n.); his explanation is convincingly rebutted by R. Meiggs, *Ostia*, p. 486. The harbour, according to ps.-Acro, is the Lucrine in Campania, built under Octavian and known as *portus Iulius*, cf. Virg. *G.* II. 161–4, Suet. *Aug.* 16. 1, Dio Cass. XLVIII. 50, al. In his autobiography Agrippa claimed that he had devised it (Philarg. on Virg. *G.* II. 161–4); its use however appears to have been short-lived (Strabo, V. 244–5). Yet the details of Virgilian geography are absent from this passage, and such details would be indispensable if H. had intended the passage to be read in the light of Agrippa's engineering exploits, even in the tortuous manner of Immisch (pp. 91–3).

65 *regis opus* has caused much doubt. If it resembled *C.* I. 2. 15 *monumenta regis* (= *Regia*, the residence of the King, i.e. Numa Pompilius), it should point to a person who could be named, even if H. had avoided naming him; thus Ov. *Fast.* VI. 259 *regis opus placidi* = Numa, Aus. *Mos.* 289–90 *constratum...pontum, | regis opus magni* = Xerxes. But specific references to Caesar, let alone Augustus or

Commentary

Agrippa, are not intended if my arguments, 63–9 n., 64 n., prevail. Nor can H. be thinking solely of the enterprises of any one oriental monarch, as would be implied in Lucullus' nickname *Xerxes togatus*, 63–4 n. If the text is sound, then, *regis* ought to be generic. This usage, the 'collective singular' of the grammarians, has been much debated, cf. the standard grammars and such discussions as Riemann, *Étude sur... Tite Live*[2], pp. 42–50, Löfstedt, *Pereg. Aeth.* pp. 178–9, A. H. Salonius, *Vitae Patrum*, pp. 73–6. The Augustans, it is often noted, greatly extended and invigorated this usage. Yet no study of the relevant authors has surveyed the more remarkable instances. Many cases of H.'s generic use of the sing. are listed in D. Bo, *Hor. Op.* III, 360–3. But these scarcely transcend the conventional categories and in fact throw doubt on the present passage. *regis opus* cannot be 'the work of the king' or 'of a king' in the same generic sense in which *Romanus* 'the Roman' (*A.P.* 54) lays stress on the collective notion. The meaning should be '(truly) royal work', whether the king is an eastern *rex* or a Roman grandee, e.g. *C.* I. 4. 13–14 *pauperum tabernas | regumque turres*, II. 14. 11–12, *S.* II. 2. 45.

I doubt therefore if *regis opus* expresses this notion, whereas *C.* II. 15. 1–2 *regiae | moles* expresses it perfectly. Meineke's emendation *regium opus* may well hit the mark, cf. ps.-Acro *hoc est regium opus, quod nullus facere potest nisi rex*. I have obelized *regis* rather than put *regium* in the text because of the paucity of elisions in this part of the first foot. I have only once noted such an elision in the *Ars*, 234 *non ego inornata*. My colleague Mr E. J. Kenney reminds me of the rarity of a middle syllable elided between two shorts, not to mention the vowel (*regi-*) here preceding; cf. J. Soubiran, *L'élision dans la poésie lat.* (1966), 226.

65–6 *sterilisue...aratrum:* like the harbour of the preceding verse, work on the *palus* of this passage is said by Porphyrion to be one of the projects which *diuus Caesar...instituerat...facere*: he identifies it with the plans for the draining of the Pomptine Marshes, cf. Plut. *Caes.* 58. 9, Dio Cass. XLIV. 5. 1, Suet. *Caes.* 44. 3, but Caesar is excluded by the arguments set out in 63–9 n. Although again ps.-Acro ascribes the operations to Augustus—*ut Pontinam paludem exsiccaret*—there is no evidence that this area had been made into agricultural land in the Princeps' time. A claim for Augustus is not among those so often made in ancient history, from the second century B.C. to the fifth A.D. The marshes were in fact not extensively drained until recent engineering techniques could be applied. Cf. Mommsen, *CIL*, x, 684, V. Orsolini-Cancelli, *Le paludi Pontine*, etc. (1934), *idem, Enciclopedia Italiana*, s.v. *Pontina Regione*.

65 *-ue:* a variant reading, *-que*, appears in some MSS as well as in the citations of Priscian and Servius. The two particles are of course frequently confused by scribes, as at *C.* III. 4. 3 (on which I accept Bentley's view), *Ep.* I. 8. 5, II. I. 69, *A.P.* 250. Either *-ue* or *-que* could be used to specify one of a set of possibilities, e.g. *S.* II. 2. 82–6, Virg. *A.* II. 36–7, VII. 605; Housman, Manilius, v, p. 150. But in the present passage, *-que* sandwiched between *siue* (63) and *seu* (67) is not tenable since it indicates one of three topics, not an adjunct to the preceding. Rather compare *C.* IV. 2. 10 ff. *seu...deuoluit..., seu... canit..., siue...dicit..., ...-ue* (*que* uar.)...*plorat*; Man. III. 149 ff., [Ov.] *Hal.* 68–71 (cf. J. A. Richmond's edition, 1962, pp. 96–7), or, in the same clause, *Aetna* 359–60 *siue peregrinis...propriisue | ... causis.*

†*diu palus*†: *palŭs* for *palūs* was noted by ancient grammarians, who base the shortening, unique in classical Latin poetry, on this one example. F. Skutsch, Γέρας: *Abhand....August Fick gewidmet* (1903), p. 147 n. 1, called it iambic shortening. Vollmer, in the second edition of his text, p. 345 (followed by Klingner, p. 325), lists it under *correpta uocabula iambica*, contrasting *honŏr*, etc. with *honōs*, *Ep.* I. 18. 102, *A.P.* 69. But, as Housman said, reviewing Vollmer's edition in *CR*, XXII (1908), 89, 'he defends palŭs (-ūdis) by the analogy of honŏr (-ōris), and attributes both to *Iambenkürzung*; the same influence, I presume, which leaves honōs long and shortens calcăr'. A. Kiessling (1889) had been more critical, but when Housman saw that Kiessling's edition was to be revised by Heinze he knew that we should have *palŭs* back again; 'and we have' (Housman, *C.Q.* XXII (1928), 7). F. Sommer doubtfully suggested the analogy of *lacus* (*Handbuch²*, p. 363) and K. Meister (cit. Heinze) that of nominatives in *-us* of '*o*' stems; neither analogy is plausible. Finally in *Glotta*, VIII (1917), Vollmer wondered if *palŭs* might not be a local pronunciation of a local name for the Pomptine marshes; he convinced Immisch, who remarked (p. 91 n. 18), 'zur Textänderung ist daher kein Anlaß'.

On the contrary, nothing would be better than a wholly convincing emendation. But the simplest change, J. M. Gesner's *palus diu* for *diu palus*, involves a shortening of *u* in *diu* before the initial vowel of *aptaque*, for which the formula *si mĕ amas*, in the conversational context of *S.* I. 9. 38, is scarcely sufficient warrant. Thus Bentley holds the field with *palus prius* for *diu palus*, excellent indeed but too uncertain to be put in the text. The passage still awaits emendation.

66 The metonymy in *alit* and *graue sentit aratrum* holds the poetic tone on the level set by *debemur*, etc. The territory, so long a swamp, now is busy 'feeding' the towns, and 'experiences' the weight of the plough. The order of clauses ('ὕστερον πρότερον') gives the same impression: first the result, then the heavy labour that lends animate features to the new soil, formerly sterile now fruitful. Hence the imagery is much more concrete than, say, Liv. v. 40. 5 *plebis turba quam nec capere tam exiguus collis nec alere...poterat*; the Horatian passage is set in a misleading context in *TLL*, I. 1710. 47. For *graue... aratrum*, see *S.* I. 1. 28 the ploughman *duro...aratro* turning *grauem terram*, Virg. *G.* I. 162 *graue robur aratri*, Ov. *Met.* VII. 118 *pondus graue...aratri*; for the metaphor in *sentiet*, *C.* III. 23. 5 *nec pestilentem sentiet Africum | fecunda uitis*, Virg. *G.* I. 47–8 *illa seges demum uotis respondet auari | agricolae, bis quae solem, bis frigora sensit*, and generally Virgil's technique of humanizing nature.

67–8 The course of a river in the countryside is changed. Both Porphyrion and ps.-Acro apply this to the Tiber, the former naming Agrippa, the latter Augustus as the person who *hunc...deriuauit*. H. however is not talking of the Tiber, because, as C. Fea noted (*ad l.*), *iniquum frugibus amnis* is a river in the country, not in the city. Besides, the ancient commentators allege that the area concerned was the Velabrum at Rome. This, as again Fea remarked, is demonstrably false: the region had been drained by the *Cloaca Maxima* centuries earlier and Agrippa's sanitary operations, dated to 33 B.C. (Dio Cass. XLIX. 43. 1, Plin. *N.H.* XXXVI. 104), are excluded by H.'s wording. Later work by Augustus on the course of the Tiber was undertaken after H.'s death, cf. *CIL*, VI, nos. 1235–6, Suet. *Aug.* 30. 1; A. Michaelis (cit. above 63–9 n.), p. 427.

68 *doctus iter melius* continues the metaphor: the river has learned a lesson, as *Ep.* I. 14. 29–30 *riuus, si decidit imber, | multa mole docendus aprico parcere prato*. The accusative 'retained' with a passive verb is poetic, and a poetizing and Silver usage in prose, see *S.* I. 6. 76–7 *puerum...docendum | artes*, *C.* III. 6. 21 *motus doceri gaudet Ionicos*, 8. 5, 9. 10, Tac. *Agr.* 26. 2 *Agricola iter hostium ab exploratoribus edoctus*; Kühner–Stegmann, I. 298, C. F. W. Müller, *Syn. des Nom. und Akk.* 145–6.

mortalia facta peribunt takes up (*debemur morti nos*) *nostraque*, 63; the following verse returns to the topic of language. The rhetoric is as precise and direct as Lucr. v. 311 *denique non monumenta uirum dilapsa uidemus...?*, but the Horatian overtones are richer. Seneca may be contrasted, *Ad Polyb.* I. 1 *quid enim immortale manus mortales fecerunt? septem illa miracula, et si qua his multo mirabilia sequentium annorum exstruxit ambitio, aliquando solo aequata uisentur.*

facta makes the transition from the 'doing' or 'making' of 63 ff. to speech, *sermonum*, 69. The context excludes the classical notion of *factum*, deed (286–7 n.): the meaning must be the thing made, not done. Hence *mortalia facta = mortalium opera*, cf. Sen. *Ep.* 91. 12 *omnia mortalium opera mortalitate damnata sunt; inter peritura uiuimus.* The unusual meaning prompted emendation of *facta*, notably Bentley's *cuncta*, which he later found in the cod. Galeanus; he therefore ascribed the antithesis 'works–speech' to a *nasutus interpolator.* Yet it is inherent in the passage as a whole and *cuncta . . . nedum sermones* makes a weak progression, *sermones* being part of *cuncta.* Scanning the article in *TLL* I find no parallel save one, long since noted: Ov. *Her.* 10. 60 *non hominum uideo, non ego facta boum,* apparently modelled on Homer, *Od.* x. 98 ἔνθα μὲν οὔτε βοῶν οὔτ' ἀνδρῶν φαίνετο ἔργα. Virgil's language, *G.* 1. 118, is more conventional: *hominumque boumque labores.*

peribunt, that is, *non stabunt,* contrast *stet* (69); the force of the verb, as *C.* 1. 16. 19–21 *cur perirent (urbes) | funditus imprimeretque muris | . . . aratrum exercitus,* Pl. *Most.* 147–8 *aedes meas quin . . . ruant, | cum fundamenta perierint.* The tense 'gnomic' as *Ep.* 1. 18. 4 *scurrae distabit amicus.*

69 looks back to 61, the impermanence of words. *nedum* takes up the implied negative in *peribunt,* 68. It occurs only here in H. and is rare in all Latin verse: J. H. Walden, *HS,* 11 (1891), 116, B. Axelson, *Unpoet. Wörter,* p. 96. Hence Aldus' implausible *sermonum haud* for *nedum (ned) sermonum.*

sermonum: not *uerborum* but their use, 'diction'; pl. because the variety in the use of words is contrasted with the variety of *facta. sermo = loquendi consuetuod:* Cic. *Off.* 1. 111 *sermone eo debemus uti, Att.* VII. 3. 10 *elegantiam s.,* Petron. 132. 15 *s. puri . . . gratia,* Quint. *I.O.* 1. 6. 43 *quid est aliud uetus s. quam uetus loquendi consuetudo?* The only other instance of this notion of the pl. known to me is Varro, *Men.* 399 *in sermonibus Plautus (poscit palmam). sermones* there stands beside *argumenta* and *ethe;* it is therefore likely to be 'diction', not 'conversations', contrasted with 'subject-matter' and 'ethos', cf. my remarks *Varron,* Fondation Hardt, IX (1963), 176. H. Dahlmann (*AAM* (1953), no. 3, 117 n. 2) plausibly compares Quint. *I.O.* x. 1. 99 *Varro Musas, Aelii Stilone sententia, Plautino dicit sermone locuturas fuisse si Latine loqui uellent.*

stet 'stands firm, lasts', of buildings, etc., *C.* III. 3. 42–3 *(dum) stet Capitolium | fulgens,* Enn. trag. fr. 84 (Jocelyn) (*Andromacha*) *cui nec arae . . . stant, fractae et disiectae iacent,* Cic. *Lael.* 23 *nec domus nec urbs ulla stare poterit,* Virg. *A.* 11. 56 *Troiaque nunc staret;* metaphorically, as *Ep.* 11. 1. 176 *cadat an recto stet fabula talo,* Enn. *Ann.* 500 *res . . . Romana,* Cic. *Phil.* 2. 24 *res publica,* Virg. *A.* IV. 539 *gratia facti* (cf. A. S. Pease, *ad l.*).

honos et gratia: a metaphor describing social standing, some instances at *TLL*, VI. 2. 2212. 49–51. For *honos* applied to wording, see 71, 243 *tantum . . . accedit honoris, Ep.* II. 2. 112 *(uerba) honore indigna ferentur.* The alternative formations *honos* and *-r* are noted by Serv. *Virg. A.* I. 253 *plerumque poetae 'r' in 's' mutant causa metri; -os enim longa est, -or breuis . . . sed ecce in hoc loco etiam sine metri necessitate 's' dixit.*

uiuax 'retentive of life, enduring'. Thus the evergreen ivy but not the *breue lilium, C.* I. 36. 16; *uiuacis oliuae,* Virg. *G.* II. 181. The adjective, going with the predicate *stet,* probably qualifies *honos* as well as *gratia;* the biological metaphor, 60 ff., is not far away. Cf. Ov. *Pont.* IV. 8. 47–8 *carmine fit uiuax uirtus, expersque sepulcri | notitiam serae posteritatis habet.*

70–1 The metaphor of 60–1 is now turned differently: old words are reborn and current perish.

70 One, almost perfunctory, verse glances at archaisms; in the *Florus* the procedure is the opposite; moreover old words, as well as new ones above, are here seen as stages in the life of language; above 46/5–72 n. Cicero's position in rhetorical theory, and Varro's in grammatical theory, may be remembered: Varro, *L.L.* IX. 19 *idem, ex sermone si quid deperiit, non modo nihil impendunt ut requirant, sed etiam contra indices repugnant ne restituatur?*, Cic. *De Or.* III. 153 *quae* (i.e. *prisca . . . ab usu cotidiani sermonis iamdiu intermissa) sunt poetarum licentiae liberiora quam nostrae; sed tamen raro habet etiam in oratione poeticum aliquod uerbum dignitatem,* etc. Contrast Gell. I. 10, where mention is made of Caesar's determined embargo on *inauditum . . . uerbum.*

cecidere, cadentque: cf. *cadunt,* 61. This recalls a Lucretian phrase, in a like context, III. 969 *nec minus ergo ante haec quam tu cecidere cadentque,* and without the doublet v. 327–8, *quo tot facta uirum totiens cecidere neque usquam | . . . florent?* The polyptoton as 58 *licuit semperque licebit, Ep.* I. 2. 43 *labitur et labetur,* II. 1. 160 *manserunt hodieque manent* or, still closer, *C.* II. 13. 20 *rapuit rapietque.* (For the device, cf. Hofmann–Szantyr, pp. 70 f.) Here however the two verbs are not in the same syntactic group, the second clause spills over into the next verse, and the order is chiastic: *cecidere* and *cadentque* in the middle, the logical opposites *renascentur* (70) and *sunt in honore* (71) on opposite sides, in two different types of clause.

71 *sunt in honore,* cf. *honos et gratia* (69): this again recalls Lucretius, see v. 1273 ff. *nam fuit in pretio magis ⟨aes⟩ aurumque iacebat | . . . | nunc iacet aes, aurum in summum successit honorem. | sic uoluenda aetas commutat tempora rerum: | quod fuit in pretio, fit nullo denique honore,* etc. For *in honore esse,* see Cic. *N.D.* I. 16, Ov. *Fast.* III. 138, *Met.* X. 170, al., of persons, Cic. *Cat.* III. 2, Caes. *B.C.* III. 59. 3, al. In the more frequent use with adjectives or pronouns, *in* is optional.

uocabula, unlike *S.* II. 3. 280, *Ep.* II. 2. 116, and many other instances elsewhere, has not *rerum* juxtaposed or implied in the context; hence 'words' rather than 'terms'.

si uolet: usus—like *utilitas* and *consuetudo*, and whether denoting 'need', 'practice' or 'usage'—is often credited with an active force. This suits what H. wants to do in this passage: to lay stress on the impersonal or 'natural' features of language. Cf. *S.* I. 3. 102 *fabricauerat usus, Ep.* II. 2. 119 *produxerit usus*, below 72; Lucr. V. 1029 *utilitas expressit nomina rerum*, Varro, *L.L.* VI. 78 *his (uerbis) . . . consuetudo est usa*, 82 *consuetudo communis . . . etiamnunc seruat*, IX. 1 *quoad patiatur consuetudo*, X. 74 *non repugnante consuetudine communi*, Cic. *De Or.* III. 39, 170, *Or.* 155 *an dabat hanc consuetudo licentiam?*, 159 *eadem consuetudo non probauit.*

usus: if my observations, 69 and 70–1 nn., are just, *usus* does not here denote the need for new terms expressed by *si forte necesse est*, etc., 48 ff. Even less does it denote 'necessity', *nécessité*, not only *besoin*, as M. Ruch, *REL*, XLI (1963), 248–54, assumes. H. is now talking of the process that leads to the *obscurata uocabula, Ep.* II. 2. 115, and to their revival.

I suggest, then, *usus* = usage, and so, as far as I know, did all commentators from Porphyrion to the beginning of this century, cf. Porph. *hoc est ratio loquendi: usus nihil enim aliud est quam regula sermonis Latini*; ps.-Acro *idest consuetudo siue ratio loquendi: ratio enim usu et consuetudine uincitur*. What moved R. Reitzenstein (*M. Terentius Varro und Johannes Mauropus von Euchaita* (1901), p. 54 n. 1) and R. Heinze—followed by Rostagni, Immisch (p. 77 n. 11), Steidle (*Studien*, p. 39 n. 74), and more recent writers such as P. Grimal (*Essai sur l'Art Poétique d'Horace* (1968), pp. 90 ff.)—to render *usus* by 'need, requirement, χρεία'? Heinze offers three arguments: (1) 'usage' would be inept in the present context which, he says, deals with the coinage of new words; thus, too, Reitzenstein, *loc. cit.*; (2) *usus* resumes *necesse est* (48); (3) H. does not employ *usus* = usage but does employ *usus* = need, notably in the parallel passage, *Ep.* II. 2. 119. These arguments seem to me partly erroneous and partly irrelevant. (1) As is argued at the beginning of this note, the present context does not concern the coinage of new words. The proposition 'obsolete words will revive if need so wills' would make some sense outside this context; the proposition 'current words will perish if need so wills' makes no sense in any context. (2) *usus* does not resume *necesse est* (48). (3) H., it is true, does not elsewhere employ *usus* = *consuetudo* and in two apparently similar passages he does employ *usus* = need. But the similarity is misleading: at *Ep.* II. 2. 119 the context *is* the coinage of new words and *genitor produxerit* in the same verse suggest the meaning 'need', χρεία; so does *fabricauerat* at *S.* I. 3. 102. Elsewhere in H. *usus* = use, or (once, *S.* II. 6. 75) expediency. Yet *usus* in the language of the grammarians and rhetoricians is a set term for 'practice' and in relevant contexts closely approaches *consuetudo*, συνήθεια, 'usage'. There was no reason therefore why H. should not employ an established word in an established meaning, and employ it once only. Cf. Varro, *L.L.* x. 73 *usui⟨s⟩ species uidentur esse tres—una consuetudinis ueteris, altera consuetudinis huius, tertia neutra⟨e⟩, 78 contra usum ueterem*, Cic. *Inv.* I. 57 *in usu dicendi, De Or.* I. 109, *Or.* 160, Quint. *I.O.* v. 10. 5, 14. 33 *uerbis quam maxime propriis et ex usu*, VIII. 2. 2 *omnia quae sunt in (sine, sm̄ MSS) usu...reformidant*. F. Solmsen was right therefore to reject Heinze's explanation, cf. *H*, LXVI (1931), 246 n. 2; *usus* in this passage = 'usage', *consuetudo*.

72 Usage is proclaimed as the principle governing language. συνήθεια was certainly so proclaimed by the Stoics (cf. Diocles of Magnesia *ap.* Diog. L. VII. 59 = *SVF*, III. 214. 13), perhaps also by the Peripatetics (cf. Solmsen, below on *norma*, citing συνήθεια *ap.* Demetr. *Interpr.*); in different ways the grammarians enunciated a similar principle, cf. Sext. Emp. *Math.* I. 84 ff., Varro and others. Does the concurrence of H. and Demetrius point to Neoptolemus, as Solmsen suggested? Too little is known about the early post-Aristotelian Lyceum to do more than ask this question. It needs to be remembered however that H. is not inculcating usage as apt for one particular style only—the plain—as do *Ad Her.* IV. 11 *attenuata (oratio) est quae demissa est usque ad usitatissimam puri consuetudinem sermonis*, Cic. *Or.* 76 *summissus est et humilis, consuetudinem imitans*, and others. If writers on the Horatian tradition of the sixteenth and seventeenth centuries had remembered this (for example, Wesley Trimpi, *Ben Jonson's poems; a study of the plain style* (Stanford, 1962), they would have avoided some awkward traps.

Consuetudo governs language. This is recognized by Cicero and Varro as valid within certain limits, cf. Cic. *De Or.* III. 170 *si aut uetustum uerbum sit, quod tamen consuetudo ferre possit, aut factum uel coniunctione uel nouitate, in quo item est auribus consuetudinique parcendum*, Varro above 71 n. on *si uolet*. The role of *consuetudo* is stressed at *Ad Her.* II. 45 *quam rem* (i.e. *nomen et uocabulum*) *consuetudo optime potest iudicare*, Quint. *I.O.* I. 6. 3 *consuetudo uero certissima loquendi magistra, utendumque plane sermone ut nummo, cui publica forma est* (cf. above 59 n.), 44, 45 *consuetudinem sermonis uocabo consensum eruditorum sicut uiuendi consensum bonorum*, Gell. XII. 13. 16 *consuetudo uicit, quae cum omnium domina rerum, tum maxime uerborum est.*

Usage, H. says, has *arbitrium...et ius*, hinting perhaps at Pindar (*ap*. Plat. *Gorg.* 484 b), νόμος ὁ πάντων βασιλεύς. I do not know the age of the anonymous Latin tag, *usus tyrannus*, cf. Cic. *Leg.* III. 2 *legem... mutum magistratum* (A. Otto, *Sprichwörter*, 192); for the wording, Ter. *Heaut.* 25–6 *arbitrium uestrum, uestra existimatio ualebit*, Cic. *Off.* I. 6 *iudicio arbitrioque nostro*, Liv. XXIII. 23. 4 *ne penes unum hominem iudicium arbitriumque de fama...senatoris fuerit*, Ov. *Her.* 12. 73–4 *ius | ...et arbitrium*, Sen. *Med.* 137–8, Suet. *Cal.* 14. 1, al. *ius* too is recognized in the latitude allowed to the writer or poet, e.g. Varro, *L.L.* IX. 5 *eorum* (i.e. *oratoris et poetae*) *non idem ius*, 6 *ego populi consuetudinis non sum ut dominus, ut ille meae est*, cf. *potestas* above 10.

For *norma loquendi*, F. Solmsen (*H*, LXVI (1931), 246) has appositely compared Demetr. *Interpr.* 87 and 91, where συνήθεια is said to be the standard, κανών, for metaphors and compound words, and generally of all ὀνομασία. Also *ibid.* 86 πάντων δὲ καὶ τῶν ἄλλων ἡ συνήθεια καὶ μάλιστα μεταφορῶν διδάσκαλος, 95, 275.

quem penes: this preposition occurs frequently in phrases expressing power or sovereignty such as this and Liv. XXIII. 23. 4 (cit. above); the only other instance in H. is *penes te es?* (*S.* II. 3. 273), 'are you in your right mind?', i.e. 'in your possession'. Cf. Paul. Fest. 22 (M.) *apud et penes in hoc differunt quod alterum personam cum loco significat, alterum personam et dominium ac potestatem.* The archaic 'anastrophe' of prepositions of more than one syllable is common after relative pronouns even in Ciceronian prose. H. like other Augustan poets has it with nouns as well; Tacitus makes much of this anastrophe, cf. Kühner–Stegmann, I. 586, Hofmann–Szantyr, 215 f.

(b) Norms of diction in poetic genres, 73–85 (88)

The tradition. This is another topic which literary theory and rhetoric approached in different but comparable ways. In Greek τὰ μέτρα may denote 'verse', words included, not merely 'rhythms', thus Ar. *Rhet.* III. 2, 1404 b 14, contrasting ἐν δὲ τοῖς ψιλοῖς λόγοις 'prose'. Hence writing on poetic composition or style, Aristotle (*Poet.* 6, 1449 b 34) defines λέξις not simply by σύνθεσις τῶν ὀνομάτων but by σύνθεσις τῶν μέτρων; this, Rostagni explains, is σύνθεσις τῶν ὀνομάτων ἐν τοῖς μέτροις, words so put together as to fit a predetermined metre. But writing on rhetorical style

Aristotle assigns a chapter to prose rhythm, *Rhet.* III. 8; the context is the use of words, singly and in composition, cf. *Prol.* 94. Rhythm continues as a property of 'composition' in rhetorical discussion, e.g. in the *De Compositione*, περὶ συνθέσεως ὀνομάτων, of Dion. Hal. Moreover when the topic of periodic or rhythmic speech is set in larger treatises its place in the sequence conforms to the Aristotelian, *Rhet.* III. 7–8; words, style, and rhythm are found in close vicinity in Demetr. *De Interpr.* 1–35, also *Ad Her.* IV, 26, Cic. *De Or.* III. 171 ff., especially 184, *Or.* 149 ff., 168 ff., Quint. *I.O.* IX, chs. 3–4.

Yet W. Steidle has been right to deny that this passage is concerned with metre *per se* (*Studien*, pp. 46–8); that topic comes later in the *Ars.* H. here is concerned with poetic genres defined by metre and subject. Ps.-Acro (on *A.P.* 73) probably has this in mind: *docet quomodo singulae* res *quibus* metris *scribendae sint.* It is not then *one* poetic style that is in question but as many as there are genres. Research on poetic genres was a speciality of Alexandrian scholarship. Apollonius was not by any means the only writer on genres, εἴδη, though he was the Alexandrian specifically called ὁ εἰδογράφος.

A further Hellenistic feature seems to be the emphasis on literary history; and that includes the originators of poetic genres and metres. H.'s material contains some features in which the Alexandrians were known to differ from Aristotle, cf. below 75–8 n., 79 n. Research had not however ceased; *adhuc sub iudice lis est,* H. remarks àpropos of the origins of the fashionable elegiac genre, see 77 n.

Too little is known about Alexandrian εἰδογραφία to determine the details of the tradition on which H. has drawn. He mentions the chief genres in this order: epic, elegy, iambic verse, comedy, tragedy, and lyric; it will cause no surprise that his subdivisions for lyric verse are both highly selective and in a traditional vein (83, 84, 85 nn.). As for the division of the genres as a whole, generalizations are hard to establish. It is true, scholars have asserted for some time that the Horatian material is based in some way or other on the (Aristotelian and ultimately Platonic) distinction between 'narrative' and 'dramatic'; cf. J. Kayser, *De veterum arte poetica quaest. sel.* (Thesis, Leipzig 1906), H. Färber, *Die Lyrik in der Kunsttheorie d. Antike* (1936), H. Dahlmann, *Varros Schr. de poematis*, etc. *AAM* (1953), no. 3, pp. 146 ff. Nevertheless the late compilations on which Dahlmann and his predecessors draw subsume their material under these (to them) irrelevant headings, whereas H., happily, does not. Nor for that matter does Quintilian (*I.O.* x, ch. 1) and probably others, as P. Steinmetz points out, *H*, xcii (1964), 460 ff. The Horatian arrangement of the genres is partly chronological but chiefly according to metre, even to the extent of attaching comedy and tragedy (in that order) to Archilochus, because they concur in using iambic verse. To assert similarity between H. and the modes of the compilers, their schematism has to be projected on to the canvas of the *Ars*. Moreover H.'s order has to be changed, for drama in this section comes before, not after, lyric, unlike the arrangement of the compilations; the discussion of tragedy and comedy, *A.P.* 89 ff., of which Dahlmann avails himself, is not part of the present section. That H.'s metrical arrangement would have suited some Alexandrians and a writer like Neoptolemus is not without plausibility. But Dahlmann's assumption, p. 153, that Neoptolemus too had the layout wrongly asserted for H.—I mean (*a*) non-dramatic: epic, elegiac, iambic, lyric; and (*b*) dramatic: tragedy and comedy —is not only unproven but unwarranted.

Nor does the Roman evidence help us much. There had been an interest in poetic genres at least since Accius' *Didascalica*; but the much-quoted fragment about the difference of *genera* (Funaioli, *Gram. Rom. Fr.* p. 27, fr. 8, cit. below 86 n. on *uices*) is no basis for a comparison with the *Ars*; for the post-Horatian evidence see P. Steinmetz, *H*, xcii (1964), 462.

Horace. What then does H. do with the traditional material, as far as we can recognize it? At 73 he introduces the metrical topic of the genres brusquely and unconnectedly as the difference of subject-matter seems to demand. It is only later that he reaps the poetic benefit of this procedure. [I cannot find the connexion with 71 *usus* asserted by Heinze and Immisch (pp. 94 f.), nor the particular contrast stated by K. Witte, *Gesch. d. röm. Dicht.* etc. II. 1 (1931), 246.]

H. adopts a mock-serious lecturing style, just as he does in the subsequent passage on metre, 251 ff. But in both cases he amuses himself, and any reader who can be amused, by a jump from an elementary lecture to something, to his mind, really important—here it is the style and tone of different types of poetry. Nor is the humour empty, for in his opinion elementary expertise and higher criticism are intimately connected.

H. seems to show some interest in literary-historical research. But in fact he is mocking the reader, who is undeceived presently. H. is drawing the outlines of a normative poetics based on the (metrical) genres. Hence what begins as a historical essay ends in a demand for the appropriateness of writing which he has hinted at already in the earlier portions of the poem.

Some commentators have missed references to Roman poetic genres—mistakenly, for H. is concerned to point to the original Greek genres for the benefit of his Roman readers. But as Steidle, *Studien*, p. 47, remarks, there may well be some implied opposition to neoteric-Hellenistic tendencies; cf. 77 n. on elegy. We need to note what H. omits, not only what he acknowledges.

73–4: the hexameter and epic poetry. The hexameter is the heroic metre, called in fact by that name: Ar. *Rhet.* III. 8, 1408 b 32 τῶν δὲ ῥυθμῶν ὁ μὲν ἡρῷος σεμνὸς κτλ. It is also the appropriate metre for narrative, *Poet.* 24, 1459 b 31 τὸ δὲ μέτρον τὸ ἡρωικὸν ἀπὸ τῆς πείρας ἥρμοκεν. εἰ γάρ τις ἐν ἄλλῳ τινὶ μέτρῳ διηγηματικὴν μίμησιν ποιοῖτο ἢ ἐν πολλοῖς, ἀπρεπὲς ἂν φαίνοιτο· τὸ γὰρ ἡρωικὸν στασιμώτατον καὶ ὀγκωδέστατον τῶν μέτρων ἐστὶν κτλ. It has been appointed by nature, *ibid.* 1460 a 2 διὸ οὐδεὶς μακρὰν σύστασιν ἐν ἄλλῳ πεποίηκεν ἢ τῷ ἡρῴῳ, ἀλλ᾽ ὥσπερ εἴπομεν (4, 1449 a 24 on iambus) αὐτὴ ἡ φύσις διδάσκει τὸ ἁρμόττον αὐτῇ αἱρεῖσθαι. The name remained down to the compilations of late antiquity, as in this passage of Terentianus Maurus based on H., 1646–8 *leges quippe datas heroica carmina poscunt,* | *quis acta Homerus heroum cum scriberet* | *uersibus ostendit.*

73 *res gestae* does not here denote the public record of official action as in Ennius (*Scipio,* Varia fr. 2 Vahlen) *columnam quae res tuas gestas loquatur* or in the *Res Gestae Divi Augusti,* and as *TLL,* VI. 2. 1945. 53 ff. might suggest. Because of its context in this and similar places, it applies to public actions, ancient or contemporary, as a subject for heroic epic: *Ep.* I. 3. 7–8 *quis sibi res gestas Augusti scribere sumit?* | *bella quis et paces longum diffundit in aeuum?,* II. I. 250–1 *nec sermones ego mallem* | *repentes per humum quam res componere gestas.* The word *facta* lacks political colour but is otherwise close in meaning, as in *S.* I. 10. 42–3 *Pollio regum* | *facta canit pede ter percusso* (tragedy, distinguished from *forte epos*), *Ep.* II. I. 6 *post ingentia facta deorum in templa recepti,* below 286–7 n.

regumque ducumque, the former the βασιλῆες of heroic epic, as above in *regum facta,* Virg. *E.* 6. 3 *cum canerem reges et proelia*; the latter may refer to generals, leaders in war (*C.* II. 2. 21 *magnos...duces,* IV. 15. 29 *uirtute functos...duces...canemus,* and *duces* in the historians) and thus to historical epic.

-que...-que may here have epic tone, in some other passages it lacks it, cf. above 11 n.

tristia bella (Virg. *A.* VII. 325, *Culex* 81, al.) likewise in pl. and at end of line Virg. *E.* 6. 7; cf. *C.* I. I. 24–5 *bella...matribus* | *detestata.*

74 *quo...numero* 'verse, metre', in sing. as *Ep.* II. I. 158 *numerus Saturnius,* Cic. *De Or.* III. 185 *anapaestus, procerior quidam numerus,* even more frequently in pl. as 270 *Plautinos...numeros,* 211 *numerisque modisque,* and the 'Plautine epitaph' *ap.* Gell. I. 24. 3 *numeri innumeri.*

scribi like *scriptor* often of poetry.

possent 'is (to be) achieved', not 'might be achieved', an idiom not always recognized, cf. *C.* III. 3. 40–4 *dum...stet Capitolium... triumphatisque possit* | *Roma ferox dare iura Medis, Ep.* II. I. 106–7 *per quae* | *crescere res* posset, *minui damnosa libido,* 'is to be made to grow', II. 2. 131–5 *qui uitae* seruaret *munia...,* posset *qui ignoscere seruis...,* posset *qui...puteum uitare patentem,* 'knows how to...'.

monstrauit 'reveal, make known', in Greek κατέδειξε, Aristoph. *Ran.* 1032 ff. Ὀρφεὺς... τελετάς θ᾽ ἡμῖν κατέδειξε, φόνων τ᾽ ἀπέχεσθαι ..., | ...Ἡσίοδος δὲ | γῆς ἐργασίας...,ὁ δὲ θεῖος Ὅμηρος |...χρήστ᾽ ἐδίδαξεν κτλ., cf. ὑπέδειξεν Ar. *Poet.* 4, 1448 b 36 (Ὅμηρος) τὰ τῆς κωμῳδίας σχήματα πρῶτος ὑπέδειξεν (and Bywater's n.); so too in the passage of the *Ars* related to that of the *Frogs,* below 404 (*per carmina*) *uitae monstrata uia est,* and 49 *monstrare...abdita rerum*; with inf., Lucr. v. 1106, and in the satirical passage *S*. II. 8. 51–2 *inulas ego primus amaras | monstraui incoquere*, cf. *TLL*, VIII. 1442. 82 ff.

Homerus: Aristotle did not ascribe the 'invention' of the hexameter to Homer, and Alexandrian scholars tended to name Apollo, or Orpheus and other mythological personages. Thus a measure of scepticism remained in the learned tradition, which persisted all the way down to the compilations of late antiquity. Thus *Frag. Berol.* (*GL*, VI. 633. 2 ff.) *hoc creditur ub Apolline inuentum uel ab eius sacerdote Phemonoe, et heroum idcirco appellatum quod Homerus tali metro res gestas heroum scripsit*, Mallius Theodorus (*ibid.* 589. 20 ff.) *inuentum primitus ab Orpheo . . . permulti ab Homero* (*adserunt*), *qui profecto . . . metri huius . . . aut repertor aut certe approbator fuit*. Rostagni's point is therefore worth making that H. does not here attribute the hexameter to Homer, but rather its application in epic poetry. But there may be the same point in 77 *auctor*, 79 *Archilochum*; and 83 *Musa* anyway evades this question. H. concerns himself with poets evolving genres in certain metres, not with inventors of rhythms.

75–8: the elegiac couplet, elegy and epigram. This account agrees closely with that attributed to the περὶ ποιητῶν of the Alexandrian scholar Didymus, an older contemporary of H., which agreement may, but need not, bear out the well-known reference to the poet's own time—*adhuc sub iudice lis est* (78). Didymus is said by Orion (*Etymologicum*, col. 58. 7 ff., ed. Sturz (1820), cf. *Etym. Gud.* and *Etym. Magn.*) to derive ἔλεγος from the εὖ λέγειν of the lament, θρῆνος, for the dead, H.'s *querimonia*; this etymology is met elsewhere. Other equally unconvincing derivations of course occur (cf. A. Severyns, *Recherches sur la Chrestom. de Proclos*, II (1938), 99 ff.). The elegiac couplet is next likened to a team of horses, the second horse not keeping up with the first, H.'s *impariter iunctis* (75 n.), 'as though it were expiring and dying away concurrently with the fate of the dying person': ὅθεν πεντάμετρον τῷ ἡρωϊκῷ συνῆπτον, οὐχ ὁμοδραμοῦντα τῇ τοῦ προτέρου δυνάμει, ἀλλ' οἷον συνεκπνέοντα καὶ συναποσβεννύμενον ταῖς τοῦ τελευτήσαντος τύχαις. Later, Didymus continues, elegiac verse was addressed to all. As for the 'inventor', three incompatible views are mentioned, one party favouring Archilochus, another Mimnermus, and a third Callinus on grounds of age. Didymus' description of the metre is highly metaphorical and a poetic source is not by any means excluded. For the ancient view on 'lament' and 'elegy', see A. E. Harvey, 'The classification of Greek lyric poetry', *CQ*. n.s. v (1955), 168–72.

A contemporary note is, I believe, implied in H's. concentration on lament and votive epigram, to the exclusion, here as well as at 402,

Commentary

of narrative and amatory elegy. Considering the attention paid to love *lyric* a few verses below (85) and the popularity of love *elegy* at the time, the omission can scarcely be accidental, cf. *Prol.* 205, 225.

75 *uersibus impariter iunctis:* Ovid often expresses the idea of the unequal pair, hexameter and pentameter, simply and elegantly by saying that the verses thus joined *are* unequal, *Am.* II. 17. 21–2 *carminis...genus impar sed tamen apte | iungitur herous cum breviore modo*, III. 1. 37, *A.A.* I. 264, *Pont.* IV. 16. 11, 36, *Trist.* II. 220. He lacks H.'s characteristic energy and compression: 'in verses unequally joined'. This is called *hypallage* by K.–H. There is a case for saying that H. expressed succinctly some such imagery as that cited from Didymus above (75–8 n.), which does not make Didymus H.'s 'source'.

The adverb *impariter* seems to have been coined for the occasion: Q. Terentius Scaurus *ap.* Charis. *Inst. Gr.* II. 13 (*GL*, I. 202. 26 ff.) quoting this verse *in commentariis in artem poeticam libro X 'aduerbium' inquit 'figurauit'.* [Scaurus is the earliest known Horatian commentator, not editor, of the time of Hadrian; for the commentary, see Wessner, *R-E*, V A. 674. 43 ff.] At any rate the *TLL* does not record the word before this passage, and afterwards not again until Boethius, who required it as a mathematical term.

querimonia: an archaism. In Plautus as well as in republican and subsequent prose it denotes 'complaint' or 'dispute'. It often has a legal flavour; as late as the Justinian Code it is used for a suit in law (Heumann–Seckel, *Handbuch zu den Quellen des röm. Rechts*, s.v.), cf. *querella*. In verse after Plautus *querimonia* is exceedingly rare—according to the materials of the Latin Thesaurus only at *Ciris* 462, *Carm. Epigr.* 2121. 11, Aus. 391. 3 (p. 257 P.), all denoting 'lament'. Perhaps H. picked up the old and full-sounding word in spite of its prosaic overtones. He used it here and *C.* II. 20. 22 for 'lament', *C.* I. 13. 19 for 'quarrel', and *C.* III. 24. 33 for 'complaint'.

76 *inclusa est:* the readings *iunctis–iunctus–iuncta (est)* are rightly explained by Keller, *Epil.* 742, as a mechanical transposition from 75 *iunctis.* For the verb 'frame, enshrine' (in rhythm or verse), and its grammar, see *S.* I. 10. 59 *pedibus quid claudere senis*, II. 1. 28 *me pedibus delectat claudere uerba*, Cic. *Or.* 229 *numeris sententias*, Ov. *Pont.* IV. 16. 36, et al., *TLL*, III. 1309. 81 ff.; *includo* too is used by Cic. *De Or.* III. 184 where the metaphor is noted, a contrast between *uerba uersu includere* and *oratio...uere soluta*; for later instances, see *TLL*, VII. 1. 954. 73 ff.

uoti sententia compos: votive epigrams, *epigrammata consecrationum*, as the grammarian Sacerdos paraphrases (*GL*, VI. 510. 1); ps.-Acro's scholium *postea etiam laetae coeperunt scribi*, persuaded older commen-

166

tators (wrongly as it happens) that the love elegy was involved. From
sensit se uoti compotem esse the *sententia* itself becomes *uoti compos*.
Commonly it is *uoti damnatus, reus*, etc. but *uoti compos* occurs in Augustan and Silver Latin although it does not happen to be recorded
before this passage, *TLL*, III. 2137. 29 ff.; it was sufficiently established
to be shortened *u. c.* in inscriptions, *TLL, ibid.*

77 *exiguos elegos* marks the contrast to the long epic poem. The
adjective is probably loaded, casting a slur on Callimachean pride
in the small and highly wrought poem.

emiserit 'put out, publish', as *Ep.* I. 20. 6 *non erit emisso reditus tibi*
(sc. *liber*, cf. Sulp. Sev. *ap.* Mart. *Prooem.* 2), Cic. *Fam.* VII. 33. 1 *si
quando aliquid dignum nostro nomine emisimus*; *TLL*, V. 2. 508. 43 ff.

auctor 'originator' rather than 'author'; ps.-Acro *quis...inuenerit
elegiacum metrum.* Thus more often with *primus*, but cf. Vell. I. 8. 1
certamen...auctorem Iphitum (habuit), etc., *TLL*, II. 1205. 31 ff. *auctor*
is then likely to be predicative, 'as originator'.

78 *grammatici certant:* not without sarcasm as at *Ep.* I. 19. 40
grammaticas ambire tribus, and cf. II. 1. 51 *ut critici dicunt.*

adhuc sub iudice lis est: the famous tag sounds legal, as it is meant to
do. But it only sounds legal. Formulas taken straight and unchanged
from law, philosophy, literary theory, are rare in II. His customary
procedure is to modify them so that they carry no more than a
suggestion, legal, philosophical or literary. In fact even the slightly
haphazard collection of passages in *TLL*, VII. 2. 599. 59–62 makes one
suspect that *sub iudice* is a poeticism; a renewed search in the materials
of the *Thesaurus*, for which I am obliged to Dr W. Ehlers, confirms
that suspicion. Two idioms may be distinguished. Either *sub iudice*
may be qualified by an adj. or noun, and can replace the much more
common *apud iudicem*. So even lawyers occasionally write—Gai. *Inst.*
IV. 104, 105, 109 *sub uno iudice*, Afric. *ap. Dig.* XLIV. 1. 18 *sub eodem
iudice*. But the bulk of the instances comes from poets, or poetizing
writers of prose. Thus Ov. *Met.* XIII. 190 *sub iniquo iudice*, Val. Max.
IV. 6. 1 *magno, Laus Pis.* 29 *legitimo*, Sil. XIII. 603 *sero*; with a genitive,
Juv. 4. 12 *sub iudice morum*; or, with nouns in apposition, Ov. *Met.* XI.
156 *iudice sub Tmolo*, Luc. X. 227 *Libra*, Calp. *Ecl.* 2. 9 *Thyrsi, Laus Pis.*
65 *populo*, Stat. *Theb.* VII. 509 *me.* Or else there is no attribute or
apposition; this idiom seems entirely restricted to verse and poetic
prose. It occurs first in the present Horatian passage, next in Juv. 7.
13 *si dicas sub iudice*, and Tac. *Ann.* III. 36. 3 *quam (Anniam) fraudis sub
iudice damnauisset. lis* occurs in a genuinely legal context at *Ep.* I. 16. 42
quo multae...secantur iudice lites. But at *S.* II. 3. 103 *litem quod lite
resoluit* the word simply means 'controversy, problem'.

79–82: iambus, first in iambic poetry properly so called, then in the dialogue verse of drama.

79 *Archilochum:* as at *Ep.* 1. 19. 23 ff. Archilochus is credited with a large poetic posterity, though the offspring in each case differs; but the *Ars* focuses only on genre and metre, and makes do without the distinctions of the more personal account in *Ep.* 1. 19. H. agrees with the tenor of post-Aristotelian (originally Alexandrian) scholarship, in crediting Archilochus with the ἰαμβικὴ ἰδέα, not, as Aristotle had done at *Poet.* ch. 4, Homer on account of the *Margites*.

proprio is traditionally understood 'which thus became his property' and Rostagni claims that the word confirms Archilochus as the originator of iambic verse, in contradistinction to elegy. But Steidle, *Studien*, p. 48 n. 7, notes that ownership is expressed by *Archilochum...rabies armauit iambo*; so that *proprio* goes more easily with *rabies*, cf. 81 *aptum*, 82 *natum*. The iamb then 'belongs' to indignation. Hence an endorsement of the popular etymology of ἴαμβος from ἰάπτω, which could claim Aristotle's adherence, *Poet.* 4, 1448 b 32 ὅτι ἐν τῷ μέτρῳ τούτῳ ἰάμβιȝον ἀλλήλους. *Epod.* 6. 11 ff. and *Ep.* 1. 19, 30–1 also describe Archilochus the hater.

80 The order comedy–tragedy is one of the features distinguishing this passage from the more cut-and-dried accounts of most of the later handbooks, in which the major genre of tragedy precedes comedy. The primacy of tragedy is not invariable however; note, for example, the sequence comedy–tragedy in Pollux 4. 53 (1. 216 ed. Bethe) and Marius Victorinus (*GL*, vi. 50. 10). All H. need have in mind here is the easy and natural transition from the 'attack' of Archilochus' iambics to that of comedy. According to Rostagni, H. was also remembering Aristotle's assertion that tragedy used trochaic tetrameters in its dialogue before it changed to iambic trimeters (*Poet.* 4, 1449 a 21). For this I see no evidence in the present passage. Elsewhere H.'s context diverges, as it does below 275 ff., and I have argued that the origins of drama at *Ep.* ii. 1. 145 ff. have different, Hellenistic, affiliations, cf. *Varron*, Fondation Hardt, ix (1963), 187 ff.

socci...coturni: the 'sock' or slipper of comedy stands for the genre as at 90; so does *coturnus*, the buskin of tragedy, with a like metonymy, *C.* ii. 1. 11–12 *grande munus | Cecropio repetes coturno*, Virg. *E.* 8. 10 *Sophocleo...carmina digna coturno*, cf. *TLL*, iv. 1087. 68 ff. Cf. below 280 *magnumque loqui nitique coturno*, but in comedy *Ep.* ii. 1. 74 *quam non adstricto percurrat pulpita socco* (Plautus). The antithesis is fully established, cf. Ov. *R.A.* 375–6 *grande sonant tragici: tragicos decet ira coturnos; | usibus e mediis soccus habendus erit*, *Pont.* iv. 16. 29–30. The spelling *coturnus* for *cothurnus* κόθορνος is suggested by the best MSS of Virgil, H.'s cod. R, and others.

grandes, pace Rostagni, is not proleptic with *cepere:* 'so that tragedy became grandiose'. I find no allusion to Ar. *Poet.* 4, 1449 a 20 f. ὀψὲ ἀπεσεμνύνθη, τό τε μέτρον ἐκ τετραμέτρου ἰαμβεῖον ἐγένετο. *grandes* is an attribute of *coturni* denoting their size and metaphorically the elevated nature of tragedy, cf. the instances just cited; the adj. is applied to style from Cicero onward (*TLL*, vi. 2185. 52 ff.), and is so used at 27 above.

81–2 Three characteristics of the iambic (trimeter) are asserted: its aptness for dialogue, for overcoming the hum of the audience, and for embodying action. The first and third are known from Aristotle: *Rhet.* iii. 8, 1408 b 33 ff. ὁ δ' ἴαμβος αὐτή ἐστιν ἡ λέξις ἡ τῶν πολλῶν. διὸ μάλιστα πάντων τῶν μέτρων ἰαμβεῖα φθέγγονται λέγοντες, cf. iii. 1, 1404 a 31 ff., *Poet.* 22, 1459 a 12 ff., and especially 4, 1449 a 24 ff. iambic as the metre 'apt', οἰκεῖον, for conversation, 24, 1460 a 1, iambic as κινητικόν and πρακτικόν. These and later doctrines, Theophrastean and other, are adapted to the conditions of Roman rhetoric by Cic. (*De Or.* iii. 182, *Or.* 189, 191), Quintilian and later writers. H.'s second characteristic may ultimately be based, as Rostagni asserts, on the sharp rhythmical character of the metre (Aristotle's κινητικόν?) but is indebted to later discussion. For Cicero like H. goes beyond Aristotle in asserting, *De Or.* iii. 182 *sed sunt insignes percussiones eorum numerorum et minuti pedes,* and likewise Quint. *I.O.* ix. 4. 136 *sunt (iambi) e duabus modo syllabis eoque frequentiorem quasi pulsum habent, quae res lenitati contraria est,* cf. *ibid. aspera. . . iambis maxime concitatur.* Neither Cicero nor Quintilian however makes H.'s additional point, which is owed to observation in the Roman theatre, and a mark against drama in the *Augustus* (*Ep.* ii. 1. 182 ff., particularly 200–1).

81 *alternis aptum sermonibus:* the phrasing as *Ep.* ii. 1. 146 *uersibus alternis opprobria rustica fudit,* the iambics in dialogue or conversation as Ar. *Poet.* 4, 1449 a 26–7 πλεῖστα γὰρ ἰαμβεῖα λέγομεν ἐν τῇ διαλέκτῳ τῇ πρὸς ἀλλήλους, Cic. *De Or.* and *Or.* cited in the preceding note.

82 (*populares*) *uincentem strepitus* as *Ep.* ii. 1. 203 *tanto cum strepitu ludi spectantur.*

natum rebus agendis, cf. 377 *animis natum inuentumque poema iuuandis.* Both the metaphor, 'destined, designed', and the construction with dat. gerundive, are fully established in archaic and classical Latin; for the construction see Hofmann–Szantyr, 377. *rebus agendis* recalls Aristotle's πρακτικόν (cited 81–2 n.). For the implied reference to the dialogue of drama, see 179 *aut agitur res in scaenis aut* acta *refertur.*

83–5: lyric verse. H. selects four of the major groups into which the Alexandrians seem to have divided lyric verse—hymns or other cult poems and ἐγκώμια, next ἐπινίκια, ἐρωτικά, σκόλια; three of them are strongly represented in H.'s own verse. There is some emphasis in the wording (83 n.), and perhaps in the final position, on the Horatian genre, the lyric.

L. Mueller (ed. 1891, 83 n.) is puzzled by the lack of a connective particle at 83, but the genres are introduced without such external links also at 73, 75, 79, 80.

83 *Musa dedit:* for lyric verse the learned tradition had no early representative of the standing of Homer or Archilochus to offer. The few tentative assignments in Proclus' account, for example, are restricted to such subdivisions as the dithyramb. Hence here the divine inspirer receives a mention; hence too a particular emphasis on the inspiration of the lyric poets. The two passages that spring to mind differ in scope and phrasing: *Ep.* II. 1. 133 *uatem ni Musa dedisset,* and *A.P.* 406–7 *ne forte pudori* | *sit tibi Musa lyrae sollers et cantor Apollo.* The grammar, 'the Muse has given to the instrument to sing' etc., is only partly paralleled by 323–4 *Grais dedit ore rotundo* | *Musa loqui,* *C.* II. 16. 39 ff., *S.* II. 3. 191 (and similar instances, *TLL,* v. 1. 1689. 2 ff.) in that the indirect object here is impersonal. The paraphrase in ps.-Acro and Schol. Vindob., *Musa dedit referre diuos . . . fidibus* (abl.), is however implausible.

diuos puerosque deorum recalls Greek formulas such as παῖδες θεῶν Pindar, *Is.* 3. 19, *Ne.* 9. 27, *Py.* 4. 13, and the whole phrase e.g. in Plato, *Leg.* x. 910 a θεοῖς καὶ δαίμοσιν καὶ παισὶν θεῶν, Polyb. III. 47. 8 θεοὺς καὶ θεῶν παῖδας. Cf. *C.* I. 12. 1–3 *quem uirum aut heroa . . . quem deum?,* IV. 2. 13–14 *seu deos regesque canit, deorum sanguinem*; also *A.P.* 114 *diuus . . . heros,* 227 *deus . . . heros.* The two metrically convenient variants are combined for rhetorical effect as by Sil. III. 625 *o nate deum diuosque dature*; at *Apocol.* 9. 5 Seneca is punning, '*censeo uti diuus Claudius ex hac die deus sit*'. *puer,* like Greek παῖς, is a poetic alternative for *filius* (Cic. *Am.* 70 *deorum . . . filii*) rarely used without implication of age, as it is here, and *C.* II. 18. 32–4 *aequa tellus* | *pauperi recluditur* | *regumque pueris,* IV. 8. 22–3 *Iliae* | *Mauortisque puer,* more often with such an implication, e.g. the Dioscuri *C.* I. 12. 25, or Bacchus *C.* I. 19. 2. *iuuenes* at *C.* II. 12. 7 is similar, though this is denied by K.–H.

Words like hymns and encomia are avoided as are most kinds of terminology in the *Ars.*

84 *epinicia,* the songs of victory selected as in ancient handbooks, and apparently in the Alexandrian edition of Simonides (though not

of Pindar or Bacchylides), according to kinds of contests; two victors
are picked out, both amenable to Roman sentiment, the boxer and
the racehorse. The runner is ceebrated as victor in Greek *epinicia*;
thus Pindar and Bacchylides celebrate the horse tellingly named
Φερένικος (Pindar, *Ol.* 1. 18 ff., *Py.* 3. 74, Bacchy. 5. 37–40, 182–6).
The same selection is made in *C.* IV. 2. 17–18; IV. 3. 3–6 prefer the
boxer and the charioteer. *A.P.* 84 *equum* could be gen. pl. (K.–H.),
but both the balance of the sentence and the parallel passages from *C.*
IV make for the acc. In *pugilem uictorem et equum certamine primum* the
second word is more likely to be a quasi-adjectival apposition balanc-
ing *primum* than a predicative with *referre.* Nouns in -*tor* specially
fulfilled that function from the Augustans onward, cf. Hofmann–
Szantyr, p. 157, para. 92; such locutions as *exercitus uictor* stand out
(*TLL*, v. 2. 1397. 34).

85 *iuuenum curas: hoc est amores quos lyrici celebrant* (Porph.), the
predecessor of love elegy (above 75–8 n.), ἐρωτικά in Alexandrian
parlance. *cura,* a tell-tale word in this context, is close in sense to
amor, cf. *Epod.* 2. 37. The word, so found from Plautus onward, is
familiar from love elegy (*TLL*, IV. 1474. 80 ff.).

libera uina denotes drinking songs, σκόλια or παροίνια. Λυαῖος
suggested λύειν to the Greeks and at a remove *soluere* to the Romans,
cf. *Epod.* 9. 38 *dulci Lyaeo soluere;* so *Liber*–Ἐλεύθερος suggested
liberare. A frequent motif, e.g. *S.* I. 4. 89 *condita cum uerax aperit praecordia Liber, Ep.* I. 5. 16 ff. *dissignat, recludit, eximit, solutum.* 'As though
he contrasted the lightheartedness of the banquet with the young
lover's cares' (Wickham). Cf. Stat. *Silv.* I. 6. 41 *non sic libera uina tunc
fluebant,* 45 *libertas reuerentiam remisit.*

86–8 Two forceful rhetorical questions present a résumé, and mark
a new context. It is only by looking back from this point that the
preceding section, lines 73–85, falls into place. The little passage
balances the abruptness by which the reader has been startled at 73.
There without warning a new argument was presented to him—new
in the method of conventional teaching. Homer had brought together one kind of metre and one kind of subject-matter, thus
creating a 'genre'; other metres and subjects followed. But it is only
now, at 86, when the slow building up of the context has already
established it, that these differences are given names: *descriptas uices,*
genres, and *operum colores,* styles. These genres and styles, we are told
briefly and vigorously (87), call for talent and technique. Technique
—that is, talent made effective—appeared in the initial part of the
poem; there it was proclaimed as the foundation of all artistic
endeavour. Technique will remain a major motif throughout the

poem. Where there is that sort of technique, *ars* in the Horatian sense, 'appropriateness' will follow. This idea is slowly made to impinge on the reader's attention: 86 *descriptas seruare uices*, and earlier in 74 *possent*, 79 *proprio*, 81 *aptum*, 82 *natum*; in the next section cf. 92 n. In more mechanical language, the present three verses are a 'link passage' or 'gliding transition': *descriptas uices* as well as *operumque colores* sum up the genres of the preceding passage and point forward to the stylistic discussion of the following passage; cf. P. Cauer, *RM*, LXI (1906), 235.

86 *descriptas. . .uices operumque colores:* the words are distributed over the two limbs of the phrase, instead of *operum descriptas uices et colores*, i.e. *descriptas* goes with both the following nouns (though of course taking its gender from the adjoining *uices*) and *operum* is meant to accompany *uices* as well as *colores* as G. T. A. Krüger suggested (15th ed. 1908); cf. some of the instances noted by Housman, *Man.* I. 269–70 n., e.g. Hor. *S.* II. 2. 121–2. To understand *numerorum* (Heinze) or even *generum* with *uices* and connect *operum* only with *colores* deprives both the preceding and subsequent section of their joint reference.

descriptas codd. and schol., *discriptas* by conjecture frequently from the sixteenth century onward, see app. crit. *describo* is not here 'describe' (the meaning alleged by ps.-Acro and many others) but 'define, lay down, determine, establish'; *discribo* is 'distribute, apportion, assign'. The fashion of increasing the domain of *discribo* by emendation was started by Buecheler in 1858 (the article reprinted *Kl. Schr.* I. 135–40), and still mars Heinze's note on this passage. Ciceronian idiom however resists wholesale emendation and prepares the ground for H., e.g. *Fin.* III. 74 *natura, qua nihil est* aptius, *nihil* descriptius, *Sen.* 5 *cum ceterae partes aetatis bene descriptae sint, extremum actum tamquam ab inerti poeta esse neglectum,* where J. S. Reid's note explains the unsuitability of a verb denoting 'assignment'. Cf. Vahlen, Cic. *Leg.* III. 12 n., Keller, *Epil.* 743, Vetter, *TLL,* v. 1. 664. 7, Housman, *Man.* II. 828 n., III. 539 n.

seruare: not 'preserve', e.g. 329, 332, but as often = *obseruare,* 'heed, adhere to', *Ep.* I. 16. 41 *qui consulta patrum, qui leges iuraque seruat,* II. 2. 131–2 *munia recto | more.*

uices (sc. *operum*) is rightly paraphrased *uarietates* by ps.-Acro. *uices* 'may denote the states into which a thing passes by change, as well as the changes themselves' (Wilkins), e.g. *C.* III. 29. 13 *gratae diuitibus uices,* IV. 7. 3 *mutat terra uices,* Ov. *Met.* XV. 238 *quasque uices peragant. . .docebo*; also Lucan, V. 445 probably an imitation (cit. Keller) *oblitus seruare uices (pontus).* It is possible that H. tactfully renders a term like διαφοραί applied to all the genres in the same way as Proclus applies διάφοροι τομαί to the subdivisions of lyric verse, *Chrest.* 32. 319 b 32 (Severyns, p. 40) περὶ μελικῆς ποιήσεώς φησιν ὡς πολυμερεστάτη καὶ διαφόρους ἔχει τομάς. Such a term would serve to introduce subdivisions at the beginning of an exposition, as perhaps it did in Accius' *Didascalica*, book IX, fr. 8 (Funaioli, *Gram. Rom. Fr.* p. 27) *nam quam uaria sint genera poematorum, Baebi. . .nosce.* H. uses it as a final clue to solve the puzzles posed by the preceding section, which started *in medias res* and now as it were gets its title.

operumque colores: these are not the *colores* known from the Elder Seneca and other experts on rhetoric, cf. R. G. Austin, Quint. *I.O.* XII. 1. 33 n., *TLL*, III. 1721. 62 ff. (where *Ad Her.* IV. 16 is badly misplaced, see below). The 'colouring' here is the 'tone' or 'style' appropriate to different genres of poetry. So used—with a slight technical implication and the metaphor almost faded—the word is not on record before this passage and 236 *tragico. . .colori*; H. too talks of the *color* of life (*S.* II. 1. 60, *Ep.* 1. 17. 23), and again the metaphor is not found so muffled in earlier extant writing, cf. *TLL*, III. 1720. 24, 1721. 18. But much earlier *color* was applied to the style of rhetorical composition, with the metaphor still kept active, e.g. *Ad Her.* IV. 16 (*exornationes*) *si rarae disponentur, distinctam* sicuti *coloribus. . .reddent orationem,* Cic. *De Or.* III. 96 *ornatur. . .oratio. . . quasi colore quodam et suco,* 217 *hi sunt actori,* ut pictori, *expositi ad uariandum colores.* For all these usages there seem to be analogies in Greek χρῶμα, cf. Ernesti's *Lexicon Techn. Gr. Rhet.* s.v.; though not on record before the time of Augustus they are likely to antedate it considerably and to have influenced Latin usage.

87 *ego* is deprecating and mock-modest, cf. 25–6 n. H. seems to direct against himself what he is censuring in others. *si nequeo: per naturam; ignoroque: per artem quam non didici,* Comm. Cruq. For the metrical anomaly, see 263 n, for position of *si,* 1–2n.

poeta salutor: in H.'s context Ennius' celebrated *Enni poeta salue* offers no likely explanation. This looks like an audience's acclaim of professional status where there is no professional expertise, cf. Pers. 1. 75 *euge, poeta.* I doubt if H. has in mind an actual greeting such as *Ep.* 1. 10. 1–2. Nor is ps.-Acro's assertion of a Grecism convincing: *hoc secundum Graecos, qui cum nomine salutant officii,* χαῖρε ἰατρέ. Jocular greetings from young Marcus, as at Cic. *Att.* II. 12. 4 καὶ Κικέρων ὁ φιλόσοφος τὸν πολιτικὸν Τίτον ἀσπάζεται, lend no colour to that assumption.

88 takes up *ignoro,* 87, the amateurishness of Latin poetry, to H.'s mind the cardinal fault of Roman practitioners, as 261 ff., *Ep.* II. 1.

108 ff., 167. Hence false shame makes them seem to prefer amateur status. Wilamowitz's transposition, *praue nescire pudens* for *nescire pudens praue* (*Kl. Schr.* IV. 565), does not improve the verse. *pudens praue* denotes false shame, as *S.* II. 3. 38–9 '*caue faxis | te quicquam indignum; pudor*' inquit '*te malus angit*', *Ep.* I. 16. 24 *stultorum incurata pudor malus ulcera celat.*

nescire...discere: cf. 418 (*mihi turpe*) *quod non didici sane nescire fateri.*

(c) Styles of diction exemplified by drama, 89–118

The present section unlike the preceding is close to a specific chapter of the Aristotelian *Rhetoric*, III. 7. There style is analysed in terms of an 'appropriate' relationship between the tone of writing and (i) the given situation, τοῖς ὑποκειμένοις πράγμασιν ἀνάλογον, (ii) the emotions portrayed, παθητική, and (iii) the character, *ethos*, of the kinds of persons concerned, ἠθική. The key term throughout is appropriateness, τὸ πρέπον or the like.

I have analysed this section carefully in *Prol.* 97–9. My conclusion has been that (i) is the fundamental part of the tradition behind 89–98, and (ii) and (iii) stand in the same manner behind 99–107 and 108–18 respectively. In all three cases there are post-Aristotelian nuances in the tradition, quite apart from H.'s own way of forming the matter afresh; I have discussed what makes in favour of the assumption that these nuances are early Hellenistic.

(i) *Style and dramatic circumstance*, 89–98. H. again proceeds in his own poetic manner. For him too appropriateness is a key term. The word can now be put (92 *decentem*); its bearing can be understood because the idea has long been instrumental in shaping the argument, though without being expressed as a term. Moreover the poem has been gradually moving towards the topic of style. The *colores*, casually thrown in at 86, are now before the reader, cf. 86–8 n. H. deftly takes up the two chief kinds of drama, comedy and tragedy, which until now have appeared only as a case of metre, an offshoot of Archilochus' iambics, 80–2. Now they are made to exemplify his doctrine of style. *uersibus*, 89, and *carminibus*, 91, are still double-edged words; they may concern metre or style. But the next step leads to situations intermediate between tragedy and comedy, and here H.'s language leaves no doubt that he is talking of the tone or style of the plays.

89 is ultimately from Ar. *Rhet.* III. 7, 1408 a 13 μήτε περὶ εὐτελῶν σεμνῶς, cf. above and *Prol.* 97 f. A similar tradition is restated by Cic. *Opt. Gen. Or.* 1 (*itaque et in tragoedia comicum uitiosum est et*) *in comoedia turpe tragicum.* The distinction between the two dramatic genres was a smaller problem to the Greeks than to the Romans. Aristotle exemplifies from the tragic playwright Cleophon. Ancient scholia preserve traces of this kind of criticism: thus Schol. Soph. *Ajax* 1126 τὸ δὲ τοιοῦτο κωμῳδίας μᾶλλον ἢ τραγῳδίας (cit. K.–H.). In archaic Roman drama, where both genres were cultivated by the same authors, the problem was more serious. The matter is discussed by H. D. Jocelyn, *The Tragedies of Ennius* (1967), 24, 38 ff. Apul. *Flor.* 16. 63 is noteworthy: *ioca non infra soccum, seria non usque ad coturnum.* So is Euanthius, *De Fab.* 3. 5 (Donat. *Comm. Ter.* ed. Wessner, I. 19) *tum illud est admirandum quod et morem* (i.e. ἦθος) *retinuit* (*Terentius*), *ut comoediam scriberet, et temperauit affectum* (i.e. πάθος), *ne in tragoediam transiliret.* Cf. below 93–5.

res (*comica*): the term for subject-matter, as 40, 310, al.

non uult (*res*): a frequent metonymy, as 190 *fabula*, 348 *manus et mens.* When literary theory becomes a subject for poetry, its key terms easily acquire animate status—which does not restrict such a status to poetry, cf. 90 n. on *indignatur.*

90 is ultimately from Ar. *Rhet.* III. 7, 1408 a 12 ff. ἐὰν μήτε περὶ εὐόγκων αὐτοκαβδάλως λέγηται μήτε κτλ. εἰ δὲ μή, κωμῳδία φαίνεται. Similarly Cic. (above 89 n.). At *Or.* 36 Cicero reports a reader's admiration for Ennius *quod non discedit a communi more uerborum*, which the opponent preferring Pacuvius counters in more familiar fashion: *multa... neglegentius.*

indignatur: for the metonymy Vahlen, *Op. Ac.* I. 126, compares ps.-Long. *Subl.* 21 τὸ πάθος... ἐμποδιζόμενον ἀγανακτεῖ. Steidle, *Studien*, p. 50, sees in *indignatur* a reference to tragic pathos, unlike the *non uult* of comedy.

priuatis (*carminibus*): Aristotle, *op. cit.* 1408 a 12 f. said αὐτοκαβδάλως and εὐτελής. The counterpart to H.'s wording is ἰδιωτικός, as in the definition of tragedy probably to be ascribed to Theophrastus, ἰδιωτικῶν πραγμάτων ἀκίνδυνος περιοχή, cf. *Prol.* 98 n. 3.

socco as 80 but now the two types of drama are distinct.

91 *dignis* 'apt' or 'only worthy of', without laudatory intent as frequently, e.g. 282–3.

carminibus, though like 89 *uersibus* applied to style, still carries the notion of metre from the last section. Cf. Porph. *humilibus uerbis non uult tragoedia impleri*.

narrari: the *cena Thyestae* later exemplifies the Horatian rule that horrific subjects be restricted to narrative on the stage, cf. 186.

92 was expunged by Lehrs and Ribbeck, also by Prinz (*Rev. de l'instr. pub. en Belgique*, VI (1863), 295); transposed to an unsuitable place (after 98) by L. Mueller, or (after 86) by A. Y. Campbell, *Hor. Carm.*[1] (1945), 'Horatiana Alia' *in calce libri*. Objections are raised to its placing and grammar. About the placing Wickham says, 'the line sums up what is being said in a maxim; cp. v. 31'. Sums up what? 73–91 say Heinze and others, 89–91 as well as 73–88 Steidle, *Studien*, p. 50. But though the maxim fits both contexts, it would be hard to jump back to the subject of metre and genre, once it has been replaced by the *colores*. 89–91 therefore are summed up, if the wording is acceptable. But can *singula quaeque* take the place of *utraque*, referring to only two items? *quisque* certainly can do so with *suus*, e.g. Cic. *Q. Rosc.* 32 *suam quisque* (each of two) *partem iuris possideat*, cf. Hofmann–Szantyr, p. 201. But I cannot match the easy extension to *singula quaeque* and the material of the *TLL*, which I have consulted, suggests no parallel. Quintilian may so have understood the Horatian passage when he said, *I.O.* x. 2. 22 *sua cuique* (i.e. *oratio* and *declamatio*) *proposita lex*, suus decor *est: nec comoedia in coturnos adsurgit, nec contra tragoedia socco ingreditur*. The problem is not fully resolved, but the case against the verse is not decisive.

The MSS (C apart) divide between *decenter* and *decentem*, the latter supported by Bentley. *decentem* with *locum* provides the notion of the 'apt place' which would here be required, and if the verse is genuine, eases the transition to the occasional 'changes of place' or 'level' allowed in the next few verses, 93 *tollit* and 95 *pedestri*. It is therefore more to the point than *sortita decenter*. Appropriateness, *decorum*, would be the technical term for the πρέπον of the Greek theorists already employed by Cicero; *locum...decentem*, like *decent* at 106, preserves the pictorial language of *uices*, 86, and of the raising and lowering of style in this passage. I take *locum...decentem* to be the grammatical object of both *teneant* and *sortita*, placed 'ἀπὸ κοινοῦ'. Peerlkamp's objections to this reading are based on such inapposite parallels as 19 *sed nunc non erat his locus*; his punctuation (after *sortita*, which attaches his reading, *decenter*, to 93) would deprive this verse, and indeed section, of the final pointer to 'aptness'.

93–8 illustrate the mutual encroachment of the two genres which H. considered admissible. This doctrine is a refinement of the Aristotelian notions, for *Rhet.* III. 7 is restricted to the two extreme cases, tragic or comic. Greek as well as Roman scholia occasionally offer criticism of this kind, cf. 89, 94, 95 nn.

93 Bentley, *C.* I. 34. 6 n., overstates the difference between *interdum*, in this verse, and *plerumque*, 95; cf. 14 *plerumque*, 'often, occasionally'. The angry father is not exceedingly rare in comedy nor, as ancient criticism suggests, is *pauper et exul* unduly frequent in tragedy. I doubt therefore if Rostagni's conclusions, 95 n., are justified, which here assert only an occasional rising of the comic tone, but a frequent lowering of tone in the Euripidean type of tragedy, 'avvicinata a un comune dramma borghese'.

uocem comoedia tollit: the drama still personified as at 89–90. The tone of the voice is mentioned, but only because the level of the voice expresses the level of the style, H.'s subject. 'He raises his voice' sounds natural enough in English, but *tollit uocem* is unusual and poetic in Latin, *tollitur* (*in caelum*) *clamor, querella, gemitus, ululatus,* etc. having a different implication: *tollo*, with *uocem*, seems a direct word a poet uses in the place of the more circumlocutory prose of the rhetoricians, none of whom, to my knowledge, has *uocem tollere* for either volume or pitch of voice (*Ad Her.* III. 19 ff., Cic. *De Or.* III. 213 ff., Quint. *I.O.* XI, ch. 3). Virg. *A.* VI. 492–3 *tollere uocem | exiguam* is probably formed on the model of *tollere clamorem*, and *clamor* follows suit in the next line. Stat. *Silv.* I. 6. 81 *tollunt innumeras* ad astra *uoces* is not fully relevant and the material of the *TLL* offers no further instance with *uox* until Gell. XVI. 19. 14 *uoce sublatissima.* But the archaic compound *attollere* is used with *uocem* by poets, poeticizing historians and Silver writers. *TLL*, II. 1151. 79 ff. cites it first from Sen. *Ep.* 75. 2 *nec supploderem pedem...nec attollerem uocem, sed ista oratoribus reliquissem.* I note particularly, for its relevance to H., Quint. *I.O.* XI. 3. 65 *attollitur autem* (*uox*) *concitatis affectibus, compositis descendit pro utriusque rei modo altius uel inferius.*

94 *iratusque Chremes* is often identified with Chremes, the angry father of Ter. *Heaut.* v. 4 (e.g. by A. di Benedetto, 'Echi terenziani in Orazio', *Rend. dell' Acc....di Napoli*, XXXVII (1962), 42 f.). This is not impossible but the similarity is slight. The angry father is a stock figure in New Comedy and the name Chremes must have occurred frequently. H. knew how to direct attention to a specific scene of comedy when he wanted to, as he did at *S*. II. 3. 259 with the beginning of Terence's *Eunuchus*. The short-lived chagrin in the *Heauton*, as Wickham says, cannot easily be described by *tumido delitigat ore*. Again a similar scene at *S*. I. 4. 48 ff. *et pater ardens | saeuit*, etc. belongs to a different play. So does the Chremes of *Epod*. I. 33. And *S*. I. 10. 40–2 alludes to work by Fundanius.

tumido delitigat ore: impassioned bearing and style here obviously condoned, but elsewhere frequently frowned upon by literary critics. For example, Gell. II. 23. 21 *uersus sunt hi Caecili . . .consarcinantis* uerba tragici tumoris; Euanth. *De fabulis* 3. 5 (Donat. *Comm. Ter*. ed. Wessner, I. 20) *illud quoque inter Terentianas uirtutes mirabile quod eius fabulae eo sunt temperamento ut neque* extumescant ad tragicam celsitudinem *neque*, etc.; Donat. *Comm. Ter., Andria Praef*. I. 5 καταστροφή paene tragica, *et tamen repente ex his turbis in tranquillum peruenitur*; *Ad*. 638 *pepulisti:* elatum uerbum et tragico coturno magis quam loquelae comicae accommodatum; *ibid*. 789, on the other hand, impassioned speech is approved, even admired: *pro rei magnitudine*, etc.; *mira* αὔξησις *quam imitatus Vergilius in Orpheo*, etc. *uide hic gradus doloris et iracundiae in tantum auctos ut iam crescere non possint*, etc. And in his note on the next line of Terence, Donatus cites this Horatian verse to illustrate his point.

delitigat: only here in classical Latinity; like *denato* (*C*. III. 7. 28) and *deproelior* (*C*. I. 9. 11) possibly a Horatian coinage. For formation and context *desaeuit* may be compared (a word not on record until Virgil), *Ep*. I. 3. 14 *an tragica desaeuit et ampullatur in arte?* St Jerome, citing the present passage, probably from memory, put the more usual *desaeuiet* instead of the rare *delitigat*. To H.'s ear *de* must have been an expressive, and to his mind a meaningful, prefix; the number of *de* compounds is large, see D. Bo, *Hor. Op*. III, 385. Moreover, H.'s ἅπαξ λεγόμενα, as far as verbs are concerned, apart from four (*ampullari, Graecari, iuuenari*, and *scurrari*), are all compounds, see D. Bo, *op. cit*. III. 393–4. This is clearly an important aspect of the poet's verbal imagination.

95–8 (1) In many editions these lines are marked off from 93–4 by a semicolon (earlier even by a full stop), but 93 *et* (*comoedia*) and 95 *et* (*tragicus*) should be seen to correspond. (2) Punctuation in the rest of the passage has in my opinion been settled by Peerlkamp and Vahlen, yet editors do not regard it as settled. I am persuaded by Vahlen's argument (*H*, XII (1877), 189–90) that Telephus and Peleus can scarcely be said to express their sufferings *plerumque*. To avoid that, Bentley's and certain other editors' punctuation should be abandoned. The clause 95 should not be allowed to run on to 96

Commentary

Peleus; a comma after 95 *pedestri* (as in Heinze's and Klingner's editions) restores sense as well as balance with 93. Occasionally, H. is saying, comedy raises its voice and (i.e. when) Chremes makes his complaints; occasionally (cf. *plerumque*, 95 n.) a tragic personage (i.e. tragedy) lowers the level of style when (*cum*) Telephus and Peleus give up their high-flown language. Vahlen noted also that *plerumque...cum* are related at 95–6 as they are at 14–16. (3) For the punctuation of *pauper...uterque*, erroneous, I believe, in all recent editions, see 96 n.

95 *tragicus:* not adjectival, with *Telephus et Peleus* (used, they say, like *S.* II. 5. 91 *Dauus...comicus* or Cic. *Pis.* 47 *tragico illo Oreste aut Athamante*), but a noun, the tragic actor or *dramatis persona*, as Plaut. *Pers.* 465–6 *tragici et comici* | *numquam aeque sunt meditati* (like *tragoedi* or *comici*, *Poen.* 581, *Rud.* 1249), and probably Petron. 132. 13 *quidam tragici*.

plerumque: see 93 n. *interdum*.

sermone pedestri like *sermoni propiora* of satire, compared with comedy at *S.* I. 4. 42, 45 ff.; cf. *S.* II. 6. 17 *saturis musaque pedestri, Ep.* II. 1. 250–1 *sermones...* | *repentes per humum, A.P.* 229 *humili sermone.* This is Horatian language for Aristotle's ἐὰν δὲ ἐλεεινά, ταπεινῶς (λέγειν), *Rhet.* III. 7, 1408 a 18–19. Demetr. *Interpr.* 28 ἁπλοῦν γὰρ εἶναι βούλεται καὶ ἀποίητον τὸ πάθος, ὁμοίως δὲ καὶ τὸ ἦθος, cf. P. Shorey, *CP*, 1 (1906), 293–4.

96 *Telephus et Peleus:* Telephus is one of the favourite personages of Greek and Roman tragedy; he figures in the list of those few about whose houses αἱ κάλλισται τραγῳδίαι συντίθενται (Ar. *Poet.* 13, 1453 a 19), cf. Schwenn, *R-E*, IV A. 366, H. D. Jocelyn, *The Tragedies of Ennius*, pp. 404 ff. Peleus is a subject of tragedies by Sophocles, Euripides, and Pacuvius, cf. Lesky, *R-E*, XIX. 304 f.

pauper et exsul uterque: Heinze comments, '*uterque:* aber *pauper* geht mehr auf Telephus, *exsul* mehr auf Peleus'. But either the two adjectives apply to both or they do not. I am tempted therefore to go further than Heinze, and say that, although Telephus left his country to find his healer, he was not like Peleus exiled. Ennius' *regnum reliqui saeptus mendici stola* (fr. 282 Jocelyn) and ... *squalida saeptus stola* (fr. 281), or similar Greek passages, do not make him *exsul*. Telephus is *pauper*, πτωχός, in Aristophanes; it is Peleus who is *exsul*, e.g. ἐκβέβληκεν, Eur. *Tro.* 1128 and ἐκβεβλῆσθαι...ἐξεληλάσθαι, schol. *ibid. uterque* should therefore go with *proicit* and to signify this, the punctuation proposed by Marcilius, Gesner, Doering, and especially Peerlkamp, should be restored, a comma before *uterque*, thus: *cum, pauper et exul, uterque* | *proicit*. In fact this verse may be claimed as a variation of a 'double zeugma', *uterque proicit* ~ *proiciunt*, cf. *CR*, LVIII (1944), 43–5. *et*, not *aut*, predominates in this locution; there is no need for Bentley's conjecture. I note that in two of the more extreme cases *uterque* occurs, and is subdivided in the same manner as it is here, cf. Tac. *Ann.* I. 55. 9 and III. 63. 16, and my remarks *CR*, LVIII (1944), 44.

97 *proicit*, like *abicit*, may emphasize the notion of casting aside, abandoning, *S.* II. 3. 100–1 *aurum | in media. . .Libya*, 7. 53 *proiectis insignibus*. The nuance at 462 differs.

ampullas 'bombast': *idest irata uerba, inflata, grandia; omittit orationem tumidam et inflatam* (ps.-Acro). The same notion is claimed by L.–S.–J., but the two references cited come from Latin literature, Cic. *Att.* I. 14. 3 *nosti illas* ληκύθους and Plin. *Ep.* I. 2. 4 *Marci nostri* ληκύθους; and in both cases the context seems to make for 'cosmetics, embellishments', cf. D. R. S. Bailey, *Cic. Letters to Atticus*, 14 (I. 14). 3 n., although J. H. Quincey, *CQ*, LXIII (1949), 32–44, especially 38, 42, and P. Thielscher, *Festschrift F. Dornseiff* (Leipzig 1953), 334–71, especially 356, are inclined to deny it. Nevertheless this meaning is implausible at Virg. *Cat.* 5. 1, and is excluded here by H.'s concern in this passage with bombast and sonorous language; a decision between enunciation (*sonus raucae uocis*) and style (*tumor tragicus*), which worries R. E. H. Westendorp Boerma (*Cat.* 5. 1 n.), is hardly called for. That λήκυθοι 'bombast' existed in Greek is shown by the comments of ancient grammarians and by Callimachus, who applied μοῦσα ληκυθίζουσα to tragedy (fr. 215 with Pfeiffer's note); but the notion is likely to be older. Porphyrion clearly has Callimachus' tag in mind when he says, *hoc a Callimacho sustulit, quod dicit* —. Unfortunately the rest of the scholion is lost, but the lacuna of 14 letters after *dicit* in cod. P would accommodate one of the variants of the Callimachean fragment, either μοῦσαν ληκυθίαν or λ. μ., cf. Pfeiffer *ad l.*, Thielscher, *op. cit.* 360–2. At *Ep.* I. 3. 14 *an tragica desaeuit et ampullatur in arte?* the context is identical with that of the *Ars*, and requires the same meaning, 'bombast'. The verb *ampullatur*, which occurs only here, renders Greek ληκυθίζειν, and is likely to be a Horatian coinage *Graeco fonte*. It seems necessary therefore to posit two metaphorical notions in Latin as well as in Greek, as was seen by C. Zangemeister, *De Hor. vocibus singularibus*, Thesis, Berlin 1862, 27 f. The origin of one of them, ληκύθιον–*ampulla* = bombast, is still obscure; it has been discussed by Quincey and Thielscher in the articles cited above.

sesquipedalia uerba: the long word being descriptive; perhaps a glance at Aristophanes' measuring the length of tragic words (*Ran.*

799 καὶ κανόνας . . . καὶ πήχεις ἐπῶν), the compound words of tragedy (*Ran.* 836 ff.), and the comedian Crates' ἔπη (ἐπεὶ codd.) τριπήχη (Ath. x. 418 c; *Com. Gr.* Crat. *Lamia* fr. 2 Meineke (II. 241), fr. 18 Kock (I. 136). But there must have been talk of this kind in Hellenistic polemic and, as commentators note with regard to Gell. xix, ch. 7, such compounds were a typical feature also of archaic Roman tragedy.

98 The *si* clause qualifies 95 *tragicus plerumque dolet* (as K.–H. and some older commentators say) but may qualify also 96–7 *Telephus . . . cum . . . proicit.* The position may be compared to 19 *sed . . . locus* over against 14–16 *plerumque . . . adsuitur pannus* and 16–18 *cum . . . describitur.* Moreover, having assigned to this passage an intermediate position between the simple antithesis comedy–tragedy (89–92) and the discussion of emotion (99 ff.), H. so turns the sentence at the end that the *si* clause becomes transitional. Ps.-Acro rightly notes, *hic uersus et superioribus et sequentibus iungi potest.* Peerlkamp, erroneously, used this transitional character to attach 98 to 99 ff., preferring the inferior reading *curas* for *curat,* thus: *si curas . . . non satis est,* etc.

There is a deliberate spondaic rhythm up to the fourth-foot caesura, and a long word covering the middle caesura. Note too that, although *cor* is governed by *tetigisse* and does not go with *curat,* the assonance *curat cor* obtrudes, recalling such locutions as Pacuv. tr. 276 *lapit cor cura,* and the like, *TLL,* IV. 934. 31 ff. Is H. echoing an archaic verse in this affecting context?

curat, that is *tragicus,* is specified by *Telephus et Peleus.* The variant reading *curas* was probably prompted by a misunderstanding of the long period; it may point to a different division of sentences; cf. above.

tetigisse: the meaning as at Cic. *Att.* II. 19. 1 *minae Clodi . . . modice me tangunt,* Virg. *A.* I. 462 *mentem mortalia tangunt,* Liv. III. 17. 3 *si uos urbis . . . nulla cura tangi.* For the aoristic perf. inf. see 455 *tetigisse timent,* *S.* I. 2. 28 *sunt qui nolint tetigisse nisi illas,* and 168, 347, 434 nn.: the metrically convenient alternative to the pres. inf., as Lucr. III. 69, Cat. 69. 2, occasionally in Virgil and frequently in Ovid and Silver Latin. Cf. Norden, Virg. *A.* VI. 78–9 n., A. Engel, *De Hor. sermone metro accommodato,* Thesis, Breslau 1914, 46 f., Hofmann–Szantyr, 351 f. For Persius' variation of this verse, cf. below 102–3 n.

querella: for the spelling, see F. Sommer's *Handbuch der . . . Formenlehre*², 204–5 with bibliography. The (false) analogy with diminutives in -*ĕlla* seems to have largely prevailed in antiquity, if one may judge from the frequency of this spelling in our oldest and most careful manuscripts, and from the opposition of the grammarians. The

MSS of H. are divided between *-ela* and *-ella*. I adopt the spelling of the competent orthographer of cod. R and of the best Virgilian codices.

(ii) *Style and emotion*, 99–111 (113). Aristotle's second point in *Rhet.* III. 7 is emotion, πάθος, 1408 a 16–25. I have argued, *Prol.* 98 f., that this is the fundamental theory underlying this section. Aristotle lays down that style should be παθητική, and that it should be apt, οἰκεία, by which he means appropriate to the emotions involved—angry language when there is a feeling of outrage, etc. Then reaction will be right; the listener sympathizes with the emotions thus expressed: συνομοπαθεῖ, a 23. Clearly that is H.'s doctrine in the central piece, 101–7, especially 106–7. I note 106 *decent* as restating Aristotle's οἰκεία; later, 112, *absona* echoes this demand.

This passage however is instructive to those concerned with the tradition on which H. has drawn. Since the Aristotelian book and chapter underlying this tradition are preserved, it will be seen that H.'s material is more elaborate than that of the *Rhetoric*. Evidence for this more sophisticated tradition exists only in scattered pieces in different contexts; so a comparison with Ar. *Poet.* ch. 17 and with Roman rhetoric shows, note in particular Cic. *De Or.* II. 189 f., III. 217 ff., *T.D.* IV. 43, Quint. *I.O.* VI, ch. 2. W. Kroll, *Sokrates*, VI (1918), 88, 93, has noted the Peripatetic character of some of the Ciceronian passages. The value of these parallels, however, is no more than illustrative; apart from the *Ars* itself there is no evidence in the extant tradition for a coherent theory of this kind. Yet the character of the theory does not differ in principle from the rest of the Aristotelian tradition on which H. seems to have drawn: it takes Aristotle's argument a stage further—in the direction of Hellenistic thought on Greek poetic styles, as I have argued in my Prolegomena.

The same sceptical conclusion applies to the rest of the literary tradition in this section, although there the Aristotelian *Rhetoric* leaves us in the lurch. In the *Ars* the stylistic doctrine of sympathy is buttressed on either side by theories supporting it. It is prefaced, with extreme brevity, by a demand for emotional 'involvement', H. translating the Greek term *psychagogia*, 99–100 n. It is followed, 108–11 (13), by some abstract observations on the nature of language. These observations make language dependent on the speaker's reactions to external happenings. They are said to be a guarantee of his sincerity; sincere speech will in turn evoke an emotional response that has similar psychological roots. For the theory, see 108–11 (13) n.

As a whole then the passage on style and emotion had been divided by H. into three related divisions: 99–100 on *psychagogia*, 101–7 on emotional style and sympathy, and 108–11 (13) on the psychology of style. These may have come from one original context. But H. has treated them in his poetic manner. He has set them down as distinct, giving each his due, and he has left it to the reader to supply the links between *animum auditoris agunto* (100), the emotions of Telephus and Peleus, as well as other emotions which connect the audience with the *dramatis personae* (101–7), and finally a view of language that seeks to explain these connexions, 108 ff.

99–100: formal perfection and emotion in poetry. The distinction in literary criticism between *pulchrum* and *dulce*, καλόν and ἡδύ, is taken for granted by Dion. Hal., *Comp.* chs. 10 ff.; but his topics are technical, rhythm and the like, whereas H. is attempting to derive the effect of poetry from the emotions which the poet is expressing. Rostagni has noted that the duality is at home in the *Poetics*, but it needs to be added that Aristotle is not there concerned with poetic style but largely with two related qualities of the μῦθος, the coherence of plot construction and the pleasure arising from the painful emotions of ἔλεος and φόβος; cf. commentators on *Poet.* 14, 1453 b 12; 23, 1459 a 21, particularly G. F. Else, *Aristotle's Poetics: The Argument*, 402, 447 ff., 651 ff. Whatever their difficulties, these terms, and ψυχαγωγεῖν as well, do occur in the *Poetics*. We are dealing with a post-Aristotelian theory, which in this instance applied Aristotelian terms to the discussion of style. Commentators rightly note that the topic reappears later in the *Ars*, specially 319 ff., 333 ff., also at some length *Ep.* II. 1. 208 ff.

99 *non satis est. . .sunto:* the beginning of the verse resembles a set formula, and suits the style of instruction; *S.* I. 10. 7–8 continues less concisely, *ergo non satis est risu diducere rictum | auditoris; et est quaedam tamem hic quoque uirtus,* etc.

pulchra 'well made': as J. Tate, *CQ*, XXII (1928), 67, says, something which satisfies 'the canons of art'. He refers to *Ep.* II. I. 69–72, about the poems of Livius Andronicus: *sed* emendata *uideri | pulchraque et exactis minimum distantia miror.* Just so H. refuses, at *S.* I. 10. 6, to admire *Laberi mimos ut* pulchra *poemata.*

dulcia: the opposite term to *pulchra;* in J. M. Gesner's paraphrase, *quae afficiunt animum* as opposed to *quae placent recto iudicio. dulce* is to *pulchrum,* in this philosophy of art, as *dulce* is to *decorum* in H.'s patriotic philosophy: *dulce et decorum est pro patria mori.*

sunto: in rhyme with 100 *agunto,* cf. 176–7 n. on *seniles–uiriles,* also 241–2 *speret idem. . . | ausus idem.* The homoeoteleuton underlines the quasi-legal language of enactment to which Rostagni draws attention. Cf. for content and wording 335 *quidquid praecipies* esto *brevis,* etc.

100 *quocumque uolent:* as *Ep.* II. I. 213 *et modo me Thebis, modo ponit Athenis,* preceded 210 ff. by *ille. . .poeta,* meum qui pectus inaniter angit, | *irritat, mulcet, falsis terroribus implet,* | *ut magus.*

animum. . .agunto literally render ψυχαγωγεῖν. The 'attraction' of poetry—not as in the theory inappositely cited by Heinze from Sext. Emp. *Adv. Math.* I. 297 οἱ δὲ (ποιηταί) ἐκ παντὸς ψυχαγωγεῖν ἐθέλουσιν, but here set beside *pulchra.* Contrast at 333 *delectare: prodesse,* 334 *iucunda: idonea vitae,* 343 *dulci: utile,* Neopt. Par. (fr. 10, *Prol.* 55) *ap.* Philod. *De Poem.* V, col. 13. 10 ff. [μετὰ τ]ῆς ψυχαγω[γί]α[ς]: ὠ[φελεῖ]ν κτλ.

101–7: Style and sympathy, ὁμοπαθεῖν. Since apart from the *Ars* no sizeable discussion of this topic is extant (Ar. *Poet.* ch. 17 comes closest to it) it cannot now be known how style, voice, and gesture were accommodated in this tradition. The stray passages mentioned above, 99–111 (13) n., can tell us only that they were so accommodated; H. uses 'features', *uultus,* to good effect, but he is likely to have been instigated to do so by his material. More however cannot be said, for Ar. *Poet.* ch. 17 is concerned primarily with plot-construction, not with diction, and the rhetoricians who glance at this topic are talking about oratorical delivery, although Cic. *De Or.* III exemplifies from tragedy. H. alone talks explicitly of the style of drama. It may be remembered too that H.'s belief in poetic sincerity differs from the balanced view expressed in *Poet.* ch. 17, cf. the next note.

101 selects laughter and tears as representative of the whole range of emotion, though other emotions are touched on in 105–7. But 102 ff. show that emphasis is laid on the *ita* clause, the misery of tragic heroes. The most telling parallel comes from Ar. *Poet.* 17, 1455 a 29 ff. This too mentions the gestures, σχήματα, of the tragic hero, which the playwright when he composes is advised to mime in order to be convincing. πιθανώτατοι γὰρ οἱ ἀπὸ τῆς αὐτῆς φύσεως οἱ ἐν τοῖς πάθεσίν εἰσιν· καὶ χειμαίνει ὁ χειμαζόμενος καὶ χαλεπαίνει ὁ ὀργιζόμενος ἀληθινώτατα. διὸ εὐφυοῦς ἡ ποιητική ἐστιν ἢ μανικοῦ· τούτων γὰρ οἱ μὲν εὔπλαστοι οἱ δὲ ἐκστατικοί εἰσιν. For laughter in the rhetorical context, see Quint. *I.O.* VI, ch. 3; for tearful emotion, Ar. *Rhet.* III. 7, 1408 a 18 ἐλεεινά, and the passages of Cicero and Quintilian cited above.

adflent is probably an emendation by the anonymous of Worcester Library, *grammaticus bibliothecae Vigorniensis*, first accepted by various scholars in the sixteenth and seventeenth centuries, and later confirmed with strong arguments by Bentley against the MSS' *adsunt* (*assunt*) or *adsint* (*assint*) and Marcilius' reported *adflant*. Many editors from Orelli to Rostagni and D. Bo (1959) have refused the emendation, Wickham adding insult to injury by ascribing it to Orelli. Yet no number of instances of *adsunt* in Latin literature can heal the limp in *ita flentibus adsunt* | *humani uultus* after *ut ridentibus arrident*. The only other way has been tried by Housman, that is to preserve *adsunt*, and find the tears in *humani uultus*. But Housman's *humiduli uultus* (*JP*, XVIII (1890), 129–30) fails, not only because of the false note of the adjective but because *humani uultus* is required unchanged for *ridentibus* as well as for *flentibus*. I doubt if *flere* repeated in the next line makes against *adflent*.

For the verb see *TLL*, *adfleo*: it occurs twice in Plautus, *Pers.* 152, *Poen.* 1109, as Bentley knew without that assistance. The idea (though not its application) is commonplace; so is the antithesis of laugh and cry. Bentley again cited Ov. *Met.* III. 459–60 *cum risi, arrides; lacrimas quoque saepe notaui* | *me lacrimante tuas*, Sen. *De Ira*, II. 2. 5 *inde est quod arridemus ridentibus et contristat nos turba maerentium.* For other instances see Keller and Holder's note.

102 *humani uultus* directs attention to human features expressive of emotion, cf. Cic. *De Or.* III. 216 *omnis enim motus animi suum quemdam a natura habet* uultum et sonum et gestum; *corpusque totum hominis et* *eius* omnis uultus omnesque uoces, *ut nerui in fidibus, ita sonant ut a motu animi quoque sunt pulsae.* Facial expression is taken to be prompted by emotion, as is speech (104, 108 ff.). Moreover features are said to express fellow-feeling. τὸ φιλάνθρωπον denotes something similar in Ar. *Poet.* (13, 1452 b 38, 1453 a 2, 18, 1456 a 21) and *Rhet.* (II. 13, 1390 a 20). But in H.'s context this feeling, which in Aristotle is a reaction to suffering, is extended to joy and, at 108 ff., to all contingencies.

102–3 *dolendum est | primum ipsi tibi:* Aristotle's οἱ ἐν τοῖς πάθεσιν may be compared in the passage cited 101 n. The rhetoricians were divided as to the desirability of feigned emotion in oratory; Cic. *T.D.* IV. 43 reports from a Peripatetic source (though not necessarily Aristotle, fr. 80 R.) *oratorem denique non . . . probant (iidem Peripatetici) sine aculeis iracundiae, quae* etiamsi non adsit tamen uerbis atque motu simulandam arbitrantur, *ut auditoris iram oratoris incendat actio.* Cicero himself thought otherwise, *Or.* 132, and particularly *De Or.* II. 189 *neque fieri potest ut* doleat is qui audit, *ut oderit, ut inuideat, ut pertimescat aliquid, ut ad fletum misericordiamque deducatur, nisi omnes illi motus quos orator adhibere uolet iudici,* in ipso oratore impressi esse atque inusti uidebuntur; he then explains why *fictus dolor* will not do. Contrast however the more specific and perhaps less personal discussion, *ibid.* III. 215–23, where at 215 *animi permotio* is allowed *quae maxime* aut declaranda aut imitanda *est actione*; then various emotions are instanced from tragedy; they can be expressed *arte ac moderatione* (217) and especial importance is assigned to facial expression: *ibid.* 221 *animi est enim omnis actio, et* imago animi uultus, indices oculi, *actio* being *quasi sermo corporis quo magis menti congruens esse debet* (222). He ends by saying that that language is understood by all: *iisdem enim omnium animi motibus concitantur et eos iisdem notis in aliis agnoscunt et in se ipsi indicant.* Cf. Quint. *I.O.* VI. 2, especially 26 *ut moueamur ipsi,* 34 *nec agamus rem quasi alienam, sed* adsumamus parumper *illum dolorem,* XI. 3. 73 the emotional effect on the stage of masks. Persius casts a new and stronger light on these notions by joining, sensitively, these two verses of H. with 98 *tetigisse querella,* see Pers. 1. 90–1 *uerum, nec nocte paratum, | plorabit qui me uolet incuruasse querella.*

laedent 'hurt', a strong word to make H.'s point.

103 *tum tua* in BCK, our best tradition, though *tunc tua* (cett.) is by no means excluded in classical Latin verse. In doubtful instances it may be remembered that H. like other poets before Persius and Martial uses *tum* much oftener than *tunc*. Cf. Hofmann–Szantyr, 520, where Housman's discussions, in his Lucan and Juvenal, of *tum* before gutturals, and the evidence from the Manilian codices (v, pp. 177–8), are overlooked; see also W. V. Clausen, Persius (ed. 1956), 1. 9 n.

104 *Telephe uel Peleu* brings the reader back to the events of tragic drama and the two *personae* are addressed as though they were real— a fiction upheld in the rest of the verse.

mandata: for assignment of roles to *dramatis personae*, as 176–7 *ne forte seniles | mandentur iuueni partes.* The adverb *male* may grammatically go either with *mandata* or *loqueris*, the context seems to me to demand that it goes with the participle as at 441 *male tornatos . . . uersus, Ep.* II. 1. 233 *uersibus . . . male natis.* In Ar. *Poet.* 17, cited above 101 n., the playwright is told to mime when he composes. The gestures will be those that are relevant to the emotions of his personages; miming will make him feel their emotions so that he can be most plausible in what he lets them say or do. In the *Ars* we are still in the context of style, *colores,* cf. 106 *uerba* and 111–13. Moreover H. dramatizes the tragic poet's failure. He involves him only at a remove as it were, since the playwright is ultimately responsible for 'assigning ill-fitting speeches', *male mandata.* H. addresses the *dramatis persona,* concentrating attention on him. Telephus' or Peleus' words do not carry conviction because they are not inspired by the emotion occasioned by his calamities. This failure will then be imparted to his audience. Lambinus, though aware of this interpretation, connected *male* with *loqueris,* the addressee then being not the imaginary mythical hero but the actor playing the part, and H.'s topic, contrary to his indications, not style but gestures and acting; likewise more recently Rostagni and Steidle, *Studien,* pp. 64 ff.

105 *aut dormitabo aut ridebo:* a use of the first person singular unlike those mentioned at 25–6 n. Here as at 103, 153, 188, H. identifies himself with the audience in the theatre. Whether the homoeoteleuton was emphasized would be known better if the mode of pronunciation of elided vowels could be determined, cf. 87 *nequeo ignoroque.* For the wording, see Cic. *Brut.* 278 *tantum afuit ut inflammares nostros animos, somnum isto loco uix tenebamus;* Steidle, *Studien,* p. 64 n. 64, cites Tac. *Dial.* 21 *in quibusdam antiquorum uix* risum, *in quibusdam autem uix* somnum *tenere.*

maestum and 106 *iratum* qualify *uultum,* as 105 *tristia* and 106 *plena minarum* qualify *uerba;* but 107 *lasciua* must surely be construed like *seria* in the same verse, used as a noun with *dictu,* cf. *seria,* noun, 226, *S.* I. 1. 27, II. 2. 125. This makes one wonder if *ludentem,* which scarcely suits *uultum,* is not, as G. T. A. Krüger proposed, used as a noun, and *seuerum* likewise.

106 *decent,* 92 *decentem,* 112 *absona:* cf. 99–111 (113) n.

108–11: the psychology of style. What conceptual reasoning there is in this section was called Epicurean by Usener (*Epicurea*, p. 380, *de loquellae origine*), Kiessling and L. Mueller in their commentaries, and M. Pohlenz, *NGG*, N.F. III. 6 (1939), 197 (*Kl. Schr.* I. 85). Like Heinze however I fail to find a clear parallel in Lucr. v. 1056 ff.; H. is not concerned with the early beginnings of speech. Heinze and others call the doctrine Stoic, citing Porph. *Abst.* III. 3. According to Rostagni it is a mixture of Stoic and Epicurean. The distinction between *logos* internal (ἐνδιάθετος) and external (προφορικός) seems to have been something of a commonplace from the second century B.C. onward; Theon of Smyrna, not very helpfully, ascribes it to νεώτεροι (p. 72. 25, ed. Hiller). It had been developed from Platonic (e.g. *Soph.* 189 f., 262 f.) and Aristotelian (e.g. *An. Post.* 76 b 24) beginnings in the context of certain controversies between the schools, on which see Pohlenz, *NGG*, N.F. III. 6 (1939), 191 ff. (*Kl. Schr.* I. 79 ff.), *Die Stoa*², I. 39, II. 21. Labelling by schools of philosophy therefore calls for the specific disagreements that prompted those controversies; but those are the disagreements with which H. is not concerned. Indeed, if one may judge from his context of emotion and sympathy, there is a case for noting the Peripatetic nuance in H.'s presentation, as W. Kroll, *Sokrates*, VI (1918), 93, and Steidle, *Studien*, p. 65 n. 68, have done. (Cicero's rather splendid passage, *De Or.* III. 216, comes to similar conclusions as H., but is based on a different, musical, metaphor.)

H. avoids the Roman counterpart of λόγος ἐνδιάθετος, restricting himself to *intus* (108). But what is 'inside' is emotion, *animi motus* (111), and it becomes clear only at 111 that philosophers might have recognized this as λόγος προφορικός. His own concern is to link appropriateness of emotional styles with real emotion—a doctrine of poetic sincerity, a rarish thing in ancient literary criticism. Hence he relates emotion to language. That is what he requires for his purpose. As in an earlier passage where a metaphysic of nature was involved

Commentary

(above 12–13), he seems to have been careful to blunt philosophic doctrine and sharpen his poetic point.

108–9 Nature as a craftsman is familiar from the Attic and Hellenistic philosophers; cf. F. Solmsen, 'Nature as craftsman in Greek thought', *Jour. of the Hist. of Ideas*, XXIV (1953), 473–96. To 'fashion' in particular is one of the key terms in these contexts. Here Nature is said so to fashion or arrange the human mind that it responds to the external stimulus of human conditions and then, through language, expresses that emotion. Poetry thus expressing emotion will adequately represent the human conditions that have engendered the emotion. The style of such poetry will be appropriate and convincing. H. says of mankind (*nos*) what Aristotle said of one of two kinds of competent dramatists; the εὐφυής is 'impressionable', εὔπλαστος, whereas the μανικός succeeds because he is 'ecstatic', *Poet.* 17, 1455 a 33. The rhetoricians offered the ideal of the εὐφαντασίωτος, Quint. *I.O.* VI. 2. 30.

108 *format...natura...nos: format* perhaps corresponds to Greek πλάττει or διατίθησι. Cf., in admittedly very different contexts, Ar. *Gen. An.* I. 22, 730 b 29 ff. ἔοικε τοῖς πλάττουσιν, οὐ τοῖς τεκταινομένοις (ἡ φύσις)· οὐ γὰρ δι' ἑτέρου θιγγάνουσα δημιουργεῖ τὸ συνιστάμενον, ἀλλ' αὐτὴ τοῖς αὑτῆς μορίοις, *SVF*, II. 329. 33 αὕτη (ἡ φύσις) τὰ σώματα τῶν ζῴων καὶ τῶν φυτῶν συνίστησι...καὶ τεχνικῶς ἅπαντα διαπλάττει κτλ. For other instances, see Solmsen's paper cited in the last note.

prius, for emotion precedes, speech follows, *post* (111).

intus perhaps recalls (λόγος) ἐνδιάθετος.

109–10 *ad omnem | fortunarum habitum* 'with regard to every condition that may befall', 'every case of good or ill luck', whereas below, 112, *fortunis* includes this nuance as well as such 'human conditions' as age, sex, etc. of 114 ff., cf. W. Kroll, *loc. cit.* (above 108–11 n.). *fortunae* not infrequently in pl. to stress the variety of happenings, *TLL*, VI. 1. 1176. 71 ff. *habitus* = external condition, cf. *Cons. ad Liv.* 57 *si non habitu sic se gessisset in omni. habitus* with *fortuna* stresses the kind of happening which H., intent on *omnem*, is wanting to stress. For this locution cf. Liv. IX. 18. 2 *ex habitu nouae fortunae nouique... ingenii quod sibi uictor induerat*, Val. Max. V. 1. 9 *in pristinum fortunae habitum restituit*, Curt. III. 12. 14 *pro habitu praesentis fortunae.* The combination of pl. *fortunae* with *habitus* seems to be unique; at any rate *TLL*, VI. 3. 2485. 35 ff. offers no parallel.

iuuat–110 angit take up the emotions from 105–7.

110 *deducit et angit,* a rhyming doublet as *Ep.* I. 7. 20 *spernit et odit,* II. 1. 22 *fastidit et odit.*

111 *effert* recalls (λόγος) προφορικός.

interprete lingua, a Lucretian phrase from a very different context, VI. 1149 *animi interpres...lingua.* Cic. *Leg.* I. 30 *interpres mentis oratio* expresses another notion.

112–13: superficially a 'gliding transition'. In fact, as K.–H. observe, 112 generalizes and sums up the lively incursion into emotive language. Once again it is only at the end of a context that its scope becomes fully apparent. At the same time the summing up is used as a transition to the next topic; H.'s postulate relates to ethos as well as to emotion.

112 *fortunis* fulfils the same function: both the style of πάθος up to (114) and ἦθος (114 ff.) are subject to the same law of appropriateness; *fortunis* can refer to either (above 10 n.). It is not therefore, as Heinze thinks, identical with *fortunarum,* 109.

absona recalls 104 *male...mandata,* and negates 106 *decent.*

113 Here, as at 154, Roman audiences in the theatre are represented as a source of poetic instruction. At 321 they are credited with partial insight. Elsewhere their insufficiency is noted; *S.* I. 10. 76 and *Ep.* II. 1. 185 contrast the *equites,* men of taste, with the *indocti.* Altogether, then, *interdum uulgus rectum uidet, est ubi peccet* (*Ep.* II. 1. 63); references to audiences and readers differ in accordance with the differing purposes of a poem or passage. In this verse the knights jocularly (as at Plaut. *Poen.* 832) give a lead to the 'infantry', *pedites,* and the archaic formula *equites peditesque* is used (Cic. *Leg.* III. 7 *censores...equitum peditumque prolem discribunto,* Liv. I. 44. 1, etc.; *TLL,* v. 2. 710. 73 ff.). It is remarkable that Bentley emending to *patresque,* and Peerlkamp commending the emendation, should have missed the point.

(iii) *Style and human types,* 114–18. Aristotle's third criterion for appropriate style in *Rhet.* III. 7, 1408 a 25 ff. is what he calls *ethos.* The words for appropriateness here are ἁρμόττουσα and οἰκεῖα (1408 a 26, 31) and the desired language is called ἠθική. Ethos in this chapter denotes a type of person either in γένος—physiological differences according to age, sex, country of provenance—or in ἕξις—disposition according to station in life such as rustic and cultured; cf. *Prol.* 99. These distinctions fit the conditions of the law courts better than those of the stage but they have some relation to ancient literature. Aristotle's discussion of character in *Poet.* ch. 15 shows that they could be applied to the stage, although he there insists that goodness of character, τὸ χρηστόν, should be the foremost of four considerations; the other three—ἁρμόττον, ὅμοιον and ὁμαλόν—impinge in various ways on the ἁρμόττον of the Rhetoric. The tradition behind the treatment of 'character' in the *Ars* again shows combined what in Aristotle is separated according to 'rhetorical' and 'poetic'.

Discussion from the Hellenistic age onward was chiefly determined by the rhetorical criterion of appropriateness, which was rarely questioned (e.g. Philod. *Poem.* v. 31. 35 ff.), although writers on literature and rhetoric respectively had their own axes to grind. Both the likeness and unlikeness of viewpoint may be seen in the ancient sources often adduced in this context and extensively cited by K.–H. and Rostagni. In the pseudo-Dionysian *Art of Rhetoric*, compiled perhaps in the first century A.D., seven 'special and rhetorical characteristics' are distinguished: country, district, family relationship, age, temper, status, and occupation (Dion. Hal. *Op. Rhet.* II. 1, 377. 16 ff. edd. Usener and Radermacher, cf. Theon, *Progym.* 10, *Rhet. Gr.* II, pp. 115 f. ed. Spengel). On the other hand Plutarch's comparison of Aristophanes and Menander, though employing appropriateness as a criterion, tones down classification. Attention is paid to types as a tool of criticism; Aristophanes is said to lack Menander's gift for discrimination between 'son, father, rustic, god, old woman, *heros*' (853 d). It is a reasonable conclusion of K. Ziegler (*Tragoedia, R-E,* VI A. 1974–5) and others that this interest in typology of character goes back to the Hellenistic age, and reflects conditions of dramatic production. This is clearly so in the case of New Comedy. Too little is known of Hellenistic and Roman tragedy to commend K. Latte's view (*H,* LX (1925), 3 n.) that the typology does not apply to Greek (Hellenistic) tragedy, and indeed that H. had misrepresented his Greek 'source'. The demand is that the farmer (e.g. in Euripides' *Electra*) should be what he is, but that, say, the 'merchant' (e.g. in Sophocles' *Philoctetes*) might be more 'true to type'. Again Latte argues that Greek tragedy does not pay attention to differences of country or district, and is therefore upset by verse 118, emphasizing distinctions between Colchian and Assyrian, or Theban and Argive, cf. his remarks *op. cit.* p. 3 n. 1. But all H. is doing is to extend rhetorical προσωποποιΐα to the 'characters' of drama, cf. ps.-Acro cited below 118 n. These demands differ from Ar. *Poet.* 6, 1450 a 20 ff., as I noted *Prol.* 111.

H. shares the interest in character. His interest is more marked than Aristotle's in the *Poetics*, where ethos comes second in importance to plot. This passage is the first in the *Ars* of a number dealing with this topic; they are so spaced in the poem as to create one of its recurring motifs or patterns, cf. *Prol.* 110 ff., 139 ff., 250 ff. Even at this early stage it is seen that the poem has several such patterns. H. cuts through the dreary classification of the textbooks, and of the textbook which probably he himself had used. On the other hand he eschews the casualness of Plutarch's list of types. The poet forms a series of sharply focused instances, each a pair of contrasted types. The predominance in this passage of general, and the lack of individual, features must be remembered in constituting the text, cf. 114 n.

114 *diuus* (-*os*) is the transmitted reading of all early MSS. *Dauus* (*da(u)us, dauos*) is known from cod. K¹ (and Vat. Lat. 3866), eleventh century; it appears as a correction in the second or third hands of some MSS, is in an interpolated Servius scholium (*Aen.* XII. 18), and was frequently sponsored in the Italian Renaissance. Some critics have thought that the distinction between *diuus* and *heros* is not so great as those that are mentioned in the sequel. Orelli however explains, I think correctly, the Horatian distinction between *diuus* and *heros*; the Olympian gods have *tranquillitas*, but not the tragic heroes *quippe qui . . . uel aestuant uel mortalium aegrimoniis malis conflictantur*. *Dauus* can boast Meineke's support but is no longer found in recent editions, with the exception of Klingner's, who professes himself persuaded by Miss H. Kornhardt, *P*, xciii (1938), 476–82. This is a good paper but it fails in its main contention—to establish *Dauus an heros* as here representing comedy and tragedy. The instances cited by her (*S*. i. 10. 40, ii. 5. 91, *A.P.* 94–6, 237) differ in scope, and spoil her just observation that in this passage H. is discussing types, not individuals. Five times over he employs generic words to describe *genera hominum*. Why prevent him from completing the sextet by placing at the very outset a proper name, however typified? 'Gods and heroes' in poetry were thought to require an 'appropriate diction' of their own; so much follows from Philodemus' polemic against this doctrine, *Poem*. v. 32. 11. If Plutarch can mention θεός and later ἥρως among his types (above 114–18 n.), he clearly could, or thought he could, perceive a difference in style between *diuus* and *heros*. Why then not H.? Earlier emendations, *diuusne...an Irus, Dauusne... herosne, Dauusne...Erosne*, are open to the same charge. Most of H.'s instances seem to be deliberately chosen to fit both types of drama. No specific drama is in view; the reference to Menander's *Heros* which was alleged for some time will not convince, even if *Dauus* is read, cf. A. Hallström, *Eranos*, x (1910), 155, A. Körte, *RM*, lxvii (1912), 478, N. Terzaghi, *Athenaeum*, 1 (1913), 170.

115 ff.: an *ethologia*, as below in a more sustained form, 156–78.

115 *maturus*, like *C*. iv. 4. 55 *maturosque patres*, sets the tone of the metaphor continued in *florente iuuenta feruidus*, cf. 62 *iuuenum ritu modo nata uigentque*, Lucr. v. 888–9 *aeuo florente iuuentas | occipit*; Prud. *Perist.* v. 47 *iuuentae feruidae* probably derives from H.

115–16 *florente iuuenta | feruidus:* the epithets are traditional. For a poet as economic in technique as H. to combine two metaphorical notions produces a touch of colour and imagery that contrasts with the simple *maturus*. The epithets are latent imagery, a kind of poetic shorthand. The imagery may be spelt out fully in a whole poem, such as the Soracte Ode, *C*. i. 9; for a discussion in these terms see S. Commager, *The Odes of Horace* (1962), pp. 270 ff.

116 *matrona potens:* sarcastically repeated by Juv. i. 61.

117 *sedula nutrix:* cf. Ov. *Met*. x. 438 *male s. n.*, et al. The stock contrast travelling merchant vs. farmer, as at *C*. i. 1. 11–18. For the allusion see above, 114–18 n.; for the wording Ov. *Fast*. v. 499 *angusti cultor agelli*.

uirentis, not *uigentis* (uar.l.), *agelli*. Although Cic. *Fin*. v. 39 says *dicimus arboremque et nouellam et uetulam et uigere et senescere*, the traditional epithet describing the flourishing nature of plants, fields and the like is *uirens*; e.g. *C*. ii. 5. 5–6 *circa uirentes... | campos*, Virg. *E*.

7. 59 *nemus*, G. III. 146–7 *ilicibusque uirentem* | ...*Alburnum*, A. VI. 679 *conualle uirenti*, Val. Fl. II. 598–9 *uirentibus*...*tumulis*, Sil. X. 560–1 *uirenti stramine*, Aus. *Mos.* 416 *rura uirentia*.

118 Cf. ps.-Acro *nam Colchus non nisi saeuus inducendus est, Assyrius astutus, callidus. ne inducas Argis natum timidum aut Thebis facias [im]peritum*. Since the pairs are antithetic the contrast in the former will be *ferox* and *mollis*. *Assyrius* is often used in wider connotations in Latin verse, either for Syrian, as Cat. 66. 12 *uastatum fines iuerat Assyrios*, Virg. *E.* 4. 25 *amomum*, Hor. *C.* II. 11. 16 *nardo*, or Parthian, as Lucan VIII. 92 *Assyrios*...*casus*, or 'oriental', as Virg. *G.* II. 465 *Assyrio fucatur lana ueneno* (Phoenician purple). A wide connotation must be in mind here.

(III. Subject-matter and character in poetry, exemplified by drama and epic, 119–52)

The tradition. The presence of a new traditional topic and its identification is dryly reported by the scholiast Porphyrion (on 119) *hoc aliud praeceptum est. nam poeta scripturus aut secundum consensum debet aliquid describere aut, si historiam tamquam tritam non uult attingere, debet conuenienter noua inducere.*

I have analysed this difficult section in *Prol.* 7–9, 100–10, 246. The first clearing of the ground had been done by J. Vahlen, *Ges. Phil. Schr.* II, 757 ff., an analytical operation of considerable deftness, which modern scholars ignore at their peril, e.g. G. Williams, *JRS*, LIV (1964), 194, arguing that H. did not wish a break to be noticed here. I too had argued that this is true in a sense; precisely in what sense remains to be seen after it has been established what the features of H.'s traditional material were. A procedure that fails to distinguish between these two questions is open to the major logical incoherence which has marred Horatian studies for more than half a century, and which my *Prolegomena* were written to combat.

H.'s traditional material is here concerned with the 'subject-matter of poetry'; it is no longer concerned with diction and style. That alone shows the presence of a different topic. The same change is shown by another feature: Aristotle's *Rhetoric*, which so far, all the way from 73, has accompanied the reader, suddenly fails us, and is replaced, though less extensively, by the *Poetics*, particularly parts of chs. 9, 14 and 17. Of the six 'elements' constituting tragedy which Aristotle set out in *Poet.* ch. 6, we are now dealing with the 'story' or 'plot', μῦθος. But again it is Aristotle with a difference, for what we read in the *Ars* is an account of the subject-matter of *poetry*, not *tragedy*; genres are adduced for exemplification, and epic is adduced no less than tragedy.

Other important differences from Aristotle need to be noted and I will attempt to specify them in my notes. The most striking is the replacement of μῦθος *per se* by a discussion of μῦθος through the medium of characters, *personae*. This I presume was a feature of H.'s Hellenistic material which the poet has seen fit to preserve—a marked increase in 'ethos', which has already been noted in the preceding section.

Horace. The poet shapes this material in his own manner. He administers a shock to the reader who has happily settled down to viewing diverse human types in the context of style from 114 onward. Some readers are shockproof; those who are not are suddenly faced with the subjects, no longer the styles, of poetic speech. But for all that, they are let down gently; for although the context has changed, talk is still about people—only this time the characters are individuals, not types: the *personae* appearing in poetry. By combining what has been called an 'abrupt' and a 'gliding transition' H. makes the willing reader see something which is new but also something which is already familiar; talk of content is new whereas talk of characters is already familiar. The former is the sense which I attach to the proposition that there is a break here; the latter is the sense which I attach to the opposite proposition, that there is no break here. At the same time H. remains concrete, individual, and finds his way to the more remote abstractions of 128 ff. after he has already established them in a more familiar idiom.

For the stages of the way I refer the reader to my notes below and to my discussion in *Prol.* 103 ff.; J. H. Waszink's clarifying remarks (in *Mnem.* Ser. IV, XXI (1968), 402–7) may be compared. Briefly, 119 distinguishes traditional and 'invented' subjects, the former pursued 120–4, the latter 125–7 with an especial injunction, in that case, to safeguard consistency, or unity, of treatment. Now, 128–30, the two types of subject are confronted, and 'invented' subjects are described as generalities (128 *communia*) to which individual features must be given (*proprie dicere*), just as three verses above 'untried subject' and 'new character' were interchangeable terms. This forming of a new character H. describes as hard and it is that difficulty which moves him to give preference to traditional subjects, where the characters are already formed. I have suggested and suggest again that before an elucidation of the crucial verse 128 is attempted, this verse must be seen as part of the whole section. The opposite way starts with an elucidation of 128, and attempts to make the rest of the section conform. This has been proposed (not for the first time, as he thought) by one of the reviewers of my *Prolegomena*; the outcome is, I believe, that the coherence of the whole section is put in jeopardy; see below 128 n.

H.'s preference for traditional subjects has been described as a failure of creative imagination. This is a large subject, beyond the scope of this commentary. It is however relevant to note that it may be described in a different way, H.'s way. For what follows, it seems to me, is a piece of Horatian irony to which attention needs to be drawn. Once again the poet has a surprise in store for the reader, who has just been told that it is easier to dramatize a song of Ilium than to venture on new subjects. Now he is told how to make traditional subjects his own. At 131 ff. we learn that to do so the poet must avoid four faults: (*a*) a pedestrian and unselective account, 132; (*b*) a faithful rendering of the words of an original, 133; (*c*) an anxious reproduction of the whole of an original, 134 f.; (*d*) a larger initial promise than he can fulfil in the course of his work—the demand for unity, already known from the first part of the *Ars*; here, in terms of dispraise, reference to a 'cyclic epic' is made, 136–9. After so many paths blocked, what remains? Homer's poetic procedure, 140 ff., in which the problems of traditional and new subjects, of poetic multiplicity and unity are solved. One wonders how much conviction this private ownership of the *publica materies* carried for the Pisos, or those whom he addresses in the generic singular as 'writers' (120). Perhaps, even forgetting the Matine Bee, one may recall Iullus Antonius and Pindar (*C.* IV. 2).

There are then three different motifs or patterns of thought in this section which H. is able to pursue at the same time. In musical language, the main subject is new, and pursued all the way from 119 onward: *fama* and *fingere*. But there is a descant known from the previous section: that is 'character'. This motif reappears at 120, immediately after the new subject has been established, and when the motif reappears it is seen to fit that subject. Finally there is the motif of 'unity', which played a dominant part in the initial section, but is now restricted to two strongly marked codas, 127 and 152, which are thus related to each other and to the first part of the *Ars*.

(1) Traditional and new subjects (characters) in poetry, 119–30

The new section opens with a command, in the brief style which the poet enjoins for precepts (335 n.), *aut. . .sequere aut . . .finge*. For the address, *scriptor*, see 120 n. H. contrasts the subjects of the mythical tradition often described as 'true' and not distinguished from history in Hellenistic and Roman theorizing, here called *fama*, and subjects 'made up', 'formed', by the writer, here called 'fiction' (*finge*). This is more clear-cut than the familiar Roman and Hellenistic triad, *historia* (= *fama*)–*uerisimile–fictum* (*falsum, fabula*), or in Greek ἱστορία–πλάσμα–μῦθος, which itself replaced Aristotle's speculative antithesis of οἷα ἂν γένοιτο (κατὰ τὸ εἰκὸς ἢ ἀναγκαῖον) and τὰ γενόμενα, *Poet.* ch. 9. The comparison was made by Rostagni; cf. his introd. pp. xlvii, lxvi f., F. W. Walbank, *Historia*, ix (1960), 216 ff., and my paper *Proc. Camb. Phil. Soc.* n.s. v (1960), 14 ff. Aristotle had encouraged the use of new subjects, *Poet.* 9, 1451 b 23 ff.; later in the same work he repeated this encouragement but forbade manipulation with the kernel of a received myth, e.g. the murder of Clytemnestra by Orestes should remain unchanged but the details are open to change, *ibid.* 14, 1453 b 22 ff. τοὺς μὲν οὖν παρειλημμένους μύθους λύειν οὐκ ἔστιν, λέγω δὲ οἷον τὴν Κλυταιμήστραν ἀποθανοῦσαν ὑπὸ τοῦ Ὀρέστου..., αὐτὸν δὲ (i.e. the poet) εὑρίσκειν δεῖ καὶ τοῖς παραδεδομένοις χρῆσθαι καλῶς (cf. *Prol.* 104 f. n. 3).

119 *famam sequere:* 'tradition', that is the 'mythical record', not rumour as opposed to historical fact, Aristotle's παρειλημμένοι or παραδεδομένοι μῦθοι, Lucr. v. 328–9 *facta uirum...* | *...aeternis famae monumentis insita.* It is surprising that, because of *sequi, TLL,* vi. 1. 210. 18, while noting the difference of meaning in the previous column, should bracket Lampr. *Alex.* 48. 8 with H.; yet Lampridius conveys precisely the opposite, *uulgi magis famam...quam historiam, quae rumore utique uulgi uerior reperitur.*

sibi conuenientia: consistency, or appropriateness to each other, either of successive incidents of a story or manifestations of a character, as 316 *reddere personae scit conuenientia cuique.* If the former, it recalls Aristotle's τὸ εἰκὸς ἢ τὸ ἀναγκαῖον (*Poet.* ch. 9) and τὰ μέρη συνεστάναι τῶν πραγμάτων οὕτως ὥστε μετατιθεμένου τινὸς μέρους ἢ ἀφαιρουμένου διαφέρεσθαι καὶ κινεῖσθαι τὸ ὅλον (*ibid.* 8, 1451 a 32). If the latter, it recalls his ὁμαλόν (*ibid.* 15, 1454 a 26 ff.). Aristotle demands consistency in both: χρὴ δὲ καὶ ἐν τοῖς ἤθεσιν ὁμοίως ὥσπερ καὶ ἐν τῇ τῶν πραγμάτων συστάσει ἀεὶ ζητεῖν ἢ τὸ ἀναγκαῖον ἢ τὸ εἰκὸς κτλ. (*ibid.* a 33). So does H. But it marks the difference between the two positions that H. formulates this demand from the viewpoint of character as the next few verses will show, Aristotle all the way to ch. 15 from the viewpoint of plot-construction.

finge: Aristotle's εὑρίσκειν, the πλάττειν–πλάσμα of Hellenistic and subsequent literary theory. H.'s pair cuts across the triad of the theorists. *sibi conuenientia* takes account of *uerisimile.*

120 The new context is emphasized by the address to all would-be poets (the Pisos of course included), which then seems to carry the subsequent series of injunctions; the Pisos are not here the only addressees. Cf. Vahlen, *Ges. Phil. Schr.* II. 761.

scriptor: of poets, cf. 38 n. That verse also parallels the style of injunction, *sumite materiam . . ., qui scribitis*, etc. For enjambement and final position of voc., though in more extended form, see 103–4 *tum . . . laedent,* | *Telephe uel Peleu.* This position seems to me much superior to the alternative punctuations, either full stop at end of 119, attaching *scriptor* as nom. to the following sentence (much favoured in the last century by competent editors, sometimes with the false argument that *scriptor* is required to define *reponis*), or without punctuation attaching *scriptor* as nom. to the two verbs in 119 (K.–H., Klingner, and Villeneuve, translating, 'suivez en écrivant').

† *honoratum* †: an unsolved problem. Early commentators used to identify the word with a Homeric epithet, τιμήεις or the like— nonsensically since the τιμή denoted by *honoratus* was what the Homeric Achilles did not receive, and the next two verses show that this is the situation in H.'s mind. For the same reason this clear indication cannot be evaded by Lambinus' argument (in an otherwise admirable note, later elaborated in F. Ritter's commentary) that it is the will of Zeus thus described (Hom. *Il.* I. 506 ff., II. 4, etc.); or indeed that *honoratus* renders a traditional epithet like φαίδιμος. It was then proposed by J. W. L. Jeep (in E. T. A. Krüger's commentary, 15th ed. 1908), and accepted in *TLL*, VI. 3. 2948. 64 ff., that *honoratus = fama celebratus*, which indeed would meet the objection. Yet the one instance cited in corroboration fails to convince, for Cic. *Div.* I. 88 *Amphiaraum . . . sic honorauit fama Graeciae, deus ut haberetur*, so combines *fama* with *honorauit* that there can be no doubt as to its meaning; and besides *fama* lacks the connotation required in the *Ars*. Bentley emended *honoratum* to *Homereum* (cf. Sen. *Tranq. An.* 2. 12 *Homericus Achilles*). But quite apart from its unlikely form—avoided in the alternative proposal *Homeriacum*—this is against the scope of the passage; for *fama*, not Homer, is in question and Homer is later said to take his own line with regard to the *fama* of the Trojan War, below 131 ff. Nor will Peerlkamp's *cothornatum* convince; *fama*, not the stage, is H.'s point of orientation. J. S. Reid's *inoratus* (in Wilkins' note) is excluded because of *inexorabilis* in the next verse. This seems to leave two avenues to explore; one to lead to a word meaning *notus* taking up *fama*, the other to lead to a word negating *honoratus* literally understood, that is 'lacking in honour', not something like *honore actum* (A. Y. Campbell, *Hor. Carm.*[1] (1945), 'Horatiana Alia' *in calce libri*. J. P. Postgate's *honore orbum* (*CQ*, IV (1910), 108 ff.) may be right in sense though scarcely in wording.

Commentary

reponis: according to Porph. of repeated theatrical performances. A reference to the theatre is likely in a passage midway between the mention of spectators at 113, and 125 *siquid inexpertum scaenae committis,* 129 *Iliacum carmen deducis in actus.* Although *re* = 'again' is not obligatory in Latin and particularly Horatian usage, the contrast with 125 (just cited) favours the notion *re* = *post alios,* and so Immisch, p. 100, has proposed. At 190 *fabula quae posci uult et...reponi,* the context denotes repeated performance but the wording is doubtful.

Achillem: the large number of post-Aeschylean tragedies on the subject of Achilles rules out any identification with a specific play; for Roman versions see H. D. Jocelyn, *The Tragedies of Ennius,* pp. 161 f. For the endings *-em* and *-en,* over which here as elsewhere the MSS divide, see Housman, *JP,* xxxi (1910), 260; cod. R² and the best Virgilian MSS offer *-em.*

121–2 Aristotle had remarked that Achilles' ethos was inconsistent, unstable: fr. 168 (Rose) Ἀριστοτέλης φησὶν ἀνώμαλον εἶναι τὸ Ἀχιλλέως ἦθος. This is not the point made here, as G. F. Else has noted (*Ar. Poet.: The Argument,* p. 463 n. 30). H. may say *fama* but he has in view only one aspect of the *fama* of Achilles, the hero and his unyieldingness: Hom. *Il.* ix. 255–6, 385 ff., xx. 467, xxiv. 39 ff. Cf. *Epod.* 17. 14 *peruicacis...Achillei, C.* i. 6. 6 *Pelidae...cedere nescii.* His irascibility and ungovernable temper are a commonplace in Greek and Roman moralizing; e.g. (omitting Ar. *Poet.* 15, 1454 b 14 παράδειγμα σκληρότητος because the text is dubious) Plat. *Rep.* iii. 391 c ὑπερηφανίαν θεῶν τε καὶ ἀνθρώπων, Plut. *Quom. adul. poet.* 19 c καλὸν γὰρ εἰκὸς οὐδὲν εἶναι μετ' ὀργῆς καὶ αὐστηρῶς λεγόμενον κτλ., Cic. *T.D.* iii. 18 *itaque non inscite Heracleotes Dionysius ad ea disputat quae apud Homerum Achilles queritur...'corque meum penitus turgescit tristibus iris...'* (19) *...sic igitur inflatus et tumens animus in uitio est,* iv. 52, Sen. *Ep.* 104. 31. But Plutarch also says about Achilles, *Quom. adul. poet.* 31 b–c τὸ γὰρ ἐπισφαλῶς πρὸς ὀργὴν ἔχοντα καὶ φύσει τραχὺν ὄντα καὶ θυμοειδῆ μὴ λανθάνειν ἑαυτόν...θαυμαστῆς ἐστιν προνοίας.

121 A series of graphic adjectives or nouns juxtaposed without connective particles. This is a frequent and effective procedure in an *ethologia,* e.g. below 163–5, 172–3, *Ep.* i. 1. 38. The two long words *iracundus, inexorabilis* set the tone, the second leaving the verse without the common fourth-foot break after weak middle caesura.

impiger: Achilles the fighter, as Hom. *Il.* 1. 165–6, ἀλλὰ τὸ μὲν πλεῖον πολυάϊκος πολέμοιο | χεῖρες ἐμαὶ διέπουσι.

Some earlier commentators supplied *sit* at the end of this verse.

Commentary

It seems more likely that the adjectives qualify the two clauses in 122.

122 K. Latte remarks (*H*, LX (1925), 3), that this sounds like a verse from a tragedy adapted by H.

iura...nata: cf. Hom. *Il.* I. 295 f. ἄλλοισιν...ἐπιτέλλεο, μὴ γὰρ ἔμοιγε | σήμαιν᾽· οὐ γὰρ ἔγωγ᾽ ἔτι σοὶ πείσεσθαι ὀίω, et al. *nata*, not *lata* as at *Ep.* II. I. 153 *lex...poenaque lata*, where *nata* is an (erroneous) variant, but 'come into being, exist'; thus of inanimate objects, *S.* II. 3. 8 *iratis natus paries dis atque poetis*, *C.* I. 27. 1 *scyphis*; of verses *Ep.* II. I. 233 *incultis...uersibus et male natis*; with a double entendre, *C.* III. 21. I *o nata mecum consule Manlio* (*pia testa*); also the tag *pro* (*ex*) *re nata*. The usage is not restricted to verse.

arroget armis: with the dat. of the matter to which something is assigned, as *Ep.* II. I. 35 *chartis pretium quotus arroget annus*, *C.* IV. 14. 40; thus in poetry and later prose, first on record in H.; *TLL*, II. 652. 25 ff.

123 ff. Cf. Quint. *I.O.* XI. 3. 73 *ut sit Aerope in tragoedia tristis, atrox Medea, attonitus Aiax, truculentus Hercules*. Quintilian's list differs from H.'s except for Medea. The names are chosen to remind readers of tragic personages that are well known, not of specific titles. As in the case of Achilles, emotions contradicting one chosen aspect of a 'traditional' character are deplored. K. Latte, *H*, LX (1925), is too ready to identify these examples with extant Greek plays or known titles, frequently Euripidean.

123 *Medea ferox:* so Avien. *Orb.* 1216, Claud. 3. 153, *atrox* in Quint. (last n.). Commentators report an Alexandrian verdict on the tears of the Euripidean Medea (922, 1005 ff.): these were out of keeping with her character, *Argum. Med.* μέμφονται δ᾽ αὐτῷ τὸ μὴ πεφυλαχέναι τὴν ὑπόκρισιν τῇ Μηδείᾳ ἀλλὰ προπεσεῖν εἰς δάκρυα κτλ., cf. *Schol. Med.* 922. Too little is known of the Medea plays of Ennius and Accius to judge the relevance of this criticism with regard to Roman dramatic conventions. Ovid's *Heroides* 12 offers a different Medea; but the road from that poem to his *Medea* drama may be less straight than is sometimes assumed. Certainly Seneca's *Medea*, like his other heroines, has her ethos more rigidly set than her Greek counterpart.

inuictaque beside *ferox* hardly without a critical nuance: 'unyielding'; as address to Achilles, *Epod.* 13. 12, humorously combined with *durus*, *S.* I. 7. 29. The conventional usage is religious, an epithet applied to gods and heroes (*TLL*, VII. 2. 187. 11 ff.), the Roman people, an *imperator*, but not formally accepted by emperors until Commodus (*ibid.* 186. 46).

flebilis Ino is contrasted with Medea. Ino's sufferings were proverbial, Ἰνοῦς ἄχη, *CPG*, I. 94–5, II. 463 (6*a*). Although *Schol.* Aristoph.

Vesp. 1413 (εἰσήγαγε δ᾽ Εὐριπίδης τὴν ᾽Ινῶ ὠχρὰν ὑπὸ τῆς κακοπα-θείας) fits H.'s description, the number of dramatizations, Greek and Roman, of the legend of Ino, Athamas, or Phrixos, is considerable, cf. Eitrem, *R-E*, XII. 2297–8, s.v. *Leukothea. flebilis = lacrimosa*, a frequent poetic usage, in prose from Apuleius; *TLL*, VI. 1. 890. 49 ff.

124 *perfidus Ixion:* explained by Porph. as a reference to Ixion's murder of his father-in-law. The type of legend associated with Ixion is called παθητική by Ar. *Poet.* 18, 1456 a 1; for Euripides' version of the legend see Plut. *Quom. adul. poet.* ch. 4; the versions of Aeschylus, Sophocles and later, but not apparently Roman, dramatists are briefly discussed by Waser, *R-E*, X. 1374 ff. Latte's denial of later adaptations (*H*, LX (1925)) is erroneous.

Io uaga (thus also Val. Fl. VII. 111). Dramatizations, apart from the well-known appearances (here hardly relevant) in Aesch. *Supp.* and *Prom.*, are attested for the fourth-century tragedian Chaeremon (Nauck², p. 784) and in Rome for Accius (Ribbeck², frs. 386 ff.). The wanderings of Io also formed the subject of poems in the Hellenistic-neoteric manner, Callimachus and Calvus.

tristis Orestes: Latte, *H*, LX (1925), would like to identify the play with Euripides' *Orestes*; at any rate, he thinks, it suits Euripides better than it does the *Choephoroe*, let alone Soph. *Elec.* Perhaps so; yet uncertainty persists, not only because of the large number of competitors but because, as Rostagni points out, Orestes' *tristitia* in Euripides was apparently found wanting by Hellenistic critics; Aristophanes of Byzantium (*Argum. Orest.*) objected to its 'untragic' ending: τὸ δρᾶμα κωμικωτέραν ἔχει τὴν καταστροφήν, cf. *ibid.* τὸ δρᾶμα τῶν ἐπὶ σκηνῆς εὐδοκιμούντων, χείριστον δὲ τοῖς ἤθεσιν· πλὴν γὰρ Πυλάδου πάντες φαῦλοι ἦσαν. *S.* II. 3. 132 ff. and Virg. *A.* IV. 471 ff., often cited, are not concerned with Orestes' *tristitia* but with his madness; but see Ov. *Tr.* V. 22 *tristis Oresta*.

125 *si quid* here has an adversative function, taking up 120 *si forte* and corresponding to the second *aut* clause, 119. In H.'s style logical particles are reduced to a minimum, the coherence being in the form of sentence and thought. The prosaic *sin* does not occur in H. at all; two *si* clauses are related similarly, for example, 47 *si*–48 *si forte*, 102 *si*–104 *si*.

inexpertum may be active, *quod non expertum est scaenam*, so K.–H.; or passive, 'untried', as Virg. *A.* IV. 415 *ne quid inexpertum. . .relinquat*. At the only other place where H. employs the word it happens to be active: *Ep.* I. 18. 86–7 *dulcis inexpertis cultura potentis amici:* | *expertus metuet.* Here however, as Rostagni has argued, the passive sense in *si quid*

Commentary

inexpertum scaenae committis better fits the parallel *famam sequere . . conuenientia finge,* 119.

126 defines a new subject by a new *dramatis persona;* so the instances 120 ff. have already indicated. *formare* like 119 *finge* expresses the creation of new 'parts' or characters. The Hellenistic affiliation is seen in *Schol. A* on Hom. *Il.* xx. 40, ὡς παραδεδομένοις δηλονότι χρώμενος καὶ οὐκ αὐτὸς πλάσσων τὰ ὀνόματα. The comparison was made by R. Heinze, *Virg. Ep. Technik*[3], 376 n. 2; for other links with Homeric scholia see above 43 n., and below 148 n. Aristotle uses πεποιημένα (ὀνόματα) with regard to characters (opp. γενόμενα or γνώριμα), or εὑρίσκειν with regard to μῦθοι (*Poet.* 14, 1453 b 25). The process of creation is there described as the construction of a plot in which happenings or actions are related by logical probability or necessity; the individual features of characters are subsequently added—freely so in comedy, less freely for the most part in tragedy. This job of individualizing is described as 'the subjoining of names', ὀνόματα (*ibid.* 9, 1451 b 10, 13, 15, 20, 22; 17, 1455 b 12–13). Although the more usual Hellenistic nomenclature seems to be the word for mask or part, πρόσωπον, Lat. *persona,* i.e. τὰ τοῦ δράματος πρόσωπα, the Homeric scholium, cited above, and others show ὀνόματα persisting. Ciceronian instances of *persona* abound, but the verbs employed point to the difference of metaphor—not *formare* but *capere, suscipere, gerere, imponere, tenere,* and the like.

persona = *dramatis persona* as at 192, 316, but 'mask' at 278.

seruetur = *conseruetur,* contrast *seruare* 86 n.

ad imum used as noun = *ad finem* as *Ad Her.* III. 18. 30 *utrum ab summo an ab imo an a medio . . .incipiamus,* and the tag of the rhetoricians *a summo ad imum, TLL,* VII. 1. 1403. 22. The locution here expresses the (Aristotelian) coherence of character. It looks back to the poetic unity of 1 ff., 8–9 *uni . . .formae,* 23 *simplex . . .et unum,* and looks forward to 152 *medio ne discrepet imum.*

127 *ab incepto:* cf. 14 *inceptis grauibus,* 152 *primo.*

processerit: here not of 'advancement' but, since *ab incepto* and *ad imum* precede, of progress in time, the metaphor underlying *aetate procedere.* But the word also = 'come forth, come out of a house' and hence is used for the appearance of actors on the stage, e.g. Pl. *Amph.* 117 *ego huc processi* (*prae-* codd. Non.) *sic cum seruili schema, As.* 6–7 *quid processerim huc . . . | dicam.* The two notions combined, 'progress on the stage', 'in the play', would suit the passage well.

sibi constet: consistency of character, *Ep.* I. 14. 16 *me constare mihi scis, TLL,* IV. 528. 66 ff.; hence the *uox propria* here, where talk is of consistency.

128 This verse has been described as one of the hardest in Latin literature. It is certainly the most frequently discussed of the *Ars* and no agreement has been reached on its meaning or function in this passage. The number and diversity of the opinions offered are too large to be accommodated in a note. I therefore offer a fuller discussion in Appendix 1 and here restrict myself to explaining the passage as I see it.

difficile est proprie communia dicere: apart from *est* each word is controversial; nor is the function of the sentence agreed. I will try therefore, first, to determine the content and function rather than the wording; *uerba sequentur.*

Having distinguished two poetic procedures, *famam sequi* and *fingere*, H. goes on first to describe the former, next the latter (120–4, 125–7). Creation of new subjects is a 'venture'; 125 *audes* is a strongly emotive word. There is a risk attached to new subjects and while a *periculum* may be *dulce* and can be faced, this can hardly be so here. For *difficile* coming soon after *audes*, and coming without any qualification to the contrary, creates a presumption that the venture is not encouraged. The presumption becomes a near-certainty when the aspiring poet is told 'rather' to dramatize *Iliacum carmen*—i.e. *famam sequi*—than create new subjects; the words *rectius...quam* seem to me to clinch the matter. We thus get an uninterrupted run from 119 to 130. I now paraphrase that passage. Either follow tradition or create new subjects. If you follow tradition do this; if you venture to create new subjects do that. (But [128]) creation of new subjects is hard and (therefore) the method of dramatizing a traditional subject is preferable to that of free creation. I conclude that any attempt, at 128, to replace the creation of new subjects by the other member of the pair—use of traditional subjects—leads to logical contortion.

Now *uerba sequuntur*. First *difficile*. Provided my paraphrase is right, 'difficult' is H.'s word; if *sed facile* (Peerlkamp) were transmitted in its place, it would have to be emended. Moreover *difficile* should have its full and weighty meaning—'hard', and therefore deprecated. 'Hard but worth trying' is unacceptable if the context determined above carries conviction.

Next *proprie communia dicere*. All I have asserted so far is the required sense, 'new subjects'. One of the ps.-Acronian scholia has the merit of offering the required general sense, although few will accept its verbal explanation. It identifies *communia dicere* with 'untouched subjects' (that is, *fingere*), saying: '*communia dicere*' idest intacta; nam quando intactum est aliquid, commune est; semel dictum ab aliquo fit proprium.

How then can *communia dicere* bear or imply the meaning 'new subjects', and what sense, if any, does *proprie* make?

The social metaphor, 'common, ordinary' as opposed to 'propriety', even if it were possible on linguistic grounds, is excluded by the context. So is the quasi-legal notion by which Isocrates contrasts the deeds, πράξεις, of the past, inherited by all as common property, κοιναί, with their timely and appropriate use in speech, which is the property, ἴδιον, of the 'wise' (*Pan.* 9). The fully legal notion distinguishes common property, *commune*, from personal, *proprium* (Heumann–Seckel, *Handlexikon . . . des röm. Rechts*; cf. *TLL*, III. 1977. 81 ff.). Such was the road signposted by one of ps.-Acro's authorities; it was therefore taken by many scholars of the Italian Renaissance, and indeed by many others later. Yet it is *fama*, not *fingere*, that by definition must be 'common property' and thus, unhappily, ps.-Acro's *communia idest intacta* will not do as a verbal explanation, if we continue to adhere to the point made earlier.

The contrast between κοινά and ἴδια appears in rhetoric also apart from the Isocratean concept. The rhetoricians expressed the 'common character' of their general arguments by κοινά, and distinguished them from ἴδια, specific ones, cf. Ar. *Rhet.* I. 1, 1355 a 27, II. 18, 1391 b 27, chs. 20 ff. As the logic of rhetorical proof developed, the application to individual data became more complicated and the experts came to work out procedures on 'how to specify general thoughts in speaking', περὶ κοινῶν διανοημάτων, πῶς αὐτὰ ἰδιώσομεν λέγοντες (Hermog. Περὶ μεθόδου δεινότητος 29, p. 445 ed. Rabe, and other passages assembled in Ribbeck's commentary (1869), pp. 219 f.). Cicero theorizes on *communes loci* and *theses* frequently, and as frequently uses *communia* and *propria* in these contexts, cf. *Inv.* II. 48 ff., *De Or.* III. 106 ff., 120, *Or.* 46, 127 et al. Quintilian too discusses the matter. It is possible that Roman readers may have felt reminded of their rhetorical exercises when they first read this passage. Yet the rest of the sentence will surely have undeceived them: a user of *communes loci* can scarcely be described as putting forward *ignota indictaque primus*. Yet H. appears to identify *communia dicere* and (*proferre*) *ignota indictaque*.

This leaves us with the words as terms in logic, introduced by Aristotle into literary theory and, I believe, employed by H. in this passage. Aristotle's reason for so introducing this term into *Poet.* ch. 9 was in fact a logical and perhaps polemic one. What he saw as the greater generality of poetic statement in comparison with historical induced him to call poetry more philosophic than history; polemic intent with regard to Plato's case against poetry may have provided a motive for this mode of reasoning. He defines καθόλου, universal or general, as the *kind* of thing that is said or done by a *kind* of person in accordance with probability or necessity; καθ' ἕκαστον, particular, is the opposite term. Generality of statement too is the basis of the definition of καθόλου as distinct from καθ' ἕκαστον in *De Interpr.* 7, 17 a 39 ff.; the qualification κατὰ τὸ εἰκὸς ἢ τὸ ἀναγκαῖον however is absent. In *Prol.* 103 f. I said that this was the idea underlying *A.P.* 128, but that the Greek wording behind the Latin *communia* and *proprie* was κοινόν (not καθόλου) and ἰδίως (not καθ' ἕκαστον).

These words, which are simpler and less cumbersome, were used by Aristotle as well, and at any rate κοινόν is put by him beside καθόλου as a convertible term (Bonitz, *Index Arist.* 356. 20 ff., 399. 29 ff.). As early as the first generation after Aristotle the pairs are interchangeable, not only κοινόν associated with καθόλου but ἴδιον associated with καθ' ἕκαστον—Professor H. Cherniss reminds me of Theophr. *Metaph.* 20, 8 b 20–7, and of course later parallels can be cited. This is the Greek nomenclature behind H.'s wording.

In Latin, *commune* and *proprium* are used freely by Cicero and later writers, in the context of rhetorical or logical definition, to render Greek κοινόν and ἴδιον, e.g. Cic. *Top.* 29 (on defining terms in rhetoric) *sic igitur ueteres praecipiunt: cum sumpseris ea quae sint ei rei quam definire uelis* cum aliis communia, *usque eo persequi dum* proprium *efficiatur, quod nullam* in aliam rem transferri potest; *Part. Or.* 41, 123.

Aristotle's *Poetics* ch. 9 then remains the background to H.'s pronouncement. A Hellenistic philosopher, intent on the moral lessons of poetry, could, in more traditional fashion, suggest that the proper reading of poetry should consist in the application of particular poetic instances to other similar ones. By chance the opinion of Chrysippus, the great Stoic systematizer, is preserved. 'Chrysippus rightly taught (says Plutarch, *Quom. adul. poet.* 34 b) that one ought to transfer what is useful (in poetry from one particular instance) to others like them', ἐπὶ τὰ ὁμοειδῆ, *SVF*, II, fr. 100. Plutarch, although not easily ready to accept Stoic doctrine, agrees. Poetic sayings have a general application, which should not be allowed to remain attached to one particular instance. The young must be taught by a training in 'sharp hearing', ὀξυηκοΐα, how to elicit moral generality from poetic particulars; the term κοινότης needs to be noted although poetic utterance is accepted as particular, not general. At 34 c he says, λόγον κοινοῦν καὶ δημοσιεύειν τὴν χρείαν δυνάμενον οὐ χρὴ περιορᾶν ἑνὶ πράγματι συνηρτημένον ἀλλὰ κινεῖν ἐπὶ πάντα τὰ

Commentary

ὅμοια, καὶ τοὺς νέους ἐθίζειν τὴν κοινότητα συνορᾶν καὶ μεταφέρειν ὀξέως τὸ οἰκεῖον, ἐν πολλοῖς παραδείγμασι ποιουμένους μελέτην καὶ ἄσκησιν ὀξυηκοΐας κτλ. Here the reader is advised to take the direction from poetic particulars to moral generalities.

H. is taking the opposite way, from generalities to particulars. He is thinking of new subjects or types of character as generalities which tradition has not yet particularized, cf. *Prol.* 106–7. Like Aristotle he can talk in terms of 'general' and 'particular'. But he is not a philosopher and is aware of the particularity of the poetic process. So, unlike Aristotle, he knows (and perhaps his Hellenistic forebears knew) that to put universals in a particular manner is hard—*difficile est proprie communia dicere.* That may account to a certain extent for his startling advice, to prefer old subjects to new.

tu = scriptor, 120 n.

-que 'and therefore', as L. Mueller noted. The adversative nuance emphatically proposed by G. Williams, *JRS*, LIV (1964), 190, though implied by many of his predecessors (see below Appendix 1 (i)), is possible on general grounds, but is excluded by the context discussed above. Parallels for the normal usage are scarcely called for and *tuque* at *C.* II. 12. 9, cited by Mueller, is slightly different in function, cf. Fraenkel, *Horace*, 219 n. 4. Mueller's second instance, however, 183 *-que*, does a similar job, although there is no change of grammatical subject as there is here.

129 *rectius . . . deducis*, as commentators say, = *rectius facis si deducis.* For this idiom, see above 40 n. on *potenter* (ii). The pres. tense continues 120 *si . . . reponis*, 125 *si quid . . . committis et audes* but at 131 ff. the fut. is used as frequently as before. For the tenses in *rectius deducis . . . | quam si proferres*, see *C.* III. 16. 22 ff. *nil . . . gestio . . . quam si . . . dicerer.*

Iliacum carmen hardly, with Heinze and others, only a reference to Trojan mythology because *carmen* is not only *fama* but an actual poem; cf. Immisch, p. 108, Steidle, *Studien*, p. 75 n. 8. But that does not necessarily make it the *Iliad*; see 131 ff. and compare, as L. Mueller suggests, Ath. VII. 277 e ἔχαιρε δὲ Σοφοκλῆς τῷ ἐπικῷ κύκλῳ ὡς καὶ ὅλα δράματα ποιῆσαι κατακολουθῶν τῇ ἐν τούτῳ μυθοποιΐᾳ.

deducis not here compose or sing (K.–H. *ein ilisches Lied anzustimmen*). There may be a reminder of *deduco*, the metaphor first recorded from H., then from the other Augustans (*TLL*, v. 1. 282. 55 ff.), *tenui deducta poemata filo* and the rest; but the acc. *in actus* seems to demand 'spin' or 'turn into'. *diducis* is an emendation eloquently

207

defended in C. Fea's edition (1827). Immisch, p. 100 n. 22, linked *diducis* with the verb διαλύσῃ, which occurs in a comparable, not identical, argument in Philodemus (below 131 ff.), but several scholars have rightly refused the conjecture, e.g. C. Jensen, *SBBA* (1936), 24 n. 2, Steidle, *Studien*, p. 75 n. 8. The metaphor of spinning is sufficient to account for *de-* and exclude *di-*, as it does in slightly different contexts in Man. II. 10, III. 396 (cf. Housman's nn.).

in actus: the notion 'act (of a play)' though fully established at that time and so employed elsewhere in the *Ars* (189, 194) would be weak in this context; the meaning is more likely to be 'dramatic poems', cf. *TLL*, I. 450. 61 ff. and note Man. v. 468–9 *mille alias rerum species in carmina ducent;* | *forsitan ipse etiam Cepheus referetur in actus.* This interpretation is also supported by Ar. *Poet.* 26, 1462 b 4 (on epic) ἐκ γὰρ ὁποιασοῦν μιμήσεως πλείους τραγῳδίαι γίνονται. Because of difference of context, Immisch, p. 108 n. 25, plausibly questions the relevance of another Aristotelian remark, which is often cited in this connexion, *Poet.* 23, 1459 b 2 ἐκ γὰρ Ἰλιάδος καὶ Ὀδυσσείας μία τραγῳδία ποιεῖται ἑκατέρας ἢ δύο μόναι.

130 *proferres* combines the notions of bringing to light or creating, as above 58, *Ep.* I. 6. 24, II. 2. 116, and producing works of art, *C.* IV. 8. 5, making known, Cic. *Phil.* I. 16, publishing works of literature, Cic. *Att.* xv. 13. 1 *eius (orationis) custodiendae et proferendae arbitrium tuum,* or performing on the stage, Pl. *Am.* 118 *ueterem . . . rem nouam ad uos proferam.*

ignota indictaque restates 119 *finge,* 125 *inexpertum,* etc., 128 *communia* (as explained above). For *indicta* cf. *C.* III. 25. 8–9 *dicam insigne, recens, adhuc indictum ore alio,* Virg. *A.* VII. 733 *carminibus nostris indictus.*

(2) How to make a traditional subject the poet's own: Homer and the cyclic epic, 131–52

131 ff. The problem of originality is now raised, but it is raised within the setting of a tradition—the central problem of Roman poetic practice and theory. It is no accident that Alexandrian conceits make an appearance, for the Alexandrians, and especially Callimachus, had raised and solved that problem in a way which was relevant to the New Poets and the Augustans in Rome. Callimachus had barred the road to the forms which for H. were the most seriously poetic—great epic, drama, and the archaic type of lyric. H. writes with these genres in view. As so often, therefore, when H. makes use of Callimachean language, he turns it upside down; he employs it to affirm what Callimachus had denied. A Hellenistic tinge is noticeable not only in the stylistic character of these verses but in the technical precept that opens the section. For *publica materies priuati iuris erit*, etc. seem to echo Philodemus' words spoken not many years earlier in a similar connexion (*HV*², IV. 195 and *HV*², VII. 87, the two fragments convincingly combined by C. Jensen, *Philodemos, Über d. Gedichte*, V (1923), pp. v f. n. 2; the immediately relevant part of one fragment had been compared with *A.P.* 131 by Heinze *ad l.*). Philodemus said ἂν τὰ κατ' Εἴλιον [ἢ] Θήβας κοινῶς παρ' ἑτέρου λαβὼν ὥσπερ διαλύσηι καί πως πάλι συντάξας ἰδίαν κατασκευὴν περιθῆι. That this opinion is not an unusual one in Hellenistic letters is shown for example by Demetr. *Interpr.* 113, a comparison of prose and poetry, Θουκυδίδης μέντοι κἂν λάβῃ παρὰ ποιητοῦ τι, ἰδίως αὐτῷ χρώμενος ἴδιον τὸ ληφθὲν ποιεῖ. The rhetoricians thought likewise, as Steidle (*Studien*, p. 80) has reminded us, cf. ps.-Dion. Hal. *Ars*, 10. 19 (ed. Us.– Ra. II. 373) μίμησις γὰρ οὐ χρῆσίς ἐστι τῶν διανοημάτων ἀλλ' ἡ ὁμοία τῶν παλαιῶν ἔντεχνος μεταχείρισις. καὶ μιμεῖται τὸν Δημοσθένην οὐχ ὁ τὸ ⟨Δημοσθένους λέγων ἀλλ' ὁ⟩ Δημοσθενι- κῶς κτλ. Philodemus however seems to do little more than rephrase the observation of an earlier critic. The identification of this earlier critic with Neoptolemus of Parium is not a foregone conclusion, but a matter on which it is wise to keep an open mind; cf. Appendix 2.

The verses now following are negative; by a method of exclusion H. leads the reader to the creative (Homeric) ideal of poetic economy; this is reached at 140. The transitional character of 131–5, particularly 132 *orbem*, has been stressed by P. Cauer, *RM*, LXI (1906), 233–4.

131 In his first instance H. amusingly combines the language of Roman law with that of literary theory; the legal and poetic spheres were prefigured in the κοινόν (δημόσιον) and ἴδιον of Alexandrian criticism. *publica materies* suggests both spheres, *priuati iuris* is more definitely legal.

publicus, older *poplicus*, is 'that which belongs to the *populus*', hence Cic. *Rep.* 1. 39 *est igitur...res publica res populi*. The counterpart to *publicus* is *priuatus*, e.g. *Dig.* 1. 8. 1 *hae autem res quae humani iuris sunt aut publicae sunt aut priuatae*; for instances such as roads (cf. below 132) and rivers, see W. W. Buckland, *A Text-book of Roman Law*³, p. 183; the *ager publicus* is another type of instance. But in Ov. *A.A.* III. 480 and Juv. 7. 53, though sometimes cited in this connexion, *publicus* lacks the Horatian meaning.

materies, according to ps.-Acro, by *poetica licentia pro materia...; materies enim lignum est*. The evidence however does not suggest a difference of meaning between the two words, cf. *TLL*, VIII. 448. 29 ff., although ancient grammarians say otherwise. The difference perhaps is stylistic; for in spite of the difficulty of establishing the true reading in many cases, *materies* appears to have an archaic and poetic flavour, as is said in *TLL, loc. cit.* The MSS suggest *-am* above 38, but *-em C.* III. 24. 49. For the gen. *iuris*, see Hofmann–Szantyr, 62 (B).

132 *uilem patulumque:* for the words cf. *Prol.* 109 n. 2 and Juvenal's *carmen triuiale*, 7. 55. They recall such Callimachean language as ἐχθαίρω τὸ ποίημα τὸ κυκλικόν, οὐδὲ κελεύθῳ | χαίρω τίς πολλοὺς ὧδε καὶ ὧδε φέρει | ...σικχαίνω πάντα τὰ δημόσια (*Epigr.* 28), οἶμον ἀνὰ πλατὺν ἀλλὰ κελεύθους | ἀτρίπτους εἰ καὶ στεινοτέρην ἐλάσεις (*Aetia*, 1. fr. 1. 27–8 Pf.).

In *orbis* H. deftly uses the notion of a circular piece of ground, hinting at sameness and completeness of movement (*in orbem ire*, and the like), but equally at the epic κύκλος (cf. Callimachus' ποίημα κυκλικόν and below 136), to whose unremitting and tediously complete narrative Aristotle had objected, *Poet.* chs. 8 and 23; Proclus called it the ἀκολουθία τῶν ἐν αὐτοῖς πραγμάτων (*Chrest.* 20. 319 a 32, Severyns, p. 37). Finally there is also the Alexandrian nuance of conventionality, cf. Callim. above and Pollian. *Anth. Pal.* XI. 130. Pollianus is concerned with style, not with subject-matter and arrangement. Equally the school of Aristarchus labelled certain stylistically obnoxious passages κυκλικῶς, thus e.g. *Schol. A*, Hom. *Il.* XV. 610 ff. ἀθετοῦνται στίχοι ε'·...καὶ κυκλικῶς ταυτολογεῖται κτλ., cf. Aristonicus, *Sign. Il.* ed. Friedländer (1853, repr. 1965), p. 265. Stat. *Silv.* II. 7. 51 *trita uatibus orbita* (cit. Rostagni) is comparable for the wording but not for the content, contrasting the great Greek epics with a Roman.

133 A second instance follows: a traditional subject fails to become personal when there is close translation; cited by Jer. *Ep.* 57. 5,

Boeth. *In Isag. Porph.* II. I. I (ed. Brandt, p. 135. 6 ff.), *Tract. Vind. ad l. H.* however is not here concerned with style but with the effect on the poet's subject if the new work remains tied to the wording of an older. Ever since Lambinus commentators have compared Cic. *Opt. Gen.* 14. The likeness is indubitable: *nec conuerti ut interpres; non uerbum pro uerbo; genus omne uerborum uimque seruaui.* Yet *ibid.* 23, naturally, even *rerum ordo* is said to be preserved since Cicero is talking about a translation of Aeschines and Demosthenes. H. on the other hand has in mind a Greek subject so re-created that the *rerum ordo* is bound to differ from the Greek source. Cf. *Ep.* I. 19. 24–5 *numeros animosque secutus* | . . . *non res et* . . . *uerba, ibid.* 29 *rebus et ordine dispar.* Other cases, such as the proems of Cicero's philosophical works, would be more relevant. For these and the school exercises of *paraphrasis,* see H. D. Jocelyn, *The Tragedies of Ennius* (1967), pp. 25 ff.

fidus with *interpres* is less usual in Latin than may be suggested by the phrase, 'a faithful translation'. The adj., according to *TLL,* VI. I. 703. 72 ff., in this connexion, denotes any person *qui in certa condicione fidem praestat,* e.g. *in re narranda.* H.'s point seems to be that this is *fides* wrongly shown; he has transferred the epithet from such instances as *Ep.* I. 8. 9 *medicis* and *C.* IV. 9. 40–1 *bonus atque f.* | *iudex.* The poet in question, unlike the Horatian poet, has 'trusted' another person, not himself: *Ep.* I. 19. 22 *qui sibi fidet.*

134 The third fault is straightforward imitation; *in artum* is at the opposite pole from *patulum* (132). Use of a *traditional* theme must be *original.* While in one sense of the word no literature is more imitative than Augustan poetry, in another none is more creative than Virgil's or H.'s work. That is the sentiment which inspired *o imitatores, seruum pecus* (*Ep.* I. 19. 19, cf. *ibid.* 12 ff.) and *libera per uacuum posui uestigia princeps,* etc. (*ibid.* 21 ff.). I doubt if there is here a reference to the fable of the fox (*Ep.* I. 7. 29 ff.) but *desilies* . . . *in artum* creates a vivid image which would suit a fable. The imitator imprisons himself and cannot escape. For the wording, commentators cite Cic. *Fam.* VIII. 16. 5 *ne te sciens prudensque eo demittas unde exitum uideo nullum esse.*

135 *pudor,* more likely, as Rostagni says = 'timidity, lack of confidence' (cf. *Ep.* II. I. 258–9 *nec meus audet* | *rem temptare pudor quam uires ferre recusent* and I. 19. 22 *qui sibi fidet*) than ps.-Acro's *quia pudendum est inchoata deserere.*

operis lex: the concept of a 'poetic law' has a Latin stamp. In earlier Greek it would be the ἀρετή or φύσις of a kind of art or literature; in later, νόμος where it occurs is often felt to be metaphorical, e.g. Lucian, *Hist. Conscr.* 8 ποιητικῆς μὲν καὶ ποιημάτων ἄλλαι ὑποσχέσεις καὶ κανόνες ἴδιοι, ἱστορίας δ’ ἄλλοι. ἐκεῖ μὲν γὰρ ἀκρατὴς ἡ ἐλευθερία, καὶ νόμος εἷς, τὸ δόξαν τῷ ποιητῇ κτλ. Characteristically the Romans applied the notion of law over a wide non-legal range so that *lex* comes close to *ratio*, 'procedure'; the only field where the evidence is reasonably well known is that of the 'law of nature'. Other applications are still insufficiently documented. It seems however to be the case that the legal concept appealed to Cicero and H. Cicero applied it widely, e.g. *lex uitae, amicitiae, ueri rectique, philosophiae, historiae, orationis* (*De Or.* III. 190 *hanc . . . ad legem . . . formanda oratio est*), *uersuum* (*Or.* 198 *in illis* (*sc. uersibus*) *certa quaedam et definita lex est*). At an early stage of his poetic career H. talks of 'law' with regard to satire, *S.* II. 1. 1–2 *in satura . . . nimis acer et ultra | legem tendere opus*, here the word denotes the procedure in single works but the *lex* clearly is the law of the genre and there is punning in the poem: *lex* oscillates between the poles of poetry and legality (*Prol.* 174). At *Ep.* II. 2. 109 the metaphor is thought to be sufficiently established to justify the adj. *legitimum*: a poem is 'lawful', so at *A.P.* 274 are metre and sound. In the present passage, even more than at *S.* II. 1. 1–2 the law directs an *opus*; the nuance is in *uetet*: it forbids something, i.e. free movement within the genre. An unnecessary and unwholesome limitation is imposed by the work that the imitator has undertaken. M. Nicolau, *RP*, 3ᵉ sér. IX (1935), 350–2, suggests that the legal term *lex operis* (sc. *faciendi*) actually applies to regulations imposed on a contractor for public works. He cites Ulp. *Dig.* XXXIX. 2. 15. 10 *legem dandam operis talem nequid noceat uicinis*. For *lex* in poetry, see Juv. 7. 102 *sic ingens rerum numerus iubet atque operum lex*, Quint. *I.O.* x. 2. 22 *sua cuique* (poetry and history, oratory) *proposita lex, suus decor est*, and the occasional references to *carminis lex* and the like in Servius, Donatus, and other ancient commentators (cf. Steidle, *Studien*, p. 85 n. 39).

136–9 Fourthly, it is a fault to begin in the manner of a 'cyclic writer', that is, with a proem ill adapted to the rest of the work. Censure of this fault leads on to actual precepts; Homer's technique is presented as the ideal poetic technique. The link between faults and virtues is made by connecting the avoidance of a cyclic proem in this passage with the acceptance of a Homeric in the next (140 ff.). The proem is not discussed *per se* but as the beginning of a poem; its discussion, as Steidle (*Studien*, p. 85) has noticed, ushers in narrative technique. The proem must be an organic part of a work of poetry; cf. above 14 ff. *inceptis grauibus*.

The form of proems was a standard topic of rhetorical instruction.

Commentary

It belongs to the *partes orationis*, one of the oldest subjects of the curriculum, cf. *Prol.* 82. Hence the material on the rhetorical side is considerable. Cicero quotes an Academic philosopher asking, *cur de prooemiis et epilogis et de huius modi nugis—sic enim appellabat—referti essent eorum* (i.e. *rhetorum*) *libri* (*De Or.* I. 86). I select for mention Plato, *Phaedr.* 266 d–e, *Rhet. ad Alex.* 29, 35, 36 f., Ar. *Rhet.* III, ch. 14; *Ad Her.* I. 6–11, III. 7, 11–12, Cic. *Inv.* I. 20–6, *De Or.* II. 315–25, Quint. *I.O.* IV, ch. I. On the literary side however information is scanty. Writers on rhetoric like to refer to the Homeric proems, see below 140 n. This shows the standing of those proems and, by contradistinction, the lower standing of the cyclic proems; but it shows no more. Philodemus (fr. v of Pap. 1676, *HV²*, XI. 149. 2 ff.) discussed epic proems, and referred, as H. does, to the beginning of the *Odyssey*. T. Gomperz rightly drew attention to this fragment and he compared *A.P.* 140 ff.; but I wish I could be as certain of its meaning as he seemed to be, *SBAW*, CXXIII. 6 (1891), 53 f. Lucian, *Hist. Conscr.* 23 satirizes high-flown, melodramatic, lengthy proems, and concludes like H. with the risible mouse (cf. below 139 n.), but H.'s example, at 137, is neither unduly melodramatic nor is it lengthy. Aristotle and Cicero are closer to H.'s argument, Ar. *Rhet.* III. 14, 1415 a 12 ff. calling an epic proem a δεῖγμα τοῦ λόγου, and Cic. *De Or.* II. 325 stressing the need for an organic connexion between proem and body of speech, *cohaerens cum omni corpore membrum*; cf. *Inv.* I. 26 *separatum*, *Ad Her.* I. 11. H. is still more specific. Cyclic poets promise (the whole story of) a memorable happening—*fortunam Priami...et nobile bellum*—after which the (unselective) story will fall flat. Inability to select and dullness resulting, that was Aristotle's indictment of the cyclic epic; in his view Homer's principle of selection pointed the way to unity as well as variety (*Poet.* chs. 8 and 23). As elsewhere in the *Ars*, the tradition on which H. relies seems to bring together ideas from the *Poetics* and the *Rhetoric*; in this case, it appears, the principle of Homeric unity and rhetorical interest in the arrangement of literary works.

136 *ut scriptor cyclicus olim:* the wording, I believe, implies a particular instance of a cyclic poem, which H. proceeds to cite. For the contrary view see 137 n. Bentley, from inferior MSS, adopted *cyclius* allegedly for reasons of euphony. But Aristotle and Callimachus use κυκλικός in this literary context and that too is the form in the Greek grammatical tradition; κύκλιος on the other hand qualified words like χορός. Pollianus' use of κύκλιος (in *Anth. Pal.* XI. 130) for the writers of the epic cycle seems to be exceptional and late—the time of Hadrian; for his usage again considerations of euphony were claimed

Commentary

for a long time. But Porph. on 146 has *cyclicus poeta* like the best Horatian paradosis.

137 '*fortunam Priami cantabo et nobile bellum*' is erroneously explained by ps.-Acro as the beginning of a poem of Antimachus (cf. below 146–7 n.). The line used to be identified with the beginning of the *Lesser Iliad*, Ἴλιον ἀείδω καὶ Δαρδανίην εὔπωλον, | ἧς πέρι πολλὰ πάθον Δαναοὶ θεράποντες Ἄρηος (Kinkel, *Ep. Gr. Fr.* ι. 39, Allen, ed. Hom. v. 129) unconvincingly, since the similarities are in fact slight. The sort of thing H. has in mind is a proem corresponding to '̔ἡγεό μοι λόγον ἄλλον, ὅπως Ἀσίης ἀπὸ γαίης | ἦλθεν ἐς Εὐρώπην πόλεμος μέγας' (*ap. Ar. Rhet.* III. 14, 1415 a 17), optimistically ascribed by some editors to Choerilus. No convincing Greek counterpart has been found, but the remains of cyclic epic verse are scanty. I should not be inclined therefore to jump to Rostagni's conclusion that H. himself has fabricated an example embodying his Aristotelian creed. Aristotle was struck by Homer's achievement, τῷ μηδὲ τὸν πόλεμον...ἐπιχειρῆσαι ὅλον (*Poet.* 23, 1459 a 31–2), and censured the *Cypria* and *Lesser Iliad* for being περὶ ἕνα...καὶ περὶ ἕνα χρόνον καὶ μίαν πρᾶξιν πολυμερῆ (*Poet. ibid.* a 37 ff., cf. ch. 8). That H. had in mind some such strictures as Aristotle's I have no doubt, but the wording of the preceding verse seems to make it sufficiently clear that H. latinized one specific proem of a cyclic epic not now extant, which he contrasted with the beginning of the *Odyssey*, below 141–2.

nobile, according to *TLL*, ii. 1848. 45, only here in classical Latinity an epithet of *bellum*, cf. Claud. *Eutrop.* ι. 336–7 *quid nobile gessit* | ...? *quae bella tulit?*, Cypr. Gall. *Exod.* 530 *nobilis duelli*.

138 *tanto...hiatu:* Pers. 5. 3 *fabula seu maesto ponatur hianda tragoedo*, and Juv. 6. 636 *grande Sophocleo carmen bacchamur hiatu* traduce the grand style (cf. Greek χάσκω); the nuance here is a larger promise than the writer can keep. Prop. ii. 31. 6 *carmen hiare* lacks either nuance.

quid dignum, as *S.* ii. 3. 6 *dic aliquid dignum promissis*.

promissor: probably a Horatian coinage, attaching a comic dignity to the poetaster; the suffix -(*t*)*or* proved a fertile source of new words. Quint. *I.O.* ι. 5. 6 is likely to have this passage in mind: *occurrat mihi forsan aliquis: quid hic promissor tanti operis dignum?* Likeness with the first part of the poem assists understanding: an account of all Priam's fortune and the great war is announced but the author defaults, cf. 14 *inceptis grauibus...et magna professis*, 45 *promissi carminis auctor*, *Ep.* ii. 1. 52 *quo promissa cadant* (*Enni*).

139 *parturient* is the transmitted text, *-iunt* in one out of numerous quotations (Jer. *Adv. Iov.* ι. 1) and some Renaissance MSS, supported by Bentley and such lively critics as Peerlkamp and L. Mueller. The fut. tense however should remain in possession. If the verse stood by itself, -iunt might be preferred. But the tense is influenced by the context.

parturient...mus answers the preceding question (*quid dignum...feret?*) with a Greek proverb, transposed to the fut. tense to suit the tense of the question. For the proverb see *CPG*, I. 378. 4, II. 733. 4 ὤδινεν ὄρος, εἶτα μῦν ἀπέτεκεν alluded to by the first two words in Lucian, *Conscr. Hist.* 23, in a similar though not identical setting. Immisch, p. 112 n., has drawn attention to the parallel, but his conclusions are implausible. Lucian objects to προοίμια λαμπρὰ καὶ τραγικὰ καὶ εἰς ὑπερβολὴν μακρά where the body of the narrative is puny, H. objects to a proem (however short) announcing a large subject when its execution must fall short of the expectation raised; cf. 136–9 n., 137 n., and below 143 *non fumum ex fulgore*. Phaedrus, IV. 23 (24) has made a short fable out of the proverb, the moral being *qui, magna cum minaris, extricas nihil.* The proverb made into a skit, in Sotadean metre, on the minute body of Agesilaus and ascribed to the Egyptian King Tachos, is cited by Athen. XIV. 616 d ὤδινεν ὄρος, Ζεῦς δ' ἐφοβεῖτο, τὸ δ' ἔτεκεν μῦν. This, if historical, dates the proverb back to the fourth century B.C., but I should be loath to spin Hellenistic literary affiliations out of its metrical form, as Immisch, p. 25, is inclined to do. One might note however that the proverb makes better sense in Lucian's context than in H.'s and Lucian may therefore preserve its original application. The age of the proverb, its Greek provenance, and the literary contexts in Lucian and the *Ars* might possibly point to a common Hellenistic source.

The verse ending *ridiculus mus* recalls, with implied compliments to Virgil, *exiguus mus* of the *Georgics* (I. 181). It reproduces the monosyllabic ending, with the concomitant stress on the final syllable of the preceding word (if a stress pattern is accepted) and the homoeoteleuton -ŭs -ūs. Quint. *I.O.* VIII. 3. 20 cites the Virgilian line and, noting the apposite adj., comments *et casus singularis magis decuit, et clausula ipsa unius syllabae non usitata addidit gratiam. imitatus est itaque utramque Horatius: 'nascetur ridiculus mus'.* In his note on Virg. *A.* VIII. 83 *conspicitur sus* (cf. III. 390 *sub ilicibus sus*) Servius says, *Horatius 'et amica luto sus'* (*Ep.* I. 2. 26). *sciendum tamen hoc esse uitiosum, monosyllabo finiri uersum nisi forte ipso monosyllabo minora explicentur animalia, ut...* (*A.P.* 139). *gratiores enim uersus isti sunt secundum Lucilium.* It is possible but far from certain that the reference to Lucilius indicates a remark by the satirist on Ennius' metre, cf. F. Marx, Lucil. fr. 1209 n. It is however likely that verses ending in a monosyllable were a feature of archaic Latin hexameters; in Homer they are used for a very different effect. Virgil may have selected certain types for metrical experiment. The burlesque type is not the only type. Cf. L. Mueller, *De re metr.*[2] pp. 253 5, and the careful analysis by Joseph Hellegouarc'h, *Le monosyllabe dans l'hexamètre latin*, etc. (1964), pp. 55 f.

140–52: Homer's narrative art. In rhetorical nomenclature this is the field of ἀρεταὶ διηγήσεως, *uirtutes narrationis*, instructively discussed in J. Stroux's book, *De Theophrasti Virtutibus Dicendi*, ch. IV. For narrating the true or alleged facts of a case Isocrates made three demands which achieved doctrinal status in rhetorical theory; conciseness in the selection of factual material, συντομία ἐν τοῖς πράγμασιν, clarity, σαφήνεια, and convincing treatment, πιθανότης. The extant sources are fairly numerous; for examples I refer to Anax. *Rhet.* chs. 30 f., ps.-Cornutus, *Rhet.* 365 ff. (*Rhet. Gr.* I. 2, ed. C. Hammer, pp. 71–4, 365–70), or the brief survey, Cic. *De Or.* II. 326–30, and the more substantial, Quint. *I.O.* IV, ch. 2. Complete discussions on the literary side are lost, but relevant evidence is found in the Homeric or other scholia, and occasional remarks elsewhere. From these one gathers that the literary critics applied the rhetorical categories to poetry and particularly to the criticism, textual and aesthetic, of the Homeric poems; see the studies cited by Marie-Luise von Franz, *Die ästh. Anschauungen der Iliasscholien*, Thesis, Zürich 1943. Proems and narrative techniques were important features of those discussions. The material in the *Ars* may tentatively be brought under the following heads: (*a*) 140–2, proems, cf. above 136–9 n.; (*b*) 143–5, clarity and unity of narrative; (*c*) 146–50, brevity, and arrangement of narrative detail; (*d*) 151–2, consistency in fictional narrative, cf. above 119 n.

H. has raised these precepts to a poetic level by the expedient of concentrating theories into images, and of so foreshortening their sequence that a unified picture of a poetic ideal arises. The outline runs from the rejected, cyclic, proem to its valid counterpart, the Homeric (*a*). The difference between cyclic and Homeric is then restated and developed in the images of smoke and fire, continued in the romantic concept of Homer's *speciosa. . .miracula* (*b*). Then again something concrete is offered, two instances, immediately rejected, of cyclic narrative technique, contrasted with the Homeric procedure, graphically described as *ad euentum festinat* and *in medias res* (*c*). He concludes with the most theoretical assertion of the series, 151–2, returning in a circle to the first verse of the section, 119: Homer has mixed truth and fiction; his narrative forms a unity (*d*).

Commentary

140 *rectius* unlike 129 = 'more in accordance with (poetic) principle', as at 309 *scribendi recte*, 428 '*pulchre, bene, recte*'. What H. says about Homer is related to the motif of unity in the first part of the poem, cf. above p. 130 (4).

hic qui nil molitur inepte is contrasted with 138 *hic promissor*. Homer need not be identified either by name, as at 74 above, or by pedestrian description, as *Troiani belli scriptorem*, *Ep.* I. 2. I. Here he is identified by praise and by quotation (141–2). This is significantly like Lucretius, praising but not naming Epicurus, e.g. v. 4 ff. *eius . . . qui talia nobis* | *. . .praemia liquit*, etc. But in his brevity and matter-of-fact way of talking, H. differs from Lucretius. Aristotle's description, which does contain Homer's name, may otherwise be compared, *Poet.* 8, 1451 a 22 ff. ὁ δ' Ὅμηρος ὥσπερ καὶ τὰ ἄλλα διαφέρει καὶ τοῦτ' ἔοικεν καλῶς ἰδεῖν, ἤτοι διὰ τέχνην ἢ διὰ φύσιν, which is followed by the Homeric principle of unity. Cf. 23, 1459 a 30 f., on the same principle, καὶ ταύτῃ θεσπέσιος ἂν φανείη Ὅμηρος παρὰ τοὺς ἄλλους κτλ. For the wording Rostagni compares Strabo VI. 276 τὸ μυθωδέστατον δοκοῦν εἰρῆσθαι τῷ ποιητῇ οὐ μάτην φαίνεσθαι λεχθέν, and similar expressions in the Homeric scholia.

141–2 A paraphrase in two verses rather than a close translation of Hom. *Od.* I. 1–3. *Ep.* I. 2. 19–22 has a different paraphrase. Homer took pride of place in discussions of proems. In Ar. *Rhet.* III, ch. 14 the two Homeric proems are quoted together with a third, sometimes identified with Choerilus', cf. 137 n. Philod. (above 136–9 n.) makes reference to the proem of the *Odyssey*. Quint. *I.O.* x. 1. 48 holds that Homer had established *legem prohoemiorum*, and explains how Homer's proems satisfy Quintilian's own rhetorical categories. H.'s criterion differs as indicated above 136–9 n.

141 Homer's ἐπεὶ Τροίης ἱερὸν πτολίεθρον ἔπερσεν is summed up by *domitor Troiae* at *Ep.* I. 2. 19, but here rendered *captae post tempora Troiae. moenia*, for *tempora*, is the wording of what is otherwise a quotation of the two Horatian verses in the *Periocha Odyssiae* which goes under the name of Ausonius; Bentley, finding the reading in the first hand of one and the second hand of another unimportant MS of H., sponsored it; but it is better explained as an interpolation, perhaps from the *Periocha*. None of Bentley's instances parallels the wording, or likens the locution to Virgil's *post eruta . . .* | *Pergama* (*A.* XI. 279–80). Bentley also considered *funera* for *tempora* and Peerlkamp emended to *Troiae post moenia captae*, grammatically but not otherwise plausible. No change is, I think, required. For *tempora* after prepos., see Ov. *Met.* VIII. 365–6 *citra Troiana . . .* | *tempora*, for the variation *Troiana* and *Troiae*, compare *C.* I. 28. 11–12 *Troiana . . .* | *tempora*

testatus with Ov. above, and at *Met.* XI. 757–8 *nouissimae Troiae* |
tempora (cit. Keller *ad l.* and *Epil.* 748).

142 *mores,* here and *Ep.* 1. 2. 20, is said by many to render the
Homeric text of Zenodotus, νόμον for νόον (*Schol. A, Od.* 1. 3). So it
may. But νόον is close to what later ages would describe as ἦθος and
Quint. *I.O.* VI. 2. 8 remarked ἦθος, *cuius nomine. . .caret sermo Romanus;
mores appellantur,* etc. Hence *mores* may be a moralizing Roman way
of rendering νόον.

uidit flatly renders Homer's ἴδεν. . .καί. . .ἔγνω, *Ep.* 1. 2. 20 has
inspexit.

143–4 Imagery instead of Aristotelian argument about unity and
diversity. The cyclic poets make a large blaze of their subject at the
outset but the fire quickly dies down, and all that remains is the
smoke of an inarticulate story. The Homeric procedure is the opposite. There is the smoke of the proem, which leaves it doubtful what
the reader is in for; then a good fire (the 'oneness' of Achilles' or
Odysseus' story), which in turn produces the unexpected and bril-
liant 'fairy tales', the θαυμαστά of his episodes. Aristotle has the basic
ideas of unity and diversity, main narrative and episodes (note *Poet.*
23, 1459 a 37 διαλαμβάνει τὴν ποίησιν); he also marks the fantastic
element. But the place where he attends to θαυμαστόν is outside the
argument on unity. H., or his authority, has brought these two
topics together; interest in 'the fantastic' is a Hellenistic and Roman
feature and the analysis *uerum–uerisimile–falsum* is post-Aristotelian;
see above 119 n. and below 151–2 n.

143 *fumum ex fulgore:* Rostagni's reference to Lucian, *Tim.* 1. 1
καπνός. . .ποιητικὸς ἔξω τοῦ πατάγου τῶν ὀνομάτων, is not entirely
in point here; cf. Aug. *Conf.* 1. 17 *nonne ecce illa omnia fumus et uentus?.*
H. is not talking of insubstantial poetic fog but is concerned with
poetic *oeconomia.* He is alluding to a Roman proverb (Otto, *Sprichwörter,* p. 137 n. 667, *TLL,* VI. 1. 1542. 7 ff.): where there is smoke
there is fire. As Palinurus in Pl. *Curc.* 53 f. remarks, *flamma fumo est
proxuma;* but *fumo comburi nil potest, flamma potest.* In telling their story
the cyclic poets do not get the fire really going.

ex fumo dare lucem as in Livy's metaphor, x. 24. 13, where however
it is applied to war: *quem ille obrutum ignem reliquerit ita ut totiens
nouum ex improuiso incendium daret. fumum* and *lucem dare* are parallel:
produce *fumus* and *lux.* But *lucem* is 'light' not fire; the metaphor is
switched midway; the cyclic procedure 'befogs' the reader, is un-
clear. *nubes,* καπνός, *nebula,* at 230 n., differ. *parum claris lucem dare,*
below at 448, is 'clarify', without this imagery.

144 For *miracula* cf. θαυμαστόν, Ar. *Poet.* 24, 1460 a 12 ff., for the word, Ov. *Met.* II. 193–4 *sparsa...in uario...miracula caelo | uas-tarumque uidet* (Phaethon)*...simulacra ferarum*, Min. Fel. *Oct.* 20. 3 *ut temere crediderint etiam alia monstruosa, mera (mi-* codd.) *miracula: Scyllam...Chimaeram...et quicquid famae licet fingere.* The highly laudatory epithet, *speciosus*, recurs with *fabula* below 319–20, with *uocabula rerum*, *Ep.* II. 2. 116, cf. 150 *nitescere.* 'Brilliant fantasies' such as metamorphoses, *paradoxa* and the like, were among the popular Hellenistic and Roman genres, and 'tales', or *fabulae*, were among the approved genres of Hellenistic and Roman literary theory (cf. above 119 n.). H. seems to be saying that romantic fiction, so far from being excluded from the Homeric poems, is effectively set in the strict and clear unity of the poems as a whole.

dehinc, although the temporal sense cannot be excluded, may be spatial, carrying on the imagery of *ex fumo...lucem*: *dehinc*, i.e. *ex luce, miracula promat.* Cf. *TLL*, v. 389. 29 ff.

145 The verse consists almost entirely of Greek names, like Virg. *G.* III. 550, IV. 336, *A.* v. 826. *-que et* does not conform to the rare type of conjunction noted 196 and 214 nn. *-que* attaches *Scyllam* closely to *Antiphaten* and thus removes both together from the third part of the sentence introduced by *et.* For the use of *cum*, cf. Virg. *A.* X. 124 *Assaraci duo et senior cum Castore Thymbris*, XI. 604. But the spacing is more *recherché*, for *-que (et)* and *cum* seem to be used to space the mythological personages in two different ways—an apparent order, *a/b Antiphaten Scyllamque* and *b/c cum Cyclope Charybdis*, but also a natural order, *a/c* and *b/d*: two cruel monsters, Antiphates, the king of the Laestrygonians (*Od.* X), and the Cyclops (*Od.* IX), and next Scylla and Charybdis (*Od.* XII). Bentley was ready to divorce Scylla from Charybdis, and replace her by Circe, in order to avoid the spacing of the two associated names over the whole verse. For the Greek ending *Antiphaten* see Housman, *JP*, XXXI (1910), 245 ff. *Charybdin* though likely is not equally certain, cf. Housman, *Man.* IV. 605 n.; *TLL, Onom.* II. 382. 53 ff.

146–7 *nec reditum...ab ouo* are related to 148 *semper...festinat* as 143 *non fumum ex fulgore* are related to *sed ex fumo dare lucem*, i.e by antithesis. But instead of *sed* (143), 148 presents an asyndeton. In 146–7 therefore H. is not talking of Homeric poems but of cyclic; and on similar grounds to Aristotle's, he rejects them as unpoetic, quasi-historical; cf. *Poet.* chs. 8 and 23, cited above 137 n. Nor were these criticisms restricted to epic verse. Ps.-Cornutus, *Rhet.* 65 (p. 365, *Rhet. Gr.* I. 2 ed. Hammer), deplores 'starting too far back', ἐὰν... πόρρωθεν ἄρχῃ, καθάπερ ἐν τοῖς προλόγοις πεποίηκεν Εὐριπίδης. If scholars had paused to consider the layout of these verses, they might not have been ready to ascribe to H. certain views on the 'Homeric' *Thebaid*; cf. Appendix 3.

146 'Homer does not begin the tale of Diomede's return with the death of Meleager.' The stylistic point made in the preceding note helps to reject the following explanation: Homer does not begin *his* tale of Diomede from the death of Meleager. The verse is rather 'a compressed expression for "nor does he act like the writer who began, etc."' (Wilkins *ad l.*, cf. Dacier, H. Schütz, and others). Who was the prolix writer who practised genealogy in a unilinear, cyclic, narrative *ab interitu Meleagri*, Diomede's great-uncle? This cannot now be known without new evidence; Porph. and ps.-Acro *ad l.* mention the name of Antimachus, which produces many difficulties of interpretation. Did the poem tell of Diomede's return from Troy to Greece, or to Aetolia after the campaign of the *Epigoni* against Thebes? This question cannot be answered with any certainty, cf. Appendix 3. Nevertheless the word *reditus* = νόστος suggests a comparison with the return of *Odysseus* on the Homeric side, just as there is a comparison with the *Iliad* in the next verse. Hence there is a balance—no more—in favour of a return from Troy. So that the verse would then imply something like this: when Homer tells of a νόστος (as he does in the *Odyssey*) he does not start the narrative with a long account of the hero's ancestors, as did the cyclic poet in the case of Diomede. Roman readers may have had some interest in the Aetolian hero because of his close relation with Italic mythology, known from Virgil and Ovid, and earlier from Lycophron and Timaeus, cf. Bethe, *Diomedes*, *R-E*, v. 820 ff. and Hülsen, *Diomedis Campi*, *ibid.* 829.

147 'Nor does he begin the tale of the Trojan War with the twin egg', another genealogical story tracing the Trojan war to the birth of Helen and (?) the Dioscuri. This is often referred to the *Cypria*, one of the old cyclic epics. But in spite of the harmonizing narratives of K.–H. and Rostagni *ad l.*, and in spite of the arguments of M.-R. Sulzberger, *Études Horatiennes* (Brussels, 1937), p. 225, the reference is highly suspect, as will be seen from the evidence surveyed by A. Rzach, *R-E*, xi. 2379 ff. For neither was there much in the *Cypria* of the story of the actual *bellum Troianum*, nor does the poem seem to have contained the celebrated twin egg. There are other perhaps more debatable points against the identification, cf. Steidle, *Studien*, p. 91 n. 41. For the *geminum ouum*, see Bethe, *R-E*, v. 1113; contrast *S.* ii. 1. 26–7 with the present verse: *Castor gaudet equis, ouo prognatus eodem | pugnis.*

Although our scanty evidence allows of no plausible attribution, I find it hard to be persuasded that H. had no specific examples in

Commentary

mind, as L. Mueller and among others Steidle, *Studien*, p. 91 n. 41, have thought possible.

148 *semper. . .festinat:* for the implied antithesis, see 146–7.

ad euentum 'issue, outcome' as shown by Cicero's definition, *Inv.* I. 42 *euentus est exitus alicuius negotii,* and other instances, *TLL*, v. 2. 1018. 31 ff., ps.-Acro *ad l.* Homer hurries to the issue: this is the counterpart to the avoidance of irrelevant detail prior to the chief events of the narrative, commended 146–7. For the background of rhetorical theory, see above 140–52 n. Philod. *Poem.* v, cols. 3–4 is aware of a theory applying the rhetorical terms συντομία and ἐνάργεια to poetry. Ps.-Plut. *De vita et poesi Hom.* 162 discusses the layout of the Iliad and Odyssey in similar terms, cf. W. Kroll, *Stud. z. Verst. d. röm. Lit.* (1924), 134 f. This discussion clearly derives from a tradition close to H.'s, cf. οὐ γὰρ πόρρωθεν ἐμβαλὼν τὴν ἀρχὴν τῆς Ἰλιάδος ἐποιήσατο κτλ. τὸ δ' αὐτὸ καὶ ἐν τῇ Ὀδυσσείᾳ πεποίηκεν, ἀρξάμενος μὲν ἀπὸ τῶν τελευταίων. . .χρόνων κτλ. Note too such terms as ἐνεργότεραι καὶ ἀκμαιότεραι (πράξεις), ἀργότερα, συντόμως, δεινότερα καὶ πιθανώτερα. This way of looking at poetry is Alexandrian and is perpetuated in the Homeric and Virgilian scholia. *Schol.* on *Il.* v. 8 makes reference to the three ἀρεταὶ διηγήσεως (140–52 n.) to illustrate the selection of detail in that passage. *Schol. A, Il.* I. I asks διὰ τί εὐθὺς ἀπὸ τῶν τελευταίων τοῦ πολέμου ἤρξατο; The answer is, ὁ ποιητὴς οἰκονομικῶς. . .ἤρξατο μὲν ἀπὸ τῶν τελευταίων, διὰ δὲ τῶν σποράδην αὐτῷ λεχθέντων περιέλαβε καὶ τὰ πρὸ τούτου πραχθέντα. Thus *Schol. T, Il.* I. I puts this procedure down to ἀρετὴ ποιητική; similarly *Schol. L, Il.* I. 8 where the expression ἐξ ἀναστροφῆς, 'by inversion', is used. Terms like κεφαλαιωδῶς and κατὰ τὸ συμπέρασμα (*summatim,* the latter not in this meaning noted by L.–S.–J.) and κατὰ τὸ σιωπώμενον (*ex silentio*) are working tools of the scholiasts, e.g. at *Il.* II. 553, IX. 224, and often elsewhere, not always convincingly, applied. Cf. W. Bachmann, *Die ästh. Anschauungen Aristarchs,* etc. II (1904), 8–9. Virgil's commentators noted that the poet worked in the same tradition, Serv. Dan. on Virg. *A.* I. 34 *ut Homerus omisit initia belli Troiani, sic hic non ab initio coepit erroris.* Thus too Don. *Ter. An.* praef. II. 2 *hunc enim orbem et circulum poeticae uirtutis non modo secuti sunt tragici comicique auctores sed Homerus etiam et Vergilius tenuerunt.* For these and other links with Homeric scholia see 43, 126 nn., and M. Mühmelt, 'Griech. Grammatik in der Vergilerklärung', *Zetemata*, XXXVII (1965), 115 f.

in medias res: the sentence continues but the tail-end of this verse has become proverbial—and trite. In its context the saying *is* memorable; the work-a-day Greek critics had often expressed it but lacked

221

Horatian panache. The matter may be put in two different ways. Either omission and summary procedure are stressed, as when at *Schol. A, Il.* XVI. 432 Zenodotus is censured for overlooking this Homeric technique. Or simple inversion is stressed, as *Schol. Il.* I. 8 ἐξ ἀναστροφῆς (prec. n.), or *Schol. A, Il.* XV. 56 ὅτι ὡς ἐπίπαν πρὸς τὸ δεύτερον πρότερον ἀπαντᾷ. Aristarchus worked with both principles and often criticized his predecessors in this manner—more often in fact than we can now know: contrast the bland wording of *Schol. Od.* XI. 177 with Pap. Oxy. 1086 (VIII. 1918), col. I. 11–18 (cf. S. E. Bassett, *HS*, XXXI (1920), 47, A. Gudeman, *R-E*, II A. 638. 19 ff., and my remarks, *CQ*, XL (1946), 21). In Latin literature *in medias res* and the like commonly denote 'inversion', whether in the structure of a whole work or of a phrase or paragraph. Thus Cic. *Att.* I. 16. I *respondebo tibi* ὕστερον πρότερον Ὁμηρικῶς, Quint. *I.O.* VII. 10. 11 *ubi ab initiis incipiendum, ubi* more Homerico *a mediis uel ultimis*, Plin. *Ep.* III. 9. 28 *succurrit* quod praeterieram . . . *sed quamquam praepostere* reddetur. facit hoc Homerus *multique illius exemplo*, Serv. *Virg. A.* praef. 92 ff. (ed. Harvard) *hanc esse artem poeticam ut* a mediis incipientes *per narrationem prima reddamus*, etc. *quod etiam Horatius sic praecepit in arte poetica . . .* (43–4). *unde constat perite fecisse Vergilium.* Mühmelt, *loc. cit.* (prec. n.), compares Don. *Ter. An.* Praef. II. 2 *hanc esse uirtutem poeticam ut* a nouissimis argumenti rebus incipiens *initium fabulae . . . narratiue reddat spectatoribus*, etc. But H. seems to have in mind not only the ὕστερον πρότερον of Homer's dramatic unity but, to judge from 150, also Homeric brevity and conciseness.

149 *non secus ac:* the most usual grammar in this locution. It is sad that no recent editor feels persuaded by this instance and by *C.* III. 25. 12 (*non secus*) *ut* even to question the oddity (*orationis scabritiem* according to Meineke) of the only remaining instance of *non secus* in H., I mean *C.* II. 3. 1–2 *rebus in arduis* | . . . *non secus in bonis*, where Bentley introduced *ac bonis* from one or two late MSS, and Housman introduced *ut bonis*, in *CR*, IV (1890), 341.

rapit, a favourite with H., = *rapide fert* or *agit*, a kind of ψυχαγωγία, cf. Cic. *Or.* 128 *quod* (τὸ παθητικόν) *cum rapide fertur, sustineri nullo pacto potest.* The listener is propelled into the middle of the story and accepts it as though he knew the beginning—a telling metaphor in the context of brevity and fast narrative.

150 Here links are made, not only with the beginning of this section (see 151–2 n.) but with the first part of the poem: compare *relinquit* with 41–3 on *ordinis uirtus*, and with 1 ff. on a work of art, the parts of which do not cohere—unity unattained.

desperat: a vigorous Ciceronian word in a Ciceronian construction;

the word is rare in verse: 'deest poetis praeter singulos locos Buc. Eins. Stat. Iuv., binos: Sen. Sil. Auson., ternos: Hor. Lucani Mart., quinque: Ov., frequentat Cic. (77ies)', *TLL*, v. 1. 739. 39 ff.

tractata: of poetic handling also *Ep.* ii. 1. 209.

nitescere: cf. 41 *lucidus (ordo)*, 144 *speciosa (miracula)*—concepts of poetic sophistication, not Aristotelian metaphors; the only metaphor of light I have noticed in the *Poetics* is a censorious one (24, 1460 b 4–5 ἡ λίαν λαμπρὰ λέξις. Homer here becomes a sophisticated, Horatian poet.

relinquit encourages the view above taken of 148.

151–2, as both Heinze and Rostagni have noticed, bring together the two strands from the beginning of this section, 119, *famam sequi* and *fingere*. The former is identified with *uera*, the latter with *falsa*; for this pair see above 119 n. Homer is credited with both. Rostagni has made another important point. H. is tying *uera* and *falsa* to the achievement of an over-all unity. Even *speciosa miracula* he accepts only if they become part of the body poetic; see Steidle, *Studien*, pp. 91 f. And this is no mere theory. As he does throughout the *Ars*, H. here has attempted to do what he prescribes: these verses not only complete this section with its imaginative touches so that it becomes a unity, but join it with the early motifs of the poem, cf. 150 n.

151 Heinze has (mistakenly, I believe) separated this verse from its Aristotelian context. H. is restating doctrine which is related to Aristotle's. Homer, according to *Poet.* 24, 1460 a 18–19, 'has taught others' (i.e. other poets) 'to make false statements in the right way', δεδίδαχεν δὲ μάλιστα Ὅμηρος καὶ τοὺς ἄλλους ψευδῆ λέγειν ὡς δεῖ. But as H. puts the matter it contradicts the Aristotelian conception to a certain extent. In *Poet.* ch. 9 all poetry *is* a purveyor of *uerisimilia*, οἷα ἂν γένοιτο καὶ τὰ δυνατὰ κατὰ τὸ εἰκὸς ἢ τὸ ἀναγκαῖον (1451 a 37–8). This cuts across the simple distinction between factual truth and poetic falsehood. H. is closer to the Hellenistic separation of *uera* from *uerisimilia* or *falsa* mentioned in 119 n. Yet Aristotle himself allowed an exception to his rule, in ch. 21, 1460 a 11–b 5, on which Rostagni and G. F. Else (*Ar. Poetics*, etc. pp. 621 ff.) have written convincingly. H. takes 'poetic lies' for granted, just as he takes variety for granted in the initial section on unity: he treats *falsa* as an artistic problem. In the next verse he acknowledges that Homer has so fitted them into the unity of his story as to leave visible no joint between *famam sequi* and *fingere*, cf. above 119, 125–7.

ueris...remiscet: the abl. appears to have been the case in original use with such verbs of joining as *misceo* and *iungo*, but the dat. appears early and, where a distinction between the two can be made, is seen to be the prevalent usage in classical Latin, cf. Hofmann–Szantyr, p. 115. The few instances of the rare compound are in fact indistinct; *C.* IV. 15. 30 *Lydis remixto carmine tibiis, pace* Heinze, is no certain instance of the abl., nor is Sen. *Const.* 7. 4, and Sen. *Ep.* 71. 16 *naturae remiscebitur* is dat.

ita–sic: as against 225–6 *ita–ita–ita.* Cf. Virg. *A.* XII. 10 sic *adfatur regem atque* ita *turbidus infit* as against *E.* I. 22, *A.* III. 490 and other instances of repeated *sic* or *ita*.

152 *primo . . . medium, medio . . . imum*, the words in emphatic (chiastic) order, pointedly state the basic law of unity at the close of the section; cf. 119 *sibi conuenientia*, 126–7 *ad imum | . . . ab incepto . . . sibi constet*, but also 8–9 *uni . . . formae*, 23 *simplex . . . et unum*, et al. For the wording cf. 148 *in medias res*, Cic. *Fin.* V. 83 *mirabilis et apud illos* (i.e. *Stoicos*) *contextus rerum; respondent extrema primis, media utrisque, omnia omnibus*, Quint. *I.O.* VII. 10. 11 (cit. 148 n.), Euanth. *De Fab.* 3. 7 (Donat. *Comm. Ter.* ed. Wessner, I. 20) *media primis atque postremis ita nexuit ut . . . aptum ex se totum et uno corpore uideatur esse compositum.* Cf. Ar. *Poet.* chs. 8 and 23, and the passages cited above 8–9 and 23 nn.

ne belongs to a large group of instances in which the distinction between final (*ne*) and consecutive (*ut non*) proves too neat and tidy, cf. Hofmann–Szantyr, pp. 641 ff. and the evidence discussed from different points of view by R. G. Nisbet and W. G. Kirk, *AJP*, XLIV (1925), 27 ff., 260 ff. Here antecedent *ita–sic* could lead to a simple *ut non* of result, but *ne* emphasizes that the result is designed by Homer; cf. below 225–7 *ita–ita–ita . . . ne*, *Ep.* I. 13. 12–13 sic *positum seruabis onus*, ne forte *sub ala | fasciculum portes librorum*.

primo and *medio*, though indistinct in form, are likely to be datives with *discrepet* (like the equally indistinct cases below 219, *S.* I. 6. 92, II. 3. 108, *C.* I. 27. 56), since the first indubitable abl. with that verb is not recorded before Apul. *Apol.* 69 *quantum lingua eius manu discrepet* (*TLL*, V. 1. 1348. 73) whereas the first indubitable dat. belongs to the Ciceronian period: Nigid. *ap.* Gell. VII. 6. 10 (*TLL*, V. 1. 1346. 74), followed closely in time by the remaining Horatian instance *Ep.* II. 2. 193–4 *quantum simplex . . . nepoti | discrepet.* The position is not stated clearly in *TLL*.

IV. Drama, 153–294

The tradition. Until now our sources have rendered discussion of the literary tradition at any rate possible. In the present section the sources largely fail us. The strictly rhetorical material becomes on the whole irrelevant; it has no business with drama as a poetic genre. As for Aristotle, I have suggested, *Prol.* 110–19, that the *Poetics* can still do useful service, for it can remind the reader of the placing of some of the subjects which H. has taken from the tradition. That applies to the discussion of characters with which Ar. *Poet.* ch. 15 deals after the plot, and H. at a comparable place from 153 to 178, although the content is manifestly under the influence of *Rhet.* ii, chs. 12–14. It applies to the miscellany of rules as well—in the *Poetics* chs. 17–18, before Aristotle proceeds to thought and diction; in the *Ars* 179–219, if not only the chorus but music is here included. After that place the *Poetics* is little use to the student comparing the two major works on literary criticism that have come down to us from antiquity. The passage on metre in drama has some slight Aristotelian parallels, cf. *Prol.* 118 f. But the historical remarks (so far as they are historical and not educational) on the dramatic genres, 220–50 and 275–94, are closely tied to the Hellenistic position and very little to the Aristotelian, cf. *Prol. ibid.* These affiliations apart, what I think we can gather is again a matter of placing. In the *Poetics* observations on the genre of tragedy form the main substance of the book and virtually alone account for its arrangement. H. on the other hand seems to be relying on a scheme of things in which a more general discussion of style and content preceded detailed observations on the dramatic genres: *Prol.* 99 ff., 138.

Horace. Up to 152, drama, though often adduced by way of example, has not been the main topic. From 153 to 294 it is. The three introductory verses, 153–5, set a new theme and this is not abandoned until the end of the section. Whether the new context is meant still to exemplify the preceding section, or whether this is a fourth large group of subjects I find hard, and not very profitable, to determine, cf. *Prol.* 7–10.

Having brought 'character' into the discussion of other topics, H. now discusses character study in drama *per se.*

Some readers profess themselves surprised by the weight given to *mores*, e.g. G. Williams, *JRS*, LIV (1964), 194, 'an odd proposition for H. to embrace so devotedly'. Why odd, one wonders. What could be more Roman than this passion for *mores*? And what more Horatian, in ¦*Odes*, *Satires*, and *Epistles* alike, than this perceptive eye for typical human features? A further motif is continued in the section on character—appropriateness. Here it is called *decor* (157), the fitting detail, in a setting remarkable for descriptive appropriateness in focusing the four ages of man.

After (1) character, 156–78, there follow miscellaneous rules, all but one negative and getting briefer each time: interdicts against (2) horrors enacted on the stage, 179–88, (3) plays longer than five acts, 189–90, (4) an unmotivated *deus ex machina*, 191–2, and (5) more speaking parts than three, 192. The next paragraph is the exception—an injunction not an interdict, and longer than (1)–(5): (6) the appropriate function (*apte* 195) of the chorus, 193–201. The treatment of music (7) follows, 202–19, remarkable for its absence of a ruling, positive or negative, though there can be no doubt of H.'s sentiment. As I noted in *Prol.* 115 f., H. looks back nostalgically to a golden age of the art; τὸ πρέπον and perhaps a ruling are implied.

If H. had adopted a simple unilinear arrangement, he would have placed next, (8) metre of drama, (9) tragedy, (10) comedy, and (11) Satyric drama in Greece and (12) Rome. As it is, the layout is as follows: after music, and separating music from its counterparts, rhythm and metre, there follow (8) the epilogue to tragedy, Satyric drama, 220–50; (9) the metre of dramatic dialogue, 251–74, which turns into a harangue against the Roman neglect of *ars*, so that the established major genres can now be set against the background of an antithesis—Roman potentiality vis-à-vis Greek perfection; (10) Greek tragedy, 275–80, and comedy, 281–4, (11) Roman tragedy and comedy, 285–94. These are clear indications of H.'s imaginative and poetic ordering of topics;

for comments on this arrangement, see the remarks introducing the sections at 251, 275, 281, 285.

In the latter part of this large section H. has made full use of the motif of *ars*, technical mastery. It is brought to the fore with great delicacy; in the end it becomes the dominant feature and paves the way to the next large part of the poem (at 295) in which *ars* is set against *natura*. In the present section a further major motif appears, Roman versus Greek closely entwined with the theme of *ars*: *exemplaria Graeca*.

(1) Introduction, 153, Characters, 154–78

153 One vigorous line introduces the new series of instructions. For the imp., cf. 38, 119. There is no telling whether the line introduces the first topic only; *quid*, rather than *quae*, does not (as Immisch p. 122 suggests) settle the question. Düntzer and several nineteenth-century editors placed a comma after this verse and a full stop after 155; thus, too, many recent editors. Kiessling in particular argued that the transition from epic to drama is made clear only if the *si* clause shares the first sentence. This is implausible, and refuted by H.'s use of *audi* to introduce a new topic. Whether or no the indirect question precedes the imp., such sentences are self-contained with a full stop after *audi* or the indir. question. They do not drag after them a tail two lines long:

S. I. I. 14–15	ne te morer, audi
	quo rem deducam.
Ep. I. 2. 5	cur ita crediderim, nisi quid te detinet, audi.
14. 31	nunc age, quid nostrum concentum diuidat audi.
17. 16–17	iunior audi
	cur sit Aristippi potior sententia.
II. 2. 95–6	mox etiam, si forte uacas, sequere et procul audi
	quid ferat et qua re sibi nectat uterque coronam.

The passages below 268, 385, 426, cited by F. Klingner, *BVSA*, LXXXVIII. 3 (1937), 30–1 n. 2, apropos of initial *tu* differ in form and scope.

tu continues the instruction offered to 'the poet' or 'poets', *scriptor* 120 n. and *qui scribitis* 38 n. Rostagni and some of his predecessors assume gratuitously that the elder of the two sons of Piso is here addressed. But the reader has not yet been told that any especial interest attaches to the elder son and he is not so told here. The young man has so far been addressed only as one of the family,

6 *Pisones*, 24 *pater et iuuenes patre digni*, and likewise later in this section, 235 *Pisones*, 292 *Pompilius sanguis*. He does not receive separate mention until 366 *o maior iuuenum*. Cf. Vahlen, *Ges. Phil. Schr.* II. 761, 766.

ego et populus mecum: that is, spectators critical and uncritical; 113 *equites peditesque*, cf. *Prol.* 260 n. 1 and above 113 n. There is however an obvious nuance here: H. lets his opinion be known as at 103 *me*, 105 *dormitabo aut ridebo*, 182 *spectator* compared with 188 *incredulus odi*. But H. represents himself as part of an audience, and what is studied is the reaction of the audience. The implication seems to be that artistic competence so far from losing an audience will result in a success. If another view seems to be expressed with startling frankness in the *Augustus*, *Ep.* II. 1. 182 ff., this relates to an audience with which H. cannot identify himself.

Characters

In two earlier passages 'character' was one motif, the main division of the *Ars* another. Thus at 112–18 character diversified the topic of diction, and the *mores* belonged to classes or types—such impersonal features as sex, social status, etc. At 120–7 *mores* diversified the topic of content; subject-matter was put in terms of *personae*, personages of *fama* or fiction. Now the poet offers a series of pen-portraits, a spirited *ethologia*. Although at 115 'age' was said to be one of the features characterizing diction, there is no incongruity when it makes another appearance. For *mores* now are to show the lifelikeness that keeps the spectator interested—typical traits which the 'four ages' may be thought to exhibit. The playwright must make them as lifelike on the stage as they are in this poem.

The tradition on which H. is likely to have drawn combines once again elements from Aristotle's *Poetics* and *Rhetoric*. For a discussion of possible links with Ar. *Poet.* ch. 15, see *Prol.* 140 n. 1; for a comparison of the passages on character, *ibid.* 251 f. That the placing of this topic agrees with the *Poetics* has been said above. And for the relation of this piece to the style of Aristotle's and Theophrastus' characters, and in particular to Ar. *Rhet.* II, chs. 12–14, see *Prol.* 111–13 and my notes below.

Commentary

Are the four ages, replacing Aristotle's three, H.'s innovation? Or are they older, possibly going back to a time when (as I have suggested) rhetorical and literary teachings were combined? We have no way of telling. G. Williams' remarks (*Tradition and Originality*, etc. (1968), p. 333) do not provide an answer. 'There is no reason' (he says) 'to interpose some Hellenistic prose treatise between H. and Aristotle: the dramatist would find H. almost useless—except as an inspiration—and would turn to Aristotle for analysis.' Whichever the answer, the quartet, instead of the trio, is not, as K.–H. and others maintain, an argument against Peripatetic and (ultimately) Aristotelian derivation of H.'s description. The four-age schema occurs frequently but, as F. Boll pointed out in his learned discussion of this topic (*Kl. Schr.* 171), H. differs from many in that he does not make the often-repeated comparison with the four seasons.

What matters is the close similarity of H.'s style in this section with Peripatetic typology. There was a poetic challenge here. The poet accepted it and produced this memorable piece. Juvenal lacks this background. His hard-hitting but prolix and often repulsive caricature of old age, 10. 190–288, may be contrasted. Juvenal here continues some of the gross features of Roman satire; thus compare Juv. 10. 205 with Lucil. fr. 332 (Marx). For H. the typology of the Lyceum provided one stimulus; the character-studies of comedy and perhaps satire another. These one-sided, sharply focused portraits form a poetic excursus which goes a long way beyond what was needed to illustrate the topic of the *ars*.

Four ages are distinguished, *puer* 158–60, *iuuenis* 161–5, *uir* 166–8, *senex* 169–74. This sequence, it has often been noted, is chronological, and thus differs from Aristotle's logical schema: youth, old age, maturity—the extremes and the mean. Two introductory verses, 156–7, and four concluding, 175–8, inculcate the regulative theme, *decor* 157, and *aptis* 178, if the line stands, the final word of the section.

229

154 *plosoris* (*plaus-*): Bentley replaced this word by *fautoris* in order to avoid the near-repetition at 155 *plaudite*; Peerlkamp and Meineke adopted even stronger measures. But *plosoris*, or *plausoris*, is shielded by the subsequent *sessuri*, a collocation like *Ep.* II. 2. 130 *sessor plausorque*. As for the sequence *plosoris* (or *plaus-*)–*plaudite*, repetition without emphasis is found in Latin writers in varying degrees; the studies noted by E. J. Kenney, *CQ*, n.s. IX (1959), 248 n. 1 may be compared. Housman thought that H. was 'as sensitive to iteration as any modern' (Lucan, p. xxxiii). Here however there is, I think, some emphasis and the near-repetition may be desired: the spectator, ready to applaud, must be kept in his seat until the *uos plaudite*. We have no means of knowing how strong, in that case, the emphasis is meant to be. It would be even stronger if *plausoris*, not *plosoris*, were the right reading. Although the archetypes of our MSS had *plosoris* or *plusoris*, an ancient variant *plausoris* seems to be attested by ps.-Acro *ad l.*, and occasionally is added by later hands in various codices. *plausor* only is attested at *Ep.* II. 2. 130. For the vowels, see F. Sommer, *Handbuch*², p. 79, Stolz–Leumann, pp. 79 f.

Professional claques are mentioned for example by Petron. 5, Suet. *Nero* 20. But H. is not talking of a hired claque. If the dramatist is competent, he maintains, then the spectator will be ready to stay for the final curtain, cf. above on *ego et populus mecum*. The passage of the *Augustus* cited in the same note shows that this was a real problem. Terence is said to have dealt with it by letting the play run on without pauses, Don. *Eun.* praef. 1. 5 *quia* tenendi spectatoris causa *uult poeta noster omnes quinque actus uelut unum fieri ne* . . . ante aulaea sublata fastidiosus spectator exsurgat; for Donatus' *fastidiosus spectator*, see *Ep.* II. 1. 215. Nero solved the problem by more forcible means: Suet. *Nero* 23. 2 *cantante eo ne necessaria quidem causa excedere theatro licitum est*, etc.

eges: not 'you need' but 'wish for', as *S.* I. 1. 59 *qui tantuli eget, quanto est opus*, Pl. *As.* 591 *quia tui amans abeuntis egeo*, Liv. III. 28. 10 *sanguinis se Aequorum non egere; licere abire*.

aulaea: the drop-curtain of the Roman stage: refs. *TLL*, II. 1460. 57 ff., cf. W. Beare, *The Roman Stage*³ (1964), App. E. The later evidence is not yet fully clarified, but in Ciceronian and early imperial times the curtain was raised so as to conceal the stage and mark the end of the performance: Cic. *Cael.* 65 *mimi. . .exitus. . .aulaeum tollitur*, the earliest known instance; the same term is used by Virg. *G.* III. 25, and in the graphic description Ov. *Met.* III (not X, Beare, p. 268), 111–14. Hence Porph. *donec aulaeum leuetur* renders H.'s notion correctly. The curtain is 'kept down' *aulaea premuntur*, during the performance, Hor. *Ep.* II. 1. 189; *aulaeo misso,* Phaedr. v. 7. 23, the lowering of the curtain marks the beginning of the performance.

-laea: the standard spelling for words derived from Greek -αῖος (Prisc. *GL,* II. 70, Serv. *Virg. A.* I. 697), in the present passage C Porph., *-lea* M; *-lea* appears frequently even in good MSS, *TLL,* II. 1459. 61 ff., 75 ff., but see Housman, *JP,* xxxiii (1914), 59.

manentis: transitive in archaic, poetic and Silver usage.

155 *sessuri:* Augustan poets frequently concentrate in a fut. part., attrib. or pred., what in earlier prose would have been a whole clause, e.g. *qui sedeat*; Silver and later writers, especially Tacitus, follow suit, cf. Hofmann–Szantyr, 390. This usage has a good deal of force, which may be intensified by a subordinate clause, *donec* in this verse.

donec in combination with *usque* (154) appears to be archaic (Pl. *Mil.* 269, *Mos.* 116, *Rud.* 716, Ter. *Ad.* 718, Cato), occasionally it occurs in Silver and Late Latin. In H. it is found here only, not in his lyrics nor in other elevated Augustan and post-Augustan verse (*TLL,* v. 1. 2003. 62 ff.).

cantor: Roman dramatic pieces closed with a request for applause. The identity of the speaker or speakers of this request has been much debated after the fundamental but divergent remarks by Bentley, Ter. *An.* 981 n., and G. Hermann, *Opusc.* I. 302. The matter is not solved by the indications in the MSS of Plautus and Terence (as Bentley thought), nor by Porph. *ad l.,* *is qui agit.* Even less is it solved by the much-quoted passage Cic. *Sest.* 118, which rests on the pun, *cantor* in a play and *cantor* 'hired brawler' (of Clodius); it does not prove (as Hermann thought) that *cantor* elsewhere = *histrio* or *actor,* and it does not make reference to the final *plaudite* of a play. Nor, as Wilkins remarks *ad l.,* does any other passage suggest this equivalence. We are left therefore with the two established meanings, 'singer' and 'piper' and I am not aware of independent evidence to settle the question.

uos plaudite or a similar address marks the end of a Roman tragedy and comedy: Quint. *I.O.* vi. 1. 52 *cum uentum est ad ipsum illud quo ueteres tragoediae comoediaeque cluduntur 'plaudite',* Porph. *consummatio et comoediae et tragoediae est.* The meaning was sufficiently established for Cicero's metaphor, *Sen.* 70 *neque enim histrioni ut placeat peragenda fabula est. . .neque sapienti usque ad 'plaudite' ueniendum est.*

156 *aetatis. . .mores:* as Ar. *Rhet.* II. 12, 1388 b 31 τὰ δὲ ἤθη ποῖοί τινες κατὰ. . .τὰς ἡλικίας, b 36 ἡλικίαι δέ εἰσι νεότης καὶ ἀκμὴ καὶ γῆρας. *pueritia* completes the series, poetically rewarding rather than relevant to drama.

notandi was misunderstood by Heinze in one of the comments that do not improve on his predecessor's work. For, as Kiessling explained, the word here means 'describe, represent', cf. C. Becker, *Das Spätwerk des Horaz*, p. 100 n. 4. Although *notare* is not condemnatory in this passage, it often retains the nuance with which the censor's black mark or *nota* is associated; thus it expresses moral censure (*S.* I. 3. 24, 4. 5, 106 al.) or artistic (below 449 on poetic faults). But censoriousness is largely absent from the descriptions of moral stances in Aristotle's *Ethics*, and of the Three Ages in the *Rhetoric* which appear to have stimulated H. in this section; this applies even more to the amusing foibles of Theophrastus' *Characters*. Nor is there overt moralizing in the rhetorical sketching of characters which, as Immisch (p. 123) points out, is called *notatio*; *Ad Her.* IV. 63 *notatio est cum alicuius natura certis describitur signis quae ⟨sunt⟩ sicuti notae quae naturae sunt attributa.* [*Characterismos* is the Greek name which links this procedure with Theophrastus' *Characters*; Immisch (p. 123) used that name, cf. my *Prol.* p. 112 n. 1. But in strict rhetorical terminology *characterismos* depicts physical features only, the *effictio* of *Ad Her.* IV. 63. *notare* in the *Ad Her.* (and perhaps in H.) corresponds to Greek *ethopoeia*, which the author of *Ad Her.* illustrates by a circumstantial account worthy of Theophrastus. Rutilius Lupus too has the relevant illustration under the same heading, I. 21, not where Immisch looked for it, under II. 7 *characterismos*. Quint. *I.O.* IX. 3 brushes these distinctions aside; they are too petty to count among his *schemata*.]

157 *naturis:* it has not been observed that this is the term used *Ad Her.* IV. 63. The passage (cit. last note) ties *alicuius natura* to *ethopoeia*; *natura* presumably renders φύσις, less likely τρόπος or ἦθος. The author connects *natura* as closely with the definition of *notatio* as does H.—a decisive argument against *maturis* (ς, Bentley) for MSS *naturis*. The conjecture, though admirable, is one which Bentley would not have published, had he been as aware of the literary and rhetorical background as he was of so many things. The same notion, Immisch points out p. 124, is ascribed to philosophy by Cic. *De Or.* I. 53, with *naturae* pl. as in H., cf. *Or.* 70. H. echoes the pair *naturis . . . et annis* in 166 by *aetas animusque*. Two other points have been made against *maturis*, rightly I think. The layout of the section does not encourage a division into two, *mobiles* and *maturi*; at the end, 176 ff., H. still envisages four diverse types. And finally an observation which could be set aside if *maturis* were wholly convincing: there seems to be no other case of displaced *et* in the *Ars*, but *maturis* displaces *et*, as M. Haupt noted, *Opusc.* I. 122. A. Michaelis, *Comm. . . . in hon. Theodori Mommseni*, p. 429, was ill advised to deny this observation on the basis of a dubious conjecture, for with *naturis* in the text *et* is used normally.

mobilibus...naturis..et annis 'to the characters changing with the changing years'. '*mobilibus*': *currentibus, quia semper* '*labuntur anni*' (*C.* II. 14. 2), rightly says ps.-Acro; and rightly too Lambinus, '*non leuibus, aut inconstantibus, ut quidam putat, sed quae variatis aetatibus immutantur*'. *mobilis* can indeed be 'inconstant' but in scores of instances it is *quod* '*moueri potest uel mouetur*' (*TLL*, VIII. 1197. 43). Thus in particular *Ep.* II. 2. 172 *puncto...mobilis horae* (174 *permutet*), *Anth. Lat.* 931. 97 *fuga mobilis aeui*, et al. Note too the verses of a late author steeped in classical Latin verse, Cyprian of Gaul (about A.D. 500), *Gen.* 331–2 *festinos menses et tempora mobilis anni | inrequieta iubens consuetos uoluere cursus.* The section headed '*respicitur inconstantia*', in *TLL, ibid.* 1199. 65 ff., unfortunately, not only contains the present passage, but separates H.'s *mobiles anni* (1200. 18) from his *mobilis hora* (1199. 44).

decor, ps.-Acro *puero...*τὸ πρέπον *idest decus tribuendum est,* cf. above 86 *descriptas...uices operumque colores,* 92 *locum...decentem,* 112 *fortunis absona dicta,* below 178 *in adiunctis aeuoque...aptis,* 316 *conuenientia cuique.* Quintilian often so used the word, e.g. *I.O.* 1. 8. 17 *quae in decore rerum, quid personae cuique conuenerit,* X. 1. 27 *in personis decor petitur,* XI. 3. 69 *decoris illa sunt, ut sit primo rectum et secundum naturam.*

158 *reddere uoces* 'speak', that is 'render words' which the child has heard and learned: ps.-Acro *qui iam potest loqui.* Thus *Ep.* I. 18. 13–14 *puerum...dictata magistro | reddere uel partes mimum tractare secundas, C.* IV. 6. 43 *reddidi carmen,* II. 33–4 *condisce modos, amanda | uoce quos reddas*; thus, with a different nuance, the *fidus interpres* above 133 *nec uerbo uerbum curabis reddere.* The little boy therefore can now speak and walk. Answer and walk would be the odd notion suggested by two passages often quoted (the second as early as ps.-Acro), and defended by Wilkins: Cat. 64. 166 *nec missas audire queunt nec reddere uoces (aurae),* Virg. *A.* I. 409 *ueras audire et reddere uoces.*

158–9 *pede certo | signat humum* aptly depicts the child's deliberate manner of walking; the imprint of feet on the shore, Ov. *Am.* II. 11. 15 *litora marmoreis pedibus signate, puellae. signare uestigia* is how Virgil describes the first cart-drill of bullocks, *G.* III. 169–71 *coge gradum conferre iuuencos: | ...illis...rotae ducantur inanes | per terram, et summo uestigia puluere signent.* Prosaic usage, for example in Cicero, is *uestigium ponere* or *facere.*

159 *paribus colludere:* the verb is common as a metaphor for 'collusion', and then often construed with *cum,* but is very rare in its literal meaning. This is the only known instance in classical Latin of *colludere* thus used with the dat. (cf. other compounds with *con*-); *TLL*, III. 1658. 28 records one other instance, from late Latin.

iram: the child's unreasonableness, sudden explosions of temper which as suddenly die down: Ter. *Hec.* 310 *pueri inter sese quam pro leuibus noxiis iram gerunt* (cit. A. di Benedetto, 'Echi terenziani in Orazio', *Rend. Acc. di Napoli*, XXXVII (1962), 57). Cf. *gestit*, 160 *temere*, *mutatur*. The *iuuenis* too is of course changeable, see 163, and Aristotle's εὐμετάβολος. H. says about himself: *irasci celerem, tamen ut placabilis essem*, *Ep.* I. 20. 25.

160 *concipit* I had conjectured before I noticed that Peerlkamp had so emended *colligit* (*conl*-) and had in turn been forestalled by the *editio Zarottina* of 1474, perhaps from a MS source. Surprisingly no edition since Peerlkamp prints it; Wilkins mentions the emendation only to reject it. Yet I think the MS reading *colligit* (*conligit*) cannot stand and the change to *concipit* is small; Peerlkamp cites Ov. *Met.* v. 446 *conceperat* MNF λ, *collegerat* (*conl*-) H, Heinsius, VI. 341 *concepit* ε'Fϛ, *collegit* BMN ϛ. All the instances of *colligo* assembled by Peerlkamp, and in *TLL*, III. 1613. 64–7 and 70, presuppose a slow and lengthy growth of the emotion. Thus Lucr. I. 722–5, Mount Etna working up its anger before an eruption, Virg. *A.* IX. 63–4 *collecta fatigat edendi* | *ex longo rabies*, Lucan I. 206–12, the lion crouching *dubius totam dum colligit iram*, | *mox*, etc., II. 93–4 Marius in Africa: *Libycas ibi colligit iras.* | *ut primum fortuna redit*, etc. Two other passages appear in a later section of *TLL* (= *cohibere, inhibere, ibid.* 1616. 61–2), wrongly, because Val. Fl. VII. 335 belongs to the previous section, whereas Sil. IX. 477 requires emendation. Anger long felt makes nonsense of a child's emotion, quick to flare up and quick to subside. That is what *concipere* expresses: '*percipere, affici*' (*TLL*). Cf. Cic. *T.D.* IV. 21 *ira acerbior...corde concepta*, Ov. *Met.* I. 166 *ingentes animo... concipit iras*, Val. Max. VII. 2. 5 *si quid irae conceperant*, et al.

mutatur in horas: like the *puella infans*, *Ep.* II. I. 100 *quod cupide petiit, mature plena reliquit.*

161–5 *iuuenis:* the νέοι of Ar. *Rhet.* II. 12. The age envisaged is about sixteen, cf. 161 n. While the typology is very similar to that in Aristotle and his successors, the colour is Roman.

161 I print *imberbis* (*inb*-) with BR and the majority of the MSS in spite of the homoeoteleuton -*is iuuenis*; Bland. Vet. and some eleventh-century MSS offer *imberbus*, C after correction. At *Ep.* II. I. 85 -*es* is in all MSS. Both forms were known, ps.-Acro *inberbus et inberbis sicut inermus et inermis*, cf. Keller, *Epil.* 750. Charis. I, *GL*, I. 95 (p. 122. 9 ed. Barwick) prefers -*us* but also cites -*is* from Livy. *TLL*,

Commentary

VII. 1. 424. 63 ff. offers the evidence, from which *-is* appears as the current post-Ciceronian form, *-us* in Lucil. and Varro, whereas Cicero's usage is doubtful.

tandem is said sympathetically, as befits an *ethopoeia*. Cf. Stat. *Silv.* V. 2. 68–9 *quem non corrupit pubes effrena, nouaeque | libertas properata togae*, Mart. IX. 27. 11 *iam paedagogo liberatus*.

custode remoto, that is at the age of *c*. 16 when the *toga uirilis* replaced the *praetexta*; ps.-Acro ⟨*custode*⟩ *idest paedagogo*. For the nuance in Latin *custos*, 'guardian', see *R-E* s.v. *Paidagogos*, XVIII. 2380, *TLL*, IV. 1575. 17 ff., e.g. Pl. *Mer.* 91 *mihi paedagogus fuerat, quasi uti mihi foret | custos*, *Pseud.* 865 *his discipulis priuos custodes dabo*, Cic. *Rep.* IV. 3 *ad militiam euntibus dari. . .custodes a quibus primo anno regantur*, Virg. *A.* V. 546 *custodem. . .comitemque impubis Iuli*, Hor. *A.P.* 239 *custos famulusque dei Silenus alumni*, *S.* I. 4. 118–19 (H.'s father) '*dum custodis eges, uitam . . .tueri | . . .possum*', I. 6. 81–2 *ipse mihi custos incorruptissimus omnis | circum doctores aderat*.

162 The passion for horses, hunting, and athletics is notably absent from Aristotle's account, although comedy offers such features. Ps.-Acro cites part of Ter. *An.* 56–7 *quod plerique omnes faciunt adulescentuli, | ut animum ad aliquod studium adiungant, aut equos | alere aut canes ad uenandum (aut ad philosophos)*; cf. *Phor.* 6–7 *adulescentulum | ceruam uidere fugere et sectari canes*.

For some characteristic remarks, see Polyb. XXXII. 15. 8 f., Plut. *Aem. Paul.* 6. 9 f., Cic. *Fin.* I. 69 *si. . .gymnasia, si campum, si canes, si equos, si ludicra exercendi aut uenandi, consuetudine adamare solemus*, etc., Hor. *C.* III. 12. 7 ff., 24. 54 ff., Tib. IV. 3 (Sulpicia), et al.; H. Blümner, *Die röm. Privataltertümer* (Müller's *Handbuch*, IV. 2. 2, 1911), pp. 512 ff.

163–5 H. has concentrated the descriptive features by subdividing the verses antithetically, unconnected in the middle of the line, except for the last. This dialectic scheme is not applied in Aristotle.

163 *in uitium flecti*: cf. Ar. *Rhet.* II. 12, 1389 b 3 (ἅπαντα ἐπὶ τὸ μᾶλλον καὶ σφοδρότερον) ἁμαρτάνουσι, and a 6 εὐμετάβολοι; the moral metaphor is not in Ar. The metaphor, *flectere*, was current since Enn. *Ann.* 259 *dictis nostris sententia flexa est* (cf. *TLL*, VI. 1. 892. 80 ff.) and the archaic adj. *flexanimus*, Pacuv. tr. 177 *o flexanima atque omnium regina rerum oratio*, applied to literary and moral subjects. So was the imagery of wax, known from Greek philosophy. For the imagery Juv. 7. 237–8 and others may be compared. The virtue of the passage does not, however, lie in the metaphor but in its wording, 'waxen so as to be modelled into the likeness of vice'. The pass. inf. *flecti*, 'epexegetic', explains the scope of *cereus*. For this type of inf. with

235

adj. or noun see Hofmann–Szantyr, 350 f.; some Greek influence is undeniable, but development in Latin literature, particularly Augustan verse, is the important feature. Cf. below 165 correspondingly *relinquere pernix.*

monitoribus: one of the descriptive nouns in -(*t*/*s*)*or*, half a dozen in these verses; cf. (in addition to *censor*) *prouisor, dilator, laudator, castigator.* Some of these agent nouns were archaic or poetic, but new ones seem to have been added steadily. The usage is complex and the material insufficiently known. Three lines of development may be distinguished. (*a*) Poets and poetizing writers of prose use rare instances of these formations, or fashion new ones, e.g. *prouisor* (164 n.), *dilator* (172 n.). (*b*) The descriptive conciseness of these nouns seems to have induced Cicero and other writers of classical prose to extend this usage; some of these nouns reappear in verse, e.g. *assentatores* (420 n.), cf. G. B. A. Fletcher, *Annotations on Tacitus* (1964), p. 64, apropos of Tac. *Hist.* I. 72. 1, *ibid.* 73, *Hist.* II. 76. 5. (*c*) Administrative language very early had *praetor, lictor,* etc. But later official jargon drew increasingly on these nouns; some of them had literary antecedents, e.g. *prouisor* (164 n.).

asper at the end of the line is contrasted with *cereus* at its beginning: however easily influenced for the worse, the *iuuenis* is impatient of overt guidance. Cf. above 161 *tandem custode remoto,* and Ar. *Rhet.* II. 12, 1389 a 11 ff. on the φιλονικία of the young, also b 5 εἰδέναι ἅπαντα οἴονται καὶ διϊσχυρίζονται.

164 Ar. *Rhet.* II. 12, 1389 a 14–15 φιλοχρήματοι δὲ ἥκιστα διὰ τὸ μήπω ἐνδείας πεπειρᾶσθαι, b 1 μήπω πρὸς τὸ συμφέρον κρίνειν μηδέν. In the *Ars* an antithetic pair: the young are slow to make money, (but) ready to spend it.

prouisor here, it seems, for the first time; next in literature known from Tac. *Ann.* XII. 4. 1, in a style even more elevated. But in the fourth and fifth centuries a provincial governor was commemorated in an inscription as *prouisor...prouinciae,* Dessau no. 1263 (*CIL*, XIV. 2917), another as *ordinis prouisor,* Dessau no. 1276 (*CIL*, X. 3860). See above 163 n. on *monitoribus* (*c*).

165 *sublimis* 'high-minded', like Greek μεγαλόψυχος, but also 'feeling superior' or 'desiring superiority', a double entendre which even the materials of the Latin Thesaurus cannot parallel; contrast *superbus,* one of ps.-Acro's 'synonyms'. It is likely to be a perceptive transference from such Greek terms as Ar. *Rhet.* II. 12, 1389 a 12 φιλότιμοι...μᾶλλον δὲ φιλόνικοι· ὑπεροχῆς γὰρ ἐπιθυμεῖ ἡ νεότης, ἡ δὲ νίκη ὑπεροχή τις. Cf. a 30 μεγαλόψυχοι· οὐ γὰρ ὑπὸ τοῦ βίου πω τεταπείνωνται κτλ., b 11 φιλευτράπελοι· ἡ γὰρ εὐτραπελία πεπαι-

Commentary

δευμένη ὕβρις ἐστίν. The thought then is Aristotelian but the power of catching in a single word the characteristically mixed state of youthful idealism and conceit is Horatian.

sublimis is a noble and antique word, at home in Roman tragedy (H. Haffter, *Glotta*, XXII (1935), 251 ff., H. D. Jocelyn, Enn. trag. fr. 3 n.), perhaps also in Ennian epic (Norden, Virg. *A*. VI. 719 n.) and, probably paratragic, in comedy (cf. Haffter, *loc. cit.*). It never quite shed the traces of this ancestry. From Varro onward it is often used as a poetizing word for 'highly placed': *R.R.* II. 4. 9 *antiqui reges et sublimes uiri*. *Sublimis* 'elated' often retains the metaphorical character of 'elevation, height', cf. Varro, *Men.* 1 *sublimis speribus*, Virg. *A*. X. 143–4 *quem. . . sublimem gloria tollit*, XII. 788 *sublimes armis animisque refecti*. Ovid too makes some poetic capital out of its connotations, notably *Met.* IV. 420–1 (elated by, proud of), *Pont.* III. 3. 103 *mens tua sublimis supra genus eminet ipsum* (great, elevated) and, of poetry, *Am*. I. 15. 23 *carmina sublimis. . .Lucreti*. Silver Latin continues these various notions. Ironies like Apul. *Met.* IV. 10 *sublimis ille uexillarius noster* occur. But H.'s double entendre is not to my knowledge repeated anywhere in Latin.

cupidus: cf. Ar. *Rhet.* II. 12, 1389 a 3 ff. ἐπιθυμητικοὶ κτλ.

amata relinquere pernix: cf. Ar. *Rhet.* II. 12, 1389 a 6–7 εὐμετάβολοι δὲ καὶ ἀψίκοροι πρὸς τὰς ἐπιθυμίας καὶ σφόδρα μὲν ἐπιθυμοῦσιν, ταχέως δὲ παύονται. The changeability of the boy, 160 n., is still remembered. An expressive phrase; contrast Ar.'s prosaic ταχέως δὲ παύονται. *amata* may be anything desired (cf. 164 neut. *utilium*), but may also hint at Ar.'s ἀκολουθητικοί εἰσι ⟨τῇ⟩ περὶ ἀφροδίσια (ἐπιθυμίᾳ) καὶ ἀκρατεῖς ταύτης (*ibid*. a 5), cf. *cupidus*. *pernix* occurs in poetry, historiography, and Silver prose. For the inf. see 162 n.

166 *aetas animusque*: the pair as 156 *aetatis cuiusque. . .mores* 157 *naturis. . .et annis*, *Ep.* I. 1. 4 *non eadem est aetas, non mens*. Virg. *G.* III. 100 had applied *animos aeuumque notabis* to horses.

167 *opes et amicitias*, etc.: contrast 164 *utilium tardus prouisor*. *opes* here defines *amicitiae* as 'useful connexions'—not the only aspects of Roman *amicitia*, cf. Cic. *Lael.* 55; contrast Ar. *Rhet.* II. 12, 1389 b 1–2, the young μήπω πρὸς τὸ συμφέρον κρίνειν μηδέν, ὥστε μηδὲ τοὺς φίλους. The wide range of *amicitia* is instructively discussed by P. A. Brunt, *Proc. Cam. Phil. Soc.* (1965), pp. 1 ff.

inseruit honori: cf. Cic. *Off.* II. 4 *posteaquam honoribus inseruire coepi meque totum rei publicae tradidi*, although Wilkins denies the relevance of this parallel. What is in point here is not the φιλοτιμία of the young but the seeking of public office and position. Unlike the pl. *honores* (e.g. *C.* I. 1. 8, III. 2. 18, *S.* I. 6. 11), *honor* denotes this *type* of position, *Ep.* I. 18. 102–3 *honos an dulce lucellum | an secretum iter et fallentis semita uitae*, Cic. *Brut.* 281 *cum honos sit praemium uirtutis iudicio . . .ciuium delatum ad aliquem*, Verr. I. 11 *quaestura primus gradus honoris.* Cf. *TLL*, VI. 3. 2927. 47 ff.

168 The *animus uirilis* differs from the others in showing steadiness and cautious 'commitment', cf. Ar. *Rhet.* II. 14, 1390 a 1–2 οὔτε πᾶσι πιστεύοντες οὔτε πᾶσιν ἀπιστοῦντες κτλ.

For the idiomatic perf. inf. *commisisse* see 98 n. *tetigisse. caueo* with inf. occurs in archaic literature and Silver prose; in classical writing it is largely restricted to verse, but see Cic. *Att.* III. 17. 3.

mox mutare, the reading of the best MSS, is much superior to *permutare*, uar.l. Keller, *Epil.* 750, cites Serv. Virg. *G.* I. 24 *Horatius mox . . . (C.* III. 6. 47–8) *idest postea;* ps.-Acro in his note on the present verse paraphrases *postea. . .mutare*. In *CQ*, XXI (1927), 62 H. J. Rose said that at *A.P.* 168 and 184 '*mox* simply means later'; he was right (as regards those and such other passages as 221), but ancient grammarians like Servius and ps.-Acro were aware of H.'s usage. Keller, *ibid.*, makes an attempt to explain the textual variant as a gloss p̄ (*post* explaining *mox*) misread as p = *per.*

169 Cf. Ar. *Rhet.* II. 13, 1389 b 16–17 καὶ τὰ πλείω φαῦλα εἶναι τῶν πραγμάτων.

senem circumueniunt incommoda, for the military metaphor, cf. Enn. trag. fr. 16 (Jocelyn) *multis sum modis circumuentus, morbo exilio atque inopia*, Sall. *Iug.* 7. 1 *his difficultatibus circumuentus*, Sen. *Dial.* II. 8. 3 *damna. . .quae sapientem, etiamsi uniuersa circumueniant, non mergunt*, Apul. *Met.* IX. 38 *tot malis circumuentus senex*; al. *TLL*, III. 1179. 82 ff.

uel quod. . . (171 *uel quod*), in the prosaic calculating *concinnitas* adapted to hexameter verse by Lucretius, e.g. I. 742–6 *primum quod . . .deinde quod*, II. 435–6 *uel cum. . .uel cum*, III. 807 ff., IV. 314–15, even in such elevated passages as I. 931 ff., II. 3–4.

170 Cf. Ar. *Rhet.* II. 13, 1389 b 26–9 τῶν πρὸς τὸν βίον ἐπιθυμοῦσι. καὶ ἀνελεύθεροι· ἐν γάρ τι τῶν ἀναγκαίων ἡ οὐσία, ἅμα δὲ. . .ἴσασιν ὡς χαλεπὸν τὸ κτήσασθαι καὶ ῥᾴδιον τὸ ἀποβαλεῖν, 1390 a 15 δουλεύουσι τῷ κέρδει. *quaerit*, cf. Ar.'s τὸ κτήσασθαι but also a pun, *quaerere–inuenire–uti* as *S.* I. 1. 37–8 (*formica) non usquam prorepit et illis utitur ante | quaesitis sapiens*, etc., *Ep.* I. 7. 57 *et quaerere et uti. inuentis. . .timet uti* a picture of ἀνελευθερία.

171 *timide gelideque:* cf. Ar. *Rhet.* II. 13, 1389 b 31 ff. κατεψυγμένοι γάρ εἰσιν. . .ὥστε προωδοπεποίηκε τὸ γῆρας τῇ δειλίᾳ· καὶ γὰρ ὁ φόβος κατάψυξίς τίς ἐστιν.

ministrat 'manages', an archaic, poetic and Silver prose usage.

Commentary

172–4 The qualities are now singly expressed, in descriptive adjectives or nouns in -(t)or.

172 *dilator:* this expressive noun, probably a Horatian coinage, is found here only in classical Latinity. August. *Serm.* XL. 5, cit. *TLL*, v. I. 1166. 25, is likely to be inspired by H.: *o male dilator, o crastini male appetitor.*

† *spe longus†*: Bentley impugned the phrase and sought to emend it. L. Mueller obelized it. Modern editors do not; presumably they understand it, though they do not say how, or if they do they fail. A. Y. Campbell, in *Bull. Lond. Inst. Class. St.* v (1958), 65, readily admitted that emendations had failed, but his own attempt (*speculator*) will convince few. Wilkins (1892) honestly confessed puzzlement. The words must apply to the *senex* himself; and while *spe* may be 'expectation' rather than 'hope', the *spes* cannot be that of others —τὰς ἐλπίδας χρονίζει (T. G. Tucker, *CQ*, VII (1913), 106). Old men, Ar. said, had their hopes disappointed, *Rhet.* II. 13, 1390 a 4 δυσέλπιδες διὰ τὴν ἐμπειρίαν, unlike the young (12, 1389 a 18 ff.), who are εὐέλπιδες, ὥσπερ γὰρ οἱ οἰνωμένοι κτλ. καὶ ζῶσι τὰ πλεῖστα ἐλπίδι. This would demand words denoting 'slow to conceive hopes', or indeed 'without hopes', the very opposite of the *spes longa* often quoted from *C.* I. 4. 15 *uitae summa breuis spem nos uetat incohare longam,* II. 6–7 *spatio breui | spem longam reseces.* Bentley therefore proposed *spe lentus,* but his parallels do not bear out the meaning posited; as Wilkins said, *lentus* = 'tenacious of hope'. And words denoting 'disappointed' or the like do not fit the *ductus* of the transmitted letters. Peerlkamp, for example, considered and rejected *spe tardus*; other attempts such as *spe serus* or *spe lapsus* (Caes. *B.G.* v. 55. 3) fail for the same reason. There remains the possibility canvassed by Peerlkamp and Heinze: *spe longus* = *spei longus,* 'holding long to his hopes', attached as an attribute to *dilator* = *qui in longum tempus differt.* But granted that the Latin will bear this construction (which I doubt), the *senex,* however attached to life, can scarcely be thought to reckon with a long life. Neither Soph. fr. 63 (Nauck²) τοῦ ζῆν γὰρ οὐδεὶς ὡς ὁ γηράσκων ἐρᾷ nor Cic. *Sen.* 24 *nemo enim est tam senex qui se annum non putet posse uiuere* bears out this reasoning. '(*Le vieillard*) *semble compter sur une vie sans fin*', is what J. Hardy distils from the Ciceronian remark (*Musée Belge*, XXV (1921), 229), regrettably, because to my mind he talks sound sense on the second part of this verse, ⟨*p*⟩*auidusque futuri.*

⟨*p*⟩*auidusque futuri:* thus Bentley. The MS reading is often compared with the passages of Sophocles and Cicero cited above, and defended by reference to Ar. *Rhet.* II. 14, 1389 a 32 ff. καὶ φιλόζωοι,

239

Commentary

καὶ μᾶλλον ἐπὶ τῇ τελευταίᾳ ἡμέρᾳ, διὰ τὸ τοῦ ἀπόντος εἶναι τὴν ἐπιθυμίαν, καὶ οὗ ἐνδεεῖς τούτου μάλιστα ἐπιθυμεῖν. So too ps.-Acro explains, *idest cupidus futuri quia semper senex timore mortis uiuere desiderat; nam timor mortis desiderium uitae est.* But, as J. Hardy said in the paper cited in the last note, *auidus futuri* is not φιλόζωος, and Cicero's words in another place of the *De Sen.* (72), supposed by A. Delatte, *Musée Belge*, XXVI (1922), 153, to corroborate the MS reading, in fact make against it; for the words are *ita fit ut* illud breue uitae reliquum *nec auide appetendum senibus nec sine causa deserendum sit.* Another defence, attempted by H. Nettleship, *JP*, XIX (1891), 296 and Heinze *ad l.*, seems to me untenable for a different reason. Epicurus taught that to be happy the wise man did not require the next day; on the contrary, ὁ τῆς αὔριον ἥκιστα δεόμενος ἥδιστα πρόσεισι πρὸς τὴν αὔριον (fr. 490, Usener, *Epic.* p. 307). Epicurean literature is full of that doctrine, e.g. Philod. *De Morte*, 38 f., and Seneca especially in his letters. A man so versed in Hellenistic philosophy as H. will have known that doctrine, but does he express it here? Seneca remarks, *Ep. 13. 17, occurrunt tibi senes qui se cum maxime ad ambitionem, ad peregrinationes, ad negotiandum parent. quid est autem turpius quam senex uiuere incipiens?* Such is the application of Epicureanism to old age—hardly relevant to the *iners senex* of this verse. Nor is an earlier time of life any more relevant, in spite of the apparent similarity with H.'s phrasing: Sen. *Ep. 32. 2 quam breuiorem inconstantia facimus (uitam), aliud eius subinde atque aliud facientes initium, ibid. 4 auidos futuri,* 101. 8 *cupiditas futuri exedens animum.* The defence of the MS reading based on Epicurean doctrine therefore fails, and by the same token Bentley's emendation is commended, not as a rendering of the Aristotelian passage cited at the beginning of this note, nor as repeating the sentiment of *S.* II. 2. 110–11 *an qui contentus paruo* metuensque futuri | *in pace . . . aptarit idonea bello.* Rather *iners ⟨p⟩auidusque futuri,* as the same critic observed, is the Horatian version of Ar. *Rhet.* II. 13, 1389 b 29–30 καὶ δειλοὶ καὶ πάντα προφοβητικοί.

The second part of the line does not then contain an antithesis—*iners ⟨sed⟩ . . .* ; all the descriptive terms for the *senex* seem to be similarly focused: a man inactive now, afraid of the future, living in the past.

173 *difficilis, querulus:* Ar. *Rhet.* II. 13, 1390 a 21–3 ὅθεν ὀδυρτικοί εἰσι, καὶ οὐκ εὐτράπελοι οὐδὲ φιλογέλοιοι· ἐναντίον γὰρ τὸ ὀδυρτικὸν τῷ φιλογέλωτι. Cf. *S.* II. 5. 90 *difficilem et morosum (offendet garrulus),* Ter. *Heaut.* 535 *hunc difficilem inuitum seruaret senem,* Cic. *Sen.* 7 *nec difficiles nec inhumani senes,* 65 *morosi . . . et iracundi et difficiles senes,* Sen. *Dial.* IV. 19. 4 *senes difficiles et queruli; TLL,* V. 1. 1087. 54 ff.

Commentary

173–4 *laudator temporis acti* | *se puero:* cf. Ar. *Rhet.* II. 13, 1390 a 6 ff. ζῶσι τῇ μνήμῃ μᾶλλον ἢ τῇ ἐλπίδι κτλ. ὅπερ αἴτιον καὶ τῆς ἀδολεσχίας αὐτοῖς. διατελοῦσι γὰρ τὰ γενόμενα λέγοντες. ἀναμιμνησκόμενοι γὰρ ἥδονται. *laudator* also below 433, frequently in Cicero, but not to my knowledge before him. *tempus actum* is 'the time spent' (e.g. Sall. *Iug.* 6. 1 *pleraque tempora in uenando agere) se puero*; first recorded in this passage with the time but not the action indicated (*TLL,* I. 1401. 29); contrast Val. Fl. III. 627 *temporis acti,* but cf. e.g. Cens. 16. 5 where (*tempus*) *ante actum...et uenturum* take up *ibid.* 16. 4 *praeteritum...futurum.*

castigator censorque minorum: castigator, an archaic and rarish word, first known from Plautus, but here only in classical Latin verse. The context lends a 'censorious' notion to both terms; *censor* metaphorical but restricted to literary criticism, *Ep.* II. 2. 110. The rhyme *-or -or(que)* is probably emphatic, cf. *-it et -it,* 110 n.

175–8 round off the descriptive part by linking up with the two introductory verses, 156–7, and stressing the principles underlying the description. The points of principle are H.'s approach to age, familiar from the lyrics (*eheu fugaces, Postume, Postume, labuntur anni*), but here merely implied; the idea of ἀκμή in *ferunt* and *adimunt*; and finally appropriateness, *aptis* (178), if that verse is genuine.

175 *anni* resumes 157 *annis; commoda* sums up the advantages of each age.

ferunt, contrasted with 176 *adimunt.* For H.'s imagery cf. *C.* II. 5. 14–15 *dempserit...apponet, Ep.* II. 2. 55 *praedantur.*

uenientes (glossed '*crescentes*' by ps.-Acro) is likewise contrasted with 176 *recedentes.* For the metaphor in H. of years rising to, or approaching, an acme, and then falling or receding, see *S.* II. 6. 40 *fugerit, Ep.* II. 1. 147 *recurrentis, C.* IV. 11. 19 *adfluentis.* Thus elsewhere in Latin poetry, e.g. Ov. *A.A.* I. 61 *adhuc crescentibus annis.*

176 *ne forte* (*mandentur*) used to be considered an independent prohibitive clause; many of the earlier editions placed a full stop after *uiriles* at the end of 177. But independent prohibitions with *ne* are very rare at this date, even in the form which orders and prohibitions will commonly take, the 2nd pers. sing. Such sentences therefore should not be accepted lightly. The more colloquial language of the hexameter poems is not necessarily relevant to the lyric poems. In the usage of the *Odes, neu* and *nec* (unless they continue *ne*) introduce independent prohibitions in the second person after a preceding jussive subjun. at *C.* I. 2. 51, II. 11. 3–4; but such instances of *ne* as *C.* I. 33. 1, III. 29. 6 still require discussion, see *Proc. Camb. Philol. Soc.* n.s. xv (1969), 4–6.

Commentary

The type *ne forte...mandentur* is not truly independent, nor is it explained by calling it an 'extension' of the independent prohibition (Hofmann–Szantyr, 336). This type is in fact dependent, although an apodosis is as it were suppressed. 'Lest the role of an old man be given to a youth...' (sc. *hoc dico* or the like), and then there follows a main clause. In this idiom it does not matter whether the second or third person is used, or the *ne forte* clause precedes or follows the statement qualified by it; in each case a colon is probably the best way of indicating the logical tie. At *C.* IV. 9. 1 *ne forte credas interitura quae* (colon, 4), *Ep.* I. 1. 13 *ac ne forte roges* (colon *ibid.*), II. 1. 208 *ac ne forte putes* (colon, 209), and perhaps in this passage *ne forte...* | *mandentur* (colon, 177), the *ne* clauses precede the statement; below 406–7 *ne forte pudori* | *sit*, etc., and possibly again the present passage, follow the statement (colon, 406), before *ne*. Klingner's Teubner edition marks the colon in all cases. To the present instance I have added the word 'perhaps' because the *ne forte* clause here may either pronounce on the preceding verses, or introduce the following verse. The nature of *ne forte*, etc. makes it unlikely that this clause has a Janus face. Some editors conceal the position by printing two colons (Vollmer and Klingner, *adimunt: uiriles:*) or a colon and semicolon (K.–H. and others *adimunt: uiriles;*). A choice will depend on the view taken of 178 (see below).

Since I regard the grammatical note in K.–H. as confused, it seemed worthwhile to show that the instances of *ne forte* (whether in the second or third person) form a syntactical group. Similar Horatian *ne* clauses without *forte* require further discussion, see *Proc. Camb. Philol. Soc.* cited above. In *HS*, LXIX (1965), 30, G. P. Goold has applied the name 'parenthetical clause of purpose' to a related idiom. But these *ne forte* clauses are not parentheses like *ut ita dicam*, or *ne dicam stulte* below 272, or perhaps even Ov. *A.A.* I. 428 *ne didicisse iuuet*, the passage which prompted Goold's note. Whereas all these cases are 'elliptic', and might be so called, only some of them form parentheses. It is to the latter cases that the name 'parenthetic' truly applies.

177 The fourfold division is preserved still, cf. above 157 n., but the types are now interwoven; *senex* is contrasted with *iuuenis*, and *puer* with *uir*.

mandentur, etymologically 'hand over', may denote *munus deferre*, *TLL*, VIII. 263. 8 ff. Applied to dramatic parts *mandare* is not recorded except here and above 104. *Ep.* I. 19. 8–9 shows the connexion between this and the less specialized usage: *forum...* | *mandabo siccis*, *adimam cantare seueris*.

uiriles rhymes with *seniles* at the end of the previous verse, two of the

Commentary

opposed terms of this section. Two verbs are similarly placed above
99–100 *sunto–agunto*; cf. the rhyming repetition of the same word at
241–2 *speret idem*... | *ausus idem*. These rhymes are formal means of
bringing out features of the content; there is less scope for that in a
verse-technique that employs rhyme habitually. Such homoeoteleuta
were noticed by the Greek literary critics, cf. Eustath. on Hom. *Il.*
XXII. 383–4 (cit. Orelli) ἔχει δὲ κάλλος καὶ τὰ ἐν τέλει στίχων δύο
πάρισα, τὸ 'τοῦδε πεσόντος' καὶ '"Εκτορος οὐκέτ' ἐόντος'.

178 was excised by O. Ribbeck (ed. 1869, pp. 211 ff.). Ribbeck
did textual criticism by doctrine, and his doctrine led him often
astray; but his doubts here have some justification. He impugns (*a*)
adiunctis, (*b*) *aeuo*, (*c*) *morabimur* (*-tur*), (*d*) the validity of the verse as
a whole. There is also the ἀπὸ κοινοῦ position of *aeuo* to be considered.

adiunctis, though rejected by Ribbeck as inadequate or superficial,
is in fact a Ciceronian word for 'inherent' qualities and features.
Textual work in the *Ars* is a tricky business without the technical
vocabulary of the literary critics and rhetoricians. Now, of course,
TLL, I. 712. 31 ff. provides the evidence.

aeuo, said Ribbeck, in H. is not 'age', *aetas*, but either 'life' or
'stage of life' (*Lebenszeit*). But *Ep.* I. 20. 26 *forte meum si quis te percontabitur aeuum* means 'if someone asks you my age', not 'my stage of
life', though of course any person's 'age' may be *described* as 'a stage
of life'. II.'s *aetas animusque* (above 166) may be set beside Virgil's
poeticism *animos aeuumque* (cited there) and similar passages are listed
in *TLL*, I. 1167. 22 ff.

Ribbeck may be right however about *morabimur* (*-tur*). 'We shall
remain in (i.e. firmly adhere to) what is suitable for each age' is an
odd way of putting the matter. The usage does not seem to be covered
either by Virg. *A.* IX. 439 *Volcentem petit, in solo Volcente moratur*, or by
the other passages cited *TLL*, VIII. 1500. 54 ff., although the compiler
of the article does not seem to have sensed any incongruity. If the
verse is genuine, *morabimur* (*-tur*) becomes suspect. Moreover MSS
and editors divide over *morabimur* or *-tur*, cf. Keller, *Epil.* 751. Rostagni,
defending *morabitur*, understands *iuuenis* and *puer* as grammatical
subj. from the preceding verse—a hard and unlikely collocation. Nor
is *morabitur*, sc. *scriptor* any more plausible. As regards *morabimur*
Heinze remarks that H. never includes himself in precepts in the fut.
tense; I can quote no instances of precepts in 1st per. pl. fut. to
disprove him, although H. frequently joins others in an apparently
companionable 'we', cf. notes on 11–12, 24, 25–6, 153 *ego et populus
mecum*, 331, 347.

in adiunctis aeuoque... *aptis* has *-que* displaced from *aptis* to *aeuo*, which in turn depends 'ἀπὸ κοινοῦ' on *adiunctis* and *aptis*. The prosaic order would be *in adiunctis aptisque aeuo*. This idiom is common with verbs (e.g. *C.* ii. 19. 32 *pedes tetigitque crura*) and subjects or objects of sentences; for some Horatian instances see Klingner's 3rd ed. of H., p. 337, for a discussion of various types of 'dislocation' in Latin verse, see Housman, *CQ*, x (1916), 149 f. The ἀπὸ κοινοῦ construction is much less frequent with other parts of the sentence. The present case recalls the *rarum illius figurae genus* 'quo substantiuum ad duo adiectiua pertinens secundo demum adiungitur eique praemittitur, ut Hor. Serm. i. 6. 101 sq. *ducendus et unus | et* comes *alter* (si tamen substantiuum est *comes*)', etc., Housman, *Man.* iv. 726 n. But here of course *aeuo* is governed by *adiunctis* and *aptis*. The rarity of the construction however is no point against Horatian authorship. Cf. also above 86 n.

Finally, Ribbeck's case against the verse as a whole. That 178 looks back to 156–7 is no case against it, for so do 176–7. But the passage as it stands turns back to the beginning twice over and the circle would be closed sufficiently by 176 *ne forte*–177. In that case *ne forte* etc. would round off the section after a colon at *adimunt* (176), cf. 406–7. The stress on *aptum*, appropriateness, adds but little since this principle is already inherent in the preceding three verses.

The upshot of my lengthy discussion is this: 178 is suspect, but the suspicions are not definite enough to condemn this verse as an (ancient) interpolation. Cf. 449, 467 nn.

(2) Action and reported action on the stage, 179–88

The tradition. For its relation to Ar. *Poet.* 14, 1453 b 1–11, see *Prol.* 114. Unlike Rostagni, I see no connexion here with the topics of Ar. ch. 15, though there may be some with ch. 11, 1452 b 11–13. In the tradition on which H. has drawn, Aristotle's argument has been moved out of the context of the *Poetics* to another; Aristotle was concerned with the effect of the plot, the Horatian tradition, it seems, with the permissibility of horror on the stage. Cf. Philostr. *V.A.* vi. 11. 113 τὸ ὑπὸ σκηνῆς ἀποθνήσκειν ἐπενόησεν (Αἰσχύλος), ὡς μὴ ἐν φανερῷ σφάττοι, *Schol.* Soph. *Ajax* 815 ἔστι δὲ τὰ τοιαῦτα παρὰ τοῖς παλαιοῖς σπάνια· εἰώθασι γὰρ τὰ πεπραγμένα δι' ἀγγέλων ἀπαγγέλλειν· τί οὖν τὸ αἴτιον; φθάνει Αἰσχύλος ἐν Θρήσσαις τὴν ἀναίρεσιν Αἴαντος δι' ἀγγέλου ἀπαγγείλας·

Commentary

ἴσως οὖν καινοτομεῖν βουλόμενος . . . ὑπ' ὄψιν ἔθηκεν τὸ δρώμενον ἢ μᾶλλον ἐκπλῆξαι βουλόμενος κτλ., *Schol. A*, Hom. *Il.* vi. 58 ὅθεν κἂν ταῖς τραγῳδίαις κρύπτουσι τοὺς δρῶντας τὰ τοιαῦτα (sc. μισητὰ καὶ ὠμά) ἐν ταῖς σκηναῖς κτλ. (cit. Orelli, Heinze, Rostagni). The first scholium's ὄψις and ἐκπλῆξαι seem to imply an idea of vision similar to H.'s. Hamlet's vivid expression, 'amaze the very faculties of eyes and ears' in the scene with the players does not so distinguish sight and hearing. Cf. 181 n.

Horace. After the descriptive rhetoric of the preceding piece, there is now a change of subject—marked, as often, by a brusque new beginning—and a change of style: prescription instead of description.

179 *agere* with partic. *actus* (e.g. *Didasc.* Ter. *Phor.* '*incipit Terenti Phormio: acta Ludis Romanis*'), noun *actus*, and *actor*, the conventional word for 'perform, act'. The 'polyptoton' *agitur–acta* contrasts action on the stage with action reported in speeches.

scaenis, the generalized pl., known from Virgil and others; contrast a few lines below, 183 *in scaenam*, 125 *siquid . . . scaenae committis*, 260, al.

180–2 correspond to 179 *agitur*, 182–4 to *acta refertur*. Ar. *Poet.* 6, 1449 b 26 is more definite: δρώντων καὶ οὐ δι' ἀπαγγελίας.

180 expresses ψυχαγωγία by the more vivid metaphor of 'stirring the mind', as *Ep.* ii. 1. 210–13 *ille . . . poeta, meum qui* pectus *inaniter angit,* | *irritat, mulcet, falsis terroribus implet,* | *ut magus*, etc. At *Poet.* 6, 1450 b 16 ἡ δὲ ὄψις ψυχαγωγικὸν κτλ., Ar. is not talking about the sense of vision but about the stage-setting. For *irritant* cf. Sen. *Ep.* 58. 26 *quae nos accendunt et irritant*, 87. 33 *non irritantem tantum animos sed attrahentem*, 113. 18 *omne rationale animal nihil agit, nisi primum specie alicuius rei irritatum est.*

segnius: Nazar. *Pan.* 32. 4 *ad animum* languidius *accedunt quae aurium uia manant quam quae oculis hauriuntur*, Pac. *Pan.* 24. 4 *non auribus modo, quarum sensus est leuior, sed coram oculis.* Cf. Lucr., 181 n. on *fidelibus.*

demissa per aurem: cf. Cic. *De Or.* ii. 357 *ea, quae perciperentur auribus* (in memorizing), Virg. *A.* iv. 428 *cur mea dicta negat duras demittere in aures*; *demittere* is frequently so used with *pectus, animus* or the like, e.g. Sall. *Iug.* 102, Ov. *Met.* ix. 468.

181 *oculis subiecta*: this is not the proverb 'eyes are more reliable

245

than ears' and similar commonplace sayings (see below, *fidelibus*, or such sentiments as are expressed by Cic. *Fam.* VI. I. 1, 4. 3) nor a philosophical doctrine of vision. Peerlkamp noted that *demissa* seems to indicate a stronger sense impression than *subiecta*, and proposed an exchange of the two words. This was rightly rejected by Wilkins. Yet even a false conjecture by an acute textual critic is often valuable because it points to something in need of explanation. In fact *oculis subiecta* recalls the 'vivid style', ἐνάργεια or ὑποτύπωσις of the rhetoricians; in Greek it is often expressed by πρὸ ὀμμάτων τιθέναι. Quint. *I.O.* IV. 2. 64 *cum quid ueri non dicendum sed quodammodo etiam ostendendum est, sed subici perspicuitati potest*; VI. 2. 32 quae *a Cicerone illustratio et euidentia nominatur* (the Ciceronian passage closest to this description, though scarcely what Quint. has in mind, is *Part. Or.* 20 *illustris est autem oratio si*, etc. *est enim haec pars orationis quae rem constituat paene ante oculos*), IX. 2. 40 *illa uero, ut ait Cicero*, sub oculos subiectio (Cic. *De Or.* III. 202) . . . cum res non gesta indicatur sed ut sit gesta ostenditur . . . *quem locum proximo libro* (VIII. 3. 61 ff.) subiecimus euidentiae . . . *ab aliis* ὑποτύπωσις *dicitur* . . . *ut* cerni *potius uideatur quam* audiri. Action on the stage is the most vivid presentation and H. describes it by using the terminology that the rhetoricians had developed for their *euidentia*. Dramatic presentations *oculis subiecta* are therefore more vivid than *demissa per aurem*. Here again there is a mixture of literary and rhetorical categories which characterizes the *Ars* throughout. Theophrastus disagreed with this kind of assessment, *ap.* Plut. *De Aud.* 38 a περὶ τῆς ἀκουστικῆς αἰσθήσεως ἦν ὁ Θεόφραστος παθητικωτάτην εἶναί φησι πασῶν. οὔτε γὰρ ὁρατὸν οὐδὲν οὔτε γευστόν . . . ἐκστάσεις ἐπιφέρει κτλ., with Plutarch's comments. Great value is of course attributed to the ear when H. contrasts listening to poetic drama with the watching of spectacles, *Ep.* II. I. 188, cf. Fraenkel, *Hor.* 393 n. 3. St Augustine's remarks, *Conf.* I. 10, use traditional language in a far from traditional spirit.

fidelibus: proverbial in Greek, *CPG*, II. 744 ὠτίων πιστότεροι ὀφθαλμοί. Thus Herod. I. 8 ὦτα . . . ἀπιστότερα ὀφθαλμῶν et al. Cf. Lucr. V. 102–3 (noted by Mr E. J. Kenney), Sen. *Ep.* 6. 5 et al.

182 *ipse sibi tradit*: a more direct way of expressing the immediate character of sense impressions than (say) Cic. *De Or.* II. 357 *quae essent a sensu tradita atque impressa*; *ibid. si etiam commendatione oculorum animis traderentur*.

182 *non tamen*–**84**, and the instances that follow, correspond to the rejection of 'fearsomeness by way of spectacle', τὸ φοβερόν, διὰ τῆς ὄψεως, and, even more, 'the monstrous', τὸ τερατῶδες, rejected by Ar. *Poet.* 14, 1453 b 8–10. But the motive differs. Aristotle rejects them because they do not provide the pleasure akin to tragedy, H. because of a sense of fitness: 183 n. *digna*, 188 n. *incredulus odi*.

182 *intus* 'indoors, offstage', i.e. inside the house which fronted the stage according to the Graeco-Roman convention. *intus* is contrasted with *promes in scaenam, coram populo, palam*, 183–6, and it is the conventional term in comedy, e.g. Pl. *Cas.* 751 *gladium Casinam intus habere ait*, 756 *perspicito prius quid intus agatur*.

183 *digna geri:* not 'worthy to be done' but displaying the derivation from the root of *decet, decus*, i.e. **decnos*, 'fitting': ps.-Acro *quae debent intus agi*; *TLL*, v. 1. 1143. 15 paraphrases that notion by '*decens, aptus, conueniens*', yet subjoins the present instance under the wrong heading, 1152. 69. This meaning as well as the inf. appear frequently, e.g below 282–3 *uim | dignam lege regi*, *S.* 1. 3. 24 *improbus hic amor est dignusque notari*, 4. 3 *siquis erat dignus describi quod malus ac fur*, 24–5 *utpote pluris | culpari dignos*, *Ep.* 1. 10. 48.

promes . . . tolles still an address to the putative poet, 119 n., 153 n.

184 *ex oculis* cf. 181 *oculis*.

mox, probably = *postea*, 168 n.

facundia praesens, as commentators say, = *f. praesentis nuntii*, but the presence of the reporter or report is emphasized; he or it, not the action, is presented.

185 Dramatic incidents in this verse and the next are again too readily identified with known plays, e.g. by K.–H. *ad l.* and K. Latte, *H*, LX (1925), 3. For tragic versions of the Medea legend, see Lesky, *R-E*, XV. 54 f., Eur. *Med.* ed. D. L. Page, pp. xxx ff. Ar. *Poet.* 14, 1453 b 28–9 refers to the killing of the children, but Aristotle's point is unconnected with H.'s; Keller's ref. to Aristotle in his app. crit. is misleading. Enn. tr. 234–6 (Jocelyn) seems to imply that the murder of the children was not shown on the stage, as Eur. *Med.* 1251 ff. certainly implies. Whether conclusions may be based on artistic representations (for which see Lesky, *op. cit.* 61 ff.) is a different matter. In Seneca's (presumably recited) tragedy the question does not strictly arise; but as far as it does, Seneca did not pay attention to this Horatian rule, cf. Sen. *Med.* 967 ff.

ne in virtually the whole of the transmission, although Bentley had to sponsor it against vulgate *nec*; continued by independent *neue* 189, and *nec*, 191, 192. It is more likely to begin a subord. clause than a new independent one, proposed by Peerlkamp.

186 A stock example of a horrific play, hackneyed and insipid to Persius' mind, 5. 8–9 *si quibus aut Procnes aut si quibus olla Thyestae | feruebit saepe insulso cenanda Glyconi*. For Atreus and the *cena Thyestae*, see 91, where *narrari* need not imply that *acta refertur*. In Seneca's tragedy the doors of the house are said to be opened at 901–2; Atreus describes the *cena* supposed to be held offstage, 908 ff.

187 The verse is arranged in chiastic order with *uertatur* in the centre: both dramas contained metamorphoses. Tragedies on the theme of Procne are discussed by G. Radke, *R-E*, xxiii. 247 f.; cf. Persius, cited in the previous note. Cadmus' metamorphosis is mentioned at Eur. *Bac.* 1330 ff.; for the tenuous traces of his Cadmus tragedy, K. Latte, *R-E*, x. 1468. 11 ff., Eur. fr. 448 (Nauck²). But Eur. fr. 930 (Nauck²) οἴμοι, δράκων μου γίγνεται τό ⟨γ'⟩ ἥμισυ· | τέκνον, περιπλάκηθι τῷ λοιπῷ πατρί, cited by Hermogenes for its bad taste (κακόζηλον), is not by him assigned to the *Cadmus*; cf. Nauck *ad l.* But even if it were, as K.–H. and Rostagni remark, it is likely to come from a messenger's speech.

Procne, although this spelling, unlike *Progne*, here occurs only in φψ apart from Renaissance MSS of the *Ars*; hence 'Progne non Procne', pronounced S. G. Owen, Ovid, *Trist.* p. xv, referring the reader to this verse and two others, and was punished accordingly by Housman *CR*, xvii (1903), 390, cf. *CQ*, xxii (1928), 3 ff. The MSS of Virgil in capitals all have *Procne* at *G.* iv. 15, cf. Housman, *CQ*, xxii (1928), 9.

188 *ostendis:* cf. 181 *oculis subiecta*, Quint. *I.O.* ix. 2. 40 *ostenditur*, cit. 181 n.

incredulus odi: cf. *Ep.* ii. 1. 89 *liuidus odit*. For *odi* as a (stronger) term for 'reject, spurn', see *Ep.* i. 7. 20 *spernit et odit*, and Fraenkel, *Hor.* 263. Ps.-Acro may but need not be right in assuming that the adj. gives the reason for *odi*: *idest non credens sic debere fieri, ac per hoc sperno atque contempno.* A difference of principle between H.'s various instances in this section is implausibly asserted by Rostagni and K. Ziegler, *R-E*, vi a. 1973.

(3) The 'five-act law', 189–90

The evidence such as it is has been discussed with divergent results by various scholars, especially by R. T. Weissinger, 'A Study of Act Divisions in Classical Drama' (*Iowa Studies* ix, 1940) and W. Beare, *The Roman Stage*³ (1964), ch. 25, both of whom seem to me to assert too much. *actus* is 'part of drama', but the principle of the division is not certain. It is at any rate likely that it corresponds to the 'prologue, episode, and exodus' in the suspect ch. 12 of Ar. *Poet.*; that is, the original principle of division was the presence of choruses. A different type of division would be obtained on the basis of *Poet.* ch. 7 with its 'beginning, middle, and end'. The divisions in classical tragedies differ in number, notably in Sophoclean and Euripidean. Division of plays into 'parts', i.e. something like acts, is known from Hellenistic theory, and that presupposes such divisions applied to classical tragedies (Eur. *And.* hypoth. ἐν τῷ δευτέρῳ μέρει, *Vita Aesch.* ed. Wilamowitz, § 6 ἕως τρίτου μέρους). The division does not suit Old Comedy. As for New Comedy, the Bodmer papyrus of Menander's *Dyscolus* has four indications of ΧΟΡΟΥ which account for five parts or acts. E. W. Handley (*The Dyskolos of Men.* (1965), p. 4) thinks it 'probable that for Menander that number was the rule'. This reasonable guess is now borne out by Menander's *Aspis* and *Samia* from the same papyrus codex (where ΧΟΡΟΥ is preserved before the places that would correspond to the beginnings of 'Acts' ii, iii, v, and iv, v respectively; the Sorbonne papyrus is equally marked before 'Acts' iv and v); the indications in *Aspis* and *Samia* are discussed by Rodolphe Kasser in *Pap. Bodmer XXV* (1969), p. 22. What is certain however is that the Mytilene mosaics illustrating scenes from Menander (of which Professor Handley kindly reminds me) do not go beyond the number five; one of the mosaics has μέρος α′, four β′, two γ′, one δ′, two ε′, cf. G. Daux's publication, *Bull. Corr. Hell.* xci (1967), 474–6. For what it is worth it may also be remembered that Apuleius, *Flor.* 16. 64, reports happenings 'in the third act' of a comedy by Philemon. This evidence is descriptive, whereas H., and perhaps his Hellenistic authorities, are prescriptive: a successful play must have neither more nor less than five acts. Beare, *The Roman Stage*[3], pp. 208, 215, does not put this point clearly. The presence of act divisions in Hellenistic theory and practice, and the possibility of a Hellenistic precedent for H.'s prescription, make it hazardous to assert (Beare, *op. cit.* p. 209) that 'the case for the law rests on Latin evidence alone'. In the generation before H. both Varro and Cicero show themselves sufficiently conversant with act divisions of various kinds to apply them metaphorically to topics other than drama, cf. *TLL*, I. 450. 78 ff., 451. 3 ff.). As for Plautus' technique, the small but important remains of the new papyrus of Menander's Δὶς ἐξαπατῶν allow instructive comparisons with the *Bacchides* in this regard, cf. E. W. Handley, *Menander and Plautus: a Study in Comparison* (Inaug. Lect. London 1968), p. 14 with nn. 11 and 12. Terence seems to have worked according to a model of continuous action (see above 154 n. and C. C. Conrad, *The Technique of Continuous Action in Roman Comedy*, 1915); some modern scholars claim the plausibility of act divisions in his comedies, but Donatus and Euanthius found it hard to apply such divisions (see G. E. Duckworth, *The Nature of Roman Comedy*, 98–101, H. D. Jocelyn, *The Tragedies of Ennius*, pp. 18 f. and the refs. *ap.* Beare, p. 209). Nothing definite can be known about the structure of republican tragedy. The fivefold division however fits Senecan tragedy and the structural principle is not invalidated by the reasonable surmise that Seneca's plays were written for recitation.

189 *neue . . . neu:* cf. *S.* II. 5. 89 *neu desis operae neue immoderatus abundes.*

productior: the quasi-adj. is established in Cicero in the sense here required; the compar. Cic. *Or.* 178, *T.D.* III. 38, and in Silver Latin, cf. G. B. A. Fletcher, *Annot. on Tac.* 41.

actu = quam actum: for an acc. of extent thus cast into an abl. of comparison, see Kühner–Stegmann, II. 466 f. For the word in a wider sense applied to drama, see 129 n.; here it denotes each of the (five) 'acts' of a play, Greek μέρος; but πρᾶξις with this connotation, asserted by Rostagni, 189–90 n., is unknown to me except in late Greek lexicography. *actus* is so used by Varro and Cicero (above 189–90 n.). Ter. *Hec.* 39 *primo actu placeo* perhaps need not denote more than the 'beginning of the play', cf. *Ad.* 9 *in prima fabula*; the expression is indistinct.

190 is clear enough in its general purport: 'if a play is to succeed'; cf. 153–5, *spectare* 'watch a performance', Ter. *And.* prol. 27, *Heaut.* prol. 29, *Hec.* prol. 3 and 20. The wording is however dubious. (1) *et spectanda* aCRφ Porph. ps.-Acro or *et exspectanda* BK, *exs-* in ras. ψ; *et spectata* δπ λl; (2) *reponi* joined to *posci*. As for (1), *ex* is a dittography of *et*; *-andus* and *-atus* are frequently confused, e.g. above 37, *S.* I. 10. 39, cf. Keller, *Epil.* 751 f.; thus elsewhere, e.g. Ov. *Am.* II. 11. 15,

and the emendations at *Am.* II. 9. 1 and *A.A.* 1. 114 discussed by
G. P. Goold, *HS*, LXIX (1965), 35 f., 61.

At first sight *spectata* looks convincing and -*anda* a tautology, so for
example Wilkins *ad l.* In fact *posci* on grounds of quality cannot be
explained except on the assumption of a previous performance and
it is *spectata* that is already inherent in *posci*; no thought here of a
recitation before the acceptance of the play. That makes for *spectanda*
and for repeated performances as at *S.* 1. 10. 39 *nec redeant iterum atque
iterum spectanda theatris.* It also makes for *spectanda* placed ἀπὸ κοινοῦ
in both clauses as suggested by K.–H. and illustrated (though for
spectata) with many instances from the *Epistles* in Ribbeck's edition,
pp. 225 f. As for (2), *reponi*, 120 *reponis Achillem* differs in meaning.
It is true, *pono* 'put on' (a dramatic performance), is the word used
by Asinius Pollio, Cic. *Fam.* X. 32. 3; but it would be weak next to
posci, often = demand a song or poem, e.g. Ov. *Fast.* IV. 721–2 *Parilia
poscor:* | *non poscor frustra*, Prop. IV. 1. 74 *poscis ab inuita uerba pigenda
lyra.* Here *posci* is a demand for a dramatic performance, cf. *postu-
lantibus*, Apul. *Flor.* 16. 64 (recitation of a comedy by Philemon).
Having been demanded once, *posci*, it should be demanded again—
not *reponi* but *reposci*, the proposal reported but not approved by
Lambinus, and later proposed afresh by Wyttenbach and Ribbeck;
Peerlkamp too favoured it but rewrote the whole line gratuitously.
Hence Terence's *iterum referre*, *Hecyram ad uos refero*, and *refero denuo*
(*Hec.* prol. 1. 7, prol. 2. 21, 30) or similar notions are, then, here
expressed by *reposci*. For simple verb and compound in such collo-
cation as *posci–reposci*, cf. *A.P.* 101 *ridentibus arrident. . .flentibus adflent*,
Ep. I. 1. 98 *petiit. . .repetit*, 7. 55 *it, redit*. For *sc* confused with *n* in
these two verbs, see Prop. I. 17. 11 *reponere: reposcere* Baehrens'
'necessary correction' (D. R. Shackleton Bailey, *Prop.* 51), but Ov.
Met. XIII. 235 *reposco: repono* ς, Bentley, edd.

(4) The 'deus ex machina', 191–2 (inciderit)

The mechanism of the stage-device known as μηχανή or
machina is discussed in Pickard-Cambridge's *Theatre of Dionysus*,
pp. 127–8, al. (see μηχανή, Index), its relevance to the structure of the tragic plot in A. Spira's *Unters. zum Deus ex machina
bei Soph. und Eur.*, Frankfurt, 1960. The device was suspect
because of its potential violation of dramatic coherence: Ar.
Poet. 15, 1454 b 1 ff., Antiphanes fr. 191 (Kock). Hence by
comparison—ὥσπερ οἱ τραγῳδοποιοί and the like—the

machina illustrates artificial and illogical solutions of difficulties, a knot cut but not untied; thus the activities of gods and divine personages (Plato, *Crat.* 425 d, Polyb. III. 48. 8–9, Cic. *N.D.* I. 53). A witness out of the blue, ὥσπερ ἀπὸ μηχανῆς (Demosth. XL. 59), is half-way between comparison and metaphor, and Anaxagoras' cosmic Reason μηχανῇ (Ar. *Met.* A, 985 a 18) is metaphorical. Ar. *Poet. ibid.* restricts the device to events ἔξω τοῦ δράματος in the past or future which could not be known to the *dramatis personae* but only to divine omniscience. H. too wishes to restrict the *machina*; it should be used only if the dramatic knot cannot appropriately (see *dignus* below) be untied without it.

191 *nec* codd. (*non* in *Flor. Nostr.*). In independent clauses of prohibition classical poetic usage occasionally varies *neu* with *nec*, e.g. Cat. 61. 119 ff. (126 ff.) *ne taceat...nec...neget.*

dignus: scarcely a dramatic knot 'worthy' of divine intervention (to which phrase in the context of Greek tragedy I cannot attach any meaning) but one to which such an intervention 'is appropriate', cf. 183 n. As elsewhere H. refuses to specify; his refusal has evoked surprise (e.g. *CR*, XXXIV (1920), 10). Since this instruction simply demands appropriateness, it is possible that H. echoes something like the Aristotelian ruling, but it does not follow that the reminiscence is 'distorted' (Bywater, Ar. *Poet.* 15, 1454 b 2 n. on ἀλλὰ μηχανῇ).

uindice, not in its legal sense, as for example Dacier thought: 'cette expression est heureuse, elle est prise du Droit Romain, qui appelle *uindicem* un homme qui met un esclave en liberté'. Rather note Proclus (cit. Orelli) on Plato *Alcib. I* 105 a (ed. Creuzer 142, ed. Westerink p. 64) ὥσπερ ἐν ταῖς τραγῳδίαις ἐκ μηχανῆς πολλάκις θεούς τινας εἰσάγουσιν οἱ ποιηταὶ τῶν παρόντων πραγμάτων διορθωτάς, 'to set right present embarrassments'. διορθωτής is the Greek term for the Roman office of *corrector. uindex* happily renders some such notion, combining protection and the obviating of difficulties, cf. Pl. *Trin.* 644–6 *honori posterorum tuorum ut uindex fieres, | tibi pater...facilem fecit...uiam | ad quaerundum honorem,* Ov. *Her.* 9. 13 (Hercules) *respice uindicibus pacatum uiribus orbem.*

nodus is not before this passage known as a term for the dramatic knot; it appears to be a translation of Aristotle's δέσις. The untying of the knot, which is beyond human power to deal with, makes it *dignus uindice.* Compare *explicare* in Porph. *ad l.* The critics of the tragedians used the same language when they said, as Cic. does in the passage noted 191–2 n., *cum* explicare *argumenti exitum non potestis, confugitis ad deum.* Next after H. *nodus* seems to appear in Apuleius. R. Kassel (*RM*, cv (1962), 96) has made sense of Apul. *Flor.* 16. 63, on the subject of Philemon's comedies. *argumenta lepide implexa* (Kassel, *inflexa* MS) are now seen to denote the tying of the dramatic knot, and Kassel is surely right in sponsoring Colvius' excellent emendation (ed. 1588) *ac nodos* (*adgnatos* MS) *lucide explicatos.* Later still is Don. *Ter. An.* Praef. II. 1 (p. 37. 19 ff. Wessner) (*periculumque Charini...et*) *totus error inenodabilis usque ad eum finem est ductus, ibid.* p. 38. 3 (*dum*) *nodum fabulae soluat, ibid.* on 404 *haec scaena nodum innectit erroris fabulae.* In spite of the paucity of ancient instances *nodus* with this connotation must have been sufficiently established to be continued in a Romance language: *dénouement* is *disnodamentum.*

(5) The rule of Three Actors, 192 (nec...laboret)

The evidence has been surveyed by Pickard-Cambridge, *Dram. Fest.*[2] (1958), 135–56 with bibliog. (*ibid.* 138 f. on κωφὰ πρόσωπα and παραχορήγημα); for Menander add E. W. Handley, *The Dysk. of M.* (1965), pp. 25–30, for Roman comedy H. W. Prescott, *CP*, xviii (1923), 23–34, C. M. Kurrelmeyer, *The Economy of Actors in Pl.* (Graz, 1932), H. D. Jocelyn, *The Tragedies of Ennius* (1967), pp. 20 f. In fact two rules are conflated *breuitatis causa*: the number of speaking actors to be restricted to three; if a fourth *persona* appears at all, it should be *muta.* (Cf. Martial's parody, vi. 6 *comoedi tres sunt, sed amat tua Paula, Luperce,* | *quattuor; et* κωφὸν *Paula* πρόσωπον *amat.*) These precepts differ from the brief factual remark in Ar. *Poet.* ch. 4; they may have a Hellenistic basis, cf. *Prol.* 114 and *Schol.* Aesch. *Cho.* 899 ἵνα μὴ δ' λέγωσιν. H.'s prescriptive procedure is best explained as an attempt to normalize the technique of Roman drama by the example of Greek. Ancient commentators and *grammatici* were aware of the differences between H.'s rules and Roman practice: ps.-Acro, *loquentes...non amplius quam tres, licet aliter reperiatur in comoediis et tragoediis*; Diom. *GL*, I. 491. 2 adds (after asserting *quia quarta semper muta,* i.e. in the Greek theatre), *at Latini scriptores complures personas in fabulas introduxerunt, ut speciosiores frequentia facerent.*

> *nec:* cf. 191 n.
> *persona:* cf. 126 n.
> *laboret:* cf. 25 n.

(6) The Chorus, 193–201

The first three verses, like Ar. *Poet.* (see 193 n.), extend an actor's part to the chorus—thus in a sense making up for the restriction at 192, and also establishing a link between the two precepts. The demand is the Aristotelian one: an organic connexion between choral passages and the action of the play. The remaining six verses, 196 ff., prescribe the sentiments proper for the chorus. 193–5 therefore restate Aristotle's view, cf. *Prol.* 115 and my notes below; 196 ff. have no Aristotelian precedent but express the moralistic view of poetry that is found throughout the *Ars*. The two groups together show the same complexion of Aristotelianism restated which I regard as the Hellenistic feature of the Horatian tradition. Presumably we owe it to H. himself that the two diverse elements appear as a unity with a Roman colouring and Augustan moral rhetoric.

That Roman archaic tragedy contained some choruses even in lyric metre is suggested by our scanty evidence. F. Leo's arguments concerning these matters (particularly *Gesch. der röm. Lit.* 71, 101 f., 193 ff., 229) remain fundamental for future discussion. But his conclusion that lyric choruses were always replaced by recited metres is implausible in Ennius' tragedies and, as Leo himself admits, it fails for pre-Ennian tragedy and Pacuvius; for discussion and bibliog. see H. D. Jocelyn, *The Tragedies of Ennius* (1967), Introd. pp. 19, 30 f., fr. XCIX n. Jocelyn, *op. cit.* p. 19, rightly notes that H. would have spoken differently if there had been no Roman tragic choruses. Roman playwrights and critics were aware of the problems of dramatic structure posed by the Greek tragic chorus; this is shown by a fragment from Accius' *Didascalica ap.* Non. 178. 20 (Funaioli,

Commentary

Gram. Rom. Fr. p. 26, fr. 6) *sed Euripidis, qui choros temerius in fabulis*, cf. below 195 n. The problem does not arise for Seneca's tragedies if they were recited, not performed on the stage; but the structural aspect concerned him as much as his Greek predecessors. It is a fair guess that H.'s precept applied to contemporary conditions because it is similar in principle to those parts of the *Ars* which more clearly show contemporary preoccupations. More than that cannot be said since there is next to no evidence.

193 *actoris partes* 'the role of an actor': *partes* as at 177 (*seniles*) *mandentur...partes*, 315 *partes...ducis*. This is almost a translation of, though not necessarily a direct borrowing from, Ar. *Poet.* 18, 1456 a 25–6 καὶ τὸν χορὸν δὲ ἕνα δεῖ ὑπολαμβάνειν τῶν ὑποκριτῶν.

officiumque uirile: where *officium* varies *partes* as it does 314–15 *iudicis officium* and *partes ducis.* The wording comes close to συναγωνί-ζεσθαι, which Aristotle has in the sequel of the passage just cited, see below 195 n. There is a double entendre here: 'a full actor's part' and 'to the best of his ability', *si uir esse uolet* (Otto, *Sprichwörter* 373), *pro uirili parte.*

194 *defendat* continues the metaphor in 193: let the chorus not allow itself to be edged out of it. Also cf. *S.* 1. 10. 12 *defendente uicem... rhetoris atque poetae.*

neu not *nec* here continues a jussive subjun., as at Cic. *Man.* 69 *ut maneas...neue pertimescas*, cf. Hofmann–Szantyr, 338; this continuation provides variety and is much employed in verse, e.g. *C.* I. 2. 50–1 *hic ames dici...princeps,* | *neu sinas*, etc., *S.* I. 10. 9–10 *ut currat sententia neu se* | *impediat*, II. 5. 24, *Ep.* I. 18. 109–10; after imp. *S.* II. 5. 24, *Ep.* I. 11. 23. Also *neue, C.* I. 2. 47.

intercinat: an ἅπαξ λεγόμενον in Latin literature (apart from Porph. on 202, cit. *TLL*), probably coined by H. *Graeco fonte*, to render, as Rostagni and others suggest, something like ἐμβόλιμα ᾄδουσιν, in the sequel of the Aristotelian passage cited 193 n.: 1456 a 29 ff. διὸ ἐμβόλιμα ᾄδουσιν πρώτου ἄρξαντος Ἀγάθωνος τοῦ τοιούτου. καίτοι τί διαφέρει ἢ ἐμβόλιμα ᾄδειν ἢ εἰ ῥῆσιν ἐξ ἄλλου εἰς ἄλλο ἁρμόττοι ἢ ἐπεισόδιον ὅλον; For musical interludes as act-divisions on the Roman stage see Donatus on Ter. *An.* (ed. Wessner) Praef. II. 3 *animaduertendum ubi et quando scaena uacua sit ab omnibus personis, ita ut in ea chorus uel tibicen obaudiri possint; quod cum uiderimus ibi* actum esse finitum *debemus agnoscere.*

medios...actus: obj. instead of prep. + acc., cf. 424 n. H. favoured this

255

idiom as Lambinus showed *C.* II. 7. 23–4 n., cf. D. Bo, *Hor. Opera*, III, 116 f. Such lists tend to differ because editors are inconsistent in their use of tmesis. The idiom is familiar from Tacitus, e.g. *Ann.* II. 9. 1 *flumen Visurgis* Romanos Cheruscosque *interfluebat*; the point however is not that the construction 'becomes very common in Tacitus' (Wilkins *ad l.*). Rather against the tendency of a highly developed language that favours the analytic expedient of prepositions, Silver prose and Tacitus in particular adopt this archaic and direct manner of speech from poetry, cf. E. Löfstedt, *Syn.* I², 291 ff. on similar constructions with the abl. Caution however is enjoined by instances without preposition in ordinary prose, cf. G. B. A. Fletcher, *Annot. on Tac.* (1964), p. 63, on Caesar's usage, apropos of Tac. *Hist.* I. 61. 1 *Italiam irrumpere*.

195 The chorus, Aristotle said in the passage cited above 193 n., must take the part of an actor. He continues, καὶ μόριον εἶναι τοῦ ὅλου καὶ συναγωνίζεσθαι μὴ ὥσπερ Εὐριπίδῃ ἀλλ᾽ ὥσπερ Σοφοκλεῖ. τοῖς δὲ λοιποῖς τὰ ᾀδόμενα οὐδὲν μᾶλλον τοῦ μύθου ἢ ἄλλης τραγῳδίας ἐστίν. There follow the remarks about ἐμβόλιμα cited above 194 n. I doubt if that is the sentiment expressed by Aristoph. *Ach.* 443, as Dacier repeats from the scholium on the verse of the *Ach.*; but it is certainly that of the scholium *Ach.* 443 οὗτος (Εὐριπίδης) γὰρ εἰσάγει τοὺς χοροὺς οὐ τὰ ἀκόλουθα φθεγγομένους τῇ ὑποθέσει...οὔτε κτλ. For Roman criticism cf. Accius cited 193–201 n. For the limitations of Aristotle's criticism, see Rostagni's note. Unlike Aristotle, H. does not specify his criticism.

proposito conducat: cf. *Schol.* cited in the preceding note ἀκόλουθα... τῇ ὑποθέσει, Ar., cited in the same note, μόριον τοῦ ὅλου.

haereat apte: the verb brings out the organic connexion. Choral passages must be 'inherent' in the plot; the simple verb as against *inhaerere*, e.g. Cic. *Fin.* I. 68 (*uirtutes*) *semper uoluptatibus inhaererent*. *apte* continues the motif of 'appropriateness', here restating the sense but not the wording of the Aristotelian passage.

196–201 Principles for the handling of choral passages either in dialogue or song are laid down. They well exemplify the state of affairs in the *Ars*. The whole passage makes sense in Greek as well as Roman terms. The instances of piety and conventional good sense are clearly taken from Greek tragedy. They are fitted on to the Aristotelian doctrine of *A.P.* 193–5, from which however they differ in their moralizing. Some of the instances can be paralleled in the tragic scholia and in moral theory (below 196 n.); Hellenistic provenance is not therefore unlikely. In one case or possibly two quotation from actual choruses seems to be intended, and it is possible but cannot be proved that these quotations were part of the Hellenistic context (below 198, 199 nn.). On the other hand these demands can be read in Roman and Augustan terms, and as part of a Horatian poem should be so read. One may compare the *officia* recommended as subject-matter for poetry, below 312 ff. One may also recall the ideology inherent in virtue (196), (ancient Roman) simplicity of life (198), justice and law, peace and trust (199–200).

196 *bonis faueat:* commentators appositely cite *Schol.* Eur. *Phoen.* 202 ἐπίτηδες δ' οὔκ εἰσιν ἐγχώριαι αἱ ἀπὸ τοῦ χοροῦ, ἀλλὰ ξέναι καὶ ἱερόδουλοι, ὅπως ἐν τοῖς ἑξῆς ἀδεῶς ἀντιλέγοιεν πρὸς τὴν Ἐτεοκλέους ἀδικίαν κτλ. (*Phoen.* 526). ἀεὶ γὰρ ὁ χορὸς παρρησιαζόμενος τοῦ δικαίου προΐσταται. πῶς οὖν ἔμελλον τὸν βασιλέα ἐλέγχειν, εἰ ὑπ' αὐτοῦ ἐβασιλεύοντο; Cf. Ar. *Prob.* xix. 48, 922 b ἔστι γὰρ ὁ χορὸς κηδευτὴς ἄπρακτος· εὔνοιαν γὰρ μόνον παρέχεται οἷς πάρεστιν.

-que et: the archaic equivalent of Greek τε καί which survives in classical Roman poetry and archaizing prose, cf. Hofmann–Szantyr, 515, my remarks *JRS*, XLI (1951), 48, G. B. A. Fletcher, *Annot. on Tacitus* (1964), pp. 81 f. The Augustans, and H. in particular, avail themselves of its twofold advantages: one, metrical, adding a syllable (*uerumque prudens et*) or providing a lengthening of the preceding syllable (*faueatque et*) or avoiding hiatus (*teque et*); the other, stylistic, joining closely the parts of a clause or sentence. The conjunction is used frequently when more than two parts are joined, cf. 145, 156, 199, et al. For joining two parts, it occurs only five times in H., and not earlier than the *Epistles*: once in *Ep.* I, twice in *C.* IV, and three times in the *Ars*, cf. 214, 444 nn.

consilietur: the verb does not occur again in the sense of *dare consilium* until late Latin writing: *TLL*, IV. 440. 24. *C.* III. 3. 17 differs.

amice like (*coniurat*) *amice* below 411; the variant *amicis*, without regard to the earlier obj. *bonis,* is faulty, *amici* perhaps an intermediate stage.

197 *amet* †*peccare timentes*†: so printed because I disbelieve this reading which is offered by most MSS; and in spite of the fact that the faulty *paccare* and *pecare* point to *pacare* or *placare*, I cannot fully establish either the emendation *p(l)acare timentes* or the more likely one *p(l)acare tumentes*. (*a*) *amet peccare timentes*, 'befriend those afraid to commit a fault', needs to be rejected because it almost duplicates 196 *bonis faueat*, and duplicates it clumsily and moreover in the wrong place: even at 196, where Peerlkamp put it (exchanging the two halves of the verses), it would be lamentably weak. Men 'afraid to do wrong' are scarcely commended in H.'s ethics; cf. *Ep.* I. 16. 52–3, which (Professor Goodyear reminds me) makes against the reading, not, as Rostagni, Schütz and others have thought, for it. (*b*) *amet pacare* (or *placare*, H. Fuchs, *H*, LXX (1935), 248) *timentes*, 'choose to pacify the fearful', may call to mind *Ep.* I. 4. 12 *inter spem curamque, timores* ~~inter et iras (cf. Doederlein, Keller, Epil. 753,~~ K.–H.). But I doubt, as others have done, whether 'pacify' is a tenable verb with 'fearful'; Sen. *Ep.* 59. 8, *pace* Keller (app. crit.), does not bear out the locution: *nihil stultitia* pacatum *habet; tam superne illi* metus *est quam infra; utrumque* trepidat *latus*. A more plausible verb than *pacare* or *placare* is wanted; *recreare* 'encourage' (A. Y. Campbell, Hor. *Carm*.[1] (1946), 'Horatiana Alia' *in calce libri*) is the right notion beside *timentes*, and possibly the apt verb, cf. Cic. *Cat.* III. 8 et al. (*c*) Bentley argues for *pacare tumentes*, which he found, doubtless as an emendation, in one of the late MSS which often instigated his feats of erudition (cod. Pulmanni). *tumentes* could express other emotional disturbances than anger, cf. *S.* II. 3. 213 *purum est uitio tibi, cum tumidum est, cor?*, Stat. *Theb.* IX. 79. So Cicero had used the word, e.g. *T.D.* IV. 29. But next to *iratos* it is likely to point to the same emotion, cf. Norden, Virg. *A.* VI. 49 n. on *rabie . . . corda tument; ira* and *tumor*, as Bentley's citations show, are often conjoined, as at Virg. *A.* VIII. 40 *tumor omnis et irae*. If that is so, *p(l)acare tumentes* after *regat iratos* probably makes too explicit and wordy a doublet to be considered Horatian.

198 *dapes laudet mensae breuis:* one of the variations of μέτρον ἄριστον familiar *inter alia* from choral moralizing in Greek tragedy and from the precepts of Roman men of letters. The metaphor *mensae breuis* sharpens the language of what might well be its Greek source, 'a modest board', cf. H.'s *uiuitur paruo bene*, etc., in particular *Ep.* I. 14. 35 *cena breuis iuuat*. ἀρκεῖ μετρία βιοτά (βορά Nauck dub.) μοι σώφρονος τραπέζης, began a Euripidean chorus, *TGF*[2] fr. 893 Nauck (Athen. IV. 158 e); its sequel enlarges on the principle of μέτρον: τὸ δ' ἄκαιρον ἅπαν ⟨?τόδ'⟩ | ὑπερβάλλον τε μὴ προσείμαν. Wilamowitz noted the striking similarity of wording (*H*, XLV (1910), 391, repr. *Kl. Schr.* IV. 258). He suggested that Athenaeus got this fragment from a moral tract of Chrysippus, cited a little later (159 a). The fragment must certainly have come from a Stoic author to Philo. *Quod omnis probus liber*, 145 (VI. 41 edd. Cohn and Reiter). Wilamowitz finally asserted its provenance from 'the literary tract which H. followed in the *Ars*'. This derivation, however probable, is quite unprovable. What needs to be noted is the convergence of a literary tradition with Hellenistic moral theory.

199 (*laudet . . . ille salubrem*) *iustitiam legesque et apertis otia portis:* Wilamowitz *loc. cit.* (last note) suggested that this too was based on a Greek choral passage, 'aber davon scheint jede Spur verloren'. A few

Commentary

years earlier T. Zielinski (*P*, LX (1901), 1) had compared *iustitia–leges–otia* with their Greek counterparts Δίκη–Εὐνομία–Εἰρήνη, Hesiod's three *Horai*, *Theog.* 902, and had guessed at provenance from a Greek tragic chorus in which the three divinities had been praised in song. K.–H. and Rostagni are probably right not to reject this possibility in view of Pind. *Ol.* XIII. 6–7 Εὐνομία . . . κασίγνηταί τε, βάθρον πολίων ἀσφαλές, | Δίκα καὶ ὁμότροφος Εἰρήνα, τάμι' ἀνδράσι πλούτου.

salubrem (198): wrongly suspected by Peerlkamp, probably extends to *leges* and *otia* as well as to *iustitiam*. 'Healthy' = 'beneficial' is said by Lewis and Short to be more usual in the case of *salutaris* than of *salubris*. But *salubris* is well established in that sense, even in prose, e.g. Cic. *Dom.* 16 (*sententiam*) *rei p. saluberrimam*, *Or.* 90, Liv. II. 3. 4. In fact both aspects of the word fit and are probably meant to fit the context. Law and order (under the new regime) 'benefit' industry and social life as much as they 'give health' to crops and human beings. Virgil called Octavian *auctorem frugum tempestatumque potentem*, cf. Hor. *C.* IV. 5. 17–20, Ov. *Fast.* I. 704 *pax Cererem nutrit*, but also the fulsome rhetoric of the contemporary inscription of Halicarnassus (*Inscr. Brit. Mus.* 894, ll. 9 ff., Ehrenberg and Jones, *Documents . . . of Augustus and Tiberius²*, no. 98a, p. 84), not inappositely cited by K.–H. at *C.* IV. 5. 17, εἰρηνεύουσι μὲν γὰρ γῆ τε καὶ θάλαττα, πόλεις δ' ἀνθοῦσιν εὐνομίᾳ ὁμονοίᾳ τε καὶ σωτηρίᾳ κτλ.

apertis . . . portis: the open city gates, a token of peace. Ps.-Acro, *idest pacem quia in pace portae patent, ut 'panduntur portae'* (Virg. *A.* II. 27) *et contrario 'quae moenia clausis | ferrum acuant portis'* (Virg. *A.* VIII. 385–6); Serv. on *A.* II. 27, the first of Acro's two passages, *signum pacis est, ut Sallustius 'apertae portae, repleta arua cultoribus'* (Maurenbrecher, Sall. *Hist.* I, fr. 14). *C.* III. 5. 23–4 may be set beside Sallust: *portasque non clausas et arua | . . . coli*. Also cf. Ov. *Met.* XV. 598, Sil. XVI. 694 *portis bellabit apertis (Carthago)?* For similar phrases with *moenia*, see G. B. A. Fletcher, *Annot. on Tac.* (1964), p. 44.

200–1 were transposed to the place before 198 by L. Mueller in order to bring together all references to action and plot. This is erroneous, see below.

200 *tegat commissa:* the request for secrecy brought about by the continuous presence of the chorus in Greek tragedy: instances naturally abound. But the Roman moral code too is involved, cf. *S.* I. 3. 95 (*si*) *prodiderit commissa fide*, 4. 84–5 *commissa tacere | qui nequit*, *Ep.* I. 18. 38 *commissumque teges et uino tortus et ira*, *ibid.* 70, et al.

deosque precetur et oret: a familiar doublet; for H.'s use of this or similar locutions, see *S.* II. 6. 13 *hac prece te oro*, *Ep.* I. 13. 18 *oratus multa*

prece, Ep. 1. 7. 95 *(te) obsecro et obtestor,* 9. 2 *cum rogat et prece cogit.*
In spite of the set character of the locution Peerlkamp punctuated
after *precetur,* eliciting out of *fortuna* (201) an obj. of *oret. Fortuna,* he
added, was a deity in her own right, not a gift of the gods. So she was
often, but here the degree of personification is restricted to *redeat* and
abeat. For in this passage, as Rostagni saw, H. glances at Aristotle's
'reversal of fortune', peripety, *Poet.* chs. 9 ff. Moreover here *fortuna* =
'good fortune'.

201 *ut . . . superbis:* this recalls a 'happy ending' on the non-tragic
Odyssean pattern criticized by Ar. *Poet.* 13, 1453 a 33; set ἡ διπ-
λῆν τε τὴν σύστασιν ἔχουσα καθάπερ ἡ 'Οδύσσεια, καὶ τελευτῶσα ἐξ
ἐναντίας τοῖς βελτίοσι καὶ χείροσι beside *ut redeat miseris, abeat fortuna
superbis.* H. may have thought it desirable to moralize tragic peripety
but it does not follow from this verse that he did. For he does here no
more than lay down the line the chorus is to take. Explicitly then this
is not a statement on the plot (cf. 200–1 n.) but on what the chorus
should say or sing.

(7) Music in Drama, 202–19

The tradition. Of the many strands recognizable in Plato's
writing on music in the *Republic* or *Laws* only two have some
relevance to H. (1) The assumption is made *Rep.* IV. 424 C,
ascribed there to Damon, and perhaps of Pythagorean origin,
that changes in music are to be resisted as corrupting the
social fabric; changes in music are accompanied always by
important changes in the body politic. (2) Certain musical
instruments, notably the *aulos,* and technical elaboration of all
instruments, are vehicles of this corruption, and should therefore be banned (see below 202 n.). But although these assumptions can be recognized in H., his context and, I believe, the
context in which they were set in the tradition on which he has
drawn, are not Platonizing. The context of Cicero's *De Legibus*
equally differs from H.'s; Cicero preserves the Platonic
mould, although he relaxes Plato's most uncompromising
demand, see Cic. *Leg.* II. 37–9; cf. Quint. *I.O.* I. 10. 31.

What I regard as the true affiliations, Aristotelian and
Hellenistic, I have set out in *Prol.* 115–17. At *Poet.* 6, 1449 b 3–
4 music, like diction, is said to belong to the medium in which

the tragedian works: εἶτα μελοποιΐα καὶ λέξις· ἐν τούτοις γὰρ ποιοῦνται τὴν μίμησιν. Thus music is one of the six constituent 'parts' of tragedy (*ibid.* 1450 a 10) and in fact 'the greatest of its sweetenings', μέγιστον τῶν ἡδυσμάτων (b 16), cf. *Pol.* VIII. 5, 1340 b 16–17 ἡ δὲ μουσικὴ φύσει τῶν ἡδυσμάτων ἐστίν. As a poetic ingredient however it sinks to the penultimate place in the scale and, apart from a brief remark at the beginning of ch. 24, Aristotle does not return to it. Yet, as I pointed out *Prol.* 115–17, there is an Aristotelian precedent. Music is discussed in educational terms, as a social and historical phenomenon, in *Pol.* VIII, chs. 5–7; some of these social and historical implications are found also in this section of the *Ars.* But the Horatian sentiment echoes more significantly the feelings of Aristoxenus and perhaps other early Peripatetics. The sentiment may be described as resignation and a yearning for lost simplicity. 'So, Aristoxenus said, let the few of us by ourselves remember what music was like; for now the theatres have become utterly barbaric and that vulgar music has proceeded to destruction and ruin' (*ap.* Ath. XIV. 632 b, Wehrli fr. 124; cit. *Prol.* 116 n. 3).

Horace. In his literary criticism H. rejects scholastic matter that resists the poetic process; equally he steers clear of musical theory and recalcitrant philosophical argument. A neglect of this technique is liable to prejudice our view of H.'s poetry—a neglect that has, for example, inspired G. Williams' unjustified censure of this passage (*Tradition and Originality*, etc. 336–41); for details see below 202 and 203 nn. H. selects one or two concrete instances and builds them up into patterns suggesting the progression from simplicity to corruption. Again he starts without an overt transition although a link with the preceding section on the chorus is quickly sensed and soon (204) made explicit. The same attitude as in the foregoing precepts is noticed: appropriateness of artistic procedure is related not only to aesthetic but moral principles. The present section however differs from the earlier ones;

Commentary

it avoids legislating, and simply traces the historical process
by which music is said to have lost its early innocence and
goodness. This process is, *more Aristotelico*, related to moral and
political change (cf. *Ep.* II. 1. 93 ff., 161ff., for similar changes).
The loss of a simple musical ethos is regretted in terms reminiscent of Aristoxenus and perhaps other Greek theorists, but
is more historical and less sentimental. A comparison with
Cic. (*Leg.* II. 37–9, mentioned above) shows not only that H.
draws on a different tradition but suggests a different
approach. H. presents two types of society and two types of
music; without argument or preaching he leaves the contrast
to exert its own inherent effect. Once more he changes from
instruction to a picture; and the picture is one of prevailing
conditions. He goes *in medias res*, starting *tibia non, ut nunc*. The
villain of the piece is *tibia*, corresponding to the Greek αὐλός.
I avoid the variously misleading terms 'flute, clarinet, oboe',
and render *tibia* by 'pipe'.

202 Much restrictive criticism of Greek music was tied to the
rejection, for drama, dithyramb, etc., of the αὐλός (*tibia*), or at any
rate its more spectacular varieties. Either encroachment of the *aulos*
on 'song', or of music on poetry, are opposed, as in the celebrated
'hyporchema' of Pratinas, and in the context *ap.* Ath. XIV. 616 e ff.
where the piece is preserved. Or else objection is made to the complexities of the new music for the *aulos*, as in the revealing piece of
Pherecrates (fr. 145, Kock, *Com. Att. Fr.* I. 188). This piece is cited by
ps.-Plutarch (*De Mus.* ch. 30), who says, accusingly, αὐλητικὴ ἀφ'
ἁπλουστέρας εἰς ποικιλωτέραν μεταβέβηκε μουσικήν· τὸ γὰρ παλαιὸν
κτλ. Philosophers opposed that kind of music on ideological grounds,
e.g. Plato, *Rep.* III. 399 d, cf. *Laws*, III. 700–1, especially 701 a 3 θεατροκρατία, Ar. *Pol.* VIII. 6, 1341 a 21–2 οὐκ ἔστιν ὁ αὐλὸς ἠθικὸν ἀλλὰ
μᾶλλον ὀργιαστικὸν κτλ., ps.-Plut. *De Mus.* ch. 15, Ath. XIV. 616 e ff.
Aristoxenus' part in these discussions is conjectural. Varro discussed
the technical advances in the making of *tibiae* on which H. frowns,
see below 203 n. Keller (app. crit.) says, rashly, '*Varronem sequitur
Flaccus*'; Immisch, p. 123 n. 40, is more cautious.

Where poetry is concerned H. habitually decries the old, not the
new; here he decries the new. Two motives may account for this.
Morals are concerned: what underlies the musical decline is said to

be a moral decline. On this topic H. often accepts the familiar Roman pattern of degeneration. More important perhaps, H., like many poets before and after him, regarded music as an accompaniment of poetry. The new music however did not merely want to assist poetry, as the old had done—204 *adesse choris erat utilis*; ultimately it invaded even the style of speech: 217 *facundia praeceps*.

tibia non ut nunc is not simply 'something of a verbal stratagem', nor is it without 'real relevance to the contemporary Roman scene' (G. Williams, *Tradition and Originality*, etc. p. 337). The section begins with this abrupt contrast between past and present, soon shown to be a contrast between a golden age of innocent simplicity and the corrupt sophistication of contemporary music—not that H. was himself a stranger to sophistication. For *nunc* compare Cic. *Leg.* II. 39 *quae solebant* quondam *compleri seueritate iucunda Liuianis et Naeuianis modis*, nunc *ut eadem exsultent et ceruices oculosque pariter cum modorum flexionibus torqueant* (Vahlen, *Ges. Phil. Schr.* II. 765 n. 24, Immisch, pp. 132 f.); Varro's reports on the history of αὐλός–*tibia* seem to have stressed the difference between the old and the sophisticated modern instruments (*apud antiquos*, cit. 203 n.). The Ciceronian passage shows that it was precisely the changes in the music of the first century B.C. that are likely to have suggested to H. certain similarities with the earlier Greek development, and may have moved him to set down this composite picture of Greek and Roman.

orichalco uincta: G. Williams (*Tradition and Originality*, etc. p. 337) reproves H., who, he thinks, 'has (not surprisingly, since music was a very esoteric subject after the fifth century B.C.) mistaken the meaning of "bound by copper", for this must refer to a use of copper rings to occlude the holes, which represented, like the increase in the actual number of holes (*foramine pauco*), an increase in the musical range of the instrument (far more than in its volume) associated with the name of Pronomus of Thebes in the fifth century B.C.'

This argument seems to fail on several counts. (1) The purpose of keywork to act as keys, i.e. on an ancient instrument to produce different modal scales, must have been well known; there is nothing esoteric about it. (2) Dr J. G. Landels of Reading University has acquainted me with the forthcoming publication, in the *Annual of the British School at Athens*, LXIII (1968), of the *aulos* recently acquired by his university. The Reading instrument, Dr Landels informs me, is the first instance known to him (excepting possibly the 'Maenad pipes' in the British Museum, and an instrument from Dodona in the National Museum at Athens), of an *aulos* with metal casing which does not seem to be keywork. If this interpretation is correct, it would be of considerable interest, since the literary evidence for such casing is inconclusive; cf. Landels on Pindar, *Pyth.* 12. 25–7 and the comic writer Alcaeus, fr. 20 (Kock, *Com. Att. Fr.* I. 761), in *Hesperia,* xxxiii (1964), 392 n. 4 and in the forthcoming article mentioned above. *orichalco cincta* need not therefore refer to keywork, in which case a reference to the 'brassy tone' of the instrument cannot be excluded. (3) In spite of this new information the phrase is more likely to have the conventional meaning of 'metal bands occluding the holes' because of the context indicated by the next verse (203 n.). (4) Even so H. does not incur the strictures mentioned at the beginning of this note. For to assert that the poet is confusing volume of sound and range of pitch is to press him too hard. He deals with volume as well as range in the following verse; here however he is saying, humorously, something like this: there is so much brass on (the keywork of) the modern *tibia* that it might almost be a 'brass instrument', *tubaeque aemula*. Thus H. would be bringing together range and make (202) with range and volume (203) in a whimsical fashion that is not unusual for him.

The modern type of pipe was 'ringed' with metal; *uincta* in this wider sense as at *C.* iv. 11. 7 *uincta uerbenis* (*ara*). The word is not *iuncta* 'joined', as cod. K, perhaps C, some dett. and (from one of them) John of Salisbury have it; Bentley's defence of this reading is based on *iuncta* in a different context. Reinach's suggestion *cincta* is possible, but less plausible than *uincta*. For the construction commentators suggest the model of a Greek adj. like χρυσόδετος, χαλκόδετος. These bands are illustrated and their purpose (to occlude holes) discussed by T. Reinach in Daremberg and Saglio's *Dict.* s.v. *tibia,* v. 308, cf. also A. A. Howard, *HS,* iv (1893), 7, and the bibliography in *New Oxford Hist. of Music,* i (1957), 380 f., n. 6.

Various metal alloys were used for these rings. *ŏrĭchalco* (scanned as Virg. *A.* xii. 87; *auri-* in Plautus and elsewhere, connected by popular etymologizing with *aurum*), from Greek ὀρείχαλκος, 'mountain bronze'. This was an unidentified metal from Cyprus, presumably a kind of copper compound; cf. A. Schramm, *R-E,* xviii. 938 ff., *TLL,* ii. 1493. 20 ff. It is known from early Greek literature and considered a precious metal by Plato, *Crit.* 114 e. In Roman usage the word may be related to gold as in modern usage brass may be so related: it looks like the precious metal; cf. Cic. *Off.* iii. 92, Virg. *A.* xii. 87, Porph. *ad l. orichalco...quod* (*a*)*es simillimum bratteae aureae est*; A. Otto, *Sprichwörter,* p. 49 (s.v. *aurum,* 2). In the passage of H. *orichalcum* is the *uox propria,* leading from the 'brass' rings of the pipe to the trumpet, properly a brass instrument.

Commentary

203 first carries over *aemula* by enjambement from the last line, thus completing the caricature of the modern *tibia* as a 'brass' instrument, and stressing the antithesis to the primitive type. After this gay caricature no prosaic musical history should be expected, although, of course, H. is talking about a change in instrument-making. The following words suggest a verbal picture of pristine musical simplicity. They delicately hint at the size and volume of the old *tibia*, its small range, and the kind of music then possible.

aemula, of an inanimate object, would be an easy metonymy, but here *tibia* is quasi-personal.

tenuis is 'frail, slender', of shape and make (like *fragili*...*cicuta*, Virg. *E*. 5. 85), but thinness of sound (not to mention a kind of style) is indicated e.g. at Virg. *E*. 1. 2 *siluestrem tenui musam meditaris auena*, Ov. *Met*. 1. 707–8 *motos in harundine uentos* | *effecisse sonum tenuem similemque querenti*, and actually emphasized by Pomp. fr. 58–9 (*CRF³*, p. 281) *uocem*... | *tenuem et tinnulam ap*. Macr. *Sat*. VI. 4. 13 *deducta uoce*, etc., Quint. *I.O*. XI. 3. 32. I conclude that in the Horatian verse the width of the instrument as well as its volume are indicated. Experiments with bits of bamboo or reeds teach that this little pipe (with a 'small bore') is weaker in tone than a pipe with a large bore like a modern clarinet or oboe. Sophisticated *tibiae* in H.'s time had a large bore. Specimens that are roughly contemporary still survive; Dr Landels refers me to the *auloi* of Meroe (N. B. Bodley, *A. J. Arch*. 6 (1946), 217–40) and fr. F of the instruments from the Athenian Agora (J. G. Landels, *Hesperia*, XXXIII (1964), 398).

simplexque naturally refers to the unsophisticated make of the early pipes, but the simplicity of the music playable on such an instrument will not be forgotten. So in Greek, see ps.-Plut. *De Mus*. 30 ἁπλουστέρας sc. αὐλητικῆς, i.e. the music played on the (primitive) pipe.

foramine pauco, not *paruo* (uar.l. from 206, as Keller noted); *paruo* is not convincingly defended by the assumption of a highly technical and unparalleled sense for *foramine*, 'with small bore' (Landels in n. 18 of his forthcoming article 'A newly discovered Aulos' in the *Annual of the Br. School at Athens*, LXIII); nor indeed *parco* (H. Richards, *CR*, XIII (1899), 19). *paucus* sing. seems to be colloquial, possibly archaic: *Ad Her*. IV. 45 *abusio est*...'*uti pauco sermone*', *Bell. Afr*. 67. 2 *pauco tritici* (*numero*), Vitr. I. 1. 6 *pauca manu*, Gell. IV. 11. 11, XX. 1. 31, et al. All these instances come from prose, although the corresponding use of *multus* is familiar from H. and other poets, cf. D. Bo, *Hor. Op*. III. 362, Hofmann–Szantyr, 161 f. This is probably sufficient warrant and I have left *pauco* in the text; doubts remain, however. Ov. *Fast*. VI. 697 describes the invention of the same simple instrument in another way, *terebrato per rara foramina buxo*, and this may suggest that the adj. was *raro*. *r* and *p* are frequently confused both in capital and minuscule writing, e.g. Pl. *Mil.* 363 cod. B¹ *peripe propero*, CDB² *peri perpropere*, for *perire propera* (A:PERIREPROPE ⟨RA⟩); Cat. 64. 120 *portaret* for *optarit*, Virg. *G.* III. 34 cod. R RARII for PARII (cf. O. Ribbeck, *Prol.* 252); Tac. *Ann.* III. 54. 6 *prope* for *pro re*, IV. 3. 1 *corpipere* for *corripere*. Once *paro* had replaced *raro*, *paruo* or *pauco* would follow. Cf. below 259 (*iambus*) *rarus*.

Pipes with a small number of holes and consequently a small compass represent the older type. Cf. Varro *ap.* ps.-Acro. *ad l. ait in tertio Disciplinarum et ad Marcellum De Lingua Latina* (*L.L.* ed Goetz–Schoell, p. 218) *quattuor foraminum fuisse tibias apud antiquos; nam et ipsum in Marsiae* (i.e. *Marsyae*) *templo uidisse tibias quattuor foraminum . . . alii dicunt* (cf. Porph.) *non plus quam tria*; for the Greek sources see Pollux, IV. 80, Paus. IX. 12. 5, Ath. XIV. 631 e, Reinach, Daremberg–Saglio, *Dict.* v. 307 b, A. A. Howard, *HS*, IV (1893), 4 f.

204: the pipe accompanied the chorus not vice versa. Cf. ps.-Plut. *De Mus.* 30 τὸ γὰρ παλαιὸν ἕως εἰς Μελανιππίδην τὸν τῶν διθυράμβων ποιητήν, συμβεβήκει τοὺς αὐλητὰς παρὰ τῶν ποιητῶν λαμβάνειν τοὺς μισθούς, πρωταγωνιστούσης δηλονότι τῆς ποιήσεως, τῶν δ' αὐλητῶν ὑπηρετούντων τοῖς διδασκάλοις κτλ. Ath. XIV. 617 b–c, introducing Pratinas' 'hyporchema', τοὺς αὐλητὰς μὴ συναυλεῖν τοῖς χοροῖς, καθάπερ ἦν πάτριον, ἀλλὰ τοὺς χοροὺς συνᾴδειν τοῖς αὐληταῖς κτλ.

adspirare probably renders, and in directness outdoes, συναυλεῖν in such a passage as Ath. cited above: the flute 'accompanies' the chorus. I have found no Latin parallel for this usage. But the verb also carries the connotations of inspiring and helping.

Thus *adspirare* leads on to *adesse*, 'assist, accompany'. '*adspirando adesse . . .* to support by accompaniment' is Wickham's paraphrase.

utilis 'was sufficient to . . .' For this use of adjs. in *-lis*, cf. K.–H. on *C.* 1. 24. 9; for the inf., Hofmann–Szantyr, 350 f.

205 Performances make H. contrast the crowded conditions of his day, whether in theatre or hall; hence *spissa* as at *Ep.* 1. 19. 41–2 *spissis indigna theatris | scripta pudet recitare*, and *spissae . . . coronae* for the crowds of the *Campus*, below 381. The weak tone of the primitive pipe was sufficient for the small audiences, *nondum spissa nimis*, of the time. Lack of crowding and a mythical 'small theatre' symbolize primitive conditions, just as 209 *latior . . . murus* implies a larger city without much reference to enlargement of city walls. No need, I think, to speculate, like K.–H., whether H. knew about the size of the Athenian theatre in different periods, or, like Wilkins, whether

Commentary

he knew that the circuit of the Roman wall had not been altered between the time of Servius Tullius and his own.

sedilia, a poetic and Silver word, not in Ciceronian prose.

206 *quo*, etc.: ps.-Acro, 'idest ad sedilia, idest ad theatrum', etc. *sane* 'indicates the point of *nondum spissa nimis*' (Wickham).

numerabilis according to the material of the *TLL* occurs here and Ov. *Met.* v. 588, next very rarely in Silver Latin, but more frequently in later authors, especially Christian; perhaps a Horatian coinage *Graeco fonte*, cf. ἀριθμητός, εὐαρίθμητος (L.-S.-J.).

utpote paruus explains *numerabilis* (not *numerabilis...coibat*: Wickham), 'you could count them because of their small number'; to remove the comma after *paruus* (H. Schütz) would be depriving *utpote* of its function.

207 *frugi castusque uerecundusque*: cf. the *agricolae prisci fortes paruoque beati* of *Ep.* II. 1. 139, but the audience here are not *agricolae*, see below 212–13 n. For double -*que*, see above 11 n. Here the conjunctions join two solemn epithets and together effect a deliberate displacement of regular rhythms and caesuras, cf. 98 n.

208 Aristotle held that increase of wealth in Athens brought increase in leisure and hence the fine arts flourished, particularly after the Persian Wars (*Pol.* VIII. 6, 1341 a 29 ff., cf. *Prol.* 115 f.). H. has the same notion twice. At *Ep.* II. 1. 93 ff., 139 ff., it enables him to demonstrate, partly humorously, how the Greeks *positis bellis* (*ibid.* 93) had indulged in a great variety of pursuits, music and tragic drama among them; at Rome, on the other hand, the arts had developed late, and though the rusticity of early drama had yielded to Greek influence, *manserunt hodieque manent uestigia ruris*; cf. *Varron*, Fond. Hardt, IX (1963), 189. In the present passage a victorious undefined city also develops drama and music. But here the tenor is even more critical; what develops is *licentia*. Cf. above 203–19 n. on Plato and Aristoxenus.

agros extendere: unlike its English counterpart, Latin *extendere*, of territory, is a poeticism or Silver and late usage; e.g. *C.* II. 15. 2–4 *latius* | *extenta...* | *stagna lacu*. In fact these two instances are the first recorded by *TLL*, v. 2. 1974. 32 ff. Next comes Man. III. 3 (*Musarum*) *fines*.

uictor: cf. *Ep.* II. 1. 93 *positis...Graecia bellis*, 156 *Graecia capta ferum uictorem cepit*, 162 *post Punica bella quietus*.

urbem I have printed in my text. It is in one or two of the dett., and probably in others from which the early editors took it; the paradosis is *urbes* (-*is*), cf. Orelli *ad l.*, Keller, *Epil.* 754. Some commentators are as emphatic on the Greek colouring of this passage (cf. *Ep.* II. 1. 93 ff.) as are others on the Roman (cf. *Ep.* II. 1. 101 ff., 139 ff.)—neither party without justification. Some features, such as 210 *Genius* and perhaps 209 *murus*, are Roman, others, such as 219 *sortilegis*...*Delphis* are Greek, and others again, such as 208 *uictor*, and the development of the pipe, apply to both. Orelli, 202–19 n., said perceptively, '*est autem* μελοποιΐας *tragicae historia, ut ita dicam, poëtica, inter Athenas, Romam, poëtaeque* φαντασίαν *mire fluctuans*', cf. Immisch, pp. 134–5. This imagined city has composite characteristics, but though composite is still *one—urbem* not *urbes*. The sing. therefore is required, and fits *uictor* in this line, *populus* in 206, and *murus* in 209. The pl. would destroy the unity of this picture, and may owe its existence to the preceding *agros*. Bentley and the early editors before him offer *urbem* without argument, and without noting the MSS' *urbes*. Ribbeck and H. Schütz explicitly preferred the sing. to the pl., Ribbeck (p. 227) arguing more plausibly than Schütz.

209 *latior*...*murus* should be *laxior* according to Bentley because in the passages which he adduced the former denotes the thickness of the wall, the latter the width or length of the area surrounded by it. *Contra* rightly Peerlkamp, 'late amplecti *dicitur de quouis spatio tam in latitudinem quam in longitudinem*', etc. As he remarks, it would have been easy if there were an ambiguity to write *latius*; but there is none. *latior murus* in this context clearly is *murus qui latius patet*. Keller cites Ov. *Fast.* III. 181–2 *moenia*...*populis angusta futuris,* | *credita sed turbae tunc nimis ampla. angustus* 'narrow' is a double-sided term like *latus*; the context shows the relevant aspect.

uinoque diurno: not daily but during the day (*S.* II. 8. 3 *de medio potare die*), cf. below 269 *nocturna–diurna, Ep.* I. 19. 11 *nocturno certare mero, putere diurno*, II. 2. 79. For *diurnus* 'daily', see *TLL*, v. 1. 1639. 70. To make his point H. turns the *licentia* and *libertas* into an indictment, not of morals and manners as at *Ep.* II. 1. 144 ff. and below 282, but of morals and poetic style.

210 *placari Genius*: Roman colouring as *Ep.* II. 1. 143–4 *Siluanum lacte piabant* | ...*et uino Genium*; but there Roman custom is described, while in this passage the imagery only is Roman whereas the application may be indiscriminately Roman or Greek. Cf. *C.* III. 17. 14–16 *cras Genium mero* | *curabis*... | *cum famulis operum solutis.*

festis...*diebus*: cf. *Ep.* II. 1. 140 *tempore festo.*

impune: ps.-Acro, *idest non contradicente lege aut moribus.*

211 *numerisque modisque*: an emphatic double -*que* like 207; as in that verse and *Ep.* II. 2. 144 *numerosque modosque* a distortion of the caesural pattern ensues. For the juxtaposition of *numeri* 'rhythms' and *modi* 'measures' (either the tune itself or 'harmony' in the ancient sense, the mode or scale), cf. Plato, *Rep.* III. 398 d τὸ μέλος ἐκ τριῶν

ἐστιν συγκείμενον, λόγου τε καὶ ἁρμονίας καὶ ῥυθμοῦ, Ar. *Pol.* VIII.
7, 1341 b 19 σκεπτέον ἔτι περί τε τὰς ἁρμονίας καὶ τοὺς ῥυθμούς, Cic.
De Or. I. 187 *numeri et uoces et modi.*

licentia maior: the notion is the Pythagorean and Platonic one,
which relates moral and political constitution to fixed musical modes
and hence condemns musical change as morally and politically
subversive. But, as was said above 202–19 n., no reforming or utopian
zeal is implied; H. offers a detached poetic picture of *licentia*, not
without some humorous touches. Cf. e.g. Plato, *Rep.* IV. 424 c εἶδος
γὰρ καινὸν μουσικῆς μεταβάλλειν εὐλαβητέον ὡς ἐν ὅλῳ κινδυνεύ-
οντα κτλ. (mention of Damon), *Laws*, III. 700 a ff., especially 701 a,
θεατροκρατία instead of ἀριστοκρατία, Aristotle's criticism of such
doctrines, *Pol.* VIII. 7, 1341 b 20 (σκεπτέον) πρὸς παιδείαν πότερον
πάσαις χρηστέον ταῖς ἁρμονίαις καὶ πᾶσι τοῖς ῥυθμοῖς κτλ., Aristox.
fr. 124 (Wehrli) above 202–19 n., Ath. XIV. 633 b γενομένης ἀταξίας
καταγηρασάντων... τῶν ἀρχαίων νομίμων ἥ τε προαίρεσις αὕτη
κατελύθη καὶ τρόποι μουσικῆς φαῦλοι κατεδείχθησαν, οἷς ἕκαστος
τῶν χρωμένων... ἀντὶ... σωφροσύνης ἀκολασίαν καὶ ἄνεσιν (περι-
εποιεῖτο), Cic. *Leg.* II. 38–9.

212–13 For musical and theatrical audiences, see Plato, *Rep.* III.
397 d, *Laws*, III. 700 e and, *contra*, the realistic assessment Ar. *Pol.*
VIII. 7, 1342 a 18 ff. ἐπεὶ δ' ὁ θεατὴς διττός, ὁ μὲν ἐλεύθερος καὶ
πεπαιδευμένος, ὁ δὲ φορτικὸς ἐκ βαναύσων καὶ θητῶν καὶ ἄλλων
τοιούτων συγκείμενος, ἀποδοτέον ἀγῶνας... καὶ τοῖς τοιούτοις
πρὸς ἀνάπαυσιν κτλ. But here the *rusticus*, not Aristotle's city prole-
tariat, is called *indoctus*. H. judges audiences variously in accordance
with his poetic purpose, see notes on 113, 153–5, 248, 270–4, 319–22,
also *Ep.* II. 1. 182 ff., 215.

212 *saperet:* of poetic taste as *Ep.* II. 1. 68. Below 309, poetic taste,
recte scribere, is made dependent on rational *sapere*.

liberque laborum as *Ep.* II. 1. 140 *condita post frumenta*, *S.* II. 2. 119
operum uacuo, *C.* III. 17. 16 *cum famulis operum solutis.* The gen. 'free
from' like Greek ἐλεύθερος, not 'permissive with regard to', which is
much older: Pl. *Amph.* prol. 105; the present idiom is first known from
Virg. *A.* X. 154 *libera fati* (unless *fatis* is preferred), next from H. and
later poets, e.g. Lucan, IV. 384, VI. 301, Sil. V. 212, cf. Hofmann–
Szantyr, 78. H. liked experimenting with this type of construction in
place of the Ciceronian abl. or *ab*.

213 *rusticus urbano confusus:* it is commonly assumed that this applies
to the lack of separate seating before 194 B.C. (Liv. XXXIV. 44. 5,
54. 4 ff.) and again before the *lex Roscia* of 67 B.C. Perhaps *confusus*
alludes to that matter. But if so, there is a surprising lack of emphasis.

What H. censures is not indiscriminate seating but the size and nature of an audience which contained *turpes* as well as *honestos, indoctos* and *doctos.*

turpis honesto: according to the common social distinction, cf. Aristotle's φορτικός and ἐλεύθερος, 212–13 n. above; but further according to *doctus* and *indoctus*, cf. Aristotle's πεπαιδευμένος *ibid.* Elsewhere H. divorces the social from the moral connotations, *S.* I. 6. 63–4 *quod placui tibi, qui turpi secernis honestum | non patre praeclaro, sed uita et pectore puro.*

214 *priscae... arti:* the contrast old–good and new–debased is in accord with the passages cited in the preceding notes. In matters poetic this is not the contrast generally accepted by H., as I have noted above 202–19 n.

motumque et luxuriem: the two are closely related. The relation of bodily movement and ethos had been much emphasized by Plato, especially *Rep.* III and *Laws* III; cf. Ar. *Pol.* VIII. 7, 1341 b 16 (cit. *Prol.* 116 n. 2). Miming aulos-players are singled out for criticism by Ar. *Poet.* 26, 1461 b 29 ff., cit. *Prol.* 116 n. 2, where also Theophrastus' remark on σικελίζειν is noted. The combination of movement and effeminate elegance (*luxuria*) is a commonplace in these discussions, e.g. Ath. XIV. 628 ff. Cic. *Leg.* II. 39 marks the contrast between old and new in precisely these terms: *quae solebant quondam compleri seueritate iucunda Liuianis et Naeuianis modis* on the one hand, and *nunc... ceruices oculosque pariter cum modorum flexionibus torqueant.* Plin. *N.H.* XVI. 171 does not mention bodily movement but the *uarietas* and *cantus luxuria* of modern pipe music.

-que et: cf. 196 n. For *-que et* joining two verbs, see 196; two nouns as here are joined at *C.* IV. 14. 46 *Nilusque et Hister*, two pronouns below 444, *Ep.* I. 14. 19.

luxuriem is a choicer form than *-am* and is better attested here than at the only other place in H. where the acc. occurs, *S.* II. 3. 224. The abl. *-a* at *S.* II. 3. 79. Cf. Keller, *Epil.* 754.

215 *traxitque... uestem* indicates a trailing robe like that of the major tragic actors worn by the piper. *Ep.* II. 1. 207 presumably refers to the same garment. The Greek term for the tragic robe, perpetuated by the Romans, was *syrma*; its introduction is attributed to Aeschylus by Porph. (on 278) and others; for the evidence cf. M. Bieber, *R-E*, IV A. 1786 f., below 278 n. In Martial *syrma* connotes tragedy, IV. 49. 8, XII. 94. 3–4. Cf. the single verse by one Valerius *in Phormione*, *CRF*[3], p. 367, *quid hic cum tragicis uersis et syrma facis?*

uagus: ps.-Acro ...*uarie huc atque illuc sese circumfert* (*tibicen*).

per pulpita: a vivid picture of the piper moving 'across the stage', as at *Ep.* II. 1. 174 Plautus *percurrat pulpita*. For *pulpita* 'stage', cf. below 279 n.; a platform for recitation *Ep.* I. 19. 40. The *tibicen* in the Roman theatre played on the stage, the *orchestra* being used for seating; the Greek αὐλῳδός was placed with the chorus in the *orchestra*.

216 *fidibus:* the refinement of the lyre or cithara is represented as a concomitant of the more complicated types of pipe and pipe music. For the string instruments see Abert, *R-E*, XIII. 2479 ff. The partly dubious tradition as it appears in the late sources imputes these changes to the dithyrambic poets and composers; thus ps.-Plut. *De Mus.*, chs. 28–30, specially 29 Λᾶσος δ' ὁ Ἑρμιονεὺς . . . τῇ τῶν αὐλῶν πολυφωνίᾳ κατακολουθήσας, πλείοσί τε φθόγγοις καὶ διερριμμένοις χρησάμενος, εἰς μετάθεσιν τὴν προϋπάρχουσαν ἤγαγε μουσικήν. 30 ὁμοίως δὲ καὶ Μελανιππίδης ὁ μελοποιὸς ἐπιγενόμενος οὐκ ἐπέμεινε τῇ προϋπαρχούσῃ μουσικῇ, ἀλλ' οὐδὲ Φιλόξενος οὐδὲ Τιμόθεος. οὗτος γάρ, ἑπταφθόγγου τῆς λύρας ὑπαρχούσης ἕως εἰς Τέρπανδρον τὸν Ἀντισσαῖον, διέρριψεν εἰς πλείονας φθόγγους κτλ. If this information is correct, the pipe preceded string instruments in having provisions for music in a number of modes. These provisions, from the (later) technique of the lyre, could be described as 'supplied with many strings', πολύχορδος—'more probably a conscious metaphor than a "faded" use' (R. P. Winnington-Ingram, *CQ*, n.s. VI (1956), 172 n. 7). Thus the lyric fragment τερπνοτάτων μελέων ὁ καλλιβόας πολύχορδος αὐλός (fr. adesp. 947, Page, *Poetae Mel. Gr.* p. 510). Thus too the much-quoted passage of the *Republic* (III. 399 c–d) in which Plato, having restricted the available musical modes, concludes that 'provision for a large number of strings and all modes (πολυχορδίας . . . παναρμονίου) will not be required'. Here he calls the pipe πολυχορδότατον. Such passages help to explain the otherwise puzzling connexion between lyre and pipe in this verse of H.

uoces 'sounds', cf. πολυφωνία, πολυχορδία, παναρμόνιος in the preceding n.

seueris: cf. *seueritate* Cic. *Leg.* II. 39 (see 214 n.), ps.-Plut. *De Mus.* 14. 1136 b σεμνὴ οὖν κατὰ πάντα ἡ μουσική, θεῶν εὕρημα οὖσα, 28. 1140 e μετὰ τοῦ σεμνοῦ καὶ πρέποντος, et al. *C.* II. 1. 9 *seuerae Musa tragoediae*, though similar in image, applies the word differently.

217–19 were rather insensitively expunged by Ribbeck on the grounds that the transition to style is unduly abrupt. But in the wake of *numeri modique* may naturally follow diction (cf. 211 n.) and the lesson is taught that poetry once governed music—πρωταγωνιστούσης δηλονότι τῆς ποιήσεως, ps.-Plut. *De Mus.* 30—but now came to be governed by it. Cf. above 202 n. and L. Mueller 217 n., contrasting 204 *adesse*. Nor is the transition unduly abrupt:

the *et* clause here continues *sic etiam* of 216, which itself reiterates 214 *sic*.

217 *tulit* 'bore, brought forth, gave rise to'; ps.-Acro, *protulit*; a metaphor alien to neither classical verse nor prose, e.g. *C*. 1. 12. 42 *Curium tulit. . .paupertas*, Cic. *Brut*. 44 *haec. . .aetas. . .oratorem prope perfectum tulit*. Heinsius' *extulit*, for *et tulit*, is not therefore required.

eloquium. The history of the word is summed up by I. Kapp and G. Meyer, *TLL*, v. 2. 412. 28 ff., '*legitur inde a Verg. Hor. Prop. . . .; fictum putes a dactylicis poetis ex analogia uocabulorum q.s. al-, colloquium, ut "eloquentiae". . .seu "elocutionis". . .uoces metro haud aptas uitare possent, etc.; a poetis sumpserunt Vell. Val. Max. Sen. al.*' Here clearly = *elocutio*, thus used for the first time in recorded Latin, *TLL*, v. 2. 414. 16.

insolitum: not the same notion as at Cic. *Sest*. 119 *ad insolitum genus dicendi labi*, though bracketed with this passage in *TLL*, VII. 1. 1933. 26–8 because of the superficial likeness of wording. Cicero is there talking of the unusual nature of his subject, H. of the strained style of tragedy in its later stages. Although H. is talking of style, not of vocabulary only, comparison may be made with Cic. *Balb*. 36 *priscum aliquod aut insolitum uerbum*, *Brut*. 274 *uerbum. . .insolens*, Caes. *ap*. Gell. 1. 10. 4 *inauditum atque insolens uerbum*, Gell. XI. 7. 1 *uerbis. . . insolentibus nouitatisque durae*, et al.

facundia praeceps: the adj. not with *tulit eloquium*, 'carried it head-long' (K.–H.). L. Mueller wished to remove Quintilian's reference to *corrupta eloquentia* from consideration. This is mistaken and I agree with O. Immisch, pp. 136 f., that the notion of *praeceps* is derived from stylistic theory, though this does not make H. an adherent of *Hypsoslehre*. Cf. Quint. *I.O.* VII. 1. 44 *sententiae. . .praecipites uel obscurae; nam ea nunc uirtus est*, and his denunciation of *uitiosum et corruptum dicendi genus*, XII. 10. 73–6, which (at 73) *aut* praecipitia *pro sublimibus habet aut specie libertatis insanit*, Plin. *Ep*. IX. 26; cf. above 27 n.

218–19 Just as tragic style has become strained, so the thought, *sententia*, has become oracular. Hence 218 seems to indicate the function of tragic thought accepted by H., 219 its excess.

218 *utiliumque sagax rerum* (*sententia*) is the moral insight of tragedy. The construction of *sagax* represents another, probably Horatian, extension of the gen. after adjs., cf. 212 n., below *diuina*, and 407 *sollers*, Hofmann–Szantyr, 78. This time it is the type familiar from *peritus*; *sagax* so construed is first known from this passage, next in Silver prose (Col. praef. 22) and verse (Sil. III. 344). *sagax* = *acutus* occurs in the hexameter poems here only; it denotes the perceptive-ness of tragic thought.

diuina futuri (*sententia*): the chorus warns (e.g. above 196) against the consequences of present or past action. *diuinus* 'prophetic' is itself rare (*TLL*, v. 1. 1623. 76 ff.) and besides offers another Horatian instance of a gen. with adj., cf. above; there is only one other instance in recorded Latinity, *C.* III. 27. 10 *imbrium diuina auis imminentium*, *TLL*, *loc. cit.* The idea of divination leads on to the censure of this kind of *sententia* as 'Delphic'.

219 *sortilegis...Delphis:* a compressed comparison, in place of prosaic (*non discrepuit*) *sententia sortilegorum Delphorum*, cf. Wilkins *ad l.*, Hofmann–Szantyr, 826. For the abl., see 152 n. Divination by lot, common in Italy (Ehrenberg, *R-E*, XIII. 1455. 14 ff., A. S. Pease, Cic. *Div.* I. 12 n.), is sometimes said to be extended here to the Delphic oracle. Whatever may be the case elsewhere, e.g. Virg. *A.* IV. 346 *Lyciae...sortes*, prehistoric cleromancy in Delphi is attested, cf. Ehrenberg, *R-E*, XIII. 1452–3. This feature, perpetuated in the term ἀναιρεῖν, may account also for *sortilegi* as epithet for Delphi.

sententia: according to Porph. = γνώμη, but more likely = thought, διάνοια, in contrast with *facundia* and *eloquium* = λέξις above, as e.g. Cic. *De Or.* III. 24 *neque esse ullam sententiam illustrem sine luce uerborum.*

(8) Satyric Drama, 220–50

The tradition. This is a much-discussed topic for two reasons: it presents important information—or, more likely, theory— on the origins of Greek drama, and it presents a major puzzle in Roman literary history. The Roman aspect will be discussed presently under the heading of 'Horace'. On the Greek aspect I shall be brief. This account of Satyric drama and tragedy cannot easily be squared with Aristotle's. In the *Ars* tragedy is a competition *uilem...ob hircum* (220), Satyric drama is a later addition (221). In the *Poetics* (4, 1449 a 9 ff.) no attempt is made to name a prize (τράγος) which at the same time would explain the name 'tragedy'; and something 'satyr-like', τὸ σατυρικόν, is said to be the source of tragedy. There is no mention of Satyric drama strictly so called. A great deal of special pleading is required to make these two accounts agree. I accept as a basis for argument the proposition first formulated by M. Pohlenz ('Das Satyrspiel und Pratinas von Phleius', *NGG*, 1926 no. 3): H. propagated a theory different from and probably competing with the Aristotelian. Further research has suggested that H.'s theory is of Alexandrian provenance, and probably asserted a common rustic origin for tragedy and comedy; it did not operate with an original 'σατυρικόν'. For discussion, see K. Meuli, 'Altrömischer Maskenbrauch', *MH*, xii (1955), 206 ff., who cites earlier literature and briefly sets out the Hellenistic evidence, pp. 266–7; cf. the convenient summary by A. Lesky, *Die trag. Dicht. der Hellenen* (1956), ch. 1; for H. and Varro my paper in Fond. Hardt, ix (1963), 182 ff. An attempt to distinguish Aristotelian, Peripatetic, and Alexandrian theorizing has been made by H. Patzer, *Die Anfänge d. gr. Trag.* (1962), pp. 14–38. But theory apart, contemporary output shows that Alexandria under the early Ptolemies took a lively interest in Satyric drama, cf. K. Latte, *H*, lx (1925), 1 ff. The assessment of Satyric drama as a middle style, a mean between tragedy and comedy, has a Peripatetic ring. Apart from H. there is other ancient evidence for this doctrine. Alexandrian provenance is not unlikely, cf. G. Kaibel, 'Die Prolegomena περὶ κωμῳδίας', *AGG*, N.F. iii. 4 (1898), 51–3.

Horace. There is no evidence for Roman Satyric drama. Rostagni, and many others before and after him, have therefore concluded that H. cannot possibly mean what he says— that he regards it as a viable Roman genre. This is not a plausible inference; after all, our only piece of positive evidence is what H. tells us. To argue from two unknown factors —H.'s opinions, and what was or was not possible in the contemporary setting—instead of from the known—the *Ars*— that is *ignotum ex ignoto*, a suspect procedure. Some even consider their own *non sequitur* sufficient warrant to deny the contemporary scope of the *Ars* as a whole. I suggest that we cannot reasonably fail to take H.'s word for what he is trying to convey, the possibility of re-establishing an old Greek genre in the Roman setting. But whether his judgement was at fault is quite another question. For the rest we must admit that the Roman theatre of that time is insufficiently known. To talk even of performance and recitation (as I have done, *Prol.* 228) goes beyond the evidence and had best be avoided.

The least dogmatic discussions of this vexed problem that I have come across (without necessarily agreeing with specific arguments) are Lucian Mueller's introductory remarks on this section, O. Immisch, pp. 139–58, and Steidle, *Studien*, 114–29; cf. also C. A. van Rooy, *Studies in Class. Satire*, etc. (1965), chs. 6 and 7. For a wholly different view, see G. Williams, *Tradition and Originality*, etc. 341–5. I offer the following suggestions.

(1) Well-meant attempts, whether ancient or modern, to make mythological *Atellanae* into pre-Horatian Satyric drama have miscarried. For ancient attempts, cf. Porph. on 221 *satyrica coeperunt scribere ut Pomponius Atalanten uel Sisyphon uel Ariadnen*, Mar. Vict. *GL*, VI. 82. 1 ff. *ut (apud Graecos) non heroas aut reges sed Satyros inducat ludendi iocandique causa...quod Horatius his uersibus testatur* (seq. *A.P.* 220–4, cf. Diom. *GL*, I. 491. 4 ff.); *quod genus nostri in Atellanis habent*. These are literary fictions based on what mythological travesty there was in the two genres. Diomedes, as doubtless his authorities, was quite clear about the difference obtaining between *Atellana* and Satyric drama: *GL*, I. 490, 18 *Latina Atellana a Graeca satyrica differt, quod in satyrica fere Satyrorum personae inducuntur, aut siquae sunt ridiculae similes Satyris, Autolycus, Busiris; in Atellana Oscae personae ut Maccus*. Modern attempts, such as those of T. Birt *ap.* A. Dieterich, *Pulcinella* (1897), pp. 296 ff., H. Nettleship, *Lectures and Essays*, 1 (1850), 179 f., are no more convincing than their ancient counterparts. But at least they do not eliminate the Horatian evidence.

(2) In this sizeable piece H. talks with seriousness and conviction. He is commending a Greek genre and a new style for the Roman stage.

(3) The Romans produced adjuncts to tragic performances known as *exodia*, just as the Greeks had produced Satyric plays as adjuncts of tragedy. In Cicero's time mimes were

used for that purpose, earlier on *Atellanae* (*Fam.* ix. 16. 7). Atellan production, which had flourished in Sulla's time, declined but was later revived (Macr. *Sat.* i. 10. 3, cf. F. Marx, *R-E*, ii. 1921. 11 ff.); there is talk about it again from the end of the first century A.D., cf. Juv. 6. 71 f. (which I do not explain as proposed by F. Skutsch, *R-E*, vi. 1688. 29 ff.), Suet. *Dom.* 10, *Schol.* Juv. 3. 175. These changes of taste alone suggest that H. cannot have thought of mythological *Atellanae* only; there were other candidates for *exodia* as well.

(4) While the convention of an *exodium* is clearly envisaged by H., there is in this section no reference whatever to *Atellana* or mime. There are such however to *togata* (cf. 229 n., *tabernas*) and to the language of *palliata*, 237 f.

(5) There is little ground for the assumption that the staging of drama seriously diminished from the later first century A.D. onwards, cf. H. D. Jocelyn, *The Tragedies of Ennius*, pp. 48 ff. But in view of the decline of comedy even in H.'s own time, and the withdrawal of much tragic production into the reciter's hall, it may be doubted whether his proposals for Roman Satyric drama were much more unrealistic than the poetic ideal he set up for tragedy and comedy.

(6) The layout and style of the section are entirely governed by the Horatian idea of Satyric drama as a middle form between tragedy and comedy. Note especially the balance achieved in 225–33, 234–9, 245–7; his own style follows the extremes in each case and throws into relief the most difficult of all things, 240–1 *ex noto fictum carmen...ut sibi quiuis...speret idem.* The new section starts abruptly, adding one adjunct of tragedy (Satyric drama) to another (music). But it is hard to read *grata nouitate* (223) without remembering that in the last section a different kind of *nouitas* was censured; so there may be a contrast hinted at, without further elaboration.

The idea of a middle style is adumbrated three times over, (*a*) 225–33, (*b*) 234–43, (*c*) 244–50, each time with different and suggestive imagery. But the three divisions also assign their parts to the *dramatis personae* (as seen by L. Spengel, *P*,

Commentary

XXXIII (1874), 575 and T. Fritzsche, *P*, XLIV (1885), 89): (*a*) to the grand personages who have migrated from tragic to Satyric drama, *deus* and *heros*, (*b*) to Silenus, the wise old πάππος of the Satyrs, and (*c*) to the Satyrs themselves, who form the chorus of the drama. The functions and patterns add strength to each other. They are perfectly fused.

220 *carmine...tragico* followed by *ob hircum* implies a barely concealed derivation; ps.-Acro comments, *hircus fuit praemium tragoediae, unde et tragoedia dicta est* (cf. Porph.); *tragos enim Graece hircus appellatur.* Contrast such definitions as *Etym. Magnum* (s.v. τραγῳδία), κέκληται δὲ τραγῳδία...ἢ ὅτι τὰ πολλὰ οἱ χοροὶ ἐκ σατύρων συνίσταντο, οὓς ἐκάλουν τράγους κτλ. *carmine* is here applied to tragedy, as is *carmen* 240 to Satyric drama.

qui: Homer at 140 is introduced also anonymously; but there no one requires the name: the beginning of the *Odyssey* is sufficient identification. Here the name is probably omitted as an irrelevant piece of antiquarianism; in the learned tradition Pratinas had occasionally the status of the first writer of Satyric drama; the name is likely to be hidden also under *Cratini*, ps.-Acro on 1. 216, in spite of the doubts of Pohlenz, *NGG*, 1926 no. 3, 299; cf. Pickard-Cambridge, *Dith.*[2] 65 ff., 67 n. 1. For the wording apart from the name (and for the rural setting) Immisch, p. 154, compares Dioscor. *Anth. Pal.* VII. 410 Θέσπις ὅδε τραγικὴν ὃς ἀνέπλασα πρῶτος ἀοιδὴν | κωμήταις κτλ.

certauit: the later competition for a prize is here said to have been originally competition for the goat as a prize. A rendering like 'the poet who...*first* competed for a...goat soon also brought on', etc. (Loeb trans.) is erroneous; it may falsely imply the identity of 'inventors' of tragedy and Satyric drama.

uilem...ob hircum 'a mere he-goat as a prize'. Cheap local products —animals, fruit, etc.—in aetiological legends of this kind characterize primitive conditions, cf. E. Reisch, Ἆθλον, *R-E*, II. 2059. 58 ff., 2060. 49 ff. That *hircum* conceals a derivation of the word (and genre) 'tragedy' has been said above, *carmine...tragico.* The derivation is Hellenistic; another, 'dance round the he-goat', is different but not necessarily incompatible with it. For the evidence, see the bibliography in the introductory note to this section, also K. Ziegler, 'Tragoedia', *R-E*, VI A. 1924 f. The oldest known mention of the τράγος as prize occurs, under the lemma 'Thespis' (*c.* 536 B.C.), in the *Marmor Parium*, which is dated to the 260s B.C.; not much later in Dioscor. *Anth. Pal.* VII. 410, the epigram on Thespis, where however the word τράγος has been doubted: Gow and Page, *The Gr. Anth.*, *Hellenistic Epigrams* II. 252. For more hypothetical claimants, see Ziegler, *loc. cit.*, F. Solmsen, *TAPA*, LXXVIII (1947), 252 ff., H. Patzer, *Die Anfänge der gr. Trag.* (1962), 31 ff. Cf. the refs. to Varro, H. (this passage) and Virgil (*G.* II. 380) *ap.* Diom. III, 'de poem.' 8 (Kaibel, *Com. Gr. Fr.* p. 57; Keil, *GL*, I. 487. 11 ff.) and my discussion, in *Varron*, Fond. Hardt, IX (1963), 183 ff.

221 *mox* is rendered 'soon after' (*alsbald auch*) by Hand, *Turs.* III. 656, '*non ita multo post (inuentam tragoediam)*' by Orelli *ad l.*; both were still trying, though implausibly, to adapt H.'s account to Aristotle's, an attempt already wisely abandoned in the sixteenth century by Lambinus (220 n.). Rostagni, arguing with a similar preconception (as did Wickham and others more guardedly), refers *mox* not to a historical sequence of genres but, as 228 *nuper*, to the order of performances in which Satyric drama followed tragic (at any rate before the fourth century B.C. when that order was no longer invariable: *IG*, II, no. 973). This suggestion, dubious in 220–1, seems to me excluded by 222 *temptauit*, which indicates a new genre, not only a new item on the programme. H. J. Rose wrote, *CQ*, XXI (1927), 62, 'but the sense of his' (sc. Orelli's) '*non ita multo post inuentam tragoediam*' is contained in *carmine...hircum*, which in itself denotes an early stage. *Mox* is 'next', 'afterwards'. This is reasonable. A likely paraphrase seems therefore to be, 'the author who competed with a tragic song in those early days when the prize was still merely a goat, later also', etc. In this way the formal proximity of the tragic and Satyric dramas is brought out, which is H.'s point. *mox etiam* introduces something added on afterwards, and thus, as Pohlenz, *op. cit.* 302 n. 1, remarks, favours Hermann's emendation (ed. Eur. *Cycl.* praef. p. xi) προσ- for προ- in Zen. v. 40 (*CPG*, I. 137 'οὐδὲν πρὸς τὸν Διόνυσον') διὰ γοῦν τοῦτο τοὺς Σατύρους ὕστερον ἔδοξεν αὐτοῖς προ⟨σ⟩εισάγειν, *contra* Wilamowitz, Aesch. ed. mai. p. 18.

agrestis Satyros: as at Aus. *Mos.* 170, cf. 244 *siluis deducti...Fauni.*

nudauit is offered by the whole of the transmission, direct as well as indirect (Porph., ps.-Acro, Marius Vict.), with the exception of Diomedes, who has *nouauit* (below (*a*) and (*b*)). I have given the MS reading the benefit of the doubt, but *nudauit* is highly suspect. Not only would it have to refer to the tragic chorus, now stripped of its costume for the Satyr play on the poet's instructions (*nudauit* = *nudatos induxit*, K.–H.), but to a tragic chorus to be inferred from *carmine tragico*. Peerlkamp's INDVXIT for NVDAVIT expresses at any rate the required sense. But, whether *nudauit* or *induxit*, the following notions should be rejected: (*a*) *nouauit* (Diomedes), perhaps influenced by *nouitate*, 223; (*b*) an alleged practice showing tragic personae in an apparel of goatskins, because τὸ σατυρικόν was the original form of tragedy (Rostagni), but Aristotle's theory is not here in point; (*c*) 'a bold extension' of the usage whereby a poet is 'represented as doing himself an action, the doing of which he describes' (Wilkins): but there is no such extension here, for the playwright himself would presumably *inducere nudatos,* contrast *asper,* below; (*d*) *nudauit = protulit, prompsit* as *S.* ii. 8. 74 (L. Mueller); (*e*) a reference to the risqué manner of the satyrs (ps.-Acro).

asper: for here the poet *is* said to be what his characters are: he is 'unkempt', attempting Satyric jocularity, bringing on Satyrs who are *agrestes* and *siluis deductos.* Cf. *S.* ii. 6. 82, the country mouse; the excess of *asperitas* is noted at *Ep.* i. 18. 6 *asperitas agrestis...* (8) (*quae*) *uult libertas dici mera ueraque uirtus,* Cic. *De Or.* iii. 44 *neque solum rusticam asperitatem sed etiam peregrinam insolentiam fugere discamus.*

222 *incolumi grauitate:* tragic gravity being uncompromised by the *iocus* of Satyric drama. 225 ff. explain the surprising oxymoron of the 'joke with dignity untouched'.

eo quod: a prosaic element, in the *Epistles* here only, but cf. *S.* i. 3. 30, ii. 3. 120.

223–4 The introduction to Athens of Satyric drama, H. asserts, was based on the principle which he has employed earlier, 153–5 n., and employs again 248–50: the spectators must be detained, yet poetic quality and the right 'tone' must not be sacrificed. This is a hard thing to manage because of the atmosphere of rustic jollification which H. assumes for early drama.

223 *illecebris:* a different aspect in a different genre of 99 *dulcia sunto.*

grata nouitate: according to L. Mueller, not a new genre but a change of subject-matter from tragic to Satyric drama; according to Rostagni as already to Dacier, not a new genre but a renewal of the original if neglected element of (Aristotle's) σατυρικόν, as implied in the proverb οὐδὲν πρὸς τὸν Διόνυσον. The former view is unlikely because another item in the programme would be called 'different', not 'new'; the latter because 'renewal' would not be expressed by *nouitas*: as elsewhere Rostagni is attempting to square the Horatian account with the Aristotelian. *nouitas* presumably means what it says; Ovid's use of the word supports that, particularly *Met.* iv. 284 *dulcique animos nouitate tenebo.* Thus unlike the new music of the preceding section or the new subjects of 125 ff., this *nouitas* is approved provided it fulfils the conditions of the *ars.* Innovation as such is far from being discouraged by H.: cf. *Ep.* II. I. 90–1 *quodsi tam Graecis nouitas inuisa fuisset* | *quam nobis.*

morandus: as 321 (*fabula*) *ualdius oblectat populum meliusque moratur,* cf. above 154 *plausoris . . . aulaea manentis.* To hold the attention of the kind of spectator envisaged in the next verse and yet proceed according to *ars poetica* is the measure of the poet's problem.

224 *functusque sacris:* for the dramatic contests in relation to the rites of the Athenian festivals, see Pickard-Cambridge, *Dram. Fest.* pts I and II, for the City Dionysia in particular, *ibid.* pp. 62–5.

potus: cf. ps.-Acro (on 222–3) *ideo satyram admiscuit tragoediae quia spectator erat* 'grata nouitate' *retinendus, qui spectator ueniebat post sacrificia iam pransus, iam potus.* Plato, *Laws*, VI. 775 b (cit. Wilkins) legislates that intoxication be restricted to (Dionysiac) festivals when the god presented the wine.

exlex: cf. Non. 10. 10 *inlex et exlex est qui sine lege uiuit.* The word is known first from Lucilius (Marx, frs. 83, 1088, the latter instance fitting the last foot of a hexameter as here), but used by him, and later by Sisenna, Varro, and Cicero, as a term in serious political controversy, cf. *TLL*, v. 2. 1540. 6 ff. The nuance here is wholly different: it is the freedom from restriction enjoyed on these occasions, cf. above 209–11, 85 n. *libera uina.*

225–33 now turn from the imagined Greek setting to the Roman world, and place a proviso on the amusement that may be provided for the modern audience. First in a beautifully articulated period (225–30) the reader is led step by step—*ita, ita, ita: ne*—to an ideal of a Satyric play which is as much removed from the gross humour of realistic comedy as from tragic grandeur. Next Tragedy becomes a Roman *matrona* who knows how to dance on a festive occasion.

225 *uerum:* a strongly adversative word, very selectively used in classical Latin (Hofmann–Szantyr, 495) but favoured by H. in the hexameter poems; in the lyrics only *C.* IV. 12. 25. It introduces the picture of the Roman *Satyri.* Cf. *uerum* below 303, 351, 360.

ita . . . (227) *ne:* cf. 151 n.

risores, one of H.'s words in *-or,* is known, according to the materials of the *TLL,* only from this passage, the grammarians, and the late Latin *Querolus;* Firm. *Math.* v. 2. 11 *risores* is a false reading. Like *dicaces* that follows, the word oscillates between noun and adj., *dicax* has the function of a noun at *S.* 1. 4. 83 *qui captat risus hominum famamque dicacis,* 'of a wit'. Both words here are attributes of *Satyros.* Cicero describes *dicacitas* as wit, a type of *facetiae, peracutum et breue* (*De Or.* II. 218), contrasted with 'humour', *aequabiliter in omni sermone fusum;* the whole of Cicero's discussion

Commentary

provides a lively commentary to H.'s verses and may have been in his mind. Cf. *ibid.* 244 *scurrilis oratori dicacitas magno opere fugienda est*, 247 *ipsius dicacitatis moderatio et temperantia et raritas dictorum distinguent oratorem a scurra*, and his distinction between *ingenuus* and *illiberalis iocus, Off.* I. 104.

commendare (conueniet) is a hard injunction for *dicaces Satyri.*

226 *conueniet:* the fut. as frequently in injunctions, e.g. 42. Horatian Satyrs too must be 'appropriate', not only original and amusing.

uertere seria ludo 'turn seriousness to jest'; grammatically unexplained. *uertere* is thus used also at *C.* I. 35. 4 *uertere funeribus triumphos*, perhaps abl. on the model of *mutare, conuertere* (Porph. on *C.* I. 35. 4, cf. D. Bo, *Hor. Op.* III. 103), construed as *C.* I. 17. 1–2 *Lucretilem | mutat Lycaeo Faunus.* The genre σπουδαιογέλοιον is not in point, the τραγῳδία παίζουσα, not infrequently adduced by commentators, is relevant if rightly understood. Laughter, Demetr. *Interpr.* 169 says, which is combined with graces (of style) in Satyric drama and comedy, is an enemy of tragedy in spite of the many graces tragedy commands, 'since no one can imagine a playful tragedy', τραγῳδίαν παίζουσαν, 'for in that case σάτυρον γράψει ἀντὶ τραγῳδίας'. When tragedy starts jesting, it is no longer tragedy but Satyric drama. H., on the other hand, is saying that Satyric drama must retain some of the dignity of tragic style, for its major *personae* are those of tragedy.

227 *ne:* see 225 n.

deus...heros: the two most exalted kinds of tragic *personae*, cf. 114 *diuus...an heros* or, in lyric verse, 83 *diuos puerosque deorum.*

adhibebitur: K.–H. and Rostagni press the word harder than I am inclined to do. Is it more than 'summon, bring to a place' (here, the stage)? For which notion see the dictionaries.

228 *regali conspectus in auro...et ostro:* a locution reminiscent of epic verse, frequently employed in various forms by Virgil and post-Virgilian poets. K.–H. doubtfully consider the notion 'reclining on embroidered purple'; this may be commended by 229 *migret* but is, I suggest, excluded by such passages as Dioscor. *Anth. Pal.* VII. 37. 4–5 (ὅς με τὸν ἐκ Φλιοῦντος...) ἐς χρύσεον σχῆμα μεθηρμόσατο | καὶ λεπτὴν ἐνέδυσεν ἀλουργίδα (the wording is compared with H. by G. Williams, *Tradition and Originality*, etc. 343; for σχῆμα see the comment by Gow and Page, *The Gr. Anth., Hellenistic Epigrams*, II, 255); Virg. *G.* III. 17 *Tyrio conspectus in ostro*, *A.* IV. 134 *ostroque insignis et auro*, v. 132–3 *auro | ductores longe effulgent ostroque decori*, XII. 126 *ductores auro...ostroque superbi*, etc.; some later instances are cited by Keller[2]. Cf. also *C.* IV. 9. 14–15 *aurum uestibus illitum | mirata regalesque cultus*, Lucr. v. 1427–8 *ueste... | purpurea atque auro* *signisque ingentibus apta*, Virg. *A.* XI. 72 *uestes auroque ostroque rigentis*. It is true, *aurum atque uestis*, 'trinkets and clothes', familiar from comedy, imply nothing of the kind, and equally *auro et purpura* at Livy XXXIV. 3. 9, are shown by an earlier passage (*ibid.* 1. 3) to be dissociated; but the above passages and others suggest the richly embroidered purple cloak of royalty. A similar cloak probably was the long *syrma* of tragedy, cf. Bieber, *R-E*, IV A. 1786 f. Its use on the tragic stage was traditionally ascribed to Aeschylus, see below 278 n. *pallae...honestae.* For the possible cultic origin of the dress of republican Roman tragedy, see H. D. Jocelyn, *The Tragedies of Ennius*, 21. Cf. Juv. 8. 228–9 *longum...Thyestae | syrma uel Antigones aut personam Melanippes*, also Sen. *H.F.* 475 *auro decorum syrma barbarico* of Bacchus, *Oed.* 423, Stat. *Ach.* 1. 262–3 *si decet aurata Bacchum uestigia palla | uerrere.*

nuper in the tragedy or tragedies preceding the Satyric drama.

229 joins in one pregnant locution two different concepts: 'uses language befitting the cottage' and 'behaves as though he had moved from a palace to a cottage'; *migret...humili sermone* accomplishes this feat of wording. *tabernas* 'cottage', as in *pauperum tabernas*, *C.* 1. 4. 13; but at *Ep.* 1. 14. 24 *taberna* is shown by the context to be a 'tavern', in many other places, such as *S.* 1. 3. 131, 4. 71, it is 'shop'. K.–H. cite Diom. *GL*, 1. 489. 29 ff. (ed. Leo *ap.* Kaibel, *CGF*, p. 59) on the realistic Roman comedy, *comoedia togata*, of Titinius, Atta, and Afranius, to which the name *fabula tabernaria* had been applied: '*et humilitate personarum et argumentorum similitudine comoediis pares, in quibus non magistratus regesue sed humiles homines et priuatae domus inducuntur*, quae quidem olim...*tabernae uocabantur*'. Whatever the source of these remarks they reveal the literary background H. took for granted. Earlier evidence than Diomedes is cited by W. Kroll, *R-E*, VI A. 1660–2.

humili sermone, though not the *sermones... | repentis per humum* of H.'s hexameter poems, *Ep.* II. 1. 250–1.

230 In the preceding verse the tragic *persona* has left his palace (*migret*) and H. barred his road to the cottage. But now he is also warned against migrating into unduly high quarters—unlike the stylist, above 28. Such advice, however different from the *genus medium* of the rhetoricians, amounts to a middle road.

nubes et inania 'clouds and empty space', *inane* in poetic language being the 'air' or 'ether', Virg. *A.* XII. 906 *lapis...uacuum per inane uolutus*; Lucretius' *inane*, τὸ κενόν, is not in question here. This recalls the popular Greek idea of 'high' discourse, μετεωρολογία, parodied e.g. by Aristoph. *Nub.* 316–17 οὐράνιαι Νεφέλαι... | αἵπερ γνώμην...ἡμῖν παρέχουσιν, 319–20 ψυχή μου πεπότηται |

καὶ λεπτολογεῖν ἤδη ζητεῖ καὶ περὶ καπνοῦ στενολεσχεῖν, 424 τὸ χάος τουτὶ καὶ τὰς Νεφέλας καὶ τὴν γλῶτταν. But H. is hinting at a quality of formal speech which recalls ps.-Long. *Subl.* 3. 2 (Callisthenes') τινα. . . ὄντα οὐχ ὑψηλὰ ἀλλὰ μετέωρα preceded at 3. 1 by a warning that, in tragedy, πράγματι ὀγκηρῷ. . .τὸ παρὰ μέλος οἰδεῖν is unforgiveable; Quint. *I.O.* xii. 10. 16 *inflati illi et inanes, ibid.* 17 *nihil inane aut redundans.* Both conceits are combined in H. and, probably under his influence, Pers. 5. 7 *grande locuturi nebulas Helicone legunto.* Also see *TLL*, vii. 1. 827. 75 ff.

captet in later Roman rhetoric denotes the 'picking up' of tricks or devices of style, as at Sen. *Contr.* 1. 6. 11 *sententiam uirilem*, Sen. *Ep.* 100. 5 *electa uerba sunt (Fabiani), non captata*, Quint. *I.O.* vi. 3. 47 *illa obscura (dicta) quae Atellani e more captant*, x. 1. 32 *Sallustiana breuitas.* Here however there is also the oxymoron, 'get hold of something insubstantial, snatch what amounts to nothing'.

231 The verse denying triviality to the Satyrs starts with the kind of language that is deplored. *effutire*, from *futis*, 'watering can', is 'to pour out, spout, babble'; ps.-Acro, *proprie. . .est 'inepte loqui'.* *TLL*, v. 2. 229. 80 ff. shows that the word was at home in comedy and Lucilian satire, next in Cicero and Lucretius for hasty and unconsidered speech.

leuis. . .uersus is opposed to the *grauitas* of tragedy as 226 *ludo* to *seria*.

indigna = *quam non decet* as in *indignari*, 'consider improper' at *Ep.* 1. 3. 35 (below). For the inf. with *indignus*, see 183 *digna geri*, 283 *regi*, and other pass. infs., but act. *Ep.* 1. 3. 35 *indigni fraternum rumpere foedus*, so *effutire* in this verse. The parallel with ἀνάξιος need not imply a Grecism.

tragoedia is personified with more gusto than *comoedia*, above 93. 'Tragedy' is a woman, but as becomes her status in these verses she feels a little uneasy in the company of the Satyrs as would a Roman *matrona* obliged to dance at a religious festival. A very different *Tragoedia* appears at Ov. *Am.* iii. 1. 11 and she is *Romana T.* at that, *ibid.* 29.

232 *festis. . .diebus:* ps.-Acro, *sunt enim quaedam sacra in quibus saltant matronae sicut in sacrificiis Matris deum.* This comment probably moved Wilkins in his useful note to refer *festis. . .diebus* to the *Hilaria*, cf. Cumont, *R-E*, viii. 1598. That however was surely not the only occasion, cf. H. on Maecenas' Licymnia (not, it is true, a typical Roman *matrona*), *C.* ii. 12. 17 and ps.-Acro's note there; also Serv. on Virg. *G.* 1. 350, cited in Wilkins' note, makes against his contention: *saltationem aptam religioni nec ex ulla arte uenientem.* While accomplished dancing is for the stage and for entertainers (cf. *R-E*, IV A. 2247), even Sallust objects only to Sempronia's dancing a little too well, *Cat.* 25. 2 *elegantius quam necesse est probae*. For other social aspects see Macr. *Sat.* III, ch. 14, especially 5 ff. *taceo quod matronae etiam saltationem non inhonestam putabant*, etc.

moueri: middle voice, 'dance', as *Ep.* II. 2. 125 where an acc. follows (as in Persius, below) *nunc Satyrum, nunc . . . Cyclopa mouetur*, cf. K.–H. *ad l.* Ov. *Am.* III. 1. 37 *imparibus tamen es numeris dignata moueri*, addressed by *Elegia* to *Tragoedia*, uses *moueri* differently, and is perhaps independent of H. But the likeness between *Ep.* II. 2. 125 and Pers. 5. 123 is marked: *tris tantum ad numeros Satyrum moueare Bathylli*.

iussa: commentators compare Ov. *Tr.* II. 23–4 *ipse . . . Caesar matresque nurusque | carmina turrigerae dicere iussit Opi*.

233 *pudibunda*: poetic (first known from *Culex* 399 (ΓV) and this passage) and later also in prose (Plin. *N.H.* x. 44, al.). The position of *pudibunda* too should be noted; the two antithetic words, *pudibunda* and *proteruis* collide. For the latter, cf. Hes. fr. 123. 2 (ed. Merkelbach–West) καὶ γένος οὐτιδανῶν Σατύρων καὶ ἀμηχανοεργῶν, Ov. *Her.* v. 139 (*Satyri,*) *turba proterua*, et al.

234–43 *The middle style*. The verses read like an application to the new Satyric drama, and to Silenus above all, of more general principles, particularly those laid down at 47 ff. (so T. Fritzsche pointed out as long ago as 1885: *P*, XLIV, 89–90). But having made the two passages so alike, H. clearly wanted readers to notice that he has not made them the same. Not only is the application different, but here H. aims at an Aristotelian Mean and, moreover, he offers a doctrine joining rhetorical and poetic categories in the manner which, I have suggested, characterizes his literary tradition in so many places. The rhetorical categories are offered in the first part of ch. 2 (up to 1404 b 25) of Ar. *Rhet.* III, although the idea of the middle style is not there emphasized. The poetic categories are partly contained in Aristotle's references to poetry, especially tragedy, and partly in the position assigned to the three dramatic genres, Satyric drama standing between tragedy and comedy.

234–5 may be either 'I will favour not only ordinary words' but others less ordinary, though in moderation (235–9); or 'I will favour not only ordinary words' but their uncommon composition (240). K.–H. argue in the former sense, recent commentators, rightly I think, in the latter. Not all translators make this explicit, however; and older commentators muddled the argument by referring 240–3 to the content, not the style, of the plays; so still Wickham, 240 n.

234 *ego*: H.'s imaginary 'I' (cf. 25–6 n.). He identifies himself with any writer of Satyric drama, 235 *Satyrorum scriptor*, though every-one knows that he is not. This use of the 1st person does not differ from 240 *sequar* and 244 *me iudice*—a sure sign that the division proposed by G. Williams (see above 25–6) is inapposite, for he needs to assign 234 ff. and 240 ff. to one of his categories, and 244 to the other.

inornata: the general notion of formalized and artistic speech as 'embellishment' belongs to the rhetoricians from Isocrates (e.g. *Euag.* 190 d) to Cicero's *ornare* and far beyond. I note that κοσμεῖν as a *general* term is not used in the *Poetics*; the very restricted kind of figurative speech called κόσμος (Ar. *Poet.* 21, 1457 b 34, 22, 1459 a 14; precisely what kind is not known) is a different matter. In the *Rhetoric* on the other hand the general term appears in a context close to *Poet.* 21–2 (which is referred to) and to this passage of the *Ars*; Ar. *Rhet.* III. 2, 1404 b 5 ff. τῶν δ' ὀνομάτων καὶ ῥημάτων σαφῆ μὲν ποιεῖ τὰ κύρια, μὴ ταπεινὴν δὲ ἀλλὰ κεκοσμημένην τἆλλα ὀνόματα ὅσα εἴρηται ἐν τοῖς περὶ ποιητικῆς. τὸ γὰρ ἐξαλλάξαι ποιεῖ φαίνεσθαι σεμνοτέραν. . .διὸ δεῖ ποιεῖν ξένην τὴν διάλεκτον. Cf. *ibid.* 1405 a 14 κοσμεῖν and 7, 1408 a 13–14 μηδ' ἐπὶ τῷ εὐτελεῖ ὀνόματι ἐπῇ κόσμος. The use of this term therefore in the context of a poetic genre suggests the mixture of rhetorical and poetic categories to which attention has been drawn above.

dominantia: the only occurrence in classical Latin (excluding, that is, a late medical writer, Cael. Aurelianus) of this word in the sense of Greek τὰ κύρια. This is likely to be a Horatian coinage *Graeco fonte* to express 'recondite matters' (above 49). It is the use in a specific sense of a participle otherwise occasionally employed in poetic and late Latin in the general sense of 'dominating', *TLL*, v. 1. 1906. 29 ff. As Bywater says, Ar. *Poet.* 21, 1457 b 1 n., κύριον in Ar. is (*a*) 'the established and familiar name for a thing', as distinct from glosses, metaphors, and any other 'strange use' of language, and (*b*) more specifically, the literal term distinct from the metaphorical; for later Greek usage, see L.–S.–J. s.v., and P. Geigenmüller, *Quaest. Dionys. de vocab. artis crit.* (Thesis, Leipzig 1908), 15 f., 21 f. Which of the two H. has in mind is not certain. Either meaning will fit his context; there was no need for him to make this nice distinction. Cicero and others express a similar notion by *proprium*: e.g. *De Or.* III. 149 where (*uerba*) *quae propria sunt et certa quasi uocabula rerum, paene una nata cum rebus ipsis* are contrasted with metaphors and coinages. Porph. explains *dominantia* by saying *sunt quae rerum propriis uocabulis nuncupantur, ut libri, capsa, pagina*. H.'s word is an imaginative touch rendering the κυριεύειν of τὰ κύρια in Latin. In his now familiar manner H. does

285

what he teaches, offering *dominantia* in the place of the common word for 'familiar' or 'literal', cf. Steidle, *Studien*, p. 120 n. 28.

nomina (uerbaque) the two comprehensive classes of words as in the passage cited above from Ar. *Rhet.* III. 2, 1404 b 5 ff.: τῶν δ' ὀνομάτων καὶ ῥημάτων...τὰ κύρια. *S.* I. 3. 103–4 is not a clear instance.

235 *Pisones:* Mueller observes that in H.'s letters the addressee is commonly addressed once only; he attributes this exceptional use of the address to the length of this letter, in the middle of which, or nearly so, H. repeats *Pisones.* That is commonly the case (though not at *Ep.* I. 10. 1: 44), but in the *Ars* this procedure is replaced by a much more complex network of addresses, both to the Pisos and the reader, cf. Vahlen cited above 6 n., and 6, 24, 291–2, 366, also 119, 153 et al. Rather what needs to be noted is the function of these addresses in each case; H. likes to give prominence to certain words or parts of a poem by the placing of the addressee's name, cf. Fraenkel, *Hor.* 206 n. 1 and the other observations listed in his index under 'name of the person addressed carefully placed'. One can readily see why the poet as a pretended *Satyrorum scriptor* and advocate of a new Roman genre might wish to give prominence to this particular precept. Beyond that nothing can be known; no personal predilection of the Pisos provides part of the poem's substance. But then what do we know about the personal predilections of the Pisos?

Satyrorum scriptor: like Greek Σάτυροι for the play, e.g. Aristoph. *Th.* 157 ὅταν Σατύρους τοίνυν ποιῇς. *scriptor* here means no more than 'if I wrote'. 120 *scriptor* is dissimilar.

amabo 'in that case I should favour...', cf. below 317 *iubebo*, *Ep.* I. 14. 44 *censebo*, 19. 9 *mandabo...adimam.*

236 goes from the choice of words to the style, *color*. Satyric drama must not be realistic in style and ethos unlike comedy, the reverse of tragedy.

enitar with inf. as *C.* III. 27. 47; the appearance of this construction, apart from H., in Terence, next in Sallust, the declamations of ps.-Quintilian, Gellius, and late prose (*TLL*, v. 2. 598. 67 ff.), suggests an archaism.

tragico...colori, cf. *colores* above 86 n.

differre with dat. in H. is certain here and *S.* I. 4. 48; for *discrepare*, see 152 n.

237 (*nec sic differre*) *ut nihil intersit:* ps.-Acro, *ut sit inter seueritatem tragoediae et leuitatem* (*len-* codd.) *comoediae medio temperamento figurata.* But H.'s poetic point is that he avoids the mechanical description of a middle style and, probably not without amusement, produces this

Commentary

tortuous qualification 'and not so to differ...that there is nothing between...'.

Dauus (no evidence here for the spelling *-uos* in spite of Keller, *Epil.* 756) appears as a typical slave of comedy, *S.* I. 10. 40, II. 5. 91. Whether he belonged to the comedy which ps.-Acro claims to identify (238 n.) is unknown.

et for the faulty *an*, which seems imported from 239, is only in Bland. Vet. and BC.

238 Ps.-Acro, *non dicit de Pythia Terentiana* (that is, the *Eunuchus*) *sed quae apud Lucilium* (*Caecilium* Orelli) *tragoediographum inducitur ancilla per astutias accipere argentum a domino, nam fefellit dominum suum et accepit ab eo talentum.* Likewise Comm. Cruq., adding *in dotem filiae.* Ribbeck accepted Orelli's emendation *Caecilium*, and placed the scholium among the fragments of Caecilius, *CRF*³, fr. 287. The MS reading was however defended by J. Becker, *RM*, n.s. V (1847), 38 f. For there are indications that Lucilius offered something resembling a scene, or scenes, from a comedy in Book XXIX of the *Satires*, cf. C. Cichorius, *Unters. zu Lucil.* 171 ff. It is then possible still that part of that Satire was based on a comedy to which reference is made here, just as H. based part of *S.* II. 3 (259 ff.) on a scene from Ter. *Eun.* But these guesses are rendered dubious by *tragoediographum.*

emuncto...Simone: again *emungo* demonstrates what, H. says, should be avoided; all commentators remark on the stylistic character of the word. It is a vulgarism that belongs to the language of comedy (and satire), *TLL*, V. 2. 543. 78 ff. Greek ἀπομύσσειν may be compared, Poll. II. 78 ἤδη δέ τινες τῶν κωμικῶν τὸ ἐπὶ κέρδει ἐξαπατᾶν ἀπομύττειν εἶπον, Men. (ed. Koerte) fr. 427 γέρων ἀ⟨πε⟩μέμυκτ' ἄθλιος, λῆμφος. Simo is known as a *senex* from Pl. *Most.* and Ter. *An.*

239 *custos famulusque dei Silenus alumni:* in extant Satyric drama Silenus is the father of the Satyrs; the older characteristics of Silenuses were less paternal. The evidence, literary and archaeological, for this Dionysiac demon was presented and discussed by E. Kuhnert, 'Satyros und Silenos' in Roscher's *Lexikon*, IV (1909–15), 444 ff., more recent discussion and bibliography in A. Lesky, *Trag. Dicht.* etc. (1956), 8, 23 ff. and the 2nd ed. (1962) of Pickard-Cambridge, *Dith.* 116 ff. Silenus as teacher of Dionysus is familiar from Satyric drama; S. the sage too is known from the fifth century B.C. onward; Plato's famous comparison of Socrates with statuettes of Silenus (*Symp.* 215) may hint at this notion. For H.'s wise and idyllic S., Diod. IV. 4 should be compared, φασὶ δὲ καὶ παιδαγωγὸν καὶ τροφέα συνέπεσθαι κατὰ τὰς στρατείας αὐτῷ (sc. Διονύσῳ) Σειληνόν, εἰσηγητὴν καὶ διδάσκαλον γινόμενον τῶν καλλίστων ἐπιτηδευμάτων,

287

Commentary

καὶ μεγάλα συμβάλλεσθαι τῷ Διονύσῳ πρὸς ἀρετήν τε καὶ δόξαν (cit. Orelli). In Latin literature this type of Silenus appears in Nemes. *Ecl.* 3. 27 and 59, the prophet and sage in Cic. *T.D.* 1. 114 and Virgil's Sixth Eclogue.

240–3 Earlier commentators were put on the wrong track by the scholiasts, especially by ps.-Acro's reference (on 240) to subject-matter instead of to style: *idest fingam carmen quod ex nota possit esse materia*, etc. This error went into Cruquius' and Lambinus' commentaries, persisted until the nineteenth century and was defended as late as 1891 by Wickham, though not by Wilkins; K. Latte restated it in 1925, *H*, LX. 7. There had been occasional protests (Vico, Wieland, Duentzer), but the spell was broken by Orelli, who stated clearly that H. was talking about style, not subject-matter. Earlier attempts at expunction or transposition (the latter as late as 1922 in A. O. Prickard's *Una forcatella di spine*, 12) were based on the mistaken interpretation.

The contrast between ordinary words and their effective combination is repeated from 47–8. Its purpose differs, however. In the earlier passage H. is talking of diction in general terms, here of the ideal mean in the style of Satyric drama. In the earlier passage the notion of art concealing art is either absent or unstressed; here it is strongly emphasized. Finally, in the earlier passage the problem is how to give freshness to a familiar vocabulary, here how to raise the poetic weight of ordinary words by an artifice concealed to the audience. Immisch, pp. 78 and 80, neglects the marked difference between the two passages of H., just as he neglects the differences between the other passages which he offers as illustration, pp. 78 ff. The passages are, Ar. *Rhet.* III. 2, 1404 b 24–5, Philod. *HV*², IV. 151 (Hausrath, *JB f. kl. Phil.* Supp. XVII (1890), 275), Dion. Hal. *Comp.* 3. 11 ff., 20. 145, 25. 135–6, ps.-Long. *Subl.*, ch. 40, *Anth. Pal.* VII. 50, Agrippa *ap.* Don. *Vit. Verg.* § 44, and H.

Of these *Anth. Pal.* must here be jettisoned; though the writer talks of Euripides' misleading simplicity, he does not talk of plain words in a less plain composition. So must Philodemus because his context is unhappily lost: πόημα...γί[νεσθαι ἐ]ξ ἰδιωτικῶν [τε καὶ ε]ὐτελῶν, συ[γ]κει[μένων] δὲ καλῶς, χ[ρ]ησ[τόν]. This, apart from the Romans, leaves us with Aristotle on the one hand, and Dionysius and Longinus on the other—two different doctrines. For Dionysius and to a lesser extent Longinus are concerned with euphony, rhythm, hiatus, and what was known as rhetorical composition, σύνθεσις. This was part of rhetorical teaching and may be as old as the rhetoricians' interest in euphony and the effect of composition. Aristotelian teaching may however have made an impact on such later critics as Longinus as well. Aristotle has been cited above 47–8 n. He has his own notion of style; he is talking of familiar words in an effective context; rhetorical *compositio* does not enter. Agrippa and H. argue on the basis of the Aristotelian tradition, unconcerned here as to euphony and the rest. Both envisage a position intermediate between two extremes of style and a pointed style concealed by art. Agrippa calls Virgil *nouae cacozeliae repertorem, non tumidae nec exilis* (sc. the two extremes) *sed ex communibus uerbis atque ideo latentis* (i.e. *cacozelia* concealed); he has an axe to grind—Virgil's alleged affectation. So Aristotle emerges as H.'s closest ally. The Aristotelian position in *Rhet.* III, ch. 2 may be stated as follows. An element of strangeness in everyday language (1404 b 10), regulated by appropriateness (b 17–18), its poetic character made acceptable by seeming naturalness (b 19), composition concealing its artistry by the use of ordinary words, first achieved in Euripides' poetry (b 24–5). Compare H.'s position. Satyric drama requires language less heightened than that of tragedy, everyday language but not the realism of comedy (234–9), the poetic level of the style made acceptable by a naturalness concealing art and suggesting that it is in anyone's reach (240–2), achieved by effective composition consisting of ordinary words (242–3).

240 *ex noto fictum:* the adj. as in *notum . . . uerbum* above 47, but here used as a noun, cf. the more established *de medio*, below 243, which perhaps assisted the transference, cf. Aristotle, in the passage mentioned above, *Rhet.* III. 2, 1404 b 24–5 ἐάν τις ἐκ τῆς εἰωθυίας διαλέκτου ἐκλέγων συντιθῇ.

carmen sequar: for the 1st person see above 234 n. *ego.* The verb = 'pursue, aim at' as *Ep.* II. 2. 143 *uerba sequi . . . modulanda*, Pers. 5. 14 *uerba togae sequeris.* Hence . . . *fictum carmen sequar* = *carmen fingam,* 331–2 *speremus carmina fingi | posse*, 382 *uersus . . . fingere*, and the like, cf. *TLL*, VI. 1. 773. 82 ff. L. Mueller defined *carmen* by content and arrangement, not diction, Wickham by plot. But the sense that is intended must be naturally inherent in the context.

240–1 *sibi . . . | speret:* as Virg. *A.* XII. 241–2 *mihi . . . | sperabant* Ov. *Met.* II. 631 *sperantemque sibi*, cf. J. Vahlen, *Op. Ac.* II. 248.

241 *speret idem* is mockingly echoed by *ausus idem* in the same place of the next verse; for the 'rhyme', see 176–7 n. These men hope, dare, toil—and fail. They are deceived by the art concealing art—H.'s ideal of art becoming nature. Impressively put, with a rare personal touch, *Ep.* II. 2. 124–5, after the hard work prescribed in the preceding verses, *ludentis speciem dabit, et torquebitur, ut qui | nunc Satyrum* *nunc agrestem Cyclopa mouetur.* Cf. Ar. *Rhet.* III. 2, 1404 b 18 ff. λανθάνειν... καὶ μὴ δοκεῖν λέγειν πεπλασμένως ἀλλὰ πεφυκότως, followed by κλέπτεται δ' εὖ ἐάν τις κτλ.· ὅπερ Εὐριπίδης ποιεῖ καὶ ὑπέδειξε πρῶτος, *Anth. Pal.* VII. 50. 3–4 (on Euripides) λείη μὲν γὰρ ἰδεῖν καὶ ἐπίρροθος· | ἢν δέ τις αὐτὴν | εἰσβαίνῃ, χαλεποῦ τρηχυτέρη σκόλοπος. For instances from Cicero and Dionysius, see Rostagni, 240 n.

sudet multum: a well-established metaphor from athletic training, cf. the athlete, below 413, *sudauit et alsit* (where at 416 the poet fails to put in the training required), *Ep.* II. 1. 168–9, metaphorical as here, *creditur, ex medio quia res accersit, habere | sudoris minimum (comoedia).*

frustraque: 'adversative' *-que,* in grammatical parlance; for a similar use of *et,* see *TLL,* v. 2. 893. 4 ff. Cf. Hofmann–Szantyr, 481; the complex cases discussed by Fraenkel, *Horace,* 219 n. 4 differ. In fact, it is not *-que* but the context that is adversative and this is thrown into strong relief by the simple connective particle: 'sweat and fail'. Cf. Wilamowitz's enlightening remarks, Eur. *Her.* 509 n.

242 *ausus idem:* cf. 241 n. *speret idem.*

series iuncturaque pollet: The two nouns together, 'texture and combination', realize some of the potentialities of the simple Greek 'σύνθεσις'. They are a sophisticated version that seems to echo *in uerbis serendis* (45) and *iunctura* (48), as has often been noted. This version befits a sophisticated poet. Thus two pronouncements on diction are tied together; one is general (46 ff.), the other specific. But just like *callida...iunctura* 46–7, this locution attaches an especial virtue and effectiveness to *iunctura,* which Aristotle's simple ἐάν τις... συντιθῇ did not possess. The same is true for the emphasis placed on σύνθεσις by the rhetoricians. Here as at 47–8, H.'s *iunctura* has nothing to do with euphony, rhythm, and the other features of that 'composition' which Cicero calls *coniunctio* (e.g. *De Or.* III. 175) and Quintilian *iunctura* (e.g. *I.O.* IX. 4. 22 *in omni porro compositione tria sunt genera necessaria, ordo iunctura numerus*). For H.'s *iunctura* and Pers. 5. 14, see above 47 n.

243 *tantum,* repeated from the preceding verse, is highly emphatic: placed rightly in the right context ordinary words will receive 'standing'.

de medio sumptis, an occasional synonym (with *de* or *e*) in rhetorical theory for *uerba usitata* or similar terms, Cic. *De Or.* III. 177, *Or.* 163, al. (*TLL,* VIII. 594. 5 ff.).

accedit honoris, cf. 70–1 *cadentque | quae nunc sunt in honore uocabula, Ep.* II. 2. 112–13 *(quaecumque) honore indigna ferentur | uerba mouere loco.*

244–50 The new poetic Mean has a third aspect—the tone of the

Commentary

Satyrs who form the chorus of the drama. The Mean they must attain lies between two townish extremes to which their rusticity may incline them, the sentimentality fit for the young men of the Forum and the vulgarity of the city plebs.

244 *siluis deducti...Fauni:* the abl. after *deducti* without the preposition common in prose, as at *Ep.* I. 2. 48, and after many compounds with *a, de, ex,* cf. D. Bo, *Hor. Op.* III. 98 ff. The Satyrs, like the primitive men, *siluestres homines* (391), belong to the countryside, are *agrestes*, 221. H. makes the twofold identification, common at the time, of (goat-like) Satyrs with the Greek goat demon Pan and, in turn, of Pan with the Italic Faunus. Like Pan the *Fauni* belong to the countryside in Augustan verse: *C.* III. 18. 1 ff., cf. I. 4. 11, Virg. *G.* I. 10, Ov. *Fast.* II. 193, III. 315. H. even makes Faunus commute between Pan's Arcadia and Italy, *C.* I. 17. 1–2 *uelox amoenum saepe Lucretilem | mutat Lycaeo Faunus.* Elsewhere the two are conjoined, *Ep.* I. 19. 3–4 *ut male sanos | adscripsit Liber Satyris Faunisque poetas.*

me iudice seems to resolve any doubts as to the identity of *Satyrorum scriptor* (235); it is H. the critic, cf. Steidle, *Studien,* 127 f.

245 Urbanized Satyrs or Fauns are deplored. K. Latte, *H,* LX (1925), 8, has compared H.'s *Satyri–Fauni* with the Satyr of Dioscorides' epigram on Sositheus, the Alexandrian writer of tragic and Satyric drama of the time of Ptolemy Philadelphus: *Anth. Pal.* VII. 707 (no. XXIII, Gow and Page, *The Gr. Anth., Hellenistic Epigrams,* I, p. 88, 5–6 κἠμὲ τὸν ἐν καινοῖς τεθραμμένον ἤθεσιν ἤδη | ἤγαγεν εἰς μνήμην πατρίδ' ἀναρχαίσας. For the text see Gow and Page, II, 256, who consider emending πατρίδος ἀρχαῖσας, and support G. Hermann's point that both dramatic genres may be alluded to. The two genres also may have been in Dioscorides' mind at *Anth. Pal.* VII. 411 (no. XXI, Gow and Page, I. 87) τὰ δ' ἀγροιῶτιν ἀν' ὕλαν | παίγνια. Latte regarded Neoptolemus of Parium, H.'s reputed authority, as a near contemporary of Sositheus, and suggested that H. had here been drawing on an Alexandrian feature of his 'source'. This is at any rate a possible date for Neoptolemus (cf. *Prol.* 44, 149), and a plausible though not inevitable provenance of H.'s urbanized Satyrs.

uelut innati triuiis: as in the preceding verse classical prose would favour a preposition; the case is likely to be dat., cf. *TLL,* VII. 1. 1692. 65; the certain instances of the abl. are late Latin. H. imagines the woodland Satyrs behaving 'as though they had been born in a common (Roman) street': *triuium* suggests *plebecula,* cf. Cic. *Mur.* 13 *non debes...arripere maledictum ex triuio* (Otto, *Sprichwörter,* 351 f.). *uelut* makes *innati* into something resembling a hypothetical clause, *uelut si innati essent,* for which the historians and poets sometimes

Commentary

ventured *uelut* without *si*, e.g. Sall. *Iug.* 53. 7, cf. Hofmann–Szantyr, 675. H. resourcefully favours the participle in the place of a whole clause, see for *uelut(i)* S. II. 1. 33–4 *uotiua . . . ueluti descripta tabella | uita senis*, II. 3. 98 *ueluti uirtute paratum* (cf. Hofmann–Szantyr, 385).

   ac paene forenses either may enlarge on *innati triuiis* and = *uulgares*, as in ps.-Acro's note and Greek ἀγοραστικοί, cf. Cic. *Clu.* 40 *pharmacopolam circumforaneum*, Cael., Cic. *Fam.* VIII. 1. 4 *subrostrani*, Liv. IX. 46. 13 *forensis factio . . ., omnem forensem turbam excretam*, Paul. Fest. 45 *canalicolae forenses homines pauperes dicti quod circa canales fori consisterent.* Or else *forenses* may be the eloquent and well-informed frequenters of the Forum, as Varro, *Men.* 147 *forenses decernunt ut Existimatiu nomen meum in sanorum numerum referat*, Vitr. VI. 5. 2 *forensibus . . . et disertis*, and especially Quint. *I.O.* x. 1. 55 *musa illa rustica et pastoralis non forum modo uerum ipsam etiam urbem reformidat.* The word is indistinct but *concinnitas* makes in favour of the latter notion. The next two verses look as though they took up the two locutions in converse order: 246 corresponding to *paene forenses*, and 247 to *triuiis innati*; so it was proposed by Doederlein (ed. 1858) and Krüger (15th ed. 1908), later less clearly by others. Without this antecedent the later division would be unconvincing and abrupt. With the antecedent the later division has the further function of explaining the indistinct *forenses*. If that is so, *Satyri triuiales* and *forenses* are distinguished as two styles were before, a way of talking reminiscent of the 'double zeugma' discussed above 96 n. A disjunctive *aut* for *ac*, *pace* Wilkins, is not only not required in this figure of speech, but would be objectionable before the double *aut* 246–7.

   246 *nimium teneris . . . uersibus:* one of the two new extremes to be avoided; *tener* has literary connotations: Steidle, *Studien*, pp. 123 f. For the wording *nimium teneris*, cf. Prud. *Perist.* III. 24.

   iuuenentur happily alludes to the Satyrs as young men—a feature, it seems, of Satyric drama, where they are contrasted as his τέκνα with Papposilenus, cf. Soph. *Indag.* 47 παῖδας δ' ἐμούς, 147–8 τοιοῦδε πατρός . . . | οὗ πόλλ' ἐφ' ἥβης μνήματ' ἀνδρείας ὕπο κτλ., Eur. *Cycl.* 13, 100–1, etc. Hence νεανιεύεσθαι and μειρακιεύεσθαι would be apposite verbs in Greek. In Latin, Varro, *Men.* 550 has *tu quoque adhuc adulescentiaris*, Laberius even more daringly, *CRF*[3], fr. 138 *incipio adulescenturire et nescioquid nugarum facere*. H.'s very apt *iuuenentur* is an ἅπαξ λεγόμενον, probably his coinage, on a Greek basis, as in many other instances. Here however the Latin antecedents may also be seen. The word is certainly not the recommended 'ordinary' kind, *de medio sumptum* (243)—a likely instance, therefore, of *exemple joint au précepte* (J. Marouzeau, *RP*, n.s. L (1926), 110–11). It may also suit *nimium teneri uersus*; contrast *crepent* in the context of *immunda dicta* of the following line.

247 rejects the other extreme, smutty jokes, the language of the gutter; *dicta* may have both connotations. This is the world of *mimus* and *comoedia*.

immunda...ignominiosaque are aptly strong words applied to talk. I have found no other instance.

crepent 'to noise, shout, utter, prattle', cf. 231 *effutire*, and *S*. II. 3. 33 *siquid Stertinius ueri crepat, Ep*. I. 7. 84 *sulcos et uineta crepat mera*, Lucr. II. 1170-1 *crepat, antiquum genus ut pietate repletum | perfacile angustis tolerarit finibus aeuum*. Cf. the likely colloquial nuance in *C*. I. 18. 5 *quis post uina grauem militiam aut pauperiem crepat?* (*increpat* in the weaker MSS), and above 246 n. on *iuuenentur*.

248-50 again deliver a Horatian judgement which appears to be made dependent on the reaction of the audience. But unlike 113 *equites peditesque* and 153 *ego et populus mecum*, these verses proclaim only the knights, and their judgement differs markedly from the *plebecula*. Arbuscula, at *S*. I. 10. 76-7, despised 'the others': *satis est equitem mihi plaudere... | contemptis aliis. Ep*. II. 1. 182-6 *indocti stolidique* in the middle of a play call for 'a bear or boxers', and are willing to fight it out *si discordet eques*; but there, in the sequel, even the *eques* gets his share of criticism. Of the two extremes rejected in 245-7, only the *immunda dicta* are taken up. I conclude that, although the *uia media* between tragedy and comedy was taken seriously by H., it was the proximity of comedy from which he wanted to remove the New Satyric drama. The 'comic' character of the *exodia* was part of the literary scene and thus H.'s procedure supports the practical nature of his proposals.

248 *offenduntur:* of taste, cf. 352, 376; in the former place as here of poetic taste, thus in the instances cited from other authors by Steidle, *Studien*, p. 124 n. 49.

equus–pater–res: H.'s epigrammatic manner gives especial standing to these judges, who fulfilled the social qualifications, and are now supposed to have taste as well. H. notices social aspects in accordance with the varying scope of his poems; see below 366 ff. on the poetic attempts of a young *nobilis*, and contrast for example *Epod.* 4. 5-6 with *S*. I. 6. 10 ff. The poet could not have written as he did if 'cultured leisure' had not been within the purview of this class; see, for example, C. Nicolet, *L'ordre équestre à l'époque républicaine*, 1 (1966), part ii, ch. 7, 'Les chevaliers et les activités libérales'. *equus, pater, res* are humorously juxtaposed, but in fact *equus* (equestrian status) depended on *res* (the census, cf. Juv. 3. 154-5 *de puluino surgat equestri, | cuius res legi non sufficit*) and *pater* (a free-born father, cf. below 383 n.). For the latter condition and its relaxations, see Mommsen, *Röm. Staatsrecht*, III. I. 451, 500, 517 ff., A. Stein, *Der röm. Ritterstand* (1927), ch. 3, C. Nicolet, *op. cit.* (1966), especially pp. 101–2 n. 73. The long standing of an equestrian family is not in point, whereas it is in such passages as Cic. *Planc.* 32, Ov. *Tr.* IV. 10. 7–8. Emendations intended to introduce senators (*pater, et quibus est*, G. Waddel, *Animad. crit.* etc. (1738), p. 85 or, more idiomatically, *patres, equus et quibus et res*, Peerlkamp) also introduce a false note; here as elsewhere, approvingly or not, H. sets the *eques* apart from the rest. The threefold division of Stat. *Silv.* IV. I. 25–6 (cit. Ritter) is equally off the point.

249 *ciceris...et nucis:* the food of the poor *asse... constat*, Mart. I. 103. 10; distributed by donation, *S.* II. 3. 182. Again this manner of talking suits the passage; at *S.* I. 6. 115, practising low living and high thinking, H. himself returns home *ad porri et ciceris...laganique catinum. nucis* also comprises chestnuts, almonds, etc.

fricti: the usual way of preparing chick-pea, nuts and the like; cf. Pl. *Bac.* 767 *tam frictum ego illum reddam quam frictum est cicer, Poen.* 326 *frictas nuces.* The latter passage shows that, as Wilkins notes, *fricti* is likely to be attrib. ἀπὸ κοινοῦ with *nucis* as well as *ciceris.* My colleague Professor U. Limentani tells me that fried, or rather roasted, chick-peas survived as a standard dish in rural Latium as late as 1935, and may still do so; cf. Ignazio Silone, *Vino e pane* (Milan, 1955, 1st ed. 1935), p. 138, *c'era quasi sempre un piattino* di ceci abbrustoliti *nel sale.*

250 *aequis...animis:* the rendering 'equanimity' is usually reasonable next to *accipio*, e.g. Sall. *Cat.* 3. 2, and with other verbs too is often shown to be so by the context, as Cic. *Att.* II. 4. 2 *animo aequo, immo uero etiam gaudenti ac libenti* (cit. Orelli). In many instances however *aequus* with *animus, mens*, etc. is 'favourable', e.g. Ter. *An.* prol. 24 *fauete, adeste aequo animo, Hec.* 28 *aequo animo attendite*, Caes. *Civ.* III. 6. 1 *quodcumque imperauisset se aequo animo facturos*, Virg. *A.* IX. 234 *audite o mentibus aequis.* This adds a livelier complexion to *accipiunt...donantue corona.* Wilkins' advocacy is therefore justified, although his instances (*oculis aequis, aequus Iuppiter*) are too far from this passage.

donantue corona: (not -*que*). In Athens a victorious poet's success in the competition was marked by a crown of ivy, see Pickard-Cambridge, *Dram. Fest.* 99 n. 7. H. however may not be referring to actual custom, either Greek or contemporary Roman. *corona*, in spite of *Ep.* II. 2. 96, is most likely to be metaphorical because (*a*) H.'s way of talking seems to overstate the influence of the *equites* or any other group on the award of the prize, cf. the works cited by Steidle, *Studien*, p. 125; (*b*) *Ep.* II. I. 181 *palma negata*, like *corona* above, seems to continue republican allusions to poets' victories, when 'there is no clear evidence for poetic competitions during republican times' (H. D. Jocelyn, *The Tragedies of Ennius*, pp. 22 f.); Varro, *L.L.* v. 178 and Plut. *Cato Min.* 46. 4, cited by Rostagni, talk of gifts or prizes for actors, not playwrights. The 'crown' was sufficiently established as symbolizing poetic victory for H. to refuse to take it from Lucilius: *S.* I. 10. 48–9 *detrahere . . . | haerentem capiti cum multa laude coronam.* This does not prevent us from contrasting the end of this section with the imaginary Greek prize-giving of the *hircus* at its beginning, 220.

(9) The metre of dramatic dialogue; 'ars' in Greek and Roman poetry, 251–74

The tradition. The Greek literary tradition on the subject of metre is virtually unknown. It is true there are a few relevant remarks in Hephaestion and his scholiasts. But they are sadly depleted, and in any case represent technical writing by experts in metre. They do not represent literary theory. The only glimpses we get of that theory are in ch. 4 of the *Poetics*, and in the discussion of prose rhythm in *Rhet.* III, ch. 8, neither of much use. No Hellenistic writing on this subject is preserved. Thus there is no Greek evidence against which to set H.'s metrical study; tenuous reflections of earlier work in the late grammarians do not supply sufficient evidence. That is regrettable, for his discussion of the Greek trimeter and the Latin senarius seems to presuppose not only Greek practice but Greek theory.

Horace. H. writes not as a historian of archaic Roman poetry but as a poet-critic. His lack of fairness in dealing with the old Roman playwrights has often been deplored. But he is not even attempting to understand the principles of their technique. He is establishing a different and more exacting set of principles. Hence the charges of careless workmanship or lack of insight. As for the placing of this section I have pointed out earlier (153–294 n.) that H. has avoided the mechanical order, which might be reminiscent of prosaic exposition: miscellaneous rules, chorus, music, metre, the three dramatic genres of Satyric drama, comedy, tragedy. His own arrangement demands more flexible and less superficial reading. It leads from miscellaneous rules, chorus and music to Satyric drama, treated as another technical problem, how to cope with an *exodium* to tragedy. Only then does he move on to metre, again discussed as a problem of technique. This problem is known as a recurring motif from earlier sections, that of *ars*–τέχνη. And it is *ars* which provides the criterion for an assessment of metre, first in the dialogue of drama, next in all its various forms. Metre carries ancient poetry, and Roman achievement here is found wanting, Greek works become *exemplaria*. Thus Roman vs. Greek *ars* becomes the dominant theme from 263 onward and after 274 the subject of metre is allowed to fall away. (The structural importance of the motif 'Roman vs. Greek' was first emphasized by P. Cauer, *RM*, LXI (1906), 238 f.) The two major genres of drama, comedy and tragedy, are set against this background; so there again are two topics, the straightforward technical ones of the genres and the continuing motif of *ars*. And it is this motif which makes the link with the final large section of the poem, where it remains a dominant feature.

H. has built the subject up into a little sketch on metre, with the Iambus personified as its main agent. In his customary fashion he begins abruptly; the links with what precedes and what follows are not on the surface. The start is jocular, the mild bathos of an elementary definition, but the reader is quickly shocked into recognition of the paradox that at any rate in Horatian terms the simple short–long of the iambus involves the status of Roman poetry.

251 begins in lecturing style. The initial remark is so elementary that its purpose should have deceived no one. It is the technique of surprise which H. practises in many ways. And it is made plain presently that the real purpose was not elementary at all, but a

Commentary

pointer to a difficult technical problem, humorously disguised as elementary instruction. It has even been suggested, amusingly, that this verse is a 'memoria technica line, used in schools' (E. H. Blakeney's translation (1928), p. 82).

syllaba longa breui subiecta: conversely *Anth. Lat.* 480. 4 *at praelata breuis longae concludet iambum.*

252 *pes citus:* cf. *C.* I. 16. 24 *celeres iambos*, Ov. *Rem.* 377–8 *iambus* | *seu celer, extremum seu trahat ille pedem* (i.e. scazon), Prud. *Epil.* 7 *citos iambicos*, Sid. *Ep.* VIII. 11. 7, Sacerd. *GL*, VI. 518. 13 *eius uelocitas* (seq. *A.P.* 251–2), Ter. Maur. 1383 *iambus, pes uirilis acer et raptim citus*, 2182–3; cf. Arctinus *ap.* Diom. *GL*, I. 477. 12 προφόρῳ ποδί. Contrast above 79–82, where H. combines Aristotle's λεκτικόν with a hint at the energy of the metre, *natum rebus agendis*; Aristotle, as K.–H. remark, regarded the trochee as a 'running' or speedy rhythm, *Rhet.* III. 8, 1409 a 1. Having obtained the initial effect of comic bathos, H. is going to say why 'short–long' and 'rapid' are worth talking about.

unde: the assertion being that because of its tempo metra consisting of two feet were formed.

trimetris: for the nomenclature, see Rufinus, *GL*, VI. 556. 14 f. *Varro in eodem septimo de lingua Latina...senarium*, etc., 18 ff. *trimetros uersus iambicos...M. Tullius (Or.* 184, 189) *senarios dicit. Quintilianus et trimetros et senarios nominauit (I.O.* IX. 4. 75) *et Flauius Caper...trimetros ...senarios appellauit.*

accrescere 'grow, be annexed, adhere', with dat. as ps.-Sall. *In Tull.* 4 *quid tibi litibus accreuerit*, Plin. *Ep.* II. 8. 3 *ueteribus negotiis noua accrescunt.* According to Wilkins, '*accrescere* denotes the gradual adhesion of the name to that which is not properly denoted thereby'. The word however is oddly used of the acquisition of a name in spite of K.–H.'s explanation and I am not sure that a gradual process is implied. I have left the word in the text with misgivings. Peerlkamp proposed *accedere* (thus in some dett., presumably by conjecture; cf. Stat. *Ach.* II. 22 *discedere*] *descendere* E *decedere* R *decrescere* Q²ς), L. Mueller *succrescere.*

iussit: the iambus assuming the command as it were. Dramatically personified, the iambus remains grammatical subj. up to 262, cf. Steidle, *Studien*, p. 49.

253 *nomen:* Ribbeck for no good reason replaced the word by *momen* (from Lucr. et al.), undeterred by Bentley's verdict (cit. Housman, Man. I. 34 n.), '*qui* (sc. Scaliger) *saepius hoc uerbum (momen) ingerit, numquam feliciter*'. Cf. Vahlen, *Op. Ac.* I. 57.

iambeis: commentators note the ἅπαξ λεγόμενον for Greek

297

ἰαμβεῖον, in place of the cretic form *iambicis*. Of the major MSS of H. only cod. B gets this wrong: *iambis*. For the Latin spelling of adjs. derived from -εῖος, see Housman, *JP*, xxxiii (1914), 56.

After *iambeis* no strong punctuation is to be entertained; see below 254 n. *non ita pridem*.

cum: concessive, implausibly explained as causal by Wickham: in spite of its six beats, because of its fast tempo, it is called trimeter.

senos...ictus: as *pede ter percusso* (*S.* i. 10. 43) denoting the rhythmic beat, cf. Ter. Maur. 2191–3 *iambus ipse sex enim locis manet, | et inde nomen inditum est senario; | sed ter feritur, hinc trimetrus dicitur*; he adds cautiously (2195) *quae causa cogat, non morabor edere*. Iuba on the other hand, *ap*. Prisc. *GL*, iii. 420. 13 ff., gives a reason, which is in fact implied in Terentianus' *ter feritur*. Contrast χρόνοι in a Greek definition such as *Schol. A*, Hephaest. (ed. Consbruch), p. 117. 21 ff. τὸ ἰαμβικὸν μέτρον κατὰ συζυγίαν μετρεῖται. καὶ ἔστιν ἡ συζυγία ἢ δίϊαμβος ἐξ χρόνων, and compare Quint. *I.O.* ix. 4. 51 *tempora... metiuntur et pedum et digitorum ictu*, below 274 n. *digitis*, Mar. Vict. *GL*, vi. 80. 2 *tria tempora*; Fortunatianus, *GL*, vi. 286. 15, uses the term συζυγίαι.

For punctuation after *ictus*, see below 254 n. *non ita pridem*.

254 *primus ad extremum:* the nom. as at *Ep.* i. 1. 54 *Ianus summus ab imo*, with Bentley's note. The words *non ita pridem* that follow are not contrasted with *primus*, as was asserted by Immisch, p. 162 n. 52. Hence the problem which he sought to solve by the assumption of a temporal meaning of *primus* does not arise. Even if *primus* = *primum* (cf. Housman, *Man.* i. 226 n.) and here meant 'first, originally', *non ita pridem* could scarcely express the second stage, *non multo post*.

similis sibi: i.e. iambic first to last. This is the trimeter consisting of pure iambuses, an artificiality not now known from the whole of any Greek poem but from Cat. 4 and 29, *Catal.* 6, 10, and 12 of the Virgilian corpus, *Priap.* 83, 85, and Hor. *Epod.* 16, which are not unlikely to have Hellenistic antecedents. Earlier students of metre may have talked of an 'age of pure iambics' (Wickham), as H. does here and Ter. Maur. 2182 ff. did some centuries later. Others seem to be avoiding historical pronouncements of this kind, e.g. Mar. Vict. *GL*, vi. 80. 1 ff., Fortunat. *GL*, vi. 286. 14 ff., Sacerd. *GL*, vi. 518. 1 ff., Rufin. *GL*, vi. 556. 18 ff.

non ita pridem: an unsolved problem both in wording and punctuation. The problem has been much debated, cf. H. Schütz, Ribbeck, Wilkins *ad l*. Now most editors (though not Villeneuve) accept the text as if it conveyed a tenable meaning. O. Immisch and A. Y. Campbell reject current views on the passage, but their own suggestions carry little conviction (Immisch, pp. 162–3, n. 52; Campbell, *Bull. Inst. Class. Lond.* v (1956), 66–7).

(*a*) H. Weil, *RP*, XIX (1895), 20–2 first suggested attaching *non ita pridem* to the preceding context. The meaning, as Immisch objected, would seem to be 'not for such a long time' rather than 'not so long ago'. Three punctuations may be canvassed: a full stop after 253 *iambeis* (Weil), or after *ictus* (Lejay in Plessis–Lejay's small edition of H.), or after 254 *pridem*. A break after *iambeis* would blunt the contrast between *trimetris* and *senos*. A break after *ictus* would remove the phrase *primus ad extremum similis sibi* from *senos…ictus*, which it seems to qualify. A full stop after 254 would leave *non ita pridem* at the close of the sentence—a collocation unexampled in the many instances of *pridem* that I have seen. Weil's suggestion seems to be ruled out on these grounds.

(*b*) is the vulgate: a full stop precedes *non ita pridem*. But H., of all Romans, would not suggest that the alleged change from all-iambic senarius to classical trimeter was made 'not so long ago'. For that technique must be Greek not Roman, and he knew his Archilochus. Klingner's argument (*BVSA*, LXXXVIII (1937), 35 n. 2) does not eliminate this difficulty. Nor can *non ita pridem* refer to 252 *iussit* (K.–H.). The words therefore seem to be corrupt. The required sense is either 'later, afterwards', *mox* in Terentianus Maurus' account of the same metre, 2196 (which seems influenced by the Horatian theory), or else the very opposite of the MSS reading, 'a long time ago'. But no plausible emendation on these lines has occurred to me. I hope it will occur to others.

255 *paulo* (not *paulum* π) placed between *tardior* and *grauiorque* probably applies to both; the restricted number of spondees change only a little of the lightness and speed of the *pes citus*. This marks an intermediate position between an entirely iambic run and the 'slowness' of the senarius of Roman tragedy censured at 258 ff. *paulo* with a comparative (the type *paulo maiora canamus*) probably has a colloquial nuance, cf. H. C. Gotoff, *P*, CXI (1967), 67 n. 4.

256 *stabiles*: of rhythm, Quint. *I.O.* IX. 4. 83 *quo quique* (*pedes*) *sunt temporibus pleniores* longisque *syllabis magis stabiles, hoc grauiorem faciunt* orationem, breues celerem *ac mobilem, ibid.* 97 (*dochmius*) *stabilis in clausulis et seuerus,* 111 (paeon starting with long syllable) *merito laudatur: nam et primam stabilem et tres celeres habet.*

in iura paterna recepit: the spondee is being 'adopted' into the iambic family, and can now enjoy the rights, *iura paterna*, of the iambus' *patrimonium*, as though he were a natural son, cf. W. W. Buckland, *A Text-book of Roman Law*[3], 122: 'the *adoptatus* acquired the rights of a natural son'. The witty adj. *paterna* should not be weakened by the conjecture *alterna*, cf. Wilkins *ad l.*; for the construction, see *TLL*, I. 810. 31 ff., *adoptare* and *recipere* being construed alike.

257 *commodus* 'obliging', as *C.* IV. 8. 1–2 *donarem pateras grataque commodus* | . . .*meis aera sodalibus, Ep.* II. I. 227 where the adj. is used in the same adverbial function. *patiens* 'tolerant', as *S.* II. 5. 43 *ut patiens, ut amicis aptus.*

non ut = *non ita ut*, not on the terms that' (Wickham), 'except that he would not', cf. *Ep.* I. 16. 6 *sed ut*, and R. G. Nisbet's remarks *AJP*, XLIV (1923), 29.

257–8 *de sede secunda* | . . .*aut quarta:* pairing of iambic feet—the συзυγίαι and διίαμβοι of the Greeks, above 253 n.— and the resulting difference in the treatment of the feet is a topic much discussed by the grammarians, e.g. Sacerd. *GL*, VI. 518. 24 ff. *in secunda uero et quarta parte (nam de sexta nulla ratio est quoniam in omni metro pes nouissimus indifferens est) illos ponere debemus qui ex breui incipiunt, iambum, tribrachyn, anapaestum, ibid.* 526. 20 ff. *quamuis H. usque ad trimetrum praeceperit, cum de sexto pede uel septimo iambico nullam fecerit mentionem,* Ter. Maur. 2196 ff., particularly 2209–10 *dum pes secundus, quartus et nouissimus* | *semper dicatus uni iambo seruiat,* Fortunat. *GL*, VI. 286. 19 *sed iambus, ut ait H., spondeum in partem (paterna iura* Keller from H., implausibly) *recipit, qui pes omnia paene metra ornat atque disponit*; Iuba *ap.* Prisc. *GL*, III. 420. 7 ff. *ideo in secundo et quarto et sexto loco iambus non recipit nisi a breui incipientes, quia in his locis feriuntur per coniugationem pedestrem metrorum; et uult extrema pars pedum iambicorum celerior esse quomodo et ipsi iambi,* Mar. Vict. *GL*, VI. 81. 28 ff., et al. H. omitted a mention of the final foot. Critics such as Peerlkamp remove a good word from H.'s text (see below on *socialiter*) in order to provide an unnecessary mention of the last foot.

socialiter 'in the partnership', which Peerlkamp uncritically replaced by *sextaue sed*, cf. preceding note. The adv. qualifies *non ut . . . cederet*. Wilkins' proposal, attaching *socialiter* to *commodus et patiens*, deprives the *non ut* clause of an amusing poetic touch. The word is not based on the notion of a partnership in business, *societas* (for which see Manigk, *R-E*, III A. 772. 34 ff.) but on association or partnership in the family. *socius* had the general sense of 'associate'; and *iura paterna* would have implied a sharing throughout. *socialis* is used several times by Ovid for partnership in marriage, e.g. *Tr.* II. 161 *Liuia sic tecum sociales compleat annos*; Seneca used it to denote a share in the *societas humana*. The adj. occurs as early as Cicero in the political sense of alliance, which is not here applicable. The adv., according to the materials of the Latin *Thesaurus*, is restricted to this passage in classical Latin (Rostagni compares Greek κοινωνικῶς), but it reappears in St Augustine and other Christian writers. Cf. *sociabilis* in Livy and later prose, *sociabiliter* in late Latin.

hic 'he', the *iambus* personalized (not 'here', i.e. 'in these places', F. Schultess, *RM*, LVII (1902), 468) now marks the transition to metre in Roman drama, which will presently attach itself to the major motif of technical sufficiency, Greek vs. Roman. *tragicus iambus* in Rome, and the neglect of the restriction in the second and fourth feet, are noted in most of the metrical passages cited above, and in others.

259 (*Acci*) *nobilibus trimetris* sounds like a quotation; it may be one of the contemporary *critici* speaking, cf. *Ep.* II. 1. 56 *alti* concerning the same Accius, in a burlesque passage, cf. *Prol.* 194. Victorius' *mobilibus* had best be forgotten. Like Immisch (p. 163), I am unconvinced by K.–H.'s rendering of *nobilibus*, 'which everybody knows'. For *nobilis* descriptive of persons or their works, see Bentley, *C.* I. 29. 14 n.

rarus: pred., points to the opposite extreme to that of 251 ff. The pure iambic trimeter was all lightness and speed; it could do with a little gravity. Accius and Ennius on the other hand neglect the 'statutory rights' of the iambus, 257–8. L. Mueller notes that the distribution of spondee and iambus in Seneca's tragedies largely conforms to Horatian precept and perhaps Augustan technique. So already Bentley, 260 n., '*Quod cum ex Senecae Tragoediis jam licet cognoscere, tum ex Fragmentis quae ex Ovidii, Varii, Gracchique Fabulis hodie supersunt*'.

260 The grammatical subject in the criticism of Ennius (260–2) is *hic*: the iambus, where it appears (not *hic. . .rarus*, the rarity of the i., K.–H.), 'prosecutes' Ennius. Bentley's emendation and repunctuation of the verse, already proposed by Marcilius and commended by Dacier, are therefore beside the mark; cf. Peerlkamp *ad l.* In H.'s literary criticism *pondus* is a laudatory term, below 320, *Ep.* I. 19. 42, II. 2. 112; and as laudatory it may have been intended by the critic who apparently applied it to Ennius (cf. 259 n.), but Lucilius, *S.* I. 10. 54, *ridet uersus Enni grauitate minores*: for this sounds like an ironical quotation in the manner of *Ep.* II. 1. 50–1 *Ennius et sapiens et fortis et alter Homerus,* | *ut critici dicunt.* Cf. Ov. *Tr.* II. 424 *Ennius ingenio maximus, arte rudis*, Quint. *I.O.* I. 8. 8, on archaic poetry in general, *ueteres. . .Latini. . .plerique plus ingenio quam arte ualuerunt.* Archaism quickly reversed these judgements.

Parody too is suggested, not by the sequence of four spondees, which occurs fairly often in this poem (G. E. Duckworth 'Metrical Patterns in H.', *TAPA*, XCVI (1965), 92), but by its combination with the archaic order *cum magno pondere* which Bentley defended against *magno cum* in some dett. Not only Virgil, as commentators say, would probably have written *magno cum pondere* but Cicero, in a line equally full of spondees, has *obuertunt nauem magno cum pondere nautae* (*Arat.* 132, cit. Keller).

261–2 specify certain archaic features that, in Augustan criticism, are interpreted as lack of care and lack of skill. These singly or combined inspire H.'s censures of Lucilius in *S.* 1. 4 and 10 and of archaic poetry in *Ep.* ii. 1. Cf. *Prol.* 156 ff.

261 For criticism of hasty work, *operae celeris nimium,* and shoddiness, *curaque carentis,* the instances cited in the preceding note may be compared

262 *ignoratae . . . artis:* cf. particularly above 87 *cur ego si nequeo ignoroque poeta salutor,* and the poems mentioned above. ars–τέχνη was a watchword among the Callimacheans and the New Poets in Rome. Hence amateurism—or seeming amateurism—becomes an 'ugly charge'.

premit . . . crimine: cf. Liv. iii. 13. 1 *premebat reum . . . crimen unum* (cit. Orelli), Ov. *A.A.* iii. 12 (*Helenes sororem*) *quo premat . . . crimine, Met.* xiv. 401 *criminibusque premunt ueris* (*Circen*). *crimine turpi* ends a hexameter also at Lucr. iii. 49, Ov. *Met.* xiii. 308 (cit. Keller).

263–74 one of the central passages of the poem. I print it as a separate paragraph, for without dropping the metrical topic, H. explores the poetic standards of Roman archaic tragedy, using the foil of Greek artistic sufficiency, just as he does in the letter to Augustus.

263–4 is a 'gliding transition'. The device of an (apparent) apology or admission ('I admit that, etc.', Wilkins) bridges the gulf between the narrow topic of dialogue metre and the wider of Roman critical standards. In reverse order, H. imputes to Roman 'judges' the preceding twofold allegation against archaic Roman dramatists: 263 lack of artistic perception, cf. 262 *ignoratae artis*; 264 undue permissiveness, *uenia . . . indigna,* cf. 261 *curaque carentis.* But what was a disjunctive *aut–aut* above (261–2) is a simple *et* here: undue permissiveness follows lack of perception.

263 *immodulata* is not known again before Calcidius; it was perhaps coined by H. on the basis of something like Greek ἄρρυθμος, an expressive long word covering the middle of the line. It moves talk from the restricted topic of iambus and spondee to any kind of metrical insufficiency. The verse is commonly and not unreasonably interpreted as a parody—a metrically incoherent hexameter on an occasion when H. is damning metrical incoherence in poets and critics. Wilamowitz put the matter strongly; at *Gr. Verskunst*, 9, he suggests that 'Horaz mit *non quivis*,...in neckischer Absicht einen solchen Nichtvers gebaut hat'. In what way '*Nichtvers*', *immodulatum?* The absence of a middle caesura, it is plausibly said, though Wilamowitz uses the (to me dubious) term 'the caesura which makes a Greek or Latin verse'. The *im-* of *immodulata* is scarcely meant to fulfil the function of a separate word, cf. Norden, Virg. *A*. VI. 426 n. 3. At *Prol.* 267 n. 1 I suggested that judgement on the present verse and on 87, where parody is not unlikely, is contingent on 377, where no such purpose is apparent. Two verses in the *Sermones* (II. 3. 134, 181) show this and other anomalies, but cannot be explained as metrical parodies either. In such an accomplished craftsman as H. there may be more motives than that of parody to account for these anomalies. Metrical parody may account for *A.P.* 87 and 263; for the third instance in this poem see 377 n. In a well-known note (Lucr. VI. 1067) Lachmann distinguishes two types of verses without middle caesura—one in which elision tones down the caesura, e.g. 87 *nequeo ignoroque*, and another in which there is no such elision, e.g. the present verse, *uidet immodulata*. Only the latter he considers a true absence of middle caesura. The relation of elision and caesura is still an open problem. But comparison of the present unelided verse with the elisions at 87 and 377 suggests that for H. at any rate elision plays a secondary part in this matter. The metrical effect does not differ in the three instances of the *Ars*: *nequeo ignoroque*, *uidet immodulata*, *natum inuentumque*.

quiuis...iudex: those who judge, the audience, cf. 265 *omnes*—not primarily professional critics. At 86–7 the critics were not blamed, here part of the fault lies with the audience. The function of criticism receives further notice in the final part of the poem, where H. avowedly talks as a teacher, and where criticism is assigned an important place. Cf. *Ep*. II. 2. 109–10 *at qui legitimum cupiet fecisse poema,* | *cum tabulis animum censoris sumet honesti.* For an untutored sense of poetic rhythm, see below 265–7 n.

264 Peerlkamp, followed by H. Schütz, replaced *et* by *nec* assuming 263–4 to be an interlocutor's objection to which 265 replies in the same sense as 11 replies to the objector of 9–10. This is now rightly discounted: *uenia indigna* is H.'s own comment on Roman poetry and its reception; it is the basis for his appeal to informed criticism.

et: probably 'and therefore'.

Romanis: it is not until 268 that *Graeca* points the antithesis.

indigna poetis: the noun according to some commentators first dat.

with *data*, next understood as abl. with *indigna*. This is not impossible but unnecessary, nor need the supposed abl. *poetis* be severed from the dat. *Romanis. indigna* is *quae non decebat* (Lejay). Poets can be unworthy without an indication what they are unworthy of, e.g. *Ep.* II. 1. 231 *indigno non committenda poetae*; so can an indulgence, *uenia*, be.

265 *idcircone*, according to Peerlkamp's implausible suggestion, begins H.'s answer to a protest. The word introduces a question in conversational tone. *idcirco*, avoided altogether by some poets (Lucr., Cat., Tib., Mart.), is rarely used by others, cf. the statistics *TLL*, VII. 1. 172, B. Axelson, *Unpoet. Wörter*, 80 n. 67. The three other passages, all in the hexameter poems, belong to the same matter-of-fact contexts as this passage.

uager: for the 1st pers. sing. see above 25–6 n. H. lays down the law, but in his wording he identifies himself with those wishing to be poets and willing to be taught. So all the way down to 274; at 272 he says *ego et uos.* Cf. 35 *siquid componere curem*, et al. The verb like the adj. *uagus* metaphorically describes freedom from strict principle (K.–H. cite *S.* II. 7. 74 *uaga . . .frenis natura remotis*); thus Cicero calls oratory, unlike dialectic, not bound by strict logical principle *uagum illud orationis et fusum et multiplex . . .genus* (*Brut.* 119), cf. *De Or.* I. 209 *ne uagari et errare cogatur oratio* (speech in terms undefined), *Rep.* II. 22 *non uaganti oratione sed defixa in una republica.*

licenter: freedom from the *leges* of *ars poetica.* Cf. *Ep.* II. 2. 109 *legitimum . . .poema, A.P.* 10 *quidlibet audendi . . .potestas,* 51 *dabiturque licentia sumpta pudenter,* 58 *licuit semperque licebit,* et al. Altogether *si licet* and similar words are used to remind H.'s readers of principles in the worlds of nature, morality—and art.

265 *an omnes-***267** *cautus?* A sentence which has given much trouble; Bentley's and Peerlkamp's notes show the lines of earlier discussion. What was needed however was not emendation but attention to subject-matter, the literary theory which H. is opposing. The poet himself offers sufficient guidance: there seems to be an offer either to abandon the principles of *ars* altogether (*licentia*), 'or' (not 'although', 'so that', 'and') reconsider his denial that everyone is a judge of poetic rhythm (263). Should he now rather believe *omnes uisuros peccata . . .mea*, and conform to prevailing standards, an almost literal reversal of *non quiuis uidet immodulata poemata iudex*? His answer is that avoidance of uninformed criticism is insufficient. Commentators have always remarked that H. clearly disagrees with Cicero's acknowledgement of a natural and untutored sense of poetic rhythm, *De Or.* III. 196 *at in his (numeris) si paulum modo offensum est, . . .theatra tota reclamant,* cf. III. 98; *Or.* 173 *in uersu quidem theatra tota exclamant si* *fuit una syllaba aut breuior aut longior,* cf. *Par. Sto.* 3. 26. Steidle, *Studien,* p. 132 n. 9, has shown that Greek critics share this view. They hold a doctrine asserting the same natural appreciation of rhythm. He cites Philod. *HV²,* IV. 113 (ed. Hausrath, fr. 47, Jensen, *Philodemos,* etc. p. 150) and particularly Dion. Hal. *Comp.* 11. 55 f., like Cicero reflecting on the reaction of audiences in the theatres, and inferring from their impulsive criticism in the theatres that there exists φυσική τις ἀπάντων...ἡμῶν οἰκειότης πρὸς ἐμμέλειάν τε καὶ εὐρυθμίαν κτλ. H. criticizes this kind of assertion.

266 *tutus* is explained by the rest of the sentence.

et I take to be explanatory.

267 For *cautus* combined with *tutus* (266), see above 28 n. *tutus.*

intra spem ueniae: with *cautus* this produces a concise and vivid image, literally 'careful within (i.e. not to stray beyond) hope of pardon'. This notion of *intra* seems to be derived from *intra fines* and the like, *TLL*, VII. 2. 37. 19 ff. There are such instances as Ov. *Tr.* III. 4. 25–6 *intra | fortunam debet quisque manere suam;* but Cic. *Fam.* IX. 26. 3 *non modo non contra legem...sed etiam intra legem,* is not as similar as Lejay's note might suggest, cf. *TLL,* VII. 2. 37. 66 ff. The characteristic Horatian *audacia* I cannot parallel.

denique: cf. above 23.

culpam 'censure', cf. above 31 n. The poet then would merely avoid being faulted.

268 *non laudem merui:* H. mitigates his harsh condemnation of Roman poetic standards by talking in terms of personal doubt. Would *he* be justified in accommodating himself to the domestic scale of criticism? The answer is that he would not. His motive would be wrong, avoidance of (uninformed) censure, not poetic achievement, which he calls *laus:* in the style of the *Odes, C.* IV. 8. 28 *dignum laude uirum Musa uetat mori.* This motive he ascribes to the Greeks a little later in the poem, 324 *(Grais) praeter laudem nullius auaris,* where the idealized Greek scale of values is contrasted with the Roman. In the present passage the Romans are said not to care enough for poetry to take the trouble which alone earns *laus;* hence *exemplaria Graeca.* Quint. *I.O.* XII. 1. 8 *non praecipue acuit ad cupiditatem litterarum amor laudis?* Ausonius' couplet, III. 4. 33 (ed. Peiper, p. 23, cit. Keller), indicates the likely provenance of the antithesis *culpa–laus,* i.e. morals: *deliquisse nihil numquam laudem esse putaui, | atque bonos mores legibus antetuli.*

uos: cf. 270 n. *uestri proaui.* The address, I believe, is rightly explained by Rostagni against many contenders: not only the Pisos but the Romans.

exemplaria Graeca: a further widening of the horizon: *Romanis* (264) now finds its counterpart. With extraordinary sparseness of expression it is implied that (*a*) the only way to true poetic mastery is the way of ancient Greece, (*b*) the Greeks have avoided not only chance criticism but have acquired glory, (*c*) the Greeks alone have poetic *exemplaria* to offer. *exemplar*, 'pattern', is what the copyist imitates but also what the artist or writer sets down. It is moreover Cicero's word in his Latin *Timaeus* (4 and 6) for the 'paradigm' of the demiurge in Plato's cosmological myth (*Tim.* 28 a and c). In Cic. *Rep.* II. 11 it expresses the ideal 'form' of a state. In H. it is sometimes a moral paradigm, *Ep.* I. 2. 18 *utile proposuit nobis exemplar Vlixem*, I. 19. 17 *decipit exemplar uitiis imitabile*; or a poetic, *Ep.* II. 1. 58 *Plautus ad exemplar Siculi properare Epicharmi*; below 317 n. *exemplar uitae morumque*. His use of *exemplum* also may be recalled. Alexandrian critics seem to have proposed κανόνες of classical writers; but their outstanding poetic practitioners knew how to differ in spirit from the great models. Now, for the Augustan Romans, those classical writers become '*the* Greeks', *Graeci*. They are to help the New Poets to transcend the spirit of Roman permissiveness, *spem ueniae*. In spite of this emotional pressure there is a dry, almost humorous, touch in *exemplaria...uersate*. For *exemplaria* are copies of books, *TLL*, v. 2. 1325. 20, cf. 1324. 31 ff., and the next verse shows realistically that they are to be 'handled' day and night.

269 The essence of the Horatian, Augustan, creed is put in a brief and imperious precept, one of the most strictly balanced in H.: a¹bcba² (*uos exemplaria Graeca* |) *nocturna uersate manu, uersate diurna*. Its form and wording closely resemble the by no means solemn verse *Ep.* I. 19. 11 *nocturno certare mero, putere diurno*. Since *Ep.* Book I is likely to antedate the *Ars*, the present passage would be an echo of that in the *Ep.*; the flippant appears to precede the more serious use of a happy pattern. Imitation and self-imitation are among the outstanding features of Latin, especially Augustan, poetry. Sometimes allusion is intended, often it is not. In the present case, just as in Virgil's *inuitus regina* over against its flippant Catullan antecedent, clearly there is 'imitation'; yet no overt allusion seems to be intended since such an allusion would be out of keeping with the desired effect. Nor on the other hand is the echo likely to be accidental, though J. Vahlen (*Op. Ac.* I. 341) maintains it is. H. uses a pattern and a form of wording remembered from another poem, and puts it to an entirely different use. Repetitions of whole verses are a different matter again, see 421 n.

nocturna...manu...diurna: the adverbial use of the adj. is largely poetic and often emotional—*ibant obscuri*; for H. cf. P. Lejay's large

edition of the *Satires*, 1. 6. 128 n., for adjs. with *manus*, Heinze, 7th ed.,
C. II. 13. 2 n. The midnight oil even more than work by day is an
affectation familiar from the *Kunstfleiß* of the Callimacheans and
their Roman successors, cf. Callim. *Epigr.* 27 (= *Anth. Pal.* IX. 507),
3–4 χαίρετε λεπταί | ῥήσιες, Ἀρήτου σύμβολον ἀγρυπνίης, Cinna, fr.
11. 1–2 (Morel, *FPL*, p. 89) *haec tibi Arateis multum inuigilata lucernis* |
carmina, and the other passages cited by Steidle, *Studien*, p. 134 n. 15,
Pfeiffer, Callim. *loc. cit.*, Gow and Page, *The Greek Anth.*, *Hellenistic
Epigrams*, II. 209. H. has avoided the emphasis of such phrases as
nox lucubrata.

uersate . . . uersate marks the emphasis. '*uersare*' is not the *uox propria*
for 'turning a roll'.

270–2, as was said above, adds Roman comedy to the indictment,
the style of its wit as well as its metre. Defenders of Plautus will say,
fairly enough, that this shows *la même méconnaissance de la métrique de
Plaute que celle d'Accius et d'Ennius* (Lejay *ad l.*). But H. is not writing
literary history; he writes as a poet enunciating in his poetry the
principles of a new poetics.

270 *at* introduces an objection. H. puts indirectly—not by direct
interlocution—what others may say of his strictness: 'but your ancestors (you might say) . . .'; a form of Horatian brevity. Peerlkamp's
division into dialogue of the section 263–74 is particularly implausible in this line and the next; there is no indication of an (imaginary)
change of speaker before 271 *nimium*.

uestri, the reading of all known major MSS, continues the address
of 268 *uos*. *nostri* would suit direct interlocution, which has already
been rejected; H. himself would scarcely refer to his *proaui*. Whom is
H. addressing? Not the Pisos, as has often been thought. But the last
address to the Pisos (235) is no longer in view: *ne dicam stulte* would
be a boorish way of referring to their ancestors. *uestri* like *uos* (268)
denotes neither the ancestral Pisos nor critics as different from poets
(Immisch, taken to task by Steidle, *Studien*, pp. 133 f.) but all whom
it may concern—his Roman readers. This is the same polemic against
archaic standards which animates all his critical writing from the
first literary satire to the *Augustus*.

Plautinos . . . numeros: a straight denial of the archaizing taste of the
preceding generation, notably that of Cicero and Varro. The acid
remarks on Plautus, *Ep.* II. 1. 170–6, may be remembered. Commentators note that the conjunction of Plautine rhythms in this verse and
his wit in the next recalls the celebrated epitaph on Plautus, Gell. 1.
24. 3 *scaena est deserta, dein Risus Ludus* Iocusque | *et Numeri innumeri
simul omnes conlacrimarunt.*

271 *sales* extends the censure to Plautus' wit. It is instructive to see H. and Cicero differing on this topic in spite of their adherence to a similar theory; cf. Cic. *Off.* 1. 104 (cit. below 273 n.). To Lucilius at *S.* 1. 4. 7 the epithet *facetus* is granted, although he is *durus componere uersus*; at *S.* 1. 10. 65 the same archaic satirist is *comis et urbanus*, but note *ibid.* 7 ff.

nimium patienter begins the reply to the objection: 'too indulgently'; for the usage, cf. 257 *patiens, Ep.* 1. 1. 40 *patientem . . . aurem.*

272 *ne dicam* often emphasizes what it apparently apologizes for: Ter. *Ad.* 375–6 *est hercle inepta, ne dicam dolo, atque | absurda*, Cic. *Deiot.* 2 *crudelem Castorem, ne dicam sceleratum et impium*, Ov. *Her.* 15 (16). 285 *nimium simplex Helene, ne rustica dicam*, cf. *TLL*, v. 1. 976. 58 ff.

stulte is a hard word even if the mitigating *ne dicam* is taken more seriously than I am inclined to do. *sapientia prima (est) | stultitia caruisse* (*Ep.* 1. 1. 41–2): *stultitia* always implies obtuseness, e.g. *Ep.* 1. 1. 47 *ne cures ea quae stulte miraris et optas.* The reproach of 262 *ignoratae . . . artis*, the alternative there of *incuria*, is still in mind, and likewise it is distinguished from *nimium patienter.* These nuances confirm what I suggested above (270 n. *uestri*); H. can talk in general terms about ancient Roman *stultitia* but would not say to the Pisos that their ancestors were *stulti.*

ego et uos bring the 1st and 3rd persons of 263 ff. together; for the 1st pers. see above 265 n. *uager* and 25–6 n.

273 resumes, chiastically, *sales* of 271. *urbanum* is the hallmark of elegant wit—*lepidum, come*—as opposed to crude jocularity. Thus Cicero's analysis of types of wit, *Off.* 1. 104 (cf. above 271 n.) *duplex omnino est iocandi genus; unum illiberale petulans, flagitiosum obscenum, alterum elegans urbanum, ingeniosum facetum. quo genere non modo Plautus noster et Atticorum antiqua comoedia, sed etiam philosophorum Socraticorum libri referti sunt*, etc., and more elaborately *De Or.* ii. 235 ff., in particular 270 *Socratem opinor in hac ironia dissimulantiaque longe lepore et humanitate omnibus praestitisse. genus est perelegans et cum grauitate salsum cumque oratoriis dictionibus tum urbanis sermonibus accommodatum.* This in the new Roman setting perpetuates the Peripatetic and ultimately Aristotelian position. H. emerges here as the more perceptive literary critic in the assessment of Plautine wit, which Cicero classes with Socrates' irony and Attic comedy; and unlike Cicero, H. keeps to his Aristotelian principles. Cf. Ar. *E.N.* iv. 7, 1127 b 25 on Socrates, and *ibid.* ch. 8 on the types of ἄγροικος, βωμολόχος, and εὐτράπελος, especially 1128 a 9 f. οἱ δ' ἐμμελῶς παίζοντες εὐτράπελοι προσαγορεύονται, οἷον εὔτροποι, a 14 ff. καὶ οἱ βωμολόχοι εὐτράπελοι προσαγορεύονται ὡς χαρίεντες· ὅτι δὲ διαφέρουσι καὶ οὐ μικρόν, ἐκ τῶν

Commentary

εἰρημένων δῆλον, a 22 f. (particularly relevant to Cicero and H.) ἴδοι δ' ἄν τις καὶ ἐκ τῶν κωμῳδιῶν τῶν παλαιῶν καὶ τῶν καινῶν· τοῖς μὲν γὰρ ἦν γελοῖον ἡ αἰσχρολογία, τοῖς δὲ μᾶλλον ἡ ὑπόνοια· διαφέρει δ' οὐ μικρὸν ταῦτα πρὸς εὐσχημοσύνην, *Rhet.* III. 18, 1419 b 6 ff. εἴρηται πόσα εἴδη γελοίων ἔστιν ἐν τοῖς περὶ ποιητικῆς (not now extant), ὧν τὸ μὲν ἁρμόττει ἐλευθέρῳ τὸ δ' οὔ, ὅπως τὸ ἁρμόττον αὐτῷ λήψεται. ἔστι δ' ἡ εἰρωνεία τῆς βωμολοχίας ἐλευθεριώτερον· ὁ μὲν γὰρ αὑτοῦ ἕνεκα ποιεῖ τὸ γελοῖον, ὁ δὲ βωμολόχος ἑτέρου. H.'s and Cicero's distinction of *inurbanum* and *lepidum dictum* clearly derives from Peripatetic theory; but H. differs from Cicero in its application to the type of humour represented by Plautus.

seponere poetically (as with other compounds denoting separation such as *secerno* below 397) with abl., called dat. by some, where classical prose would prefer *ab*; contrast *dicto* with Cic. *De Or.* I. 22 *seposuisse a ceteris dictionibus.* Cf. D. Bo, *Hor. Op.* III. 100.

dicto: witticism, cf. the *dicta* of Satyric drama, 247.

274 returns without a strain to rhythm and metre, from which H. had digressed by way of Plautine metre and Plautine humour, cf. 270 *numeros.*

legitimumque sonum 'lawful', because the whole section has been concerned with the *leges* of *ars rhythmica*, which need to be 'known', and which, to H.'s ear, Plautus did not know. The adj. as in *Ep.* II. 2. 109 *legitimum . . . poema.*

callemus: an archaic, poetic, and Silver word, rarely used by Cicero, 'to develop the right touch or skill for', and hence 'understand'. Because of this practical nuance the word is very apt here; cf. *callida* 47 n.

digitis . . . et aure: the scanning with finger or foot is mentioned in a well-known passage of Quintilian, *I.O.* IX. 4. 51 *tempora . . . metiuntur et pedum et digitorum ictu.* The teaching method, Ter. Maur. 2254–5 *quam (moram) pollicis sonore uel plausu pedis | discriminare qui docent artem solent*, is a different matter; it probably resembles the *pollicis ictum* of *C.* IV. 6. 36, Ov. *Fast.* II. 108 *icta . . . pollice chorda*, cf. Fraenkel, *Horace,* 404. Save for *digitis* however Quintilian's remark is not in point, for he deals with the difference between rhythm in music and the verbal arts. The writings of the rhetoricians, Cicero's and Quintilian's especially, are full of remarks on the rhythmic sense of the ear. Cic. *Or.* 203 says *(uersuum) modum notat ars, sed aures ipsae tacito eum sensu sine arte definiunt.* H.'s point on the other hand is that *ars* and *auris* must go together.

(10) Greek Tragedy (–280) and Greek Comedy, 275–84

The tradition. H. draws on an account of the origin of tragedy which ultimately belongs to the early Peripatos or Alexandria, see above 220–50 n. and 220 n. This account seems to have been designed partly to contradict and partly to supplement Aristotelian teaching. The literary evidence for Thespis is set out by Pickard-Cambridge, *Dithyramb²*, etc. (1962), pp. 69 ff., and more fully by E. Tièche, *Thespis* (1933); cf. also K. Ziegler, 'Tragoedia', *R-E*, VI A. 1929 ff. and H. Patzer, *Die Anfänge der gr. Trag.* (1962), pp. 21 ff. For Alexandrian theorizing on the origins of drama, see the papers by Pohlenz, Latte, Solmsen, and Meuli, mentioned above 220–50 n., and the partly divergent discussion of Patzer. The account in the *Ars* contains some features not now found anywhere else, see particularly 276 n. on *plaustris*, and 277 n. The account of Aeschylus, with the one important exception of 280 *magnum loqui*, concerns costume and style of performance; for the literary evidence, probably Hellenistic in origin, see Pickard-Cambridge, *Dram. Fest.* (1953), 214 ff., who interprets some of it in dogmatically negative fashion; archaeological as well as literary evidence is discussed by T. B. L. Webster, *Gr. Theatre Production* (1956), pp. 5 ff., 35 ff.; P. Arnott, *Gr. Scenic Conventions* (1962) uses actual stage practice to query some of Pickard-Cambridge's assumptions.

Greek Comedy is dealt with in three sentences. These assert that old comedy was instituted later than tragedy, that personal abuse in comedy was checked by law, and that the chorus grew silent when it was deprived of its 'right of injury'. The account in the *Ars* happens to be our earliest information concerning the end of old Attic comedy. This must be accidental since the facts in the confused later accounts, which agree with H.'s allusions, must go back to Hellenistic sources. For the evidence see A. Körte, *R-E*, XI. 1228–42, Pickard-Cambridge, *Dram. Fest.* 83 ff., 103 ff., and the works cited below 283–4 n.

Commentary

Horace. At a first reading these verses look like a rather sketchy and odd essay on the history of Greek tragedy and comedy. The very sketchiness however helps to draw attention to the true character of this piece. H. has selected and reorganized some information on the history of Greek drama which bears out certain basic contentions of his. The history of tragedy is taken to the point when the genre acquired grandeur; this is thought to be the effect of Aeschylus' work. Earlier in the *Ars* H. has considered as axiomatic the great and serious nature of tragedy. The history of comedy is taken to the point where the genre lost its political ethos of public censure. Thus the two major forms of Greek drama are brought close to the Roman scene. So that the abrupt beginning of the section on Roman drama is more apparent than real, 285 *nil intemptatum nostri liquere poetae.*

The scope of the piece may be defined by two facts. One is its quasi-historical character, which sets its aside from the 'precepts', 153 ff., 179 ff. including Satyric drama. The other is its position between two sections on Roman drama, both highly critical of its techniques. Immediately after the homily on metre, which provokes the reference to *exemplaria Graeca*, H. shows how the exemplary Greek genres and their salient features were established. The exemplary Greek genres thus established form the background for the final judgement on Roman drama.

With a severe economy of selection and expression H. has concentrated his account of tragedy on the features that made for grandeur, σεμνότης—the (alleged) evolution of the genre from Thespis to Aeschylus. Old comedy based on *libertas* won high renown, *non sine multa laude*; but the very manner of its public criticism destroyed the genre. He does not mention new comedy; but its non-political character may be implied by contradistinction.

275, not 220, is H.'s comment on the 'invention' of tragedy. *ignotum* as at 130 denotes something new in poetry, in the earlier passage (on tragic plots) *ignota indictaque* combined with *primus,* in

311

this (on a new genre) *ignotum* with *inuenisse* stress the innovation. *camenae* denotes the genre, as Bentley, in the *Phalaris*, reminded Boyle. *tragicae genus . . . camenae* of tragic poetry or poems, as *S.* II. 6. 17 *saturis musaque pedestri* or *sermones*, *C.* IV. 9. 6–8 of lyric verse, et al.

276 *dicitur:* H. leaves the responsibility for this statement to his authorities.

Thespis as the earliest tragedian is not known from Aristotle's *Poetics*, though Themistius, *Or.* 26. 316 d quotes Aristotle on Thespis; as the list in Pickard-Cambridge, *Dith.*[2] 69 ff. shows, he first appears in the entry of the *Marmor Parium* of the middle of the third century B.C., referred to above 220 n. (on *uilem ob hircum*). Thespis appears in a similar way in the roughly contemporary epigrams of Dioscorides, *Anth. Pal.* VII. 410 and 411, but the text of the former is dubious, see Gow and Page, *The Gr. Anth., Hellenistic Epigrams*, II. 251 f. I note that these two references of the third century B.C. are the only ones certainly antedating H.; others have been assumed, and are discussed in the works cited above 275–84 n.

plaustris, the wagon of Thespis, which owes its fame to this passage. Apart from authors themselves dependent on H., such as Diomedes, Donatus, and probably Sid. *C.* 9. 236, this information does not appear in ancient sources. The vehicle is often said to owe its existence to an erroneous connexion with 'the jokes from the wagon' at the Anthesteria and Lenaea, e.g. *Suda* and Phot. τὰ ἐκ τῶν ἁμαξῶν, Pickard-Cambridge, *Dith.*[2] 82, *Dram. Fest.* 7. But the fact that a piece of information is unique, or combined with others that are erroneous, does not falsify it. The obvious parallel with the strolling players of later ages (P. Arnott, *Gr. Scenic Conventions*, p. 6) cannot be ruled out. To H. the wagon presumably suggested the informal, perhaps rural, character of early tragedy, which is a feature of some Alexandrian accounts.

uexisse poemata 'he carried the tragedies about (on his wagon)', ps.-Acro *tam multa scripsisse quae posset plaustris aduehere.* ς, Donatus, also Bentley read *qui* (= *eos qui*; with *canerent* governing *poemata*) for *quae* at 277, the relative pronoun transposed to the beginning of the next verse as e.g. at *Ep.* I. 17. 52–3. This is elegant but probably to be resisted. For it removes the grotesque element that is a part of Roman Satire. The legendary past in particular evokes a certain genial whimsicality from H., e.g. at *S.* I. 3. 99 ff., *Ep.* II. 1. 139 ff.

277 *quae:* Bentley *qui*, see above on *uexisse poemata*.

canerent agerentque: on the assumption that *agere* refers to the *one* actor then employed and *canere* to the chorus, commentators talk of grammatical attraction of *ageret* into the pl. of *canerent*. But *canerent ageretque* would be risible prosiness, and in any case the chorus shared in *actio* in a wider sense. H. Schütz's explanation strikes me as plausible: H. generalized the singers and performers, without labouring the distinction between the two classes. The instances cited by Hofmann–Szantyr, 16, differ.

peruncti faecibus ora: the internal acc. with the part. is rare enough in the hexameter poems to be noted, cf. below 384, and D. Bo, *Hor. Op.* III. 118. This is the primitive disguise that in H.'s account precedes the use of masks, 278. *faex* is τρύξ, wine-lees, and the word may hint at τρύξ (thus Porph.), and a vintage-festival. (The relevant reading in *Anth. Pal.* VII. 410. 3, Gow and Page cit. above 276 n., is unfortunately dubious.) This is the kind of detail that can be freely elaborated and the Alexandrians elaborated it. *Suda*, s.v. *Thespis*, reflects a fuller account: first white lead, next purslane hung over the face, then 'masks of linen only', ἐν μόνῃ ὀθόνῃ, cf. Pickard-Cambridge, *Dith.*[2] 71 no. 14, 79 f., *Dram. Fest.* 177. Other kinds of early make-up are mentioned without reference to Thespis, Pickard-Cambridge, *Dith.*[2] 74.

279–80 Porph. on 278 *Aeschylus primus tragoediis coturnos et syrma et personam dedit; horum enim trium auctor est.* This summary omits *pulpita* (279) and, even more important, *magnumque loqui* (280). Contrast Ar. *Poet.* 4, 1449 a 15 ff. καὶ τό τε τῶν ὑποκριτῶν πλῆθος ἐξ ἑνὸς εἰς δύο πρῶτος Αἰσχύλος ἤγαγε καὶ τὰ τοῦ χοροῦ ἠλάττωσε καὶ τὸν λόγον πρωταγωνιστεῖν παρεσκεύασεν. But Aristotle is not here dealing with ὄψις.

278 *post hunc:* there is no mention of Choerilus and Phrynichus or the younger tragedians: Thespis inaugurated and Aeschylus completed the genre. This is not the picture in Ar. *Poet.* ch. 4. But even with regard to the external features of the genre there was a tendency to ascribe to Aeschylus what belonged to various innovators over a long period of time; the tendency is noticeable in the ancient *Life* of Aeschylus. Cf. Pickard-Cambridge, *Dram. Fest.* 175, citing *Anec. Par.* ed. Cramer, I. 19 εἰ μὲν δὴ πάντα τις Αἰσχύλῳ βούλεται τὰ περὶ τὴν σκηνὴν εὑρήματα προσνέμειν. This tendency goes back a long way and these attributions were controversial in Alexandrian scholarship. H.'s attributions are part of that picture.

personae: H. does not allow for intervening stages between Thespis and Aeschylus in the introduction of the mask; contrast *Suda*, s.vv. Χοιρίλος and Φρύνιχος. But the Epitome of Hesychius is more specific, s.v. Αἰσχύλος (cf. Wilamowitz, Aesch. ed. mai. p. 14, no. 41): πρῶτος εὗρε προσωπεῖα δεινὰ καὶ χρώμασι κεχρισμένα ἔχειν τοὺς τραγικούς.

pallae . . . honestae: 'the cloak of distinction' is shown by other evidence to be the *syrma* or full-length tragic costume; cf. above 228 n. *regali . . . auro . . . et ostro.* The tradition ascribing the introduction of this garment to Aeschylus is first found in this passage, later also in Ath. I. 21 d; Philostr. *Apoll.* VI. 11, *Soph.* I. 9; *Vita Aesch.* (Wilamowitz, Aesch. ed. mai. p. 5), § 14 τῷ σύρματι ἐξογκώσας; *syrma* Porph. on 278: cf. Pickard-Cambridge, *Dram. Fest.* 214 ff. Our oldest witness, long before H., does not say Aeschylus introduced a distinctive costume for his heroes, but what he says is not incompatible with such a view: Aristoph. *Ran.* 1061 ἱματίοις ἡμῶν χρῶνται πολὺ σεμνοτέροισιν.

repertor: one of the many nouns in -(*t*)*or* in H.; this is archaic, poetic and Silver prose but not Ciceronian or Caesarian.

279 *instrauit:* an archaic and poetic word, not found in Cicero but in later prose, expressing realistically 'to spread something on', with dat. *pulpita* here as elsewhere in H. is 'platform, stage', not however stage buildings—*scaena*, above 215, *Ep.* I. 19. 40, II. 1. 174. The primitive theatre is made of wood not stone: *tignis* is beams, which may but need not be uprights; they are uprights in Caesar's celebrated bridge across the Rhine, *B.G.* IV. 17. 3 ff., but defined by an adj. as cross-beams, in Trebonius' elaborate earthwork, *B.C.* II. 15. 2 *trauersaria tigna iniciuntur.* The context of this verse suggests that the *tigna* more likely than not are uprights: 'he spread a platform upon beams of no great size (*modicis*)'. I infer that H. is describing a primitive raised stage of modest size. (Prud. *Perist.* x. 1016 *tabulis superne strata texunt pulpita* seems to be based on H.)

The passage has been looked at askance by scholars demanding archaeological evidence for a raised stage in the fifth century B.C., perhaps a sanguine expectation in the case of perishable wooden structures. Hence W. Dörpfeld and E. Reisch, having found no such archaeological evidence, concluded, in *Das gr. Theater* (1896), p. 348, that this passage provides no evidence either; half a century later Pickard-Cambridge still felt committed to that procedure, and even denied the probable meaning of *tignis*, cf. *Theatre of Dionysus*, p. 72. But H. was no archaeologist. The passage is neither evidence for a raised fifth-century stage, nor need it imply that H. inferred from the raised stages of his day the existence of a raised Aeschylean stage, 'only a modest one' (Pickard-Cambridge, *loc. cit.*). As in the rest of this passage the poet selects traditional, perhaps Alexandrian, material for his own purpose. This tradition must have suggested the existence of a primitive raised stage in the time of Aeschylus and, not unreasonably, H. accepted it. He may well have been right. Cf. the

Commentary

cautious remarks of T. B. L. Webster, *Greek Theatre Production* (1956), p. 7.

280 combines with obvious deliberation (though it has not seemed obvious to all commentators) exalted speech and exalted stance, *magnum loqui* and *niti coturno*. This apparently is a feature of the ancient literary tradition concerning Aeschylus. H. puts it in a kind of pun, but this is by no means far-fetched, for it simply expresses the harmony of scenic and poetic effect. M. Pohlenz noticed (*NGG*, 1920, 148 n. 2, also K.–H. *ad l.*) that precisely this implication—in the comic form, grandeur of speech befitting grandeur of costume—is found in Aristoph., writing *Ran.* 1060–1 about Aeschylus, κἄλλως εἰκὸς τοὺς ἡμιθέους τοῖς ῥήμασι μείζοσι χρῆσθαι· | καὶ γὰρ τοῖς ἱματίοις ἡμῶν χρῶνται πολὺ σεμνοτέροισιν.

docuit: Aeschylus established a style of poetry and performing, cf. above 74 n. *monstrauit Homerus. docuere* 288 differs.

-que...-que: the archaic formula (see above 11 n.) effectively serves here to juxtapose speech and stance.

magnum...loqui: the neut. adj. *magnum*, or pl. *magna*, like μέγα or μεγάλα in Greek, easily passes from adj. to adv. use, cf. *TLL*, VIII. 148. 55 ff. The words could mean 'speak loudly', as Pl. *Mil.* 822–3 *an dormit...?—non naso quidem,* | *nam eo magnum clamat*, Virg. *A.* IX. 705 *magnum stridens contorta phalarica uenit*. This view has been taken; indeed the grammarian Gavius Bassus (*De Origine Vocabulorum, ap.* Gell. v. 7. 1) derived, equally wrongly, the use of theatrical masks from an alleged 'megaphone effect', and the word *persōna* from *per-sŏnare*, cf. Pickard-Cambridge, *Dram. Fest.* 193 f. But the ancient literary tradition often combines the grandeur of Aeschylus' style and décor (e.g. in Aristoph. cited in the last note), and this is what H. seems to have in mind. *TLL*, VIII. 135. 26 separates this passage from the adv. use 148. 55 ff., erroneously, I suggest; compare for example *S.* 1. 4. 44 (*os*) *magna sonaturum* (*TLL*, VIII. 148. 69). Ar. *Poet.* 4, 1449 a 20 simply says of tragedy ὀψὲ ἀπεσεμνύνθη, although Themistius imputed more definite opinions to him, cf. above 276 n. The later literary tradition, first in the Lyceum and Alexandria, was less reticent than the *Poetics*.

niti...coturno: K. Schneider, *R-E*, Supp. VIII. 195 f., confidently ascribes to Aeschylus a *coturnus* with a sole. The matter seems less certain. The ancient tradition is unanimous in ascribing the introduction of the high-soled tragic boot (κόθορνος, cf. ὀκρίβας, ἐμβάτης) to Aeschylus; the evidence is assembled by Pickard-Cambridge, *Dram. Fest.* 216, 230 n. 3. Archaeological remains however suggest that this kind of boot is certainly Roman (*coturnus* becoming a metonymy for tragedy, above 80 n.), probably also Hellenistic, though not, it appears, before *c.* 200 B.C.; there is no evidence for it from the fifth century. 'That Aeschylus did something to improve the footwear of his actors is quite probable', says Pickard-Cambridge, *loc. cit.* T. B. L. Webster considers some possibilities, *Greek Theatre Production*, pp. 37 f., 44, *Miscell. . . .in memoria di Augusto Rostagni* (1963), p. 533. It remains hard to explain, if the ascription also goes back to the Hellenistic age, how a kind of footwear then newly introduced could have been dated back more than three centuries.

281 *successit. . .his:* that is, Thespis and Aeschylus, or tragedy in its established form. No comic writer is named; comedy arrives in the wake of tragedy. Since H. perhaps accepted a common origin for tragedy and comedy, it should be noted that the word *successit* need only denote the institutional form of *uetus. . .comoedia*, which was known to have come in after tragedy: Ar. *Poet.* 5, 1449 b 1 f. καὶ γὰρ χορὸν κωμῳδῶν ὀψέ ποτε ὁ ἄρχων ἔδωκεν, ἀλλ' ἐθελονταὶ ἦσαν. *Suda* s.v. Chionides, Χιωνίδης Ἀθηναῖος. . .ὃν καὶ λέγουσι πρωταγωνιστὴν (?) γενέσθαι τῆς ἀρχαίας κωμῳδίας, διδάσκειν δ' ἔτεσιν η' πρὸ τῶν Περσικῶν. The year 486 B.C. is alluded to; for the manner of computation see Körte, *R-E*, XI. 1226 f. with bibliography; the documents are listed by Pickard-Cambridge, *Dram. Fest.* 70 ff., 103 ff.

282 *laude:* as above 268 n. *laudem*, 271 *laudauere*, cf. *Ep.* II. 1. 168 ff.

in uitium libertas excidit: libertas is the free speech used in ὀνομαστὶ κωμῳδεῖν; thus *S.* I. 4. 3 ff. *si quis erat dignus describi. . .multa cum libertate notabant*, and the (assumed) parallel with archaic Roman conditions, *Ep.* II. 1. 145 *Fescennina. . .licentia*, 146 *opprobria rustica*, 147–8 *libertasque. . .lusit*, 149 *in rabiem coepit uerti iocus*; in a different context Quint. *I.O.* XII. 9. 13 *frequenter etiam species libertatis deducere ad temeritatem solet.* 'Freedom of speech exceeding into defect' makes a vigorous image out of the Aristotelian idea of faults being virtues overdone.

283 *dignam:* cf. *digna* 183 n.

lege. . .lex is emphatic. The instances of 'polyptoton' in the lists of D. Bo, *Hor. Op.* III. 402 ff., show what H. could do with words repeated but differently inflected. *Ep.* II. 1. 152–3 concerns the same matter: *quin etiam lex | poenaque lata*, but there is no such rhetorical effect.

283–4 *lex etc.:* a number of minor Greek sources purvey information similar to this; thus the late *Prolegomena* to comedy, the *Life* of Aristophanes, *Suda* s.v. Antimachos, and the scholia to Aristophanes. In all of them a connexion is established between a decree or decrees (*lex*, ψήφισμα) restricting public censure of citizens by the comic

Commentary

chorus and the decline of the chorus in middle and new comedy. For the evidence, see A. Körte, *R-E*, XI. 1233–6, P. Geissler, *Chron. d. altattischen Kom.* (1925), p. 17, K. J. Maidment, *CQ*, XXIX (1935), 9 ff. Occasionally a decree is specified, more often it is not, and the accounts are confused and unintelligent. Yet the basic information on a decree interfering with the right of public criticism on the comic stage cannot have been invented by these late compilers; it must go back to a time when the facts were readily available, presumably the early Hellenistic age. That however does not make the alleged connexion between legal enactment and dramatic output more than an implausible historical shorthand for a complex literary and social phenomenon. The transition from one type of comedy to another was not 'caused' by a decree.

Instigated by these Greek models, Roman grammarians, perhaps Varro, seem to have brought some legal provisions against *Fescennina licentia* into connexion with the development of Roman comedy; H. makes reference to this connexion at *Ep.* II. 1. 145 ff., cf. *Prol.* 174 for the *mala carmina* of *S.* II. 1. 82–3. In the present passage H. is not attempting to vie with the literary scholars on their own ground. He is not going into the question of *choregia* with which the compilers grapple unsuccessfully; this point is rightly made by Steidle, *Studien*, p. 140, against Heinze's pronouncements. What interests H. is that the poets obeyed a law restricting excessive personal criticism on the stage—and the comic chorus grew silent *sublato iure nocendi*; a convenient myth to account for the loss of public criticism that marks the difference between the two major types of ancient comedy, political and non-political. Hence too the difference in his treatment of post-classical tragedy and comedy. Tragedy retained its chorus, however unrelated to the plot; so that H. finds it worthwhile to legislate for it, 193 ff. He makes no such attempt for comedy. All comic production was 'new comedy' in that sense, although a chorus need by no means be absent from it. This brief section on comedy therefore ends on a negative note, *chorusque...obticuit*, etc. On the other hand the preceding historical sketch of tragedy ends on a positive note, *magnumque loqui nitique coturno*. These features in H.'s view are fundamental to later Roman developments.

turpiter: G. L. Hendrickson, *AJP*, XXI (1900), 132, has made a case for connecting the adv. not with the adjacent *obticuit* but with *nocendi*, to express something like αἰσχρολογίᾳ λυπεῖν. He aptly compares Cic. *De Or.* II. 236 *haec enim ridentur...quae notant...turpitudinem...non turpiter.* Cf. also K.–H. The word-order is ambiguous.

obticuit, an archaic and poetic word, lends emotion to the alleged

317

incident. Euanthius, *De Fab.* 2. 4 (*Com. Gr. Fr.* p. 64. 57, Don. ed. Wessner. I., 16. 18) *lata lege siluerunt* is probably based on H. As in the whole passage on comedy, H. seems to acknowledge that unrestrained public criticism is compatible only with certain social and political conditions. One may perhaps recall Tacitus' remarks on a related topic, *Dial.* chs. 36 ff.

iure nocendi: although *ius* here is no more than 'facility, opportunity for an action', the word carries enough of the legal connotation of 'right' to produce the ambiguity of a pun with *nocendi*. There is as little a 'right of injury' as there is a 'right of perishing', below 466 *sit ius liceatque perire poetis.*

(11) Roman drama, 285–94

For obvious reasons no distinction between a Greek literary tradition and the poet's use of it can be made in this section. H. now sets Roman drama against the background of Greek. The new subject seems to come in abruptly, but has in fact been prepared in the preceding section (see above 275–84 n.). After the adaptation of the Greek dramatic forms (265 n.), national themes follow. There is high praise for this attempt and a patriotic note can be sensed. But satisfaction is shattered, just as it was when Roman adaptations of Greek tragedy came up for judgement, *Ep.* II. 1. 164–7; *limae labor* is found wanting. Thus the simple plan according to literary genres is at the end of this large section conjoined with the motif of *ars*, the true concern of an *ars poetica*. This motif, in the strongly contrasted form of Greek *ars* vs. Roman *ignorata ars*, was sounded in the preceding context on metre, 263 (258) ff. Now a whole constituent part of this poem closes with an appeal, which is given personal resonance by a renewed and solemn address to the Pisos as *Pompilius sanguis*. Traditional Roman nobility is asked to take poetry seriously.

285 *nil* includes Greek dramatic forms adapted by Roman poets. Neither adaptations of Greek mythological tragedy nor of Greek new comedy are specified in the next few verses.

intemptatum: Ep. II. 1. 164 *temptauit quoque rem, si digne uertere posset* is comparable but sounds matter-of-fact in comparison. The reason lies partly in the spondees of this line and partly in the wording. *intemptatum* seems to be a new word in Augustan poetry. It is known only from two places before this: the Pyrrha Ode, *C.* I. 5. 12–13 *miseri quibus* | *intemptata nites*, and Virg. *A.* x. 39–40 *haec intemptata manebat* | *sors rerum*, for the variant reading at *A.* VIII. 206 is less likely than *intractatum*; then follow other poets and writers of Silver prose, cf. *TLL*, VII. 1. 2112. 15–16. K.–H. suggest that the word was modelled by H. on Greek ἀπείρατος or the like. In view of the dates of the poems, and H.'s fondness for new, or probably new, compounds with *in-* (cf. C. Zangemeister, *De Hor. voc. singularibus* (cit. above 53 n.), 14 ff.) that is at any rate possible. *nostri* has greater warmth than the *uictor* of *Ep.* II. 1. 156. Note also the verb *liquere*; of the nine other occurrences in H. of the simple verb instead of the compound, seven come in the *Odes* and two in parodic contexts of the Brundisium poem and the Bore (*S.* I. 5. 35, 9. 74). Martial parodies this verse, and perhaps 287, at II. 14. 1 *nil intemptatum Selius, nil linquit inausum.*

286–7 *uestigia (Graeca)* | *...deserere:* this is not quite the Callimachean metaphor of the untrodden poetic path, noted in Steidle's *Studien*, p. 141, cf. *Prol.* 109 n. 2, 181, Pfeiffer on *Aetia* I. 1. 25; but it doubtless hints at it.

ausi: the creative venture, above 9 n.; notably of the pioneer, above 125, *S.* II. 1. 62–3 *est Lucilius ausus* | *primus in hunc operis componere carmina morem.*

celebrare: the great genres as *C.* I. 7. 6, 12. 2.

domestica facta: the notion is 'home', with its emotional overtones; the contrast is *externa, aliena, peregrina,* and here *Graeca* comes in the same category. The Greeks, *exemplaria Graeca* a few verses earlier, are now *externi* as it were. *facta* in Latin verse (like *acta* for a different metrical antecedent, contrast Ov. *Met.* XIV. 108 with xv. 750) often has a full poetic sound: 'achievements'; for H. see *S.* I. 10. 42–3 *Pollio regum* | *facta canit pede ter percusso, Ep.* II. 1. 6 *ingentia f.*, 130 *recte f. refert*, 237 *splendida f.*; cf. above 73 *res gestae*; 68 *mortalia f.* differs in meaning. In the next verse, however, not only serious drama but also comedy, *togata*, is indicated, cf. 288 n.

288 H. calls drama on Roman topics either *praetexta* or *togata*. The verse is more difficult than it seems because the meaning of these terms is not agreed. According to L. Mueller they are two names for the same object, serious Roman drama, the former on Greek mythical subjects, the latter Roman 'histories'. This distinction is implausible, although it must be admitted that 287 *celebrare domestica facta* and 289 *uirtute...armis* point to serious drama; these words partly precede

319

and partly follow *praetextas* and *togatas*. Nevertheless the clear division
uel . . .uel, immediately after Greek tragedy and comedy, makes it
exceedingly hard not to accept the same distinction here. *celebrare
domestica facta* therefore must apply to both topics, tragedy and comedy on Roman themes, or else be tied more closely to *praetextas*; 289
uirtute and *armis* are in any case contrasted with *lingua*, and belong to
a different context.

From the (*toga*) *praetexta* of Roman magistrates the adj. seems to
have been applied to *fabula* to denote a serious drama on national
themes. Asinius Pollio, at Cic. *Fam.* x. 32. 3 and 5, uses the short form
praetexta before H.; Paulus, Fest. 223 M. *praetextae*, may at any rate
represent Festus and possibly Verrius Flaccus. *praetextata* on the other
hand is the technical term of the grammarians, formed, it has been
suggested, on the model of *palliata* and the like. *togata*, in Varro, fr. 306
(Funaioli, *GRF*, p. 322), is a comedy on a Roman theme; Cic. *Sest.*
118 calls such a play by Afranius by that name. Now *togata* was not a
very accurate term, for though it distinguished the Roman garment
from the Greek *pallium*, few of its personages actually wore a *toga*.
Hence, W. Kroll (*R-E*, vi A. 1661. 10 ff.) concluded, later Roman
scholars tried to improve nomenclature, and used *togata* as a general
term for Roman plays on national subjects, whether serious or not.
Certainly Diom. *GL*, i. 489. 14 ff. cites and criticizes the present
verse of the *Ars* for the *communis error* of its nomenclature: *praetextata*,
he pronounces, is a kind of *togata*, and H. should have called his
togata by the name of *tabernaria*. For similar evidence, see Kroll, *loc. cit.*,
Beare, *Rom. Stage*[3] (1964), Appendix D. The earlier history of these
names then is obscure, but Diomedes' criticism of H. shows that
traditionally *praetextas* in this verse was understood as serious drama
on Roman themes, and *togatas* as comedies on Roman themes; which
confirms the most natural interpretation. *praetexta* was first attempted
by Naevius (Leo, *Gesch. der röm. Lit.* i. 89 ff., Fraenkel, *R-E*, Supp.
vi. 627. 19 ff.), later by the well-known archaic tragedians; it
remained a live genre down to the time of drama, acted or recited,
in the first century A.D. and probably later. Leo's further suggestion
(*op. cit.* p. 92), imputing to Naevius the creation also of *togata* is open
to considerable doubt (cf. Fraenkel, *op. cit.* 631. 38 ff.). Of the three
standard authors of that genre, Titinius is undated, Afranius and
Atta link the generations of the Gracchi and Sulla. Sen. *Ep.* 8. 8
talks of the genre with familiarity, but of contemporary *togatae* in his
time or in that of H. nothing is known.

docuere 'produced', differs from the notion of the verb at 280. It
renders Greek διδάσκειν (*TLL*, v. 1. 1729. 45 ff.), as in Cicero and

probably Accius, cf. Cic. *Brut.* 229 (Accius, fr. 20, Funaioli, *op. cit.* p. 30) *Accius isdem aedilibus ait se et Pacuuium docuisse fabulam.*

289 If Virgil's *excudent alii* and Lucretius' *patrii sermonis egestas* are at all comparable, H. draws precisely the opposite conclusion from similar facts, cf. Steidle, *Studien*, p. 142. Rome, H. is asserting, has the potentiality to match her status in the world by her poetry. Cf. *Ep.* II. I. 32–3 *uenimus ad summum fortunae*, etc., 61 *Roma potens.*

289 *foret:* a convenient metrical stand-by for *esset*, only here in the *Ars*, rare in the *Odes* and the other *Epistles*, but frequent in *Satires* I.

-que (codd. BCK) rather than *-ue* (rell.) is suggested by the combination *uirtute–armis*. So I had written when I noticed that Peerlkamp and L. Mueller had sponsored *-que*; but they have been ignored. Cf. Liv. VII. 6. 3 *an ullum magis Romanum bonum quam arma uirtusque esset?*—also such locutions as *ui et armis, armis animisque, TLL*, II. 593. 17 and 29.

potentius: the word seems to have been fertile ground for punning—'power' in its different connotations: Virg. *A.* I. 531 *terra antiqua, potens armis atque ubere glaebae*, Ov. *Fast.* III. 281 *armisque potentius aequum est*, *Met.* VI. 678. Here the potency of arms and poetry are conjoined; for the latter cf. *C.* III. 30. 10–12 *dicar...ex humili potens*, IV. 8. 26–7 *lingua potentium | ualum.*

290 *lingua Latium:* cf. *Ep.* II. 2. 121 *Latiumque beabit diuite lingua.*
unum, for the enjambement, see next note.

290–1 *unum | quemque:* presumably the line division serves to put emphasis on 'one and all', as Rostagni suggests. The same enjambement occurs at *S.* I. 9. 51–2 *est locus uni | cuique suus*, *Ep.* II. 2. 188–9 *mortalis in unum | quodque caput*, thus obviating Orelli's explanation of *malitiosa ironia* in this passage. *unus quisque* is not in the class labelled tmesis in such passages as 424–5 *inter-|noscere* and even less than *S.* II. 3. 117–18 *unde-|octoginta.*

291 *limae labor et mora:* the πόνος and ἀγρυπνίη of the Callimacheans, the trouble and time demanded by *ars*–τέχνη, a motif known from all parts of this poem. But here it is not only a demand for what the Romans lack but also expresses confidence that it is a goal worth attaining, *foret...potentius..Latium*. The file, *lima*, recalls the fine arts considered at the beginning of the poem; *limatus* however described an ideal of style before H., e.g. Cic. *Brut.* 93 *limatius dicendi...genus*, *De Or.* I. 180 *(homo) oratione maxime limatus.* Thus *S.* I. 10. 65–6 *fuerit limatior idem | quam rudis et Graecis intacti carminis auctor.* The *Augustus* expresses a similar sentiment to the *Ars: Ep.* II. I. 166–7 *nam spirat tragicum satis et feliciter audet, | sed turpem putat inscite metuitque lituram.*

292 (*uos o*) *Pompilius sanguis:* the fourth address by name in the poem (cf. above 6 n.) and easily the most solemn, invcking the royal line of Numa Pompilius. This does not exclude but rather intensifies a general application, as Rostagni notes. Porph. *ad l. quia Calpus filius est Numae, a quo Calpurnii Pisones traxerunt nomen.* F. Münzer, *R-E*, III. 1365. 12 remarks that the plebeian *gens Calpurnia*, especially through the Pisonian family, attained influence in the first century B.C.; he assumes that the fanciful genealogy belongs to that time. For other refs. see *ibid*. The first Piso to put a portrait of Numa on his coins was Cn. Piso, cos. 23 B.C., who is a modern, and I think unlikely, candidate for the place of the *pater* of H.'s dedication, cf. 24, 366, 388, and *Prol.* 239.

The nom. of the address, *Pompilius*, and the vocative particle *o*, add to the archaic solemnity (over-solemnity, it would seem) of phrasing, see J. Svennung, *Anredeformen*, etc. (Lund, 1958), p. 270, Hofmann–Szantyr, 25. So too does *sanguis*, cf. Virg. *A.* VI. 835 (*tu*) *sanguis meus*; but the epic poet's solemnity befits the subject. Persius magnifies what in H. is a studied incongruity between the elevated address and the pedestrian subject of *labor* by his own strongly derisory note, 1. 61–2 *uos, o patricius sanguis, quos uiuere fas est | occipiti caeco, posticae occurrite sannae.* Behind the Virgilian pattern stands Ennius, *Ann.* 113 f. (V.²), *o pater, o genitor, o sanguen dis oriundum, tu*, etc.

carmen reprehendite: the critical sense of the New Poets. Doubtless H. means what he says, but the solemnity is so great that a humorous bathos is inevitable and can scarcely be unintentional. It will not be a coincidence either that the very tone of his pronouncement puts laborious art in its place, whereas, in the sequel, heavy irony devalues *ingenium* beyond all recognition.

293 *multa dies* looks back to 291 *mora*, and *multa litura* to *limae labor*; *multa* is emphatically repeated as *C.* II. 16. 23–4 *ocior ceruis et . . . ocior Euro*, and in the style of satire, *S.* II. 3. 325 *mille . . . mille*. For *multus* sing. see 203 n.; for *dies* fem. in H. and other hexameter verse, see *TLL*, V. 1. 1024, E. Fraenkel, *Glotta*, VIII (1917), 60 ff. (repr. *Kl. Beitr.* 1. 63 ff. *dies* here approaches the sense of duration, *spatium temporis*; Fraenkel, *Kl. Beitr.* 1. 64 n. 2, compares Lucr. III. 908, IV. 1031, Virg. *A.* IX. 7 *uoluenda dies. multus(-a) dies* is 'noon', 'afternoon' from Plautus onwards (Pl. *Ps.* 1158, Liv. III. 60. 8, Stat. *Silv.* 1. 5. 45); the notion 'much time' is not known before this passage, later only rarely in poetry or poetic prose, as Sil. III. 382, XIII. 853, ps.-Quint. *Decl. Mai.* 6. 11 (ed. Lehnert, p. 121. 5).

coercuit 'keep within bounds, check, control'. The vocabulary of literary criticism is bound to be metaphorical, e.g. the verbs

employed below 445–9 and *Ep.* II. 2. 122–3 draw on law, politics, the
army and agriculture. *coercere* is applied to the 'flow' of his youthful
rhetoric by Cic. *Brut.* 316 *ut nimis redundantes nos et supra fluentes...
reprimeret et quasi extra ripas diffluentes coerceret.* But it may connote
'pruning', e.g. Quint. *I.O.* IX. 4. 5 *cur uites coercemus manu?* Quint.
employs both metaphors, cf. *I.O.* IX. 2. 76 *uerba ui quadam ueritatis
erumpentia...coercere,* X. 4. 1 *exultantia coercere,* XII. 1. 20 (with reference
to Cic. *Brut.* 316 cited above) *abscisurum* and *coercuisse.* The corresponding term in the next verse is *castigauit.*

294 *deciens* 'many times', as below 365 *d. repetita placebit, Ep.* I.
18. 25 *decem uitiis* with K.–H.'s note; cf. *TLL,* V. 1. 168. 55 ff.; for the
spelling, see Keller, *Epileg.* 418 on *C.S.* 21. The word could be
ἀπὸ κοινοῦ with *praesectum* as well as with *castigauit* but is more likely
to qualify *praesectum,* thus continuing *multa dies et multa litura,* cf. *ad
unguem* below.

castigauit, often of moral 'correction', but in a literary context
paralleled only from Symm. *Ep.* I. 4. 1 (*TLL,* III. 533. 11).

praesectum...ad unguem: p̄fectum and p̱fectum are easily confused in
minuscule script; compare also *perspectum* cod. π (second p *in ras.*).
perfectum, in most of the MSS, ps.-Acro, *Tract. Vind.,* could be taken
for the transmitted text, whereas *praesectum* may look like a clever
Carolingian emendation. But *praesectum* is in some of the best MSS,
not only B and apparently C, which often form a group, but Bland.
Vet.; contrary to appearances this reading may be much the older.
ad unguem recalls Greek εἰς ὄνυχα, δι' ὄνυχος, which do not however
contribute to the present problem; for evidence see Erasmus, *Adagia,*
I. 5. 91, Casaubon on Pers. I. 65, O. Jahn, *ibid.,* Wyttenbach on Plut.
Quomodo sent. profectus, 86 a; also A. Otto, *Sprichwörter,* 357.

praesectum...ad unguem 'by the well-pared nail', is at first sight
attractive; *ungues ponere* (297) is thought to point back to it, and
the reading is accepted with little or no argument by all recent editors. They have the support of the best critics in the Horatian field;
Bentley, before him Lambinus, and later Meineke and Munro, all
print *praesectum,* mistakenly, I think—if, as they assume, that word
qualifies *ad unguem.* It makes sense neither to the stonemason nor to
the Latinist. Take first the stonemason or worker in marble. Ps.-Acro
comments, '*ad unguem*': *tractum a marmorariis qui iuncturas marmorum
ungue pertemptant. alibi* (*S.* I. 5. 32–3) '*ad unguem | factus homo*'. *ad
unguem autem ad perfectionem, ad examen, hoc est ad perfectum iudicium.*
Likewise ps.-Acro and Porphyrion on *S.* I. 5. 32, *Schol.* Pers. I. 64,
Corp. Gloss. V. 560. 9 (ed. Goetz) *ad unguem: ad plenum, ad perfectionem.*
So far therefore from having to pare his nails, the mason needs them

for testing a true join, if he tests it that way. Nor is the case saved by Wilkins' assertion that a recently pared nail is 'more sensitive to irregularities'. The Latinist is served no better by this reading. *ad unguem*, 'to a nicety', accepts an attribute as uncommonly as *in annos* (above, 60); in both cases the attribute offered by the MSS should put the editor on his guard. Cf. *S.* I. 5. 32–3 *ad unguem* | *factus homo*, Col. XI. 2. 13 *dolari ad unguem*, Apul. *Socr.* prol. 3 (107 H.) *ad unguem coaequatum*, Aus. *Ecl.* 3. 3 (ed. Peiper, p. 90) *explorat ad unguem*, Macr. *Sat.* I. 16. 38 *ad unguem, ut aiunt, emendatum*, Boeth. *Mus.* V. 2 (p. 352. 20 ed. Friedlein) *ad unguem expolitae*, et al. Ennodius was fond of this mode of speech; Otto, *Sprichwörter*, 357, cites six instances: *ad unguem polita conuersatio*; *politi sermonis*; *ducta uita*; *docti*; *fabricantur* (twice). There are others, especially *Dict.* 3 (7). 6 (p. 7. 21 ed. Vogel, p. 444. 21 Hartel) *nobilitatem metalli, nisi ad unguem manus ducat artificis*. *in unguem* may be compared: Virg. *G.* II. 227–8 *omnis (uia) in unguem* | *...quadret*, Cels. VIII. 1. 3 *suturae in unguem committuntur*, 'fit together exactly', Vitr. IV. 6. 2 *in unguem...coniungantur*. It is true Ter. Maur. 344 says *poliuit usque finem ad unguis extimum*, 'to the tip of the nail', 'to the nicest nicety'; but even if Terentianus were a source of classical Latinity, these words would not explain *praesectum ad unguem*. Nor do I see why Bentley should have drawn encouragement from Sid. *Ep.* IX. 7. 3 *non impacto digitus ungue perlabitur*. For this only shows the metaphor in action, as does Pers. I. 63–5 (not uninfluenced by H.) *carmina molli* | *...numero fluere, ut per leue seueros* | *effundat iunctura ungues*. These passages do not parallel *praesectum...ad unguem*.

In his edition of 1811 Carlo Fea made the archaeologist's point about masonry against Bentley and brought the reading *perfectum* back into the text; he was followed by Orelli, Schütz, Keller (*Epil.* 759 f.), and a few others. His explanation was, '*quod non castigauit adeo, ut expolitum, leuigatum, perfectum dici possit usque ad experimentum unguis*'. Ps.-Acro would have agreed, for he paraphrased *cum iam perfectum uideretur*; and *perfectum* seems to have been a term for a true join; Porph. on *S.* I. 5. 32 *iuncturas marmorum tum demum* perfectas *dicunt si unguis superductus non offendat*. Whether *perfectum* thus used is what they call proleptic or not, it makes tenable grammar. What gives one pause is the ordinariness of the word in the midst of very vigorous phrasing. Also, why scribes should corrupt the common *perfectum* to the uncommon *praesectum* is hard to see. *perfectum* is more likely to be an old gloss.

So the problem is open still. *praesectum* may well be right, but only if sense and punctuation remove it from *ad unguem*. Censure a poem, H. says, which has not been reduced to right proportions and (when

it has been reduced) has not been tested to a nicety. Peerlkamp
tried to find the Latin for the words that I have put in parenthesis;
but the metre tripped him up: *resectum* cannot replace *praesectum*.
praeseco is a (prosaic and not very common) word for pruning and
cutting, e.g. Varro, *L.L.* v. 104 *brassica ut p⟨r⟩a⟨e⟩sica, quod ex eius scapo
minutatim praesicatur*, Plin. *N.H.* xvii. 115 *praesectam (uitem)*. I know
of no other instance where it is applied to style, but it recalls a similar metaphor *abscidere* (see 293 n.), and *coercere* suits all these contexts.

V. The Poet, 295–476

The tradition. Scholars who deny that a tradition lies behind
the initial and final parts of the poem are deceived by H.'s
manner. So I suggested at the beginning (above p. 75); and
so I suggest still. Traditional teaching is more easily apparent
when technicalities of style or dramatic forms are discussed;
that is one difference between this and the preceding parts of
the *Ars* from 42 onward. The caricatures of the painting at
the outset, and of the mad poet at the end, concentrate theory
into vivid imagery; that is another difference, although descriptiveness is not by any means absent from the rest of the
poem. Yet in spite of these and other divergences, the presence
of traditional thought cannot well be doubted. After all, a
certain piece of evidence for such a tradition is a fragment of
Neoptolemus of Parium (*Prol.* 55, no. 10) on ψυχαγωγία and
χρησιμολογεῖν which appears to be restated in H.'s *et iucunda et
idonea dicere uitae* (334) and *qui miscuit utile dulci* (343). And it
is this fragment that clearly belongs to the context denoted by
'The Poet'; it does not fit any of the technical sections on
unity, style, subject-matter, or poetic genres. What remains
in this section cannot be verified in the same way, but its
traditional character stands to reason: *mimesis*, the origins of
poetry, genius and art.

What this however implies for the structure of H.'s traditional lore, remains controversial. The structural principle is
a product of the classifying pedantry of the Hellenistic age—I
am referring to the distinction between τέχνη (in this case

ποίημα and ποίησις) and τεχνίτης, *ars* and *artifex*. The distinction has its uses for classifying, but conveys little meaning. It derives from Attic philosophy, where it has some substance. There is no pedantry in the motive that caused Plato to write one work on political science, calling it Πολιτεία, and another on the political expert, calling it Πολιτικός. It seems reasonable (cf. my remarks *CQ*, XL (1946), 23, and H. Dahlmann, *AAM*, no. 3 (1953), no. 10 (1962)) in the same way to contrast Aristotle's Περὶ ποιητικῆς with his Περὶ ποιητῶν, Praxiphanes' Περὶ ποιημάτων with his Περὶ ποιητῶν, and Varro's *De poematis* with his *De poetis*. It is reasonable also to note, as Dahlmann has done, that before H.'s *Ars*, and in the field of rhetoric Quintilian's *Institutio*, no single work survives that combines these two aspects in the same manner. But this may be no more than an accident. For what does the title of Heraclides' lost work Περὶ ποιητικῆς καὶ τῶν ποιητῶν imply if not a combination of two similar aspects? It would not be so reasonable therefore to conclude dogmatically that Neoptolemus did not combine these aspects, and that no one else did until H., who was not after all given to tedious classifying, decided to make this innovation. What we know of H. is his penchant not for introducing but for playing down such distinctions where he used them. We cannot be certain therefore, but the balance of the scanty evidence does not favour Dahlmann's conclusions, as I have argued, *Prol.* 36 ff. The holocaust of a vast Hellenistic literature on poetic theory has to be borne in mind. The onus of proof rests with those who propose to restrict the possibilities suggested by the evidence. Quintilian's attempt lies in a different field, rhetoric, and thus calls for a different kind of argument.

It is one of E. Norden's great merits to have asserted the traditional basis of H.'s argument in the final part of the *Ars*, cf. *H*, XL (1905), 497 ff. Before the Neoptolemic material was rediscovered Norden recognized that *A.P.* 306–8 contain a table of contents, and that these contents can be identified as Greek literary commonplaces. (That H.'s touch makes them

lose their commonplace character concerns H., not his traditional theory.) In spite of serious overstatements and misunderstandings Norden also identified the places where these
traditional doctrines appear in H.'s poem: *mimesis* in 309 ff.,
dulce and *utile* 333 ff., *perfectus poeta* 347 ff., and finally
uesanus poeta 453–76, with two other traditional matters inter-
spersed, the origins of poetry 391–407, and *natura an arte*
408 ff. Norden never attempted to take his enquiry beyond
'source criticism'. But seeking to clarify not H.'s sources but
his poetry, we can now ask what the poet has made of such
apparently unpromising material. A first foray into this territory was attempted by P. Cauer, *RM*, LXI (1906), 239–43.

Horace. H. has instilled life into desiccated Hellenistic abstractions. The present section is, poetically, perhaps the
hardest but also, because of its insight, variability and wit,
the most rewarding part of the poem. It is introduced by a
passage moving delicately from the last 'technical' section to
this, 295–308. The motif of artistry is the link, and *ars* is now
split dialectically into *studium* and *ingenium*, an unreal contrast
but profitable for satire and censure of contemporary abuses.
This leads to a new table of contents, *partitio*, in the humorous
personal form of 306–8. Three traditional topics of scholastic
dispute are indicated: (1) *poeta fit.* How is he formed? (2)
What is his aim? (3) What constitutes his excellence, what
nullifies him? Commentators have professed inability to trace
the topics of H.'s summary in the subsequent verses. But it
should cause no surprise that H. refrains from marking the
reappearance of these topics at the beginning of each corresponding 'section', for this rather than the converse is his
practice. (I mention a less complex instance from the lyrics. At
C. I. 12 the initial question, *quem uirum aut heroa . . ., quem deum*,
foreshadows the layout of the poem, but the principle of
division is not reaffirmed explicitly in the sequel; H. had good
reason for departing from his Pindaric model in this and other
respects, cf. Fraenkel, *Horace*, 292 f.) An earlier part of the *Ars*

may be recalled. At 40–1 a similar table of contents is offered, and is there followed by the first of its items (41 *ordo*, which came last in the preceding *partitio*), but the remaining items are not marked so clearly. Just so the first topic follows here immediately, and cannot be missed. Hence commentators do not miss it at 309–22 (how the poet learns to become a *doctus imitator* of reality), but get restive when they come to H.'s more imaginative glosses, cf. 323–32 n. The second topic should however be unmistakable because H. starts off pointedly with *aut prodesse uolunt aut delectare* (333) and the difficulty is merely one of terminology: does *quid deceat* (308) denote the poetic aims of *prodesse* and *delectare* (333)? I argue below that it does, and suggest that this second topic is taken up at 333–46. The greatest difficulty has been found in the third topic (308), poetic *uirtus* and *error*, which fills the rest of the poem, 347–476. I have undertaken a first charting of the ground in *Prol.* 255–9; detailed comments will be made below.

(1) Transition and Introduction, 295–308

These verses clearly introduce a major section of the poem. So at an early stage in the job of analysis P. Cauer noted, *RM*, LXI (1906), 233. The similarity with other major breaks is undeniable. The extensive transition before and after 119 will be recalled—*mores* before and after, but attached to style up to 118, to subject-matter from 119. Thus here workmanship is the subject, but attached to Roman amateurism, in the 'technical' section up to 294, and to the qualities of the poet, in the general argument from 295. The present passage however forms part of a larger imaginative and personal setting; thus this is probably to be regarded as a more important turn of events than 119. For the personal note the transition at 153 (*tu, quid ego et populus mecum desideret, audi*) may be compared, although again this passage is more emphatic.

The preceding antithesis contrasted *incuria* with care and enterprise (261 ff., 285 ff.). Now a new antithesis takes its place, overstated so as to score a dialectical point: talent without art, art without talent. Democritus' doctrine of inspiration in poetry is made responsible for the alleged poetic success of untutored, *soi-disant* geniuses. But the same doctrine is said, satirically, to provide the reason for H.'s self-imputed failure as a poet. If he cannot now write (lyric) poetry, he claims at any rate to be able to teach the would-be poet how to acquire professional standing (306). Thus some matters of principle in poetry are proposed for discussion (307–8). These, I have suggested above, turn out to be the guiding lines for the highly complex poetic involutions in the rest of the poem. In rhetorical speech the division of the subject into subordinate topics was called *partitio*. 307–8 have the function of such a table of contents but, in accordance with the style of a poetic *sermo*, it is brought in obliquely. H. offers a similar division at 40–1. The topics have been set out above in the introductory note to this part of the poem.

295–8 In a lyric poem which is emotionally attuned to the idea of inspiration, H. is quite ready to claim it, thus *C.* III. 4. 5–6 *an me ludit amabilis | insania?*, etc., 25. 1–2 *quo me, Bacche, rapis tui | plenum?* This poem moreover professes to be didactic; hence H. sometimes satirizes *ingenium*, at other times, in a matter-of-fact way, makes it a condition of *ars*. Here, in a *sermo* on literary theory, looking at poetry from outside as it were, he burlesques the Democritean (and Platonic) notion of inspiration. This I believe is a mark against any contention (such as O. Immisch's) that would find in the *Ars* Platonic, in particular Middle Platonic, influences. For a number of crucial Platonic passages, see Rostagni's note, cf. the discussion and some references to the vast literature in P. Vicaire, *Platon: critique littéraire* (1960), pp. 213 ff.; for Democritus' aesthetic doctrine, Diels–Kranz, *Vorsokratiker*, II⁸, 68 B 17, 18, 21, A. Delatte, *Les conceptions de l'enthousiasme chez les philosophes présocratiques* (1938), pp. 28 ff., E. R. Dodds, *The Greeks and the Irrational* (1951), p. 82, W. K. C. Guthrie, *Hist. of Gr. Phil.* II (1965), 476 f. In particular Cic. *De Or.* II. 194 (= fr. 17, Diels–Kranz, in addition to *Div.* I. 80, and *A.P.*) joins Democritus with Plato in asserting that no *poeta* can be *bonus* without *inflammatio animorum* and *quidam afflatus quasi furoris*; *sine furore* without qualification occurs in the other passage, *Div.* I. 80. Something like ἐνθουσιασμός and ἱερὸν πνεῦμα (fr. 18) is the Greek behind the wording of Cicero and H.

295 The tone of the verse is set by the carefully balanced order of words—a symbol perhaps of *ars* rather than *ingenium*—starting with the key word *ingenium*, and interweaving *ingenium...fortunatius* with its counterparts *misera...arte*. What arises from it is the celebrated pair φύσις–τέχνη. Later it is shown that the antithesis is oversharp: 410 *nec rude quid possit uideo ingenium*.

misera...arte: the nuance of the adj. is seen e.g. at *S.* i. 6. 129 *misera ambitione grauique*, ii. 8. 18 *diuitias miseras*, *C.* iii. 29. 58–9 *ad miseras preces | decurrere*. Its meaning largely depends on the context, in this case the opposite term, *fortunatius*.

fortunatius perhaps hints at Greek antitheses apart from τέχνη–φύσις, which underlies the whole poem, and this section in particular; I am thinking of τύχη–φύσις, τύχη–τέχνη. Ps.-Acro rightly paraphrases *Democritus felicius putat ingenium arte*, cf. Delatte, *op. cit.* (above 295–8 n.), p. 45. *ingenium* (φύσις) is *fortunatum* because *fortuna* (τύχη, εὐτυχία) attends it. Native genius 'succeeds' where laborious art fails; *ars* is *misera*. Ar. *E..N.* vi. 4, 1140 a 17 ff. argues in the opposite way, in favour of τύχη–τέχνη: καὶ τρόπον τινὰ περὶ τὰ αὐτά ἐστιν ἡ τύχη καὶ ἡ τέχνη, καθάπερ καὶ ᾽Αγάθων φησὶν ᾽τέχνη τύχην ἔστερξε καὶ τύχη τέχνην᾽.

296 *excludit...Helicone:* Mt Helicon is an appropriate locale for restrictive practices since it had acquired symbolical significance for poets as diverse as Hesiod, Callimachus and Ennius, and others. The details, apart from Hesiod, are still dubious, cf. Pfeiffer, *Callim.* i. 9–11, O. Skutsch, *The Annals of Q. Ennius*, Inaug. Lect. 1951 (London (1953), pp. 5 ff., A. Kambylis, *Die Dichterweihe*, etc. (Heidelberg, 1965). In reporting the exclusion of poets who are not *furiosi*, H. treats Mt Helicon simply as a shorthand for poetic endeavour, cf. *Ep.* ii. 1. 218.

sanos...poetas: Plato, *Phaedr.* 245 a ὃς δ᾽ ἂν ἄνευ μανίας Μουσῶν ἐπὶ ποιητικὰς θύρας ἀφίκηται..., ἀτελὴς αὐτός τε καὶ ἡ ποίησις ὑπὸ τῆς τῶν μαινομένων ἡ τοῦ σωφρονοῦντος ἠφανίσθη, summarized Sen. *Tranq. An.* 17. 10 *frustra poeticas fores compos sui pepulit, Ion* 534 a οὐκ ἔμφρονες ὄντες, al. Cf. the *uesanus poeta* below 453 ff., *S.* ii. 3. 322 (in the Stoic vein) *quae (poemata) si quis sanus fecit, sanus facis et tu, Ep.* i. 19. 3–4 *male sanos | adscripsit Liber Satyris...poetas*, ibid. 9 *seueris*.

297 *bona pars* 'a good many': somewhat colloquial, according to Wilkins. So it may have been. But more likely it was an archaism, cf. Ter. *Eun.* 123 *bonam magnamque partem* and Porph. on *S.* i. 1. 61 *bona nunc pro magna dictum, ut saepe Ennius et alii ueteres*. This need not exclude survival as a colloquialism and some of the instances (cited *TLL*, ii. 2091. 80 ff.) may probably be so explained: Cic. *De Or.* ii. 14 *bonam*

Commentary

partem sermonis, Hor. *S.* 1. 1. 61 *at bona pars hominum*, Pers. 2. 5 *at bona pars procerum*. In other passages the stylistic level excludes colloquial usage, thus *C.* IV. 2. 46, Lucretius V. 1025, VI. 1249, Virg. *A.* IX. 156–7. Moreover occasionally (though not in this verse) there is punning with the familiar meaning of *bonus*, e.g. Virg. *loc. cit. melior quoniam pars acta diei*, | *quod superest*, etc. For *C.* IV. 2. 45–6 *tum meae* . . . | *uocis accedet bona pars*, see Fraenkel's remarks, *SBHA* no. 2 (1932–3), p. 8. Also cf. Mart. VIII, Praef. *pars libri et maior et melior*.

ungues: cf. 298 *barbam*, the imitation of external features, as *Ep.* 1. 19. 17 *decipit exemplar uitiis imitabile*. Physical neglect was the foible of 'the philosophers', especially the Cynics. Ps.-Acro, *non uult poetas philosophorum more incedere*. Commentators cite Tatian, *Ad Graec.* 102, on the Cynics, κόμην ἐπιείμενοι πωγωνοτροφοῦσιν ὄνυχας θηρίων περιφέροντες.

ponere 'deponere', cf. D. Bo, *Hor. Op.* III. 388.

298 *barbam:* cf. πωγωνοτροφοῦσιν (prec. n.), *S.* II. 3. 35 *(me) iussit sapientem pascere barbam*. Cod. B has *barbas*, probably no more than a dittography before *secreta* but, it seems, a variant reading which gave rise to ps.-Acro's comment on sing. and pl.

secreta petit loca: cf. *C.* 1. 1. 30–2 *me gelidum nemus* | *nympharumque* . . . *chori* | *secernunt populo*, III. 4. 6–7 *uideor pios* | *errare per lucos*, 25. 12–14, IV. 3. 11, *Ep.* II. 2. 77 *scriptorum chorus omnis amat nemus et fugit urbes*, Tac. *Dial.* 9. 6 *ut ipsi* (sc. *poetae*) *dicunt, in nemora et lucos, id est in solitudinem, secedendum est* and the passages cited by Gudeman *ad l.* Quint. *I.O.* X. 3. 22–3 adopts the commonsensical approach which H. humorously opposes to the romantic.

balnea uitat: both cleanliness and sociability are in point.

299 *nanciscetur:* for the grammatical subj. see 300 n.

enim: elliptic and ironical: and they must be right, for . . .

pretium nomenque poeta[e]: cf. 400–1 *sic honor et nomen diuinis uatibus atque* | *carminibus uenit*, Cic. *Off.* III. 82 *uiri boni et splendorem et nomen*. For *nomen* E. Norden, *loc. cit.* p. 498 compares Cic. *De Or.* 1. 64 *orator* . . .*hoc cum graui dignus nomine*, Quint. *I.O.* XII. 1. 24 *donabimus oratoris illo sacro nomine*. For the emendation *poeta*, see 300 n. *(poeta)* | *si.*

300–1 The structure of these verses is passed over by commentators though they require explanation. They contain two disparate notions skilfully and wittily combined: (1) The inspired poet's head is incurable, his head because the mind supposedly resides in the 'acropolis' of the body (Plato, *Tim.* 70 a, Cic. *N.D.* II. 140, al.); he is mad. (2) The poet's head is not submitted to the barber, long hair being a sign of poetic genius (madness).

300 This verse and the two following allude to the medicinal use of hellebore, Latin *ueratrum*. As a supposed purgative remedy against madness it is mentioned from the Hippocratic writings onwards, see Stadler, *R-E*, VIII. 165 ff. Celsus, not long after H., writes, II. 13 *at ubi longi ualentesque morbi sine febre sunt*, ut comitialis, ut insania, *ueratro quoque albo utendum est. id* . . . *(datur) optime* uere, *tolerabiliter autumno* . . . *illud scire oportet* . . . *medicamentum* . . . *non semper aegris prodesse, semper sanis nocere*, cf. Plin. *N.H.* xxv. 47 ff., specially 60 *melancholicis, insanientibus*. The firmly established belief gave rise to colloquialisms, in Greek ἐλλεβοριάω, in Latin *elleborosus* = 'mad', see Pl. *Mos.* 952, *Rud.* 1006. For hellebore in comedy and satire, see A. O'Brien Moore, *Madness in Ancient Literature* (Princeton Diss. 1924), pp. 36 ff.

(*poeta* |)*si* Peerlkamp for (*poetae* |)*si* codd., (*poetae* |)*qui* Ribbeck. Recent editors accept the MSS' reading without comment but I am not persuaded that the subj. of this clause can be indefinite 'someone', alleged by Heinze; I am not aware of any plausible Horatian parallel. Even less can *bona pars* be continued as subj. beyond the sentence which, in present tenses—*curat, petit, uitat*—describes the antics of wayward geniuses. It is not the many, *bona pars*, who *will* acquire the title of poet; rather *enim* introduces a further contingency in general terms: either 'the poet if he' or 'the man who'. Both emendations meet this requirement, but it makes against Ribbeck's *qui* that it comes into collision with *qui purgor* two lines down; a reference is not likely to be intended, however, since *qui* . . *commiserit* and *qui purgor* are not entirely in logical balance and one hesitates to introduce negligent repetitions of a word by conjecture, frequent though they are. Peerlkamp's *poeta* for *poete* (*-ae*) supplies the grammatical subj. At the same time it provides an explanation for the genitive, added to complete the locution *pretium nomenque*, which may but need not contain *poetae*, as is shown by the instances cited above.

tribus Anticyris: the habitat of hellebore was widespread, but at Anticyra, Ἀντίκυρα, in Phocis on the gulf of Corinth, and in Malis near Mt Oeta the plant grew in abundance; Hirschfeld, *R-E*, I. 2427. 47 ff. A third Anticyra is attested, cf. Hirschfeld, *op. cit.* 2428. 25, Oldfather, *op. cit.* XIII. 1225. 66 ff., on Strabo IX. 434, Liv. XXVI. 26. 1–2, but no ancient author appears to mention that hellebore grew there. Reference to the three Anticyras cannot therefore be ruled out, but is unlikely. Nor need it be assumed since the name had become a metonymy for the plant, *S.* II. 3. 82–3 *Anticyram* . . . *illis destinet omnem*, Pers. 4. 16 *Anticyras* . . . *sorbere meracas* cf. Hor. *Ep.* II. 2. 137 *elleboro* . . . *meraco* and *Schol.* Pers. *ad l. merito pluraliter Anticyras dixit, ut appareat eius tam magnae insaniae unam sufficere non posse*, ps.-Acro on *tribus Anticyris*: *tribus* . . . *potionibus* . . . *aut multo helleboro*. 'If a commentator came across the phrase "ten Karlsbads would not cure

Commentary

you", he would hardly think necessary to determine the geographical position of all ten' (Wilkins). In bald prose the sentence would run somewhat like Petron. 88. 4 *Chrysippus, ut ad inuentionem sufficeret, ter elleboro animum detersit.* Hellebore was supposed to render the mind alert and inventive, thus Carneades' reputed use of the drug, Val. Max. VIII. 7 extr. 5, Plin. *N.H.* xxv. 52, Gell. XVII. 15, Mart. Cap. IV. 327. The Stoic Chrysippus was thought to be strongminded enough to drug himself three times over for that purpose; thus Petronius just cited, Lucian, *Hermot.* 86, *Ver. Hist.* II. 18, *Vit. Auct.* 23. In view of this anecdote, Immisch, p. 195, and H. Fuchs (in Dahlmann and Merkelbach, *Studien zur Textgesch. und Textkritik* (1959), 71–2) have good reason for seeing in H.'s *tribus* an allusion to 'Chrysippus' cure'.

301 *tonsori Licino:* an individual in an apparently individual case; H., as in *tribus Anticyris* above and often elsewhere, prefers an instance to an empty logical class. The individual is unknown, though identified by ps.-Acro and Comm. Cruq. with a personage prominent under Caesar. The identification probably reflects research *de personis Horatianis* but is unlikely for all that, on chronological and other grounds, cf. F. Münzer, *R-E*, XIII. 503. 18 ff.

o ego: with the common hiatus as at *Epod.* 12. 25, *S.* II. 3. 265, *Ep.* I. 19. 19. In exclamations consisting of interjection and personal pronoun the type *o ego* is poetic and very rare, cf. *TLL.* v. 2. 272. 59 ff. *Epod.* 12. 25 *o ego non felix,* the present passage, and *Ciris* 424 *o ego crudelis* are the earliest known instances instead of the established *o me*+acc.

laeuus is usually taken to mean 'maladroit, dull, foolish', but the Virgilian passages often cited do not in fact support that meaning; cf. R. G. Austin, Virg. *A.* II. 54 n. on *si mens non laeua fuisset* in the passage of the *Aeneid* and *E.* I. 16 as 'a formula for human self-deception'. Indeed 'deluded, perverse' would be an acceptable notion for *laeuus* here. But the basic metaphor is of course 'unlucky, unfortunate', and that suits the delightful hide-and-seek of this passage better still. With a glance at 295 *fortunatius* and *misera,* the poet's cure is represented as the poet's bad luck. Without the cure he would be quite mad—but no one would make better poems.

302 *purgor bilem:* reflexive, construed like *lauor,* retains the acc. appropriate to the active, as at *S.* II. 7. 38 *nasum. . .supinor,* Virg. *A.* VII. 113; cf. commentators on *C.* II. 13. 38 *laborem* (-*um* variant) *decipitur,* contrast *S.* II. 3. 27 *morbi purgatum te illius. purger* ς and Peerlkamp, unnecessarily since H. mixes ind. and subjun. even in the same descriptive rel. cl., e.g. *S.* I. 3. 9–11. If inspired poetry involves

333

madness, that is, a surplus of (black) bile supposed to cause the melancholia of genius, then (H. suggests sarcastically) he would rather be rid of it, and be sane. διὰ τί πάντες ὅσοι περιττοὶ γεγόνασιν ἄνδρες ἢ κατὰ φιλοσοφίαν ἢ πολιτικὴν ἢ ποίησιν ἢ τέχνας φαίνονται μελαγχολικοὶ ὄντες; ask the so-called Aristotelian *Problemata*, xxx. 1, 953 a 10 ff.; Ar. *Poet.* 17, 1455 a 32–4 (cit. above 101 n.). Cf. above 295–8 n., 296 n. R. Klibansky, E. Panofsky, and F. Saxl bring together some of the basic texts on this notion in *Saturn and Melancholy* (1964), ch. 1. But such subtle permeations of philosophic and poetic thinking as appear in this passage are beyond the scope of that study. See the instructive discussion by D. W. Lucas, Ar. *Poet.* (1968), Appendix II, pp. 279 ff., also H. Flashar, *H*, LXXXIV (1956), 12–18, *idem*, *Melancholie und Melancholiker* (1966), and the works cited by Lucas, *op. cit.* pp. 286–7.

uerni temporis: spring, according to Celsus II. 13 (cit. above 300 n.) is the most profitable season for administering hellebore. Porph. *omnes enim uerno tempore purgationem sumunt, quod uocatur* καθαρτικόν.

sub . . . horam: often like ὥρα = 'season' in poetry and Silver and late Latin, *TLL*, VI. 3. 2964. 1 ff. First known from H., thus *C.* I. 12. 15–16 *uariisque mundum | temperat horis* (*Iuppiter*), III. 13. 9, *Ep.* I. 16. 16. The circumstantial poeticism clashes with the realistic *purgor bilem*: this suits H.'s patent irony.

303 *non alius faceret meliora poemata* suppresses such a protasis as *nisi purgarer* and rushes to self-indictment. This ironic diminution of his own status H. has practised throughout his career from *S.* I. 4. 13 ff. onwards, ever-changing in accordance with the scope of the poem. Few instances are as amusingly and disarmingly ambiguous as the present one. Other users of the drug than H. have suffered other strange effects. The cure may have put Chrysippus in a productive frame of mind, see above 300 n. on *tribus Anticyris*; but the poor playwright at *Ep.* II. 2. 137 emerged wholly disillusioned, and the poet Attius had his offspring affected genetically, producing an epic poem 'drunk with hellebore', Pers. 1. 50–1 *Ilias Atti | ebria ueratro*.

uerum, 'but indeed', cf. above 225 n.

304 *nil tanti est* is often elliptic in colloquial usage (Doederlein *ad l.*), so that the sentence has to be completed from the context, 'nothing is worth so much (as . . .)'. Thus Cic. *Att.* II. 13. 2 *quare . . .* φιλοσοφῶμεν. *iuratus tibi possum dicere nihil esse tanti* (sc. *quanti philosophari*), v. 8. 3, XIII. 42. 1, Sen. *Contr.* VII. 3. 10, Sen. *Ben.* II. 5. 2. Hence here, as Doederlein said, understand something like *quanti sanum fieri purganda bile*. Madvig, *Opusc.* II. 190, *Lat. Gr.* § 294 n. 3, and many commentators take *nil* in these locutions to be a strong negative. The notion then becomes, 'that (sc. to be an inspired poet) is not by any means worth it'—not a probable Horatian sentiment nor borne out by Cicero's usage.

ergo draws an unexpected and humorous conclusion: since he will not give up his sanity and therefore cannot write (true) poetry, he proposes to teach poets rather than be one. This is crazy logic, but it allows H. to be sane and yet write (though not 'poetry') and it puts Democritus in his place, for his doctrine abhors teaching.

fungar uice cotis: commentators cite the saying of Isocrates, which is likely to have been in H.'s mind, *ap.* Plut. *Vit. Dec. Or.* 4. 838 e πρὸς τὸν ἐρόμενον διὰ τί οὐκ ὢν αὐτὸς ἱκανὸς (λέγειν) ἄλλους ποιεῖ, εἶπεν ὅτι καὶ αἱ ἀκόναι μὲν (?⟨αὐταὶ⟩) τεμεῖν οὐ δύνανται, τὸν δὲ σίδηρον τμητικὸν ποιοῦσιν, criticized for its *non sequitur* by Sext. Emp. *Math.* ii. 19. Cf. other Greek refs. in P. Shorey's paper, *TAPA*, xl (1909), 188 with n. 4, though I doubt the impact of Pindar, *Ol.* 10. 20–1 θήξεις δέ κε φύντ' ἀρετᾷ ποτὶ | πελώριον ὁρμᾶσαι κλέος ἀνὴρ θεοῦ σὺν παλάμᾳ.

305 Cf. Isocr. cited above.

ualet: cf. 40 n.

exsors ipsa secandi: for the faulty but probably ancient variant *exsortita secandi*, see Keller, *Epil.* 760. The word appears first in Augustan verse, then in Silver and late Latin, *TLL*, v. 2. 1881. 56 f. The stylistic level of the word is high, cf. Virg. *A.* vi. 428 *dulcis uitae exsortes*, and its Greek counterpart ἄμοιρος, which perhaps influenced *exsors*, though it did itself not entirely escape a tarring with the prosaic brush in the Hellenistic age: Aristo *ap.* Philod. *Poem.* v. 20. 4 [τῶν χρησ]τῶν [διανο]ημάτ[ων ἀ]μο[ίρ]ου[ς]. The present context is realistic—the whetstone, etc.—but as often in such contexts of the hexameter poems H. prevents the level of style from falling.

306 Here the poem reaches what in a speech or tract would be a *partitio*, cf. above 295–476 n. By way of parody, a lecture and its subject are announced; in the next two verses the subject is further specified. This comes at the end of a sentence, not about poetry but about H. declining to be a poet. The mixture of fun and seriousness is H.'s way of accommodating an utterly prosaic thing—a table of contents. By relating it to the personal paradox of this *sermo*—H. writing poetry on poetry, and therefore by definition not poetry—he draws the *partitio* into the poetic situation of his *Ars*.

E. Norden suggested that the announcement of the subject corresponds to similar announcements in all ancient handbooks on *artes*: the task (ἔργον, *officium*) of the *artifex* is defined in the part of the book concerned with the *artifex*. The matter is more complex than that. For the problems inherent in the placing of this announcement, see the discussions *Prol.* ch. 2, and above 1–40 n., 295–476 n.

munus et officium: the current term for the 'profession' of the *artifex* appears to have been *officium*, Greek ἔργον. For this notion Norden, *loc. cit.*, has cited instances from diverse *artes*. For the poetic *ars* I note Isid. *Et.* VIII. 7. 10 (cf. Dahlmann, *AAM*, no. 10 (1962), p. 575) *officium autem poetae in eo est ut,* etc. Rhetorical theory is much more fully preserved and earlier sources can be cited, e.g. *Ad Her.* I. 2 *oratoris officium est,* etc., Cic. *Inv.* I. 4 *de genere ipsius artis, de officio, de fine,* etc., *ibid.* 6 *officium autem eius facultatis uidetur esse,* etc., Quint. *I.O.* XII, pr. 4 *mores ei* (sc. *oratori*) *conabitur dare et assignabit officia,* cf. 1, pr. 22. H., who is not writing a straightforward *ars* but a poetic letter reflecting an *ars*, adds a little more colour—*munus et officium.* Though the former is sometimes defined by the latter, each of the two words had its own emotional overtones. For *munus*, as A. Meillet has suggested, belongs to a class of words with a predominantly juridical and religious significance, see J. Pinsent, *CQ*, n.s. IV (1954), 158–61. *officium* on the other hand came to stress social and moral obligation. These differences made it worthwhile to combine *munus* with *officium*, e.g. Cic. *Rep.* II. 69 *illum...uirum cui praeficias officio et muneri,* *Fin.* IV. 36 *omne officium munusque sapientiae,* *T.D.* III. 15 *totumue corpus statu cum est motum, deest officio suo et muneri.*

nil scribens ipse, i.e. H. writing in the style of *sermo,* see *Prol.* 183, 204 n. 4, 242.

docebo. For the nuance in the 1st person, see above 25–6 n.

307 The verse as a whole expresses the training of the poet. H.'s language is reminiscent of the formulas of the *artes*, but is more concrete than they are. The *opes* on which the poet is told to draw are in fact *quid alat formetque poetam.* Prosaic speech would convey something like *qua copia mentes poetarum alantur.*

unde parentur opes may refer to the whole *materia* of an *ars*, and provide matter as well as expression, arrangement, and the rest, e.g. Cic. *Inv.* I. 9 *quare materia...rhetoricae uidetur artis ea quam Aristoteli uisam esse diximus; partes autem eae quas plerique dixerunt, inuentio* (concerned with *res*), *dispositio, eloquentia, memoria, pronuntiatio.* Or else it may be the store of subjects, ideas, principles, which the rhetoricians express by *res* or *instrumentum.* *opes* suggests *copia,* 'store, equipment', which again is used in both these senses: Quint. *I.O.* X. 1. 5 *ei* (sc. *oratori*) *uelut opes sint quaedam* parandae *quibus uti ubicumque desideratum erit possit? hae constant* copia rerum ac uerborum, 3. 3 *illic* (sc. *in scribendo*) opes *uelut...aerario conditae unde...proferantur.* H.'s notion of *opes* seems to be the narrower of the two. He is in fact concerned with *res*, subject-matter, at 310, 312 ff.; 311 *uerba* are a concomitant of *res*.

alat: cf. Cic. *De Or.* III. 48 *praecepta...quae puerilis doctrina tradit et subtilior cognitio...litterarum alit*, *Brut.* 126 (*Gracchus orator*) *non...solum acuere sed etiam alere ingenium potest*, Quint. *I.O.* I. 8. 6 *utiles tragoediae; alunt et lyrici*, 8 *quae maxime ingenium alant atque animum augeant*, VIII, pr. 2, X. 1. 31 *historia quoque alere oratorem quodam uberi* (*moueri* codd.)...*suco potest*, X. 5. 14, et al.

formetque, not 'to delineate, set down' (Norden), as in *orator quem informare uolumus*, but 'form the mind' of a person, the poet. Thus *formare* is used of shaping the intellect or *mores*, not only in the vigorous image Cic. *Brut.* 142 (*flebile*) *penetrat in animos eosque fingit format flectit*, but not infrequently in poetry and Silver writing, *TLL*, VI. 1. 1104. 5 ff. For the person himself so shaped *formare* is first attested *S.* I. 4. 120–1 *me | formabat puerum dictis*, later too in poetry and Silver prose, e.g. Quint. *I.O.* I. 1. 10 *oratorem institui, rem arduam, etiam cum ei formando nihil defuerit*, XII. 6. 7. *informare* is more rarely so used in classical Latin, cf. *TLL*, VII. 1. 1479. 30 ff. Cic. *Or.* 33, there mentioned, I do not regard as different from *Or.* 7 and 37, the 'sketching' of the ideal orator.

308 *quid deceat, quid non:* for the pattern cf. *Ep.* I. 6. 62 *quid deceat, quid non, obliti*, where *deceat* however is 'seemliness'. Norden and in his wake Rostagni equate *decet* with τέλος, the poet's aim, later said to be *utile* and *dulce*. I believe this to be right with the proviso that the term is still quite indistinct at this place. (As so often it is not that Norden and Rostagni go wrong but that they do not allow enough for H.'s flexibility.) *decet*, like πρέπον, is a value term, which can be attached to the most various approved aims, thus Cic. *Off.* I. 94 (on *decorum*) *huius uis ea est ut ab honesto non queat separari; nam et quod decet honestum est et quod honestum est decet. qualis autem differentia sit..., facilius intelligi quam explanari potest.* In the same way it is hard to separate *decet* from *finis*, the right aim being what it is proper to aim at. Norden therefore (*loc. cit.* 501 f.) rightly refers to Cic. *Inv.* I. 6 *in fine* (distinct from *officio*) *quid effici conueniat consideratur*, etc. Yet it is not here but only at 333 ff. that *quod effici conuenit* is seen to be produced by the poet *qui miscuit utile dulci.*

quo uirtus, quo ferat error: if it is asked how this notion differs from the *deceat* of the first half of the verse, the answer, I suggest, is that poetic virtue (ἀρετή) need not differ at all from poetic appropriateness (τὸ πρέπον). H. however distinguishes, conveniently for him, between the approved effects of poetry and the ideal *uirtus* of the *perfectus poeta* and the *error* personified and caricatured in the *uesanus poeta*. Norden (*loc. cit.* 502 ff.) and Rostagni again put this rightly if rigidly. H.'s apparently inconsequential involutions have to be shown to make unforced sense if these divisions are to have any relevance to his poetry.

(2) 'opes', the acquisition of the poet's equipment, his philosophy ('sapere'): his values and education, 'res' and 'uerba', characters and moral criteria, 309–18; Greek and Roman poetic substance contrasted, national ethos accounts for difference in attainment, 319–32

H. attaches himself to a rationalistic theory of poetry. Good poetry (*scribere recte*) demands understanding, *sapere*, in two different ways, which are later seen to be related (311, 317 ff.). It demands the technical expertise (*sapere*) taught in the earlier sections of the poem. But the primary demand is for the knowledge (*sapere*) which philosophy teaches, soon to be narrowed to moral theory. Although the ethos of the *Poetics* is related to the *Ethics*, Aristotle did not instruct the poet to take up moral theory. Nor is *Socraticae chartae* (310) an unambiguous reference to Plato and other Socratics; 'books of moral philosophy' may be all that is in mind, see 310 n. H. demands a theory of *ethos* adapted to the specific needs of the poet, just as Cicero's or Quintilian's demands are largely adapted to the specific needs of the orator; cf. *Prol.* 129 ff., and for rhetoric, Cic. *De Or.*, especially I. 45 ff., III. 46 ff., *Or.* 14 ff., Quint. *I.O.* XII, ch. 2.

309 *scribendi recte:* according to principles or rules that may be stated, as in *legitimum...poema* Ep. II. 2. 109, *legitimum...sonum* above 274. *rectum,* τὸ ὀρθόν, is what is right, not only in moral but in aesthetic theory, cf. 140, 319, 363, and the *species recti* above 25, *S.* 1. 4. 13.

sapere, more strongly than *sapientia,* keeps a link with *sapor,* 'taste' and the like, cf. 46 n. *callidus,* 218 *sagax.* The archaic wisdom of the old 'poets' however is called *sapientia,* 396. Others professing other *artes* also demanded 'philosophy', notably Cicero and Quintilian in their rhetoric. This does not, as has been thought, make H. a Ciceronian. The demands of the two writers differ, as the sequel will show.

principium et fons: the first noun, like Greek ἀρχή, stresses beginning and principle, the second 'derivation' from the fountainhead. Norden (*op. cit.* 498 n. 2) has shown the pairing to be Greek also, Strabo, I. 18 πηγὴ καὶ ἀρχὴ φράσεως...ῥητορικῆς ὑπῆρξεν ἡ ποιητική. Cf. Plut. *Quomodo adul. ab am.* 56 b on ethos, ἀρχὴν καὶ πηγὴν τοῦ βίου. In Latin *Ep.* I. 17. 45 *atqui rerum caput hoc erat, hic fons*, Cic. *De Or.* I. 42 *ab illo fonte et capite Socrate*, II. 117, al.

310 *rem...ostendere:* the verb is 'reveal', cf. 70 n. *monstrauit Homerus.* Words are separated from subject-matter, although in good poetry the two coalesce inseparably. Priority is given to *res* derived, as moral principles, from what H. calls *Socraticae chartae.*

Socraticae...chartae (spelt *cha-* in BCK, Porph. cod. M, s. x, *ca-* cett.; R, the best orthographer, has *ca-*, but *cha-* in all other places in Horace). For these words, cf. *Prol.* 131 n. 1 advocating the notion 'moral theory', although the wider notion of *Socratici*—Minor Socratics as well as Platonists, Aristotelians, and Stoics—cannot and need not be excluded. Lucilius in an unknown context employed similar wording (fr. 709 (Marx) †*nec sic ubi Graeci?*† *ubi nunc Socratici carti?* (*charti* G, *carthi* L). The unique and archaic *cartus* preserves the gender of Greek ὁ χάρτης. When the word reappears in Varro, Cicero, Catullus, it is feminine, cf. Varro *ap.* Char. *GL*, I. 104 *Varro...ait uocabula ex Graeco sumpta, si suum genus non retineant, ex masculino in femininum Latine transire et 'a' littera terminari uelut...* χάρτης, *charta.* H. is certainly not correcting the style of the archaic poet, as Rostagni suggests. For even in its corrupt state the Lucilian verse can be seen to be so different from H. as to render even an allusion dubious. This applies emphatically to the far-flung guesses of G. C. Fiske, 'Lucilius and H.', *Wisc. St.* VII (1920), 460 f. If anything, the Lucilian context may be closer to Prop. II. 34 (*b*). 27 *Socraticis...libris*, as F. Marx suggested (*ad l.* Lucil.). The Propertian passage should be added to those set down *Prol.* 131 n. 1 as another possible instance for the notion 'moral philosophy'.

poterunt (*ostendere*): emphatic for *ostendent*, cf. *possent*, 74 n. Rostagni, following Heinze, ignores this idiom in saying '*poterunt*...e non già *ostendent*, appunto perchè si tratta d'un esempio soltanto'. The contrary is the case.

311 *uerba...rem...sequentur:* one of several instances in which H. repeats a topic, or expresses a sentiment, already pre-empted in a different part of the poem so that light falls on it from different quarters, cf. *Prol.* 244 ff., 261 ff. Here, as Norden *loc. cit.* 500 f. has seen, 40–1 may be compared, *cui lecta potenter erit res | nec facundia deseret hunc nec lucidus ordo.* In both cases H. inculcates his creed—the poet must have something to say; if *ars* is at his command, the rest will follow. But, in the context of *ars*, at 40, unity is the thing aimed at and the rest will follow from the right choice of task, whatever it be. In the context of *artifex*, in this passage, the poet's equipment is to the fore and the choice of poetic 'substance' is prescribed.

The Elder Cato said *rem tene, uerba sequentur* (H. Jordan, p. 80; for a possible Greek background of the saying, see Dion. Hal. *Lysias*, ch. 4, especially p. 13. 7, ed. Us.–Ra.). H. applies the *praeceptum paene diuinum* (Jul. Vict., Halm, *Rhet. Lat. Min.* 347. 17) to a different purpose, which would have surprised the old Censor; so perhaps did Asinius Pollio (*ap.* Porph. *ad l.*) *male hercule eueniat uerbis nisi rem sequuntur*. H.'s *res* has two aspects: the principles, soon revealed as moral, which the poet gets from his early study of philosophy, and the 'subject-matter' on which he will draw in writing poetry. Cicero' and Quintilian's demands for philosophical rhetoric have a similar two-sidedness.

prouisam (*rem*): a technical term of the Greek literary critics, made to fit language not so technical. The *materia, instrumenta*, etc. of the textbooks may be compared. The Greek term is προνοούμενα (-ησάμενα), discovered by C. Jensen in Philod. *Poem.* v. 3, in none of three instances fully preserved but lines 14, 24, 25 confirm each other, since clearly the same word is used; cf. Jensen, pp. 115 f. Philodemus is attacking a theory—hardly Neoptolemus', as Jensen (at first) and Rostagni thought—which burdens the poet with an unnecessarily encyclopaedic store of knowledge. This recalls certain features (no more) of the philosophic 'provision' demanded by H. for the poet, and by Cicero and Quintilian for the orator. The only parallel for the literary use of *prouisum* that I can find in the collections of the Latin *Thesaurus* is Quint. *I.O.* x. 7. 8 *ut . . . nostram uocem prouisa et formata cogitatio excipiat.* But of course the general notion of 'provisions' was well established: *Ep.* i. 18. 109–10 *prouisae frugis . . .* | *copia*, also *frumentum prouisum* in the historians, and *prouisum* generally in Cicero and others, e.g. *Lael.* 6 *multa . . . prouisa prudenter.* H. may have extended the meaning under Hellenistic influence.

non inuita: personified as at *Ep.* ii. 2. 113 *uerba mouere loco, quamuis inuita recedant*, extending without strain the metaphor in Cato's *sequentur*.

312–16 reveal the kind of *sapere* demanded of the poet—moral principle and a knowledge of typical human features derived from ethics. H. shows none of Cicero's desire to make rhetoric into an intellectual discipline by basing it on philosophy and thus to heal the breach between speech and thought; thus Crassus at *De Or.* iii. 56–81, though the same speaker restricts the orator's philosophy to moral theory at i. 69 *qua re hic locus de uita et moribus totus est oratori* *perdiscendus; cetera si non didicerit, tamen poterit,* etc. Even less does he show Quintilian's educational fervour, *I.O.* xii, ch. 2. The abstractions of moral theory are avoided; H. makes the reader contemplate the affections and obligations in the social setting: love of country, family, friends (cf. Plato, *Rep.* iii. 386 a, gods, family, friends); obligations of senator, judge, military leader. The philosophers systematize such traditional moral qualities as are set out in the *Ars* and in Lucilius' long fragment on the virtues (frs. 1326–38, cit. *Prol.* 131 n. 2). Thus Panaetius, restated by Cic. *Off.* 1. 58 *patria...parentes... liberi totaque domus...bene conuenientes propinqui,* has been compared with Lucilius (F. Marx *ad l.*) and may be compared with *A.P.* 312–13. But there is nothing specifically Stoic in H.'s account of social relationships and obligations of magistrates, cf. *Prol.* 136 n. 4. In particular I find no trace of the ever-widening circles of social *officia* that are a significant feature of Stoic accounts. If there was such an order of things, H. has broken it up and rearranged it with a light touch: *patria* away from *parens* and *frater,* who however are closely connected through the ἀπὸ κοινοῦ position and the assonance *amore...amandus*; *amicis* away from *hospes.* Rather the multiplicity of relationships is brought out: *quid...quid, quo...quo, quod... quod*; H. is fond of marking a variety of aspects in this way, e.g. above 307–8 *unde...quid... | quid...quid, quo...quo,* or *Ep.* 1. 16. 41–3.

312 *didicit:* the training of the student; at 318 he emerges so trained, and is ready to apply the principles.

quid debeat has been made much of by those finding a Stoic *uir bonus* in this verse. But if 'he owes' is more than 'what is owed' it is as awareness of principle, at most something like Quint. xii. 1. 28–9 *si sit ad proelium miles cohortandus, ex mediis sapientiae praeceptis orationem trahet?...quae certe melius persuadebit aliis qui prius persuaserit sibi,* etc. Cf. above 101 *ut ridentibus arrident,* etc.

314 *conscripti...officium:* the origin of the formula *patres conscripti* is controversial, cf. Brassloff, *R-E,* iv. 891 ff. But whatever its origin, it is a generic term for the body of senators, the singular being either municipal (*Lex Iul. Mun.* 108, 127) or else, where it occurs in Roman literature, a stylistic freak. The only instance of the sing. cited in *TLL,* iv. 374. 54 ff. appears to be jocular, Cic. *Phil.* 13. 28 *Asinius quidam senator uoluntarius lectus ipse a se...mutauit calceos, pater conscriptus repente factus est.* The present instance is unique, *conscriptus* used not only in the sing. but without its otherwise inseparable *pater.* The point is not easily seen since the genial irony suitable in *praeclare senator* (*S.* 1. 6. 110) does not fit the tone of this passage.

iudicis: cf. H.'s father pointing to a juror as an example of rectitude, *S.* I. 4. 123 *unum ex iudicibus selectis obiciebat.*

315 Regulus and other *exempla* of the *Odes* are relevant.

profecto: an expressive and unusual word for H., occurring in his verse here only, and again in Virgil only once, although B. Axelson, *Unpoet. Wörter,* 94 shows that other poets did not object to it. The word 'expresses personal conviction', R. G. Austin, Quint. *I.O.* XII. 2. 18 n., citing Landgraf on Cic. *Rosc.* 30, Seyffert–Mueller on Cic. *Am.* 2. *profecto* serves to switch *ille,* the apprentice poet, back to *qui didicit,* thus showing that the intervening piece was a digression, apparently exemplifying, in fact putting in descriptive terms what has been more briefly put in abstract language.

316 The preceding examples have prepared the reader for the next step—the *sapere* provided by moral theory turns out to concern character, just as the *fama* and fiction of 119 was put in terms of characters. *mores* are a pervasive motif of the poem; here as at 126 H. says *persona*—the Achilles of the stage (cf. *fabula* 320) or the Aeneas of epic poetry. Appropriateness too returns. The same term *conueniens* is used in an earlier passage soon related to character, 119 *sibi conuenientia finge,* etc.

Affiliation with philosophical doctrine has been considered. If *Socraticae chartae* relates to Plato, one may be inclined to refer to the knowledge of psychological types demanded from the user of λόγος in *Phaedr.* 271. Others may feel reminded of Cicero's *personae, Off.* I. 107 ff., 115 ff., types of character which doubtless are Panaetius' πρόσωπα in a Latin dress. But neither is put with the doctrinal implications that would justify calling them Platonic or Stoic. Certain Aristotelian implications however are noticeable. For this reason I have suggested, *Prol.* 140 n. 1, 251–2, that the passage is based on a Peripatetic theory, developed from the relevant ch. 15 of the *Poetics,* especially 1454 a 16–17 ἓν μὲν καὶ πρῶτον ὅπως χρηστὰ ᾖ (τὰ ἤθη). Rostagni draws attention to the typical, anonymous features of the examples 312 ff.; that too may be claimed as an Aristotelian feature. I am doubtful however whether *conuenientia* can be plausibly equated with ἐοικότα, and this with τὸ εἰκός of *Poet.* ch. 9, as Rostagni suggests. Cf. *exemplar uitae morumque,* 317 n.

317 *respicere* 'to scrutinize' (for the purpose of copying). This is not the usual meaning of this or similar verbs—contrast e.g. *S.* II. 3. 299, *Ep.* I. 1. 105—but the meaning is tied to the context. The Platonic metaphor βλέπω πρὸς..., expressing the 'orientation' of the artist or thinker, may be compared, especially the scrutinizing of the eternal model by the artist-demiurge of *Tim.* 28 a. Cic. *Tim.* 4

renders that passage by *speciem*...intuebitur *atque id sibi proponet exemplar*; about Phidias he says, *Or.* 9 *nec uero*...*cum faceret Iouis formam*...contemplabatur *aliquem e quo similitudinem duceret, sed ipsius in mente insidebat species pulchritudinis*...*quaedam*, quam intuens in eaque defixus *ad illius similitudinem artem et manum dirigebat*. The metaphor has to be noted though it does not necessarily stamp the Horatian passage as Platonic. Cf. next note.

exemplar uitae morumque: for *exemplar*, see above 268 n. L. Mueller suggests that this is a hendiadys for *morum uitae*, cf. however Stat. *Silv.* III. 3. 203–4 *uiam morum longaeque examina uitae* | ...*poscam*. In any event no realism is intended; likeness to life will be introduced presently, *uiuas hinc ducere uoces*. Something like Lambinus' paraphrase must be near the mark: *ueram et perfectam speciem uitae humanae morumque intueri*. But although *exemplar* may render Greek παρά-δειγμα, no attempt is made to reproduce Plato's theory of Forms. Nor is Middle Platonic doctrine expressed in the clear terms of Cic. *Or.* 9 (cit. prec. n.), which places the 'Form' in the artist's mind. H. himself however (as has not escaped commentators) assists our search at *Ep.* I. 2. 17–18 (*Homerus*) *rursus quid uirtus et quid sapientia possit,* | *utile proposuit nobis* exemplar *Vlixem*. Homer's Odysseus offers a better model for morality than the moralists, *ibid.* 3–4 *quid sit pulchrum turpe, quid utile quid non,* | *planius ac melius Chrysippo et Crantore dicit* (*Homerus*). This generality of the exemplar rather suggests to me the Aristotelian notion of καθόλου (*Poet.* ch. 9). For the approved moral features of the exemplaria of 312 ff. Aristotle's μίμησις βελτιόνων may be cited. Cf. Ar. *Poet.* 2, 1448 a 1 ff. ἐπεὶ δὲ μιμοῦνται οἱ μιμούμενοι πράτ-τοντας, ἀνάγκη δὲ τούτους ἢ σπουδαίους ἢ φαύλους εἶναι (...κακίᾳ γὰρ καὶ ἀρετῇ τὰ ἤθη διαφέρουσι πάντες) ἤτοι βελτίονας ἢ καθ' ἡμᾶς ἢ χείρονας ἢ καὶ τοιούτους, ὥσπερ οἱ γραφεῖς κτλ., a 17 ff. on tragedy and comedy: ἡ μὲν γὰρ χείρους, ἡ δὲ βελτίους μιμεῖσθαι βούλεται τῶν νῦν, 15, 1454 b 10 ff. ἐκεῖνοι (good portrait-painters) ἀποδιδόν-τες τὴν ἰδίαν μορφὴν ὁμοίους ποιοῦντες καλλίους γράφουσιν, et al. This kind of μίμησις, rather than the Hellenistic μίμησις βίου to which Rostagni refers, seems worth considering tentatively as a background for H.'s *exemplar uitae morumque*.

iubebo: cf. *docebo*, 306 n.

318 *doctum* because, at 312, *didicit*.

imitatorem, μιμητήν, e.g. Ar. *Poet.* 25, 1460 b 8 ff. ἐπεὶ γάρ ἐστι μιμητὴς ὁ ποιητὴς ὡσπερανεὶ ζωγράφος ἢ τις ἄλλος εἰκονοποιός, ἀνάγκη μιμεῖσθαι...ἢ...οἷα ἦν ἢ ἔστιν, ἢ οἷά φασιν καὶ δοκεῖ, ἢ οἷα εἶναι δεῖ.

uiuas hinc ducere uoces: cf. Virg. *A.* VI. 848 *uiuos ducent de marmore uultus*; not an ambiguous *ueras . . . uoces* (ς), the vulgate up to Bentley's time, rejected by him. The proverbial *uiua uox* (A. Otto, *Sprichwörter*, 378) sets the spoken word vis-à-vis the written or read. Here on the other hand the *uerba* bring to individual life the general types of moral theory (*res*): *uiuae uoces* are the words, apt and true to life, that willingly follow *res* (311). *uiuos . . . uoltus* (Peerlkamp) therefore misses the mark.

319–32 If *res* and *uerba* are not as closely associated as 310–11 postulated, the poem will not be 'appropriate'. This problem of unity is present throughout the poem, but is here put in the general terms that suit the chapter on 'the poet'. Some consequences of this dissociation of *res* and *uerba* are now considered, 319–22, and next the root of the trouble is diagnosed, 323 ff. In each case the context begins abruptly and the reader is left to relate these conclusions to the premisses of 309 ff.

319 *interdum* doubtless in the familiar sense of *modo* 'at times', as 93; the two alternate at *S.* 1. 9. 9.

speciosa locis: a difficult locution; the text has been doubted and no agreement on the meaning of the words has been reached.

(1) Porphyrion reasonably comments on the merits of *res*, but the shortcomings of diction and composition according to him are wanting in this *fabula*, whereas H. seems to be saying the opposite. Peerlkamp therefore rewrote the line, ⟨*haud*⟩ *speciosa locis, morata sed apte*. Yet, quite apart from his unacceptable wording, since *morataque recte* seem to be sound, *-que* must remain a guide to the sense of the verse. Hence no antithesis is likely to be intended and the first part probably contains laudatory language. Porphyrion's text may have been corrupt or he misunderstood the passage. What then does *speciosa* mean? Archaic Roman drama, in H.'s scale of values, would qualify under *res* but fail under diction and composition. Does *speciosa* describe this state of affairs? Not without some obliqueness, for the word is so much closer to *uenus, pondus, ars*, which the very next line denies to the *fabula*. The adj. is a highly approving term in H. (except of course when outward appearance only is denoted as at *Ep.* 1. 16. 45 *introrsus turpem, speciosum pelle decora*), see 144 Homer's *speciosa . . . miracula, Ep.* 11. 2. 116 *speciosa uocabula rerum*. The same approval would be denoted here, limited though its range is by *locis*. But I doubt if that limitation would be sufficient unless an ironical undertone can be felt—'making a splendid show with its *loci*', and hence *oblectat populum*. With this explanation *speciosa* may perhaps stand, though misgivings remain because the word itself may not remove the verse far enough from 320.

Commentary

(2) What does *locis* mean? Schütz, followed by Wilkins, equates it with the sources or headings of (dialectic) argument, the τόποι of Aristotle's *Topics*, cf. Cic. *Top.* 7. Others have equated it with epigrams, *sententiae*, γνῶμαι, Quintilian's *uberes loci popularesque sententiae* (v. 13. 42), *locis speciosis* (VII. 1. 41), et al. Finally K.–H. derive *locis* from *loca*, 'places, passages', *Ep.* II. 1. 223. Of these only the second notion is at all acceptable; the first is ruled out because *loci*, i.e. *sedes argumentorum*, cannot without comment become the 'psychological principles' demanded by Schütz and (with less conviction) by Wilkins; the third because it makes the difference between 319 and 320 a matter of degree not of quality.

The meaning may therefore be, 'make a splendid show with its (edifying) maxims'. But doubt lingers.

morataque recte: for the adv., see above 309 *scribendi recte. morata* looks back to the types of character 312 ff. and to 316 *personae... conuenientia cuique.* Porph: *ad l. bene instituta; unde in consuetudine dicere solemus bene moratum eum qui rectos mores ediderit.* Cf. Cic. *Div.* I. 66 *o poema (Enni) tenerum et moratum atque molle*, Quint. *I.O.* IV. 2. 64 *in oratione morata debent esse omnia cum dignitate quae poterunt*, Ennod. *Dict.* 7. 9 *bene morata oratio.* It seems to me hazardous to separate these instances from the Horatian, as is done in *TLL*, VIII. 1476. 35 and 43 ff.

320 *fabula* may be 'tale', e.g. the *Iliad* at *Ep.* I. 2. 6 *fabula qua Paridis propter narratur amorem*, or 'drama', as above. Here 321 confirms the latter.

nullīus: here, at 324, and *Ep.* I. 17. 22 the archaic *-īus* is preserved, but *nullĭus Epod.* 16. 61, *Ep.* I. 1. 14—all in hexameters. For other instances of *-īus*, see D. Bo, *Hor. Op.* III. 88.

ueneris–pondere–arte indicate different aspects of the poetic sufficiency which is missed when content and form are not in balance.

nullius ueneris 'without charm', cf. 42 n., Ernesti, *Lex. Tech. Rhet.* vol. I under Χάρις, vol. II under *Venus*, P. Geigenmüller, *Quaest. Dionys.* (1908) under ἀφροδίτη and χάρις.

sine pondere 'lightweight'; *pondus*, contrary to Callimachean and neoteric poetics, is a recommended quality at *Ep.* II. 2. 111 ff. *quaecumque parum splendoris habebunt, | et sine pondere erunt et honore indigna ferentur, Ep.* I. 19. 42 *nugis addere pondus.* But at 260 above a double entendre deflects the praise, *pondus* being 'heaviness' as well as 'weight'. In the highly Horatian context of Pers. 5. 19–20 all *pondus* can do is to give apparent solidity to smoke, *dare pondus...fumo.* Writing ἐλαφρῶς, when large poems are concerned, is deplored by Philodemus as much as is writing εὐτελῶς (*Poem.* v. 4. 31 f.). Callimachus' οὐλαχύς may be contrasted, and so may his and the Roman

Callimacheans' polemics against the large and weighty epic. These poets did not find charm and art where the critical scales registered weight.

As for *pondus*, to satisfy the scope of this passage we must expect the theorists to recognize weight as a quality of diction and of subject-matter, *pondus uerborum* and *pondus sententiarum*. This is the case in rhetoric; see Ernesti, *op. cit.* under βάρος and *pondus*, and Geigenmüller, *op. cit.* under the same headings. In the unreal distinctions of ancient theory, both *uerba* and *sententiae* or *res* must have their due weight to please an audience. Demosthenes was praised for his care in weighing *uerborum...pondera* (Cic. *Or.* 26); *Antonius in* uerbis... *eligendis, neque id ipsum tam* leporis *causa quam* ponderis...*nihil non ad rationem et* tamquam *ad* artem *dirigebat* (Cic. *Brut.* 140). Hence the two kinds of *pondus* tend to appear in close proximity; thus Cic. *De Or.* II. 73 *omnium sententiarum grauitate, omnium uerborum ponderibus est utendum,* Or. 197 *et uerborum et sententiarum ponderibus utemur. nam qui audiunt haec duo animaduertunt et iucunda sibi censent, uerba dico et sententias,* Part. Or. 19, Quint. *I.O.* x. 1. 97, et al. Yet the rhetoricians are content to censure the violation of appropriateness in their various styles, thus for *uerba sine re*, the passages cited 322 n., and conversely for *res sine uerbis* Quint. *I.O.* x. 1. 130, 2. 23. H., on the other hand, by one of his dialectical turns, allows us to share his own insight into poetry. Roman audiences desire the right thing, poetic drama that has something to say, that offers more than empty words however pretty. But they desire the right thing in the wrong way. They mistake, as it were, *res* for *uerba*, enjoying poetry that is poetically unformed (*sine arte*), words lacking the *uenus* and *pondus* which alone can convey the subject, or in modern parlance—they enjoy prose and think it poetry.

321 As in the middle section popular approval is considered a criterion of value, but a limited one.

ualdius: ualde has a colloquial note, which should not be overrated, for the word occurs not only in Cicero's letters and dialogues but in the speeches. It is rare in verse and the comparative is very rare, cf. E. Wölfflin, *Lat. und roman. Komparation*, 9 f., B. Axelson, *Unpoet. Wörter*, 36 f., J. B. Hofmann, *Lat. Umgangssprache*[2], 75 f., 192 where this passage may be added to the only other instance in H. of the comparative, *Ep.* 1. 9. 6; the positive does not occur in H. Probably K.–H. make too much of the nuance 'more strongly' in both passages.

populum: contrast 113 n., 153 n. *ego et populus mecum.* Here the *populus* have a very partial view of the Horatian truth; they are said to prefer poetic 'substance', however inartistic, to melodious trifles.

mŏratur: mōrataque two verses above is unlikely to be a deliberate assonance. *moratur* applies the same test as 154 *aulaea manentes*, 223 *grata nouitate morandus.* If this kind of *fabula* is archaic tragedy, H.'s view may be borne out by continued performances of Ennian and other old drama.

322 *inopes rerum:* the adj. is established in Ciceronian rhetoric as denoting 'weak style'; but the gen. (current with *inops* in both prose and verse) qualifies the assessment, this being art without substance (for *rerum* cf. *rem*, 310). At the opposite end of the scale H. sets up small and delicate poems, which suggest the Alexandrian and neoteric fashions of poetry. Since he identified *res* with moral theory and with ethos, *inopes rerum* is likely to hint at the absence of these qualities.

nugaeque canorae: H. at times talks of his own verse as *nugae* or the like, never without an element of irony or apologia, *S.* I. 9. 2, *Ep.* I. 19. 42, II. 2. 141, cf. *S.* I. 10. 37, al. Here the notion differs: *nugae* are declined as an ideal different both from the poetry of *os rotundum* that now follows, and the *morata recte fabula* which he has already rejected. For *canorae* both Heinze and Rostagni mention the Hellenistic critics who found the criterion of good poetry in εὐφωνία not διανοήματα, cf. C. Jensen, *Philod. über die Gedichte*, v. 146 ff. If that is the implication here, the two words together, *nugae canorae*, and the context, suggest it; *i nunc et uersus tecum meditare canoros* (*Ep.* II. 2. 76) does not. Cf. Cic. *De Or.* I. 51 *quid est enim tam furiosum quam uerborum uel optimorum atque ornatissimorum sonitus inanis, nulla subiecta sententia nec scientia?*, Quint. *I.O.* IX. 3. 74, *ibid.* 100 *sunt qui neglecto rerum pondere et uiribus sententiarum, si uel inania uerba in hos modos deprauarunt, summos se iudicent artifices*, etc., IX. 4. 113 *si quidem relicto rerum pondere ac nitore contempto tesserulas, ut ait Lucilius* (cf. frs. 84–5 Marx) *struet*, etc.

323–32 At the beginning there is another apparent hiatus in thought. No attempt is made to define poetry which is neither *morata recte fabula* and no more, nor *uersus inopes rerum* and no more. Instead of describing the coalescence of *res* and *uerba* in abstract terms, H., as unexpectedly and impressively as at 268, sets up the Greek poetic ideal, and then as a contrast, equally unconnected, a satiric sketch of Roman tuition in arithmetic follows. Concentrating as ever on focal points or motifs, H. leaves the reader to divine the relations between these points. Thus here, (1) the ideal of Greek *ingenium* and poetry, (2) Roman concern for property built into their education. A logical link between the two would call for unpromising topics. Instead of offering an argument H. brusquely interrupts the little sketch (330 after the first word, *semis*), and with great force (3) asks the question to which the whole of this section tended—can we really hope for serious poetry from minds trained to think seriously of nothing but material gain? The question remains unanswered, the antithesis unresolved; but its resolution is less in doubt than that of a similar antithesis, *Ep.* II. 1. 93–117, cf. *Prol.* 198 ff. In the present passage humour turns out to be misleading; 330–2 show the underlying seriousness.

323 *Grais:* the verse expresses personal conviction. It gives great prominence to 'the Greeks': *Grais* heads its first division as it heads the second. The solemn word *Grais* occurs only here in the *Ars*, not *Graecus* as on the other three occasions, 53 *Graeco fonte*, 268 *exemplaria Graeca*, 286 *uestigia Graeca*—a fact which does not predispose one in favour of A. Ernout's suggestion on H.'s use of these words, 'avec lui disparaît l'antique distinction établie entre *Graius* et *Graecus*', *RP*, XXXVI (1962), 216, repr. *Philologica*, III (1965), 89. H. uses both but observes a stylistic distinction.

ingenium . . . ore rotundo: the first requires no comment in the context of ancient literary theory. It recalls the first word of the final part of the *Ars* (295); it is there, but not here, opposed to *ars. ore rotundo* is not self-explanatory, though *prima facie* there is an expectation that the rounded quality is related to *ars*, as Lambinus, Ernesti, and more recently Rostagni have urged; cf. Lambinus on *S.* II. 7. 86, 'rotundum valet idem, quod cultum, politum, perfectum', Non. 60. 8 ff. (M.) *est rotundum collectum et per omnem circuitum sine offensione asperi aut anguli leue*, 164. 2 *rotunde positum eleganter, concinne uel collecte.* This is borne out by a number of Greek and Latin passages cited by Lambinus and Ernesti. Cf. Plato, *Phaedr.* 234 e τὸν λόγον ἐπαινεθῆναι . . . οὐκ ἐκείνῃ μόνον ὅτι σαφῆ καὶ στρογγύλα (the corresponding Greek term), καὶ ἀκριβῶς ἕκαστα τῶν ὀνομάτων ἀποτετόρνευται, Dion. Hal. *Demosth.* 19. 1010 (ed. Us.–Ra. I. 168), where a passage of Isocrates is criticized as formless and unconcentrated: he is told to make his words στρογγυλώτερα. The rounded quality of style is therefore a matter of technique, as it is in the judgements of Cic. *Or.* 40 *praefractior nec satis, ut ita dicam, rotundus, Brut.* 272 *uerborum . . . apta et quasi rotunda constructio.* Cf. above 26, 31 nn. *rotundum* may be effortless as Heinze says, but it is the effortlessness of art that has become nature. For *ore*, cf. Aristoph. fr. 471 (Kock) χρῶμαι γὰρ αὐτοῦ τοῦ στόματος τῷ στρογγύλῳ, and for the origin of the metaphor, Dem. *Interpr.* 20 (cit. Orelli), a rounded rhetorical period is in need of στρογγύλου στόματος. H. then joins with *ingenium* not simply the complementary term *ars*, but the outcome of *ars* in poetry, the mastery that can forget art, a flowing style.

dedit (Musa loqui): cf. 83 n. *Musa dedit (referre).*

Commentary

324 *praeter laudem nullius auaris* is beautifully turned: they may be *auari* (a fault), but the gain they want to make is *laus* (a virtue by definition). This is an oxymoron also because *uatis auarus | non temere est animus*, *Ep.* II. I. I19–20; the poet is said not to be swayed by gain, *ibid.* 120 ff., *Prol.* 199. *auaritia*, properly speaking, is a hideous aberration in H.'s and all contemporary moralizing. As for *laudem*, cf. 268 *non laudem merui*. The Greeks, not only one or two of their poets, can be said to be involved because it is a matter of values—an essay in national psychology and Roman self-criticism, cf. above 323–32 n. *auaris* thus becomes a concept linking H.'s glorification of the Greeks with his criticism of Roman values. φιλοτιμία in turn is a popular topic in Greek moral theory; many passages are in point but especially Orelli's citation of Xen. *Mem.* III. 3. 13 on the Athenians. Rostagni compares Cic. *T.D.* 1. 3 ff. for the connexion between *laus* and artistic excellence.

nullius: cf. 320 n. The gen. belongs to neut. *nullum* as Ov. *Met.* I. 17 *nulli sua forma manebat*, al. In the comparable locution *nullius egentem*, *Ep.* I. 17. 22, it is masc.

325–30 H.'s change of poetic mood at the beginning and end of this little paragraph has been noted above, 323–32 n.

325 *Romani pueri* not only omits an adversative particle (as commentators note) but scores an especial effect by the comic bathos after the high flight of the last two verses. This effect persists in the sketch that follows, the sort of thing the genre *sermo* can accommodate.

assem: a unit divided into 12 *unciae*. Volus. Maec. 7 (*Metrol. Scr. Rel.* ed. Hultsch. II. 62) *diuiditur item as in duodecim partes duodecimas, uocantur singulae unciae, Lib. de Asse* 1 (*ibid.* p. 72) *quicquid unum est et quod ex integrorum diuisione remanet, assem ratiocinatores uocant,* 4 (*ibid.* p. 73) *cuiuslibet integrae rei in duodecim partes diuisae semper duodecima pars uncia dicitur.*

326 Division into a hundred parts, often (as in Orelli's *uel minutissimas*) regarded merely as an approximate description of 'long calculations', *longis rationibus* in H. It is true, Roman computation of fractions was largely duodecimal; yet interest was computed in percentages, *centesimae*, cf. Hultsch, 'Arithmetica', *R-E*, II. 1115. 52 ff., J. Tropfke, *Geschichte der Elementar-Math.* I³ (1930), 156 ff., 195. This fact, alongside H.'s censure of commercialism, renders a literal meaning of *centesimae* more probable, cf. K.–H. *ad l.*

dicat: Bentley *dicas.* But the idiomatic use of the 3rd person makes decisively against that change, *C.* I. 27. 10–11 where a person present is addressed, *dicat Opuntiae | frater Megillae.*

327 *filius Albini:* ps.-Acro's comment, *faeneratoris cuiusdam aurari filius* looks like improvisation.

quincunce 'five twelfths'.

remota est 'is deducted', perhaps a way of avoiding such prosaic words as *deducere* Cic. *Leg.* II. 53, *Off.* I. 59, Liv. VI. 35. 4, *detrahas* Volus. Maec. 8, *sublata Lib. de Asse* 14, et al. G. T. A. Krüger suggested that *remouere* like 329 *redit* was probably derived from, and still hinted at, operations on an abacus. For *remouere* as a financial term see 329 n.

328 *superat:* intrans., rather than the literal *superest* (dett.), is a more idiomatic manner of expressing a numerical 'remainder'. Cf. Prop. IV. 2. 57 *sex superant uersus*, Germ. 573 *quantum superet...noctis*, cf. Man. III. 423 *quodque his exsuperat demptis. Liber de Asse* 14 has *remanet* for the total after subtraction. Bentley's subjun. *superet* (dett.) is of course possible and occurs in the instance cited above 326 n. *dicat* (*qua pereat sagitta*) but in this lively sketch direct speech is not convincingly removed.

poteras: though *poterat* (α $\delta^2\pi^1$, Bentley) would be possible after *dicat*, the 2nd person shows the teacher turning to the pupil—a realistic touch. 'You might have told me by this time' (Wilkins) hints at a moment's hesitation; the 'imperf. of neglected duty' (A. Palmer), a much-favoured idiom, e.g. below 376 *poterat duci quia cena sine istis*, S. II. 1. 16 *et iustum poteras et scribere fortem*, negative *ibid.* 6–7 *peream male si non | optimum erat.*

triens: $\frac{5-1}{12} = \frac{1}{3}$, *Lib. de Asse* 14 *sublata uncia de quincunce remanet triens.*

eu: a long-established Greek colloquialism (of the kind '*bravo, bon*') as the old comic writers show; grammarians acknowledge it but after archaic comedy, unlike *euge*, it happens to be recorded only from this passage, cf. *TLL*, v. 2. 981. 82 ff., 1033. 48 ff., J. B. Hofmann, *Lat. Umgangsspr.*[2], pp. 23, 26. Contrast below 428 n.

329 *rem...seruare:* for the verb, see 86 n. The expression is much more emphatic at *Ep.* I. 1. 65–6 *rem facias, rem, | si possis, recte, si non, quocumque modo, rem*, though 330 shows that the sentiment here is no less strong.

redit: ps.-Acro *additur*; commonly *additur* but also *applicatur, confertur*, e.g. Volus. Maec. 8; the verb often means 'comes in as revenue', but does not necessarily do so here. H. Düntzer extended the financial notion to 327 *remota est*, i.e. 'disburse' (*P*, IX (1854), 382), which does not seem to be on record.

fit 'is the total', like *esse* and *facere* technical in computation, cf. *TLL*, VI. 1. 100. 71 ff., where this passage should be added.

330 *semis:* i.e. $\frac{5+1}{12} = \frac{1}{2}$.

an: the reader is pulled up suddenly by this rhetorical question on Roman materialism. (Pers. 1. 79–82 uses a similar type of indignant question in an entirely literary context.) This like many questions introduced by *an* rests on an assumption to be understood from the context, an ellipse from which H. obtains poetic capital, see 323–32 n. *an* is 'argumentative' (Kühner–Stegmann II. 519 f., D. Bo, *Lexicon Hor., an*); it suggests a reason for an assertion by denying its logical opposite, often in the form *an uero, an existimas, an censemus,* etc. Here *an* appears only in a small but outstanding portion of the paradosis, B, Bland. Vet. and two other Blandinian codices. Achilles Statius restored it by emendation; Bentley defended it and it is now established in all recent texts. Otherwise, *ad* cett., *at* ς (thus the variants e.g. *S.* I. 1. 88), *et* a weak attempt by Cunningham and Peerlkamp to avoid Bentley's decision.

aerugo: Greek ἰός. Applied to envy, this metaphor does not appear to be recorded before *S.* I. 4. 101 (*TLL,* I. 1066. 4); H. may have taken it from Greek, where Aesch. has it in an impressive verse, *Ag.* 834; K.–H. also cite Antisthenes, cf. below 331 n. But ἰός also attached to avarice; K.–H. cite Plut. *Superst.* 1, and again H. is the first to be known to use it so in Latin, later Martial, Sen. *Ep.,* Hier. *Ep.* 1. *robigo,* rust (of indolence), is applied to *ingenium* by Ov. *Tr.* V. 12. 21.

et: explanatory, cf. above 266.

cura peculi may hint at Virg. *E.* 1. 32 *nec spes libertatis erat nec cura peculi* (Heinze thinks the reader would remember that the Virgilian speaker is a slave, hence consider this *cura* illiberal). For φιλαργυρία as a disease, see ps.-Long. *Subl.* 44. 6 νόσημα μικροποιόν.

331 *imbuerit:* Antisth. *ap.* Diog. La. VI. 5 has κατεσθίεσθαι in a similar metaphor, ὥσπερ ὑπὸ τοῦ ἰοῦ τὸν σίδηρον, οὕτως ἔλεγε τοὺς φθονηροὺς ὑπὸ τοῦ ἰδίου ἤθους κατεσθίεσθαι.

speremus or *-amus* MSS. Either mood is grammatically possible but there is a slight preference in favour of the subjun. not as a '*lectio difficilior*', but because of its frequency in questions with this type of *an,* conveniently set out in D. Bo's *Lex. Hor.* under *an.*

carmina fingi: for the locution see 240, *Ep.* II. 1. 227, *C.* IV. 2. 32; below 382 *uersus.* The metaphor in 'fiction' differs, cf. 8, 119, 338.

332 *cedro . . . cupresso:* cf. Porph. *libri enim qui aut cedro inlinuntur aut arca cupressea inclusi sunt, a tineis non uexantur,* Vitr. II. 9. 13; for the lasting character of cypress wood, see Theoph. *H.P.* V. 4. 2, Plin. *N.H.* XVI. 212. Cedar oil as imagery for enduring works of literature, not infrequent in Latin verse after H. (*TLL,* III. 736. 57 ff.), is not attested before him; its realistic character is Horatian (which does not prove Horatian origin) especially in the highly metaphorical setting of this sentence.

cedro et leui: an isolated case in the *Ars* of a final long vowel elided before short, according to A. Michaelis, *op. cit.* (above 63–9 n.), 428. This over-simplifies a complex phenomenon, cf. 137, 330, 419, 427, not to mention 'prodelision' before *est*.

seruanda 'preserve', *conseruanda*, cf. 86 n.

(3) The poet's scope: instruction and delight, 333–46, cf. above 308 'quid deceat, quid non'

In rhetorical theory *docere, mouere,* and *delectare* are the *fines* (τέλη) of the craftsman, cf. E. Norden, *op. cit.* p. 502. That poetic theory in the Hellenistic age, and in particular H.'s probable 'source', imputed these aims to the poet is shown by Neoptolemus of Parium *ap.* Philod. *Poem.* v. 13. 8 ff., cf. *Prol.* 55 (Neopt. no. 10), 128 f., 135: καὶ πρὸς ἀρετὴν δεῖν τῷ τελείῳ ποιητῇ μετὰ τῆς ψυχαγωγίας τοῦ τοὺς ἀκούοντας ὠφελεῖν καὶ χρησιμολογεῖν, the supplements are noted *Prol.* 55. H. is seen therefore to work with traditional concepts in this part of the poem as well, cf. above 295–476 n. Moreover he adopts the same 'Peripatetic' compromise as Neoptolemus, although naturally this compromise means to him his unique blend of seriousness and humour, hardly what it meant to the Hellenistic *littérateur*. Whether Neoptolemus like H. linked *prodesse* with instruction and *delectare* with 'fiction' is not known. The scope in poetry of τὸ θαυμαστόν was certainly a topic of discussion as early as Ar. *Poet.* 24, 1460 a 11 ff., 25, 1460 b 22 ff.; Plut. *De aud. poet.* 16 f. is well known, for other evidence see Rostagni, 333–46 n. The outstanding feature of this section however is attention to the way the poet actually works. Here as elsewhere *artifex* impinges on *ars: breuitas* for instruction, cf. 335 n., verisimilitude for 'fiction', cf. 338 n. That this kind of topic could be shifted between *ars* and *artifex* is shown by Philodemus' remark, *Poem.* v. 4. 13–16. In the artificial language of Hellenistic and Roman literary theory, to bring together moral content and imaginative

Commentary

range is, in a sense, the aim of poetry and explains the promise of classical status.

333–4 *aut . . . aut . . .* | *aut . . . et . . . et:* the style, Rostagni points out, is again deliberately *ex cathedra*; the precept 119 *aut . . . aut* may be compared. Precision is apt for this kind of subject and H.'s style pictures the subject.

333 *prodesse:* ὠφελεῖν in Greek, e.g. Neopt. *loc. cit.*

delectare: Greek ἡδονή, τέρπειν, etc., cf. Neopt. *op. cit.* no. 11, al.; I. Bekker, *Anec.* 116 equates τέρπειν with ψυχαγωγεῖν, cf. Bywater on Ar. *Poet.* 6, 1450 a 33. Hence *delectare* may render either word. Neoptolemus happens to use ψυχαγωγία, *loc. cit.* In Eratosthenes' extreme pronouncement the same term is used, *ap.* Strabo 1. 15 ποιητὴν πάντα στοχάζεσθαι ψυχαγωγίας, οὐ διδασκαλίας.

334 *iucunda* is related to *delectare* as ἡδύ to τέρπειν in Greek theory.

idonea dicere uitae is a valid but rather roundabout way of putting the matter and it is instructive to note the Neoptolemic counterpart [τοὺς] ἀκούοντ[ας] ὠ[φελεῖ]ν καὶ χρησι[μο]λ[ογεῖ]ν. The last word, apparently a neologism, would be called uncertain, were it not for Philodemus' reference to it a few lines below (23–4), ὠφελήσεως καὶ χρησ[ιμ]ολογίας. The closeness to the Hellenistic original needs to be noted.

335 *praecipies* continues *prodesse* and *idonea dicere uitae*, 333–4; the fut. tense as often in precepts throughout the poem, e.g. 3–4, 40–1, 68, etc.

esto breuis: for *breuitas* in literary theory, see above 25 n. It has often been noted that this injunction expresses H.'s own practice, in this very passage as e.g. 23, 45, 92, 99–100, 102–3, 119–20. There are of course other aspects of Horatian terseness. *S.* 1. 10. 9–10 *est breuitate opus*, etc. does not only apply to teaching but to the style of *sermo*. Above 26–7 are comments on the difficulty in preventing brevity degenerating into obscurity, 148–9 concern the rapidity of Homer's narrative. *S.* 1. 4. 18 expresses H.'s personal predilection.

335–6 *ut cito dicta* | *percipiant animi dociles teneantque fideles:* in spite of K.–H.'s comparison with *S.* 1. 10. 9–10 *ut currat sententia neu se* | *impediat uerbis lassas onerantibus aures*, the adv. *cito* is, as Lambinus noted, more likely to qualify *percipiant animi* than *dicta:* the mind seizes brief speech fast and then retains it. The predic. force of *dociles* and *fideles* is no obstacle. The image is developed out of the archaic mode of instruction placed in the hearer's mind: ὦ Πέρση, σὺ δὲ ταῦτα τεῷ ἐνικάτθεο θυμῷ, or σὺ δὲ ταῦτα μετὰ φρεσὶ βάλλεο σῇσι. Cf. Lucil. fr. 610 (Marx) *tu si uoles per aures pectus inrigarier.*

337 Bentley considered the verse unattractive and ambiguous, and proposed its deletion; Peerlkamp and L. Mueller agreed without arguing the case. Bentley's arguments will not bear scrutiny, but it is true that the verse is otiose in a sense, in that it secures a point negatively which has already been made in positive terms—not a serious obstacle when the imagery adds to the fullness of the picture. The wording is Horatian.

superuacuum occurs in poetry, historiography, and Silver Latin for *superuacaneum*, H. and Livy apparently being the first to be known to use it; Paul. Fest. 294 (M.) *superuacaneum superuacuum*. It is a metaphor for 'supernumerary, pointless, idle'. Thus *Ep.* I. 15. 2–3 *mihi Baias* | *Musa superuacuas Antonius (facit)*, 'pointless' because the cure is not available at Baiae. So too *C.* II. 20. 24 *(sepulcri) mitte superuacuos honores*, pointless because his poetry will not die.

pectore: as S. II. 4. 90 *memori...pectore*, Ep. I. 2. 67–8 *adbibe puro* | *pectore uerba, puer*, al.; see also above 335–6 n. *animi* and *pectore* alternate as at *C.* II. 19. 5–6, Lucr. I. 924–5 *pectus...mente*, II. 45–6 *animo...pectus*, v. 103 *in pectus templaque mentis*, al.

manat: ps.-Acro, *idest effluit...pectus enim, quod iam uarietate...* *plenum est, ea quae superuacua audierit, non retinet*.

338–42 take up *delectare* (333) just as *praecipies* (335) took up *prodesse* (333). Reference is made to the Hellenistic and Roman doctrine distinguishing literary forms according to their assumed degree of factual truth: ἱστορία (*fama, uerum*), πλάσμα (*fictum* or *argumentum, uerisimile*), and μῦθος (*fabula, falsum*), where πλάσμα and μῦθος inevitably get entangled, and may be conflated. Rostagni has drawn attention to the importance of this doctrine to ancient literary history; for discussion and bibliography, see Rostagni *ad l.*, and above 119, 151 nn. The present passage differs from the two earlier in that 'fiction' is here tied to entertainment and *delectare*, whereas *uerum* is tied to instruction and *prodesse*, both therefore to general topics appropriate to the *poeta* section. Thus once again the sections of the poem are seen to impinge on each other, and thus to be related. Although this theory was well known in Roman literary theory as early as the *Rhet. ad Her.* and presumably earlier, it here appears in close connexion with Neoptolemus' triad, *prodesse–delectare–prodesse et delectare*. This connexion constitutes not indeed a certainty but a balance of probability in favour of Hellenistic rather than Roman provenance for the Horatian tradition. The earliest actual mention of the triad ἱστορία–πλάσμα–μῦθος that is at present known occurs in Asclepiades of Myrlea (*ap.* Sext. Emp. *Math.* I. 12. 252) which dates it at all events back to the second century B.C.

Commentary

338 *ficta* as a word Latinizes Greek πλάσμα, the label for the intermediate genre between *historia*, that is *gesta res*, and *fabula*, *quae neque ueras neque ueri similes continet res*, *Ad Her.* 1. 13. In the same work, and in Cic. *Inv.* 1. 27, it is called *argumentum*, and defined as *ficta res*, *quae tamen fieri potuit*, cf. Quint. *I.O.* 11. 4. 2 *argumentum*. But in H., who uses fixed doctrine for his own poetic purposes, no clear distinction is made between the two genres which are *non uera*: *fictum* and *fabula*.

uoluptatis causa: Ar. *Poet.* 24, 1460 a 11 ff. describes τὸ θαυμαστόν, the realm of ἄλογον, as ἡδύ. In Hellenistic terminology marvellous and irrational happenings were assigned to μῦθος, 'tale', in its new, non-Aristotelian, significance. And τὸ ἡδύ followed suit, cf. *Schol. Dion. Thr.* p. 449. 14 (ed. Hilgard) ἱκανὸς δὲ ὁ μῦθος δυσωπῆσαι δι' ἡδονῆς...ἡ δὲ ποιητικὴ ἔχει μὲν τὸ προσαγωγὸν ἐκ τῆς ἡδονῆς. In rhetorical theory, understandably enough, all three kinds of narrative, *historia, argumentum,* and *fabula,* were claimed as sources of diversion and entertainment, Cic. *Inv.* 1. 27 *quod delectationis causa non inutili cum exercitatione dicitur et scribitur.*

proxima ueris, Greek εἰκότα. *Ad Her.* and Cic. *Inv.* (cit. above under *ficta*) *ueri similes* and *quae...fieri potest,* Quint. *I.O.* (cit. *ibid.*) *argumentum, quod falsum sed uero simile,* ps.-Acro *ad l. uerisimilia.* The criterion of probability in matters of *fictum* or *fabula* was known to the Latin scholiasts as it had been to the Greek; for evidence from ancient Virgilian exegesis, see R. Heinze, *Virg. Ep. Technik*[3], p. 246 n. 1. H. avoids a prosaic term like *uerisimilia* and replaces it by something describing a concrete, spatial notion, 'close to the truth'. The occurrence of this locution in didactic verse probably suggests that it is at home there: Germ. *Phaen.* 26 *plaustraue, quae facies stellarum proxima uero* (Z, *uera* O, *uerae* Barth), *Aetna* 177 *Aetna sui manifesta fides et proxima uero est.*

339 *ne* Bentley, as against *nec* BC al., rightly since *neu* follows in the next verse, though there B alone offers *non* (N̄). Bentley compared 185 *ne.* In both instances *ne* may be *ita ut non.* The ellipse probable in *ne forte* (176 n.) need not necessarily be assumed.

quodcumque uolet: uelit uar.l. Either is possible, cf. Hofmann–Szantyr, 562; the frequency in late Latin of the subjun. in such a rel. cl. (urged by F. Klingner, *BVSA,* LXXXVIII, 3 (1936), 43 n. 1) does not itself make against this construction when the rel. cl. is set in a final one. But the generalizing notion of the fut. indic. may well be aimed at, cf. *C.* 1. 28. 25–9. Scribes would be tempted to turn *uolet* into the normal grammar of *uelit.*

poscat...credi with object cl. and inf.; for the inf. cf. *C.* 1. 4. 12 *seu poscat agna* sc. *immolari*; for this construction after other verbs of asking, see Kühner–Stegmann, I. 681 f.

fabula: scarcely 'drama' as 320, but, as K.–H. suggest, 'tall story', *falsum,* cf. above 338–42 n.

340 *neu*, though parallel to the general case introduced by *ne* and continuing, in *extrahat*, the personification of *fabula*, introduces in fact an instance of such a *fabula*.

Lamiae: the child-eating ogress of ancient fairy tales, see Schwenn, *R-E*, XII. 544. 35 ff., Porph. *haec ad infantes terrendos solet nominari*. This is an instance adroitly selected and presented from a well-stocked narrative store; Sext. Emp. *Math.* I. 264 shows the traditional background in offering as examples of μῦθος the Titans, Pegasus, Gorgo, as well as metamorphoses; so does ps.-Long. *Subl.* 9. 14 in his account of τὸ μυθικόν in Homer, and *ibid.* Zoilus on the χοιρίδια κλαίοντα of Circe. H. tells as it were the story in one verse, *uiuum puerum extrahat aluo*—the gruesome detail, not perhaps surprisingly, restricted to this verse, cf. Schwenn, *R-E*, XII. 545. 49—and the comic *pransae*, 'for lunch', the concise part. as *S.* I. 5. 25, 6. 127.

extrahat + abl., for which construction many instances are cited by D. Bo, *Hor. Op.* III. 100.

341–6 The attempt to ensure success for the right kind of poem continues, H. making a new appeal. So far the groups approached have been *ego et populus mecum* (153), the *populus* without H. (321), the *nucis emptor* (249), knights of special standing (248), the ancient Romans (270) and *Pompilius sanguis* (292). The case most like the present is 113 *equites peditesque* and the different parties imagined at 249–50. Here H. builds up the three scholastic types of poetry into a contest between moralists, aesthetes, and compromisers. The contest is pictured as a Roman voting procedure, with the compromisers finally winning every vote, and with H. giving, at 345–6, his own assessment of the result, so that after all *ego* is added to *populus*.

341–2 *centuriae seniorum* and *Ramnes* survived as names to H.'s day and beyond. However jocularly and archaically, they point to actual voting arrangements in the centuriate assembly. What Liv. I. 43. 5 calls the *discrimen aetatium* is an enduring feature of the original 'Servian' army and civic order, cf. Livy, *ibid.* 1–2 *octoginta confecit centurias, quadragenas* seniorum ac iuniorum...; *seniores ad urbis custodiam ut praesto essent, iuuenes ut foris bella gererent.* The age limit was 46, Mommsen, *R.St.* I. 3. 508, III. 262. The age groups survived for voting purposes: Livy, *ibid.* 12, a passage roughly contemporary with H., and much debated, since it involves later changes in the centuriate order; for discussion and bibliography see Ernst Meyer,

Commentary

Röm. Staat und Staatsgedanke[4] (1964), pp. 497–504. The *centuriae seniorum* then correspond to the '*pedites*' of 113, but only to the *seniores* among them. Their adversaries are not the *iuniores* of the '*pedites*' but young Roman knights—the famous *sex centuriae* or *sex suffragia* preserving the old Etruscan tribal designations of *Ramnes Luceres Titie(nse)s*; cf. Mommsen, *op. cit.* III. 106–8, Rosenberg, *R-E*, I A. 138 f. (*Ramnes*), Klotz, *R-E*, II A. 2024 (*Sex Suffragia*). Mommsen, *op. cit.* III. 254 n. 3, says the *Ramnes* here represent the centuries of knights. So they do, but H. neglects the *seniores* and singles out the young, whom he had neglected in the first group. Thus he obtains a double grouping that serves his purpose of a humorously overstated contrast, not only between '*pedites*' and *equites*, but strait-laced bourgeois and young men of fashion. These two groups aptly approve of the two invalid extremes, the one of *prodesse*, the other of *delectare*. The antithesis 319–24 may be recalled, *morata...recte fabula* and *nugae...canorae*.

341 *agitant*: Porph. *ea quae nugatorie dicuntur exagitant senes*. But the use of the simple verb is illustrated by *C.* II. 13. 40 *timidos agitare lyncas*, III. 12. 10–11 *agitato* | *grege*, i.e. 'chase, startle, attack'. At Cic. *Mur.* 21 *insectatur* (*legationem*) follows *agitat* (*rem militarem*). The nuance below 456 *agitant pueri* (*uesanum poetam*) differs slightly.

expertia frugis: i.e. *poemata* (342). *frux* in a metaphorical sense is not known before this passage without a defining gen., and occurs in H. here only, *TLL*, VI. 1. 1454. 3 ff., 37 ff.

342 For *celsi...Ramnes*, cf. Pers. 1. 4 *Troiades*, 31 *Romulidae*, and particularly 20 *ingentes trepidare Titos* with Lydus, *Mag.* I. 9 καὶ Τίτους (ἐκάλεσαν) τοὺς ἐκ προγόνων εὐγενεῖς, ὥς φησι Πέρσιος ὁ ᾽Ρωμαῖος, and *Cecropides, Teucrorum proles, Troiugenae* in Juvenal's Eighth Satire. *celsi*, an expressive archaic word, with its noun *Ramnes* frames the line: 'erect' and 'disdainful', in H. here only. As Wilkins says, it may be pred. or attrib. Cf. Varro, *Men.* 9 *cedit citus celsus tolutim*, Cic. *T.D.* v. 42 *celsus et erectus et ea quae homini accidere possunt omnia parua ducens*, *De Or.* I. 184, Liv. VII. 16. 5 *celsique et spe haud dubia feroces in proelium uadunt*.

praetereunt: cf. Mart. I. 25. 2–4 *profer opus*, | *quod nec Cecropiae damnent Pandionis arces* | *nec sileant nostri praetereantque senes*. But K.–H. mention that *praeterire* denotes rejecting a candidate in an election, Cic. *T.D.* v. 54 *cum sapiens et bonus uir...suffragiis praeteritur*, *Planc.* 8, Caes. *B.C.* I. 6, al. This suits H.'s setting.

austera poemata: still strongly metaphorical in H.'s time. Instances of the metaphor before H. seem to apply to persons (*TLL*, II. 1559. 59 ff.) except for the oxymoron Cic. *De Or.* III. 103 *ut suauitatem habeat*

357

austeram et solidam, non dulcem atque decoctam. H. also has *austerum...*
laborem, S. II. 2. 12.

343–6 H. now adds his voice to that of the *seniores* and *iuniores*.

343 *omne tulit punctum* completes the metaphor of voting; cf. *Ep.* II.
2. 99 *discedo Alcaeus puncto illius.* Porph. on 343 *punctum...ideo quod*
antiqui suffragia non scribebant sed puncto notabant; ps.-Acro on 343 *usus*
est hoc uerbo etiam Cicero in Fundaniana, on II. 2. 99 *suffragio, iuxta legem*
tabellariam; Cic. *Planc.* 53, *Mur.* 72, *T.D.* II. 62, cf. Mommsen, *R.St.*
III. 404.

miscuit utile dulci: cf. 334 *simul et...et*; *ibid.* notes on *iucunda* and
idonea...uitae. dulci abl., as is shown by *S.* II. 4. 55, 65.

For the tense of *tulit* and *miscuit*, see 373 n.

344 *delectando:* cf. 333 *delectare.*

monendo: cf. 333 *prodesse.*

345 This is humorous in style, but in fact the promise of wide and
lasting fame in the next verse means what it says. The apparently
flat 'mixture' of *utile* and *dulce* reveals what elsewhere in this poem
and in the *Odes* would be called glory.

Sosiis: the publishers or booksellers get the cash, writers the fame;
earnings by the author, known from the first century A.D., are not
here indicated. For the name cf. *Ep.* I. 20. 2 *Sosiorum pumice mundus,*
Porph. on *Ep.* I. 20. 2 *Sosii illo tempore fratres erant bibliopolae celeberrimi*
but on 345 he says *antea...erant*, and there is no other information
on them. The length of the first vowel, in spite of ps.-Acro's assertion,
is not certain. Dio Cassius transliterates the names of C. Sosius and
Q. Sosius Senecio by Σόσιος or Σόσσιος, cf. *R-E* III A. 1176, 1180;
W. Schulze, *Eigennamen*, p. 425. But note *Sosis* in ps.-Acro's report
and codd. BCK al. (Keller, *Epil.* p. 764).

mare transit: the acc. as *Ep.* I. 6. 59, cf. D. Bo, *Hor. Op.* III. 117.
At *Ep.* I. 20. 13 sales to Africa or Spain are forecast when the book
has been well read at home; they are pictured there as flight or exile.
C. II. 20. 13–20 sounds a different note. Cf. Marquardt–Mau, *Das*
Privatleben d. Römer, 828. E. Auerbach, *Literary Language and its Public*
in Late Antiquity (Eng. Tr. 1965), cites this and similar passages at p. 238,
and comments on 'the wide range of the literary public in the first
imperial century'.

346 *longum:* proleptic, unlike *S.* II. 2. 118, *Ep.* I. 3. 8, II. 1. 159; not
longum noto (H. Schütz). The adj., redundant with *prorogat*, strongly
emphasizes the length of time.

Commentary

(4) ('poeta perfectus' and 'poeta uesanus', 347–476, cf. above 308 'quo uirtus, quo ferat error')

In a sense this section corresponds to the 'table of contents', 308 *quo uirtus, quo ferat error. uirtus* is perfection or ideal, the fulfilment of the true nature of a thing or person, Greek ἀρετή. This is the notion underlying the *summus orator* of Cicero: *Or.* 3 (*quod eloquentiae genus*) *summum et perfectissimum iudicem*, 7 *in summo oratore fingendo talem informabo qualis fortasse nemo fuit. non enim quaero quis fuerit, sed quid sit illud quo nihil esse possit praestantius*, etc., 8 *nihil esse in ullo genere tam pulchrum quo non pulchrius id sit unde illud ut ex ore aliquo quasi imago exprimatur*, etc. Quintilian's *perfectus orator*, *I.O.* XII, may be compared. Greek influence would at this stage of Roman development suggest the Greek notion of ἀρετή, or τέλος, which H. has in mind at 308 *quo uirtus...ferat*. E. Norden, *H*, XL (1905), 504 n. 2, quoted Stoic writings for τέλειος ῥήτωρ and his counterpart, ἀτελής. He was able to note Philod. *Rhet.* I, p. 5, II, p. 127; ἀρετή (or τέλος) as a literary term however was not noted by him because he wrote before Jensen had made available large portions of Philodemus' *Poem.* v. There not only τέλειος appears in literary nomenclature, e.g. 7. 29 f. τ[έ]λ[ει]ος δὲ καὶ ἀγαθὸς ποιητής, but ἀρετή of poem or poet, thus Praxiphanes 9. 28–30 Πρα[ξ]ιφάνης...λέγει περὶ τῆς ἀρετῆς ἐν [τ]ῶι πρώτωι περὶ ποιη[μά]των, Neopt. 13. 8–10 πρὸς ἀρε[τὴν δεῖν τ]ῶι τελείωι ποι[ητῆι] κτλ., also Philod. 22. 35–23. 1 τῆς ἀρετῆς ἐστηκότες ὑπόκεινται σκ[οπ]οί, et al.

But for an understanding of H. it is essential to clarify what is meant by the statement that this 'section' corresponds to 308 *quo uirtus quo ferat error*. In making this statement, *H*, XL (1905), 502 ff., Norden was intent on laying bare the doctrinal structure hidden behind the *Ars*. So he subdivided 347 ff., (1) 347–407 on the postulate of perfection, (2) 408–52, followed by the satirical epilogue 453–76, on how to fulfil this postulate. Norden pointed to certain structural similarities with rhetorical criticism. But that procedure, by analogy, may tell us something about the Horatian tradition, little about H. For the poet that literary tradition is no more than a stimulant, which prompts his reactions. In the final part of the poem, perhaps more than anywhere else, he is concerned to be specific and particular, not general and abstract. Hence he breaks up the large and lumpy abstractions which his tradition offered him. That procedure enabled him to instil life into the small constituent parts thus resulting. A unity arises not from subject headings but from the inward relation of these elements. For that reason, at *Prol.* 258–60, I have followed the Horatian hints rather than the hints of the literary tradition, and have separated off eight contexts, each with a traditional core to it, and all related to the announcement, *docebo...quo uirtus, quo ferat error.* Below I number H.'s 'subsections' according to the small contexts which he has created. Disconcertingly to the reader who demands a prosaic argument, H. does not aid him by placing each context under the heading of an overriding abstraction. Thus he does not say, as does Norden, *loc. cit.* p. 502, '347–407: although faultlessness is unattainable (347–65) yet mediocrity condemns the poet (366–78, 379–90). For poetry is something majestic and sacred (391–407).' The matter is more complex, and more interesting, than that. The unity of this and other pieces of poetry can be described but it cannot be restated by a somewhat trite logicality. This is no harsh criticism of Norden, whose contribution to unriddling the *Ars* is second to none.

(a) Two notions of poetic fault, 347–60

As an approach to the ideal of *perfectus poeta* the notion of faults is considered. What is the kind of perfection to be aimed at? Which faults (*delicta, uitia*) are venial, which nullify a poet? To let an exclusion of ἁμαρτήματα precede ἀρετή seems to have been a method adopted elsewhere in technical discussion; cf. ps.-Long. *Subl.* 1 ff., Quint. *I.O.* XII. 1. 19 ff. But the early chapters of Longinus deal with actual faults, not with oversight. That problem, as Norden realized (*loc. cit.* pp. 504 f. n. 3),

is dealt with in a later place of Longinus, ch. 33, which needs
to be compared with the present section.

347 *sunt*, etc.: this is not an interlocutor's protest, answered at
351 ff., as Keller thought.

delicta: also 442, like *culpa*, is a stronger word and less terminological
than *uitium*, cf. 31 *in uitium ducit culpae fuga*, 354 *peccat*. I am unable
here to find the difference in meaning between *delicta* and *peccata*
asserted by Rostagni; the difference lies in the context.

(delic)ta ta(men): Quintilian says at *I.O.* IX. 4. 41 *uidendum . . .ne
syllaba uerbi prioris ultima et prima sequentis consonet.* Citing Quintilian,
N. I. Herescu (*RP*, 3ᵐᵉ sér. XXIV (1946), 74f.) concludes that the
sequence *-ta ta-* is a *delictum* which H. exemplified in the manner
asserted by J. Marouzeau, *RP*, n.s. L (1926), 110 and elsewhere—
l'exemple joint au précepte. This strikes me as unlikely; see 36 n. above.

tamen according to Wickham is explained not by any single preceding statement but by the general picture of perfection drawn in
the last section. This is true, except that an idea of perfection *is* set
up in the last two verses, and perfection is now considered from a
different viewpoint. *tamen* therefore as much as the verse as a whole
makes a transition from one context to another.

ignouisse: for the perf. inf. see above 98 n. *tetigisse.*

uelimus: an unemphatic and unspecified 'we', cf. 331 *speremus*, and
contrast 11 *scimus . . .petimusque damusque*, which is more personal, and
24–5 *maxima pars uatum . . .decipimur*, 272–4 *ego et uos | scimus . . .
callemus*, which are more specific.

348–50 A poetically effective, 'incomplete', comparison brings in
two other arts to clarify H.'s point by juxtaposition and illustration.
Of these, archery is often used in philosophy, specially Stoic, to
illustrate achievement and fault. The proposition in the preceding
verse is general—'there are venial faults'—although the reference to
poetry may be assumed. Then the weaknesses are explained in the
cases of the string player and archer, but not applied to the main
topic. So that when H. returns to poetry all emphasis can fall on the
new notion of high achievement (*ubi plura nitent*, 351), which alone
matters. The negative aspect (there are venial faults in poetry as
well) comes thereafter, understated since this negative conclusion has
already been implied, and subserves the positive.

nam, explanatory and elliptic, introduces the illustrations, but the
venial character of the offence remains unexpressed until we come to
351–3, where the application to poetry is made and this notion has
its proper place.

(*sonum*) *reddit* 'render', cf. above 158 n., sc. *semper* from the corresponding clause 350, but cf. 349 n.

manus et mens, the two nouns are combined in various ways elsewhere, e.g. Cic. *De Or.* 1. 194 *ab alienis mentes, oculos, manus abstinere*, Liv. xxxix. 16. 1 *si a facinoribus manus, mentem a fraudibus abstinuissent*, but here form an alliterative pair like 42 *uirtus. . .et uenus*.

349 The verse is highly suspect. (1) *persaepe*. L. Mueller observes that this is the only instance in the *Epistles* and *Ars* (apart, that is, from *A.P.* 7 *persimilem*, which he overlooked) of an adj. or adv. compounded with *per* = 'very'; B. Axelson, *Unpoet. Wörter*, 38, notes the extreme rarity of these compounds in Augustan verse. In H. all the other instances occur in the *Satires* and one in the *Epodes*: *perfacilis permagnus permulta perpauca perraro*, and *persaepe* itself in *Epod.* 14. 11, *S.* 1. 2. 82, 3. 10. This observation would be insufficient grounds for a black mark were it not for its coincidence with the wrong sense—'very often'. Commentators render the word by '*nur zu oft*', K.–H., '*trop souvent*', Lejay; what is required is 'occasionally', cf. 350 *nec semper*, 351 *paucis* as contrasted with 354 *usque*, 356 *semper*, 357 *multum*, which seems to invalidate the transmitted text. But *persaepe* resists emendation. (2) A. Platt, *CR*, IV (1890), 50, objects to the whole verse because it describes not a small but a serious fault. Moreover the omission in 348 of *semper* is intolerable if the qualifying word is postponed until 350; *persaepe*, 349, cannot take its place. But if 350 immediately follows 348, *semper* can ἀπὸ κοινοῦ qualify both *neque. . .reddit*, 348, and *nec. . .feriet*, 350. I cannot counter these objections. This verse, even more than 178, is likely to be spurious. It is best explained as an old descriptive interpolation.

350 The personification of *chorda*, begun as a corollary of *manus et mens*, is complete in *minabitur arcus*—apt in both cases, the instruments as it were refusing compliance.

quodcumque minabitur here differs from *Epod.* 9. 9 and *C.* 1. 28. 25 in that an inf. has to be understood from *feriet*. Madvig, *Adv. Crit.* 1. 68 found it intolerably hard to supply *se percussurum esse*, and proposed *cuicumque* (*quoicumque*, he thought), on the basis, as he assumed, of MS evidence. This may be smoother. There is however, Wilkins noted, no such evidence in any of the major MSS, but the alteration would be slight. What makes against it is that no full acc. + inf. need be understood (for instances of the inf. see *TLL*, VIII. 1030. 11 ff.) and *quodcumque* 'whatever aim' is preferable to the personal obj. The ellipsis is easy and requires no comment. Those who think otherwise may consider L. Mueller's examples.

351 *uerum:* cf. 225 n. The particle does not here introduce an interlocutor's objection, nor indeed H.'s answer to an assumed interlocutor in 347–50.

nitent: cf. 150 n.

352 *offendar:* cf. 248 n., 376 n., and the same verb in a similar argument at Cic. *De Or.* I. 259.

maculis here first attested in application to style, cf. Quint. *I.O.* VIII. 3. 18 *in oratione nitida notabile humilius uerbum et uelut macula,* 5. 28 also with *uelut.* But the word is frequently applied to religious and moral pollution, *TLL*, VIII. 25. 84 ff.

quas . . .fudit is realistic, the metaphor not being dead as in the tag, 'he has blotted his copy-book'. In *TLL*, VI. 1. 1563. 61 this use is rightly called a trope, but the passage is oddly placed under '*res liquidas sim.*' '*quae a nasis effunduntur*'.

aut. . . | (*aut*) as though there were a logical juxtaposition.

incuria: inattention responsible for a momentary slip, not the inability to take trouble impugned 261, 290–1. This permissiveness, as Norden has shown *loc. cit.*, is embedded in speculations on the *perfectus artifex:* ps.-Long. *Subl.* 33. 4 (on Homer and other great writers) οὐχ ἁμαρτήματα μᾶλλον αὐτὰ ἑκούσια καλῶν ἢ παροράματα δι' ἀμέλειαν εἰκῆ που καὶ ὡς ἔτυχεν ὑπὸ μεγαλοφυΐας ἀνεπιστάτως παρενηνεγμένα, Quint. *I.O.* X. 1. 24 (*neque*) *omnia quae optimi auctores dixerint utique esse perfecta. nam et labuntur aliquando et oneri cedunt . . .; nonnumquam fatigantur,* 2. 9 *cum in his quos maximos adhuc nouimus nemo sit inuentus in quo nihil aut desideretur aut reprehendatur,* XII. 1. 20, see below 359 n. Longinus however regards risks as a *necessary* concomitant of greatness (33. 2), cf. Plato, *Rep.* VI. 497 d τὰ . . .μεγάλα πάντα ἐπισφαλῆ. So does, as O. Immisch, p. 190, and D. A. Russell (ps.-Long. *ad l.*) note, Pompeius Geminus, the addressee of Dion. Hal.'s essay: *Pomp.* 2. 15 (ed. Us.–Ra. II. 231) ἐν οἷς καὶ σφάλλεσθαί ἐστιν ἀναγκαῖον. These are ideas floating about during the first century; they must have been well known to H. One needs therefore to be aware of his deliberate coolness towards these aspirations. He is willing to make allowances for occasional lapses in Homer; he is not willing to share romantic admiration of 'necessary faults'. This is why O. Immisch's '*Erhabenheitslehre*' does not ring true in the *Ars*; H.'s dislike of this kind of romanticism may be one of several motives for his 'Aristotelianism'. Yet H. goes his own way. A supreme craftsman himself, he recognizes mistakes when he sees them. The reader of the *Poetics* is hardly aware that such lapses occur, provided he follow the philosopher's advice. These matters look different to a poet.

353 *humana...natura:* this simply amounts to *errare* (or *errasse*) *humanum est,* cf. A. Otto, *Sprichwörter,* 165 (3). This kind of excuse confirms the impression of the last verse, for H. argues it is human, not noble, to err.

quid ergo est? Lambinus said, '*quid ergo?*' *nonnulli libri habent* '*quid ergo est?*'. *ego nihil muto*; contrast Cruquius cited above p. 50. Bentley restored *est* from the MSS (only some *Itali* in fact offer *quid ergo?*). Although there are a few instances of *quid ergo?* preceding an affirmative clause, classical not only Ciceronian usage endorses *quid ergo?* in argument before questions, but *quid ergo est?* before an affirmative clause, cf. *TLL,* v. 2. 764. 82 ff., 765. 27 ff., 37 ff., 57 ff. The present passage (with a misprint in the ref.) is rightly listed *ibid.* 765. 49.

354–60 The distinction between habitual and occasional mistakes is now made, the former interpreted as poetic nullity set off by a few successes, the latter as excellence achieved with a few minor faults. This as before takes the form of a comparison between other arts (*ut*) and poetry (*sic*). But again the comparison prefers essentials to external neatness. The other arts contribute only the warning example of the habitual botcher; the new and decisive aspects appear only when H. returns to poetry. This is a feature of many Horatian comparisons.

354 *scriptor...librarius:* L. Mueller notes that *scriptor* in H. = 'poet', and hence to become 'scribe' receives the qualifying label *librarius,* 'writer of books'; H. avoids the prosaic *scriba.* Cicero has both, *scriptor* being scribe or author, rarely as at *Arch.* 18 used of poets. Cf. Fest. 333 (M.) *scribas proprio nomine antiqui* et librarios et poetas *uocabant; at nunc dicuntur scribae quidem librari qui rationes publicas scribunt in tabulis,* etc.

peccat idem: for the verb see above 347 n. *delicta,* for the acc. *S.* 1. 3. 115 *tantundemque ut peccet idemque,* 140 *si quid peccaro, C.* III. 27. 19–20 *quid...* | *peccet,* Cic. *N.D.* 1. 31 *Xenophon...eadem fere peccat*; cf. Kühner–Stegmann, 1. 279 f.

usque: the old adverbial usage, 'throughout', preserved in poetry and a favourite with H.

355 *quamuis est:* ps.-Acro, *pro eo quod est* '*quamuis sit*' *propter cacenfaton,* etc. The explanation is doubly implausible, because of the cloudiness of the term *cacemphaton* (see above 36 n.), and in view of the fact that of the 18 certain cases of *quamuis*+verb 13 have the indic., few of which are open to ps.-Acro's explanation. Cf. N. di Lorenzo, *Boll. Fil. Cl.* XII (1906), 13 ff.

ut citharoedus: ς (Bentley), *et c.* rell. codd. While no certainty is attainable, the anaphora of *ut,* which is *suauior* and *uiuidior* as Bentley says, is commended by a number of instances, among them those of *utque* or *et ut*, thus *ut–utque* at *S.* I. 2. 38–9, 4. 109, II. 1. 50, thus *ut–et ut* at *S.* II. 4. 13, and *ut–ut* (*–ut*) at *S.* I. 3. 129–30, II. 5. 43, *Ep.* I. 1. 20–1, 13. 13–15, II. 1. 172.

356 *oberrat:* poetic and Silver Latin, vividly pictures the shifting of the finger (*ob-*) to the wrong place *chorda...eadem,* the verb first known from this passage, next in Silver Latin.

357–60 A rigid application of the principle borrowed from the other arts—occasional mistakes venial, botching unforgivable— would be tedious and jejune. Instead H. sees the case in personal terms, concretely. He identifies the latter position with a famous botcher among poets, and in the sequel identifies the former with the supreme poet, Homer. He then dialectically reverses the position, not just condemning the botcher's work but expressing amused surprise when he gets one or two things right. By the same token he does not simply forgive Homer his occasional lapses, but professes to be annoyed when Homer, very occasionally, nods. Hence he must call himself and others to order and assert reason in the face of emotional confusion: 'an occasional nap over a long work is right and proper'. There is nothing wrong with the text, the sequence of thought is apt and lively, provided H.'s dialectical process is understood.

357 *multum:* the neut. adj. with *cessat* is used adverbially as is *idem* (354 n.), e.g. *Epod.* 17. 20 *amata nautis multum, S.* I. 3. 57, II. 3. 320, *Ep.* I. 3. 15, 6. 52, above 241 *sudet multum frustraque laboret;* also with adj. as *S.* II. 3. 147 *medicus multum celer.* Cf. such colloquialisms as Cic. *Att.* I. 1. 5 *multum te amamus.*

cessat: frequent in H. and elsewhere for 'hang back, default'; *cessator* is a shirker, *S.* II. 7. 100. The verb is used in the context of literary perfection to indicate (as it does here) lapses: Quint. *I.O.* I. 10. 4 (*oratoris*) *perfecti illius ex nulla parte cessantis,* II. 8. 10.

fit Choerilus: he becomes Choerilus as it were, not only like C., see e.g. *Ep.* I. 2. 41–2 *qui...prorogat horam,* | *rusticus expectat,* not *ut rusticus,* and below 476 n.

Choerilus: 'the obscure C. of the fourth century' (L. P. Wilkinson, *Horace*[2], p. 91 n. 1)—obscure in one sense but not in another. For C., one of the highly paid court poets of Alexander of Macedon, had entered the ancient tradition as an undoubted competitor for the position of *pessimus poeta;* cf. Crusius, *R-E,* III. 2361. 58 ff. He is mentioned in *Ep.* II. 1, where H. turns his own criticism of Alexander's regrettable taste into a tactful if pointed comparison with Augustus, 232–4 *gratus Alexandro regi magno fuit ille* | *Choerilus, incultis qui uersibus et male natis* | *rettulit acceptos, regale nomisma, Philippos,* cf. *Prol.* 208.

A considerable mythology attaches to the name; the specimens in Porphyrion's and ps.-Acro's notes on the two passages make amusing reading. The present passage can be explained fully if it is set in the context of Hellenistic criticism—another link with Alexandrianism, cf. Heinze and Rostagni *ad l.*, O. Immisch, pp. 187–92 (his discussion again vitiated by the desire to find a Platonizing doctrine of the Sublime in the *Ars*). The neo-Platonist Hermias of the fifth century in a note on Plato, *Phaedr.* 245 a ('the madness of the muses') contrasts the poetry of inspiration with the poetry of 'art' (112, pp. 98. 28 ff. ed. P. Couvreur, 1901) τί γὰρ ὅμοιον ἡ Χοιρίλου καὶ Καλλιμάχου ποίησις πρὸς τὴν Ὁμήρου ἢ Πινδάρου;. This comment classes Choerilus with Callimachus as a (Hellenistic) man of τέχνη and contrasts both with the poets of inspiration, Homer and Pindar—a significant Alexandrian echo. Philod. *Poem.*, *HV²*, VI. 174. 4 ff. is even more relevant, and was brought into Horatian criticism by Usener, *RM*, XLIII (1888), 150 and Kiessling (1889): κ[ατ]ὰ [τ]ὸ συνέχ[ο]ν καὶ κυ[ρι]ώτα[τον δὲ] τῶν ἐμ πο[η]τ[ι]κῆ[ι] δ[ια]φέρειν Χοιρί[λ]ον κ[αὶ] Ἀναξιμένην Ὁμήρο[υ], καὶ Καρκίνον...Ε]ὐρειπίδου, καὶ τοὺς ἄλ[λου]ς τοὺς πονηροὺς ἐμ ποιητικῆι [τ]ῶ̣[ν] ἀ[ρίστων], cf. T. Gomperz 'Philod. und die ästh. Schr. der Herc. Bibliothek', *SBAW*, CXXIII (1891), 37. Here Choerilus, Anaximenes, and others are confronted as πονηροί, *mali poetae*, of the epic genre with Homer as ἄριστος, *bonus* or *summus*, a striking parallel to the *Ars*.

ille: Peerlkamp proposed the punctuation *Choerilus, ille | quem...*, attractive in isolation but unlikely in the context and excluded by *ille Choerilus...qui* in the parallel passage of the *Augustus*, cited in the last n.

358 *bis terue* BK, *bis terque* cett. Although Bentley tended to change *-que* and *-ue* oftener than is warranted (cf. Housman on Man. I. 475, III. 15), I have no doubt that he was right here to correct the vulgate of his time and bring *-ue*, known to him only from Ox. Reg., into the text; cf. ps.-Acro *duos uel tres uersus elegantes*. For *bis terue* means 'at most two or three times', Cic. *Fam.* II. I. I (*-ue* or *-ne* in the MSS), cf. Mart. X. 11. 6 *terue quaterue* (*-que* MSS, cf. M. Haupt, *Opusc.* III. 584); and this must be the meaning here—for the sense cf. *Ep.* II. I. 73–4. On the other hand *bis terque* is 'several times over' as at *Epod.* 5. 33, *A.P.* 440, Cic. *Qu. F.* III. 6 (8). 6, and the passages listed in Forcellini, and Keller, *Epil.* 765, especially Stat. *Silv.* IV. 2. 58 since it would have been a poor compliment to Domitian if Statius had wished him 'another year or two' beyond Vespasian's age. Other locutions may be compared: *ter et amplius, ter et quater, ter quaterque* in H., *terque*

Commentary

quaterque in Virgil. Editors now accept the right reading, but Lejay and later Villeneuve should not have stood out.

bonum: K.–H. 359 n. on *bonus Homerus*, '*epitheton perpetuum* as different from *bis terue bonus Choerilus*'. *bonus poeta* can take the place of *perfectus* even in critical writings, e.g. Cic. *De Or.* ii. 194 *poetam bonum neminem . . . sine inflammatione animorum existere posse*, Tac. *Dial.* 10. 1 *mediocres poetas nemo non nouit, bonos pauci.* So also *bonus orator*, e.g. Cic. *De Or.* i. 118. For other instances '*de eis qui in arte sua et negotio perfecti sunt*', see *TLL*, ii. 2080. 42 ff. This will have to be borne in mind for judging the nuance of *bonus . . . Homerus* in the next verse.

cum risu: S. i. 8. 50 *cum magno risuque iocoque*.

et idem consummates the paradox, cf. 357–60 n. Some earlier editors tried to eliminate the apparent contradiction by emending *et* to *ut*, defended by L. Mueller and others, or else *ut* for *et* and *indignor* interrogative: 'but should I be annoyed when, etc.?' (O. Ribbeck, p. 240). Both are contradicted by the adversative *uerum* 360, see below.

359 *indignor:* contrast 351–2 *non . . . offendar*; ps.-Long. *Subl.* 33. 4 ἥκιστα τοῖς πταίσμασιν ('Ομήρου) ἀρεσκόμενος, ὅμως κτλ. Unlike the same verb at *Ep.* ii. 1. 76 it is here coloured by its ironical counterpart *cum risu miror*, 358. H. pretends to admire Choerilus when very occasionally he gets something right, and to feel irked, unreasonably, when Homer gets something wrong. For *indignor* Cic. *Or.* 104 may be compared, *usque eo difficiles ac morosi sumus, ut nobis non satisfaciat ipse Demosthenes; qui quamquam unus eminet*, etc. I see no point in Heinze's speculations about the difference between *indignor* and *offendar*, 352.

quandoque in H. occurs only as a conjunction, 'whenever'. It is archaic, poetic (first in verse known from H.) and Silver and late Latin. The instances in H. are restricted to *C.* iv (1. 17, 2. 34) and the present passage.

bonus: so the whole of the MS tradition but Hier. *Ep.* 84. 8 cites the verse with *magnus* instead of *bonus*. Contrast above 358 *bis terue bonum*, St Jerome's reading would remove this link. *S.* i. 10. 52 *tu nihil in magno . . . reprehendis Homero?* differs in scope; *poeta bonus* or *poeta magnus* occur in two similar passages of Cicero, the former *De Or.* ii. 194 the latter *Div.* i. 80. But *bonus* qualifying a proper name has to be distinguished from the epithet with a noun like *poeta*. It is likely to be predicative here as it is in the case of Choerilus above: Choerilus *quem . . . miror* 'when he is *bonus* on rare occasions'; Homer 'who is indeed *bonus*', or possibly 'in spite of his perfection', *dormitat*.

dormitat Homerus: Quintilian was struck by the likeness of this passage to Cicero's comment on Demosthenes, *I.O.* x. 1. 24 (not even

367

optimi auctores are perfect, cit. above 352 n.) *nonnumquam fatigantur, cum Ciceroni dormitare interim Demosthenes, Horatio uero Homerus ipse uideatur.* He repeats this at XII. 1. 22, adding *nec Cicero Bruto Caluoque* (sc. *uideatur satis esse perfectus*). For the provenance of Cicero's criticism, see Plut. *Cic.* 24. H. would scarcely have applied to Homer what Cicero said about Demosthenes, hence I regard it as *prima facie* probable that both authors were stimulated by Hellenistic criticism of Homer (thus Norden, *loc. cit.* 504 f., n. 3). Cf. ps.-Long. *Subl.* 33. 4 ἁμαρτήματα καὶ Ὁμήρου καὶ τῶν ἄλλων ὅσοι μέγιστοι, and note the likeness between the contexts of Longinus and H., and the unlikeness of their views (above 352 n.).

360 Deletion of this verse was proposed in the last century (C. Hammerstein, L. Mueller) but may now be forgotten; the verse is essential to H.'s poetic argument. It alleges a reason for Homeric faults, which quite differs from mere *incuria*: the size of his task. A large work may be a success as a whole, though it occasionally flags. This defence skirts the notion of the large poetic unity discussed *Prol.* 62 ff. Lucilius' view of Homer is relevant here, IX, frs. 344–7, cf. *Prol.* 64, *qua propter dico: nemo qui culpat Homerum,* | *perpetuo culpat neque quod dixi ante poesin:* | *uersum unum culpat, uerbum, enthymema, (?) poema.* In spite of the similarity the two contexts are not identical.

uerum: cf. 225 n.

operi longo is the prevalent reading of the MSS, *opere in longo* and *opere longo* have some MS authority in H. and in late codd. of St Jerome, who cites the line *Ep.* 84. 8. Was *operi* made to move (perhaps via *opere*) to *opere in* or the reverse? Either construction is grammatically possible, cf. Bentley's n. and the dictionaries. The question is whether the imagery is disturbed when sleep is said to steal upon the poet's *work* (360) after the poet has been said to nod on occasion (359). I do not think that either the conceit *somnus obrepit operi* or the change of viewpoint disturbs the imagery. Both are borne out by Bentley's parallel from Stat. *Theb.* VIII. 216–17 *nox . . . curas* | *obruit et facilis lacrimis obrepere somnus.*

(b) Poetic excellence clarified by a comparison of poetry and painting (cf. Prol. 258), 361–5

Again H. makes an abrupt new start. But the argument itself proceeds, for the capacity to create a poem that will stand up to repeated reading is part of poetic *uirtus*, perfection; the point is made manifest by a visual art, where the worth of a

picture is assessed by the method of 'inspection'. Having in
the first words of the section juxtaposed poetry and painting,
H. has no need to dwell on the likeness in detail. The criterion
of repeated close scrutiny is valid for both cases, and belongs
to the context of artistic perfection. A passage in Longinus
provides external support, which to my knowledge has not
yet been claimed. Ps.-Long. *Subl.* 7. 3–4 makes in fact H.'s
point, with the proviso that what in H. is poetic *uirtus* or
bonum is to Longinus' romantic mind the sublime: *haec deciens
repetita placebit*, in H.; τοῦτο γὰρ τῷ ὄντι μέγα οὗ πολλὴ μὲν
ἡ ἀναθεώρησις in Longinus.

The comparison of poetry and the fine arts, especially
painting, is as old as literary theory. Simonides, who pre-
empts various notions rationalized, or further rationalized, by
the Sophists, called a picture silent poetry and poetry a
speaking picture (Plut. *Mor.* 17 f, 58 b, 346 f, al.). As early as
400 B.C. the comparison was familiar; the author of the
Δισσοὶ Λόγοι uses it (3. 10) for a comment on the illusionist effect,
ἐξαπατᾶν, of painting and tragedy. Plato and Aristotle are
concerned above all with two aspects of the comparison, the
related or 'organic' character of the parts of a work of art or
poetry and, secondly, the character of *mimesis*, that is the kind
of reality an artefact or poem may possess. Hellenistic literary
discussion seems to have made these notions so familiar that
they could be carried into neighbouring fields: Polyb. 1. 3. 4
dilates on the organic character of history, σωματοειδῆ...
ἱστορίαν, and its unity, cf. F. W. Walbank *ad l.* In Rome these
notions were common literary property. The writer *Ad Her.*
IV. 39 can quote Simonides' dictum without much ado,
poema loquens pictura, pictura tacitum poema debet esse. Cicero, the
Greek critics of the Augustan age like Dion. Hal., and later
Quintilian and others use them freely, see H. Nettleship,
Lectures, etc. II. 54–6, K. Borinski, *Die Antike in Poetik und
Kunsttheorie*, I (1914), 97, 183 ff., R. G. Austin on Quint. *I.O.*
XII, ch. 10.

H. then may have picked up these notions from contemporary or slightly older writers, Roman or Greek; but equally, and more convincingly for the reasons I have suggested throughout this book, he may have drawn on Hellenistic literary theory. He employs the comparison twice. At the beginning of the *Ars*, 1 ff., and intermittently up to 40, painting is made to illustrate the notion of unity, or its lack. This is one of the ways in which Plato and Aristotle employ the comparison, and in my notes on the first part of the poem I have given my reasons for believing that H. uses the Aristotelian notion of artistic unity. In the present passage his aim is simpler. Mastery in painting and poetry alike can be such as to make its creations withstand and reward repeated inspection. He does not say that such a work is 'better' than that which bears inspection only once. But this clearly is the result of the comparison. 364 *quae non formidat acumen* and 365 *deciens repetita placebit* proclaim this assessment more memorably than if he had actually stated it.

Some have commended H.'s broadmindedness. He is said to acknowledge the value of impressionist painting, and demand that such pictures should be viewed from afar. But few painters, however impressionist, would agree that their pictures should 'please only once'. H. does not acknowledge the value of a painting that pleases only once. Yet the error unaccountably persists in modern writing on the history of art. Thus an otherwise competent and illuminating article by Renselaer W. Lee, '*Ut pictura poesis*: The humanistic theory of painting', *The Art Bulletin*, xxii (1940), 199. There H. is oddly said to plead 'for further flexibility in critical judgment by declaring in effect that poetry should be compared to a painting which exhibits not merely a detailed style that requires close scrutiny but also a broad impressionistic style that will not please unless viewed from a distance'.

'*ut pictura poesis*' was sufficiently memorable to serve as a base for far-reaching assertions on the relation of the arts. Of these it is innocent, if it is not actually opposed to them. In the Italian Renaissance H.'s saying was used as if it were '*ut poesis pictura*', to inculcate the superiority of painting to poetry, music, and the rest. In Lessing's *Laokoon* it was made to point the inherent difference rather than likeness between poetry and painting. The debates thus provoked tended to gain in scope and interest as the distance from the original Horatian context increased. [For bibliography and discussion knowledgeable friends refer me to A. Blunt, *Artistic theory in Italy 1450–1600* (Oxford, 1940), Renselaer W. Lee, *loc. cit.* XXII, 197–296, XXIII, 332–5, E. S. King, 'Ingres as Classicist', *Jour. of the Walters Art Gallery*, V (1942), 69–113, E. Panofsky, *Galileo as a Critic of the Arts* (1954), p. 3.]

361 The layout of the verse puzzled ancient students of the poem: the punctuation in the scholia and MSS is erroneous. Meineke's punctuation, *ut pictura, poesis erit,* etc., while avoiding a general statement (*ut pictura poesis* to be limited presently to a specific similarity) is, I think, excluded because it predicates of *poesis* what in fact only belongs to *pictura*—the distance of viewing. For H. is not discussing modes of viewing pictures but the inherent quality that makes for a repeated reading of poems (365). He leads the reader to this quality through illustrating two different ways of viewing pictures, of which only one is approved. Hence the now current punctuation is correct, *ut pictura poesis:,* etc. The exaggerated generality is a deliberate puzzle, which is not fully cleared up until 365.

poesis 'poem', the word here only in H. This is not the technical term of the literary critics, e.g. Lucil. cit. 360 n., *Prol.* 29 ff., 58 ff., 247.

erit, quae,—thus Dacier, later Orelli and other editors in the nineteenth century. This I regard as the only punctuation excluding the locution *est qui,* which the sequel shows to be excluded. K.–H. say, '*pictura* is subject'. The subject is more likely to be (*pictura*) *quaedam,* the pronoun being placed ἀπὸ κοινοῦ in the next verse. Without this assumption the nonsensical order *pictura . . ., et quaedam* (*pictura*) is obtained. The sentence then is, I think, *erit (pictura quaedam), quae, si propius stes, te capiat magis; et quaedam (quae te capiat magis), si longius abstes*; double *haec* in 363 takes up this (*quaedam*)—*quaedam*. A fuller form of this idiom would have *quidam* twice over, = 'some— others', as Cic. *Top.* 79 quibusdam *quaestionibus alios,* quibusdam *alios esse aptiores locos,* Liv. XXVIII. 12. 10 *in Hispania res* quadam ex parte eandem fortunam, quadam *longe disparem habebant,* XLI. 20. 4 quidam . . .

quidam; cf. 1. 54. 8 *multi*..., *quidam, in quibus*, etc., XXXVII. 20. 5 *pars*...*pars*...*quidam*, XXVIII. 30. 2 *maxima parte*...*quibusdam*, XLV, 10. 14 *quidam*...*alii*, etc.

362 *capiat:* as *S.* 1. 4. 28 *hunc capit argenti splendor.*

quaedam: see 361 n.; *quae iam* implausibly L. Mueller in order to avoid the grammatical difficulty discussed above.

abstes: aptes B (*apstes* Keller), perhaps an ἅπαξ λεγόμενον, since trans. *abstare*, Pl. *Trin.* 265 (K.–H. and *TLL*, 1. 198. 45), is implausible, and other alleged instances of the intrans. usage are either false (Lucan VI. 720 proposed by Wölfflin) or dubious (Hor. *Ep.* 1. 18. 58, Bentley, and Sil. XII. 480, L. Bauer). Such compounds as *abesse, amouere*, and Greek ἀφίσταμαι, may have assisted the formation; and the noun *abstantia*, 'distance' (Vitr. IX. 1. 11), existed.

This evidence does not move me to replace *abstes* by *absis* (J. P. Postgate, *CQ*, IV (1910), 110), still less by *adstes* �. With the MS readings, 362 and 361 rhyme, cf. 177 n. on *uiriles.*

363 replaces (*quaedam*)...*quaedam* by *haec*...*haec.* Chiastically *longius* (362) is followed by *obscurum* whereas *sub luce* corresponds to *propius.* This is not, as many readers, especially historians of art, have assumed, an exercise in impressionistic art criticism. The view from afar is condemned. The picture which *amat obscurum* is the picture, and later the poem, which does not stand up to repeated inspection; it is seen and discarded.

sub luce, πρὸς αὐγάς, ps.-Long. *Subl.* 3. 1 (cit. K.–H.).

364 *iudicis:* the critic, cf. 244, 263, 387, *S.* 1. 10. 38, II. 1. 84.

365 *deciens:* see 294 n.

repetita: cf. *S.* 1. 10. 72.

(c) Excellence and mediocrity in the liberal and the useful arts, 366–78

Norden's researches have uncovered at any rate one clear and suggestive parallel to these contentions, Cicero's *perfectus orator*, restated by Quint. *I.O.* XII; cf. Norden, *H*, XL (1905), 502–5 (and following his lead, Heinze and Rostagni *ad l.*), citing *De Or.* I. 117–18, II. 185, III. 213, *Brut.* 193; for a different aspect, see *De Or.* I. 259. Cicero is aware that a higher standard of achievement is demanded in poetry, and certain other arts, than in utilitarian pursuits, which are also called *artes.* He is concerned to extend to rhetoric that standard, without wishing to discourage weaker practitioners. H. does not accept Cicero's submission; rhetoric and jurisprudence, he thinks, are practical arts in which a useful mediocrity has a place; poetry is not such an art. What H. and Cicero share in this matter is not 'a common rhetorical environing atmosphere' (C. G. Fiske, *Wisc. St.* xxvii (1929), 38). Rather H.'s theorizing must be close to the original setting of the argument about poetry and the fine arts, which has little or no place for rhetoric. Cicero on the other hand must be secondary since he is extending to rhetoric the quality of the finer arts, and is hoping to compromise at the same time. The speculative setting from which the Horatian (and at the remove just stated, the Ciceronian) distinction of *artes* derives is Aristotle's analysis of τέχναι, in particular his distinction between practical and the fine arts, τἀναγκαῖα, as opposed to διαγωγή or τὰ εἰς εὐσχημοσύνην καὶ περιουσίαν and the like, e.g. *Met.* 1. 2, 982 b 23, where the practical and fine arts are grouped together over against 'theory', and *Pol.* vii. 10, 1329 b 27 ff., or, more important, viii, chs. 3 ff., where the two are set apart from each other. But H.'s model has different aims; it must have been developed in the early Hellenistic age from these Aristotelian beginnings, and is not preserved. Certain similarities with Longinus also need to be taken into account, see below 372 n.

[The specific problem of this note has not, to my knowledge, been raised before. I have however found helpful some recent work on the Aristotelian notions of τέχνη. For the triad, in the *Metaphysics*, of Arts necessary, fine, and philosophic, see W. Jaeger, *SI*, xxvii–xxviii (1956), 135 (= *Scr. Min.* ii. 488); for Ar. *Pol.* viii, chs. 3 ff., see E. Koller, *MH*, xiii (1956), 1–37, 94–124, F. Solmsen, *RM*, lvii (1964), 193–220. I have omitted Platonic references as not directly relevant, but *Epinomis*, 974 d ff. may be recalled because of the distinction between 'necessary' and 'fine' (i.e. mimetic) arts, which there appears as part of a Platonizing analysis of τέχναι. For possible pre-Socratic antecedents of the Aristotelian schema see E. Koller, *loc. cit.* 34, and the important article by F. Heinimann, 'Eine

vorplatonische Theorie der Techne', *MH*, xviii (1961), 118
n. 58.]

366 *o maior iuuenum:* for addresses to the Pisos, cf. above 6 n. The
two *iuuenes* together were addressed at 24. Here for the first time the
elder of the two is singled out and one may speculate on the reasons
for the address in this section, since H.'s placing of his addressees'
names is deliberate and adroit. Cf. below 385–90, 406–7.

quamuis+indic., cf. 355 n.

uoce paterna: cf. 388 *patris.*

367 *fingeris ad:* of training. *C.* iii. 6. 22 the young girl training
herself in objectionable *artes*, *Ep.* 1. 2. 64 the training of a horse by
the *magister.* The fashioning or training to a standard is expressed by
ad: Cic. *De Or.* iii. 58 (*artes*) *quae repertae sunt ut puerorum mentes ad
humanitatem fingerentur atque uirtutem*, cf. Sen. *Ep.* 92. 29 *non est adhuc
bonus, sed in bonum fingitur*; *TLL*, vi. 1. 733. 25 ff.

rectum: the moral notion may not be absent but only the poetic is
fully germane, cf. 25 n., 309.

(*quamuis*) *per te sapis* recalls *Ep.* 1. 17. 1 *quamuis, Scaeua, satis per te
tibi consulis.* For *sapere*, see 309 n. Lucil. fr. 617 (Marx) *tuam probatam mi
et spectatam maxume adulescentiam* may be relevant here, but its context
is unknown. Cf. below on 388.

368 (*tibi dictum*) *tolle memor: tibi* seems to be ἀπὸ κοινοῦ with *dictum*
and *tolle.* The pronouncement 368–73 is introduced not only by the
address, *o maior iuuenum*, but by this solemn epic locution: Virg. *A.*
vi. 377 *cape dicta memor*, cf. Enn. *Ann.* 198 (V.²) *et hoc simul accipe dictum*,
Virg. *A.* iii. 250 *accipite ergo animis atque haec mea figite dicta*, al. Greek
precedents such as those cited 336 n. are familiar, but neither the
Latin nor the Greek instances parallel *tollo.* At *Ep.* 1. 18. 12 *uerba
cadentia tollit* the addition of *cadentia* makes *tollo* a metaphor for
servility.

certis is more emphatic than *quibusdam.* The fairly wide spacing
certis...rebus, with the decisive adjs. interposed, also makes for
emphasis.

medium: cf. 370 *mediocris*, 372 *mediocribus.* This mean is mediocre
and not golden, but I would not call it an 'aesthetic term' (K.–H.).
So *mediocris* and *mediocritas* in the Ciceronian passages cited above
366–78 n., ps.-Long. *Subl.* 33. 2 contrasts ταπεινὰς καὶ μέσας
φύσεις with ὑπερμεγέθεις.

et explanatory: 'by which I mean...'. This serves to enlarge on
the indistinct word *medium.*

369 *recte* 'rightly', without the nuance of *rectum* 366. As frequently

Commentary

in H. the word compresses a qualifying clause into an adv.: *atque id recte conceditur*.

370 combines, as at *Ep.* II. 2. 87, two of the major 'practical' arts at Rome, jurisprudence and rhetoric. This is the view opposed by Cicero.

(*actor*) *causarum:* as Cic. *De Or.* III. 73 *Socratici a se causarum actores . . . separauerunt, Div. in Caec.* 11 *me actorem causae totius esse uoluerunt*, al. *TLL*, I. 446. 61 ff.

uirtute: the significant term *uirtus* (cf. above 308), excellence, occurs in passing, applied to oratory, not to poetry.

diserti: distinguished from *eloquens* in a much-quoted saying of the orator M. Antonius, e.g. Cic. *De Or.* I. 94 *scripsi . . . quodam in libello . . . disertos cognosse me nonnullos, eloquentem adhuc neminem, Or.* 18, al. (*TLL*, V. I. 1377. 71 f.). But elsewhere the two words are frequently synonymous, and used indifferently (*TLL, ibid.* 1377. 74 ff., 1378. 1 ff.). *diserti* is highly laudatory here.

371 The instances follow in reverse order. Messala (Corvinus at *S.* I. 10. 29), the great orator, of roughly the same age as H., probably a little younger, cf. Hanslik, *R-E*, VIII A. 135. 1 ff. But whatever the precise date, he was at least 40 years younger than Cascellius; hence in spite of the present tenses of *abest* and *scit* there is no need to assume a reference to contemporaries. Aulus Cascellius is the eminent lawyer, born *c.* 104 B.C., cf. Jörs, *R-E*, III. 1634. 48 ff. He would have been *c.* 90 about the middle of the last decennium of the century. This is possible, but is not necessary to explain the passage. His expertise (*scit*) must be known still; no more is required, cf. *Prol.* 240 n. 3.

372 *in pretio est.* In view of 299 *pretium nomenque*, 400 *honor et nomen*, 71 *sunt in honore*, the wording scarcely depreciates the value of useful mediocrity; it is the context that does. The same applies to Cic. *De Or.* I. 117 *magno honori fuisse . . . illam ipsam quamcumque assequi potuerat in dicendo mediocritatem*.

mediocribus esse poetis (sc. *non concessere columnae*): the pred. dat. usual with *licet* and inf.—thus in the two relevant Horatian instances, *S.* I. I. 19 *licet esse beatis*, 2. 51 *munifico* (*-um*, uar.l.) *esse licet*—is here transferred to *concedo*, which resembles it in meaning. *TLL*, IV. 16. 37 offers no parallel to this extension with *concedere* and dative with *esse* before Aug. *Ep.* 118. 31 (acc., uar.l.). H. and other Augustan poets extend this idiom further, perhaps under Greek influence; E. Löfstedt, *Syn.* II. 108, notes *Ep.* I. 16. 61 *da iusto sanctoque uideri*. For *mediocris* 'middling', see G. B. A. Fletcher, *Annot. on Tacitus*, 104, apropos of Tac. *Dial.* 10. 1. Again Cicero, and here also Longinus, show similarity of thought: Cic. *De Or.* I. 118 *in eis artibus in quibus . . .*

*quaeritur . . .animi libera quaedam oblectatio, quam diligenter et quam prope
fastidiose iudicamus,* 119 *non uti (orator) eis satis faciat, quibus necesse est, sed
uideatur quibus libere liceat iudicare,* ps.-Long. *Subl.* 33. 4 τὰς μείζονας
ἀρετὰς. . .τὴν τοῦ πρωτείου ψῆφον μᾶλλον ἀεὶ φέρεσθαι. G. C.
Fiske, 'Lucil. and Hor.', *Wisc. St.* vii (1920), 462, has rashly identified
H.'s own known context with the unknown of Lucil. fr. 702 (Marx)
paulo hoc melius quam mediocre, hoc minus malum quam ut pessumum.
Lucilius' context is not likely to have been that of H. in this passage
nor in that cited when Fiske had second thoughts, *ibid.* n. 85; cf.
rather *Prol.* 168.

373 Those who are said to forbid mediocrity are *homines*; up to this
point thought and wording are serious, even solemn. Then there
follows a sudden change of mood: H. is enunciating a cosmic law,
homines suggesting the pair *homines diuosque,* cf. *TLL,* vi. 3. 2875. 49 ff.,
e.g. Cic. *Q. Fr.* ii. 4. 1 *dis hominibusque plaudentibus,* a humorous twist.
Ritter suggests such mercantile patrons as Vertumnus and Janus (*Ep.*
i. 20. 1); perhaps so, but H. claims more. This in turn leads on to the
bookshops, which are more nearly concerned with the 'approval' of
books of verse, cf. above 332, 345 f. Hence the *columnae,* cf. *S.* i. 4. 71
nulla taberna *meos habeat neque* pila *libellos* and Porph. on i. 71 *negat se
libellos suos edere bibliopolis, qui uel tabernas habeant uel armaria apud pilas;*
cf. Mart. i. 117. 10. In comparison there is little plausibility in the
notices of poetic recitations said to be displayed on such pillars (ps.-
Acro on *A.P.* 373), or in the recitations themselves, supposedly indicated by the pillars of a domestic peristyle where such readings might
be given (thus J. Gwynn Griffiths, *CR,* n.s. x (1960), 104). *columnae*
then provides the comic bathos in a tricolon which is marked by
treble anaphora and, at the end, an assonance (*con- col-*): *non homines
non di, non concessere columnae.*

concessere: the 'empirical' perf., aptly, and beside *columnae* humor-
ously, represents H.'s contention as a 'law' proved by experience.
For this use of the tense, see above 10, 343 and the commentators on
S. i. 9. 60, *Ep.* i. 2. 48, 19. 48, and various places in the *Odes;*
Hofmann–Szantyr, 318 f. with bibliography.

374–8 comprise one of H's. comparisons marked by *ut. . .sic*
(*ita*) that are deliberately irregular, and thus more telling because
they draw attention to what matters in the comparison, e.g. above
60–2, 354–60. The whole sentence purports to bring out the high
standards of Cicero's *animi libera quaedam oblectatio* (372 n.). The *ut* cl.
states the desirably useless character of such 'arts' as music and
cookery. The *si* cl. is then left finally to reveal what the comparison
really aims at—in poetry the only alternative to excellence is nullity.

Commentary

374 Music: Cicero's example of a useless art, which therefore by (his and H.'s) definition demands a high standard, is acting: *De Or.* I. 118 audiences need not *in theatro actores malos perpeti* in the same way as they put up with mediocre advocates. Ar. *Pol.* VIII. 3, 1338 a 30 ff. (cit. Norden, *loc. cit.* 504 n. 1) recommends music in education οὐχ ὡς χρησίμην . . . οὐδ' ὡς ἀναγκαίαν ἀλλ' ὡς ἐλευθέριον καὶ καλήν (for the terms, see above 366–78 n.). This is clearly the method of evaluation which prompts the mention of music in this passage, although Aristotle is far from drawing the Ciceronian and Horatian conclusion as to the high degree of achievement in the liberal arts, cf. E. Koller, *loc. cit.* (above 366–78 n.), pp. 112–14. Moreover H. uses the example in his own oblique way. Music is part of an entertainment at dinner and its assessment is coupled with an assessment of the fare offered.

symphonia discors: table music, performed by slaves trained for the purpose and called *symphoniaci*, was a feature of elaborate Roman entertainment from the first century B.C. onward, cf. Abert, *R-E*, IV A. 1169. 59 ff. The conventional name has prompted H.'s Heraclitean oxymoron; at *Ep.* I. 12. 19 *rerum concordia discors* it is imputed to Empedocles' balance between the conflicting principles of νεῖκος and φιλία.

375 is even more realistic. Excellence is demanded for the perfumes supplied to guests at dinner (e.g. *C.* III. 14. 17 *i, pete unguentum, puer, et coronas*, et al.) and for their menu. This concerns the *cenarum . . . artem, S.* II. 4. 35, a parallel well established in ancient discussions of this kind, cf. E. Koller, *loc. cit.* (above 366–78 n.), p. 95. As an illustration of excellence in the liberal arts, and poetry more than any, it is highly ironical and entertaining.

crassum unguentum: Plin. *N.H.* XIII. 2. 15 says that the unguent made of cinnamon fetches prodigious prices; he adds, *unguentorum hoc crassissimum.* On the other hand he reports at ch. 4. 21, with what seems distaste, *sed quosdam crassitudo maxime delectat, spissum appellantes, linique iam non solum perfundi gaudent.* Tastes in perfumes doubtless differed and that perhaps may account for H.'s criticism of 'thick perfumes', though he speaks as if tastes did not differ. Neither usage nor Pliny's discussion bears out ps.-Acro's suggestion that *crassum = mali odoris; nam ut lenem odorem dicimus suauem, ita et crassum malum.*

Sardo cum melle papauer: dessert spoilt by Sardinian honey, which was bitter, Porph. *Corsicum et Sardum mel pessimi saporis est,* Virg. *E.* 7. 41 *Sardoniis . . . amarior herbis.* Roasted seeds of white poppy and honey for dessert *apud antiquos dabatur*, reports Plin. *N.H.* XIX. 53. 168, not much more than half a century later.

Commentary

376 *offendunt:* as S. II. 8. 12–13 *quodque* | *posset cenantis offendere.* Cf. 248, 352 *offendere* in matters aesthetic, and the Ciceronian passage mentioned 352 n.

poterat duci. . .cena: in spite of S. I. 5. 70 *iucunde cenam producimus illam,* scarcely 'prolong', which does not fit two of the three instances. On the other hand the locutions cited for *ducere cenam* 'hold a dinner' (*aeuum* or *uitam d.*) or 'take dinner' (e.g. as *pocula*) do not support it fully. Is *duci* sound?

quia in third place. In H. displacement of *quia* is rare; it occurs only in 4 out of (probably) 34 cases: once, *C.* IV. 9. 28, in the second place of its clause, three times in the third, this passage and above 295, *Ep.* II. 1. 168—all four of them in late work (*Odes* IV, *Augustus*) or work that may be late (*A.P.*).

istis perhaps with a derisory nuance. This pronoun is entirely avoided by some poets and very selectively used by others, cf. B. Axelson, *Unpoet. Wörter,* 71 f. It is not rare in H.'s hexameter poems but in the *Ars* occurs only once more, 6 *isti tabulae,* never in the *Odes.*

377 This is one of three verses in the *Ars* without a clearly marked middle caesura. Unlike the two other, discussed at 263 n., the present one cannot be accounted for by metrical parody, although, because of the sentiment in the next verse, this has been alleged e.g. by L. Mueller. If any motive can be alleged, it might be the expressive character of a long central word in an expressive line. But this matter can only be cleared up on the basis of all available instances of this not uncommon phenomenon in Latin and Greek verse.

This verse and the next contain the burden of the argument—a poem is either good or void. The structure of the present verse seems to be designed to concentrate attention on two features, the nature (*natum*) and scope (*inuentum*) of a poem, namely *animis iuuandis.* *iuuare* is not here the *iuuare* which some critics liked to divorce from *prodesse.* H.'s view is expressed at 343 *omne tulit punctum qui miscuit utile dulci,* 99 *non satis est pulchra esse poemata, dulcia sunto.* All poetry in H.'s sense is *animi libera quaedam oblectatio* (above 368–78 n., 372 n.).

(*animis*) *natum* (. . .*iuuandis*)*:* cf. 82 n. *natum rebus agendis* (*iambum*).

inuentum is tinged with the metaphorical notion of *natum,* 'destined for'. Cf. 405 *repertus.*

378 *summo. . .ad imum* substantival as 152 *medium* and *imum.* This is not Longinus' notion that the greatest poets sometimes πίπτουσιν ἀτυχέστατα (*Subl.* 33. 5), though the same passage shows Longinus discounting mediocre poetry on different grounds.

decessit (not *dis-* Lambinus) 'falls short of'.

uergit is the right reading, 'approaches' (the low mark). . . . *pergit* was a variant, which displaced the correct reading in two of the best MSS, BC; but in turn C notes *uergit* as a variant.

(d) Competence in the arts: in athletics (another 'useless art') incompetence is condemned, but in poetry it is not, 379–384, 385–90

The obvious conclusion that incompetent practitioners must refrain from practising is not explicitly drawn. This moral is only implied in the address to Piso's elder son (385), who had already been addressed in the last section (on mediocrity). H.'s advice touches on three topics (385–90), talent, informed criticism, and the much-quoted delay before publication.

379 Athletics, or games in general, now replace table music and dining as 'arts of liberal enjoyment' (372 n.). But Ar. *Pol.* VIII. 3, 1338 b 5 ff. reckons them among 'useful pursuits' because they strengthen the physique.

ludere nescit (with inf. as *scit*, 158, 316, *Ep.* II. 2. 213, al.) expresses the need for technique in games, cf. *C.* III. 24. 56 *ludere doctior* opp. *uenari.*

campestribus...armis: the adj. is not predic., as K.–H. suggest, but an ordinary attribute: 'used on the Campus Martius' (cf. above 162 n.), cf. *Ep.* I. 18. 53–4 *quo clamore coronae | proelia sustineas campestria,* Cic. *Cael.* 11 *ut exercitatione ludoque campestri uteremur,* al. *arma* elsewhere is applied to the 'tools' of the farmer (Virg. *A.* I. 177), the sailor (*A.* V. 15), the horseman (Ov. *Am.* I. 2. 16) and others (see *TLL,* II. 590, 58 ff.). Hence the meaning 'weapons for sham fights' (Wilkins) is not required; the 'weapons' are those enumerated in the next verse and others like them. Even the *proelia campestria* cited above are probably contests rather than fights, cf. Porph. *ad l. Ep. exerceri,* ps.-Acro *ibid. cum clamore circumstantium ludis.*

380 *indoctusque pilae:* cf. *nescit* and *doctior* in the previous note, and *S.* I. 5. 49 *pila...ludere*; the gen. as at Cic. *Phil.* II. 37 *indoctus ignarusque rerum* though there *ignarus* immediately precedes the gen.; cf. 218 *sagax,* 407 *sollers,* al. (D. Bo, *Hor. Op.* III. 229).

disciue: cf. *S.* II. 2. 10–13 *si Romana fatigat | militia adsuetum graecari, seu pila uelox | ... | seu te discus agit, C.* I. 8. 11 *trochiue* cf. *C.* III. 24. 57 *Graeco...trocho.*

quiescit 'abstains', as *S.* II. 1. 5 *quiescas.* The extension of meaning from 'keep silent' to 'keep quiet, abstain, cease' seems to be archaic in view of Pl. *Mos.* 1173 + inf., Ter. *An.* 691 + abl., Claud. Quad. *ap.* Gell. IX. 13. 8 (fr. 10ᵇ Peter), Gell. II. 28. 2 + inf.

381 *spissae* meaning 'crowded' (above 205 n.) is poetic and Silver Latin.

coronae: as in the similar context *Ep.* 1. 18. 53–4 (cit. above 379 n.).

risum tollant: cf. above 113 *tollent cachinnum.* The reaction of the public is once again justified.

382 *qui nescit uersus tamen audet fingere:* 379 *ludere qui nescit* suggests a similar construction here. Hence K.–H.'s and Klingner's punctuation (which repeats Bentley's), *nescit uersus, tamen* is unlikely; Rostagni rightly refrains from putting a comma. Cf. Dillenburger *ad l.* '*alii distinguunt* qui nescit, versus, *alii contra* qui nescit versus, tamen. *rectius omni interductu abstinebis, quoniam sententia est: qui nescit versus fingere, tamen audet versus fingere*'. The locution *uersus fingere* is in fact distributed over the two clauses, as K.–H. remark, oddly, in view of their punctuation. This interwoven order, a kind of ἀπὸ κοινοῦ construction, is often encountered in Latin verse; it is much favoured by H. Noun and adj. are most usually so distributed, though verb (inf. included) and object, as here, occur not at all rarely. Cf. Housman on Man. 1. 269–70, Luc. 1. 637–8, Juv. 6. 495–6, Heinze on Hor. *C.* 1. 27. 11–12. But these are not the most elaborate instances of this figure of speech.

quidni? sc. *audeas* from the preceding *audet fingere*: 'and why (should he not? After all he is...' The locution is put fully by Juv. 10. 94–6 *uis certe pila cohortes* | *...quidni* | *haec cupias?* The particle is archaic and colloquial. It introduces a strongly pointed 'rhetorical' question and ironically asserts the reverse of what the question expresses. So here: no one should in fact think he can write verses just because he is a free Roman citizen. For the origin of *quidni*, and its early use in Plautus and Terence, see Hofmann–Szantyr, 458; for its stylistic level, B. Axelson, *Unpoet. Wörter*, p. 96. Its use is very flexible; Cat. 79. 1 has the sequel of a rel. cl., Cic. *Quinct.* 69 the same linked with *enim*; at Ov. *Her.* 7. 45, 15 (16). 221 *quidni* introduces a parenthesis. H. obtains an especial effect in the present passage because *est* is understood after *liber*, etc. That brings it close to a particle like *utpote* and the irony is heightened by the certainty displayed. The effect would be lost if '*quidni?*' were ascribed to an interlocutor, as earlier commentators, e.g. Orelli, assumed.

383 accumulates four qualifications from which the absurd (but doubtless contemporary) conclusion would follow that the writing of (good) verse is a social accomplishment and tied to position: free status, free birth, equestrian census, unimpeached *mores—liber, ingenuus, equestrem (summam nummorum), uitio remotus. liber* here has none of the (Stoic) moral implications of *S.* II. 7. 92, *Ep.* 1. 106–7, al.

Commentary

For *ingenuus*, cf. *S.* I. 6. 7–8; the word here lacks the force of *Ep.* I. 19. 34 *(iuuat) ingenuis oculisque legi manibusque teneri*; it is to be defined in legal terms, although precisely what terms is open to further discussion, cf. Gai. *Inst.* I. 11 *ingenui sunt qui liberi nati sunt* (contrasted with *libertini*), Mommsen, *R.St.* III. 1. 72 ff., especially 73 with n. 2, Kübler, *R-E*, IX. 1547, and many more recent contributions. The *pater* (above 248 n.) may or may not be in point here.

census: pass. with the 'retained' acc. of the sum assessed, cf. Cic. *Flacc.* 80 *magnum agri modum censeri . . . census es . . . $\overline{CXXX}$ . . . census es mancipia Amyntae . . .; pertimuit cum te audisset seruos suos esse censum* (this apparently earliest instance of the acc. construction is omitted in *TLL*, III. 787. 21 ff., 54 ff., although *Flacc.* 80 is cited twice in the same column), Gell. VI. 13, Gai. *Inst.* II. 274; contrast *TLL, ibid.* for the more familiar abl. of the census, *Ep.* I. 1. 58–9 on equestrian census: *sed quadringentis sex septem milia desunt: | plebs eris.*

384 *summam nummorum:* ps.-Acro *hoc est: quadringentorum sestertiorum,* *Ep.* I. 1. 58 (cit. prec. n.). 'Sum of money' is rubbed in with gusto.

uitioque remotus ab omni: as *sine crimine*, 'an excellent record', a reference above all to the censor's *morum seuerissimum magisterium* (Cic. *Prov. Cons.* 46), which, if there was a *probrum*, might cause a *nota* and *ignominia*, cf. Mommsen, *R.St.* I. 3. 494 ff., II. 3. 1. 375 ff., III. 1. 251 f., 2. 875. A pun may well be intended, for the citizen who is *uitio remotus ab omni* would not necessarily be free from poetic *uitium* (above 31 n.). The point is not that 'H. does not answer the plea which answers itself' (Wickham); rather that the statement introduced by *quidni* is no plea but a sarcastic rejection.

385 *tu* is not the reader (so for example 153) but the *maior iuuenum* (366) to whom the preceding harangue was addressed. The young man has the status just described, and more; yet (it is tactfully suggested) he will be the last to draw the absurd conclusion that civic status makes a poet. Contemporary society was civilized enough to indulge a taste in poetic composition, and uncritical enough to mistake its quality. The censure implied here is one of the links with the *Augustus*, see *Ep.* II. 1. 108 ff., in particular 109 f. *pueri patresque seueri | fronde comas uincti cenant et carmina dictant,* 117 *scribimus* indocti doctique *poemata passim.*

nihil . . . dices faciesue: 'ce n'est pas un conseil, mais une louange, pour adoucir les préceptes qu'il veut lui donner' (Dacier). K.–H., insensitively, refer this to the young man's *gesamte Lebenshaltung*. This makes little sense in the context, and is refuted by *tamen* (386). *dices,* as some of the older commentators have seen (e.g. Orelli) and Rostagni has rightly repeated, concerns the poetic contingencies which H.

has mooted in a section introduced with an address to the young man; *dices* applies more to poetic speech (as it does frequently in H.), *facies* to the action of composing, *uersus facere*.

inuita...Minerua: ps.-Acro ...*et est prouerbium artificum...quia et ipsa inter ceteras artes etiam poesi praeest.* Cf. A. Otto, *Sprichwörter*, 224. Commentators rightly cite Cic. *Off.* 1. 110 *neque enim attinet naturae repugnare nec quicquam sequi quod assequi non queas. ex quo magis emergit quale sit decorum illud, ideo quia nihil decet inuita Minerua, ut aiunt, id est aduersante et repugnante natura.* The point about *ars* having been made, H. now inculcates the contrary principle, talent. This is unexpected after what precedes, but such a quick dialectical change is a favourite Horatian device, ensuring flexibility. *natura* and *ars* are but two different aspects of the ability to produce good poetry. Wickham rightly refers to the same topic in the initial part of the poem, 38–40. The criteria are the same but the different contexts need to be noted.

386 *id tibi iudicium est, ea mens* takes up 367 *et per te sapis.* The twofold *iudicium–mens* emphasizes the young man's own decision, cf. *Ep.* 1. 14. 8–9 *tamen istuc mens animusque | fert*, Cic. *Vat.* 30 *quo consilio aut qua mente*, *Phil.* III. 13 *magno consilio atque optima mente.* This notion is intensified by the change of gender *id...ea*, a kind of polyptoton more familiar with *hic*, Pl. *Poen.* 1099 *hoc consilium capio et hanc fabricam*, Cic. *Font.* 35 *hanc urbem et hoc imperium*, Virg. *A.* VI. 788 *huc geminas nunc flecte acies, hanc aspice gentem*, and with other pronouns, above 314–15 *quod...officium, quae | partes*, et al. *id...ea* should be noted because the change of gender was perhaps too obvious and rhetorical in poetry except for special effect. *is* in particular happens to be an increasingly rare word in Latin verse after Lucretius (B. Axelson, *Unpoet. Wörter*, 70 f.); H., with the exception of *C.* IV. 8. 18 (*C.* III. 11. 18 I regard as spurious), restricts it to the hexameter poems, and does not elsewhere repeat it for emphasis.

tamen allows for *natura* as well as for the *ars* inculcated earlier. H. demands criticism to check both—a motif in the preceding part of the poem (cf. 263 ff.) and even more important in the sequel, 419 ff. Ps.-Acro maintains that Piso (i.e. *maior iuuenum*) *tragoedias scripsit.* This is likely to be a mere guess, based on the poem.

olim: ps.-Acro *idest quandocumque*, cf. *C.* II. 10. 17–18 *non si male nunc, et olim | sic erit*, *S.* I. 4. 136–7 *numquid ego illi | imprudens olim faciam simile?*, II. 5. 27, *Ep.* I. 10. 42, Virg. *A.* I. 203, IV. 627; Cic. *Att.* XI. 4. 1.

387 *Maeci...iudicis:* in this form as well as *Maecii, Meci, Meti, Mettii*, etc. in the MSS and old editions. The person was identified by Manutius and Lambinus as the critic Sp. Maecius Tarpa, whom

Cicero mentioned in a critical aside as a selector of plays, *Fam.* VII.
1. 1 (55 B.C.), and H. some twenty years later at *S.* 1. 10. 37–8 *haec ego
ludo | quae neque in aede sonent certantia iudice Tarpa,* cf. Porph. *ad l.*
Bentley restored the spelling *Maeci,* and suggested the meaning 'a
renowned critic', that is, a reference to critical status, not to his
person—which is unlikely. Cf. Münzer, *R-E,* XIV. 238. 48 ff., and for
this question, and the problem of dating which underlies it, *Prol.*
p. 240 n. 4.

in (Maeci) descendat...aures: a measured term for this examination.
Parallels are equally solemn, Sall. *Iug.* 11. 7 *quod uerbum in pectus
Iugurthae altius, quam quisquam ratus erat, descendit,* Liv. III. 52. 2 *curam
in animas patrum descensuram,* and frequently in Seneca (cf. *TLL,* V. 1.
650. 62 ff.). This suggests an old stylistic precedent for the usage.
Also cf. Lucil. fr. 610 (cit. above 335–6 n.).

388 *et nostras:* 304–5 above may be compared. Kindly advice
offered by writers and critics of standing to younger friends was not
only a reality but a literary convention. Lucil. fr. 944 (Marx) *a me
auxiliatus sies* may belong to the genre, as C. Cichorius, *Untersuch. zu
Lucil.* (1908), p. 116 suggested cautiously and G. C. Fiske 'Lucil. and
H.', *Wisc. St.* VII (1920), 448, less cautiously.

nonum...in annum seems to suggest neoteric elaboration, in particular Cinna's *Zmyrna,* although there is no commendation of Cinna's
style; cf. Porph. and ps.-Acro *ad l.,* Philarg. on Virg. *E.* 9. 35,
F. Skutsch, *R-E,* VIII. 227. 19 ff. For Quintilian's reference to this
verse, see below 389 n. Cat. 95. 1–2, in his epigram on the *Zmyrna:*
nonam post...messem | quam coepta est nonamque edita post hiemem. These
verses doubtless lie behind the Horatian, but the reference is qualified, see the following notes.

388–9 *prematur...., | membranis intus positis:* Bentley's punctuation,
now generally accepted. The verb = 'conceal, confine closely', as
Epod. 1. 33 *quod...auarus ut Chremes terra premam,* Mart. III. 41(40) *quas
(opes) grauis arca premit.* A similar notion is expressed by *membranis
intus positis,* where *intus* has its familiar meaning 'inside the house'
(182 n.). This is the situation also at *Ep.* 1. 20. 1 ff., where the completed *liber epistularum* will be put on sale and thus escape from the
confinement at home, *ibid.* 3 *odisti claues et grata sigilla pudico.* But
liber...pumice mundus in that passage does not square with *membranis*
here. For there is no evidence that a fair copy was made on parchment, *membrana,* at that time, and some evidence against it. *membrana*
is shown by *S.* II. 3. 1 ff. to be used for notes and rough drafts: *sic raro
scribis,* H. is told, *ut toto non quater anno|membranam poscas, scriptorum
quaeque retexens.* This reference to parchment sheets or notebooks

is the first that is known, although it is not at all unlikely that Catullus' *palimpsesti* (22. 5) denote the same thing, for parchments like wax tables could be used more than once, cf. T. Birt, *Das antike Buchwesen*, p. 59, C. H. Roberts, 'The Codex', *Proc. Br. Ac.* XL (1954), 173. Hence the notion propagated by Wilkins and Wickham that H., in the *Ars*, is advising young Piso to complete his poem and then keep it under lock and seal for nine years rests on no evidence. Nor is this advice likely on general grounds.

389 *delere licebit* is ambiguous and, I suspect, prompted the opinion rejected in the previous note. It may be 'delete, destroy'; so Juvenal advises the aspiring poet, 7. 22 ff., where the *membrana* is either to be burned or locked up to be eaten by worms—hence, 27, *uigilata . . . proelia dele*. Or else it may be 'delete' for the purpose of correction, *S.* I. 10. 72–3 *saepe stilum uertas, iterum quae digna legi sint,* | *scripturus*. The context suggests that the latter is the case, but H. does not tell. Quintilian certainly so understood the passage, cf. *I.O., Ep. ad Tryph.* 2 *usus deinde Horati consilio qui in arte poetica suadet ne praecipitetur editio* '*nonumque prematur in annum*', *dabam iis* (to his own work) *otium, ut refrigerato inuentionis amore*, diligentius repetitos *tamquam lector perpenderem, I.O.* x. 4. 4 *Cinnae Zmyrnam* nouem annis *accepimus* scriptam, *et Panegyricum Isocratis . . . decem annis dicunt* elaboratum.

390 *edideris* 'publish' as distinct from *membranis* intus *positis*, as explained above.

nescit uox missa reuerti: cf. *Ep.* I. 20. 6 *non erit* emisso *reditus tibi* (*liber*), 18. 71 *et semel* emissum *uolat irreuocabile uerbum*; A. Otto, *Sprichwörter*, 367. *mitto* is a poetic variant of *emitto* above; the usage might have been noted by D. Bo, *Hor. Op.* III. 388.

(e) True excellence: poets the founders and civilizers of society, 391–407

The tradition. In this section some surviving evidence encourages an attempt to separate H. from the tradition on which he appears to have relied. The evidence has been assembled and discussed from very different points of view by M. Pohlenz, *NGG*, 1920, 150, F. Solmsen, *H*, LXVII (1932), 151 ff., Rostagni in the introductory note on this section, and in 'Il proemio di Suetonio *De Poetis*', etc., *Mélanges Marouzeau* (1948), pp. 509–23 (= *Scr. Min.* I. 238 ff.), H. Dahlmann, *AAM*, x (1962), 575–9; cf. *Prol.* 132–4, 147. Moreover in an important paper F. Heinimann has set this curious type of *Kulturgeschichte* in the context of

Commentary

Sophistic τέχναι, cf. 'Eine vorplatonische Theorie der τέχνη', *MH*, xviii (1961), 118 f. Writers on certain 'arts' from the fifth century B.C. onward projected these arts back into a mythical past. In each case mankind was said to have been civilized by the 'invention' of the τέχνη or *ars* for which primacy in time and rank was asserted. The Greek poets had traditionally had that primacy and it must have seemed plausible for the rhetoricians and sophists, who claimed the educative role of the poets, also to claim their early status as civilizers of the human race. This claim appears in the obviously derivative and traditional proem to Cic. *Inv.* i. 2 ff. and is referred to *De Or.* i. 33; but its basic assumptions are as old as Isocr. *Nic.* 5, cf. Solmsen, *op. cit.* p. 153; in fact these notions are likely to go back a little further still. For the inaugural speech of Protagoras in Plato's dialogue, 316 d, makes similar or even greater claims for σοφιστικὴ τέχνη: Orpheus, Musaeus, Homer, Hesiod, Simonides, were Sophists in the guise of poets, musicians, soothsayers. The speech would lose much of its satiric force if this were not a parody of Sophistic propaganda; Heinimann, *loc. cit.*, has given plausible reasons for the Sophistic provenance of these claims. Philosophers later took the same road, e.g. in the Stoic account of Sen. *Ep.* 90, which derives from Posidonius. The advocates of poetry in turn seem to have reasserted their claims. Of these three pieces of evidence remain, widely spaced in time: Aristoph. *Ran.* 1030–6, a fragment from the introduction to Suet. *De Poetis* (*ap.* Isid. *Et.* viii. 7. 1–2), and the present passage. It is not implausible that, as Dahlmann argues, the introduction to Varro's *De Poetis* contained a similar account. By their different modes of reasoning, Solmsen, Rostagni, and Dahlmann have come to ascribe the notions of the *Ars* to Neoptolemus of Parium. This is a guess, but a reasonable one, and I have discussed it, *Prol.* 132–4, 147, as part of the hypothesis that the basis of the *Ars* as a whole is derived from Neoptolemus. Unlike Aristophanes and Suetonius, H.'s account rationalizes the myths of Orpheus and Amphion in order to arrive at assertions on the earliest poets. Aristophanes' pseudo-historical account ends with Homer, and Suetonius mentions not names but genres. H. on the other hand places Homer and Tyrtaeus after the mythical personages, Orpheus, etc., but before a selective list of poetic genres. For the principle of selection, see *Prol.* and my notes below.

Horace. Here as often in this poem the invigorating shock of an apparently unconnected topic is administered at the outset: *nescit uox missa reuerti* ends the last sentence, *siluestres homines sacer interpresque deorum* begins this. But the pieces are sufficiently linked in the sequel to make this more than a superficial effect. H. is still concerned with *perfectus poeta*. That is the wider context in which he now sets the topic 'poet and society'. If poetry is merely a pastime for the *liber, ingenuus*, and rich (of 383–4), its achievement will be middling; but mediocrity has already been excluded by definition (372–3). So this social criterion for poetic quality will not do; another social criterion however will. For poetry, the very founder of civilized society (391 ff.), has its natural habitat in society (400 ff.). No need therefore for the person addressed at the end of this piece (406 f.) to be ashamed of *Musa* and *cantor Apollo*. The person so addressed is the *maior iuuenum* of 366. The two addresses are, in a sense, complementary and bring the intermediate contexts more closely together. Perfection in poetry is not a concomitant of social standing, but rather true poetry is social in origin and has always achieved its own kind of social standing. The true quality of poetry and its true efficacy go together.

391 *siluestres homines:* early man as in the parallel accounts cited above 391–407 n.: Suet. *De poetis* (Isid. *Et.* VIII. 7. 1) *cum primum homines exuta feritate*, etc., Aristoph. *Ran.* 1030–1 σκέψαι γὰρ ἀπ' ἀρχῆς | ὡς ὠφέλιμοι τῶν ποιητῶν οἱ γενναῖοι γεγένηνται, Quint. *I.O.* 1. 10. 9 (on Orpheus as an early musician, poet, and sage) *quia... agrestes animos admiratione mulceret*, cf. 393 n.; Isocr. *Nic.* 6 τοῦ θηριωδῶς ζῆν ἀπηλλάγημεν (through rhetoric), Cic. *Inv.* 1. 2 (on

Commentary

early rhetoric) *nam fuit quoddam tempus cum in agris homines passim bestiarum modo uagabantur.*

sacer interpresque deorum: for emphasis separated at the end of this verse from the name to which it belongs, *Orpheus*, at the end of the next. *interpres* is quasi-adjectival beside *sacer*; similar usages are discussed by Hofmann–Szantyr, 157 f. Cf. e.g. Aristoph. *Ran.* 1032–3 Ὀρφεύς... τελετάς θ᾽ ἡμῖν κατέδειξε... | Μουσαῖος δ᾽ ἐξακέσεις τε νόσων καὶ χρησμούς, Plato, *Prot.* 316 d τούς... τελετάς τε καὶ χρησμῳδίας (πρόσχημα ποιεῖσθαι), τοὺς ἀμφί τε Ὀρφέα καὶ Μουσαῖον al. In a different context Plato, *Ion* 534 e, calls poets ἑρμηνεῖς... τῶν θεῶν. According to Virg. *A.* vi. 645 Orpheus is *Threicius longa cum ueste sacerdos*, cf. ps.-Acro on *sacer* above, *idest sacerdos; ut poeta* (seq. Virg. *A.* vi. 645 f.). H.'s description need not imply an acceptance of that legendary figure as author of the Orphic poems so-called, rejected by Aristotle and others.

392 *caedibus et uictu foedo deterruit:* ps.-Acro *glandium esu*, Comm. Cruq. *instar ferarum*. Orelli's paraphrase *glandibus et ferina cruda* may be right. Many scholars however think that *caedibus* and *uictu foedo* together point to cannibalism, thus K.–H., Rostagni, and the writers cited by J. Haussleiter, 'Der Vegetarismus in der Antike' (*Religionsgesch. Versuche*, xxiv (1935), 77); this assessment is uncertain but cannot be excluded, see A. J. Festugière, *Harv. Theol. Rev.* xlii (1949), 218–20. Cf. Moschion, fr. 6. 14–15 (*TGF²*, p. 814 Nauck) βοραὶ δὲ σαρκοβρῶτες ἀλληλοκτόνους | παρεῖχον αὐτοῖς δαῖτας, Plato, *Laws*, vi. 782 b–c, *Epinomis*, 975 a 5 ff. ἡ τῆς ἀλληλοφαγίας τῶν ζῴων ἡμᾶς τῶν μέν, ὡς ὁ μῦθός ἐστιν, τὸ παράπαν ἀποστήσασα (ἐπιστήμη), τῶν δὲ εἰς τὴν νόμιμον ἐδωδὴν καταστήσασα, Orph. fr. 292 (p. 303 Kern) ἦν χρόνος ἡνίκα φῶτες ἀπ᾽ ἀλλήλων βίον εἶχον | σαρκοδακῇ, et al. Aristoph. *Ran.* 1032 Ὀρφεύς... φόνων τ᾽ ἀπέχεσθαι (κατέδειξε) may support this explanation, but Cic. *Inv.* i. 2 *cum... sibi uictu fero uitam propagabant* is more indistinct. In view of the large amount of Peripatetic doctrine in the *Ars*, it may be noted that neither Theophrastus nor Dicaearchus at all agreed with this account: Haussleiter, *op. cit.* pp. 59, 62.

Orpheus: cf. *Prol.* 133 nn. 1 and 2, and below 401 n.

393 H. allegorizes parts of the Orphic myth: Orpheus spellbinding wild animals really is Orpheus civilizing primitive and brutish man. For the allegory, see *Prol.* 133 n. 2. Quint.'s remarks (*I.O.* 1. 10. 9) on Orpheus and Linus, *musici et uates et sapientes*, resemble this section, except that Quintilian happens to be talking about the uses of music for the orator (*Prol.* 133 n. 1). His sources however offered the same allegory, *quia (Orpheus) rudes quoque atque agrestes animos*

Commentary

admiratione mulceret, non feras modo sed saxa etiam siluasque duxisse posteritatis memoriae traditum est. This is a familiar feature in Stoic allegorizing, cf. Heinze *ad l.* and Solmsen *loc. cit.*; which does not necessarily make H.'s or Quintilian's accounts Stoic. H., who claims credence when the imaginative situation of a poem justifies it—e.g. *C.* I. 12. 5–12, 24. 13–14—demonstrates the difference between literalness and metaphor when he writes in a lower emotional key. The doublet *dictus–dictus* and its placing at the beginning of this and the next verse give prominence to the allegorizing.

rabidos, ἀπὸ κοινοῦ with *tigres* as well as with *leones*; not *rapidos,* cf. Lachmann on Lucr. IV. 712. The adjs., like the verbs *rabio* and *rapio,* are continually confused by scribes and have to be carefully distinguished, see O. Skutsch's bibliography, *HS* LXXI (1966), 141 n. 15.

394 The prose order would be *et Amphion, conditor . . . urbis, (ob hoc) dictus (est) saxa mouere,* etc.; the attribute *conditor urbis* corresponds to the main cl. 390 f. *homines deterruit,* and *dictus* (sc. *est*) makes a good anaphora but balances only superficially the first *dictus,* which is genuinely participial.

Amphion, Thebanae conditor urbis: for the adj. cf. above 18 n. *flumen Rhenum.* In spite of *Romanae conditor arcis* (Virg. *A.* VIII. 313), *arcis* (uar.l.) does not make H.'s point as fully as *urbis*; whether *arx* or *urbs* applied was debated in mythology, cf. Homer cit. below, Paus. II. 6. 4, IX. 5. 7–8. *conditor urbis* corresponds to *homines deterruit,* a similarly magical and civilizing activity, the founding of cities: 399 n. on *oppida moliri*; Thebes according to some mythologies was reputed to be the oldest city. Orpheus and Amphion together appear at Paus. VI. 20. 18. In Hom. *Od.* XI. 262–3 Zethos as well as Amphion founded and fortified Thebes. The musical myth is probably as old as Hesiod (*Palaeph.* 42) and was given prominence in Eur. *Antiope* (D. L. Page, *Greek Lit. Pap.* I. 68), 81–2 ἄστυ . . . ἐξαρτύετε, the miracle of the building follows, 84 ff., cf. Wernicke, *R-E,* I. 1946. 2 ff. As in the instance of Orpheus, H. elsewhere tells the myth unrationalized, *C.* III. 11. 1–2. Allegorizing of a different kind is met in Tzetzes, *Chil.* I. 323 ff. φασὶ δὲ τὸν Ἀμφίονα κτλ. | τὸ δ' ἀληθές· Ἀμφίων μὲν ᾖδε κρατῶν τὴν λύραν, | οἱ λιθουργοὶ δ' ἐπήρειδον τοὺς λίθους συντιθέντες κτλ.

395 *saxa mouere sono testudinis:* cf. *C.* III. 11. 2, Eur. *ibid.* 86–9.

prece blanda: in Eur. 86 Amphion is told, lyre in hand μέλπειν θεοὺ[ς ὠι]δαῖσιν and the miracle follows. *blandus,* 'that which charms, casts a spell', a conventional epithet, here more telling than often, for incantations, *Ep.* II. 1. 135 *docta prece blandus, C.* IV. 1. 8

388

blandae...preces, *TLL*, 11. 2039. 10 f., cf. *C.* 1. 24. 13 *Threicio blandius Orpheo*, 12. 11–12 *blandum et...ducere quercus.*

396 *fuit...quondam:* cf. above 391 n. on *siluestres homines*: ἐξ ἀρχῆς, *nam fuit quoddam tempus, cum primum.*

haec points forward to the infs. 397–9, cf. 42–3 *ordinis haec uirtus erit...* | *ut, S.* 11. 5. 36–7 *haec mea cura est,* | *ne.*

sapientia: Orpheus and Linus were *musici et uates et sapientes* (Quint. cit. 393 n.). Rhetoricians, Sophists, and philosophers claimed that poetry (or music) was their own *sapientia* at an earlier stage and could still serve as propaedeutic. On the other hand the poet is advised (309) to turn to philosophy as *scribendi recte...fons.*

397–9: each verse subdivided into two complementary halves, the divisions irregular. Cf. above 195–7.

397 *publica priuatis secernere, sacra profanis:* (for the grammar see above 273 n. *seponere*), basic distinctions of Roman law. Gai. *Inst.* 11. 2 ff. *summa itaque rerum diuisio in duos articulos diducitur, nam aliae sunt diuini iuris, aliae humani. 3. diuini iuris sunt ueluti res sacrae et religiosae. 4. sacrae sunt quae diis superis consecratae sunt, religiosae quae diis Manibus relictae sunt...10. hae autem res quae humani iuris sunt, aut publicae sunt aut priuatae. 11. quae publicae sunt nullius uidentur in bonis esse;...priuata sunt, quae singulorum hominum sunt.* Cic. *Inv.* 1. 2 (see 391 n.) talks in different though still Roman terms, *nondum diuinae religionis, non humani officii ratio colebatur;* contrast Suet. *De Poetis* (see 391 n.) *seque ac deos suos nosse,* which strikes a Greek note.

398 *concubitu prohibere uago* 'restrain from', with abl. but no direct object as in the equally 'general precept'—*ex quo sunt illa communia*— Cic. *Off.* 1. 52 *non prohibere aqua profluente,* al. Their marriages were as unsettled, *uagi,* as they themselves were in their nomadic state: *concubitus* not *matrimonium* or *nuptiae,* cf. *uenerem incertam rapientis more ferarum* in the Lucretian account of *S.* 1. 3. 109.

dare iura maritis is the positive counterpart to *prohibere:* Cic. *ibid.* (391 n.) *nemo nuptias uiderat legitimas.* Cf. Gai. *Inst.* 1. 55 *quos* (sc. *liberos*) *iustis nuptiis procreauimus; quod* ius proprium ciuium Romanorum est, Just. *Inst.* 1. 10 pr. *iustas autem nuptias inter se ciues Romani contrahunt qui secundum praecepta legum coeunt,* etc. *mariti* pl. is poetic, Silver and late Latin for *coniuges,* not, as L. Mueller suggests, protective legislation for wronged husbands, in spite of *S.* 1. 3. 106 *neu quis adulter,* cf. *TLL*, VIII. 404. 65 ff., especially *Dig.* XXIV. 1. 52 *inter maritos nihil agitur* (cit. H. Schütz). The meaning of Afranius' title *Mariti* is dubious.

399 After the division of property sacred and profane, common and private, and the institution of marriage and family, there follows

Commentary

the establishment of cities and laws. To Greeks and Romans city life was civilized life and the founding of cities therefore marks the decisive stage in accounts such as these: Plat. *Prot.* 322 b 1 πόλεις δ' οὐκ ἦσαν.

oppida moliri: cf. 394 *Thebanae conditor urbis*, Isocr. *ibid.* (391 n.) συνελθόντες πόλεις ᾠκίσαμεν, Cic. *op. cit.* 1. 3 *urbibus constitutis. moliri* is more concrete than *condere* (*conditor*, 394): 'to engineer', from *moles*, with an object like cities, buildings, etc.; it is poetic and Silver Latin, cf. Virg. *A.* 1. 424 *moliri...arcem*, III. 132 *muros*, VII. 290 *tecta*, *C.* III. 1. 46 *atrium*, Ov. *Met.* XI. 199 *moenia*, al. *TLL*, VIII. 1361. 23 ff. H.'s earlier account, *S.* 1. 3. 105, had described the same thing by *oppida coeperunt munire.*

leges incidere ligno: where *ligno* is likely to be dat., cf. *TLL*, VII. 1. 907. 78 ff., especially 908. 4 f.; the Ciceronian construction is *in* + abl. Cf. *S.* 1. 3. 105 *ponere leges*, Isocr. *ibid.* (391 n.) καὶ νόμους ἐθέμεθα (καὶ τέχνας εὕρομεν), Cic. *Inv.* 1. 2 *non ius aequabile quid utilitatis haberet acceperat, 3 ut fidem colere et iustitiam retinere discerent;...ad ius...sine ui descendere.* Inscriptions of enactments on wood are an archaic touch; Porph. *aereis enim tabulis antiqui non sunt usi sed roboreis; ...unde adhuc Athenis legum tabulae axones uocantur.* Cf. Szanto, 'Axones', *R-E*, II. 2636. 6 ff., Swoboda, 'Kyrbeis', *ibid.* XII. 134. 60 ff.; Berger, 'Tabulae duodecim', *ibid.* IV A. 1918. 49 ff.

400 Accounts of the history or prehistory of an *ars* tend to explain the name of *ars* and *artifex*, thus Varro and Suet. *ap.* Isid. *Et.* VIII. 7. 3, Isidore himself on the same passage; cf. H. Dahlmann, *AAM* (1953), no. 3. 99, *AAM* (1962), no. 10. 591 ff. Thus here the names of *ars* and *artifex* are derived from the old poet-prophet who was *sacer interpresque deorum* (391). At this important place of the poem H. significantly employs not *poeta* but the archaic word *uates*, for which the New Poets of the last generation had little use. The Augustans however had come to claim it, with its overtones of inspiration, in spite of their addiction to the Callimachean discipline of *ars*–τέχνη.

sic sums up the provenance of poetry from inspiration, priestly lore, and civilizing enterprise, 391–9. Cf. Suet. *loc. cit. id genus... uocitatum est, eiusque fictores*, etc.

honor et nomen: cf. Aristoph. τιμὴν καὶ κλέος (cit. 401 n. *insignis*). The possibility of a hendiadys is suggested by *S.* 1. 4. 44 *det nominis huius* (sc. *poetae*) *honorem*, but no more than a possibility; the twofold notion 'status and title' is more likely where the two are in fact involved. So too 299 *nanciscetur enim pretium nomenque*, Cic. *Verr.* II. 87 *fuit tota Graecia summa propter ingenium honore et nomine*, *Deiot.* 14 *amplissimo regis honore et nomine*, Ov. *Pont.* III. 2. 32 *effugiunt...nomen*

Commentary

honorque rogos, Min. Fel. 6. 2 *multis honoribus ac nominibus sacerdotum*; cf. J. Vahlen, *Op. Ac.* 1. 59–60.

diuinis uatibus (atque | carminibus): the adj. may be predic. ('the name and status of *diuini*') or attrib., more likely the latter since this part of the section can scarcely culminate in a claim for anything but the ancient *uates* and *carmina*; *post hos* then begins a new line of development. The whole drift of the passage, notably 391 *sacer interpresque deorum* and 395–6 *prece blanda | ducere, quo uellet*, hints at the prophetic and miraculous character of the *uates* and his spells. The ancient notion of *uates* is therefore material and even Varro's (false) etymologizing of *uates* may have some relevance. Varro (Isid. *Et.* VIII. 7. 3) derived *uates a ui mentis . . . ; proinde poetae Latini uates olim, scripta eorum* uaticinia *dicebantur, quod ui quadam et quasi uesania in scribendo commouerentur . . . etiam per furorem* diuini *eodem erant nomine, quia et ipsi quoque pleraque uersibus efferebant*. The *honor et nomen* then was established for *uates*, the old prophet-poet, and for his *carmina. diuinis* too may be relevant and a poetic pun on 'divine' and 'prophetic' cannot be dismissed. H. uses the word in both connotations; for 'prophetic' see *S.* 1. 9. 30, *C.* III. 27. 10, and particularly above 218 *utiliumque sagax rerum et diuina futuri*, for 'divine', *S.* 1. 4. 43–4 *cui mens diuinior atque os | magna sonaturum*, and the Homeric θεῖοι ἀοιδοί, Virgil's *diuine poeta* (*E.* 5. 45, 10. 17), etc. In this passage of the *Ars* therefore the two connotations of *diuinus* seem to coalesce. As always when theories are concerned, H. no more than hints at them. But the fact that Virgil, Horace, 'and succeeding writers made *uates* once more a name of honour' (Munro on Lucr. 1. 102, cf. L. Mueller, *De re metr.*[2] 51 ff.) provides a basis for the present section; cf. also *Ep.* II. 1. 118 ff. It may moreover have prompted some sympathy with this aspect of Varronian archaism, cf. Dahlmann, *ΑΑΜ* (1962), 575–6. This possible connexion however must not be mistaken for the close and direct link between Varro and the Augustans which the same scholar has asserted in the second part of his paper at *P*, XCVII (1948), 337 ff.; cf. E. Bickel, 'Vates bei Varro und Vergil', *RM*, XCIV (1951), 260–1. Although *uates* in Virgil and H. occasionally expresses the concept of the Augustan poet in contradistinction to *poeta*, the two words are near-synonyms at 299, and in numerous places where the pale *poeta* receives some colour from its Augustan competitor. On the other hand *uates* may be humorously overstated, and thus be a source of irony. The shifting distinction between *uates* and *poeta* therefore provides an insecure foundation for large conclusions, such as J. K. Newman's dating of the *Ars* to 22 B.C. (*The concept of Vates, Coll. Latomus* (1967), pp. 79, 130).

Commentary

401 *post hos:* cf. not so much Aristoph. *op. cit.* (391 n.), where Homer, at 1034–6, ends the list of great archaic poets, preceded by Orpheus, Musaeus and Hesiod, as Ar. *Poet.* ch. 4, where (as Rostagni notes) Homer's epics, the oldest known literary documents, are preceded by hymns and encomia. The legendary Orpheus is not mentioned in the *Poetics;* fr. 7 (Rose³) from the περὶ φιλοσοφίας rules that the 'so-called Orphic poems' are not by Orpheus. H. then while not disagreeing with Aristotle is more explicit (perhaps on Alexandrian precedent) in pronouncing on prehistorical poetry before Homer and the poetic genres properly so called, cf. *Prol.* 134.

insignis: predic. with *post hos* and ἀπὸ κοινοῦ with *Homerus | Tyrtaeusque,* as H. Schütz proposed, not sc. *fuit* (K.–H., Rostagni, al.). K.–H. assume a reference to the *Odyssey* in contrast with the martial glory of Tyrtaeus in the next line. But Plut. *Alex.* 8. 2 τὴν... ᾽Ιλιάδα τῆς πολεμικῆς ἀρετῆς ἐφόδιον (which they quote) is not the only illustration to the contrary. Aristoph. (cit. 391 n.), because of his context, is more relevant and invalidates this case, 1034–6 ὁ δὲ θεῖος ῞Ομηρος | ἀπὸ τοῦ τιμὴν καὶ κλέος ἔσχεν πλῆν τοῦδ᾽ ὅτι χρήστ᾽ ἐδίδαξε, | τάξεις, ἀρετάς, ὁπλίσεις ἀνδρῶν. Cf. above 73–4. Dante still acknowledged the ancient sword-bearing Homer, *Inferno*, IV. 86 *Mira colui con quella spada in mano,* 88 *Quelli è Omero poeta sovrano.*

402 *Tyrtaeusque:* cf. Porph. and ps.-Acro *ad l.* Martial elegy is joined closely with Homer; Quint. *I.O.* x. 1. 56 *Horatius... Tyrtaeum Homero subiungit.* No other type of elegy is here mentioned, though some may be hinted in the next sentence, but cf. above 76–8.

mares animos in Martia bella: the alliteration as in Varro, *L.L.* v. 73 *Mars... quod maribus in bello praeest,* for the adj. also *Ep.*1.1.64 *nenia... maribus Curiis et decantata Camillis;* cf. *TLL,* VIII. 423. 72 ff.

403 *exacuit:* the sharpening and incitement of emotions as Cic. *De Or.* 1. 131 *ad uos exacuendos,* opp. *deterrendos, Att.* XII. 36. 2, Nep. *Phoc.* 4. 1. *TLL,* v. 2. 1139. 13 ff. offers also relevant later parallels, *Epit. Alex.* 11 *strepitu remorum... animi militum exacuebantur (exaequabantur* MS), Hom. Lat. 507 *spes exacuit languentia militis arma,* syn. *accendit.*

dictae per carmina sortes: cf. above 219 *sortilegis...Delphis.* This is the next genre, after epic and elegy—χρησμολογία. *uaticinia* of this kind persisted in historical times; hence the genre is placed here, not in the pre-Homeric section: Porph. mentions *Phemonoe,* ps.-Acro *Sibilla.* Rostagni notes that the Alexandrians classified oracles as a type of didactic verse, *Schol. Dion. Thr.* 166. 15 (ed. Hilgard). Public use and status—H.'s criterion here—qualifies them for inclusion.

Commentary

404 *uitae monstrata uia est*, the gnomic verse of Theognis, Phocylides, Solon, and the large moralistic literature of *Chriae*. A Greek term like ὑφηγητική may be in mind. Rostagni cites Diom. *GL*, 1. 482. 32 f. *angeltice* (*species poematis enarratiui*) *est qua sententiae scribuntur, ut est Theognidis liber; item Chriae,* cf. Porph. ⟨*sententiis* add. ς⟩ *sapientium quibus instructa uita est.* The metaphor of the way of life, known from Greek poetry and philosophy, is apposite here and fully established in Latin writing, cf. *Ep.* 1. 17. 26 *uitae uia si conuersa decebit,* explained by 23 *omnis Aristippum decuit color et status et res*; also in later Satire, as Pers. 5. 34–5, Juv. 7. 172. Cicero's speeches have the alliterative pair for a political persuasion, e.g. that of the Optimates, *Sest.* 140; in moral theory it continues the imagery of the parting of the ways, *Off.* 1. 118 *quam quisque uiam uiuendi sit ingressurus.*

404–5 *Pieriis . . . modis*, in H.'s usage, denotes lyrics. Lyric verse, of which choral, public, poetry is a large part, 'invited royal patronage' —a Grecizing description of a Greek genre. E.g. Ar. *Ath. Pol.* 18. 1 Ἵππαρχος . . . φιλόμουσος ἦν· καὶ τοὺς περὶ Ἀνακρέοντα καὶ Σιμωνίδην καὶ τοὺς ἄλλους ποιητὰς οὗτος ἦν ὁ μεταπεμπόμενος, ps.-Plato, *Hipp.* 228 c Ἀνακρέοντα . . . ἐκόμισεν, Σιμωνίδην δὲ τὸν Κεῖον ἀεὶ περὶ αὑτὸν εἶχεν, μεγάλοις μισθοῖς καὶ δώροις πείθων, cf. Bacchy. 5. 3–6 (Hieron), Pind. *Ol.* 1 (Hieron). 14–17, 103–5, 3. 44 (Theron), *Py.* 5. 1 ff. (Arcesilaus), et al. Without the public criterion of this section other kinds of lyric would qualify more definitely, cf. above 83–5 nn.

gratia regum | *. . . temptata* avoids the familiar *gratiam petere, appetere*; *gratiam . . . experiri* Sall. *Iug.* 102. 9.

405–6 Drama, a *ludus*, is a public spectacle as *longorum operum finis,* see above 244, *Ep.* II. 1. 140; ἀνάπαυσις in Aristotelian language, cf. E. Koller, *op. cit.* (366–78 n.), 118, 123 f.

et: explanatory, cf. ps.-Acro *ludus et . . . finis* κατὰ τὸ αὐτό *dixit.*

ne forte: cf. 176 n.

pudori, at the end, explicitly fits this section into the larger context begun with the address to the *maior iuuenum* (366, cf. 391–407 n.) and does so after the motives for this final address have clarified. The quasi-historical section (1) makes good the traditional claim of professors of *artes* that their profession is useful, *utile*, cf. F. Heinimann, *MH*, XVIII (1961) 105, 117 ff.; (2) proclaims the civilizing power of poetry, the specific form that *utile* here takes: the poet, as at *Ep.* II 1. 124, is *utilis urbi*, hence the young statesman need not feel ashamed of the art, and that in turn justifies the stringent demands made of the practitioner; (3) interweaves, in H.'s dialectical manner, the ideal of inspiration with what seemed largely a demand for *studium* (379–

84, 386–90). Now, paradoxically after his opposition to Democritean *furor* (295 ff.), *honor et nomen* of poet and poetry is seen to have sprung from the inspiration of the old *uates, sacer interpresque deorum*.

407 *Musa* and *Apollo* appear, emphatically, at the end of a section carried by the idea of inspiration. *lyrae sollers*, with the gen. construction, a Horatian favourite, extended to this adj. from *peritus* or the like, cf. Lambinus *ad l.*, Hofmann–Szantyr, 78; ps.-Acro *sollers . . . qui habet peritiam*, etc. Neither that locution nor *cantor Apollo* refers to lyric verse, as K. Latte, *H*, LX (1925), 12, and others believed. They refer to the whole of poetry, authenticated as it were in this section.

(f) Genius and artistry in literary theory, 408–18

This duality underlies the whole poem. It introduces the present part of the poem, 294–308—there in the shape of an antithesis, which H. resolves humorously in favour of his doing literary criticism since he prefers to 'cure' himself of his *ingenium* and therefore cannot write (lyric) poetry. In the sequel *ars* is strongly supported, yet *ingenium* comes to the fore several times (cf. 323, implied in 372 *mediocribus*, 385 *inuita . . . Minerua*); the last section in particular could not have been written without a firm reliance on *ingenium*. Thus before he comes to this section the reader has been exposed to varying answers to the apparently simple problem '*natura an arte*'. But more than that; the continuous dialectical switch from the one to the other must have shown that in the setting of this poem at any rate the antithesis is unreal. The bland Peripatetic compromise, '*et natura et arte*', set against this logical background, loses the character of superficiality and truism, with which it has been saddled so often. Here as elsewhere, when H. comes to put a matter in abstract terms and the language of the schools, he does so briefly, after long passages of poetic argument have made these notions real and concrete. Abstraction then acquires the nature of a summing up, which, for the reader remembering what he has read before, puts a different complexion on the abstract terms.

For the pre-Platonic position, see F. Heinimann, *MH*, XVIII (1961), 123 ff., P. Shorey, 'Φύσις, Μελέτη, Ἐπιστήμη',

Commentary

TAPA,XL(1909),185–201,D. A. Russell, 'Longinus', etc., pp. 63 f.; for the Democritean and Platonic positions, see above 295–8 n. The Aristotelian disjunction, which points the way to a compromise, is expressed at *Poet.* 8, 1451 a 22 ff. ὁ δ' "Ομηρος...καὶ τοῦτ' ἔοικεν καλῶς ἰδεῖν, ἤτοι διὰ τέχνην ἢ διὰ φύσιν. For the Peripatetic compromise reflected by H. see Neoptolemus of Parium *ap.* Philod. *Poem.* v. 11. 5–8 (*Prol.* 55, no. 2) [τὸν] τὴν τέχνην [καὶ τὴν δύν]αμιν ἔχοντα τ[ὴν ποι]η-τικήν. Longinus' notion of τέχνη as an assistance to φύσις is a different matter; but he too can talk of ἀλληλουχία repre-senting τὸ τέλειον, *perfectum* (*Subl.* 36. 4, cit. 410–11 n. *alterius...* | *altera*). In Rome the pair *natura–ars* is standard-ized in references to an *ars*, e.g. Cic. *Arch.* 1 and 15. The desiccated remains of once lively debates are enshrined in the introductions to the *artes*, the question *natura an arte* a con-ventional topic, e.g. Quint. *I.O.* II, ch. 19 starting *scio quaeri etiam naturaue plus ad eloquentiam conferat an doctrina* (cf. I, praef. 26), Vitr. I. 1. 3, al. But in the *A.P.* many topics which the humdrum types of textbook rehearsed at the outset appear in the present part of the poem—presumably their original place, though in H.'s flexible and poetic scheme not the only place, cf. above 38–41.

408 *natura* and *arte* at beginning and end provide the framework for this verse as *ingenium* and *arte* did at 295. Reasonable *artifices* like Quint. *I.O.* II. 19. 1 (cit. prec. n.) or Vitruvius (ref. *ibid.*) would tend to question the antithesis; Cicero recurs to the subject in his own way. But the *Ars* draws much of its élan from the antithesis and so H. puts the matter antithetically in the dialectical manner of the philosophers.

laudabile: cf. 268, 324, not 'laudable' but the *uirtus* or 'perfection' of 308, 370.

409 *quaesitum est:* this matter derives from the schools, is a *quaestio*, ζήτημα, πρόβλημα. Cf. *S.* I. 4. 46–7 *quidam comoedia necne poema* | *esset quaesiuere*, Quint. *I.O.* II. 19. 1 *scio* quaeri etiam *natura...an doctrina*, etc, *ibid. plurimum tamen referre arbitror,* quam *esse in hoc loco* quaestionem *uelimus.*

ego: the critic as at 306 and frequently thereafter, cf. above 24–5 n. *studium,* like μελέτη, ἄσκησις, is a technical term in these discussions.

diuite uena in conjunction with *rude* (410) suggests mining as the source of the metaphor; *uena* like Greek φλέψ may be a vein of metal or a watercourse. This does not necessarily, as K.–H. say, distinguish the imagery at *C.* II. 18. 9–10 *ingeni | benigna uena* (of his poetry) although it is true that *uena* can become a metaphor in either sense, and Ov. *Tr.* III. 7. 14 praises *raras dotes ingeniumque*, 15 leads that *ingenium* to *Pegasidas . . . undas*, 16 *ne male fecundae uena periret aquae*. The difference between the two Horatian passages is that in the present passage the image is more fully realized.

410 *rude . . . ingenium* calls for *erudire*, the job of *ars*, teacher and critic. With *diuite uena* preceding, the notion of *aes rude* may have been in H.'s mind, the metal that is not *signatum* by art. Quint. *I.O.* II. 19. 3 (comparable and probably not uninfluenced by this passage of the *Ars*) recalls the anecdote about Praxiteles carving a millstone, and adds *Parium marmor mallem rude*.

possit John of Salisbury, *Meta.* I. 8 (presumably from a MS), ς, Bentley and the best Horatian critics of the last century, *prosit* MSS and all recent editions; not an unusual variation, see e.g. *C.* I. 26. 10. *prosit* is certainly a possible notion; Quintilian has it in the same context, *I.O.* praef. 27 *haec ipsa* (sc. *bona ingeni*) *sine doctore perito, studio pertinaci . . . continua exercitatione per se nihil prosunt*, V. 10. 121 theoretical training *non magis . . . sat est quam palaestram didicisse nisi corpus . . . natura iuuatur, sicut contra ne illa quidem satis sine arte profuerint*. H.'s next verse however makes against the notion of avail, benefit (sc. to the poet to be), which is the meaning of *prosit*. The notion is rather that *studium* and *ingenium* cannot 'do' enough by themselves; each needs the other's assistance. This, many instances (most of them brought together by Bentley) show, is expressed by *posse*. Cf. Pl. *As.* 636 (*uiginti minae*) *quid pollent quidue possunt*, *Truc.* 812 *plus potest qui plus ualet*, Virg. *E.* 3. 28–9 *inter nos quid possit uterque uicissim | experiamur*, *A.* IX. 446 *si quid mea carmina possunt*, Hor. *C.* I. 26. 9–10 *nil sine te* (sc. *Pimplei*) *mei | possunt* (ps.-Acro codd. A r lemm. et comm., Bentley, *prosunt* codd.) *honores*, III. 4. 58 (*quid Typhoeus et Mimas*) *possent ruentes*, IV. 14. 9 *quid Marte posses*, *Ep.* I. 2. 17 *quid uirtus et quid sapientia possit*, 9. 6 *quid possim uidet ac nouit me ualdius ipso*. Nor is the idiom restricted to verse, see Cic. *Quinct.* 69 *quod poterant, id audebant*, *T.D.* II. 34 *hoc pueri possunt, uiri non poterunt?*, al.

sic 'to such a degree' (Wilkins), hence *sed* (Peerlkamp), is not required.

410–11 *alterius* (ĭ as always in H., cf. H. Schütz on *C.* IV. 13. 18) . . . | *altera*, but Quint. *I.O.* II. 19. 2 *si parti utrilibet omnino alteram detrahas, natura sine doctrina multum ualebit, doctrina nulla esse sine natura poterit*. Peerlkamp and others compare ps.-Long. *Subl.* 36. 4 προσήκει

Commentary

. . .βοήθημα τῇ φύσει πάντη πορίζεσθαι τὴν τέχνην (cf. H. *poscit opem*)· ἡ γὰρ ἀλληλουχία (cf. H. above) τούτων ἴσως γένοιτ᾽ ἂν τὸ τέλειον, cf. above 408–18 n.

coniurat amice, a friendly pact, whereas according to false opinion hostile relations subsist between *natura* and *ars*; so among many thought the opponent(s) of ps.-Long. (*Subl.* 2. 2) χείρω τε τὰ φυσικὰ ἔργα, ὡς οἴονται, καὶ τῷ παντὶ δειλότερα καθίσταται ταῖς τεχνολογίαις κατασκελετευόμενα. In view of the close parallel to H. in *Subl.* 36. 4 (see prec. n.), Kiessling plausibly suggests that the metaphor of a pact in both writers also rests on a precedent; I have however found no such *coniuratio* or συνωμοσία elsewhere. *coniurare*, which Cicero uses for seditious oaths only, is here used for entering into a pact, like the familiar *conspirare*; so in archaic literature and later in poets and historians (cf. *TLL*, IV. 339. 76ff.), e.g. of the military oath Caes. *B.G.* VII. 1. 1, Virg. *A.* VIII. 5, and generally Pl. *Cis.* 241, Ter. *Hec.* 198, Hor. *C.* I. 15. 7 (*Graecia*) *coniurata tuas rumpere nuptias*, Liv. XXII. 38. 4, Lucan, II. 48 *in arma* (*mundus*). The only instance noted by *TLL* of a metaphor somewhat comparable to the present is *Aetna* 359, where the winds enter into an agreement.

412 Having made the point about *ingenium*, H. again moves off in the direction of *ars*. His first example is taken from athletics, a traditional illustration, cf. above 379–81; at *Ep.* II. 1. 114–16 examples are equally traditional in this context: helmsman, doctor, carpenter. The obvious need for training made athletics a serviceable case for writers on τέχνη, underpinned in Sophistic writing and philosophy by the parallel between arts physical and intellectual. Platonic examples abound, but cf. Isocr. *Antid.* 181, Epict. III. 15. 1 ἑκάστου ἔργου σκόπει τὰ καθηγούμενα καὶ τὰ ἀκόλουθα κτλ. 2 ᾽θέλω ᾽Ολύμπια νικῆσαι.᾽ ἀλλὰ σκόπει τὰ καθηγούμενα αὐτοῦ καὶ τὰ ἀκόλουθα. . . 3 δεῖ σε εὐτακτεῖν, ἀναγκοφαγεῖν, ἀπέχεσθαι πεμμάτων, γυμνάζεσθαι πρὸς ἀνάγκην, ὥρᾳ τεταγμένη, ἐν καύματι, ἐν ψύχει· μὴ ψυχρὸν πίνειν, μὴ οἶνον ὅτ᾽ ἔτυχεν κτλ., Quint. V. 10. 121 (cit. 410 n.), al.

optatam cursu contingere metam: the relation of the goal-line (*calx*) to the (three) turning-posts expressed by the sing. *meta* is conjectural, cf. Pollak, *R-E*, III. 1421. 61 ff., Schroff, *R-E*, XV. 1311. 10 ff. Nevertheless this and other instances, cited *TLL*, VIII. 865. 1 ff., demand the meaning 'goal' and similarity with these instances (Prop. III. 14. 7, Ov. *Met.* X. 597, al.) suggests that the contestant here is a runner (*cursor*, Quint. *I.O.* II. 8. 7); *cursu* = 'by running'. The *meta*. . . *feruidis | euitata rotis* (*C.* I. 1. 4–5) is not therefore comparable. For the use of this line in Val. Fl. IV. 620 *optatam dabitur contingere pellem*, see P. Langen's commentary on the *Argonautica* and J. Stroux, *P*, xc (1935), 305 n. 1.

413 The verbs with the homoeoteleuton *tulit fecitque, sudauit et alsit*, 414 *abstinuit*, and the doublet *uenere et uino* (cf. 42 n. *uirtus*...*et uenus*)—all this to give emotional colour to the hardships borne by the athlete 'as a boy', that is 'when he was a boy', the tenses not (as H. Schütz suggests) gnomic, cf. *prius* 415. This rhetoric is at home where hardship is dramatized, even in the artless style of Epictetus, cf. ἐν καύματι, ἐν ψύχει above 412 n.

puer, cf. Prot. fr. 3 on φύσις and ἄσκησις: ἀπὸ νεότητος δὲ ἀρξαμένους δεῖ μανθάνειν, Plato, *Rep.* III. 403 c δεῖ...ταύτῃ (sc. γυμναστικῇ) ἀκριβῶς τρέφεσθαι ἐκ παίδων διὰ βίου. For παιδομαθία, cf. P. Shorey, *op. cit* (408–18 n.), p. 189.

414 *qui*–**415**: the piper too, the second instance, is a set piece in philosophical and later literary argument. Of the numerous Platonic examples, I mention *Prot.* 323 a 7 ff., because the speaker is the Sophist and his arguments are likely to hark back to contemporary debates. The αὐλητής, Philod. *Poem.* v. 8–9, comes from a literary context in which, as in H., the writer sought to determine the qualities of the 'perfect poet'. C. Jensen was able to complete the explanation of this passage and so perhaps overestimated its relevance to H. (*Philodemos*, pp. 99 ff.). But of the similarity of the wider context there can be no doubt.

qui Pythia cantat (tibicen): not Pythian songs; ps.-Acro takes this as a reference to the Πυθικὸς νόμος αὐλητικός, *carmen in Pythonem draconem compositum ab Apolline*, cf. W. Vetter, *R-E*, xvii. 840. 48 ff. Modern commentators tend to agree, although K.–H. regard as possible the meaning 'competes at the Pythian games', and Rostagni appears to accept both. But *concinnitas* with the example of the athlete favours a wording which denotes, and not only implies, a performance at one of the games. More important, plain sense favours it, for even a novice might attempt a Pythian nome, but H.'s piper is an artist who has reached the top, not a novice: he got to one of the great festivals. Hence the meaning appears to be 'competes (as a piper) at the Pythian games'. For the construction commentators cite *Ep.* I. I. 50 *magna coronari*...*Olympia*; but that extends a locution like Enn. *Ann.* 374 *uicit Olympia*, (τὰ) Ὀλύμπια νικᾶν (e.g. Epict. cit. 412 n.), *uincere* and similar verbs forming a well-established group, to which *cantare* does not seem to belong, cf. C. F. W. Müller, *Nom. und Akk.* 4 ff., Löfstedt, *Syn.* I², 259 f., Hofmann–Szantyr, 39 f. If on the other hand the present case is explained on the model of *sonare*, the acc. should rather express the content of the music, *Epod.* 17. 39–40 *mendaci*

Commentary

lyra | *uoles sonari*, Virg. *E.* 1. 5 *resonare...Amaryllida*, cf. *Ep.* II. 2. 125 *Cyclopa mouetur.* This may be grammatically more plausible, but yields an unlikely sense, the Πυθικὸς νόμος queried above. Hence either the anomalous extension of the grammar has to be condoned, *Pythia cantat* being 'competes at the Pythian games', which cannot be ruled out, or else an emendation, *certat* for *cantat*, would remove the objection. *Pythia certat*, said of a *tibicen*, might plausibly but erroneously suggest *cantat* to a scribe. Cf. *TLL*, III. 895. 20 ff., especially Varro, *Men.* 519 *in charteo stadio* ἐπιτάφιον ἀγῶνα...*certasset*, Stat. *Theb.* VI. 5–6 *primus...per arua* | *hunc pius Alcides Pelopi certauit honorem*, Apul. *Plat.* 1. 2 *tantos...progressus exercitatio ei contulit* (sc. *in palaestra*) *ut Pythia et Isthmia...certauerit.*

415 *didicit:* sc. *cantare* according to L. Mueller, sc. *a magistro* (from *magistrum*) according to Rostagni. Neither is required, cf. above 88 *cur nescire pudens praue quam discere malo, Ep.* I. 1. 48 *discere et audire et meliori credere*, II. 1. 262.

extimuitque magistrum: cf. Ter. *Phor.* 154 *patrem ut extimescam*, Cic. *T.D.* III. 38, *Phil.* 12. 30, al. (*TLL*, v. 2. 2029. 38 ff.).

416 *nec* ς, Bentley, *non* (uel *num*) Heinze, *nunc* codd. Against the MSS' reading two, in my opinion decisive, points have been made (neither of which is met by F. Klingner's defence, *BVSA* LXXXVIII, 3 (1937), 51–2 n. 1): (1) '*nulla hic temporum sed studiorum dumtaxat oppositio est*' (Bentley, cf. L. Mueller); (2) this is a quasi-comparison, which would be nullified by *nunc*, cf. Vahlen, *Ges. Phil. Schr.* II. 756 n. 11. '(As) training is required in athletics and music, (so in poetry,) *and* it is *not* enough to say', etc. For incomplete comparisons, see 374–8 n. Of the emendations *num* introducing a rhetorical question after the preceding assertion would be weak; *S.* I. 6. 15–17 differs in this and other respects. *nec* and *non* provide for the ellipse noted above under (2). The former has the advantage of providing a connexion.

satis est dixisse: for the perf. inf., see above 98 n.

ego mira poemata pango: burlesques nonsensical claims made in the grand style. Pers. I. 31 *quid dia poemata narrent* echoes H.'s rhythm and sarcasm though not his context. *pango* for 'composing, singing' is archaic and survives as an artificiality in poetry and prose. Apart from Enn. *Ann.* 299 (V.²) *tibia Musarum pangit melos*, the epigram ascribed to Ennius (*panxit...facta patrum*), Lucr. I. 25 *quos (uersus) ego de rerum natura pangere conor*, and 933 (IV. 8), all passages known to me have an archaizing or mock-heroic tinge, e.g. Cic. *Fam.* XVI. 18. 3 *an pangis aliquid Sophocleum?*, *Att.* II. 6. 2 *itaque* ἀνέκδοτα *a nobis... Theopompio genere aut etiam asperiore multo panguntur*, 14. 2 *de pangendo...*

399

fieri nihil potest, Hor. *Ep.* i. 18. 40 *nec cum uenari uolet ille, poemata panges*, Mart. xi. 3. 7–8, Val. Max. ii. 1. 10 (J. Vahlen, *Op. Ac.* ii. 135–7), Tac. *Ann.* xiv. 16. 1.

417–18: the poetaster not wanting to admit that he comes last in the race.

417 With *scabies*, 'the mange' H. descends to comic bathos after the high-sounding verse preceding. Baxter's eighteenth-century parlance hits the mark: 'Pox take the hindmost.' This is a ditty, *nenia*, from a children's game, turned into a hexameter. At *Ep.* i. 1. 59–60 *pueri ludentes . . . aiunt* the original of a similar verse in troch. sept. is cited by Porph. (*ibid.* 62); the coincidence of metre and genre is noted by E. Fraenkel, *H*, lxii (1927), 365 (repr. *Kl. Beitr.* ii. 18). The same scholiast's version of the present verse does not scan; L. Mueller *ad l.* made an attempt to rearrange it. Ps.-Acro, '*scabies*' *ludus puerorum est; habes in Suetonio Tranquillo,* '*qui nouissimus, scabiosus*' (fr. 198, *De lusibus puerorum*, p. 346 Reifferscheid). Cf. A. Otto, *Sprichwörter*, 311.

relinqui est codd. except BC¹(?)K *reli(n)qui*. Aphaeresis at the end of line and sentence is more likely in view of *A.P.* 48 *necesse est*, 102 *dolendum est*, 327 *remota est*, 353 *quid ergo est*—a feature of the hexameter poems, cf. D. Bo, *Hor. Op.* iii. 64 ff. The verb still alludes to the children's game.

418 Cf. 88 *cur nescire pudens praue quam discere malo?*

sane has caused much trouble. Ps.-Acro, nonsensically, links it with *mihi turpe*, several commentators with *non didici* (thus Heinze, without Kiessling's support, rendering *sane* by *allerdings*, 'admittedly'), Dillenburger and others with *non* = 'not properly' (cf. G. B. A. Fletcher, *Annot. on Tac.* (1964), p. 56), the majority with *nescire* = 'altogether' (Wilkins comparing the Plautine *sane sapis*). Orelli and L. Mueller have rightly stood out for *sane* (*nescire*) *fateri*, 'at least' (= *utique* Orelli) or 'simply to confess ignorance of what I have not learned'. A colloquial nuance would not have come amiss; for such a nuance in *sane*, see J. B. Hofmann, *Lat. Umgangspr.*² p. 75. But the nuance is not by any means invariable, as is shown by the evidence in B. Axelson, *Unpoet. Wörter*, pp. 94, 138, Fletcher, *op. cit.*

(g) The false critic and the false friend, 419–37

This section forms a unity with the next, each showing one aspect of poetic criticism. H. leads the reader from caricature to truth as he sees it. Willingness to accept criticism—one's own (*Ep.* ii. 2. 110) or that of others—is part of the *perfectus poeta*; willingness to accept nothing but flattery perverts critic and criticized alike. Since the Hellenistic background of the positive section (*h*) is dubious (cf. 438–52 n.), even less can be said about the present negative one. Tracts on flattery, περὶ κολακείας, doubtless abounded in Hellenistic literature, but nothing is known about κόλακες in an earlier Greek literary setting corresponding to this. Greek writings on friendship also must be relevant; some of them are reflected in Cicero's *De Amicitia*, see below 438–52 n. The preoccupation with *amicitia* of H.'s hexameter poems is striking. For friendship in the *Satires*, especially 1. 3, see the discussion by C. van Rooy, *Acta Classica*, XI (1968), 56 ff. The first literary poem, *S*. 1. 4, juxtaposes the satirist and the *liber amicus* in society. At *Ep.* 1. 18. 4 H. remarks *infido scurrae distabit amicus*, but he then proceeds to play off the obsequiousness of the flatterer against the asperities of the veracity-monger. Altogether in the *Epistles*, the poet draws a major motif both from reflections on friendship and from the practice of an *amicus* writing to *amici*, many of them much younger than he. In the present section a Roman and satirical colouring, with one dubious, one probable, and one almost certain Lucilian echo (cf. 419–20, 425 and 451, 431–3 nn.), may be stated. H. may have used a Lucilian setting for sketching a dialectical antithesis to the true critic. Wealthy dabblers in poetry gave dinner parties for the purpose of reciting their productions: this appears to be a realistic Roman touch, cf. 422 n. and, in a wider context, *Ep.* 1. 19. 37–8. The same setting provides a highly effective background for part of Persius' first *Satire*; and in other works, notably in his *Satire* 5, a common pursuit of philosophy lends a new seriousness to the worn motif of *amicitia*.

419–20 H. unexpectedly introduces a wealthy host at dinner who as it were auctions his poems for the admiration of guests bidding for his good graces. This procedure seems to recall the poetaster of the preceding verses, 416–18, also one of the rich amateurs of the earlier sections of the poem, in particular 383–4. F. Marx, Lucil. fr. 1282 n., noted the Horatian passage in commenting on the Lucilian one, in which a hawker, *scrutarius*, extols his shoddy goods, *scruta: quidni? et scruta quidem ut uendat [et] scrutarius laudat, | praefractam strigilim, soleam improbus dimidiatam*. A *scrutarius* again appears at *Ep.* II. 2. 10, though for a different purpose. Marx, noting the similarity, such as it is, between the two satirists, dubiously asked whether the fragment should be assigned to Lucilius' tenth satire, which apparently dealt with literary criticism. It is however unknown whether Lucilius' *et* points to a comparison and, if it does, what the comparison was. This is *terra infirma*. Where Marx was cautious, G. C. Fiske has incautiously asserted that 'this simile is clearly borrowed from Lucilius', see *HS*, XXIV (1913), 8, *Wisc. St.* VII (1920), 458.

419 *praeco:* not of course one of the *apparitores* but a crier or auctioneer, cf. K. Schneider, *R-E*, XXII. 1198. 11 ff. The standing of such a man differed according to the size of his business, but the realism of this verse makes it certain that he is a small trader, though clearly not the same kind of person as the attractive Volteius Mena of *Ep.* I. 7. 50; rather compare *Ep.* II. 2. 1 ff. H.'s father was a *coactor*, 'the two occupations are closely connected' (Fraenkel, *Horace*, 5); cf. the charming verses, *S.* I. 6. 85–8.

turbam . . . cogit 'he collects a crowd', ps.-Acro, *uoce hortatur populum accedere*, cf. *TLL*, III. 1519. 41–2.

qui is in fourth place, a rare collocation in H.; D. Bo, *Hor. Op.* III. 325, counts 8 instances.

420 *assentatores* 'yes-men', an expressive but prosaic word; nowhere else recorded from Latin verse, *TLL*, II. 854. 52. The length and the heavy spondees of *assentatores* are satirically exploited in this verse. H. was aware of the descriptive force of agent nouns in -(*t*)*or*, see above 163 n. on *monitoribus*, and 164, 172–4 nn. *assentator* is first known from Cicero, who seems to have appreciated its overtones and used it frequently, but only twice in the highly selective vocabulary of the speeches, cf. L. Laurand, *Études sur le style des discours de Cic.*[4], p. 289 with n. 3. For the social nuance in *assentatio*, cf. Cic. *Am.* 89 *assentatio uitiorum adiutrix procul amoueatur, quae non modo amico, sed ne libero quidem digna est*, 91 *nullam in amicitiis pestem esse maiorem quam adulationem blanditiam assentationem*, Ter. *Eun.* 252–3 cited by Cic. *Am.* 93.

iubet corresponds to the crier's *cogit*, but see 421 n.

ad lucrum ire corresponds to the crier's *ad merces . . . emendas*. Cf. Lucil. fr. 716–17 (Marx) *cocus non curat caudam (galli) insignem esse illam, dum pinguis siet. | sic amici quaerunt animum (animum quaerunt codd.), rem parasiti ac ditias*, Cic. *Am.* 31 *ut enim benefici liberalesque sumus, non ut exigamus gratiam . . ., sic amicitiam non spe mercedis adducti*

Commentary

sed quod omnis eius fructus in ipso amore inest expetendam putamus, Plut. *Quomodo adul. ab am.* 58 e οἱ δὲ κόλακες τὸν πλούσιον ὁμοῦ καὶ ῥήτορα καὶ ποιητήν, ἂν δὲ βούληται, καὶ ζωγράφον καὶ αὐλητὴν ἀποφαίνουσι κτλ.

421 does not, as H. Schütz thought when he deleted it, invalidate the following verse; it occurs however in another poem, and is not glossed by ps.-Acro. Lambinus rightly said, '*poeta locuples divitiis suis mutis ac tacitis assentatores vocat*'; after which the rich man's actions in 422–5. The verse occurs also at *S.* i. 2. 13, where it is redundant, and perhaps interpolated. This is the only verse in the *Ars* that may be so repeated, but elsewhere there are repetitions, both genuine (that is, citations as *S.* i. 2. 27: i. 4. 92, *C.* i. 19. 1 : iv. 1. 5) and interpolated (as *Ep.* i. 1. 56 from *S.* i. 6. 74). Vahlen, *Op. Ac.* i. 337–45, denies interpolations and contends for accidental repetitions by the poet; Lachmann's, Haupt's, and Meineke's treatment is more critical, cf. C. Belger, *Moritz Haupt als ak. Lehrer* (1879), pp. 267 f. The problem at *A.P.* 267 differs.

422 Lambinus plausibly continues his comment. After the mute invitation of 421–2, the actual benefits of 422: hospitality, financial pledges, legal protection. So also Pers. i. 53–4 (a passage inspired by the present) where the benefits follow a declaration of status, 51–3. The whole of Persius' context (from 30 *ecce* onward) is relevant to H.; so is Juv. 7. 43 *scit dare*.

si uero est...qui explained as above marks a climax; it is not, as Wilkins suggests, 'simply adversative'.

unctum 'a rich table', a noun, cf. ps.-Acro '*unctum*' *autem lautum conuiuium...ut alibi* (sc. *Ep.* i. 17. 12) '*accedes siccus ad unctum*'. Persius (sc. i. 53) '*calidum scis ponere sumen*'. Dinners given by rich amateurs in order to obtain audiences for their verse are a feature of Roman society, thus the instances from Martial quoted by Wilkins, e.g. iii. 50. 1 *haec tibi...est ad cenam causa uocandi*, etc.

ponere (as at *S.* ii. 2. 23, 4. 14, al., cf. D. Bo, *Hor. Op.* iii. 388) = *apponere* 'serve'. This seems to be not only a familiar poeticism, as Pers. i. 53 cit. above, but appears first in archaic Latin: Cato, *Agr.* 79 *ita ponito*, 81, 84; 80 however has *apponito*, which could be a dittography (*ita [ap]ponito*) but need not perhaps be emended. The simple verb is also colloquial, Petr. 34. 7 (Trimalchio), *heri non tam bonum posui, et multo honestiores cenabant*.

423 *spondere:* the provision of financial surety, known from H. and many other contemporary sources, cf. *S.* i. 3. 95, ii. 6. 23, *Ep.* ii. 2. 67.

leui pro paupere: ps.-Acro '*leui*' *pro tenui et egenti et uili*. But *pauper* does not call for that epithet; the adj. would be otiose, and not used with H.'s customary finesse, unless it meant 'worthless, unreliable'. (The same would apply to Peerlkamp's *uili*.) For this notion of *leuis* in combination with a synonym, see Cic. *Verr.* II. 2. 94 *Pacilius quidam, homo egens et leuis, accedit*, III. 84 *homo leuis atque egens*, *Sest.* 22 *nequam esse hominem et leuem*, *Prov. Cons.* 15 *Graecum hominem ac leuem*, al. J. Geel elegantly emended *leui* by *uelit* (cf. Schütz's n.). There is no objection to the syllabic transposition, see e.g. above 38 *iam mater* (*iā mr̄*) B for *materiam* and the numerous instances in Housman's Manilius, I. lvii f. What renders the conjecture dubious is the distinction introduced between *uelit* and 422 *possit*. But the moral connotation is probably sufficient warrant to avoid the textual change. *leui* would make the rich amateur poet seek out not only needy but worthless companions, and lends some colour to 425 *mendacem*.

eripere: sc. *pauperum* from the preceding clause so that *implicitum*, which is unlikely to be obj. by itself, can be understood as an attribute. So K.–H.; unlike H. Schütz I see no difficulty in this. '*eripere proprie de reo*', Peerlkamp referring to Graevius on Flor. I. 3. They were right, cf. Cic. *Verr.* II. I. 10 *ne actor* (i.e. prosecutor) *quidem est is cui reus . . . aut occulte surripi aut impune eripi possit*, ibid. 31, al. *TLL*, V. 2. 794. 18 ff.

artis: Bentley, *atris* codd.; *a tris* R; *at͵s* l indicate the process of corruption. '*atris* "gloomy"', like *atrae curae Carm.* IV. 11. 35. Bentley's suggestion *artis* suits *implicitum*, but is quite needless' (Wilkins). Yet Bentley had cited *atrae curae*, and had demanded something more adapted to the present context. Cf. Wakefield on Lucr. V. 1147. *atrae*, K.–H. rightly say, would be apt if sympathy should be evoked for the pauper, but the reverse is the case. Hence *artis*, which like *implicitum* denotes the toils of the lawsuit, cf. Bentley's references, especially Lucr. V. 1147 *sponte sua cecidit sub leges artaque iura*, the legal *laquei* at Cic. *Sest.* 88, *Cael.* 71, and the expressive metaphors at Amm. XXX. 4. 13 and 18.

424 *implicitum:* cf. prec. n. and Cic. *Verr.* II. 3. 82 *omnibus legibus implicatus*, 5. 150 *implicatum seueritate iudicum*, Sen. *Ben.* VI. 27. 6 *si aliqua illum lite implicares quam subinde discuteres*, al.

mirabor si sciet: for the 1st pers. sing. see 410; the fut. tense is prospective or potential, as it is called: 'I should be surprised', cf. *Ep.* I. 17. 25–6 *quem duplici panno patientia uelat,* | *mirabor, uitae uia si conuersa decebit.*

inter-|*(noscere):* tmesis between two lines, known from a different type of instances in synaphia of lyric poems, occurs in four other instances from the hexameter poems, *S.* I. 2. 62–3 *inter-est*, 6. 58–9 *circum-...uectari*, II. 3. 117–18 *unde-octoginta*, *Ep.* II. 2. 93–4 *circum-spectemus*. [D. Bo, *Hor. Op.* III. 83 subsumes under what he calls tmesis four phenomena which are quite distinct: (1) *qui-cumque*, which does not contain a quasi-preposition as prefix, (2) lyric syn-aphia, which in view of *u-xorius ue-nale* demands a different treatment from 'prepositions' used as prefixes, (3) tmesis of disyllabic prepo-sitions (also *unde-*), which differs in character from *in-*, *de-*, etc., cf. J. Wackernagel, *Syn.* II. 175, Fraenkel, *Horace*, 104 n. 3; (4) alleged tmesis of monosyllabic prefixes such as *in-*, supposed to account for middle caesura in hexameters, as above 87, 263, 377, and even in lyric verse.] *internoscere* is treated as a compound verb + acc., like *intercino* above 194 *neu quid medios intercinat actus*, and *interfundo*, *C.* I. 14. 19–20 *interfusa...* | ... *aequora Cycladas*. Thus Pl. *Men.* pr. 19–20 *(ut) mater sua* | *non internosse posset (geminos)*, Cic. *Ac.* II. 58 *oua illa non internoscere*. The verb is used in the same context as it is here, Cic. *Am.* 95 *secerni autem blandus amicus a uero et internosci...* *potest*; cf. Plutarch's essay Πῶς ἄν τις διακρίνειε τὸν κόλακα τοῦ φίλου. A more literal rendering of διακρίνω is *dinosco*, first on record in H.

425 *mendacem uerumque...amicum:* the themes of this section and the next (445–52): the *mendax* ('counterfeit') *amicus* is one of the *assentatores* of 420, the true friend is the frank critic of 445 ff. Pers. 1. 55–6 spells out the patron's urgent question, which is merely implicit in H.: *et 'uerum' inquis 'amo, uerum mihi dicite de me.'* In a comparable though non-literary setting we read *scurrantis speciem praebere, professus amicum*, *Ep.* 1. 18. 2; the flatteries of the legacy-hunter are satirized on a similar basis at *S.* II. 5. 96–9. The present section contains one almost certain Lucilian reminiscence, the false friend as a profes-sional mourner (see 431 n.); its placing within the work of Lucilius is unfortunately conjectural. I think C. Cichorius, in *Untersuchungen zu Lucilius*, 117 ff., has argued plausibly that the true friend also has a Lucilian ancestry. The subject-matter is conventional, e.g. ps.-Long. *Subl.* 1. 2 αὐτὸς δ' ἡμῖν, ἑταῖρε, τὰ ἐπὶ μέρους, ὡς πέφυκας καὶ καθήκει, συνεπικρινεῖς ἀληθέστατα, and D. A. Russell's note *ad l.*; but the equation 'true friend = true critic' is more specific. Its appear-ance in Lucilius, book XXVI (in troch. sept.) stimulated Cichorius' observations. The probable context of that book is indicated by fr. 621 (Cichorius, 113 ff.), *percrepa pugnam Popili, facta Corneli cane*. This points to advice on the writing of epic on contemporary topics and fr. 609 seems to go with it: *quid cauendum tibi censere⟨m⟩* (Lachmann, Cichorius, p. 115 n. 1), *quid uitandum maxume*. Fr. 611 is unsound in at least two places and especial caution is enjoined. Nevertheless the general notion is clear enough to be compared with H.: *porro amici est bene praecipere †tueri† bene †praedicare†*. *praedicere* is Mercerus' convincing emendation of the final word. *tueri* is scarcely sound; Cichorius' *[t]ueri* involves the change of only one letter and restores sense: *porro amici est bene praecipere ueri, bene praedicere*. The punctuation *praecipere, ueri* is more attractive: so too Fiske, *HS*, xxiv (1913), 9, *Wisc. St.* vii (1920), 458, though a single line gives little scope for argument. But whatever the answer, these fragments reveal a striking likeness to the Horatian context. Finally a Lucilian line in troch. sept. but not assigned to a book needs to be adduced, fr. 953 (Cichorius *op. cit.*) *homini amico et familiari non est mentiri meum*.

beatus: predic. ('for all his happiness', Wilkins), is sarcastically interposed between *uerumque* and *amicum*. For its meaning K.–H. refer to *Ep.* i. 18. 32, where Porph. usefully comments *beatus non uere sed qui sibi beatus uidetur ex pulchris uestibus*; at ii. 2. 107–8 *gaudent scribentes . . . et ultro,* | *si taceas, laudant quidquid scripsere beati*, where again Porph. notes *subdistingue 'scripsere' et sic infer 'beati'*. Thus too Cic. *T.D.* v. 62 *ut impenderet (gladius) illius beati* (sc. *Damoclis*) *ceruicibus*, cit. Orelli. *beatus* 'wealthy' would be inadequate here; contrast 421.

426 *tu:* the reader, not (with Rostagni and others) the elder son of Piso, cf. 120 *scriptor*, 128 *tu*, etc. Thus rightly J. Vahlen, *Ges. Phil. Schr.* ii. 756 f., K.–H. *ad l.*

seu donaris seu . . . donare uoles: not like 63–7 *siue . . . arcet . . . seu . . . mutauit* but e.g. *S.* ii. 2. 83–4 *siue . . . aduexerit annus,* | *seu recreare uolet*.

quid ἀπὸ κοινοῦ with *donaris* as well as *donare uoles*, placed in the second of two clauses, which allows a humorous emphasis in *quid . . . cui*.

427 *nolito:* for the address L. Mueller compares Lucil. fr. 1030 (Marx) *nolito . . . putare*.

ad uersus . . . ducere hints at 420 *iubet ad lucrum ire*.

tibi factos not *tibi . . . ducere* (Schütz), is the construction demanded by the sense; cf. *Ep.* i. 16. 25 *bella tibi . . . pugnata*, al. The situation is spelt out by later satirists, as Juv. 7. 36–8 *iste* | *quem colis . . .* | *ipse facit uersus atque uni cedit Homero*.

plenum laetitiae: like the κόλαξ of Attic Comedy, cf. Eupolis cit. 433 n.

428–30 In view of the appearance in Lucilius of the professional mourners (below 431 n.), one may raise but cannot answer the question whether there was not also a Lucilian precedent, lifted by H. to his own poetic level, for this delightful little sketch.

428 *pulchre, bene, recte:* Roman comedy is full of these conversational adverbs. They are used either singly, as Plautus' *eu* or *euge*, inter-

Commentary

jections derived from the Greek language of polite sociability, or in such Greek–Latin combinations as *eu, recte*; *euge, optume* and the like. One of them would do the job: *Ep.* I. 8. 15 *si dicet 'recte'*. Easy parody can be obtained from a larger number; Martial II. 27 squashes a professional parasite with six exclamations in a row. But that is farcical; H.'s satire draws its moderated effect from a nicely calculated and balanced tricolon; and neither the Greek *euge* (contrast *eu*, above 328), nor the highly colloquial *belle* are employed. Persius employs both, though he is otherwise close to H.: 1. 48–9 *sed recti finem . . . esse recuso | 'euge' tuum et 'belle', nam 'belle' hoc excute totum*, etc. and 75, 84, 87, 111. The vocabulary of aesthetic approval was stereotyped, with *'belle'* well in the lead; the cant term is ridiculed by Mart. II. 7, X. 46. Such words greeted not only declamations and pleading in law (H. Bardon, *Le vocab. de la crit. litt. chez Sénèque le Rhéteur* (1940), p. 16, S. F. Bonner, *Roman Declamation*, etc. (1949), pp. 78–9), but all recitations, discussions, and performances. Plut. *De Aud.* 45 e–46 c reminds us of the Greek background: δεῖ δὲ μηδὲ ταῖς φωναῖς τῶν ἐπαίνων ὡς ἔτυχε χρῆσθαι . . . οἱ δὲ τὰς ξένας φωνὰς τοῖς ἀκροατηρίοις νῦν ἐπεισάγοντες οὗτοι, καὶ τὸ 'θείως' καὶ 'θεοφορήτως' καὶ 'ἀπροσίτως' ἐπιλέγοντες, ὡς οὐκέτι τοῦ 'καλῶς' καὶ τοῦ 'σοφῶς' καὶ τοῦ 'ἀληθῶς' ἐξαρκοῦντος, οἷς οἱ περὶ Πλάτωνα καὶ Σωκράτην καὶ Ὑπερείδην ἐχρῶντο σημείοις τῶν ἐπαίνων, ὑπερασχημονοῦσι καὶ διαβάλλουσι τοὺς λέγοντας ὡς ὑπερηφάνων καὶ περιττῶν δεομένους ἐπαίνων . . . ὅρα γὰρ ἀληθῶς οἷόν ἐστι φιλοσόφου λέγοντος ἀπορεῖν τοὺς ἔξωθεν ὑπὸ τῶν ἔνδον βοώντων . . . πότερον αὐλοῦντος ἢ κιθαρίζοντος ἢ ὀρχουμένου τινός ὁ ἔπαινός ἐστιν. Cicero is revealing in his comments on the Roman practice: *De Or.* III. 101 *quare 'bene et praeclare' quamuis nobis saepe dicatur, 'belle et festiue' nimium saepe nolo; quamquam illa ipsa exclamatio 'non potest melius' sit uelim crebra; sed habeat tamen illa in dicendo admiratio . . . umbram aliquam . . . quo magis id quod erit illuminatum exstare atque eminere uideatur.*

429 *pallescet:* The numbness of aesthetic emotion may possibly be recalled: *S.* II. 7. 96 *cum Pausiaca torpes . . . tabella.* Persius' first Satire gives this emotion a sexual turn. It is more likely, however, as Schütz suggests, that *pallescet* in H. denotes the paleness of fear, just as the tears in the next clause probably imply pity—φόβος and ἔλεος. Cf. Ov. *Her.* 1. 14 *nomine in Hectoreo pallida semper eram.*

super his: not in ps.-Acro's temporal sense, *post haec quae dixi, pulchre, bene, recte*, nor used like *super, S.* II. 6. 103 or *Ep.* II. 2. 24. The spatial notion suggested by K.–H. is even less likely. There is no *charta* in front of the toady, for his tears to trickle on; his host's verses are surely recited, probably by the great man himself. Cf. the counterpart in 438 *Quintilio siquid recitares* and the passages there noted. *super his* goes with *pallescet* and should be punctuated accordingly; = *de his* as at *Ep.* II. 1. 152 (*fuit...cura*) *condicione super communi.*

etiam (not *et iam*, L. Mueller's text), in the place of another *super his*, thus avoids a repetitious layout. *etiam* (whether 'also' or 'even') is indeed customary in the second place of a Horatian clause (K.–H.); it is not so used in three places, where however no additional main verb occurs, *S.* I. 7. 5 *etiam* (*habebat*) *lites cum Rege molestas, Ep.* I. 18. 107 *sit mihi quod nunc est, etiam minus, C.* IV. 6. 19–20 *etiam latentem* | *matris in aluo* (*ureret*).

stillabit, like *manare*, is used transitively in verse and Silver prose, first recorded from this passage.

amicis: sc. *oculis*, an adj. as often in H. and elsewhere, takes up *amicum* (425).

430 *rorem:* a poeticism for 'moisture'; for tears as Ov. *Met.* x. 360.

saliet, tundet pede terram: in the conventions of literary criticism a listener's exaggerated bodily movements are often represented as indicating an exaggerated and depraved style of performance, or indeed of the piece performed. Thus certain passages of Greek and Roman criticism, e.g. above 214 n.; for Roman rhetoric see e.g. Cic. *Or.* 226 (Hegesias' jerky style), Quint. *I.O.* II. 2. 9. *ad omnem clausulam non exsurgunt modo, uerum etiam excurrunt, et cum indecora exsultatione conclamant,* IX. 4. 142 *lasciuissimis modis saltat;* in poetry Persius obtains some of his effects from this feature, I. 20 *ingentes trepidare Titos,* and 21 *tremulo...uersu,* cf. 82 *exsultant.* In H. these words may add to the censure of the patron-poet's recitation; cf. above 428 n.

The verbs probably indicate a reaction to comic passages after the sentimental. If the first verb means 'dance about with pleasure', thus overdoing the convention of rising to applaud (cf. Wilkins *ad l.*), the second cannot well denote what it does often, and what K.–H. suggest it does here, *gestum indignantis.* So it was rightly noted by Lambinus and others. No emendation (*Salius* L. Mueller) need be considered. The stamping of the ground in dancing comically pictured as *C.* III. 18. 15–16 *gaudet inuisam pepulisse fossor* | *ter pede terram,* I. 37. 1–2 *pede libero* | *pulsanda tellus, Ep.* I. 14. 25–6 *cuius* (sc. *tibicinae*) | *ad strepitum salias terrae grauis.*

431–3 The false friend is compared with hired mourners. H. appears to have recast a passage of Lucilius, frs. 954–5 (tro. sept.) ⟨–⟩ *mercede quae conductae flent alieno in funere* | *praeficae, multo et capillos scindunt et clamant magis.* C. Cichorius, *Untersuchungen* (above 425 n.), rightly compares H. *qui* with L. *quae; conducti: conductae; plorant: flent; in funere: alieno in funere; plura: multo magis; dicunt et faciunt: capillos*

scindunt et clamant. Lucilius' *multo* and *magis* show that he too offered
a comparison, almost certainly the same as in H. Lambinus cited
Lucilius in his note on this passage, but the close similarity was not
appreciated until E. F. Corpet's note in his edition of Lucilius,
1845; cf. F. Marx *ad l.* L. Mueller added the initial ⟨*ut*⟩ from H.,
with much probability. The number of Lucilius' book in Nonius
(s.v. *praeficae*, 66–7 M.) is shown by the metre of the fragment to be
false. Lachmann altered XXII to XXVII, Cichorius (*Untersuchungen*, 119)
more plausibly to XXVI because of the similarity of subject-matter
discussed above 425 n.

There is however a difference between the two texts noted with
much emphasis by Immisch, p. 24, Mette, *R-E*, XVI. 2467. 23, Rostagni *ad l.* In Lucilius the professional mourners are women engaged
for the purpose, *praeficae*. Ps.-Acro ascribes that name to *antiqui*, and
says the custom survived *in quibusdam prouinciis*. The first part of this
information may be traced back to Varro, *De uita populi Romani*,
book IV (*ap.* Non. *op. cit.*). He says more precisely, perhaps overstating the case, *haec mulier uocitata olim praefica usque ad Poenicum bellum*;
but naturally the name lingered, though not for long: Naev. *CRF*[3]
(Ribbeck), fr. 129, Pl. *Truc.* 495, *Frivol.* fr. 7. In all these instances, and
in the grammarians (Varro above, and *L.L.* VII. 70, Non. 145, Paul.
223, and Gellius' archaizing, XVIII. 7. 3), the mourners are, as in
Lucilius, women. H. however talks of male mourners and the reason
is not likely to be what K.–H. suggest, that the *mendaces amici* are the
point of comparison. Porphyrion's comment shows that H. had some
ancient precedents for so oddly changing the sex of the *praeficae*.
Alexandriae (says Porph. *ad l.*) *sic obolis* (W. Meyer, *sit obolis* M,
sitobolis, 'meal tickets', Immisch, *op. cit.*, though the word = 'gran-
aries' in the passages cited L.–S.–J.) *conducuntur qui mortuos fleant . . .;
hi ergo uocantur* θρηνῳδοί. Professional male mourners, black-clad and
miserable, were still known in Victorian England; but unlike their
ancient counterparts they kept decorously quiet and were therefore
called Mutes. The difference between *praeficae* and *threnodi* is indeed
striking—an Alexandrian feature like others noted in this commentary. Whether or not H. borrowed the feature from Neoptolemus (as
Immisch suggests), the evidence points to two diverse traditions
which he brought together—the Lucilian context with its *praeficae*,
and the 'foreign', Alexandrian touch of the *threnodi*. The evidence is
informative, whatever the explanation.

plorant: H. sifts Lucilius' rough but forceful rhetoric. The waste-
ful *mercede conductae* becomes simple *conducti*, and *alieno in funere*
simple *in funere*—a process of concentration. But conversely he can

afford a little more space: the expressive *plorant* replaces *flent*. Cf. 432 nn.

432 *(dicunt) et faciunt:* that is, the actions and the talk of 428–30, replacing Lucilius' *capillos scindunt et clamant*; *clamare* was already used at 428.

prope plura with great finesse replace Lucilius' unrestrained *multo . . .magis*: an intriguing example of τὸ πρέπον. Cf. *S.* II. 3. 32 *insanis et tu stultique* prope *omnes*, *Ep.* I. 6. 1–2 *nil admirari* prope *res est una . . .* | *solaque quae*, etc.

ex animo lead to the *uerus laudator*, next verse. Juvenal's flatterer (3. 101–2) *flet . . .*, | *nec dolet.*

sic: at end of verse, cf. above 12 *non ut*, 410 *sic* though not in comparison.

433 Here the *assentator* of 420, *mendax amicus* of 425, turns into a *derisor*—the noun, also at S. II. 6. 54, *Ep.* I. 18. 11, in verse since Plautus (*Cap.* 71), and in Silver prose.

uero: cf. 425.

laudatore: the noun as at 173.

mouetur: cf. Eupolis fr. 159. 9–10 (*Com. Att. Fr.* Kock) from the Κόλακες: κἄν τι τύχῃ λέγων ὁ πλούταξ, πάνυ τοῦτ' ἐπαινῶ | καὶ καταπλήττομαι δοκῶν τοῖσι λόγοισι χαίρειν.

434–7 are juxtaposed without comparative conjunctions, unlike, e.g., *ut* 431, *sic* 432. The abruptness of this final warning against *assentatio* puts in relief the true criticism, which is then made to follow just as abruptly.

reges: probably 'kings' rather than *diuites*. The same applies to *S.* I. 2. 86 *regibus hic mos est.*

multis . . .culillis 'cup, goblet', nom. and derivation unknown, the form uncertain. The word occurs only twice in recorded Latinity, here and *C.* I. 31. 11. MS tradition makes for a different form in each case. At *C.* I. 31. 11 the word is more clearly spelt *culillis* (which I have followed) A a E R ps.-Acro, *cui illis* B, as against *culullis* δπ λl φψ Porph. Here *culillis* is attested only in π ante ras. Porph. (in lemm.) *Gloss.* Γ, *cui illis* B, *cū illis* K, but *culullis* in C δ ps.-Acro Tract. Vind., *cululis* δπ λl φψ Flor. Nostr., *cucullis R²*; cf. Keller, *Epil.* 105, 772. If Porphyrion is right in saying (*C.* I. 31. 10–11) *proprie . . . calices sunt quidam* fictiles, *quibus pontifices uirginesque Vestales in sacris utuntur*, the word must have lost its original connotation of earthenware, and acquired the meaning 'cup', thus qualifying for the epithet *aureis*.

urgere 'press, solicit', as *S.* II. 6. 29–30 *urget* | *iratis precibus*, 7. 93–4 *urget enim dominus mentem non lenis, et acres* | *subiectat lasso stimulos*, cf. Pl. *Men.* 322–3 *quod te urget . . .* | *qui huic sis molestus?*

Commentary

435 *torquere mero:* the likeness with *urgere* emphasized by the same ending, again 'to press, ply', but this time specifically, put on the rack for questioning, with the oxymoron that the compulsive force is the wine. Cf. *C.* III. 21. 13–14 *tu* (sc. *testa*) *lene tormentum ingenio admoues* | . . .*duro,* cf. 15–16 *iocoso* | *consilium retegis Lyaeo, Ep.* I. 18. 38 *commissumque teges et uino tortus et ira.*

perspexisse laborent: for the tense see 98 n., for *laborent* with inf. 25 n. The MSS are divided between ind. and subjun. Either is possible (cf. Wilkins *ad l.*) and in this kind of case the better MSS may prevail.

436 *si*–**437** The second limb of the comparison is not a prosaic 'application' of the first but, as often in H., takes the argument further: 437 draws the conclusion from the testing of the friend: *numquam te fallent.*

436 *an* 'whether. . .not', cf. below 462.

si carmina condes: as *Ep.* I. 3. 24 *seu condis amabile carmen. condo* with *carmen, poema,* and the like, replaces various archaic locutions; it is known first from Cic. *Rep.* IV. 12, *T.D.* IV. 4, *Att.* I. 16. 15 (*poema*) and Lucr. V. 2; next come the Augustans in verse and prose.

437 *fallent* in the best MSS, rightly as against *fallant,* cf. *Ep.* I. 7. 25–8, Keller, *Epil.* 773.

†*animi sub uulpe latentes*†: obelized because no one to my knowledge has made satisfactory sense, either by explaining or by emending the transmitted text. If *uulpes* stands for the disingenuous flatterer, as in the Aesopean fable of the fox and the crow (166 ed. Chambry, cf. Phaedr. I. 13), then the wording is odd and unexplained. *S.* I. 3. 33–4 *at ingenium ingens* | *inculto latet hoc sub corpore* scarcely make an acceptable comparison. '"animi sub uolpe latentes" cannot stand for "animi uolpis sub eius pectore latentes": who ever said "sub me celo" meaning "sub meo pectore"? "curae sub imperatore" for "sub pectore imperatoris"?', Housman, *JP,* XVIII (1890), 34. If on the other hand *uulpes* is the animal, crafty by reputation and in looks, of the ancient fables from Archilochus onward, the present passage is wholly thrown out of gear. For to satisfy H.'s wording the craftiness must be within not without, as indeed it is in Pers. 5. 116–17 *fronte politus* | *astutam uapido seruas in pectore uulpem.* Emendations fail, though the worst illogicality is removed by such proposals as Peerlkamp's *fallent sub amica pelle latentes,* Ribbeck's *uolpes sub pelle latentes,* and others. If *animi* is correct, as it may be (*Ep.* II. 1. 249 *mores animique* = ethos), the notion in *sub uulpe* has still to be determined.

Commentary

(h) The true critic and the true friend, 438–52

The tradition. Literary theory is concentrated in 445–9: the Alexandrian critic testing a poem submitted to his judgement; 438 ff. prepare the way. This Alexandrian notion would suit a section περὶ ποιητοῦ, for it advises the poet to submit his work to judgement according to the standards of the τέχνη or *ars* concerned. As for Alexandrianism it may be recalled that Dionysius Thrax considered literary criticism, κριτική, the most advanced and valuable part of γραμματική. This notion implies that the criteria for literary judgement were those employed in the textual and expository work of the masters of the School, cf. below 450 n. But it does not necessarily ensure single-minded concentration on that κριτική. It is not known whether a demand for a critical check was part of τὸ διδακτόν, teachability, which was proclaimed already by the teachers of τέχνη before Plato, cf. F. Heinimann, *MH*, xviii (1961), 106 n. 7. Specific evidence for this feature either in Alexandrian or pre-Platonic writing on τεχνῖται is not, to my knowledge, extant.

In this section as well as the previous, honest criticism is linked with honest friendship; the true critic is the true friend. The moral aspects of flattery in friendship must have been much-vented topics in Hellenistic philosophical and popularizing writing as they are seen to be in such later works as Plut. *Quomodo adulator ab amico internoscatur* and Cic. *Am.* 88 ff. But again I know of no evidence attesting the conjunction of friendship and criticism in extant Hellenistic writing on literary theory as it is attested in H. and seems to be attested in Lucilius.

Horace. In H. certainly the true friend is the true critic and he applies the canons of Alexandrian criticism to verse that is submitted to him. H. dramatizes these issues in the activities of a person, Quintilius (Varus), 438 ff. This is an area in which human sentiment and intellectual judgement coincide, a proper topic for poetry.

Commentary

The section begins abruptly in the familiar Horatian fashion. But it is seen almost at once that the relation to the preceding section is that of a simple antithesis. Quintilius is not an *assentator*, a false friend; he is the *uerus amicus* because he is the true critic.

438 *Quintilio:* Porph. *hic erat Quintilius Varus Cremonensis amicus Vergilii eques Romanus*; ps.-Acro has *poeta* before *Cremonensis* but nothing is known of poetic production. Cf. H. Gundel, *R-E*, XXIV. 899–902. He died in 24/23 B.C., cf. 439 n. on *aiebat*. The Quintilius whose death evoked *C.* I. 24 *quis desiderio*, addressed to *Vergilius*, is identified with the same *Quintilius, sodalis Vergilii*, by Porphyrion. *Ibid.* 6–8 *cui... | incorrupta Fides nudaque Veritas | quando ullum inueniet parem?* certainly fit the character described in the *Ars*.

438–9 *si quid recitares... aiebat*, and 442–3 *si... malles | ... insumebat*, are the certain instances in H., cited by D. Bo, *Hor. Op.* III. 172, for frequentative imperf. subjun. in a *si* cl. and imperf. ind. in apodosis. Also, probably, 439–40 *negares... iubebat*, where *si* may be continued from 438. This is a distinctive and precise usage, at home in narrative or anecdote, and first known from prose authors of the generation before Augustus, see Kühner–Stegmann, II. 398. Its origins however are still debated, cf. Hofmann–Szantyr, 624, 663 f. (with older literature), S. A. Handford, *The Lat. Subjun.* (1947), pp. 176–9, and the brief but illuminating remarks of E. C. Woodcock, *A New Lat. Syn.* (1959), pp. 152 f.

438 *recitares:* cf. 429 n. *super his*, below 474 *recitator acerbus*, and *S.* I. 4. 73 *nec recito cuiquam nisi amicis idque coactus*, etc.

corrige: the verb corresponding to *rectum*, itself a literary term, cf. 367 n. *emendare* is a more technical synonym stressing the faults. E.g. Cic. *Att.* XIII. 48. 2 *laudationem Porciae tibi misi correctam*, Caecina, Cic. *Fam.* VI. 7. 4 *librum... te... correcturum*, Varro, *L.L.* IX. 16 *uerba... quae... sine offensione commutari possunt, statim ad rationem corrigi oportet*, Ov. *Pont.* IV. 12. 25 *saepe ego correxi* sub te censore *libellos*, Quint. *I.O.* II. 2. 7 *in emendando quae corrigenda erunt non acerbus*; cf. *TLL*, IV. 1035. 42 ff.

sodes: a deprecating colloquialism, 'if you please', which well suits the courteous informality of Quintilius' approach; for derivation and use, see J. B. Hofmann, *Lat. Umgangssprache*[2], 133 f. Cf. *S.* I. 9. 41, *Ep.* I. 7. 15, and the formula *dic sodes, Ep.* I. 1. 62, 16. 31.

439 *hoc... et hoc: S.* I. 1. 112 *hunc atque hunc*, cf. *Epod.* 2. 31 *hinc et hinc*, 4. 9 *huc et huc*.

413

aiebat puts the *Ars* after the death of Quintilius, 24/23 B.C., not very usefully since few doubt that date.

melius te posse: sc. *reddere* or more likely *scribere*, *S.* 1. 10. 47 *melius quod scribere possem.*

negares: hardly an independent quasi-conditional clause sandwiched between two *si* clauses. *si* 438 is probably continued and the sentence should be punctuated accordingly—a colon or semicolon after *et hoc*, though recent editors avoid putting it. For the subjun., see above 438 n. *recitares*.

440 *bis terque* 'as often as . . .', cf. 358 n.

delere, 'delete' (for later correction); above at 398 it may denote the same, or may be 'scrap' (altogether) as at *Ep.* II. 1. 69 *delendaue carmina Liui.*

iubebat: Quintilius' interventions rise to a climax (G. T. A. Krüger *ad l.*), though not in volume as it were: from the courteous *corrige sodes*, to the peremptory *delere iubebat*, to the expression of silent contempt, 443 ff.

441 *et male tornatos incudi reddere uersus:* this elegant but not outstanding verse inspired Bentley's longest note on any passage in the *Ars*. Although ingenious and learned, the note is erroneous and far too long in comparison with what it teaches. (1) Can *tornatus, limatus*, τορευτός, etc. be said to apply 'more or less', or allow such qualifications as *male, bene*? Or do they denote perfection and therefore, as Bentley thought, exclude *male* or *bene*? The answer is, they do admit of degrees, cf. Cic. *De Or.* 1. 180 (*homo*) *oratione* maxime *limatus*, and the frequent comparatives *limatior, limatius*. Moreover Peerlkamp rightly pointed to adjs. like εὔτορνος, εὔξεστος, participles like *expolitus*, also ἀποτορνεύειν and *detornatus* all of which express comparative notions in different ways. (2) Is it true that you 'turn', *tornare*, on the lathe wood, stone, ivory, glass, but that you work metal only on the anvil? If that were true, *tornatos* and *incudi* would be, as Bentley thought, incompatible. The answer is that metal, though of course less frequently, is turned on the lathe. C. Fea, *ad l.*, noted Vitr. x. 7. 3 *emboli masculi* (i.e. pistons made of metal) *torno politi*. Verses are said to be put on the lathe from Prop. II. 34 (B). 43 *incipe iam angusto uersus includere torno* onward; or else, as late as Sid. *Ep.* IX. 13. 2 *Horatiana incude formatos Asclepiadeos*, they are said to be worked on the anvil. For other instances see Bentley's n. Anvil and file concur at Ov. *Tr.* I. 7. 29–30 *ablatum mediis opus est incudibus illud,* | *defuit et scriptis ultima lima meis*, and another passage was noted by Fea for the image of metal on the lathe, Symm. *Ep.* I. 4 (*epigrammata*) *bono metallo cusa, torno exigi nescierunt; et duriorem materiem, nisi fallor, adniteris.*

Commentary

Fea and Peerlkamp therefore have explained this passage correctly and no emendations—*formatos, adornatos*, least of all Bentley's ungainly *ter natos*—seem to be required; *Ep.* II. 1. 233 *incultis . . . uersibus et male natis* is a different matter. H. is saying that the metal of the verses is badly 'finished'. Now the metal mass, as it were, must be reconstituted, and returned to the anvil, *reddere incudi*, for a new hammering and, doubtless, at the end, a new turning on the lathe, to render them *bene tornatos*—but this is not made explicit.

442 *defendere delictum:* quasi-legal, for *delictum* cf. 347 n.

uertere is still unexplained. It stands for *uertere stilum* (*S.* I. 10. 72), a highly questionable ellipse assumed by Orelli, K.–H. al.; for *auertere* according to H. Schütz, which is unexampled and not implied in the context; *uertere = euertere* does not suit *delictum*. Comm. Cruq. glosses *corrigere, mutare*, i.e. *conuertere*, certainly the sense here desired, as L. Mueller and Wilkins say; but *uertere* is not *mutare* (168, 449) nor has it here a prep. as is usual in H., such as *Ep.* I. 15. 39 *in fumum*. At *Ep.* II. 1. 154 however H. uses a simple acc., *uertere modum*, without prep. or oblique case (*C.* I. 35. 4); and an acc., *delictum*, could here be understood from the first part of the line. The parallel would lend some colour to the 'slight zeugma, *delictum* being the faulty line' (Wilkins), and the notion, in the preceding line, of starting again and reshaping (i.e. *conuertere*) into something different may help.

443 The ear tells that the three elisions in one line (the only instance in the *A.P.*) are deliberate and expressive, although it would be idle to want to define the purpose too closely. The sequence of three elisions decreases markedly from its high point in *S.* II to only 4 in *Ep.* I, to I in *Ep.* II and *A.P.* respectively, cf. D. Bo, *Hor. Op.* III. 66 n. I.

operam (sc. *nullam*) *insumebat:* cf. Cic. *Verr.* II. 3. 150 *nulla opera insumpta*, the verb infrequently used without a purposive *in* or the like, cf. next n.

inanem: pred., 'in vain', parallel to *ultra* 'beyond (reasonable limit)'; *TLL*, VII. 1. 2052. 60 cited Liv. x. 18. 14 *frustra operam insumptam*.

444 *quin* 'to prevent . . .', after the negative of the prec. l. on the model of *nil impedit quin*; commentators cite *S.* II. 3. 42 *nil uerbi, pereas quin fortiter, addam*.

sine riuali te . . . amares is proverbial, cf. A. Otto, *Sprichwörter*, 301: Cic. *Q. Fr.* III. 8. 4 *quam ineptus, quam se ipse amans sine riuali, Att.* VI. 3. 7 *licebit eum solus ames, me aemulum non habebis.* Cf. Quint. *I.O.* x. 1. 88 (*Ouidius*) *nimium amator ingenii sui*.

teque et tua: as a connective for two nouns, adjs., or pronouns, H.

rarely uses the archaic poeticism -*que et*, and always for special effect, cf. 196 n. With nouns it occurs above 214 *motumque et luxuriem* (cf. n.), *C.* IV. 14. 46 *Nilusque et Hister*; with adjs. *C.* IV. 9. 35–6 (*animus*) *rerumque prudens et secundis* | *temporibus . . . rectus*; with pronouns *Ep.* I. 14. 19 *meque et te*, and here where it makes the solipsism of authorship more pointed, 'his self as well as his works'.

445–52 The tenses now change from the imperf. reporting Quintilius' procedure to the gnomic fut., cf. e.g. 40–1 *cui lecta potenter* erit *res,* | *nec facundia* deseret *hunc*. This then is a moral drawn from Quintilius' criticism: Quintilius the man, already a somewhat exemplary figure, changes wholly into a type—the honest critic, 'an Aristarchus' (450 n.). The instances too belong to Alexandrian *ars critica*; for a dubious Lucilian echo, see 451 n.; an ideal (Peripatetic) mean of style is the yardstick for the critic (*Prol.* 189 n. 2). So it is in the *Florus*, but the compass is even smaller: two verses, *Ep.* II. 2. 122–3. How does H. represent that ideal poetically? According to D. West, *Reading Horace* (1967), pp. 59–60, 'the whole passage leaps into sense as a pruning metaphor'. This feature however is more strongly marked in the small compass of the *Florus* (West, *op. cit.* p. 54). That is where the poetic difference between two comparable passages seems to lie. In the *Ars* H. talks more in terms of theory and less in picture-language. It is only at 447–8 *ambitiosa recidet* | *ornamenta* that the metaphor comes to life. How much that colours the rest of the passage is open to question. *inertes* and *incomptis* (445–6) scarcely suggest this image, and West makes more of *durus* than I am inclined to do, 446 n. I doubt if the metaphor impinges on the rest of the verse in which it occurs, see 448 n. It does not impinge on 449. One suspects that if the whole passage drew on arboriculture, H. would have shown this by one or two of his unobtrusive touches.

445 *uir bonus et prudens:* like his counterparts, the poet (above 312) and the orator (*uir bonus dicendi peritus*), the critic must have certain moral qualities. In the background there lies the distinction between the sincere and the mendacious friend, to which is tied the distinction between the true and mendacious critic. Cf. *Ep.* II. 2. 110 *cum tabulis* animum censoris *sumet* honesti—the poet criticizing his own work. *bonus et prudens* combine truthfulness and competence, cf. *Ep.* I. 16. 32 *uir bonus et prudens*, 7. 22 *uir bonus et sapiens*.

uersus . . . inertes: not clumsy but sluggish, dull, the *uirtute carentia* of *Ep.* II. 2. 123. Calp. *Ecl.* 3. 60 calls a whole pastoral *carmen iners* (*inops* variant). Above 358 *quem bis terue bonum cum risu miror*, Quint. *I.O.* II. 4. 9 *dum satis putant uitio carere, in id ipsum incidunt uitium quod uirtutibus carent*.

reprehendet is the first of seven verbs all denoting censure of various kinds; this section is concerned with faults.

446 *culpabit:* cf. above 31 n.

duros: sc. *uersus*; nobody (according to D. West, *Reading Horace*, p. 60 with n. 41) has made full sense of this word here, because the sustained image has been missed. He explains *durus* as a metaphor from horticulture (cf. above 445–52 n.), relating to a hard woody growth. But does the word call for that explanation? Scarcely, since the metaphor is not made active. The word is known as a term in rhetoric and literary criticism (*TLL*, v. 1. 2310–11, 2314–15), perhaps on the basis of such a Greek term as σκληρός. Moreover H. elsewhere uses *durus* for (archaic) harshness and there is no live metaphorical implication; thus *Ep.* II. 1. 66–7 *si quaedam nimis antique, si pleraque dure* | *dicere credit (ueteres poetas)*, *S.* I. 4. 8 (Lucilius) *durus componere uersus*; contrast the imagery at *Ep.* II. 2. 122–3—a passage parallel to this—*nimis aspera sano* | *leuabit cultu*. Quint. *I.O.* VIII. 6. 65 in criticizing word order calls a particular instance *rectum...sed durum et incomptum*. Thus harshness (rough edges or the like) may be related to lack of finish, and *incomptum* follows next in H. If this is so, my remark *Prol.* 189 n. 2 fin. needs reconsideration.

incomptis: sc. *uersibus*; not rounded off, unfinished, 441 *male tornatos*, *Ep.* II. 1. 233 *incultis...uersibus et male natis*. Cf. Quint. *op. cit.* (prec. n.) 41 *nuda sit et uelut incompta oratio*.

allinet 'mark', cf. Cic. *Verr.* I. 17 *nulla nota, nullus color, nullae sordes uidebantur his sententiis allini posse*.

atrum | *(signum)*: Porph. *significat ac notat uersum male formatum*, ps.-Acro *notam*, etc. The humour of the double entendre is plain; as commentators point out, the blackness is that of the ink (*atramentum*, *Ep.* II. 1. 236) and of condemnation and death (*morti...atrae, C.* I. 28. 13, cf. II. 3. 16); thus the θ(άνατος) of Greek judges, in military lists of the dead, etc. Pers. 4. 13 *nigrum uitio praefigere theta*, Mart. VII. 37. 1–2 *nosti mortiferum quaestoris...signum?* | *...discere theta nouum*, Aus. *Epigr.* 87. 13 (ed. Peiper, p. 344) *tuumque nomen* θ *sectilis signet*.

447 *transuerso calamo:* ps.-Acro *non transuerso calamo sed transuerso apice*: doubtless an allusion to Aristarchus' obelus, a horizontal stroke against a verse in the margin of the MS, cf. *Anec. Paris.* (Reifferscheid, *Suet.* p. 138) *prudentiores uiri, quorum summus in hac re fuit Aristarchus, quotiens improbarent uersus...obelo (-um MS) potissime notandos (-um MS) existimarent*. Aristarchus' textual procedure was well known, cf. Cic. below 450 n. *Aristarchus*; this procedure is here supposed to be employed for literary criticism, a poetically inadequate passage is thus deleted. How readily the two types of criticism could merge may be gathered from Quint. *I.O.* x. 1. 59 *ex tribus receptis Aristarchi iudicio scriptoribus iamborum.*

ambitiosa perhaps reveals the notion 'encircling and luxuriant growth', once the following word *recidet* opens up the horticultural image; at *C.* 1. 36. 20 Damalis is *lasciuis hederis ambitiosior*, cf. D. West, *op. cit.* p. 60. In terms of literary criticism a mean is now approached from the opposite extreme; the fault is no longer a deficiency but an indefensible excess. *ambitiosa* is 'importunate, designing', first here, it seems, applied to style in what might possibly be a Horatian metaphor. Cf. Quint. *I.O.* xi. 1. 50 *tumidum ac sui iactantem et ambitiosum institorem eloquentiae*, xii. 10. 40 *affectationis et ambitiosae in loquendo iactantiae*, contrast *nihil arcessiti et elaborati.* (The word at Juv. 7. 50 is likely to have the same metaphorical notion, but 50–1 present a well-known textual crux; the simple conjecture *ambitiosum* qualifying *scribendi cacoethes* scarcely solves the problem.) The adj. appears to belong to the late Republic in any case and the transition to other spheres than political comes soon after in verse and later in Silver Latin generally. For the evidence, see *TLL*, 1. 1855. 8 ff., but the article is badly arranged.

recidet: a metaphor from horticulture (cf. *coercuit* above 293 n.) and a touch of imagery not found at *S.* 1. 10. 69–70 *recideret omne quod ultra | perfectum traheretur.* That passage however helps to explain the stylistic notion here; *Ep.* 11. 2. 122 *luxuriantia compescet* (*Prol.* 189 n. 2) helps to explain both the imagery and the application to style.

448 *ornamenta* like the *ornatus*, κόσμος, of which they are the vehicles, can be either specific figures of speech or any kind of device which raises informal to formal talk, cf. above 234 n. Here the latter seems to be intended, devices that make speech poetic, just as *ornamenta* are devices that make style rhetorical at Cic. *De Or.* 11. 122 *neminem omnium tot et tanta quanta sint in Crasso habuisse ornamenta dicendi*, 123 *si...ego* (sc. Antonius) *hunc oratorem quem nunc fingo...tradam eum Crasso uestiendum et ornandum*—a reference to the treatment of the whole of rhetorical style in *De Or.* book 111.

parum claris lucem dare: there are obscurities other than those surrounding the *ornamenta* that have just been mentioned; unlike D. West, *op. cit.* p. 59 I would argue that this clause and the preceding are as distinct as the rest of them here. *parum claris*, τοῖς ἀσαφέσι, an Aristotelian criterion by which much Alexandrian and neo-Alexandrian verse would stand condemned. Ar. *Rhet.* 111. 2 in. and *Poet.* ch. 22 in. show that the virtue of speech, which (for Aristotle) is clarity, and the virtue of poetic speech, which is 'not to be plain', are two demands that may pull in different directions, and have to be balanced. Much critical effort was therefore spent on discussing the issues so arising, see e.g. 25 n. *breuis esse laboro,* | *obscurus fio.* Cf. Quint. *I.O.* VIII, ch. 2. *lucem dare,* another touch of imagery, obscurity and light, but not necessarily the pruning metaphor. Cf. 143 n.

449 was deleted by O. Ribbeck and L. Mueller—with some plausibility, because it is not, as Rostagni suggested, a summary, nor, at first sight, does it add much to 445–8. Yet it probably contains two further notions.

ambigue dictum: not the ambiguity that is a chief source of poetic speech and thought but an accidental and faulty overlapping of meanings. So Aristotle discusses the fault of τὸ ἀμφίβολον at *Rhet.* III. 5, 1407 a 32 ff.; at *Poet.* 25, 1461 a 25, ἀμφιβολία is a chance equivocation. Quint. *I.O.* VII, ch. 9 implies a great deal of discussion of ambiguity not only by the philosophers but by literary critics and rhetoricians, although he is there concerned with subject-matter, not style. Cf. *ibid.* VIII. 5. 21, Philod. *HV*², XI. 161 (cit. Heinze, cf. Gomperz, *SBAW*, CXXIII (1891), 64).

mutanda notabit presents difficulties if it is referred to specific faults or (with Rostagni) considered a summary. It is probably best explained as a special sign (*nota*) drawing attention to anything that needs to be altered, and has not been defined earlier. For *notare*, see above 156 n.

450 *fiet Aristarchus* 'an Aristarchus', the familiar Latin idiom in the absence of an article and because *aliquis, unus, alter* would add a different nuance, as in Lact. *D.I.* V. 2. 17 *Aristophanes aliquis aut Aristarchus*; thus above 357 *sic mihi qui multum cessat fit Choerilus ille, Ep.* II. 2. 99–100 *discedo Alcaeus puncto illius* (Porph. *fio alter Alcaeus); ille meo quis?* | *quis nisi Callimachus?,* 101 *fit Mimnermus*; J. Vahlen, *Op. Ac.* I. 51, compares Mart. III. 2. 12 *illo uindice nec Probum timeto.* Aristarchus represents Alexandrian criticism (cf. 445–52 n.): the mention doubly apposite because he standardized the use of critical signs, 447 n., L. Cohn, *R-E*, II. 866 f. For the merging of textual and literary criticism, see the same note above, and Cic. *Pis. 73 te non Aristarchum sed Phalarin grammaticum habemus,* qui non notam apponas ad malum uersum *sed poetam armis persequare; Fam.* IX. 10. 1 applies textual criticism humorously to a financial account, *profert alter, opinor, duobus uersiculis expensum Niciae, alter Aristarchus hos* ὀβελίζει; *ego tamquam criticus antiquus iudicaturus sum utrum sint* τοῦ ποιητοῦ an παρεμβεβλημένοι. With a gen. it is 'the Aristarchus of...', Cic. *Att.* I. 14. 3 *quarum* (sc. *mearum orationum*) *tu A. es,* cf. D. R. Shackleton Bailey *ad l.*; again a matter of stylistic correction.

nec aEKR, *non* δπ λl φψ. Unlike many recent editors Rostagni, Villeneuve and D. Bo rightly print *nec*, the first appending an argument that would make for *non*: 'descrizione negativa, in netto distacco e opposizione con tutto ciò che precede, ch'era la descrizione positiva' —an antithesis which would be well expressed by asyndetic *non*, and so Bentley recommended. There are of course dozens of instances of this type of *non*, e.g. 268, *Ep.* II. 1. 122, 2. 13, 139. But, as H. Schütz argued, there is no antithesis, the sense being 'he will be a strenuous critic and not say...'.

451 (*cur ego amicum*) | *offendam in nugis?* : the last appeal to friendship and the last refuge for those wanting to avoid the obligation of criticizing. The two topics are tied together: such trifles do not matter, why annoy a friend by taking them seriously? Cf. Cic. *Am.* 88 (on *offensio*) *monendi amici saepe sunt et obiurgandi, et haec accipienda amice cum beneuole fiunt.* Whether unwillingness to give offence through criticism belongs to the Lucilian context of fr. 611 or 953 (above 425 n.) is uncertain. *nugae* are trifles, i.e. trifling faults; Schütz *ad l.* argues, to me plausibly, that a secondary notion, 'verses', is excluded by the next sentence.

hae nugae seria ducent | (*in mala*): the noun is now repeated in inverted commas as it were, 'what they call *nugae*' (K.–H.). Then follows the logical opposite, *seria*, still uncertain whether noun or adj.; the doubt is resolved in the next verse. Again Cicero may be compared, *Am.* 89 *molesta ueritas...sed obsequium multo molestius, quod peccatis indulgens praecipitem amicum ferri sinit.*

452 Ps.-Acro and following him Lambinus and some later commentators misunderstood the scope of this parting shot. A reference to the *assentator* and *derisor* (433) of section (*g*) would be misplaced. Neither *derisum* nor *exceptumque sinistre* will by itself convey this notion; Orelli was right to reject it. This poet is not the rich dilettante of the previous section but a poet who recites his verse without first submitting it to an Aristarchus and consequently disgraces himself, see below.

derisum semel: one débâcle may be sufficient to mar a poet's reputation. *semel* would convey nothing if *derisum* referred to the *derisor* of 433, and meant 'fooled' or 'flattered'.

exceptumque: '*proprie dicitur de histrione...in* εἴρωνα *autem illum minime quadrat*' (Orelli), cf. *TLL*, v. 2. 1251. 22–4 of public appearances: Cic. *Verr.* II. 5. 94 *excipitur ab omnibus...clamore*, Virg. *A.* v. 575 *plausu*, and then elsewhere with an abl. denoting the kind of reception. Here there follows an expressive adv. as at Suet. *Nero*, 22. 3, Nero being asked to perform *exceptusque effusius*. The adv. is the rare

sinistre, 'unfavourably'; so again Plin. *Pan.* 45. 5, Tac. *Hist.* I. 7. 2
utraque caedes s. accepta, III. 52. 3 *s.... rescripsere*.

(i) Error (cf. 308) personified: the mad poet, 453–end

The *uesanus poeta* is so clearly the *perfectus poeta* turned upside
down—a spirited caricature—that no traditional literary
theory must be looked for. To define, for what it is worth,
poetic *uirtus* as an equilibrium of *ingenium* and *ars* is literary
theory. To take one of these terms—*ingenium* in all its unreality when it is cut off from *ars*—and imagine it as a person,
that is not theory but poetic fancy. H. has concentrated one
of the ideas underlying his traditional theory into a poetic
picture, a symbol. It is not known whether he could draw on
an earlier satirist, e.g. Lucilius, for his description. What does
ingenium without *ars* look like when it is imagined as a person?
It looks like madness—imagination uncontrolled by reason.
This is the state of mind of which he now, abruptly, proceeds
to give a demonstration, a *reductio ad absurdum*. Thus the *artifex*
section, which began at 295, returns in circular motion to its
starting point, the rejection of *ingenium sine arte*. But coming at
the end of the poem, the caricature is related also to the poem
as a whole. The counterpart to this demonstration comes
at the beginning, multiplicity caricatured because it lacks
the unity granted only by *ars*. The two poetic pictures are
related to each other and form as it were a frame for the
poem: *ars* and *artifex* without the controlling force of art, cf.
Prol. 269.

Like many poems of H. the *Ars* is open-ended. No attempt
is made to bring to a close the conceptual schema of his literary
theory. Instead he draws on a dominant feature of the genre
sermo, the mixture of comic and serious, τὸ σπουδογέλοιον.
He ends with a story, the attempted suicide of the mad poet,
told with imaginative involvement—and no wonder. For what
is H. if not *ingenium*? The poem began with a paradox, see
1–40 n. So it closes with a paradox. By way of a cautionary
tale, *exemplum*, H. celebrates the *ingenium*, without which art

cannot be, but which, left to itself, would destroy art and its practitioners.

453–6, like 419–21, form a comparative sentence beginning *ut . . . qui* or in some such way but dispensing with *sic* or *ita*. With malicious literalism H. interprets Democritus' and Plato's notion of divine possession: inspiration is like an infectious or frightening disease. The relative clause is so formed as to draw attention to its descriptive features, *ut . . . quem . . . urget*, with the names of the diseases prominently displayed over two verses, cf. *S.* II. 3. 43–4 *quem mala stultitia et quemcumque inscitia ueri* | *caecum agit*.

453(–4) The diseases are rehearsed with clinical detachment, *aut . . .* | *aut . . . et*.

mala . . . scabies 'mange, scab', a term applied in antiquity to various skin diseases, some more some less dangerous. In Greek ψώρα (scab) ἀγρία may include leprosy, cf. Cels. v. 28. 16 *quo asperior est (scabies) quoque prurit magis, eo difficilius tollitur; itaque eam quae talis est agrian Graeci appellant.* H.'s *mala*, like the other very specific adjs. in this list, may convey the same notion 'dangerous'. The jingle 452 *in mala*, 453 *ut mala* may or may not be intentional.

morbus regius, or *arquatus morbus*, is jaundice, cf. Varro *ap.* Plin. *N.II.* xxii. 24. 114, Cels. iii. 24, ps.-Acro *ad l.*, with different but equally implausible explanations of the name 'royal disease'. These writers do not say whether jaundice was considered contagious.

454 *fanaticus error*: Porph. *idest qui lymphatico agitantur*, 'religious mania' and prophecy. This is a step closer to poetic inspiration: Liv. xxxviii. 18. 9 *Galli Matris Magnae . . . uaticinantes fanatico carmine*, Juv. 4. 123–4 *fanaticus oestro* | *percussus, Bellona, tuo diuinat*, cf. J. E. B. Mayor's n.; thus *oestrum* for the sting of poetic inspiration, Stat. *Theb.* I. 32–3. *fanaticus* is habitually applied to the devotees of orgiastic oriental cults, Bellona (*S.* II. 3. 220–3), Magna Mater, etc., also to Bacchants; cf. *TLL*, vi. 1. 270. 28 ff. *error* if *error mentis* = 'insanity'; and contrasted with *uirtus* = 'imperfection' (308). But the word may, as K.–H. suggest, refer to such sights in the Roman streets as the 'strolling priests' of various sects; commentators cite *Suda* s.v. ἡ Περγαία Ἄρτεμις (II. 576 Adler): τάσσεται ἐπὶ τῶν ἀγυρτῶν καὶ πλανητῶν, and Ov. *Pont.* I. 37 ff.

et is explanatory or exemplifying.

iracunda Diana: ps.-Acro *sicut lunaticum* etc., as a sign of divine displeasure, e.g. *S.* II. 3. 223 *hunc circumtonuit . . . Bellona*, cf. Greek σεληνόβλητοι, σεληνόπληκτοι, and L.–S.–J. s.v. citing *Schol.* Ar. *Nub.* 397, *Suda* s.v. βεκκεσέληνος. The scholiast's explanation is based on the equivalence of Diana and Luna, established in Roman poetry, e.g. *C.* IV. 6. 38 *Noctilucam,* Cat. 34. 15–16 *tu (Diana) . . .notho es | dicta lumine Luna.* In the cult the two separate divinities approximate to each other, cf. Wissowa, *R-E,* v. 334. 48 ff. But as to equivalence Varro expresses himself cautiously, *L.L.* v. 68 *Luna, uel quod sola lucet noctu. itaque ea dicta Noctiluca in Palatio; nam ibi noctu lucet templum. hanc ut Solem Apollinem* quidam Dianam *uocant.* So does Cic. *N.D.* II. 68 *Dianam autem et Lunam eandem esse putant.*

455 The *uesanus poeta* is the fourth sufferer from disease.

tetigisse timent: the inf. with *timent* as above 170, for the perf. inf., see 168 n. The satiric angle as *S.* II. 7. 117 *aut insanit homo aut uersus facit.*

456 *qui sapiunt* puris: those who are in their right senses and those who have the savoir of *ars poetica,* cf. 309 n.

agitant pueri 'chase', cf. above 341 n. The asyndeton is adversative.

incautique sequuntur: cf. *S.* I. 3. 133–34 *uellunt tibi barbam | lasciui pueri; quos tu nisi fuste coerces,* etc., II. 3. 130 *insanum te omnes pueri clamentque puellae.* Philo's celebrated outdoor scene *(In Flaccum,* 36) exhibits a similar feature. Carabas suffered from 'a mild form of madness' (τὴν ἀνειμένην καὶ μαλακωτέραν sc. μανίαν). οὗτος διημέρευε καὶ διενυκτέρευε γυμνὸς ἐν ταῖς ὁδοῖς. . .ἄθυρμα νηπίων καὶ μειρακίων σχολαζόντων.

457–64 A long period describing the mad poet's progress and fall. Two conditional sentences are contrasted without overt connexion, 457–60, 461–4. The former is a masterpiece of architectonic arrangement, each clause corresponding to a separate folly and the final disaster, the sequence deceptively simple in its juxtapositions. The prosaic order would be something like this, *nemo poetam uesanum, quamuis clamet, si, dum uelut auceps sublimis errat, in puteum decidit, tollere uolet.* H. has juxtaposed the stages, thus: *hic* (1) *dum sublimis. . . errat;* (2) *ueluti auceps,* with the verb drawn into the comparison so that it is the fowler who seems to have the fall, see below 458 n.; (3) the cry for help *(ciues),* implying that he belongs to the community at large; (4) the final disaster, no one will help, the madman has put himself outside the community.

457–60 The symbolical fall of the poet wandering with his head in the clouds has a precedent in the story about Thales watching the heavens while walking, Plato, *Theaet.* 174 a, Diog. L. I. 34; W. Jaeger, *SBPA,* xxv (1928), 390 (= *Scr. Min.* I. 348). The poet's fall may have been modelled on the descriptive features of the older story. Cf. too Aesop, *Fab.* 65 (ed. Chambry, cit. Rostagni).

457 *sublimis* 'head high', like μετέωρος, cf. Plato, *Theaet.* 174a Θαλῆν ἀστρονομοῦντα. . .καὶ ἄνω βλέποντα, hardly acc. with *uersus.*

The word connotes 'high-minded', cf. above 165, *Ep.* II. I. 165, and the different metaphor, *C.* I. I. 36 *sublimi feriam sidera uertice.*

uersus ructatur: Wilkins' guess (*ad l.*) that the verb had lost its coarseness in classical Latin as ἐρεύγομαι had in Hellenistic Greek is at any rate not implausible. It is true, the compound *eructo(r)* preserves its onomatopoeic notion in the few classical instances where drunken and sated speech is described as 'belching', cf. Cic. *Cat.* II. 10 *uino languidi, conferti cibo ... eructant sermonibus suis caedem;* it seems to become genteel not before Christian writing, *TLL,* v. 2. 827. 3 ff. = *proferre, promere.* But a similar verb, *euomere,* occurs as early as Enn. *Ann.* 241 (V.²) in the notion 'utter freely', and such late Latin instances as Sid. *Carm.* 23. 253 imply little more than 'mouthing'. Hence *uersus ructatur* may be 'to mouth, come out with, verses', 'blurt out' in its earlier meaning. For the dep. see Porph. '*ructatur*' *pro ructat; antiqui enim et ructo et ructor dixerunt,* etc. Paul. Fest. 263 *ructare non ructari dicendum est ... Cicero tamen* '*ructaretur*' *dixit,* Serv. on Virg. *A.* III. 632.

ructatur et errat: verses ending with two similar main verbs joined by *et* or other conjunctions have an archaic tinge and when they occur in Augustan poetry (as they do occasionally) serve a special purpose. Here the effect is probably meant to be comic: the poet spouting verses during his halting progression. Elsewhere other purposes are intended, e.g. 200 *precetur et oret,* and the verbs with homoeoteleuton 110 *deducit et angit,* though not with triple rhyme as in Ennius' much derided *splendet et horret.*

458 H. satirically identifies poet and fowler so closely that it is hard to know which of the two is *merulis intentus* and falls into a well or pit.

decidit: the verb of the *si* clause is drawn into the comparison, and thus contributes to the effect described in the last note. L. Mueller *ad l.* appositely compares the verb, *S.* II. 5. 83.

459 *in puteum foueamue:* the odd assortment of well or pit draws attention to the typical nature of the tale—'a hole in the ground like...' The point was already illustrative when the story about Thales was *ben trovato;* it simply marks the paradox that the wise man attends to things in the sky but not to things at his feet, cf. Plato, *Theaet.* 174 a πεσόντα εἰς φρέαρ Θρᾱττά τις ... θεραπαινὶς ἀποσκῶψαι λέγεται ὡς τὰ μὲν ἐν οὐρανῷ προθυμοῖτο εἰδέναι, τὰ δ' ἔμπροσθεν αὐτοῦ κτλ. Ignorance of any obstacle in one's path seems to have become proverbial for lack of practical sense, as *S.* II. 3. 59 *hic fossa est ingens, hic rupes maxima: serua, Ep.* II. 2. 135 *posset qui rupem et puteum uitare patentem.*

Commentary

licet is still rare as a quasi-conjunction in Augustan verse, e.g.
Virg. *A.* VI. 802, XI. 348, 440. In the *Ars* it occurs only here, and once
each in the *Satires* and *Epistles*, but also once each in the *Epodes* and
Odes. Though it is not unlikely that the usage gained ground in the
colloquial language of the time, the paucity of instances in each of
H.'s works does not bear out Heinze's conclusions, *C.* III. 24. 3 n.,
7th ed.

succurrite: cf. 460 n.

longum(| clamet): although the similarity of the Homeric μακρὸν
ἀυτεῖν suggests volume of voice, the situation seems to favour con-
tinued cries for help. *longum* adverbial for the time of utterance as
Pl. *Epid.* 376 *nimis longum loquor,* 665, *Per.* 167, *Ps.* 687 *nimis diu et
longum loquor,* Juv. 6. 64–5 *longum |* . . .*et miserabile gannit;* for Virg.
E. 3. 79 *longum, formose, uale . . . , inquit, Iolla* see the commentators.
These usages are not linked with H. by E. Löfstedt, *Syn.* II. 420,
Hofmann–Szantyr, 40 (*'longum* seit Hor.') and others.

460 (*'succurrite'*) *'io ciues':* the traditional cry for help addressed to
all citizens, which W. Schulze, in an outstanding paper, has traced
in various Indo-European settings, *SBPA*, 1918, 481 ff., repr. *Kl.
Schr.* (1933), pp. 160 ff. It was most often, perhaps originally, associated with an attack, especially on women, βία, *iniuria:* e.g. Eur.
Tro. 999–1000 ποίαν βοὴν | ἀνωλόλυξας . . . ; |, Pl. *Amph.* 376 *pro fidem,
Thebani ciues, Men.* 999–1000 *perii, opsecro uostram fidem, | Epidamnien-
ses, subuenite, ciues,* 1004, *Rud.* 615 *pro Cyrenenses populares, uostram ego
imploro fidem,* 617 *ferte opem* etc., Caec. *FCR*[3], frs. 211–12 *pro deum,
popularium omnium,* . . . *| clamo . . . atque imploro fidem,* Varro, *L.L* VI.
68 and Liv. XXXIII. 28. 3 on *quiritare,* Liv. III. 44. 7 *ad clamorem nutricis
fidem Quiritium implorantis fit concursus,* Ov. *Fast.* VI. 517 *dique uirique
loci, miserae succurrite matri.* To these and other instances cited by
Schulze may be added the cry of the nurse, Sen. *Phaed.* 725–6
adeste Athenae . . . fer opem. For its probable Greek provenance, see
W. H. Friedrich, *Untersuch. zu Sen. dram. Tech.* (1933), pp. 38 ff.; the
passage seems to me to affect the argument of W. S. Barrett, Eur.
Hipp. p. 39. Other emergencies also qualified; thus the Twelve
Tables on apprehending thieves, Cic. *Tull.* 50. For even less colourful
occasions, see Schulze, *Kl. Schr.* 179 n. 5, and E. Norden noting the
accident of the *uesanus poeta, ap.* Schulze, 181 n. 2. Failure to obey
such a summons probably implied a breach of *fides,* see Schulze,
182 f., unless, as it happens here, the *ciues* know that the crier or cry
need not be taken seriously; cf. *Ep.* I. 17. 58 ff., in particular 61–2
*'credite, non ludo, crudeles, tollite claudum.' | 'quaere peregrinum' uicinia
rauca reclamat.*

425

non sit: rightly explained by K.–H., Lejay, and Wilkins, as potential, not either as a prohibition or subjun. with future notion.

qui tollere curet: cf. *Ep.* 1. 17. 58–9 *nec semel irrisus triuiis attollere curat | fracto crure planum.*

461 *si curet:* adversative, '(but) if someone did care after all', with the pointed repetition and changed metrical position observed by Bentley (*tollere cúret. | si curét*), and preferred by him to the vulgate of his time *si quis curet.* The two readings were noted but misjudged by Lambinus.

462 *qui scis an . . .?* 'how do you know whether . . . not . . .?', close to affirmative sense, 'perhaps he has . . .', as in the archaic locution Pl. *Mos.* 58 *qui scis an tibi istuc eueniat . . .?* (with *an . . . non, Mil.* 448), Ter. *Eun.* 790 *qui scis an quae iubeam sine ui faciat?* Cf. Madvig, *Lat. Gram.* §453. The particle is familiar in what became a colloquial formula, *haud scio an.* This colloquialism is avoided in the *nescio an* of Ciceronian speeches. H. so uses *an* after *nescio* at *C.* II. 4. 13, and above 436 this notion is daringly extended to *perspexisse.* The question here is wholly 'rhetorical'—'perhaps then this man of genius is deliberately destroying himself?'. Thus the case of Empedocles is brought in satirically, as an *exemplum* (463–6): inspired poets and prophets must be allowed to indulge their death-wish.

prudens 'deliberately', as *S.* II. 3. 212 *cum p. scelus . . . admittis,* 5. 58, 7. 66, *Ep.* II. 2. 18.

se proiecerit should not have been set aside by F. Klingner in favour of *se deiecerit,* offered by some of the better MSS. Both readings are of course possible but the switch from *decidit* and *demittere* to *proiecerit* stresses, as Bentley said, *significationem voluntarii discriminis,* the notion of the *pro* compound. The assonance *prudens–proiecerit* makes for rather than against the reading; for the confusion of *deicere* and *proicere,* cf. *S.* I. 3. 91.

463 *Siculique poetae:* the description placed before the name Empedocles, which follows at 465—a different kind of allusiveness from 140 *hic qui,* cf. n. Empedocles in this place is *poeta,* not the φυσιολόγος to whom Ar. *Poet.* 1, 1447 b 19 denies poetic status (cf. *Prol.* 121 n. 3); so too the (probably Peripatetic) doctrine *ap. Schol. Dion. Thr.* 449. 4 ff. and 168. 10 ff. (*GG,* 1, vol. 3, ed. Hilgard), cf. Plut. *De aud. poet.* 16 c (cit. Rostagni), Porph. *ad l. E. fuit Agrigentinus physicus, qui se in craterem . . . dedit Aetnae immortalitatem affectans. Ep.* 1. 12. 20 shows that this archaic philosopher was sufficiently known to make this passage more than a recondite allusion.

464 *narrabo* ushers in an *exemplum,* as e.g. *C.* III. 7. 17 *narrat paene datum Pelea Tartaro,* 19–20 *et peccare docentes | fallax historias mouet, S.*

Commentary

1. 1. 69–70 *mutato nomine de te | fabula narratur, Ep.* 1. 2. 6; cf. *S.* II.
6. 77–8 *garrit aniles | ex re fabellas.*

interitum exemplifies inspiration leading to self-destruction.

deus immortalis: cf. Emp. fr. 112. 4–5 (Diels–Kranz, from the Καθαρμοί) ἐγὼ δ' ὑμῖν θεὸς ἄμβροτος, οὐκέτι θνητός, | πωλεῦμαι μετὰ πᾶσι τετιμένος, ὥσπερ ἔοικα | κτλ. Notions of this kind, and an element of mystifying and wonder-working, prompted a rich crop of legend and fiction, of which this is the most impressive specimen, cf. Diels–Kranz, *Vorsokr.* 31 A 16. For suggestions on the age of this legend, see Rostagni's n., Heracl. Pont. fr. 85 (Wehrli), W. K. C. Guthrie, *Hist. of Gr. Phil.* II. 131 n. 1. Cf. Diog. L. VIII. 67–75 (Diels–Kranz, *op. cit.* A 1) and *Suda* s.v. Emp. (Diels–Kranz, *ibid.* A 2). H. omits the malicious detail that Mt Etna erupting returned one of E.'s bronze sandals. The feature which he employs is more relevant to his subject, see *ardentem frigidus*, 465 n.

465 *cupit* and 466 *insiluit, perire,* mark the progress *ad interitum* of unrestrained inspiration.

ardentem frigidus: an antithesis (in chiastic order), *contentio, contrapositum,* or the like in Latin rhetoric, and a stock example for this 'figure', *Ad Her.* IV. 21 *in re frigidissima cales, in feruentissima friges,* with H. Caplan's note. Instances from late Latin verse are noted in Keller's app. crit.; Sil. IX. 497–8 (cit. L. Mueller), the wind Vulturnus getting hot *Aetnae...candente barathro,* does not share this rhetorical structure. Earlier it was regarded as a simple verbal contrast, 'getting hot in cold blood' or the like. Such an antithesis conveys sense for example in Soph. *An.* 88 θερμὴν ἐπὶ ψυχροῖσι καρδίαν ἔχεις, cf. Jebb's note, but scarcely here, where the context demands some reference to *ingenium* and, possibly, some reference to Empedocles' own teaching. The low temperature of old age (K.–H.) is irrelevant. *frigidum* is likely to be 'insensitive, dull', that is, 'lacking *ingenium*', a notion established in Cicero and later writers, and impressively in Virg. *G.* II. 483–4 *sin, has ne possim natura accedere partes, | frigidus obstiterit circum praecordia sanguis.* Servius comments on the Virgilian passage, *secundum physicos qui dicunt stultos esse homines frigidioris sanguinis, prudentes calidi.* That this states correctly the doctrines of Parmenides (in the 'Way of Seeming') and Democritus is borne out by other evidence, cf. Theoph. *De sensu,* 1–4, 58, W. K. C. Guthrie, *Hist. of Gr. Phil.* II. 67 f., 453. As for Empedocles, the evidence is incomplete. Fr. 105 places human thought in the blood surrounding the heart, αἷμα γὰρ ἀνθρώποις περικάρδιόν ἐστι νόημα. Ps.-Acro combines this feature with a doctrine of vital heat, and applies it to this passage, *Empedocles enim dicebat tarda ingenia frigido circa praecordia sanguine impediri.* Whether correct or not, ps.-Acro's ascription should have been presented with the rest of the Empedoclean evidence in Diels–Kranz. For a discussion, see my paper in *Phoenix* XXIII (1969), 138–42.

466 (*Aetnam*) *insiluit:* for the acc. see 194 n., D. Bo, *Hor. Op.* III. 117.

sit ius liceatque: above 72 the notion of *ius* is explained and enlarged by *arbitrium* and *norma*, here by *liceat* 'let poets be free to perish'—a portentous, mock-solemn, pronouncement.

467 The verse was expunged by Ribbeck and L. Mueller because (1) this is the only *versus spondiacus* in H.'s hexameter poems; (2) the axiom is extended to all, not, as in 466, restricted to poets; (3) 468 should follow 466. But (1) a neoteric mannerism, exploited with much circumspection by Virgil though avoided elsewhere by H., does not ill suit this mocking sentimentality. (2) There is no need to restrict the purview; H. is alleging a reason for the axiom of the preceding verse, cf. *Ep.* I. 20. 14–16 *ut ille | qui...in rupes protrusit asellum | iratus; quis enim inuitum seruare laboret?* (3) So far from interrupting the sequence 466–8, l. 467, as K.–H. have seen, brings talk back to *uesanus poeta* and *seruari nolit*, 463. The verse seems to be imitated in a serious context by Sen. *Phoen.* 100 *occidere est uetare cupientem mori*; but at *Ben.* II. 14. 4 the Stoic moralist argues against this permissiveness.

idem...occidenti 'the same as', like the Greek idiom ὁ αὐτός τινι, known in Latin from Lucr. II. 918, III. 1038, IV. 1174, cf. *TLL*, VII. 1. 199. 83 ff. The current, and in my view probable, explanation as a Grecism has been queried by Hofmann–Szantyr, 92.

468–9 Attempts at self-destruction are habitual with the *uesanus poeta*.

468 *nec semel hoc fecit:* as in the parallel passage (cit. above 460 n.) *Ep.* I. 17. 58 *nec semel irrisus.* Although the satire is meant to have general validity, the grammatical subject is not *un qualsiasi poeta affetto da mania* (Rostagni) but the *uesanus poeta* of 455 ff. The satire is general because the mad poet is a symbolical figure.

iam 'straight away, at last', with *fiet*, not (as in many older editions) with *erit*, cf. *TLL*, VII. 1. 106. 28.

469 *fiet homo* 'will be brought to his senses', like those *qui sapiunt* (456), *homo* being *qui sapit*. Cic. *Clu.* 199 *cuius ea stultitia est ut eam nemo hominem...appellare possit*; cf. the locution *si esses homo* and the like, *TLL*, VI. 3. 2879. 43 ff. Since however *excludit sanos Helicone poetas | Democritus* (296–7), this is a contradiction in terms; the *uesanus poeta*, like his archetype Empedocles, desires to be more not less than *homo*: a play upon the twofold notion of *homo*, both more and less than 'sense'.

ponet = deponet: cf. 160 n.

famosae mortis amorem maliciously alleges a motive for 458–9
decidit . . . | in puteum; it is the longing for a death after the manner of
Empedocles. However great H.'s irony may be, the *uesanus poeta*
himself can only long for a 'notable' death, *famosae*, not for a notorious one, as he is said to do by Wilkins and others. It is true,
'notorious' is the meaning of the word elsewhere in H. and often in
classical Latin. But occasionally, in verse and Silver and late Latin,
the reputation, *fama*, is good or neutral, *famosus* therefore 'celebrated'
or 'notable', cf. *TLL*, vi. 1. 258. 21 ff., 257. 70 ff., A. La Penna, *SI*,
xxv (1951), 212 f., D. R. Shackleton Bailey, *Propertiana*, 236, G. B. A.
Fletcher, *Annot. on Tac.* (1964), p. 57.

470–6 The *Ars* ends on a highly satirical note. Unlike true poetry
the mad poet's verses are lethal, not only to him as has just been seen,
but to the community at large.

470 The self-confessed *furor* is represented as a religious curse; the
uesanus poeta must have violated some taboo or other.

cur: ps.-Acro *nec scitur* poena propter quam *facit uersus malos insanus
poeta, an quia . . . aut quia*, etc. This well brings out the satirical logic
whereby the mad poet's verses are regarded as a consequence of
divine punishment. The only question is why he is thus punished.

uersus factitet 'with such persistence' (Wickham). A frequentative
notion is present in *factitare* and a small number of similar verbs in H.
Most of the ninety-two verbs listed by D. Bo, *Hor. Op.* iii. 384 (β) had
long since lost any frequentative force they might have had, e.g.
dubitare, cogitare, imitari.

471 *minxerit in patrios cineres:* the violation of graves often deprecated in sepulchral inscriptions, cf. C. Fea *ad l.*, O. Jahn on Pers. 1.
113–14; Plut. *Stoic. Repug.* ch. 22 cites Chrysippus on violation of
βωμός or ἀφίδρυμα θεοῦ. The style of *sermo* accommodates an
occasional lowering of verbal propriety. Cf. in a similar context Pers.
1. 113–14 *pueri, sacer est locus, extra | meiite,* Juv. 1. 131 *cuius ad
effigiem non tantum meiiere fas est.*

triste bidental: Porph. *id quod Iouis fulmine percussum est bidental appellatur. hoc expiari non potest. errant autem qui putant ab agna dictum bidental,*
cf. Non. 53. 23 *Nigidius Figulus dicit bidental uocari quo bimae pecudes
immolantur,* ps.-Acro *locus fulminis.* '*triste*' *autem quoniam propter lapsum
fulmen constituitur,* Pers. 2. 27 *triste iaces lucis euitandumque bidental.*
Other evidence is cited by Wissowa, *R-E*, s.v. *bidental*, iii. 429. 48 ff.,
Olck, *R-E*, s.v. *bidens*, iii. 426. 58 ff.

472 *mouerit* 'tamper with, disturb'. Ritter's guess that *mouerit =
demouerit:* '*non rite demouit nec praescriptis in eam rem caerimoniis*' was

revived by K.–H. and others, but does not seem to be based on evidence. Rather cf. Virg. *A.* III. 700–1 *fatis numquam concessa moueri* | . . . *Camerina*, Serv. *ad l. consultus Apollo an eam (paludem) penitus exhaurire deberent, respondit* μὴ κίνει Καμάριναν, etc., Luc. VIII. 791 *nautaque ne bustum religato fune moueret*, al.

incestus 'committing sacrilege', *sanctimoniā pollutā*, cf. *C.* III. 2. 30 (*Diespiter*) *neglectus incesto addidit integrum*. The adj. may, ἀπὸ κοινοῦ, apply to both kinds of pollution.

certe 'at any rate', an assertion after preceding doubt (*nec satis apparet cur . . . utrum . . . an*), as *C.* II. 4. 13 ff. *nescias an te . . .* | *Phyllidis . . . decorent parentes;* | *regium certe genus*.

furit: the *fanaticus error*, etc., but also the θεία μανία of the inspired poet.

uelut ursus precedes the clause of which this comparison forms a part. As elsewhere, e.g. above 458, the effect is a poetic mixture of images; it seems almost as if *recitator acerbus* has broken out of a cage with the *ursus*. The vivid humour of the *recitator* as a bear lends fresh point to the well-worn rhetorical comparison of a malefactor with a dangerous animal, cf. Ar. *Rhet.* III. 4, 1406 b 27 ff. εἰσὶν δ' εἰκόνες οἷον ἦν 'Ανδροτίων εἰς 'Ιδριέα ὅτι ὅμοιος τοῖς ἐκ τῶν δεσμῶν κυνιδίοις· ἐκεῖνά τε γὰρ προσπίπτοντα δάκνει⟨ν⟩, καὶ 'Ιδριέα λυθέντα ἐκ τῶν δεσμῶν εἶναι χαλεπόν. This εἰκών is aptly set by H. Caplan beside the *descriptio*, *Ad Her.* IV. 51 *quodsi istum, iudices . . . liberaueritis, statim*, sicut e cauea leo emissus aut aliqua taeterrima belua soluta ex catenis, *uolitabit et uagabitur in foro, acuens dentes in uniuscuiusque fortunas*, in omnes amicos atque inimicos, notos atque ignotos *incursitans*, etc.

473 *obiectos caueae . . . clatros:* not gen. ('the bars of the cage'), the dat. with *obicio* as in ordinary classical usage, e.g. Caes. *B.C.* III. 39. 2 *faucibusque portus nauem onerariam submersam obiecit*, 67. 5 *erat obiectus portis ericius*, cf. 54. 2, Cic. *Pis.* 81, *Font.* 13. For *clatri*, see Comm. Cruq. *c. sunt robusti postes et rotundi, repagula quibus obfirmatur cauea*. The word appears to be Greek κλᾷθρα, Stolz–Leumann, 76, for *t* replacing θ *ibid.* 130.

ualuit + inf.: as above 40, 305, al.

si: in 4th place of clause.

474 *indoctum doctumque:* cf. *Ad Her. ibid.* (above 472 n.) *in omnes amicos atque inimicos, notos atque ignotos*, and for this particular pair, see *Ep.* II. 1. 117 *scribimus indocti doctique poemata passim*.

recitator acerbus: outdoing even Martial's untiring reciter, III. 44. 10 ff. (cit. Orelli), not to mention the reticence enjoined at *S.* I. 4. 70–8.

475 *arripuit* and *tenet* are still appropriate to the image of the bear.

occiditque legendo: in this idiomatic construction the metaphor was all but dead, as *Epod.* 14. 5 *candide Maecenas, occidis saepe rogando*, but even by itself probably colloquial, Pl. *Ps.* 931 *occidis me quom istuc rogitas*. Here however the imagery gives fresh substance to the metaphor.

476 With startling suddenness the poet-bear changes into a leech (Porph. '*hirudo*', *haec sanguisuga appellatur*), the last word of the poem, no longer a comparison—*uelut ursus*—but an apposition, cf. above 357 n. on *fit Choerilus*.

missura: the fut. part. is attributive as above 155 (*plosoris*) *sessuri*, and with utmost conciseness further qualified by *nisi plena cruoris*. The metaphor of the leech is known from Greek, but Theoc. 2. 55–6 have a different connotation, and the wording of Call. fr. 691 is uncertain, cf. Pfeiffer *ad l.* The metaphor is established in Roman comedy for financial blood-sucking; it is probably proverbial, see A. Otto, *Sprichwörter*, 164. The *plebecula*, Cic. *Att.* 1. 16. 11, is called *illa contionalis hirudo aerari*. None of these instances resembles H.'s poetic *hirudo*.

APPENDIX 1

128–30 difficile est proprie communia dicere; tuque
rectius Iliacum carmen deducis in actus
quam si proferres ignota indictaque primus.

Of the three renderings discussed in the commentary two are ancient.
They could be sustained only if H. had talked in unconnected 'precepts', and either his context or his wording is ignored. Thus (i)
communia is equated with *fama* (119) and *publica materies* (131);
Porph. *nunc in aliud catholicum ⟨transit,* cf. 179, *uel sim.⟩ et quasi interro-
gans ait: ⟨at⟩ enim inquiunt difficile est communes res propriis explicare uerbis,*
ps.-Acro (*a*), ex Porph., *hoc interrogatiue ait: ⟨at⟩ enim dicunt difficile esse
communia propriis explicare uerbis,* cf. Commentator Cruquianus *materiam ab aliis descriptam ita proprie explicare tamquam tua sit.* Or conversely
(ii) *communia* is equated with *finge* (119) and *ignota indictaque* (130);
ps.-Acro (*b*) *'communia dicere', idest intacta; nam quando intactum est
aliquid, commune est; semel dictum ab aliquo fit proprium,* etc., Commentator Cruquianus sim. Porphyrion and ps.-Acro were available in
print from 1476 and the early commentators borrowed the one or
the other explanation. These borrowings often include some form of
ps.-Acro's additional explanation, (*c*): *communia autem dixit, quia,
quamdiu a nullo sunt acta aut dicta, singulis aeque patent ad dicendum, ut
uerbi gratia: quemadmodum domus aut ager sine domino communis est, occu-
patus uero iam proprius fit, ita et res a nullo dicta communis est.*

1 (*a*)

If *communia* = *fama* (119) and *publica materies* (131), or *uulgaria*, there is
a clash with the preceding context and, even more disturbingly, with
the following two verses. *tuque* (128) therefore must either be ignored;
or else it must be forced into conformity and, in various ways, has
been so forced by translators and commentators through the centuries. The point is not that *que* could not have an adversative nuance,
but that this nuance, if it had been intended by H., should have been
much more strongly expressed since the context pulls the other way.
The words in modern translations and paraphrases intruded to that
effect are printed in italics below; and in section 1 I have used italics
for no other purpose. (Throughout this Appendix I have also normal-
ized the spelling of the extracts.)

Madius 1550 subiungit esse communia proprie dicere, ita scilicet

432

Appendix 1

ea nouo modo exprimere, ut a nullo accepta uideantur. Cf. Luisinus' reply 1554 below under II, and Ribbeck's similar argument in this section below (b) 1869, Dacier below under II, Orelli below under III.

Achilles Statius 1553 non esse nullius laboris, aut laudis, quae sint ab aliis sumpta ita tractare, ut tractatione quidem ipsa uideantur tua.

        publica materies, etc.] quae sequuntur fere pertinent ad ipsius uim tractationis, qua fit, ut quae diximus communia, proprie tamen quodam colore splendescant iterum tractata, etc.

Sambucus 1564 publica igitur communia uocas, et peruulgata, propria eadem quidem, sed arte facta propria, etc.

Boileau Despréaux (1636–1711), remark undated (in 'Bolaeana' ed. de Monchesnay (Amsterdam, 1742), p. 93, preceded by an apparently muddled reference to Dacier's explanation) 'Il est difficile de traiter des sujets qui sont à la portée de tout le monde d'une manière qui vous les rends propres, ce qui s'appelle s'approprier un sujet par le tour qu'on y donne. M. Despréaux prétendoit avoir trouvé la solution de ce passage dans Hermogène (see below 1 (b)), et disoit mille bonnes raisons pour l'appuyer qui ont échappé à ma mémoire.'

Baxter 1701 res uulgares disertis uerbis enarrare; uel humile Thema cum dignitate tractare. 'Difficile est communes res propriis explicare uerbis.' Vet. Schol.

Fea, ed. noua (Bothe) 1827 ab aliis antea tractata, publicam materiem, ut ait 131.

Macleane 1853 ... 'proprie communia dicere'... the same as making that which is 'publica materies' 'priuati iuris'. 'communia' is usual in the sense of partnership property, and is different from 'publica'; but here it seems to have the same meaning. H. seems to have followed a Greek proverb, Χαλεπὸν τὰ κοινὰ ἰδιῶσαι.

Conington 1870 'Tis hard, I grant, to treat a subject known
            And hackneyed so that it may look one's own.

Schütz 1883 has a long and confused note on 128. He rejects 'communia = intacta' (II below), and 'communia = abstract and general subjects' (III below), which, he says, does not suit ancient drama. 'communia' and 'publica materies', he thinks, must be synonyms, and he quotes the (irrelevant) passages Demetr. 'Interpr.' 164 and Juv. 7. 53 ff. in support.

Paraphrase: 'H. hatte v. 125 ff. gelehrt, daß man bei einem bisher noch nicht dramatisch behandelten Stoffe (*neu erfunden braucht er darum noch nicht zu sein, kann es aber*) nur auf Einheitlichkeit und Folgerichtigkeit der Handlung zu sehen habe; *denn da der Stoff zum ersten Male vorgeführt wird, so hat der Dichter eine größere Freiheit in der Erfindung.*

Appendix 1

Das ist verhältnismäßig leichter; schwer *aber* einen gemeinsamen (auch von anderen bearbeiteten) Gegenstand so zu behandeln, daß er *trotz seiner Bekanntheit dennoch* als eigentümliches Werk des Dichters erscheint; *er wird dadurch zugleich eine, viel strengere, Kritik herausfordern, indem man ihn sicher tadeln wird, wenn er seine Vorgänger nicht erheblich aussticht...* Nimmst du *nun...doch* einen solchen Stoff, so wirst du richtiger verfahren, wenn du ihn einfach, wie er vorliegt, z. B. das bekannteste epische Gedicht, die Ilias, dramatisierst, *als wenn du darin Neuerungen vorbringst, durch die du dich gleichsam über Homer erheben und dadurch dir eine herbe Kritik zuziehen würdest*', etc.

Wilkins 1889 ...' *But this is comparatively easy;* the difficulty arises when you endeavour to treat familiar themes in a distinctive and individual manner. You are selecting a theme from the Iliad; then you are *wise to confine yourself to simply throwing* Homer's poem into dramatic shape, instead of attempting an *originality of handling, which would probably lead you into inconsistencies*', etc.

Wilkins 1892 (Appendix) Kiessling and Wickham approve Orelli's interpretation 'to give individual shape to common types of human character' [i.e. III below], denying the equivalence of 'communia' to 'publica materies'. It cannot be denied that this keeps better the sequence of thought.

Mewes in Orelli's 4th ed. 1892, 128 n. nescio an rectius (i.e. quam Orelli et Orelli–Baiter) comm. Cruq.: 'materiam ab aliis descriptam ita proprie explicare, tamquam tua sit', etc.   131 n. ita haec nectuntur cum prioribus, etc. haec 'publica materies', quam non differre a 'communibus' illis u. 128 satis probabile est, complectitur uniuersam copiam μύθων ab epicis et tragicis tractatorum, etc.

G. C. Macauley 1912 (CR, XXVI, 153) 'It is difficult to treat themes which have been commonly handled, in such a manner as to put upon them the distinguishing mark of your own individual genius', rephrased: 'choosing common themes and stamping upon them the mark of your individual genius is hard *enough to satisfy the poet's ambition*'.

Kroll ('Studien z. Verständnis d. röm. Lit.' p. 144 n. 11) 1924 'Schwierig *(und daher lobenswert, wenn es glückt)* ist es, das, was bereits Allgemeingut ist, individuell zu behandeln, und *darum* ist es richtiger, einen trojanischen Sagenstoff zu behandeln als einen neuen *auszugraben*'.

Fairclough (Loeb series) 1926, Blakeney 1928.

Immisch 1932 is as long-winded and as confused as Schütz (above 1883). He thinks that H. has expressed himself so badly that the passage cannot be explained without the help of the fragment of

Appendix 1

Philodemus (cited below Appendix II). Two kinds of *famam sequi* are said to be distinguished by H.; (1) the sharing of traditional subjects with earlier users of the same tradition, whence 'communia'; this is called 'hard'; (2) recourse to the Homeric fountainhead and an attempt through personal and new features to outdo earlier users of this tradition; this is commended. With 'rectius', etc. (129) understand '*ipse tuo Marte, non communiter cum antecessoribus tuis*'. 'communia', Immisch thinks, is adapted to the former alternative, 'publica materies', which becomes 'priuati iuris', to the second.

Steidle 1939 commends Kroll's interpretation. Greek literary theory and the Latin legal notions employed by H. equally suggest that 128 'communia' is to 131 'publica materies' as is 128 'proprie' to 131 'priuati iuris'. In 'tuque', as elsewhere in H., the logical nuance is unexpressed. Paraphrase: 'Schwierig ist es *schon*, in eigenartiger Form literarisches Gemeingut darzustellen, und du handelst *deshalb* richtiger, wenn du . . .'.

G. Williams 1964 (JRS, LIV, 190) says, surprisingly, 'all commentators assume that H., in saying that something is difficult, is telling the reader not to try it'. He seems to be unaware of those of his predecessors cited in this section who have made a different assumption. Perhaps their increasingly tortuous renderings and explanations, if he had known them, would have given him pause. 'tuque' (he says) could be interpreted as 'but you' and the meaning could be: 'It is difficult to say things that are common property in a way that makes them one's own, *but* you are better *occupied doing that than* . . .' The idea is then repeated and a start is made on the important theme of originality at 131 . . . If this interpretation (he concludes) is acceptable, there is no reason to find the Aristotelian doctrine of poetic universality in *A.P.* at all.

1 (b)

The rhetorical notion of κοινὰ διανοήματα, explained at 128 n., is a variation of 'communia' = 'publica materies', stated under 1. Many commentators have noted Hermogenes' chapter Περὶ κοινῶν διανοημάτων πῶς αὐτὰ ἰδιώσομεν λέγοντες (Περὶ μεθόδου δεινότητος, 29), cited in the same note. But not so many have equated the content of the Horatian passage with that of Hermogenes or other rhetoricians; thus probably Boileau (above, 1), certainly Ribbeck, Shorey and a few others.

Ribbeck 1869 (pp. 218–22) after rejecting Lambinus' rendering and citing Hermogenes and Cicero, concludes that no Roman will have understood H. otherwise than 'es ist schwer Gemeinplätze so

28-2

auszudrücken..., daß sie eine persönliche, individuelle Bedeutung erhalten'. Ribbeck recognizes however that thus understood 'communia' (128) and 'ignota indictaque' (130) are contradictory. Instead of 'tuque' (128) a contradiction would be expected: 'tamen'. Since no simple emendation can be found, a lacuna between 'dicere' and 'tuque' must be postulated.

Shorey 1906 (CP, I, 415) further adumbrates the rhetorical notion by citing, and emending, Himerius, Or. I, προθεωρία, 2, which, he thinks, is not derived from H. but perhaps from Isoc. Pan. 9 (cit. above in commentary).

G. Schmitz-Kahlmann, P, Supp. xxxi (1938-9), 2 n. links H. with the same passage of Isocrates.

II

As was said above, ps.-Acro (*b*) and (*c*) purvey the same notion— *intacta* or *non ante dicta*. The demands of the Horatian context are thus satisfied (the *fingere* of 119 being referred to), but the demands of lexicography are not. Nevertheless this notion convinced the majority of Renaissance scholars ever since it was taken over from ps.-Acro by the first commentator Landinus, but the difficulty inherent in the meaning of *communia* deterred many of their successors from the eighteenth century onwards. I cite few of these comments since they contain little that is new and calls for attention.

Landinus 1482 Communia appellat: quae a nemine adhuc dicta sunt: neque a quoquam occupati: ut agri nondum occupati communes dicuntur. Ergo communis omnibus erat Achilles et Ulyxes: cum nondum eos quisquam descripsisset. Descripsit Homerus: ergo communia proprie dixit. Deinde cum poetae Latini eadem scriberent: non iam communia: sed quae propria Homeri essent describebant. Nunc uero poeta affirmat difficilius esse quod Homerus fecit facere: quam illum imitari deducendo in actus i. in tuam fabulam Iliacum carmen i. materiam belli Troiani.

Similarly Mancinellus 1492, Badius Ascensius 1503, Parrhasius 1531, Philippus Pedimontius 1546, Robortellus 1546, Grifolus 1550, De Nores 1553, et al.

Luisinus 1554...publica materies (131)]...at Madius clarissimus philosophus, communia paulo ante pro publicis, et ab altero acceptis, et sic nobis cum illo communibus, interpretatus est, et hic publica, idest communia exponit, cuius haec uerba sunt... [above 1]...haec ille cuius ego auctoritatem libenter sequerer, si mihi scrupulus eriperetur, qui mihi in animo residet. num Horatius uerbum illud communia statim aperit, cum inquit, quam si proferres ignota,

indictaque primus. communia ergo sunt, ignota, et indicta. praeterea si communia pro ab altero dictis, atque ab altero acceptis
posuisset, subdidisset non particulam, que, sed particulam, tamen;
ut hic sensus extaret: difficile est ita explicare, quae ab altero acci-
pias, ut tua laus sit, et propria, tamen rectius ab Iliade, et facilius
argumentum sumes, quam si nouam rem aggredereris. quae si in
medium afferrem, ut eruditissimi Madii sententiam oppugnarem,
iure uideri possem ineptus. sed nosh aec quidem testata reliquimus,
ut fidi interpretis partes tueamur, qui, quod tacite ipse secum sentit,
indicet aliis etiam liberius.

Lambinus 1561, Nannius 1608.

Dacier 1681 . . .*Il est malaisé*, dit Horace, *de traiter proprement*, c'est
à dire *convenablement, des sujets communs*, c'est à dire *des sujets inventés*,
et qui n'ont aucun fondement ni dans l'Histoire, ni dans la Fable . . .
Ceux qui ont cru qu'il appelloit ici *communia* des choses communes
et ordinaires, des caractères communs et traités par d'autres poètes,
se sont infiniment trompés. Ils jettent Horace dans une contradiction
manifeste, puisqu'il conseille immédiatement après de s'attacher au
caractères connus. Cette matière est assez éclaircie, il n'est pas néces-
saire de réfuter plus au long ce sentiment qui n'a rien d'absurde.

[Dacier's opinion was called in question by a young man of
fashion, Madame de Sévigné's son Charles, and led to an exchange of
essays between them—one of the celebrated literary events of the
time, but not equally remarkable in critical terms. The essays are
reprinted in the Hachette edition of Madame de Sévigné's *Lettres*
(nouvelle éd. Paris, 1862), xi, 295–338.]

Desprez 1691 (aliter 1674) *Proprie*] 'Apta, conuenienti, et propria
ratione.' *Communia*] 'A nullo ante occupata et tractata.'

P. Francis 1746 'Tis hard a new-formed fable to express,

        And make it seem your own . . .

Metastasio 1780–2 (*Opere*, Paris; M. had however been working
on the translation and notes as early as 1749)

        Il trar primiero degli umani eventi

        Dal tesoro comun materia, e darle

        Propria forma ed acconcia è dura impresa.

The order of the words is strained; my colleague Professor U.
Limentani suggests the following paraphrase: 'It is a hard undertaking to be the first to extract a subject from the common treasury
of human events', etc.

Doering 1803.

Dillenburger 1843, but few others in the nineteenth century.

Ritter 1856–7 *communia* dixit in medio et nondum ab aliis occupata, h.e. a poeta aliquo *primum* fingenda. Haec communia noli commiscere cum uoce proxima *publica materies. proprie (in eigener Weise)*, ut tibi proprium et a communibus bonis secretum per se constare uideatur. Nos dicimus *Allgemeines individualisiren*.

publica materies: materies olim edita et publici iuris facta, qua iam unicuique uti licet. Ex hac materia pauci ita sumunt, ut *sua* (priuati iuris) proferre uideantur; illud quibus modis fieri possit statim exponit.

R. L. Dunbabin (*CR*, xxvi, 21), 1922 *communia* are said by him to be Greek literary subjects not yet appropriated by Romans, and only in that sense *ignota indictaque*.

Pasoli (p. 182) 1964 paraphrases: Dico subito che, secondo me, è difficile trattare in modo originalmente personale argomenti nuovi, che non hanno dietro di sè tradizione alcuna; pertanto tu...fai meglio a trattare in forma drammatica un argomento tratto dall'Iliade che se tu prentassi argomenti e personaggi del tutto inediti.

III

The third rendering is the only one that by-passes the antithesis *fama–fingere*, and is yet related to *fingere*, as the context enjoins; *tuque*, etc. immediately falls then into place. Nor can it be faulted on grounds of lexicography. *communia* has put many on the wrong track; in fact, with sound paragraphing (128–30 conclude the preceding context) the word is seen to point to *persona noua* (126), and a subject that is *inexpertum scaenae* (125), things *ignota indictaque* (130). 'The qualities common' (to *kinds* of people) are the moral traits, attached in the *fama* to known characters but hard to keep consistent in a newly created personage (126–8), *flebilis* perhaps though not *Ino* (123), *tristis* though not *Orestes* (124). This is expressed with Horatian brevity; the puzzle is solved without delay in 129–30. The context clearly disjoins *communia* (128) from *publica materies* (131), and keeps each meaning distinct.

This rendering is not likely to be earlier than the eighteenth century. The decisive point seems to have been made first in a French commentary of 1730 cited below, not (as is said e.g. in Plessis–Lejay's note *ad l.*) by Dumarsais, whose merit it is to have reiterated and confirmed the point.

Piat 1730 (Brocas, Paris), known to me only from Dumarsais in the essay mentioned below. Piat is there (p. 290 n. 1) cited as saying, Hic *communia* sunt mores generatim et in uniuersum spectati, nulla ratione habita huius aut huius hominis. *proprie dicere*, est mores illos, siue naturas alicui homini adscribere et illius proprias facere. cum persona aliqua ex historia desumitur, habet iam mores suos, suam indolem, suam naturam propriam ac peculiarem: nec alius poetae labor incumbit, nisi ut naturam eam, iam factam et cognitam sequatur. si noua persona effingitur, adiri necesse est naturas illas generales atque communes: atque ex iis hauriri unde huiusce personae indolem propriam conficias: quod esse difficile Horatius dicit: ideoque suadet personas iam cognitas adhiberi.

Dumarsais 1745 (*Œuvres*, III (1797), 290, in a letter addressed to M. Durand, Avocat au Parlement, for whose sons he had prepared an interlinear version of the *Ars*). The letter argues against both Dacier's and Charles de Sévigné's contrary positions (cit. above II, Dacier 1681): Ainsi *proprie communia dicere*, c'est adapter si bien un caractère à un personnage particulier, que tout ce qu'on fait dire ou faire à ce personnage, réponde parfaitement à l'idée abstraite et générale qu'on a du caractère. *communia*, c'est le caractère en lui-même dans le sens abstrait, général et métaphysique. *proprie*, c'est le caractère appliqué a un personnage et inventé pour être le tableau du caractère. Les mœurs d'un hypocrite, *communia*, ce sont les mœurs de Tartuffe, *proprie*. Du reste, Monsier, je dois le fond de cette remarque à la note que M. Piat a faite sur ce passage dans le petit Horace, qu'il fit imprimer, en 1730, chez Brocas; note qu'il ne doit à aucun autre commentateur: mais que ne trouve-t-on pas dans le fond d'un esprit judicieux? C'est l'instrument et le commentaire universel.

Batteux 1750 Il est bien difficile de donner des traits propres et individuels à ce que qui n'a rien de générique.

Gesner 1752 *proprie dicere* est ita undique describere ac finire, ut iam non commune quiddam aut generale uideatur, sed indiuiduum, in quo omnia sunt determinata, ut loquuntur Philosophi. picturae, ut proprie talis sic poeticae, maior laus si rem singularem pingat.

Dr Johnson 1776 (Boswell, *Life*, ed. Powell, III. 73–5) Dr Johnson and Mr Wilkes talked of the contested passage . . . JOHNSON [contradicting Wilkes], 'He means that it is difficult to appropriate to particular persons qualities which are common to all mankind, as Homer has done.' [In a long note Boswell denounces the Horatian passage as 'a rare instance of a defect in perspicuity in an admirable writer, who with almost every species of excellence is peculiarly remarkable for that quality'.]

Wieland 1782 Es ist vielleicht nichts schwerers, | als aus der Luft gegriffnen Menschenbildern | das eigne *Individuelle* geben.

J. H. Voss 1806 Schwer ists eigene Wesen aus Allgemeinem zu bilden.

Orelli 1838 [correct in 3rd ed. Baiter 1852 but unconvincingly altered by Mewes 4th ed. 1892] offers the fullest and best discussion of this passage. He rightly objects to the rendering cited under 1 above—cui rationi manifesto repugnat u. *tuque*; etenim si illud dicere uoluisset, pergere debuisset: '*tu tamen*', '*nihilominus tu*', etc.

Kiessling 1889 briefly restates Orelli but spoils his case by adopting Ribbeck's reference to rhetorical terminology (above under 1(*b*)).

Wickham 1891 says ...H. is glancing at the Aristotelian distinction of 'truths general' which are the proper subjects of poetry. In any case, if our view of the whole passage is correct, the special instance of the difficulty spoken of must be substantially that which Orelli explains it to be, namely, that of giving individual shape to common types of human life and character. Many editors feel so strongly the necessity of making 'communia' identical...with 'publica materies', that they are forced to take it of subjects already made public property, such as the story of the Iliad...The connected sense of the passage seems to me then to fall to pieces.

Wilkins 1892 (Appendix), see above 1.

Vahlen 1906 (repr. *Ges. Phil. Schr.* II. 759) Vorteile und Nachteile beider Wege [*fingere, fama*] werden erwogen: zuerst für das, was Horaz *fingere* genannt hat. Es ist schwierig *communia*, allgemeines, d.h. was vielen gemeinsam ist, *proprie* in einen wenigen oder einen eigentümlichen Ausdruck zu bringen* (*communia* und *propria* sind Gegensätze: Cicero *Acad. pr.* II 16, 34. *Top.* 13, 55. Derselbe Gegensatz in τὰ καθόλου und καθ' ἕκαστον, wie die Poetik des Aristoteles sie definiert, καθόλου τῷ ποίῳ τὰ ποῖα ἄττα συμβαίνει λέγειν ἢ πράττειν, καθ' ἕκαστον τί 'Αλκιβιάδης ἔπραξεν (9. 1451 b)): denn der welcher ersinnt, erdichtet, muß vom Allgemeinen ausgehen, dies aber in einen individuellen Ausdruck zu kleiden versuchen: ein Verfahren, das an Aristoteles' ἐκτίθεσθαι καθόλου τοὺς μύθους (Poetik 17. 1455 b) erinnert. Das ist schwierig, sagt Horaz, etc. [The quotations are imprecise.]

Heinze 1908 reports Kiessling but corrects his insistence on rhetorical terminology.

Lejay 1912 (in Plessis and Lejay ed. minor) individualiser des sentiments généraux, créer un type (Dumarsais, but see above Piat 1730).

Jensen 1918 (repr. Philodemos 1923, p. 120).

Rostagni 1930 restates Orelli and Vahlen, with a strong emphasis on Aristotelian doctrine.

Villeneuve 1934.

Klingner 1937.

APPENDIX 2

129–31 rectius Iliacum carmen deducis in actus
    quam si proferres ignota indictaque primus.
    publica materies priuati iuris erit, si, etc.

The parallel Greek passage (which I set down with the line-endings marked) runs as follows.

(1) ἀγαθὸ]ν εἶνα[ι] | ποιητήν, ὅμοια μόνον | ὦι βούλεται παρατέθη| κεν, οὐκ ἀποδέδειχεν ὅ|τι τοιοῦτος, ἐν ταῖς ἐπιστή|μαις διαφορᾶς πολλῆς ὑ|παρχούσης. ἀλλ᾽ ὅμω[ς], κα|θάπερ ἐπὶ τῶν κατὰ τὰς | χειρουργίας οὐχ ἡγούμε|θα <u>χείρωι</u> παρ᾽ ὅσον ὑφέμ[[μ]]|ενος ὕλην ἑτέρου τε|χνείτου καλῶς ἠργάσα|το, οὕτως οὐδὲ ποιητήν, ἐ|ὰν †ἀπόητον† ὑπόθεσι[ν] λα|βὼν προσθῆ[ι] τὸν [ἴ]διον νο[ῦν], |

(2) <u>χείρω</u> νομίζομεν, καὶ | οὐκ ἐπὶ τῶν μεικρῶν | μόνον οὕτως ἔχομεν, | ἀλλ᾽ οὐδ᾽ ἂν τὰ κατ᾽ Εἴλιον | [ἢ] Θήβας κοινῶς παρ᾽ ἐτέ|ρου λαβὼν ὥσπερ διαλύ|σηι καί πως πάλι συν|τάξας ἰδίαν κατασκευὴν | περιθῆι. τὰ γοῦν περὶ τὸν | Θυέστην καὶ τὰ περὶ τὸν | Πάριν κ[αὶ Μενέλα]ον καὶ | τὰ περὶ τὴν Ἠλέκτραν | καὶ πλείον᾽ ἄλλα Σοφ[ο]κλέ|α καὶ Εὐριπίδην καὶ πολ|λοὺς ἄλλους γεγραφότας | [ὁρ]ῶντες οὐ νομίζομεν | κατὰ τὸ τοιοῦτο τοὺς | μὲν εἶναι βελτίους τοὺς | δὲ χείρους, ἀλλὰ πολλά|κι τοὺς εἰληφότας ἀμεί|νους τῶν προκεχρημέ|νων, ἂν τὸ ποιητικὸν | ἀγαθὸν μᾶλλον εἰσε[νέγ|κ]ωνται.

The text is well preserved and offers no difficulty apart from two places underlined above. χείρωι must surely lose the final stroke to be taken up by χείρω in the parallel clause. ἀπόητον is nonsensical; the opposite sense is required but Immisch's ⟨οὐκ⟩ ἀπόητον (p. 19 n. 4) does not convince. ὕλην ἑτέρου τεχνείτου, three lines above, suggests something like ἄ⟨λλου⟩ ποιητοῦ or ἄ⟨λλων⟩ ποιητῶν.

The passage consists of two papyrus fragments from Herculaneum; (1) ἀγαθόν to νοῦν, *HV²*, vii. 87. 14–28, (2) χείρω to the end, *HV²*, iv. 195. 1–24. Attention had been drawn to (2) by T. Gomperz, *SBW*, cxxiii, Abhand. 6 (1891), 'Philodem und die ästh. Schr. der hercul. Bibl.' p. 81. The author's name and the title are lost, but Gomperz's ascription to Philodemus' fourth book Περὶ ποιημάτων has been generally and rightly accepted. Heinze quoted part of fragment (2) in his note on *A.P.* 130. C. Jensen succeeded in fitting the two fragments together, and they fit perfectly; cf. Jensen, Philodemos *Über die Gedichte*, etc. (1923), pp. v f. n. 2; *SBPA* (1936), p. 24. The likeness between the Greek and Latin contexts is close; it would be closer still if Philodemus' κοινῶς and ἰδίαν κατασκευήν could be equated with H.'s *proprie communia,* and Philodemus' τὰ κατ' Εἴλιον, διαλύσῃ, and συντάξας with H.'s preference for *Iliacum carmen,* and *deducis* (or *di-*) *in actus.* However, H. is no *fidus interpres*; the train of thought explained in the commentary and Appendix 1 must prevail over similarities in wording which may be accidental. We must allow the poet to employ *Iliacum carmen* as a link between 128 and 130; *deducis* is a metaphor in its own right; and κοινός–ἴδιος could be expressed rather by *publica materies priuati iuris erit.* Nevertheless the likeness of argument need not be fortuitous. Philodemus may well have discussed Neoptolemus in other parts of his work than book v.

APPENDIX 3

146 nec reditum Diomedis ab interitu Meleagri (orditur)

Some scholars, notably F. Ritter (ed. 1857) and K. Latte (*H,* LX (1925), 2), have concluded from this verse that H. ascribed the *Thebaid* (and Diomede's part in the expedition of the *Epigoni*) to Homer. In *Ep.* 1. 2 that poem is not mentioned. If, moreover, the present verse refers to a *Thebaid,* then it would seem to follow from the context that H. did not ascribe that poem to Homer. But there is no certainty that the verse does refer to a *Thebaid.* It is Porphyrion who so refers it, but the grounds for his assertion (and for his mention of the evidence concerning Antimachus) are unknown; Antimachus is judiciously discussed by B. Wyss, *Antim. Col. reliquiae* (1936), pp. v–ix. Another possibility cannot at any rate be dismissed out of hand; *reditus Diomedis* may belong to the Trojan cycle of Νόστοι.

THE 'ARS POETICA' AS HORATIAN POETRY

1 POETIC PATTERNS IN THE 'ARS POETICA' AND THE 'ODES'

> '*Pallida Mors* has nothing to do
> with the above.'   LANDOR

Received opinion, paradoxically encouraged by the poet's nomenclature, has it that a Horatian hexameter poem is a kind of versified prose. Levels of style in Greek and Roman literature are so marked that this notion, if it were true, would severely confine the area of H.'s experiment. If by prose we mean a vocabulary adapted to the level of Latin prose, the preceding commentary will have shown that nothing could be further from the truth. Throughout, enquiry has revealed that H. has employed a vocabulary drawn from poetry, or created on the model of the Roman poetic tradition. To save space in a book already too long I here refrain from summarizing the findings of the commentary and the listing in the index, though I may do so elsewhere. Calling the vocabulary poetic I do not, of course, mean that there are no colloquial elements in the *Epistles* and even more the *Satires*. H. accommodates a small, carefully controlled, amount of colloquial language, usually in debate, which, as a tribute to the spirit of *sermo*, includes even an occasional verbal impropriety.

The quantity may be small; but, I suspect, an optical illusion has made it *look* large. A colloquial tone is of course not infrequent. Add realism of setting, an apparently abstract argument, an apparent looseness of structure—and the case for 'prose' seems to be made. An occasional colloquialism, however, cannot invalidate the consistently poetic language that H. employs. What can be invalidated is the poet's own paradox in calling the hexameter poems 'prosaic'. Satire and Epistle alike are, for him, *sermo* 'talk'. When he contrasts *sermo* with the intensity and the high style of epic, he dubs it

445

'pedestrian' and 'unpoetic'[1]. Elsewhere he is quite ready to make large poetic claims for the satirist; the language of *rhetor* and *poeta* take their place with other strict demands.[2] No wonder that Lucilius falls short of these poetic standards,[3] that H. can class satire with the great genres[4], and the aspiring satirist is told, *saepe stilum uertas, iterum quae digna legi sint | scripturus*.[5]

The hallmark of *sermo* is the variability of tone which epic, drama, and high lyric must eschew by definition, although H. found other ways of lightening the heavy load of an exclusive style whenever he wished to do so in the *Odes*. *Sermo* is a highly poetic genre, but a mixed one. Occasionally it rises to 'poetry' in the exclusive sense of the great genres—and that applies to its vocabulary, style and tone. Very occasionally its rhetoric is pushed below a carefully judged middle level. On the whole it observes that middle level, which, as my commentary shows, is a refinement of poetic qualities (in the Roman sense), not of prosaic. If you look at *sermo* in this manner, it appears close to the comparatively large gamut from colloquial to intense expression in the lyric verse of our contemporaries. Its variability of tone and emotional level distinguishes it from the ancient selectivity of the large forms. It is one of H.'s triumphs that his middle style sounds so natural and relaxed that he makes us forget the 'poetic' provenance of much of the vocabulary in the hexameter poems. In this respect a Horatian *sermo* is quite unlike a contemporary poem, where such traditional elements, where they appear, tend to be personal and not common to all practitioners.

None of the hexameter poems quite matches the variability of the *Ars*. Clearly the poem is a *perpetuum mobile* in subject-matter, style, and tone. It is so organized as to keep the reader's mind and emotions on the move continually. Literary argument

---

[1] *S.* I. 4. 38–65, *Ep.* II. 1. 250–9 et al.   [2] *S.* I. 10. 7–19.
[3] I. 10. 50–71.   [4] I. 10. 40 ff.
[5] I. 10. 72–3.

and teaching recurs, but selectively, throughout the poem. There are the sketches that concentrate H.'s principles in pictures, and shift them from conceptual argument to visual images—the painting at the outset and the mad poet at the close, the arithmetic lesson in a Roman school, the satire on the false critic, the Satyric drama of the future, music in the primitive theatre, the shaman-poet in the dim past of human civilization, and so forth. There is the personal element, notably concerning H. as a creator of poetic language and, later, in the setting of criticism, what is clearly a personal memory of Quintilius. There is the Horatian humour, especially as a penumbra of his own personal status as a poet and critic. There is the satiric wit directed against the conditions in which poetry is produced in Rome. There is the imaginative rise to an essentially lyric level in *debemur morti nos nostraque*. All this variety will, if anything, show how real, to H., was the problem on which he pronounces in the first part of the poem—the problem of unity. And more than a theoretical problem. This poem offers a practical solution of the question asked by the poet on the level of theory. H. the critic demands *simplex et unum*. Has he achieved it himself in the very poem in which the problem is posed? Many will say, No. Those, like myself, who say otherwise, must satisfy the persistent searchers for the poetic pressure that has welded together these apparently incompatible materials. This is a question that might be asked about any poem by the same master, however different in genre and intent. The kind of pressure that unifies a Horatian lyric is not different in nature from that unifying a *sermo* poem of his, such as the *Ars*.

I am not much of a Shelleyite and might have passed by the poet's perceptive and entertaining appraisal of Wordsworth, had I not noticed it some thirty years ago in F. R. Leavis' *Revaluations*. Shelley describes Wordsworth as 'wakening a sort of thought in sense'. It seemed to me then as it seems to me now that this is not only admirably true of Wordsworth but its opposite is true of another 'philosophical' poet, though in many ways not a Wordsworthian one. Turn Shelley's description upside down: 'Wakening a sort of sense in thought' suggests as well as anything I have read about H. the curious ambivalence in his poetry between mind and emotion, between abstraction and concreteness. Every reader must have sensed his extremely tough intellectual strain. And yet, at a moment's notice, abstraction will change into sense-object or emotion, a doctrine of the moral Mean into sailing neither too close to the shore nor too far from it, or a person's anxiety or over-confidence. All the time he seems to be 'thinking' in his poetry, and yet his thought processes cannot be identified with the conceptual and argumentative procedures to which we are accustomed when we talk, or his contemporaries talked, of 'philosophical argument'. In his poems he seems to offer a philosophy, and in a sense he does. But, a few exceptions apart, he scoffs at doctrines. His philosophical truths, when you come to examine them, are a series of truisms—what anyone might accept, if only he did; which some readers have taken for more than truisms, and others have dismissed as trite, because they looked for the right thing (that is, depth) in the wrong place (that is, conceptual thought and formula). The curiously ironic detachment that the poet tends to observe in such statements should put the reader on the right track. Moral or literary problems are touched on by formula and concept; but often the poem as a whole seeks to solve them at a deeper and less explicit level.[1]

What strikes me about his thought is its unique flexibility. In many poems he will range not only, dialectically, from one intellectual position to its very antithesis, but from abstraction to concreteness, from experience to judgement, from literal to metaphorical, from individual to type, from personal to impersonal. I find the same attitude in his constant shift from

---

[1] The teaching and the delight imparted by poetry, *docere* and *delectare*, are an instance of a 'doctrine' from the *Ars*. But almost the whole poem is concerned with the sensuous and intellectual qualities of poetry. *omne tulit punctum qui miscuit utile dulci* (*A.P.* 343) is the poet's ironically pedestrian way of relating the deeper problem to the conceptual language of the schools.

seriousness to uninvolved humour—the kind of attitude that has suggested the perceptive paradox that H., 'once he has been admitted, plays about the heart-strings', *admissus circum praecordia ludit;*[1] or that H. 'can be convincingly serious only when it is certain that no one will take him quite seriously'.[2] This multiplicity is hard to understand and, once understood, hard to exhaust. Yet these aspects and moods do not fall apart, as they might do if there were no personal and unifying link. Differently related in different poems, they form a recognizable unity and structure.

H. stands apart from such poets as Lucretius and Catullus (to mention only two from the Roman world), who seem to draw their strength from a single source; they see the world as *one*, in the light of a single powerful emotion, an overwhelming idea to which we can respond simply and single-mindedly. Minerva denied that kind of strength to a poet whom she yet favoured. H. belongs to the company of those whose poetic world is as diverse as it is harmonious, and whose poetic personality while unmistakably present defies easy identification. Unobtrusively, like certain great dramatists, he slips into many opposed attitudes, as though each naturally expressed his own state of mind and manners—*mores* in the language of the *Ars*.

To say this is not to deny the integrity and inspiration of his poetry. But the *Ars*, like most Horatian works, encourages the quest for the poetic personality that has given rise not only to the contraries of thought and feeling expressed in the poem but to the manner in which those conflicts are resolved, the Horatian tone. On the basis of a single poem, however, it is easier to raise this question than to answer it. I will not therefore attempt it here.

The apt reader of this kind of poetry will be one who has trained himself to emulate some of H.'s flexibility, who has learned to relate the crossing and interweaving strands and

---

[1] Persius, I. 117.
[2] R. A. Brower, *Alexander Pope; the Poetry of Allusion* (1959), p. 162.

449

motifs. The 'solution' of the dialectic exercise tends to remain concealed; nor could the poet have made it explicit had he so wished. Its location is the structure of the poem as it evolves from verse to verse; it is here that the shifting antitheses of thought and emotion meet. Thought and wording, suggestion and tone are all inextricably involved, and cannot be caught in the net of analysis and description. Yet analysis and description can take us a long way and, I hope, will take us some way in this study of the *Ars Poetica*.

Pedestrian critics complain of 'the extraordinary difficulty in discovering anything like a connected train of thought' in some of the *Odes* (R. Y. Tyrrell). Nor is it only pedestrian critics who feel thus thwarted. Landor's famous remark on l. 13 of *Soluitur acris hiems* has often been quoted—'*Pallida Mors* has nothing to do with the above'. Yet the poem in question is but a brief lyric of moderate complexity. It cannot surprise if a lengthy and less tightly organized *sermo* evokes even more irritation or misjudgement. Clearly, the short type of ode is what we must look to, in the first place, if we want to recognize the particular Horatian kind of complexity. Abruptness, gliding transition, circular structure, block-composition —such are the terms that invite a mechanical manipulation of static 'materials'. Some of these terms have their descriptive uses; but they do not assist us to view a poem as a unity of layout and subject as well as of imagery, style, and tone.

I now attempt to illustrate from the *Odes* some of the structural devices that I find employed in H.'s *Ars* and his other long hexameter poems. The *Odes* that I have selected are much shorter and more tightly controlled than the *Sermones*; but the same kind of imagination has evolved the structure of both, though in different styles.

Few of H.'s poems are unilinear in structure—a straight progression from one point to another logically related. But just because Horatian complexity looms so large, it is well to remember that such poems exist. For sometimes the pattern of thought and emotion lends itself to a simple progression.

450

The introductory ode, *Maecenas atauis*, juxtaposes values in a series of typical human preferences, one after the other—*sunt quos...hunc...illum*, etc.—an archaic form of poetic rhetoric, on which E. Fraenkel has written instructively.[1] That series fits the mood of a poem designed to rise by way of a long factual preamble to the declaration of a personal way of life: *me doctarum hederae praemia frontium | dis miscent superis*.[2] Here the whole poem is structured by juxtaposition, because juxtaposition fits subject and mood.

This is an extreme case, though not the only one. But there are other poems whose overt structure suggests a simple logical progression, though closer examination shows it to be anything but simple. Such is the great Ode subdivided into three groups, with the headings weightily set out at the beginning, *C. I. 12 quem uirum aut heroa... | quem deum...?* It is well known that this division echoes Pindar's introductory question in the Second Olympian (τίνα θεόν, τίν' ἥρωα, τίνα δ' ἄνδρα...;). So Pindar asked, but what H. made of that question was undreamt of by the Greek poet. The tripartition comes to govern the poem as a whole. For Pindar answers his own question without delay and in the same sequence, thus defining occasion, addressee, and setting—'god' leads to Zeus who protects the district of Olympia, 'hero' to Heracles, the founder of the Olympic games, 'man' to Theron, the victor. Then he allows the question to sink out of sight, to underlie the whole poem though not to determine its order. For H. the occasion has no reality; nothing corresponds to the Olympic setting; the poem is addressed to Clio, and aimed at the emperor. Yet the poet makes the tripartite order the axis on which the whole poem turns, the cosmic context of the final prayer for Augustus. With a slight but expressive variation he first reverses the sequence, so as to rise from man to hero to god; but then, in chiastic order, he places the gods first, heroes next, and men last of all. But there is no attempt to take up

---

[1] Aeschylus, *Agamemnon*, 899–902 n., *Horace*, 230–2.
[2] *C. I. I.* 29–30.

the three 'markers' explicitly, and the possible prosaic element is thus eliminated. Instead of external links therefore the poet provides for a structuring by poetic means—the hymnic *quid prius dicam* (13), *neque te silebo* (21), *dicam* (25), *post hos prius...memorem* (33–4), and *referam* (39). Every reader will draw the obvious conclusion that *qui res hominum ac deorum...temperat* takes up *deum*, as *Alcides* takes up *heroa*. Whether *Romulum* (33) or rather *Regulum* (37) starts the last of the three divivisions seems to me an open question, not only in view of the much debated but still debatable textual difficulties at 35–6. For even if the Romulus stanza were thought to adhere convincingly to the part of the poem defined by *heroes*, it would in fact form 'at the same time a bridge to the catalogue of the Roman *uiri*'[1]—a kind of gliding transition, which relieves what would otherwise be a strict formalism of five groups of three stanzas each: invocation; *dei, heroes, uiri*; Augustus. That lack of strictness is in fact no mere avoidance, for in spite of Fraenkel's persuasive advocacy[2] I find it hard to believe that the Greek division between ἥρωες and ἄνδρες is echoed sufficiently in this Roman context. The merging of the *heroes* and *uiri* therefore may well have been induced by Roman sentiment. And the final prayer for Augustus is actually enhanced if the dividing line between *heros* and *uir* is not too clearly drawn.

We have then, in this short lyric, an apparently prosaic structure. In that way *quem uirum aut heroa* differs fundamentally from the Pindaric poem that inspired it. But the subdivisions are not worked out prosaically; they only suggest a conceptual scheme. In fact the structure is so flexible as to enhance not hinder emotion and thought.

The flexible use in a short lyric of a conceptual structure should caution readers against denying that technique in the larger hexameter poems. Thus in the *Ars* the substance of large parts of that long poem is indicated in a similar way. *A.P.* 40–1 set down *res, facundia*, and *ordo*. The sequel is

---

[1] Fraenkel, *Horace*, 296.   [2] *Ibid.* 294–6, 447.

chiastic. First *ordo*, where the word is actually repeated. Next *facundia*, which is no longer named but hinted at by *in uerbis* (46). Finally *res*, which is so far away (at 119) and arises so unobtrusively from the context that even now many scholars deny (quite wrongly, in my submission) that the topic appears at all. What matters in each case is not a cut-and-dried 'arrangement' but an order adapted to the substance and form of each context. The same technique, with its attendant difficulty to the reader, is employed at 307–8, where too a 'table' of three 'subjects' is set out. None of them, when its time comes, is verbally repeated. The first, at any rate, is alluded to, but the second, and even more the third, have to be gathered from the sequence of juxtaposed pieces. In these cases the simple conceptual scheme seems to inform a whole poem or parts of a poem, although more often than not the apparent rigidity of outline yields to a subtle play of emotion and suggestion.

Many other poems are what might be called 'open-ended'. The *ductus* of thought or feeling moves on to details—a scene, a picture, or the like—and these details are only tangentially connected with the 'subject' of the poem, although they make their own contributions to its tone and thus, indirectly, to the subject. Such for example is the amorous scene at the end of *uides ut alta*. It might be argued too that the *Ars* has an open ending, the satiric story of the mad poet. But I think it more likely that the marked similarity with the initial caricature—poem and poet going wrong from an excess of *ingenium* uncontrolled—suggests a looking back to the beginning, *humano capiti*.

Imperceptibly, towards the end, this kind of poem wheels back to something like the initial situation so that a circular movement seems to arise. This is familiar from archaic Greek writing; it has been called 'ring-composition'.

H. employs that technique in various ways. *C*. II. 10 is exemplary. *rectius uiues*; so Licinius is addressed—the first stanza, in nautical metaphor, setting out the avoidance of

453

moral extremes, and the last stanza returning to the addressee as well as to the metaphor. In between, four stanzas proclaim *aurea mediocritas* in terms leading from the social to the natural and the divine scene. Thus the intervening stanzas form a kind of panel framed by the two addresses; the panel also lends the colour and tone of moral experience to the first and last stanzas. This is not a great poem but a confident re-handling in lyric form of the moral antitheses of the *Sermones*. The poem is neither better nor worse for the truth, or truism, it contains; nor indeed for its borrowing an abstract 'rule' from moral theory. It becomes 'poetic' through viewing moral in terms of living experience, and through embodying in its structure the very nature of its subject-matter: a warning against extremes is conveyed by logical antitheses at the beginning and end, with the intervening picture of the *bene praeparatum pectus* that is reassured by sameness, in change, of nature and divinity.

Some of the love poems are fashioned in this circular manner—aptly, because the final statement is used to qualify the ironical detachment with which the poem begins; H. shows himself involved after all. In and out, involvement and detachment, emotion as well as rationality: that is the world of Horatian poetry, not only love poetry. The last two stanzas of *intermissa Venus diu* (IV. 1) explain the *parce, precor, precor* of the beginning; they also contradict the sentiment immediately preceding: *me nec femina nec puer*. In the unity of the whole poem those stanzas have more than one function. In the masterly economy of *uixi puellis nuper idoneus*, a poem of no more than three stanzas (III. 26), the switch-back effect seems to relate only to the last two lines. Until l. 10 resignation is unquestioned; but then the prayer turns about unexpectedly: *regina, sublimi flagello | tange Chloen semel arrogantem*. The poet, half humorously, half seriously, is involved still. Once you have read to the end, it it hard to look back to *uixi puellis* without a memory of the last two lines.

I have discussed no more than three instances of 'ring

composition' in the *Odes*. Despite their similarity, they all fulfil different functions. Many other instances could be adduced from lyric and *sermo* alike. But what I have said will demonstrate sufficiently that the lyric and hexameter poems derive from the same kind of structural imagination. H., the master of the small lyric form, seems to have attempted similar formal complexities in a long *sermo*.

What are the movements of thought and feeling deployed to bring about such tightly-controlled structures? It is easy to ask this question; it is not easy to answer it. For the circularity of the poems last discussed arises from apparently diverse thought-movements—often an abrupt leap, but often too one of those delicate adjustments of thinking or tone or feeling which have become known by the name of gliding transition. Such names have a certain descriptive virtue; but what they describe will often be the conceptual order of argument, not an order determined by poetic association. Nor are these 'transitions' restricted to the few poems that have been mentioned.

H.'s much deplored abruptness and his much admired 'gliding transitions' differ from each other in their effect, but seem to derive from similar thought-processes. Ideas are imaginatively, not conceptually, associated in his mind. The strategy that he adopts in revealing such associations is an integral part of every poem. It determines its unity and tone; it is not extraneous to the poem. When H. sets ideas starkly apart from each other, this abruptness—such as *pallida Mors* in the Spring Ode I. 4—is a pointer to the scope of the poem, perhaps its very germ and inspiration. The reader's imagination has to be stretched accordingly. When the opposite happens, and ideas are shown to be related before the reader can be expected to notice the link ('gliding transition'), then, too, the scope of the poem is involved. But the reader's imagination is affected differently, his attention is drawn to connexion rather than disjunction.

Any Horatian poem will show that these different forms of

455

expression are aspects of the same imaginative manner of thinking. In the love poem III. 26, to which I referred earlier, the abruptness of the final turn expresses the poignancy of the situation, the instability of human wishes. On the other hand, *me nec femina nec puer*, the third stanza from the end of the love poem IV. 1, may, with some justification, be called a gliding transition. For the stanza follows on without strain from the praise of Paulus, and prepares, by contradistinction, for the *dénouement* of the last two stanzas. Yet that transition reveals, with a difference, the same contingency of human nature.

To watch the move from one thought-complex to another is an ever-repeated and ever-new poetic experience in reading H. The step may be small or large. Sometimes the poet confirms and extends the territory just gained, or simply adds another related area without overt link and connexion. Poetically more rewarding are those daring leaps from one extreme to another, where antithetic thought is expressed by disjointedness of structure. The Spring Ode I. 4 has already been mentioned. *pallida Mors* sets the paleness of death brusquely against the colour and regeneration of spring; Sestius, like the rest of us, must make the adjustment between the permanence, in change, of nature and the *uitae summa breuis*, which is never renewed.

Often the impact of an abrupt break is mitigated, as it were, by gliding transitions that hint at a large conception still hidden from the reader. Such is the proposal, overtly abrupt, of a celebration for Caesar Augustus, *descende caelo*, III. 4. 37. For (as Fraenkel[1] has observed) the thought of the person who is now expected to keep the barbarian people in check precedes this stanza; in fact there is a continuing thought-movement that leads from the poet's charmed life in the past to the danger which, he maintains, he is ready to face among the barbarians under the protection of the Muse.

The hexameter poems lack the tautness of the Odes, their intensity and emotional range. But they have many other

[1] *Horace*, 275.

virtues. For variation of style, for venturesomeness of structure over a larger canvas, they compete with the lyrics. Perhaps no Horatian poem is so daringly successful as the *Ars* in suggesting by structure and tone the philosophy of art which it does not, and indeed cannot, express by conceptual argument. If structure has that importance, it provides sufficient inducement to an editor to break up the text into paragraphs. No division within a Horatian poem is fully self-contained. But paragraphing invites the adroit reader to attend to the fresh start as well as to the links beyond the context, major ones or minor, explicit or implied.

Transitions in the *Ars* show a large and almost inexhaustible variety. They must be seen in their own setting; many of them will be described below. Here I consider only some typical instances that recall the Odes already described. Two very special cases excepted (46 *etiam*, 347 *tamen*), the *Ars* moves from one context to the next by juxtapostion; no apparent need for external links.

A simple placing of one context beside another might express no more than juxtaposition in thought—a mere sequence or series of topics. It is striking that over a long range in the *Ars* that kind of series is exceedingly hard to find. Such seem to be, at first sight, the topics chosen to illustrate exemplary technique in the work of dramatists (from 153 onward). Appropriate character-drawing, the right mixture of reported speech and dramatic action, the number of acts, the *deus ex machina*, the number of speaking parts, chorus, music. But here other motives come into play. If H. had wanted no more than to move from one topic to another, related or vaguely related, he would have proceeded from music to metre, and then to the major dramatic genres in which these techniques materialize. But that is precisely what he does not do. By placing Satyric drama before metre, not after, he sharpens the point of both. For the former, Satyric drama, is treated like chorus and music, as a technique to be mastered by the dramatist. But when he comes to metre, the rhythmic vitality

457

of verse, he does more than that; he brings the motif of artistic potency to the fore, and thus begins the delicate jostling for position that characterizes so much of his verse. He sets Roman poetry vis-à-vis classical Greek, *exemplaria Graeca*—an incitement to fresh artistic endeavour. Which in turn enables him to confront genius and artistry, the unreal antithesis that concludes this part of the poem, and gives rise to the satiric thought-movement in the next.

The first part of the poem looks very disjointed and abrupt. I should be surprised however if 'disjointedness' can be the just comment of a reader who has made himself familiar with H.'s technique and with the literary theories that form his material. How can a lively poetic variety be achieved without declining into mere fragmentation? The answer is inherent in the progress from the initial caricature to the purple patch to the demand for *simplex et unum*. Next false variety is interpreted as a desire for the right thing without the necessary training, or without the insight that makes such a training serve the wholeness of a poetic vision, *totum*. Each of these 'paragraphs' presents a picture in its own right and yet, added to the rest, each contributes its share to the total. The abruptness of transition from one partial picture to the other draws the reader's attention to the variety as well as to the wholeness of the larger canvas.

Just as abruptly H. passes from philosophy, 'the source of good writing', and its misunderstandings (at 309–22), to the psychology of the Greeks and Romans (at 323–32). And just as effectively comes enlightenment to the reader when he senses that the implicit connexion is one of cause and effect. Were the connexion overtly expressed, a large and inconclusive argument would have resulted. For this causal chain makes a good guess but a bad proof.

H.'s imaginative procedure at its most astringent will be seen in the last sub-section of the *Ars*, beginning at 347. Drop the Horatian key—the notion of poetic excellence—and this part of the poem falls apart. But the key fits throughout.

458

Within a group of nine juxtaposed pieces a central kernel of four is explicitly held together by an address to the elder son of Piso and personal detail related to the dominant notion of poetic *uirtus*: 366 *o maior iuuenum*, 385 *tu nihil...dices*, 406–7 *ne forte pudori | sit tibi Musa lyrae sollers*. The remaining five are placed on each side of the centre-piece; the reader must take his clue from this placing. 'Abrupt juxtaposition?' 'Unobtrusive links?' I suggest that both techniques are present to a certain extent although the former predominates. H. clearly wanted to obtrude the variety of aspects in which *uirtus poetica* is involved, and has therefore underplayed their agreement.

But when it comes to turning from one large section of his literary theory to another the two procedures are differently weighted. H. still marks the new context by a more or less abrupt switch. But he assigns equal weight to a link passage, and that produces a twofold effect; the break is thus cushioned and the new subject is related to a motif common to both sections, the old and the new.

There is a likeness between two of these transitions that should not escape notice—I mean the tables of contents at 40–1 and again at 306–8. To call them by that name is not to decry them. These indications are worked so beautifully into the poetic fabric that no humdrum rehearsing of topics arises. Nevertheless topics are indicated and they are the chief topics in the two large sections on the 'poem' and the 'poet'. Since in both transitions the duality of *ars* and *ingenium* is employed as a framework, it looks as if the poet meant the likeness to be noticed—perhaps a hint, if no more, that 'poem' and 'poet' account for one strongly marked structural division among others.

'Arrangement' and 'style' arise without strain from the announcement of *ordo* and *facundia* (at 41), the former at 42, the latter at 46/5. How does the third predetermined member of the triad come into play: 'subject-matter', *res*? Having seen H.'s technique at work elsewhere we should be predisposed to recognize it in complex settings. Many commentators fail to recognize the new topic when H. ceases to speak of style (118). They willingly accept that the poet has established a link between the topics before and after this verse. But the two choices do not exclude each other. A 'gliding transition' and an abrupt break are here combined as they are elsewhere. This procedure serves more than one purpose. The desired unity of diction and subject-matter comes out unobtrusively because the demand is that diction as well as subject must be informed by *mores*. But the two settings are not the same in terms of *ars poetica*. And this difference is made to obtrude in the harsh break.

I am not equally clear in my own mind that the otherwise abrupt jump to dramatic technique (at 153) is qualified in the same manner. Although there too character study is demanded—the ages of man at 156—the break is not mitigated in the same way because 'character' does not precede the new section immediately but only at a remove.

The combination of connectedness and abruptness in the same poem, lyric or *sermo*, should put us on our guard against premature generalizing. Each method has its own function. Often several themes are entwined in an antecedent poetic vision and the reader is made aware of this complexity only in the course of the poem. A mechanical division into subjects or themes will then tend to obscure the issue.

Two lyrics in which H. speaks partly in a public and partly in a private voice will show what I have in mind. *Herculis ritu* (III. 14) and *diuis orte bonis* (IV. 5) deal with the same themes: the public occasion of a celebration for Augustus, and a private one, when an individual, Q. Horatius Flaccus, is seen to share in public rejoicing. What matters to the lyric poet is not to report two kinds of events, but to make the reader feel and understand the motives that induce a private person, and that private person H., to celebrate a public event. This is the meeting point of private and public, and in that point the unity of the poem inheres. In *diuis orte bonis* unity is achieved by a means that really does away with the individual aspect.

H. shares in the general rejoicing as a loyal and patriotic citizen, or (it may be said by a critical observer) one of the many whom the emperor *dulcedine otii pellexit*. In that sense there is no longer a valid distinction between a public and a private voice. The two 'parts' of the poem, as Fraenkel has said,[1] almost merge into each other.

But Fraenkel seems to me less persuasive in measuring *Herculis ritu* by the same yard-stick. He says truly that the transitional stanza 4 belongs no more to the first three than it belongs to the last,[2] that even stanza 5, which starts in a manner so pointedly private—*i pete unguentum, puer*—contains echoes of public concern, the social war and Spartacus. Fraenkel admires the poem, yet (291) complains of 'a faint disharmony', a clash between the two roles taken by the poet, the public and the private. Perhaps there is some dissonance, but any clash is the deliberate one from which the ode draws its strength—that in this poem H. does not submerge his individual emotion in the emotion of the many.

It may be said then that in *Odes* III. 14 and IV. 5 H. offers not a single subject, but the same two, which he has related or, in musical language, counterpointed differently. But the unity of each poem, perhaps its origin, lies in a wider entity comprising the two subjects. Hence 'unfolding one complex idea or emotion' rather than 'connecting two separate notions' might be a more plausible way of describing these poems.

Velox amoenum (I. 17) ties two or three apparently diverse strands together. The Ode has been instructively analysed by Fraenkel.[3] It consists, we are told, of two parts, separate though structurally related. One is a Greek theophany, stanzas 1–3; the other a traditional invitation to a banquet, stanzas 5–7. The poem is said not to fall apart because it is held together in the middle stanza by the role assigned to the poet himself. The bliss he enjoys through divine protection and his own craft occupy the centre of the ode, giving unity to the whole

---

[1] *Horace*, 446.   [2] *Ibid.* 290.
[3] *Ibid.* 204–7.

poem. But what is the scope of the poem, and what stays in the memory at the end? Three diverse poetic forms adroitly tied together—theophany, H. divinely protected, invitation? Or the coolness of the shade on a hot Italian day, with the animals on H.'s farm as happily sheltered from the sun as their owner and his expected musician guest? Surely, the latter. The safety of man and beast, the music of H.'s guest, and his own poetry are, with ancient religious feeling, traced to a divine source, the complex notion unfolded into the presence of Pan, who is first seen to protect the animals and then the humans who can profit by his music—you too, Tyndaris, come and sing. It is certainly instructive to track down the different literary origins of the different themes, and it is instructive to see the themes entwined; but without a lively apprehension of the complex picture as a whole, the parts will not add up. The sum total of the parts is not identical with the poem before us on the page or with the poem's image in the mind. But whichever way you go, from the parts to the whole, or from the whole to the parts, the complex unity of the ode is unmistakable.

There are Odes longer and more complex than the three with which I have operated. But restricted length and taut composition in the lyrics advantageously magnify *in parvo* the structural characteristics of the hexameter poems. Among these the *Ars* stands supreme in its concatenation of themes and motifs. There are few places in that poem where we are allowed to settle down, drowsily, to a single theme, or else have a single emotion aggrandized until it fills the horizon. H.'s poetry is multilinear, and in the *Ars* more than anywhere else.

In my *Prolegomena* (pp. 226 ff.) I have singled out a number of motifs that are used to combine with, and relate to each other, the notions of the literary critics, thus instilling principle into what had become unprincipled, unintelligent, and unpoetic. One of them is the principle of *ars*, another is that of *decorum*, appropriateness. But in saying that *ars* is 'the subject' of the poem, or else that *decorum* is, many have gone astray. They fave failed on two counts. One is the applicability of their thesis. The poem witnesses against them loudly and persistently; it has not a single subject but a large number. The other is literal-mindedness. *ars* does not appear as an abstraction with a rigidly defined meaning but as a many-sided dialectical principle, in ever-repeated interaction with its counterpart, *ingenium*. So does *decorum*, the regulator of rightness in a poetic world where style still counts, and where originality can only fulfil itself within a tradition. In spite of the appearance of conceptual argument, what is not said or only implied is as important as what is actually made explicit. The structure and the tone translate into terms of the poem what would be of little value in mere conceptual terms.

Critics are not therefore likely to prevail with a proof that *decorum* in the *Ars* is an unequivocal critical notion, meaning one and the same thing wherever it appears. But if they had remembered that a poet's terms are ever-shifting and flexible, they might have had a tenable case in urging the importance of this notion. 'Appropriateness' is a relative term and it can be related in the most various ways to the technical subjects of ancient literary theory. It may be one or several of the following: the unity of poetic texture over against the multi-plicity of subjects and tones (15–16 *purpureus...pannus*, 19 *sed nunc non erat his locus*, 23 *simplex dumtaxat et unum*); the 'proper' arrangement of topics (42 *ordinis uirtus*, 43 *debentia dici*); the appropriateness in the choice of words (46 *tenuis cautusque*), in diction vis-à-vis metre and genre (73) or emotion (101) or character (114); the consistency in the drawing of persons either 'historical' or 'fictional' (119 *famam sequere, sibi conuenientia finge*, 126 *seruetur ad imum*, 152 *medio ne discrepet imum*); the *decor*, *aptum*, *dignum* conjoined in the dramatic rules (156–7, 183, 191, 195); the middle range of Satyric drama (225, 237, 245); the *legitimus sonus* of rhythm (274). Even in the *poeta* section H. has known how to let 'the poem', and appropriateness along with it, impinge on 'the poet'. Thus certainly in the first sub-section: *conuenientia* entwined with the *opes* on which the poet is to draw (316). In the next sub-section, the 'mixture of delight and instruction' is set up as an ideal (343) in implied polemic against all those who thought that if the poet improves men, he does not do so *qua* poet. H. turns back to matters of workmanship and if, as I think is likely, this piece answers to the description *quid deceat, quid non* (308), 'appropriateness' is more than implied. In the final sub-section the wider notions of poetic *uirtus* are uppermost, although the list of faults (445 ff.) is likely to encroach on the territory of that 'aptness' with which the *poema* part has been concerned.

'Appropriateness' then, as H. uses it, is a many-sided critical principle, deployed in many parts of the poem to point the relation of a poetic technique to a standard of rightness. It does not appear as a self-contained topic in the sequence of critical theory. It does appear as a concomitant that qualifies many topics in that sequence.

The notion of 'art' is even more complex. A conventional ancient 'Arts Book' begins by persuading its putative user that the necessary guidance here offered is based on rational principles stated in the sequel. H. jettisons most of that. His introduction deals with a basic concern of all ancient art, poetry included—a unity that does not pall, and a variety that does not fail to add up. Yet 'art' is not wholly jettisoned. It must provide the one vital clue if unity is not to become uniformity, and variety fragmentation. Two subjects are thus woven together—*unum* and *ars*. But more than that: unity and 'art' are made interdependent.

Thus 'art', and its counterpart 'genius' (38–41), come to form the link of the structure, leading from the section on unity to the *Ars* proper—the teaching of arrangement, diction, subject-matter, and the advice on the genre of genres, poetic drama. Once this stage is reached, the dominant second theme, as has been noted, is appropriateness. Only rarely are the wider notions of art and genius made to shine through the fabric, as at 87–8 *cur ego si nequeo ignoroque*, etc. It is not until he comes near the end of this large part of the *Ars* that the poet returns to the wider motif. The disquisition on metre brings back *ars* (262), and *ars* casts light on the exemplary Greek forms of drama as well as on their Roman successors. Thus it forms a bridge to the last part, which is wholly built on the dialectical interplay between studied art and natural genius.

These are the motifs that are woven into the poem's main fabric throughout. *decorum*, and that mixture of craft and rationality which the Romans called *ars*, have a wide application to all artistic production in antiquity. By deploying them as structural principles in a poem on one of the arts, H. has widened the appeal and scope of that poem. The part played by other motifs is more limited. Among these two stand out—character and national psychology.

Character had traditionally a place in poetic theory. But in Aristotle's *Poetics* ethos stands as a topic by itself; there is little connexion with the rest of his theory. In H., with one possible exception (at 156), it is not a self-contained subject but an accompanying motif. What have *mores* to contribute to the various aspects of the poet's craft? A great deal, it appears. Diction had been discussed with regard to genre and emotion; in both cases appropriateness was demanded. Now (114) it is the traits of character due to natural disposition, social standing, and provenance that call for notice. But the motif does not disappear. Rather it serves to bridge the deplorable gulf which, in ancient literary theory, is fixed between diction and subject-matter. This is done so adroitly and, it appears, so naturally that readers cannot make up their minds whether there is any shift of topic at all. Some say that the poet has not abandoned the topic of character, others that he has moved from diction to *mythos*. Both are right in a sense. Character is a motif entwined with the primary topics. And it reappears once this context is ended. The rules on dramatization begin with *mores* (156). Much later H. lets it be known why he puts *mores* so high in his order of values. The *principium et fons* of good writing is *sapere* (309); and the 'understanding' taught by Socratic *chartae*, he thinks, is that of moral principle, which (for him) must lie at the root of true poetry. The poet who has learned that lesson *reddere personae scit conuenientia cuique* (316).

The traditional route of a Roman *ars* had some place for reflections on the comparative worth of Greek and Roman poetry. These are just the reflections that H. is bound to regard as illuminating. For his *Ars* is Greek to the core, though its Hellenism is of the Roman and Augustan kind; it promotes self-understanding and is meant to stimulate new poetic production. Here then is yet another motif. Although it suits the comparison between drama in Greece and Rome (275–91), it differs too much from such technical matters as diction and subject-matter to become easily part of the fabric of instruction. H. therefore treats it as a counterpoint. His study of dramatic metre reveals the unduly spondaic nature of Latin senarii compared with their ancestral Greek trimeters. Not without malice this failing is put down to negligence—H.'s customary and creative misunderstanding of archaic Roman literature, with the motif of *ars* again prominent (261 ff.). Out of the comparison the poet spins an indictment of Roman *uenia*; the vista to *exemplaria Graeca* is open. So the transition to the Greek and Roman genres is made (with all that the comparison implies, 275 ff.), and hence to the unity of form and content, where again the national comparison is prominent (319, 323 ff.). One suspects that when H. sensed the illuminating possibilities of this structure, he removed Metre from its cognate topic of Music, and consequently Satyric drama from the other dramatic forms. Irregularity of order draws attention to motive.

The national theme takes us half-way to the poem's personal and contemporary concern. H. the poet, critic, teacher, friend, theatre-goer, bows in and out from the beginning to the end of the *Ars*. The personal motif, in the various forms analysed in my note on 25–6, is employed in precisely the same manner as the other motifs that are secondary to the technical teaching of the *Ars*, though by no means secondary in importance. They bring something of the artistry and wit, the humanity and humour, of the other Epistles—sometimes even of the lyrics—to the pale artificialities of a textbook of poetics. Without these personal implications, the *Ars* would not be a Horatian poem.

At times this note enters into the very structure of the poem, most impressively at the beginning of the *poeta* section. For there the personal motif is entwined with one of the primary subjects of literary theory—*ars* versus *ingenium*—and helps to make the transition from the preceding section: *o ego laeuus,* | *qui purgor bilem* (301–2), *non alius faceret meliora poemata* (303), *fungar uice cotis* (304), *munus et officium, nil scribens ipse, docebo* (306).

Unilinear progression, logical subdivision, open endings, circular composition, transitions abrupt or unobtrusive, complexity of themes—these are the procedures on which I have now commented. They have disturbed students of the *Ars* and, for that reason, I have traced them in the shorter lyrics, where they are more easily perceived. They are traditional procedures which a poetic mind of great intellectual distinction and suppleness has put to fresh use. They are more than tricks of the trade. H.'s successful poems branch out, as it were, from a unity imaginatively perceived and realized in structure, tone, and wording. Students of the structure of his poems need to bear this in mind. Otherwise they are easily tempted to focus on the single aspect of arrangement, and to neglect subject, emotion, and expression. Most of all, this lesson has to be heeded in the *Ars*. For here we are continually tempted to remember the content—that is, literary theory—but not the practice—a poem demonstrating by example the spirit of this theory, or else remember the practice but forget the content. In the description of the *Ars* that now follows I have tried to heed this lesson.

30-2

2 THE POEM

Durch das Vernünfteln wird die Poesie vertrieben,
Aber sie mag das Vernünftige lieben.

GOETHE

Rien de plus anormal qu'un poète qui se rapproche
de l'homme normal: Hugo, Goethe...C'est le fou
libre. Le fou qui n'a pas l'air fou. Le fou qui n'est
jamais suspect. Quand j'ai écrit que Victor Hugo
était un fou qui se croyait Victor Hugo, je ne
plaisantais pas.

COCTEAU

Avoir du style et non un style.

COCTEAU

I. Unity and Art, 1-41

1. *A grotesque: no part of a painting fits any other*, 1–5
2. *A conversation on incongruity: not all variety in painting and poetry can be justified by a plea for creative freedom*, 6–13
3. *Three instances exemplifying incoherence; unity demanded*, 14–23
4. *A literary argument: faulty variety, like certain kinds of faulty style, is a virtue misunderstood; uniformity and unity; 'art' as regulator*, 24–31
5. *A cautionary tale: the bronze-founder; mastery of parts does not guarantee mastery of whole*, 32–7
6. *The poet's advice, an apparent truism: choose a poetic task adapted to your talent*, 38–40
7. *The poet's promise: if you can master your* subject, *you will be able to* express *and* arrange *it*, 40 (cui)–41. (*The technical topics of an ' ars poetica' are thereby implied—subject, diction, arrangement, which now follow in reverse order.*)

The 'Letter to the Pisos' opens with a series of violent contradictions, driving the reader from pillar to post. Such contradictions cannot seem strange to the reader of the *Odes* or
Satires. As other instances of Horatian dialectics, so this should
be scanned first in its natural sequence, and next in reverse
order, backwards from the end of the dialectical process.

(1) A grotesque: no part of a painting fits any other, 1–5

in medias res is H.'s description of Homer's procedure (*A.P.* 148). In a wider, non-narrative, sense it often applies to his own poetry, and produces a 'shock-effect', as it has been called. The realistic style of *sermo* can accommodate caricature and *grotesque*. The first four lines do not describe so much as affront: a human head set down by a painter on a horse's neck, feathers of many colours, limbs unassorted, a fish's tail but above a beautiful woman. The result of viewing such a picture, the last line adds, would be laughter.

Few readers will overlook that these verses, though ridiculed in the scheme of the poem, stand as a little masterpiece in its own right, just as does its larger companion, the poet whose unalloyed inspiration results in madness (453–76), both assigned by their creator to the same cause—lack of art. But H. is not here arguing. He clearly had the creator's love for these misshapen beauties. The caricatures of medieval architecture and the *grotesques* of the Italian Renaissance show how such fantasies can be accommodated in the larger design of another medium. The place of unnatural configurations in Roman decorative painting—*monstra potius quam ex rebus finitis imagines certae*—is adverted to, censoriously, by Vitruvius in a famous chapter (VII. 5. 3–4). The passages of H. and Vitruvius were widely known in sixteenth-century Italy.[1] The details of the present piece inspired Raphael or his colleagues to set down a monster in the *scherzi* of the Vatican's *Logge*, characteristically in the panel devoted to the Fates.[2]

[1] See Nicole Dacos, 'La découverte de la Domus Aurea et la formation des grotesques à la Renaissance', *Studies of the Warburg Institute*, XXXI (1969), 122–3. (I owe an advance notice of this publication to the courtesy of the authorities of the Warburg Institute.)

[2] Cf. K. Borinski, *Die Antike in Poetik und Kunsttheorie*, 1 (1914), 180 f., Nicole Dacos, *op. cit.* 100 ff. on *L'atelier de Raphaël. Maturation des grotesques*.

(2) A conversation on incongruity: not all variety in painting and poetry can be justified by a plea for creative freedom, 6–13

Now the address, *Pisones* (ushered in by *amici* in the previous line) with a new point which reveals that the *grotesque* is there merely to illustrate: H. is concerned with *liber*, not with *tabula* (6). Book and painting alike, if so formed, are incoherent—shapes or images—like feverish dreams. Seeming to slip back into the realistic language of the initial *grotesque*, H. employs a homely proverb to describe such works; hand and foot do not belong to the same 'form'; a hint at the description above and a sidelong glance—not at this stage recognized as such—at literary theory, for the organic metaphor had played a part in it since Plato and perhaps earlier. But such discourteous speech evokes a protest. In the best style of *sermo* an objection by an unnamed objector is quoted, but abruptly, without the customary 'someone (or 'you') might say...', and so a discussion develops. The interlocutor demands unlimited daring, the romantic prerogative of painter and poet. Believers in the proprieties called classical used to note that H. agrees but that he regards the demand as a truism when it means what the defenders do not mean (11), and as false when it means what, with vigorous realism, he describes as the mating of incompatibles, 'snakes with birds', etc. (12–13). Thus a limiting condition has to be imposed: creative liberty must not be licence. It is only some variety that emerges as faulty. What variety then does so emerge?

(3) Three instances exemplifying incoherence; unity demanded, 14–23

Three instances follow with the abruptness which a Horatian knows to be a favoured device for keeping the reader on his toes or, put differently, a device for drawing attention to connexions of substance, and away from such external links as a prosaic 'for example'.

The first instance concerns poetry: the celebrated 'purple patch', 14–19 *locus*. The piece has its place not only in the contemporary setting in which *descriptio* was a fashion. For the purpose is wider. Such descriptions were approved particularly for epic writing, larger unities by definition. And it is with larger unities that this poet is concerned. Under H.'s hands the writing prettily assumes the character of *descriptio* with its lightweight picture-painting and its imitative assonances: *et properantis aquae per amoenos ambitus agros* (17 n.). Particularities precede, but a near-technical word identifies them at the end (*describitur*, 18).

The next two instances come from the fine arts, if that is not overstating the case. For the votive tablet and the pitcher represent handicraft rather than art. But homeliness of exemplifying—and that applies to the example of sewing as well—is in the nature of *sermo* and suits the case well, the case being elementary achievement in the making of things. While the purple patch shows up topics unadapted to a poetic texture—and hence inequality of poetic tone—the votive tablet fails more grossly in a different medium; the cypress contradicts purpose and setting alike. The potter's failure is grosser still; the parts of his work do not add up to the same thing, for what began as an amphora ends as a pitcher. The instances thus get shorter and shorter; examples of failure crowd in, as it were, on the reader. By now, however, he has mastered the details, and the last line (23) summarizes briefly what has already been seen in concrete fulness. The summary may be taken to apply not only to the three instances but to what precedes them. *simplex et unum* is a basic law in nature and art.

(4) A literary argument: faulty variety, like certain kinds of faulty style, is a virtue misunderstood; uniformity and unity; 'art' as regulator, 24–31

If H. were writing a treatise he might base good poetry on variety and avoidance of uniformity, variety limited by the wholeness to be attained—unity the overriding excellence, uniformity and undue variety two opposed faults. Being a Roman critic he might exemplify this notion of 'virtues and faults' by the doctrine of style in which *uirtutes* and *uitia* loomed large. Finally he might let this striving for unity in multiplicity be ordered by that trained sensibility of workmanship which is an aspect of *ars*. In this way he would have tied together, in a manner unusual in antiquity, a plea for unity and a plea for training in *ars poetica*. As it is, H. is not writing a treatise. The abstractions of literary theory are realized through the technical problems which the poet solves, by the *manner* in which he writes about them.

The abrupt start propels the listener into a new subject, whether the exemplary doctrine of style with its 'excellences' and 'faults', or simply the doctrine of *uirtutes* and *uitia* in the context of style. That is something new in the poem, and not only because before he has told us nothing of technical criticism of poetry. It is new because H. now suggests that variability is a 'virtue', not, as one might have expected from most that precedes, a fault. This is clearly important, and hence H. marks it by a mock-solemn address to 'the father and the sons worthy of the father'; by identifying himself, humbly and humorously, with the 'greatest number of poets' who are liable to such mistakes; and by the very archaism *uates*, which the Augustans had brought back into poetic use. For six verses the reader's attention is held by talk about stylistic excellence missed through over-zealous avoidance of faults— the passage picturing the faults discussed, until it dawns on him where deception by a 'false image of truth' has led him. Style was but an example, taken from poetry, a well-known case, where learners were warned against 'opposite faults': *breuis esse laboro,* | *obscurus fio*, etc. Variability is a 'virtue', something at the root of this art. But the attempt to produce a marvel of variety—an escape from sameness—may produce a dolphin in the painting of a wood, and so forth, unnatural combinations that have been rejected before. So the *pictores atque poetae* (9) reappear; now their sins are brought home to them. It is not that variety and daring are bad; rather uniformity is a fault. But to avoid the contrary fault, undue variety, the control of art is needed. We can be told at the end what would have told us little at the beginning—a generality, an abstract rule, 'flight from fault leads to fault', *si caret arte* (31).

(1)–(4) Here, it seems, is a pause in sense and it is time to look back over the first 31 lines. Are they more than a haphazard study in variety? Variety is clearly intended and the manner of presentation does not allow us to forget it: the sequence, caricature described, followed by dialogue, followed by cautionary tales, concluded by stylistic theory and its application to the problem of variety and an implied demand for training in the art—that sequence could hardly be more diverse. This impression is strengthened by the logical antithesis which H. has built into this section. For while, in spite of the grudging admission l. 10, the first 23 lines look like a plea for unity, the end of the section makes variety a commendable aim. Reading up to this point, therefore, one would be justified in saying that H. in talking about undue variety had produced a poem (or part of it) which was all variety. And yet the progress from (1) to (4) is also a progress from grotesque variety to variety mastered by unity, and from untutored daring, which produces an 'unnatural' multiplicity, to 'art', which keeps the practitioner from oscillating between two faults—undue uniformity and undue variety. The impression therefore, as one looks back, does not so much change as add to the former view: the poem up to this point mirrors the qualities which it discusses. The poem does not only talk about multiplicity and design but its structure conveys the experience of both. Its form has coalesced with its subject. The outcome cannot be summarized, least of all in such phrases, however memorable, as *denique sit quiduis simplex dumtaxat et unum* or *in uitium ducit culpae fuga, si caret arte*. The unity of the section lies in the relation of its parts; in H.'s language, 'hand' and 'foot' do belong to *una forma*.

473

(5) A cautionary tale: the bronze-founder: mastery of parts does not guarantee mastery of whole, 32–7

Another abrupt break and the cautionary tale of the *faber* by the Aemilian School follows. The fine arts are still exemplary. This bronze-founder is second to none (32 *unus*, not *imus*) in bringing out lifelike details in his bronzes, but his skill is partial not total: *ponere totum | nesciet* (34–5). This is, as H. puts it with one of the realistic touches of his hexameter poems, like having handsome black hair and black eyes but an ugly nose. Looking back again we establish the thought-sequence. *si caret arte* the last section ended (31). 'Wholeness' is here added to the 'unity' of the earlier sections, a different thing altogether or, if you like, a different aspect of unity. The *ars* required certainly deals with parts. But if it remains partial it also remains artisanship. The true artist must be able to see and make a whole. In the last section *unum* and *ars* were brought together. In this section *totum* and *ars* are joined. The notions (ἕν and ὅλον), as my Introduction showed, are Aristotelian, but the questions asked and the answers given are not. For the juncture of unity/wholeness with *ars* is a problem for the maker. His insight and his practical training are in question. Hence an astringent demand for *ars* is already inherent in the vision of *unum* and *totum*, and it is this demand that now follows.

(6) The poet's advice, an apparent truism: choose a poetic task adapted to your talent, 38–40

(7) The poet's promise: if you can master your subject, you will be able to express and arrange it, 40 (cui)–41 (The technical topics of an 'ars poetica' are thereby implied— subject, diction, arrangement, which now follow in reverse order)

The demand that was just mentioned is put in the form of advice addressed to *qui scribitis* (38), poets. But even here the matter is complex, not simple. The pull of a dialectical mind is at work. H. is not simply saying—hence art is required to deal with the totality of a poem. His mind runs in contraries, and the contraries themselves are part of a larger vision. Paradoxically on the surface but coherently beneath it, the notion of capability in art brings *ingenium* rather than *ars* to the fore. Thus a new (antithetical) motif is introduced, and H. can warn the practitioner against undertaking work that is beyond his powers. And finally he wheels about, as it were, turning *materia*, a subject undertaken, into *res*, subject-matter, and ends by proposing the layout of a book of instruction in this verbal art—*res* (subject-matter), *facundia* (style), *ordo* (arrangement). Unity is not however forgotten, for the right choice of subject promises that style and arrangement will fall into place; thus the poet overcomes the inorganic distinction between form and content, which so disturbs modern readers. The promise is made on the understanding that *ars* has been acquired by the practitioner who has the right measure of *ingenium*.

The notion of *ars* never disappears from the poem hereafter, though it is no longer the critical topic to be debated, but an underlying motif. It comes to the surface when occasion demands it, notably, from 290 onward, where it serves to pull together the 'technical sections', two thirds of the poem, and to form a bridge to the last part, *artifex*.

(1)–(7) The introductory forty-one verses *in parvo* display the main motifs and the workmanship of the *Ars* in its entirety. From the first there is not only one topic but several, subjects come to the fore and recede; one needs to talk of motifs rather than plain subjects. *unum, totum, ars* are here so closely entwined that only the analyser and the literary historian can tell us that this combination is as unusual in antiquity as it looks natural in the poem.

H.'s poetry is not one-sided. His world is not a simple and static world; that is its strength but also its weakness. His terms are dialectically loaded; most of them seem to carry their logical opposites about them: unity and multiplicity, the whole and the parts, studied art and the spontaneity of genius. The piece, moreover, does not evolve in one unilinear progression; readers, even scholarly readers, looking for that have come to grief. The units of thought are small, like blocks sharply cut off from what precedes and follows; some critics have compared the parts of a Horatian poem to marble blocks, sharply hewn, and pushed together without much connexion. That is a misunderstanding. But those who said so did sense something real. The superficially unconnected and often antithetical contexts of a poem do reflect the dialectical cast of the poet's imagination, in this work as in many others. But that does not mean that a poem consists of unrelated parts—the fallacy against which he tilts in this piece. Rather it is the relation between contraries that moves H.'s mind, and in the flexible relation of antitheses and the implicit resolution of contradictions lies much of his art. Multiplicity and unity are thus related in the technique of many of his poems. So they are in this. But what makes the *Ars* unique is that in doing so he also talked about this very subject. The form of the poem not only mirrors his subject; it *is* his subject. H. must have been well aware that thus to relate variety and unity is what he could do best. Talk of H.'s failure to discuss his own poetry is wrongheaded. In this piece the poet not only discusses his own procedure, but he offers an instance of his procedure to illuminate a basic problem of poetic production, perhaps the basic problem—for a poet of H.'s kind.

II. The Arts of Arrangement and Diction in Poetry, 42–118

(1) Arrangement, 42–4

H. ended his 'table of contents' with *lucidus ordo* (41). When he now, 'chiastically', slips into the subject of *ordo* he is using his favourite device of a gliding transition. Favourite but not mechanical, for the transition hints at an unexpected connexion. The initial section said and implied a great deal about 'arrangement': above all the protest against the purple patch, *sed nunc non erat his locus* (19). But earlier, 'placing' was a special case of an Aristotelian unity; there were other cases. Now 'the art of placing', *more rhetorico*, becomes a subject in its own right. With dead-pan humour and a fairly outspoken insistence (*aut ego fallor*, 42 n.) he described *ordo* in truistic fashion, leaving the all-important subject, *imperatoria uirtus*, even more tersely defined than most of the critics did. Once again he is commenting on his own procedure as much as on literary theory. He demonstrates the strength and charm of the procedure by postponing, according to his precept, all that is not needful in this place (e.g. the Homeric technique, 140 ff.). This amounts to illustrating *ordo* both as the art of concentration, and as the art of the highly concentrative and undiffuse poet, Horace.

(2) Diction, 46/45–118

(a) Vocabulary, 46/45–72

'Rightness' or 'appropriateness' was an underlying but unexpressed motif in the debate on unity, up to 40. A similar quality again was to inform *ordo*; it could have been called 'sparse and circumspect'. Here, at last, at the start of the section on style, H. does use these terms (*tenuis cautusque*), and *etiam* (46 preceding, as it should, 45) vindicates this description for the order of topics as well as the choice of words. Yet, in the fashion already remarked, contradictory principles appear almost immediately. Since H. has seen fit to indicate personal involvement, the scope of this section calls for doubly careful consideration. What is the balance of contrary attitudes H. wishes to strike? The poet claims to speak of his own practice, but, at the same time, he offers a literary theory. The most unbiased view will be to regard this piece as what it claims to be—an interpretation of his own practice, made by the poet

477

himself in the theoretical terms open to him. This will tell us a great deal. The limitations will be twofold—those imposed on a poet talking about his own work, and those imposed by his critical vocabulary.

The setting differs from the rest of this poem in two respects: it has a strong personal complexion, and it sounds a sustained lyric note that is unique in the *Ars* and exceedingly rare anywhere outside the *Odes*. There is no such stress on the initial terse pronouncement (47–8 *nouum*) that diction will be out of the ordinary if ordinary words are placed in a pointed context. This provides the common basis for poetic speech. But next (48 *si forte*–59) an extraordinary emphasis is placed on the antithesis to *notum uerbum*, however refashioned by the cunning context—new coinages. The emphasis comes out in an emotional involvement which H. permits himself rarely and which therefore deserves notice. Usually when H. employs the first person in this poem, and often elsewhere, he generalizes himself in the most ingenious ways (cf. 25 n., 25–6 n.). Here however *ego* (55) really is I, Horace, who have added new words to the language, in the proud line of those who have enriched *sermonem patrium* (57). There is, moreover, a polemical point, directed against those who allow creativity in the use of words to archaic authors but not to the new, Virgil, Varius and—himself. Yet 'new words' must not be introduced for their own sake, the *Ars* deplores empty talk, *uersus inopes rerum nugaeque canorae* (322). New words must 'point to' unexplored territory: *si forte necesse est* | ...*monstrare...abdita rerum* (48–9). This is the manner in which 'appropriateness' arises out of the present context, although again this term is not mentioned. One can sense a protest in two directions, against the archaizers, who are so well known from the letter to Augustus, and those New Poets to whom a sophisticated use of words was an end and not, as H. thought it should be, a means. Such is the personal and contemporary involvement that in turn now evokes the world of the lyric poems.

The Poem

The poet's feeling for words makes them animate: they are born, live and die. Words are humanized and language shares mutability with man. Mutability, and the human emotions that it engenders, thus form the background which is to justify poetic usage, both the common stock of words and new coinages. Permanence in the ever-repeated cycle of the seasons, death leading to new birth, are religious symbols to Greek and Roman readers. In the *Odes* they often lend emotional stability to the poignant transience of the human lot:

> damna tamen celeres reparant caelestia lunae;
> > nos ubi decidimus
> quo pius Aeneas, quo diues Tullus et Ancus,
> > puluis et umbra sumus.

(C. IV. 7. 13–16)

In a sense it is true that the *Odes*, unlike the *Satires*, may conjure up death at any moment.[1] But that does not mean that there is no place for death in the world of the *Satires*. What differs is the tone. Death dryly points moral lessons in that world, and does not point them very often (*S*. II. 2. 132; 3. 122, 157; 5. 84–8, 104–6). The lessons lack depth and emotional force, as a writer on the *Odes* has remarked.[2] The *Epistles*, however, occasionally and briefly sound the lyric note: *omnem crede diem tibi diluxisse supremum* (I. 4. 13), *ire tamen restat Numa quo deuenit et Ancus* (I. 6. 27, written before the Ode just cited from book IV), *hoc sentit, 'moriar'. mors ultima linea rerum est* (I. 16. 79, cf. II. 2. 173–9, 207). But the note is never more than occasional.

In the present sections of the *Ars*, death and change yield more poetic capital than they do elsewhere in the hexameter poems. In the verses 60–9 the tone rises from a well-poised middle level to something akin to lyric intensity. First the epic simile of the changing leaves of the forest (60–2). Next the poignant Simonidean reminiscence, *debemur morti nos nostraque* (63) and three cases where Nature reasserts her power over

---

[1] F. Solmsen, *AJP*, LXVIII (1947), 342.
[2] S. Commager, *The Odes of H*. (1962), 87.

the works of man: *mortalia facta peribunt* (68). So we return to language and the conclusion is drawn, *nedum sermonum stet honos et gratia uiuax* (69). The 'excursus', as in the *Georgics*, contains the poetic substance. What inspires intensity unique in the hexameter poems is the 'life of language'. Finally a rapid fall, back to the middle style of *sermo*, 70–2: if language is thus changeable, words will die and revive under the lordship of Usage. These are notions of grammatical theory made into poetic symbols that qualify the whole of this section. H. has established an intimate connexion between the poetry written in the language and the common stock of the language in its changing aspects. On this understanding the poet's freedom to create new words is defended. The complexity of this situation is recaptured in the complexity of this piece of poetry.

(b) Norms of diction in poetic genres, 73–88

An abrupt change to a new subject—an apparently elementary disquisition on the metres of Greek poetic genres. This is a first description of the new topic. Is it a true description? Not entirely true. In the first place, the subject is metre only in a superficial sense. For the varying metre simply indicates the genres, with the diction of which H. concerns himself. Secondly, it is hard to dissociate advanced from elementary. What could be more difficult than a just appreciation of the major Greek genres and their styles? Thirdly, this is not literary history for its own sake. Rather select genres are offered as so many settings for different kinds of diction. The settings are largely defined by metre and by the 'inventor' of the genre, but the terms are generous and wide. A first reading, up to 85, fixes these apparently historical data in the reader's mind. But clearly this is done because H. demands diverse styles for diverse genres. The precedence assigned to the genres serves to establish their ideal diversity before the purpose of this exercise is disclosed. For 86–8, a 'link passage', puts it beyond doubt that the norms of diction should change according to these genres, *uices operumque colores*. A backward glance then shows literary history with an ulterior purpose. The reader addressed is the Roman poet-learner; he must train himself to observe, in his own writing, the diversity of the great Greek genres about which he has just been told. Thus the section that started as literary history is brought back to the context of diction. At the end, in unobtrusive fashion, the two earlier motifs of appropriateness and *ars* are continued, and are meant to give purpose to the literary history—*uices operumque colores* and *nequeo ignoroque*, *nescire* and *discere*.

(c) Styles of diction, exemplified from drama, 89–118

There has been a narrowing of scope as H. passed from words (*a*), which concerned all poetry, to the styles of different genres (*b*), to the diction of drama, in general terms touched on before (80–2). The layout of this section, and its key-term, 'the appropriate'—*decens*, derives ultimately from Aristotle. But, unlike the philosopher, H. regards the rightness of tone as a technical problem which the poet must learn to master from inside.

H. once again begins with an antithesis, contrasting sharply the dramatic circumstances of the two genres that are poles apart, comedy and tragedy. The contrast is intensified by the terseness and directness with which it is put: not *res comica* and *tragica* but *res comica* refusing to be expressed *uersibus tragicis*. Literal and metaphorical, fact and abstraction tend to nourish each other in H.'s imagination. Comedy and tragedy thus become agents possessing a volition of their own. Not only does the genre pass easily from the general term to a single instance—*cena Thyestae*—but to the *dramatis personae* themselves: Chremes, Telephus, Peleus. The labels 'personification' and 'metonymy' (89 n.) may have their uses but they tell us little about the way poetic language works. What needs to be noted is the nature of the Horatian style, which, without a strain, encompasses logical variables in a continuous movement from abstract to concrete or from concrete to abstract. This is an essential feature in a poem which turns the abstractions of literary theory into the concreteness of live poetry.

Having set up two contrary styles—the 'appropriate place' for comedy and another for tragedy (89–92)—H. proceeds to break down what might be a rigid and unreal distinction. Chremes, the comic type-figure, in his anger, may occasionally reach almost tragic emotion. In tragedy, on the other hand, Telephus or Peleus, in the misery of poverty or exile, may touch the spectator's heart with a realistic lament which strikes ancient feeling for style as near-comic or prosaic (93–8). Comic diction is thus raised to a level close to tragic dignity, just as tragic is lowered to near-comic realism, the hero flinging aside the *ampullae* of his lofty genre. In either case emotion (Aristotle's πάθος) is involved and diction must be related (be appropriate) to the emotions engendered by the drama. So that the passage functions as a transition from the context of 'dramatic circumstance' to that of 'emotion'.

Now emotion, pathos, comes into its own (99–113). A believer in the canons of classical art and literature may feel content with poems shaped according to the demands of formal perfection, *pulchra poemata*. Not so H., the classic *par excellence*: *non satis est pulchra esse poemata, dulcia sunto* (99); *psychagogia* is needed (100). A plea for sincerity—a rarish plea in ancient literature—colours H.'s manner of writing: *ut ridentibus arrident*. And there is an address inspired by sympathy with the *dramatis personae* of the last section: *si uis me flere... | ...tunc tua me infortunia laedent, | Telephe uel Peleu* (102–4). Hence the series of 'appropriate' styles, *tristia maestum | uultum uerba decent*, and equally anger, playful mood, seriousness (105–7). H.'s psychology demands this close link between utterance and the emotion felt. Unless the emotion is genuine, diction will not sound true (108–10). So he can turn back to the 'circumstances' of the *dramatis personae* and the attendant emotions. Words will not carry conviction unless they are inspired by emotion, and if they do not carry conviction they will sound stilted and be laughed off the stage (112–13).

As in Aristotle, 'ethos' follows after 'circumstance' and 'emotion'; the same demand is made. Diction must express character and type of person (114); that is the conclusion the reader will rightly draw from the 'link passage' (112–13) and the *intererit multum* immediately thereafter. But the brisk catalogue of antithetic types is quite different in style from the preceding plea to meet emotion with sympathetic emotion. Distinguish by their speech god and hero, old and young, and so forth.

Here the topic of diction, the *facundia* of 41, comes to a close. The next verse (119) pronounces on 'subject-matter', and wherever 'diction' appears again on the agenda it is set in a different framework.

Arrangement and Diction seen from the end of this section, 118 back to 46/45, 44–2

It is time to turn back once more, taking the long view of the whole of this section. Certain new features come into prominence, and help to clarify what H. has been trying to do. He has not only availed himself of the conceptual framework of the literary critics but has also decided to compete with them in his own way.

The evidence shows that there is a framework which relates to the notions of ancient literary criticism. To deny that there is a progression of thought from *ordo*–arrangement (42–4) to *facundia*–diction (46/45–118) is to fly in the face of the evidence. And it was arrangement and diction—two fixed points in virtually every ancient discussion of style—that were selected for mention at the end of the previous section, and there contrasted with *res*, 'subject-matter' (41). Moreover within the topic of diction there is a progression from 'words', which apply to all poetry (46/45–72), to the more selective treatment of style in the various genres (73–88), and a yet more selective piece on dramatic diction (89–118). These headings are no more but also no less important to the *Ars* than are predetermined subjects—such as a hymn or an invitation—to the lyric poems in which they occur. The scope of such predetermined matters is limited. It is worth remembering, too, that these literary terms are heavy abstractions. Unilinear progression from one abstract topic to another is a prosaic notion— not *per se* a promising poetic procedure. If H. had done no more, all that could be said is that he employed these notions but played them down, perhaps enlivening them by the technique of *sermo*—a minor achievement if achievement it be.

But then, looking back from this point, we note, as we have noted before, that H. has imposed other patterns on the one-line arrangement of the literary critics. When he has finished with his first discussion of style, he sums up the different genres and their concomitant tones by *descriptas...uices operumque colores* (86), a kind of appropriateness of diction to poetic genre. The subsequent little section he concludes by telling tragedy and comedy to keep *locum decentem* allotted to each (92); *decens* denotes what is 'becoming' or 'appropriate'. The same procedure is followed when emotion and character come up for consideration: *tristia maestum | uultum uerba decent* (105–6) starts the last sentence dealing with emotional diction, and *intererit multum* (114) introduces character-study, taking up the *absona dicta* of the 'link passage' (112). Here a large context with its technical subdivisions is guided, as it were, by the overriding principle of *decens*, which sounds less forbidding in Latin than 'appropriate' or 'becoming' in English. In any case a glance at many passages will show the light touch with which these notions are employed. Something is right in its place; something may be related to a principle; parts of a larger whole fit together—all this, in Latin, *decet*.

While it is worth noting, therefore, that the word *decens* appears after we are well into the poem (92), and its forerunners, the *descriptae uices* and the *colores*, do not appear much earlier (86), it is still true that the principle inherent in *decens* has been with us from the very first. For what are unity or wholeness (1–37) if not an appropriate (*decens*) relation of the parts of an organism, painting, poem, or what you will? Again, what is the unity of arrangement and diction, so promisingly tied to the right choice of subject-matter (40–1), if not the appropriate relation of all aspects of a poem to each other, the coalescing of word and thought, form and matter, the Horatian poet's ultimate goal? In the distinct terms of literary theory there is no clear connexion between the 'unity' of the initial part of the *Ars* and the *decens* of the present; but in a wider poetic sense there is. H. seems so to have arranged the poem up to this point that the various symbols which are used to describe the relation of unity to multiplicity, and of content to style and arrangement, suggest a regulative principle which he calls 'appropriate' (*decens*).

The same technique is used in dealing with the motif of *ars*. From *si caret arte* (31) to *ponere totum | nesciet* (34–5), to the discrimination practised in the choice of words and in *callida iunctura* (46/45 ff.), to *ignoro* (87) in the next section, and to the training which will enable the poet to meet the difficult conditions laid down for manipulating the varying styles even in the same genre—everywhere we find the same motif of *ars*, but entwined with others to which *ars* is applied.

To work in this manner, with motifs, amounts to an ordering and structuring of the poet's experience. H. applies his technique in the same way as he does in other poems—only that here that technique itself is his subject. Here as elsewhere H.'s motifs are few in number but their complexity is great. Different patterns arise according to the point of vantage from which you scan the poem. If the first 118 verses are read with a traditional literary division in mind, the reader will find unity, wholeness, and the necessity of *ars*, followed by arrangement and diction. If they are read with larger principles in mind, he will find the motifs of *ars* and *decens* qualifying the simpler division.

Nor are the terms a few simple and rigid abstractions. H.

sets art against talent, unity against multiplicity, tragic diction against comic, and so forth. In each case the unity lies in the balance that he strikes between such contraries. With accustomed agility he moves between abstract and concrete, factual and symbolic, *res comica* and Chremes, *uersus tragici* and *ampullae*. This kind of imagination, and the technique thus evolved, help to break down and build anew what was once a fairly staid literary theory. Thus poetics is drawn into action. The theory of poetry is turned into a poem that, by its quality, expresses what the literary critic can only teach in conceptual terms.

(III. Subject-matter and character in poetry, 119–52)

1. *Traditional and new subjects (characters)*, 119–30
2. *How to make a traditional subject the poet's own; Homer and the cyclic epic*, 131–52

(1) Traditional and new subjects (characters), 119–30

This major break combines with a 'gliding transition' the abrupt change of topic that is so common within the larger sections of this and other Horatian poems. The few major breaks in the *Ars* show the same combination. At the start of the last section of all, *ingenium misera* (295) marks the abrupt turn to the new topic, 'the poet', but the transitional subject is the cult of *ingenium*, which has been delicately prepared in the preceding section from 285 onward or earlier. Something at any rate like it is found at 42 and 45, where arrangement and diction mark two new contexts, cut off from the poet's choice of subject and his personal talent, on which the previous paragraph dilates (38 ff.). Nevertheless arrangement and diction were brought into the discussion of talent, at 41, and thus form a bridge from one context to the next. The abrupt break at 153, in spite of continuing attention to 'character', may serve a similar purpose.

At the outset an injunction, and an inescapable 'either–or' (119): the learner is faced with two kinds of subject, traditional or of his own making. This marks the new topic but it is shown at once from what angle the poet wants the reader to view the new topic; other viewpoints will appear presently. H. describes subject-matter in terms of its 'heroes' —not the *mythos* or *fama* of the Trojan War or the Seven against Thebes but Achilles, Medea, Ino, Ixion, Io, and Orestes—a personalized view of things which doubtless was shared by many of his contemporaries. In poetic terms this has the advantage that he can employ the notion of 'character' as a bridge to the preceding section. There ethos was impersonal as it were—status, age, calling, provenance. Here ethos is still typical—*Io uaga, tristis Orestes* (124)—but the features belong to persons as they fit certain myths of the ancient tradition. In the preceding section ethos was looked at from the viewpoint of diction, here from the viewpoint of content, story, myth. A third motif must not be overlooked. Appropriateness or consistency is a quality that ties this section to all that has gone before. So far then the evidence: 'content, myth, story' provide the basic literary theory, which is seen in terms of personal character with traits demanding consistency of treatment. This is a rich texture and the three strands are all tied together in the initial two verses (119–20): *aut famam sequere*—the literary theory—*aut sibi conuenientia finge*—the literary theory again but also the motif of consistency in daringly Horatian terseness. For *conuenientia* is the grammatical object of *finge*, and implies that the consistency which the 'inventor' has to strive for is already guaranteed by the *fama*— but next *si forte reponis Achillem*, the *fama* is expressed in terms of character. Deft character-study continues this line, each *persona* receiving no more than one telling epithet apart from Achilles whose exemplary case receives more attention. The vista is then narrowed to the stage (*scaenae*, 125, probably prepared by *reponis*, 120) and the 'inventor' receives attention. His difficulty, as H. sees it, lies in rendering *communia* (general or typical features) *proprie*, that is, making them into characters which carry a story as consistently as the set personages of a traditional myth do, where that work has been done already by *fama*. Hence H.'s advice in favour of the latter subjects.

(2) How to make a traditional subject the poet's own; Homer and the cyclic epic, 131–52

H. saw salvation not in originality *à tout prix* but in revitalizing, and being revitalized by, a tradition. His creed declares his and his friends' poetic experience. The Augustans had reacted with originality to the ancient Greek tradition. Hence the poet is told that he should prefer traditional subjects; hence too he is advised to learn how to make traditional subjects, *publica materies*, his own, *priuati iuris* (131). Such a description will fit the learner's work. But it will fit also great things, the *Aeneid* and the *Odes*, which are *publica materies* and yet eminently *priuati iuris*—a welcome reminder, though not the only one, to reprove those who complain that the *Ars* has no dealings with Roman, Augustan, or Horatian poetry.

Although the large abstractions of literary theory are seen in the background, H. here shows the poet at work. He seems to be talking of the realities of the world around him—the crowded and well-trodden round, the translator at work, the narrow hole in which the imitator gets stuck, etc. In fact these are literary symbols, which H. deftly relates to poetic faults. 'Subject-matter which belongs to all will become private property' only if certain mistakes are avoided. In each case there is a metaphor with its attendant overtones. The 'trivial and well-trodden round' suggests Callimachus' opposition to crowded roads (132), the *orbis* containing the first hint that the cyclic epic is not far away. The literal versions of the *fidus interpres* (133–4) are arraigned not because of their diction but as a failure to deal with *publica materies*; the reference is to a type of exercise much practised in antiquity. Slavish imitation is like a jump into a narrow space, the 'law of the genre' stifling instead of promoting creativity (134–5)— narrowness, whereas at first the area was too wide, and open to all (132). Finally the proem of a humdrum, 'cyclic', epic; it takes us back to the notion of unity early in the poem: 138 *tanto...promissor hiatu*, 14 *inceptis grauibus...et magna professis*. The large and unfulfilled promise, realistically set down, suggests in turn the proverb of the mountain in labour with its Hellenistic nuances (139 n.).

Having barred the escape routes, H. sets the Homeric procedure against the cyclic, not precisely an easy assignment for the aspiring poet. It is the procedure of 'him who engineers nothing foolishly' (140), the ideal exponent of *ars* and *ingenium* alike, who is great enough to be identified by description and citation. The proem of the *Odyssey* sets the tone for the rest and it is the right tone. Homeric aptness is concentrated in a vigorous image, *ex fumo dare lucem* (143)—the light of Homer's *oeconomia*, which is then shed on the *miracula* of his episodes. But there is no talk of 'unity and episodes', only imagery (143–4) and the fairy-tales conjured up by a verse consisting entirely of romantic Greek names distributed cunningly over the line (145). The *miracula*, fictional as they were known to be, are fitted without strain into the mythical events which were believed to be true to history. Only then is literary theory assigned the task of summing up in conceptual terms what has already been expressed in picture-language. Homer's poetic economy is described by *ad euentum* and *in medias res* (148–9) and his art of omission is noted (150). Finally it is claimed that 'truth' (the assumed historicity of heroic myth, the main line of his narrative) and fiction (the *miracula* admired above) form a coherent unity (151–2).

Thus *primo ne medium, medio ne discrepet imum* (152) closes the circle begun at the beginning of this section. For that is how Homer has joined *fama* and fiction (119), making the two cohere in a manner which the innovator would have to create afresh (126–7). Thus Homer performed the task, set up as an ideal (at 131), of making tradition his own. But *primo ne medium* tells us more than that. For significantly it varies the notions of the initial section. 'Unity' was there seen to arise from an organic relation of parts, continued by other notions implying 'appropriateness'. Here a similar idea appears as the inherent harmony of the mythical diversities which Homer has been able to achieve.

Homer's procedure in unifying his subject-matter is, in the first place, a narrative ideal; it belongs to the Greek epic genre or to the Latin, to Homer or to Virgil. But the earlier part of the section has shown the same notion in the setting of drama. We must go further still, for H. makes his point so generally that it has an application to poetry, whatever its genre. I for one find it hard not to see the ideal of *in medias res* realized at the beginning of this poem, though there are other instances in H. Commentators are not always aware that when they admire the dramatic impact of *humano capiti ceruicem pictor equinam* (1) and describe it by saying '*in medias res*', they are in fact describing this Homeric procedure, as H. here puts it in terms of traditional literary theory. I regard this as a telling example of Horatian complexity.

IV. Drama, 153–294

1. *Characters*, 153–78
2–5. *Interdicts*, 179–92
6. *Chorus*, 193–201
7. *Music*, 202–19
8. *Satyric drama*, 220–50
9. *Metre*, 251–74
10. *Greek drama, tragic and comic*, 275–84
11. *Roman drama, tragic and comic*, 285–94

(1) Characters, 153–78

Now there are no more pronouncements on subject-matter, nor examples from Homer. Instead the reader is addressed and his attention is called to a new topic. This marks a strong break. Drama, the genre of genres, is now under discussion, no longer as an instance of diction or content, but *qua* drama; its aspects are at first undefined. Yet other patterns of thought continue across this boundary line. Surprisingly we find H. facing the reader with a splendid series of pen-portraits: the four ages of man. It is character once again, the specific topic close to 115–16 *maturusne senex an adhuc florente iuuenta | feruidus*. But now no attention is paid to what characters say (*loquatur* 114) or to the dominant traits of individuals (120 ff.). What matters is action; *mores* must be lifelike in accordance with age. Thus the motif of *mores* is carried on; the many-sidedness of the human personality and the complexity of the poetic task are shown by the same *modus operandi*. Ethos, in this poem, is set in different poetic fields—diction, subject-matter, dramatic action. Each time the poet must adapt his creation to external factors; hence, not surprisingly, appropriateness, here *decor*, is inculcated as well: *mobilibusque decor naturis dandus et annis* (157). The pen-portraits differ in tone and intent from the 'theory' that precedes and follows them. The piece stands as an 'ethology' in its own right, both in length and emphasis, a demonstration of what is required of the poet, not only the dramatist. The same sharp eye for typical moral features which elsewhere characterizes H.'s writing is at work here; he is demanding of others what he demands of himself. Ethology was a literary form employed by the philosophers and orators. Often H. translated Aristotelian theory into poetic practice. In this passage however, just for once, he seems to enter into competition with Aristotle, or the Aristotelians, in the same field. I have tried to show in my commentary how the celebrated piece from the *Rhetoric* (II. 12–14) differs in spite of basic similarities of genre.

(2)–(5) Interdicts, 179–92

These interdicts (with one exception post-Aristotelian) mark a striking contrast to the long descriptive piece that precedes and the injunction that follows. Prescriptions must be brief, said H. elsewhere (335), and so are these. In fact, they get shorter and more imperious each time; ten lines on horrors and improbabilities enacted on the stage, two on plays longer or shorter than five acts, one line plus enjambement on an unmotivated *deus ex machina*, and the rest of the line on speaking parts exceeding three. They all restrict the working forms of a luxuriating genre. H.'s way of talking is negative, and brings out objectionable features, but there is a criterion of fitness behind these interdicts: the form that 'the appropriate' takes in this section. The visual sense has an important function in drama, but for this reason nothing must be shown on the stage that unduly strains sensibility or credibility (*intus | digna geri*, 182–3); hence H. dwells realistically on revolting incidents—Medea killing her children on the stage—or sensational and incredible ones—Atreus cooking human entrails, the metamorphosis of Procne or Cadmus. A drama must be neither shorter nor longer than five acts; this is assumed as a right mean. A *deus ex machina* must not appear unless this solution is appropriate to the kind of plot intended; *dignus* again (191). And, finally, the exclusion of a fourth speaking part. Such are the technicalities that will serve to concentrate the dramatic form. As before (153–6) the inherent appropriateness of the drama is claimed as a guarantee for its success (190).

(6) Chorus, 193–201

That the function of the Chorus must evince the same inherent quality is one of H.'s two lessons. 'Appropriateness' thus serves as a link with the preceding injunctions and the more so because the motif, now strongly expressed, is the only interdict in an otherwise prescriptive setting: the Chorus must take an actor's part and *not* sing as a mere interlude between the acts of a play *quod non proposito conducat et haereat apte* (195). H.'s second lesson is moral. The Chorus must be the mouthpiece of accepted morality and this note is sounded in language reminiscent of choral wisdom in Greek classical tragedy. There is more allusiveness here than we can now establish (196–201 nn.). But the tone of this section is clearly set; the *aptum* of literary theory turned into the sententiousness of the choral passages of *tragoedia moralis*.

(7) Music, 202–19

The step from the Chorus to music is small but the two pieces
differ widely in character. There is a jump *in medias res* when
H. (202) starts to retail as it were the rake's progress, with
tibia, the pipe, cast as a villainous character; the piper does
not take the place of the pipe until the last sentence (215).
This piece pushes descriptiveness hard against the prescrip-
tions of the last. H. is now as descriptive as he was in drawing
the four ages of man (156). But this time the picture is quasi-
historical. Society, at two typified stages of its development,
reacts quite differently to music in the theatre. In early times
simple music was condoned; the primitive audiences took it
for granted that music would play second fiddle to poetry. At
a later and more civilized stage audiences demanded more
sophistication and music invaded the domain of poetry. The
two stages are ethnically indistinct. Apart from a slight Roman
touch (in *Genius*, 210) H. may be talking of Greece or Rome
or both. But contemporary application is certain: H. starts,
tibia non ut nunc. His own judgement is not made explicit. But
clearly the narrative shows that for this poet as for many
others the verbal arts have a prior claim; music provides an
accompaniment. That and no more is its proper function. Of
the primitive *tibia* he says, *adesse choris erat utilis* (204); which is
the shape that appropriateness takes in this section. While
there is no legislating, H.'s admiration for the simplicity of
archaic music is clearly marked and so is his condemnation
of theatre-music as an art in its own right. He might have
sympathized with Goethe enjoying settings of his poems by a
second-rate contemporary, but ignoring Schubert. Modern
music is described as luxuriating—*luxuriem addidit arti* (214).
It spoils the verbal arts; what results is *facundia praeceps* (217).
The charming picture of primitive society and the garish
colours of its modern counterpart tell the same story.

The motive that induced H. to present a narrative rather
than a prescription is likely to have been not only his desire

for variation but a recognition of fact. Music in H.'s time was what it was and his objections would not have changed it. This piece of story-telling therefore may be compared to the section on ancient poetry (391 ff.). For there too an ideal is set up in a mythical past.

(8) Satyric drama, 220–50

If H. had adopted from the literary theorists a simple and unilinear scheme he would have placed Satyric drama along with the various dramatic forms, either between tragedy and comedy (280), or even after comedy (284). What he has done is more interesting and suggestive. He has talked about the *Satyri* not as a dramatic genre but as part of his instruction in the craft of framing a classical tragedy. After the Chorus, which must not be merely an accompaniment, and after music, which—in H.'s view, unfortunately—is not such an accompaniment, there follows Satyric drama. This is a different kind of 'accompaniment' of tragedy—an *exodium* or *Nachspiel*. As F. Klingner has suggested,[1] H. seeks, and obtains, the strategic advantage of a transition from the primitive feeling for what is appropriate in music to a similar one in relaxing the tension of tragedy by Satyric jest, without violating tragic dignity: *incolumi grauitate iocum temptauit* (222).

But that is not all, for the appropriateness that H. so warmly admires here appears as something very Horatian, a golden mean between the high style of tragedy and the realism of comedy, which is easy to define but exceedingly hard to achieve. In the different medium of *Singspiel*, many centuries later, Mozart achieved something similar in 'The Magic Flute'. Once again the reader can see for himself that H. is not content merely to describe or define—the style of Satyric drama should hold a balance between two opposed genres etc.—but the wording itself recaptures reality; it communicates an experience.

Three times is the notion of a poetic mean brought out by

---

[1] *BVSA*, LXXXVIII. 3 (1937), 34.

the structure of the poetry. In H.'s view Satyric drama relaxes the high seriousness of tragedy; yet it is not realistically
comic. Each group of Satyric characters is shown to achieve
its own mean in its own way, and so in each case does H.'s
style. First (225 ff.) gods and heroes, just now *personae* of
tragedy, must credibly remain gods and heroes. Yet their
diction must neither rise to tragic heights, disappearing in
clouds of grandeur, nor on the other hand descend from the
palace to the hovel. Satyric drama is like a *matrona* who
relaxes propriety just enough to agree to a dance on the
occasion of a festival. *ita...ita...ita...ne...aut* mark the
logical structure; the imagery is inseparable from the *personae*.
Next (234 ff., 239) Silenus; he lacks the grandeur of the first
group, but has his own dignity as *famulus dei*. Thus his speech
too requires a mean, but a different one. It must neither be
colloquial nor in its simplicity impinge on the realism of
comedy. This is the very centre as it were of the middle range,
and hence the occasion for a 'technical' pronouncement on
diction. If the use of ordinary vocabulary is permitted, then
anybody might hope for success in this genre. But the tone
must be raised by the context in which the words are placed—
a hard thing to achieve; *tantum series iuncturaque pollet*. So
here again is a mean: *non...nec sic...ut...ne...an*. Finally
(244 ff.), on the lowest rung of the short ladder, the chorus
of the adolescent Satyrs. Here the jocularity of this gay genre
has to be carefully assessed; *ne...aut...aut* secure the logical
structure. But once more the imagery is distinctive because
the personages are distinct. In the vernacular the Satyrs are
Fauns; by tradition they are youths. After their recent immi-
gration from the forests, they must not speak as if they were
natives of the city. Their talk must suggest neither of two
modern types—the smutty jokes of the Roman gutter, or the
delicate sensibility of the well-born.

The length and weight assigned to this topic are obvious
but this is also one of the most imaginatively organized pieces
in the whole poem. *series iuncturaque pollet* (242) reformulates

a much-heralded ruling from an earlier part of the poem. This ruling is now applied to the Satyric genre in order to inculcate what is surely a cherished Horatian conviction: the subtle touch of art that has become nature. This conviction together with the address to the Pisos (235) and the personal involvement made public by the poet (234) suggests that H. meant to give precisely the emphasis to this subject which many moderns stoutly deny it.

(9) Metre, 251–74

Metre and music have a certain resemblance of topic; Satyric drama, which H. has placed between them, resembles neither. Moreover the new context, at its very beginning, dissociates the present new topic from its predecessor. It is only in the course of the piece that the strategic gain of this placing becomes apparent. The gain does not lie in any connexion, overt or concealed, with Satyric drama, except that both are linked with dramatic techniques, the subject of the larger section to which they belong. Metre comes last before the final material point. H. makes metre the criterion of competence in the art so that the reader will accept it before he views the dramatic forms at the end of the section. The criterion is developed poetically in the course of the piece on metre.

This then is how the poet proceeds. The beginning *in medias res*—H. not saying 'now I will talk of metre' but humorously offering a lesson in the art, a trite definition of the dialogue-metre of drama, the iambus. The elementary lecturing style is reminiscent of the apparent truism on *ordo* (42). In both instances the humour lies in the manner, not in the substance. Few of H.'s readers, if any, would have to be told that an iambus is defined by 'short long'. What they do require is an ear trained to sense the application of this rhythm. Is there enough 'short long' in a trimeter consisting of iambuses and spondees? The apparent truism quickly collapses. 'Iambus' himself takes over, personified as was the pipe, *tibia*, in the

piece on music. Thus humour persists, mitigating the seriousness of the charge of ignorance or carelessness. It is hard to
resent criticism if, by an urbane conceit, 'Iambus' himself
becomes the plaintiff charging with incompetence the archaic
Roman playwrights and modern critics alike. Roman poets
and critics then turn out to be a crew of amateurs, and attention is directed to their Greek predecessors who cannot be so
described.

For poetic sufficiency, even where more than 'mere technique' is concerned, H.'s vocabulary offers two notions above
all, appropriateness and art, major motifs in this poem. In the
large section on drama the former has been well to the fore,
while the latter has been no more than implied in the technical demands made of the dramatist. In the present piece
the procedure is reversed. The 'legitimate sound' (274) implies, but does no more than imply, the right or appropriate
sound. But the motif of *ars* is made explicit at the climax of
the piece. Hence the attack on Roman *ars ignorata*, its lack of
opera and *cura* (261–2).

When H. in the *Ars* talks of Roman poetry he usually
points out its shortcomings or sets up a new ideal for its
practitioners. When he talks of Greek poetry he rarely does
so except in terms of admiration. When he mentions the names
of poets or other writers up to this point (with the one important
exception of 54–6, where inventiveness in the creation of new
Latin words is generously recognized) they are Greek, for the
avowed purpose of orientating Latin letters. Roman poetry
receives mention only in terms of censure. Yet Roman and
Greek have not before this passage been made to confront each
other. Now H. leads the way to such a comparison in
characteristically unobtrusive fashion.

'Iambus' has charged Accius and Ennius with neglect and
ignorance; 'Roman poets' are seen to be allowed an unworthy
latitude. *Romani* (264) generalizes the poets already named.
It is not until a few verses later that Roman calls forth Greek.
The different qualities of the two nations are contrasted. It is

Graeca that qualifies the word *exemplaria*. The exemplars for Romans are Greek because, it is implied but not here said, *Graeci laudem meruerunt*, not only *uitauerunt culpam* (267–8). H.'s pronouncement lacks all portentousness, partly because of the brief moment in which it flashes across the screen—the reader is required to fill the logical gap between *non laudem merui* and *exemplaria Graeca*—and partly because of the realistic, half-humorous, notion of 'thumbing', which turns the 'exemplars' into copies of books. On such an assessment comedy fails as much as tragedy; Plautus' metre is alleged to be deficient, his wit gross. Thus the thought returns to the main subject, the halting vehicle of Latin verse, by which, to Augustan ears, Roman poetic production stands condemned.

(10)–(11) Greek and Roman drama, 275–84, 285–94

Students of H. have felt puzzled by this piece, particularly its first half. Why, they ask, does H. crown a large and important section of the *Ars* by a bit of Greek literary history, archaic, incomplete, irrelevant to his subject? The question is wrongly put. The relevance, if there be any, must be poetic and imaginative; we are not dealing with arguments in conceptual terms. H. himself, in his unobtrusive and subtle way, has established links with the preceding piece. In that piece he displays Greek poetry as the great exemplar for Roman competitiveness. Now he demonstrates how the Greeks came to evolve their exemplary procedure in the field of drama. The exemplars earlier (268) derived some of their force from a logical ellipse: the reader had to account himself for the transition from *non laudem merui* to *exemplaria Graeca*, and H. had given him just enough help to do so. Now again no overt link is made between the *exemplaria Graeca* of the last piece and the specific exemplars of this. It is the virtue of this subtle procedure that once more the reader is required to work out for himself—and if he does, see more clearly—the imaginative progression of H.'s thought.

The history of Greek tragedy is, *more Aristotelico*, taken no

498

further than the point at which 'it reached its inherent nature' (as the philosopher would have put it), and thus became exemplary for later dramatists. The alleged literary data, however, are largely Alexandrian rather than Aristotelian: Thespis' innovations led to the high style of Aeschylus' language and production. Next Old Comedy is shown by the key-word *laus* to be an exemplary genre and the transition to New Comedy—the effective model for the Romans—is sketched in. Such are the exemplars.

This leaves Roman drama, tragic and comic alike, with the same double aspect that is familiar from the last piece and other Horatian poems—competitiveness with the Greeks and yet inferiority. A glance back over the whole of the last section will put many details in perspective. Above all note the following. The two motifs of *ars* and perfection or appropriateness, joined in *limae labor* and *castigauit ad unguem*, qualify the critical theory, which concerns drama. Thus, with a solemn, perhaps deliberately over-solemn, address to the Pisos, *Pompilius sanguis* (292), this section closes and, at the same time, affords a glimpse forward. *ars* was the main subject of the introduction and, later, the motif that coloured each topic of *ars poetica*. *ars* now serves to pull all these intervening subjects together, relate them to the introduction and bridge the gap between this and the final part of the poem.

V. The Poet, 295–476

(1) Transition and Introduction, 295–308

H. distrusted the common distinction between 'art' and 'genius', *ars* or *studium* and *ingenium*. Later, when he talks in the terminology of the literary theorists (408–11), he sub-scribes to the truistic compromise, 'the one cannot do without the other'. Here, and indeed elsewhere in the poem, he offers something more astringent. He so vastly overstates his advo-cacy of *ars* over against *ingenium* that antithesis becomes satire. With style following subject, a Democritean (and Platonic) panegyric on *ingenium* assigns poetry to creative madness, and bars it to those guided by prudential calculation. H. allows it to be seen how much (he thinks) there is in him of the madness he affects to despise. He is a valetudinarian, his craving for mental health forbids him now to write (lyric) poetry, but by the same token allows him to teach the *munus et officium* of poetry. Criticism is poetry *manqué*, and the poet *manqué* can lecture on what (he pretends) he cannot produce. He puts himself in the posture of a professor of this subject, and for a moment parodies lecturing style. Thus a table of contents arises, as it were, by the way.

In an earlier part of the poem (40–1) such a table con-cerned the *ars*, here the *artifex*. First comes the training of the poetic mind (307), next the approved objective of the poet with its negative counterpart attached (308 *quid deceat, quid non*), and finally the ideal figure of the poetic *artifex* and again its frustration (308 *quo uirtus, quo ferat error*). The words hint at critical terminology. But H. is not proposing to continue the lecture in these simple conceptual terms. The subsequent thought-patterns are not summarized by this division of topics but, as will be seen, they are slightly related to it.

**(2) 'opes', the acquisition of the poet's equipment, his philo-
sophy('sapere'):his values and education, 'res'and'uerba',
characters and moral criteria, 309–18; Greek and Roman
poetry contrasted, national ethos accounts for difference
in attainment, 319–32**

A first cursory reading is likely to leave the reader with the
impression of three unconnected essays in literary theory—if
'theory' is the word for the highly impressionistic skit at the
end. Such a first reading will have to be assisted by a second,
which looks back from the position reached at the end of the
section. What does each reading yield?

The first point of the 'table' is clearly taken up at the
beginning. What was announced before (307) as the *opes* on
which the growing mind of the learner can draw, is here
disclosed, paradoxically, as moral principle of a rationalistic
kind. The *principium et fons* of *scribendi recte* is *sapere*, that
'knowledge' which moral theory—'the Socratic books'—can
reveal to the student. 'Words' have been made much of, in
the preceding technical instruction, but are now demoted. At
41 they were given second place to the right choice of a task,
there called *res*. Here (311) they must take second place to *res*,
subject-matter. The poet must have something to say; poetic
substance comes first. But H. is not here describing the process
of poetic creation. He knew as well as anyone that, in a sense,
the distinction *res–uerba* is unreal. He is setting out the poet's
education. The demand is that there shall be moral principle
at the root of his mind. A person without such a principle
will not be able to gauge the right tone for his characters.
Such are the grounds for H.'s objecting to *nugae canorae* (322),
the empty tinkle of fashionable but insubstantial verse.
Poetry, he believes, is concerned with life and life with *mores*,
but *mores* with an understanding of principle.

Thus two of H.'s motifs are used to shape the present section. First *mores*, a major motif in the sections on style and
subject-matter. *mores* now reappear, in a manner disconcerting

to the amoralist among literary critics. The virtues—and by implication, vices—of man in society must be impressed on the young poet's mind (312–17). That, it is claimed, enables him to judge and represent reality, makes him a *doctus imitator*. Thus the generality and abstraction of moral theory precede the particularity of poetic production.

Closely entwined with *mores* is appropriateness, that ubiquitous concept. How to get a poetic character right has been a repeated concern before. Here it is the concern of *poeta*, this poet and all poets. *conuenientia cuique* (316) is what *Socraticae chartae* are to teach.

Then there is an abrupt break and the reader is informed that a moralistic play although it lacks artistic merit sometimes has a greater effect on audiences than the tuneful trifles that lack *res* (319–22). This clearly belongs to the preceding context; how it does, H. does not tell.

The next break is more abrupt still (323). The Greeks, we are told, are endowed with genius and rounded speech, free from greed, except the desire for glory. The Romans—and then there follows a spirited caricature of a lesson in arithmetic, which is supposed to show the young mind corroded with a desire for gain. How can such minds create true and lasting poetry? Such is the final question (330–2).

Abrupt these gyrations may be at first sight. But the abruptness is deliberate. It draws the mind away from overt connexions and opens it to others that are more complex and less explicit. Looking back from the end, we find last a leading question (330–2)—'can we hope to produce lasting poetry if our minds are early corroded by a materialistic education?' *aerugo* and *cura peculi* (330) take up the preceding satiric picture of Roman education (325–30). Without the final question that picture might have remained an affectionate skit; but with the final question humour changes to bitter sarcasm and we remember that the Roman lesson in arithmetic marked a strong antithesis to the preceding panegyric of 'the Greeks', the *ingenium* and the *ore rotundo loqui* granted them by the muse

(323–4). The Greeks are *praeter laudem nullius auari* (324). If this essay in national psychology gives a new turn to the earlier contexts, and does so by suggestion and not by argument, what is that new turn?

That the preceding two pieces are related to each other, though merely juxtaposed in syntax, has already been maintained. A moralistic play *sans art* is at times more successful with an audience than art that has nothing to say, *l'art pour l'art* (319–22). Such a play seems to possess the *res* and *mores* of the preceding context (310–18) but not the *uerba* that were there said to be spontaneously superadded (311). H. starts by making dogmatic statements. The second piece, through a kind of dialectic, breaks up rigid doctrine. *res* without *ars* may please (? in Rome), but severs form and content, which should, as the *Ars* teaches, be one and a whole. Once it is seen that this short piece stands in the middle between two contexts, everything falls into place. The implied reference to local practice raises the national problem. The Greeks fulfil H.'s poetic ideal, but the Romans do not. And, it is broadly hinted, Roman values are to be blamed for that.

In this way the backward glance reveals the poetic movement over a number of poetic contexts in a large section. The backward glance is needed because the *perpetuum mobile* of a Horatian poem is not seen to be perpetual until we have reached the final point in the process. Nor is this movement complete within a single section. Sections are not self-contained. It is precisely because H. uses an oblique technique of suggestion, rather than a straightforward technique of statement, that he can throw light from the *poeta* section on all the earlier ones. The first two-thirds of the poem deal with poetic procedures. Consequently, although unity has been a substantive issue from the first, such generalities as *ingenium* and *ars*, Greeks and Romans, the concept of character, the function and the appropriateness of poetry, the heroic figure of *perfectus poeta*—these or some of them have appeared only as accompanying motifs. In the *poeta* section they appear in their own right, substantiated by what has gone before and clarifying in turn the earlier and more technical aspects.

(3) ('quid deceat, quid non') instruction and delight, 333–46

In terms of literary theory there must be a break here. For to instruct and to delight are not activities that could be said to be within the compass of the verse that has proved an adequate summary so far: *unde parentur opes, quid alat formetque poetam* (307). But it would be within the compass of the next half-verse (*quid deceat, quid non* 308), though hardly within that of the next, poetic *uirtus* and *error*. The question, much ventilated in a moralistic society, is therefore: should the appropriate scope of poetry lie in instruction or entertainment?

In terms of a poetic ordering, however, there are some links between this piece and the preceding. For *prodesse* and *delectare* are, in a sense, inherent in the *res* (*mores*) and *uerba* of the last section. A moralistic play (319–20) will answer to the call of *prodesse*, and falsely to that of *delectare* (321), whereas, by definition, the *nugae canorae* (322) can only please—if they are *canorae*. These two aspects of H.'s procedure, separation and relatedness, are not mutually exclusive, here or anywhere in H.

The poet's opinions here seem strange to the modern mind but are closely related to ancient thinking about poetry. I have elucidated them, as far as I can, and there is no need to repeat the findings of my commentary. What H. says in this section is set down in a brisk style—the style of discourse—and the discourse spills over into the technical field of the earlier sections: poetic instruction (*prodesse*) requires brevity; poetic fiction (*delectare*) requires verisimilitude. If a poem divorces the two aspects, it will leave the public divided in taste and judgement. Thus the situation of the first section would be repeated (321); content and form, truth and fiction appeal to different groups of people, thereby destroying the inherent unity of the two. Hence H.'s concern with a synthesis, which he puts in the form—easily but mistakenly dismissed—of a Peripatetic compromise: *miscuit utile dulci*(343). *Grai*, the ideal poets, achieved a unity of content and form, talent and art. So here *prodesse* and *delectare* are joined in an ideal unity—not a weak compromise.

(4) ('uirtus' and 'error') poetic perfection and aberration, 347–476

'Poems to be preserved' were looked for at the end of the section on the *doctus imitator* (332). 'Poems ensuring long fame' were the final demand of the last section (346). On both occasions the fame sought was in specific terms, although it contained, unclarified and inexplicit, the concepts of perfection and imperfection, achievement and fault. Just as an ideal of achievement was assumed, certain large faults were thought to be excluded. Starting the last and most complex section of the *Ars*, H. makes one of his apparently simple, unemphatic, transitions; 'yet there are venial faults', he says (347). This may be described as a 'gliding transition'. Such transitions do not provide mechanical links between static doctrines but establish connexions that cannot be taken for granted—a kind of poetic thought. 'Venial fault' is the opening exploratory sally in a series of explorations, all designed to reveal poetic *uirtus* and *error*.

The word 'transition' implies a change of topic or approach. In what sense, it may be asked, is there such a change? There is, it would appear, a new topic; for (at any rate in the *poeta* section) the concept of *delictum* (347), soon to be contrasted with its counterpart *bonus* (358–9), makes a first appearance. If H. had sufficiently departed from his practice of juxtaposition, he might have marked the new beginning by a logically overriding concept, which would allow a unilinear progression. In that case we would have found not only the term *delicta* but *uirtus* and *error* repeated from 308. Then the rest would have consisted of 'sub-sections'. That procedure he has adopted here as little as at 119, where the subject changed from diction to subject-matter without any reference to 40–1. Since other aims were more important to the poet than a unilinear order, we cannot now tell how much he wished the abstractions of his 'table of contents' to impinge on the sequel. Had he cared more, he would presumably have notified his intention.

Should one therefore argue that the two concepts, at 308, of *decet* as well as *uirtus*, apply to the same thing, poetic perfection—so that the present context would simply be one of a number of juxtaposed pieces? I do not think so. The piece 309 ff. can be described in terms of *opes* and *formare poetam* (307). But the piece 333 ff. cannot be described in those terms, and hardly in terms of *uirtus* (308); but *decet* (308) does describe it. It seems to me equally true that the *uirtus* and *error* offer a suitable description of the poem all the way from the present place (347) to the end. I conclude therefore that, although no unilinear progression is intended, the pair *uirtus–error* serves as the denominator common to the series of contexts that now follows. There are no external links to bind together the members of the series. But by subject-matter, judgement, and sentiment the series is by no means unconnected. This I will now attempt to show.

(a) Two notions of poetic fault, 347–60

H. does not begin with an affirmative—poetic perfection is...
He excludes faults, negatively. But as in the realm of morals, virtue is not the absence of faults, there is no anxious hugging of the safe shore. Nor is there a romantic admiration of faults as concomitants of the sublime. What we are offered is a poetic analysis of faults; he embodies in two exemplary cases the faults of inability and occasional negligence. One of them is unforgivable, because it denies achievement by definition; the other must be forgiven, because it arises, unavoidably, in a large work: the cases of Choerilus, the proverbial botcher, and of Homer nodding. H. persuades us by the listener's reactions to Choerilus and Homer, asserting his own and gauging ours. The distinction between the two kinds of fault

is quickly made. The substance of the case lies in an oblique comparison (354–60), where all the stress falls on a paradoxical reaction to the two poets—admiration for Choerilus (when, so rarely, he gets something right) and annoyance with Homer (when, so rarely, he gets something wrong).

(b) Poetic excellence clarified by comparison with painting, 361–5

This is either a complete change of ambience or, if you will, continuity of argument in a different medium. Both apply, in a sense.

In terms of change, we suddenly hear talk of painting—'a poem is like a picture'. And what follows makes it clear that excellence is at stake, no longer faultiness. Some pictures attract more on a cursory glance from afar, others on close scrutiny. The former may please but please only once. Pictorial excellence must satisfy repeated and close inspection: *deciens repetita placebit* (365). These are H.'s words and, through the comparison implicit in the first three words—*ut pictura poesis* (361)—, it is assumed though not said to be part of the case for poetic excellence. The extremely quotable *ut pictura poesis* may suggest a theory of the arts. No such theory is advanced here, although poetry, not painting, is later set in such a context (366 ff.). The elliptic thought, which allows H. to talk of painting while he is thinking of poetry, is inherent in the poet's planning.

Yet there is continuity, barely concealed. Having admitted artistic fault only as an accidental outcome of *uirtus poetica* in a long work—Homer's but not Choerilus'—H. now lifts the quasi-argument on to a new plane. But he does not display the logical links between the two pieces. Excellence may not be faultless, but it must be such as to withstand close critical scrutiny.

(c) Excellence and mediocrity in the liberal and the useful arts, 366–78

The poetic analysis of excellence proceeds. H. makes a distinction between arts useful and liberal, and makes it first in abstract terms; mediocrity is tolerated in the former but not in the latter. This distinction is preceded by an elaborate and overwhelmingly courteous address (366–9). The elder son of Piso has his attention drawn to the importance of this issue—a well-known device not only of rhetoric but of archaic moralistic poetry. But this is not the sole personal feature. Once the distinction between the arts is made, the terms become concrete, even personal in another way. A lawyer or barrister need not be a Messala or Cascellius, paragons in their professions. Mediocrity has its uses where usefulness provides all that is required. To poetry however a (jocular) cosmic law sets narrow limits; by decree of gods, men, and bookshops, there must be no mediocrity (372–3). To see the case thus overstated has its humour; the universe is now safely divided between excellence and mediocrity.

The little section ends with a touch of malicious realism. Such realism contributes much to the *Satires*, sometimes grossly. But realism is characteristic of the genre *sermo* as a whole, and adds its share of incisive amusement to the *Epistles*. Diners, it is suggested, feel offended by dissonant table-music, thick perfumes at dinner, or bitter Sardinian honey for dessert with the roasted poppy-seeds. The ironic implication—half true, half false—is that a poem resembles the perfumes and the honey: *poema*, the elliptic comparison suggests, *si paulum summo decessit, uergit ad imum.*

(d) Competence in the arts, 379–90

This time it is appreciated without difficulty that the new topic is only apparently new. The connecting link—excellence—is easily fitted in its place, but its factual absence sets poetry cheek by jowl with odd companions, various kinds of *ludere*: now athletics, and earlier the 'artists' concerned with perfumes at table, and with other embellishments and entertainments.

Incompetence makes practitioners refrain from the sports of the *Campus*. Why not so in poetry? The answer is simple. Poetry is regarded as a gentlemanly pastime where social status, not accomplishment, counts. It is here that the elaborate address to the *maior iuuenum* (366) needs to be remembered. About that young man we know nothing—except that H. has seen fit to draw him into the poetic fiction of this letter. The *iuuenis* is not merely the recipient of a dedication. H. uses the dedication for a purpose, and the purpose concerns the poetic structure of his argument. H. has addressed this discourse on excellence in poetry to the young Piso. But more than that, he has marked the stages of the discourse by continued and varied references to him. The biographical motive for this procedure is un-known; the structural motive however is plain. At 366–7 Piso is credited with poetic insight, prompted both by his father's advice and his own powers. Yet he still seems to require exhor-tation. *hoc tibi dictum | tolle memor* marks weighty advice—the difference between the arts that tolerate mediocrity and those that do not (368–9). Now we learn a little more. *Dilettanti*, the rich and aristocratic, may think that social position absolves them from learning *ars poetica*, though they would not think similarly when *ars Campestris* is at stake. Piso, H. asserts, will not think so. Already his resolve in matters poetic is, 'nothing *inuita Minerua*' (385). But if he should produce something after all, a trio of formidable critics—Piso senior, Maecius Tarpa, and H. himself—will sit in judgement. *nonumque prematur in annum* (388), he is reminded into the bargain.

The young man therefore serves as an exemplary case. His example validates a truth for all. Just so does H. turn an in-dividual into a type when he himself speaks in the *persona* of the literary critic or countryman or lover. He draws poetic capital from the disparity of general case and particular condition.

The young Piso then is a *corpus nobile*—by no means *uile*—upon whom, and to whom, H. demonstrates the demands that

509

may generate poetic excellence, and make poetry truly noble —not noble in terms of social nomenclature. Thus such an apparently extraneous feature as Piso's own qualities becomes an integral part of the poem's substance. The young man's exemplary situation, sketched in with great tact in personal terms, individualizes the general discourse on poetic excellence. The Pisonian case serves as a link between the disparate pieces that make up this section. The importance of this link will be borne out by the following context, which has puzzled so many readers, expert and amateur alike.

(e) True excellence: poets, the founders and civilizers of society, 391–407

H. has moved close, perhaps uncomfortably close, to the 'arts' of the sports ground and, worse, to music at table, and Sardinian honey. On this showing, if the poet's *uirtus* amounts to no more, how to justify the strenuous effort, the conscientious testing, the *nonus annus*? If the reader puts this question, the sudden lifting of the tone may be H.'s answer.

siluestres homines opens the praise of the *poeta*. Simple juxtaposing rhetoric sets one of the poet's *uirtutes* beside another, from Orpheus in a primitive age to the appearance of Greek drama. Thus H. builds up the imposing picture of the poet as the civilizer of mankind, the founder and preserver of human society. The piece is wholly archaic in subject-matter and tone. It resembles an earlier one, in which an ideal of music was set up in the terms of a bygone age (202 ff.)— not what music should be but what it was. So here we are told what poetry once was, although, not unnaturally, the claims are much larger. The two pieces are alike also in pressing no conclusions. H. prescribed as little what music ought to be, as he lays down that, in these modern days, a sophisticated writer of verse ought to become a sacred *uates*. He draws a picture to look at; its severe and archaic colouring is meant to exercise what effect it can in its setting.

The implicit scope of the piece seems to be to show the

poet's impact on the society to which he belongs. The *honor et nomen* of the *uates* and his *carmina* (400–1) derive from his impact upon society as a whole. The mythical part of the story is devoted to this aspect alone and the genres that follow, from Homer's epic to the dramatists, are chosen for that purpose. H. knew as well as anyone that the poet, in the conditions of the Augustan empire, was not and could not be regarded as prophet, law-giver, philosopher. But, equally, the Augustan poet sees himself as recreating, in modern, sophisticated, conditions, certain features of the archaic *uates*. H. is not arguing a case. He allows the ideal picture to exercise its fascination. He also allows the ancient *uates* to clash with the 'excellences' inherent in the comparison with the 'arts' of the table and sports ground, and the discipline enshrined in *nonum...prematur in annum*.

Yet H.'s conclusions are more than implicit. This is the last of the paragraphs held together by an address to the *maior iuuenum*; his words at 406–7 are, 'so that you may not feel ashamed of *Musa lyrae sollers et cantor Apollo*'. The preceding paragraph ended with an exhortation (to the same person), enjoining the skill and perfection which the *liber et ingenuus* could commonly do without. Now the *uates* passage demonstrates to the young Piso that the exertions earlier demanded, so far from being unworthy of a *homo nobilis*, should really be his own. The poet's true excellence is seen to have lain in the practices of the ancient *uates* and his successors. His art eminently belonged to society, *res publica*. Poetry then is the legitimate art for the *nobilis*, because, as H. said in the *Augustus*, the true poet is *utilis urbi*.

(f) Genius and artistry in literary theory, 408–18

Many readers here complain of pedestrian and dull writing. The little section *is* pedestrian; but it is not dull. After the elevation of the section on *uates*, tone and style are made to drop back to the middle range of *sermo*. H., adopting a measure of conceptual language, states a theorem.

Why such a theorem in this place? As often before, particularly in the technical portions of the *Ars*, H. pulls together what has already been before the reader in picture or symbol, and extracts what can be formulated in the unambiguous language of theory. Holding a rationalistic philosophy, H. is not averse from using an occasional commonplace expressing that philosophy. The theorem is set down not for its own sake but as part of a poetic structure. It acts as a signpost for the reader, pointing to a route through the highly complex poetry preceding and following it.

In the preceding paragraphs H. has set before the reader a many-sided picture of poetic excellence, ordered in its later stages (366–407) by the exemplary figure of the noble learner. He now opens up another aspect of *uirtus poetica*—the equipment of the poet in a wider and more general sense than the *opes* of which he talked in an earlier section (309 ff.).

ingenium and *ars* form one of the unhappy dualities of the theorists which the whole poem is designed to explore and overcome. The pair is often dialectically split into its components; *ingenium misera* (295) and the caricature at the end of the poem are the most impressive instances. In the preceding paragraphs the two extremes have been juggled in dialectical play, with *ars* continually summoned, and *ingenium* providing the counterpoise whenever emphasis on *studium* might evoke the wrong reaction. I am thinking of such unmistakable hints as *inuita...Minerua* (385) or the magic insight claimed for the ancient *uates*, Orpheus and his kind (391 ff.). The present section eschews dialectical play and antithesis alike. H. permits himself a brief and sidelong glance at the schools of literary theory. 'The problem is raised whether a poem's excellence derives from natural endowment or art' (408–9). The warring schools are put in their place. On theoretical grounds the problem comes to naught; both contentions are as true as they are false. But on practical grounds, for the maker, the problem remains open and alive. The poem as a whole teaches how to solve it by poetic means. And even in this place the reader is left with an emphasis on art in the matter-of-fact language of the athlete and the professional performer of music.

(g) The false critic and the false friend, 419–37

This section and the next deal with the literary critic; they continue the subject of the last section. In the cut-and-dried terminology of the literary schools, *emendatio*, the correction of faults, follows *natura* and *studium*. Without criticism and *emendatio*, the theorists would say, the poet's *uirtus* cannot be realized. *emendatio* is literary criticism at its most practical. H., as in other places, first eliminates the negative; having barred aberration, next (at 438) he turns to the right road. To move from this section to the next, is to progress from the false critic, the professional admirer or yes-man, to the true critic.

Such a description would be correct in terms of literary theory but in terms of this poem it would be incomplete and misleading. H. has humanized and strengthened the austere exercise of criticism. He depicts the realities of Roman conditions, the conditions of his own time and circle. At the level envisaged by him the critical operation can be performed only by a like-minded friend, acting as the critical conscience of the poet. Poet and critic must share the same ideals and standards. As in the 10th satire of book 1, poet and critic belong to the same group of men, *doctos...et amicos* (*S.* 1. 10. 87), Virgil and Varius but also Maecenas, Messala, Plotius, et al. In the long letter to Florus (*Ep.* 11. 2. 109 ff.) the true censor is not even another person, *alter ego*; it is the critical *ego* of the poet himself.

Once these presuppositions are understood it becomes easier to see what H. is doing in these two sections. His manifest debt to Cicero and Lucilius is the token of the tradition in which he is here placing himself. The false critic is the counterfeit friend, the toady or parasite—a social phenomenon of the aristocratic world of Rome just as the κόλαξ was a feature of the Greek world.

The similarities with writings on friendship or flattery, Cicero's *De amicitia* above all, to which I have drawn attention in my commentary, are not then fortuitous. Cicero regards a flatterer as an immoralist. For a friend is seen as an *alter ego*, contradicting and exhorting if he respects you as a moral being; but the flatterer praises what he despises. So too H. thinks, except that for him the criterion is poetic *uirtus*, although his moral involvement is unmistakable.

This may be a situation for moral diatribe, but likewise for ridicule. The evidence is just sufficient, for some features at any rate, to show H. in the wake of Lucilius' *Saturae*. This spirited piece makes epistle revert to satire. One sentence in particular (431–2) may be set, word for word, beside what appears to be its Lucilian model. The same satiric spirit animates both, but H.'s rhythm, wording, and tension of word-groups combine to create a whole, where the model, followed apparently in detail, fails to do so.

The whole section may be described in similar terms: a whole created out of very diverse materials. The rich dilettante appears in the guise of a (perhaps Lucilian) auctioneer— a carefully calculated incompatibility between the aristocratic Dives and the common crier. The benefactor is incapable of knowing the true from the false friend; Dives cannot defend himself against flattery. Now for the flatterer. A tip has changed or may change hands. The recipient seems to be intoxicated with *laetitia*; his performance at the dinner-table when the patron's poems are recited suggests that he is in a trance of admiration. But the flatterer's world is a lying world. He is (as Lucilius seems to have said) like a professional mourner at a funeral; his mourning is the more *outré* the less it is *ex animo*. Dives, it is implied, must learn the justice of the royal procedure; ply with wine the man whose intentions you want to assess. The false *laudator*, or friend, needs to be distinguished from the true. The true critic, whose unbiased criticism proves his friendship, is thus before us by contradistinction.

(h) The true critic and the true friend, 438–52

The topic continues but, logically, this section presents an antithesis, which H. brings out by a different poetic form. Satire, in the last section, appropriately expresses incompatibility of pretence and pretender; the literary theory and practice, in this section, do not only express the true critic's job, but show how it is done.

There is more to it than that. H. was attracted above all by the ethos of the true critic. Since the poet sees criticism in the personal and emotional terms of friendship, he talks about a person; he seems to be recounting his own dealings with that person—*Quintilio si quid recitares* (438). 'Personal and emotional' do not mean a relaxing of critical standards. On the contrary the personal warmth that informs these verses derives from a patent admiration for the man who proved his friendship by remaining the unbribable and stern critic. The section therefore offers not only a Roman restatement of Alexandrian criticism; more than technical skill is involved. The *uir bonus et prudens* is shown at work, and the influence of a friend like Quintilius on such as H. Poetry so judged involves the whole of a person—his character as well as his mind and imagination. It is fitting that at the close of this section two tell-tale words should be made to clash. *nugae* are mere trifles, but *seria* (*mala*) point to the seriousness of the outcome when a poet has failed to obtain strenuous criticism of what is more than trifling.

(i) Error personified: the mad poet, 453–76

This is the *finale* of the poem and there can be no doubt that it answers to the description *quo ferat error* (308). But it is not of course the only section that so anwers. H.'s poetic world does not consist in a static opposition of black and white but in a continuous resolution of insufficient opposites, a world where one assertion usually brings in its antithesis. Anyone tracing the manner whereby H. builds up his picture of poetic excel-

lence, *uirtus*, will know that *error* has been present all the time
from the beginning of the *uirtus* section (at 347). *quo uirtus, quo
ferat error* (308) applies throughout. Yet the present section
differs from the rest in that the whole of this final sketch is
devoted to a caricature of poetic inspiration, a picture of error.

'Error' in what sense? Not surely in the sense that H. was
a stranger to imaginative 'madness'. This piece is too arresting
for that supposition. The satire on inspiration and the 'death-
wish' is one of the great satires in European letters. It fascin-
ates because it is written from inside the experience which it
professes to ridicule. H. is pretending to write as a detached
observer; but that is no more than a poetic fiction. He depicts
a poet whose genius is paramount, and lacks the safety device
that will restrain him from destroying himself, or destroying
others if he should survive. This cautionary story could never
have been written without a generous measure of the quality
so caricatured. Malebranche, says Voltaire, is brilliantly imaginative in attacking imagination. So is H. His *uesanus poeta* is
a welcome antidote to the neo-classical notion of Horace, the
Anacreontic versifier, or indeed to Cocteau's *fou libre* (above
p. 468).

This satire, in the scheme of the poem, endorses most effectively the anxieties that, H. asserted, made him forswear
poetry for valetudinarian reasons. Thus it links up with the
introduction to the long final portion of the *Ars* (295 ff.). H.
did not there complain that he lacked *ingenium*. He did say,
sarcastically, that he chose to be cured of a surplus of it.

Last of all there is the relation of *artifex* to *ars*. The poem
when it deals with *artifex* continually spills over into *ars*. That
is one of the unifying features of the poem, perhaps most
strongly marked at the outset and the conclusion. The *Ars*
begins with the caricature of a painting that is all variety and
daring, but lacks what would make it into a viable entity—
ars. The poem ends with the caricature of the *artifex* who is all
imagination, but lacks what would preserve him—*ars*. In both
instances the picture is gruesomely real in its unreality; it has

the force that earned the French Romantics their nickname, *les amateurs du délire*; we have seen much of that since. H. however is no Romantic. These pieces *are* caricatures—satires set in the framework of *ars poetica*. Their sharpness is mitigated, not blunted, by humour. The curse of *ingenium* is relieved by *ars* and at the base of *ars* there lie *Socraticae chartae*. H. writes as the dialectical poet. His strength lies in harnessing contradictory qualities and attitudes.

So far the poem. In my *Prolegomena* I put forward a claim: that the *Ars* would reveal its secrets when we had ceased making H. responsible for what is not likely to be his—the outlines of a trivially constructed piece of literary theory—and had begun making him responsible for what without doubt is his—the features of this Horatian poem. In my commentary and my appraisal of the poem I have tried to make good that claim; how successfully readers must judge. If I have been successful, the common charge of triteness must fail when it is directed not against H.'s poetry but against the material that he subjected to his poetic processes.

The *Ars* has now been read like any other poem in which H. rehandled a traditional form and traditional content, just as he rehandled lyric material in his own way. The evidence suggests that he did not shape but reshape an *Ars poetica*. That implies that he had such an *Ars poetica* to reshape, but it does not imply by any means that he had no other 'sources'. He raised a traditional piece of criticism to a level where it is no longer mere literary theory. His subject is ancient poetry. By recreating an *Ars* in fluid and suggestive Horatian patterns, he related it to his own verse but also to much that was alive in the poetry of his own time. Poetic patterns, through association and suggestion, hint more than they can make explicit. His *Ars* symbolizes what an ordinary *Ars* would merely theorize: the nature of ancient poetry, Greek and Roman.

By an economy of means that would be incredible if it did not seem so natural, he lightly places a new structure on the staid and unpromising sequence of 'poem' and 'poet' with some of its conventional subdivisions. The principles which he imposes suit above all Virgil's poetry and his own, but in different ways all ancient poetry. What the principles are we have seen before—unity in a shifting balance with variety, appropriateness and studied art set against inspiration, *mores* in interplay with style and subject, Roman imagination competing with the great Greek models, and finally H. himself in his varying poetic *personae*, bringing poetic experience and personal feeling to bear on an apparently self-contained critical theory and, conversely, attempting to make the 'demands' of theory stimulate new practice.

Guided by the evidence of the *Ars*, let us accept then that H. wanted to produce a genuine poem, not a piece of literary theory versified, and let us ask how far he succeeded in what he wanted to do. Such a question could not have been asked, let alone answered, before E. Norden, some sixty years ago, inaugurated a promising line of research; earlier the poem was taken for granted and poets, critics, and scholars looked to H. for practical guidance. Nor would it have been possible to subject the *Ars* to the searching literary appraisal to which we have subjected it if literary critics of our century had not applied similar procedures to poems of more recent vintage.

The *Ars*, 476 verses in all, would make a middle-length canto. This is not long by the standard of a didactic poem like the *Georgics*, or an epic like the *Aeneid* or *Metamorphoses*, but too long, and too diverse in tone and structure, to allow of the astringent and collected effect of a short lyric. The multiplicity of tone and subject belongs to a different world, the world of the *sermo*—the kind of long Short Poem in which H. excelled. In that setting it stands as the poet's most comprehensive and mature work, reminiscent of the discursive style and the panache of the *Satires*, the ironic and mannered reflections of *Epistles* book I, the personal, literary and political mode of *Epistles* book II, and, in *debemur morti*, something of the lyricism of the *Odes*. But all this a long poetic letter like the

Florus or *Augustus* could have accommodated. What distinguishes the *Epistle to the Pisos* is the unique achievement, never repeated, of making these varied effects illuminate the layout of an ancient *Ars* and a rationalistic philosophy of poetry.

The outcome was a picture of great complexity, which required a constructive imagination of a high order. A work of the length of an epic canto is formed in the highly structured image of his shorter poems. How far has H. succeeded in his ambitious design? Magnificently, it seems to me, if we apply the right criteria. In a short ode or hexameter poem the motifs are few and their interplay is restricted. In the *Ars* the number of motifs is much larger; the patterns that arise are so numerous that it is impossible to look back, and be aware of more than a few at a time. You can pick out the humdrum line of literary theory. But as soon as you do, you see it reduced to first principles by the criss-cross of *ars* and *ingenium*, or appropriateness and the rest, each valid in its own right, and each related to the others in their different styles and tones. Thus from every point of its compass, the poem assumes a different complexion.

Yet in spite of the many and varied aspects of the *Ars*, the impression that it leaves with the present reader does not fundamentally differ from what readers throughout the centuries have felt: unity is as strongly marked as variety. So in such larger Augustan works as the *Georgics*, the *Aeneid* and the *Metamorphoses*; the patterns and motifs abound, but there is a unity that defies the simple restatement of a prosaic summary. But for all its similarity, H.'s *œuvre* is not at all like that of the other Augustans. He is a different kind of poet, most of all in the incisive dialectical quality of his mind and imagination. In spite of the emphasis placed on *ars* and *decorum*, or their contraries, what stays in the mind is the balance achieved in the interplay between these contrary poetic patterns. No single argument but a poetic entity—the equipoise achieved in a long poem—may be claimed as the poet's answer to the questions posed by the literary critics.

If my picture of H.'s imagination and intelligence is a just one, it is not hard to see why the poet was attracted to literary theory, and above all to Aristotelianism. The opposed simplicities of the Stoics and Epicureans, even of Alexandrian aestheticism, would repel him; his kind of poetry was moral to the core and, at the same time, *animis natum inuentumque...iuuandis* (377). He was the poet of *quo me, Bacche, rapis?*; but he would be chary of a poetic imagination unaided by a tough intellectual fibre—a powerful motive counteracting any attraction to intuitionism which Plato or at any rate contemporary middle-Platonic philosophy might have exercised.

The introduction to the *Ars* pronounces on Aristotle's philosophy of organic unity. But altogether there is no better poetic illustration of Aristotle's 'one and whole' than H.'s poems. How to create interplay and balance between unity and daring variety is H.'s inimitable secret. In that sense he is an *anima naturaliter Aristotelica*. To critical hindsight, a lively poetic unity appears as tension resolved, variety unified. In the *Ars*, while debating this critical problem on the intellectual level, he demonstrates by his writing how to solve it. H.'s debate acquires the character of what he is debating.

But the notion of organic unity was not the only thing that attracted H. to Aristotelianism. There is the clear-cut rationality of Aristotle's and H.'s poetic theories; poetry is a form of cognition. Next, if it can be separated at all, there is the poetic entity in which alone Aristotle's 'universal' is realized, the logic of the plot. Thirdly, there is the stress on *mores*, ethos. Fourthly, there is the rhetorical concept of 'appropriate speech'.

All this does not make H. a minor Aristotle. For the *Ars* lacks the decisive feature of the *Poetics*—an explicit argument. H. offers both less and more. He offers less because the poet cannot match the philosopher's coherent reasoning. Indeed it would be fair to say that the *Ars* cannot be called a genuine piece of reasoning at all, although at times it is designed to look like an argument. But H. offers more than Aristotle because he takes reasoned arguments and uses them as material for his poetic patterns. If the *Epistle to the Pisos* is the kind of poem I take it to be, it represents imaginatively, in a way no conceptual prose could, not only views on poetry but the ancient feeling for poetry.

If we say therefore that the *Ars* lacks the logical coherence of the *Poetics*, or of any argued literary theory, we say very little. Of course it lacks it. But H. would not if he could reproduce the coherence of a piece of conceptual prose. That was not his *métier*. What he thought was his job is shown by the job he did. He was writing from inside. If his purpose may be guessed from the finished article, it was precisely the opposite of a critic's. Aristotle regarded the words of which the poetry consists as a piece of rhetoric standing in no organic relation to the logic of the plot, although certainly the words of a poem must be clear, not mean, appropriate. H., on the other hand, wrote a poem in which, in a sense, the words are the content. Thus he brought the reflections *on* poetry back to a reflection *of* poetry.

To do that he treated a traditional *Ars poetica* as he treated all other subjects. He made it into material for poetry that achieves its legitimate ends, not primarily by what it says and argues but by the devices of tone, style, and structure. A few graces of epistolary style would not have touched the substance. It was the substance that had to be broken down, and recreated in the image of his own poetry. Perhaps then there is a germ of truth in Pope's *sententia* on Horace:

> Yet judg'd with *Coolness* tho' he sang with *Fire;*
> His *Precepts* teach but what his *Works* inspire.

The *Ars* may well be seen as a poetic restatement of H.'s own poetry. He is the exemplar of the originality that may be attained within the bounds of the traditional styles and genres. A modern reader's assessment of H.'s *Ars* will therefore differ according to his preconceptions. If *ingenium* for him must be unlimited by tradition, he will condemn the *Ars*. If he can admire originality strengthened, but also limited, by tradition, he is likely to admire, if he understands it, what H. has achieved.

The *Ars* occupies a unique position in the poetry and criticism of the West. What it leaves in the reader's mind is a pre-established harmony, a natural world of poetic laws and freedoms, realized in the shape of a poem. With the underlying 'theory' the theorists had dealt better. But no one had ventured to make it the vehicle for a live poem in which originality would fulfil and transcend tradition—*ingenium* on the boundaries of *ars*. To overcome the apparent contradiction inherent in such a work, a degree of insight, resilience, and irony was called for, which few other poets, however great, could have attained. H. attained it, and thus, through the centuries, the *Ars* has withstood the literal-minded, whether they attacked it, or praised it, in the name of *méthode*, or in the name of originality and imagination.

Never before had the image of Greco-Roman poetry been caught undistorted in the mirror of a poem that represented ancient thinking no less than ancient feeling. It was never to be so again. For whereas Greco-Roman beliefs in the 'fixities' (as Coleridge might have said) of styles and genres continued to the eighteenth century and beyond, the realities of the styles and genres did not so continue. However strong and beneficial these ancient influences were, creative power often tended to diverge from the inherent virtues of the genres. Nothing can be surer than Dante's touch when he writes his poetry. But he lacks sureness when he attempts to measure the style of his *Commedia* by the yard-stick of ancient theory; this is brought out admirably in E. Auerbach's *Mimesis*.[1] Chaucer saw himself continuing the precedent of ancient poetic theory, though in fact he was striking out in a new direction.[2]

When *imitatio Horatiana* can only proclaim correctness, or

---

[1] Eng. Tr., Princeton 1953, 185–8.
[2] Cf. R. O. Payne, *The Key of Remembrance: A Study of Chaucer's Poetics*, Yale 1963.

reason, or *esprit*, H. is far away. Boileau's famous work is what many who misunderstood their H. thought the *Ars Poetica* was like. Voltaire confidently declared that '*l'Art poétique de Boileau est supérieur à celui d'Horace. La méthode est certainement une beauté dans un poème didactique; Horace n'en a point*'. And Boileau was admired not only by Voltaire but by his own friend Racine. The young Pope's *Essay on Criticism* is an astonishing Augustan performance; it has many other Horatian virtues besides—panache, wit, good sense, urbanity. But an occasional appearance of bluff heartiness marks a larger difference of tone[1] and, above all, the *Essay* lacks the complexity of the *Ars*, the mature Horatian interplay of inherited theory and individual practice.

With the coming of the German neo-classicists, and generally European romanticism, strains divided which H.'s poetry and criticism held firmly together. Schiller's *Naiv* and *Sentimentalisch*, Nietzsche's Apollonian and Dionysian, and the like, are not Horatian alternatives. *Sapientia* was mockingly turned against (romantic) poetry in Peacock's satire *The Four Ages of Poetry*, and evoked Shelley's Platonizing answer in the *Defence of Poetry*; both owe something to the *Ars*, but their aims are not Horatian.

It was not until the notions of imagination and organic form were established in the nineteenth century that a new framework for critical thought could be devised. That framework could coexist with the preconceptions of actual contemporary poetry. Ezra Pound's *Mauberley* is a poem in its own right though not proclaimed as an *ars poetica* of its time. Now the individual talent, *ingenium*, needs to devise its own *ars*, make its own nostalgic selection of widely divergent traditions, build its own shell of forms and styles—every poet his own Horace.

[1] Cf. R. A. Brower, *Alexander Pope: The Poetry of Allusion* (1959), ch. 9.

BIBLIOGRAPHY

Addenda to Bibliography in *Prolegomena*, containing writings since 1961 and a few older ones that had been overlooked. The principles of selection are the same as in the earlier volume. To save space, except in cases where larger topics have been involved, I have not repeated articles on specific passages of the *A.P.* to which reference has been made in my notes.

Anderson, W. S., *AJP*, LXXXVII (1966), 229–33, review of *Prolegomena*.
Becker, C., *Das Spätwerk des Horaz*, Göttingen, 1963, pp. 257.
Brink, C. O., 'Horace and Varro', in *Entretiens Fond. Hardt*, IX (1962), 173–205.
    'Horatian Notes: Despised Readings in the Manuscripts of the Odes', *Proc. Cam. Phil. Soc.*, n.s. XV (1969), 1–6.
    'Horace and Empedocles' temperature: a rejected fragment of Empedocles', *Phoenix*, XXIII (1969), 138–42.
Buehler, W., *Beiträge zur Erklärung der Schrift vom Erhabenen*, Göttingen 1964, pp. 159.
Clausen, W. V., 'Callimachus and Latin Poetry', *Greek, Roman and Byzantine Studies*, V (1964), 181–96.
Coulter, J. A., 'Περὶ Ὕψους and Aristotle's Theory of the Mean', *Greek, Roman and Byzantine Studies*, V (1964), 197–213.
Cupaiuolo, F., 'Studi d'estetica antica', *Paideia*, X (1955), 81–97.
    'Contributo allo studio dell'estetica antica', *Ann. Pontif. Ist. Sup. Sc. e Lett. 'S. Chiara'*, XIII (1963), 45–72.
    Tra Poesie e Poetica: Su alcuni aspetti culturali della poesia latina nell'età Augustea (Collana di Studi lat. XV, Napoli, 1966), pp. 280.
de Lacy, P., 'Stoic views on poetry', *AJP*, LXIX (1948), 241–71.
Dessen, Cynthia S., 'Iunctura callidus acri': *A study of Persius' Satires* (Illinois St. in Lang. and Lit. IX (1968)), pp. X, 117.
Eisenhut, W., 'Deducere carmen. Ein Beitrag zum Problem d. lit. Beziehungen zwischen Horaz und Properz', *Gedenkschrift für G. Rohde*, Tübingen, 1961, 91–104.
Ferrero, L., 'Tra poetica ed istorica: Duride di Samo', *Miscellanea ...Rostagni*, Torino, 1963, 68–100.
Fontaine, J., *REL*, XLI, 1963 (1964), 447–50, review of *Prolegomena*.
Fontán, A., 'Tenuis...Musa? La teoría de los χαρακτῆρες en la poesía augústea', *Emerita*, XXXII (1964), 193–208.

Bibliography

Gantar, K., 'Die Anfangsverse und die Komposition der horazischen Epistel über die Dichtkunst', *Symbolae Osloenses*, XXXIX (1964), 89–98.

Garaffoni, Cinzia, 'Riflessi della poetica filodemea', *Vichiana*, III (1966), 3–23.

Giardina, G. C., *Vichiana*, I (1964), 103–8, review of *Prolegomena*.

'Orazio e Properzio: a proposito di Hor. Ep. II 2, 91 sqq.', *RFIC*, XCIII (1965), 24–40.

Grimal, P., *Essai sur l'Art Poétique d'Horace* (Soc. d'éd. d'enseign. sup.), Paris, 1968, pp. 241.

Grube, G. M. A., *Phoenix*, XIX (1965), 77–82, review of *Prolegomena*. *The Greek and Roman Critics*, London, 1965, pp. xi, 372.

Händel, P., 'Zur Ars Poetica des Horaz', *RM*, CVI (1963), 164–86.

Harriot, Rosemary, *Poetry and Criticism before Plato*, London, 1967, pp. xiii, 168.

Heinimann, F., 'Eine vorplatonische Theorie der Techne', *MH*, XVIII (1961), 105–30.

Henss, D., 'Die Imitationstechnik des Persius', *P*, XCIX (1954–5), 277–94.

Herrmann, L., 'Les deux parties de l'Art Poétique d'Horace', *Latomus*, XXIII (1964), 506–10.

Kambylis, A., *Die Dichterweihe und ihre Symbolik: Untersuchungen zu Hesiodos, Kallimachos, Properz und Ennius* (Bibl. der kl. Altertumswissenschaften, N.F., 2. Reihe), Heidelberg, 1965, pp. 218.

Kennedy, G., *The Art of Persuasion in Greece*, London, 1963, pp. xi, 350.

Kenney, E. J., 'The First Satire of Juvenal', *Proc. Cam. Phil. Soc.*, n.s. VIII (1962), 29–40.

Koller, E., 'Muße und musische Paideia', *MH*, XIII (1956), 1–37, 94–124.

Lanata, Giuliana, *Poetica pre-Platonica: testimonianze e frammenti* (Bibl. di studi sup. XLIII), Florence, 1963, pp. xvi, 307.

La Penna, A., *Athenaeum*, XLI (1963), 449–53, review of *Prolegomena*.

Lucas, D. W. (ed. with Introduction, Commentary and Appendixes), Aristotle, *Poetics*, Oxford, 1968, pp. xxviii, 313.

Marouzeau, J., 'Quelques éléments de poétique: l'art horatien', in *Quelques aspects de la formation du latin littéraire*, Paris, 1949, 193–222.

Mette, H. J., 'Genus tenue und mensa tenuis bei Horaz', *MH*, XVIII (1961), 136–9.

Mühmelt, M., *Griech. Grammatik in der Vergilerklärung* (Zetemata, 37), München, 1965, pp. iv, 168.

Nasta, M., 'Quelques réflexions sur les termes de la poétique', *Studii Clasice* (Bucharest), III (1961), 317–36.

Newman, J. K., *Augustus and the New Poetry* (Coll. Latomus LXXXVIII), 1967, pp. 455.

The Concept of Vates in Augustan Poetry (Coll. Latomus LXXXIX), 1967, pp. 132, especially 'Dating by *Vates/Poeta* usage of H.'s *Ars Poetica*', pp. 75–81; 'The date of the *Ars Poetica*', pp. 127–30.

Otis, B., *Gnomon*, XXXVI (1964), 265–72, review of *Prolegomena*.

Paratore, E., *Biografia e poetica di Persio*, Firenze, 1968, pp. xi, 242.

Pasoli, E., 'Spunti di crit. lett. nella sat. oraziana', *Convivium* (Bologna), XXXII (1964), 449–78.

'Satura drammatica e sat. letteraria', *Vichiana*, I (1964), 3–41.

Le epistole letterarie di Orazio, Bologna, 1964, pp. xi, 235.

Reckford, K. J., 'Studies in Persius', *H*, XC (1962), 476–504.

Reiff, A., *Interpretatio, imitatio, aemulatio. Begriff und Vorstellung literarischer Abhängigkeit bei den Römern* [Thesis Köln], Bonn, 1959, pp. 125.

Ronconi, A., 'Aspetti di critica letteraria in Cicerone', *Maia*, X (1958), 83–100.

'Lucilio critico letterario', *ibid.* XV (1963), 515–25.

Ruch, M., 'Horace et les fondements de la *iunctura* dans l'ordre de la création poétique (A.P. 46–72)', *REL*, XLI, 1963 (1964), 246–69.

Rudd, N., 'Horace and the origins of Satura', *Phoenix*, XIV (1960), 36–44.

The Satires of Horace, Cambridge, 1966, pp. xi, 318.

Russell, D. A. (ed. with Introduction and Commentary), 'Longinus' *On the Sublime*, Oxford, 1964, pp. lviii, 208.

Saint Denis, E. de, 'La fantaisie et le coq-à-l'âne, *Latomus*, XXII (1963), 664–84.

Sbordone, F., 'Udito e intelletto in un nuovo testo filodemeo', *La Parola del Passato*, XLIV (1955), 390–403.

'Un nuovo libro della Poetica di Filodemo', *Atti dell'Accad. Pontaniana*, n.s. IX (1960), 231–58.

Contributo alla poetica degli antichi, L'arte tipografica, Napoli, 1961, pp. 142. [I have not seen a copy of this book.]

Solmsen, F., 'Leisure and play in Aristotle's Ideal State', *RM*, N.F. CVII (1964), 193–220.

Sörbom, Göran, *Mimesis and Art: Studies in the Origin and Early Development of an Aesthetic Vocabulary*, Uppsala, 1966, pp. 218.

Sperduti, A., 'The divine nature of poetry in antiquity', *TAPA*, LXXXI (1950), 209–40.

Bibliography

Terzaghi, N., 'Orazio e Properzio', *Rend. Acc. dei Lincei*, ser. VIII (1959), 179–201.

Vandvik, E., 'Simplex dumtaxat et unum', *Symbolae Osloenses* XIX (1939), 110–17.

Van Rooy, C. A., *Studies in classical satire and related literary theory*, Leiden, 1965, pp. xiii, 229.

'Arrangement and structure of Satires in Horace, *Sermones*, Book I, with more special reference to *Satires* 1–4', *Acta Classica*, XI (1968), 38–72.

Vicaire, P., *Platon: Critique littéraire* (Études et Commentaires, 34), Paris, 1960, pp. 448.

Recherches sur les mots désignant la poésie et le poète dans l'œuvre de Platon (Publ. de la Fac. des lettres etc., Montpellier, XXII), Paris, 1964, pp. 178.

Waszink, J. H., 'Bemerkungen zu den Literaturbriefen des Horaz', *Mnem*. Ser. IV, XXI (1968), 394–407.

Wehrli, F., 'Der erhabene und der schlichte Stil in der poetisch-rhetorischen Theorie der Antike', *Phyllobolia...P. von der Mühll*, Basel, 1945, 9–34.

Williams, G., *JRS*, LIV (1964), 186–96, review of *Prolegomena*.

Tradition and Originality in Roman Poetry, Oxford, 1968, pp. 329–57.

Wimmel, W., *Zur Form der hor. Diatribensatire*, Frankfurt a. M., 1962, pp. 77.

Witke, E. C., 'The function of Persius' Choliambics', *Mnem*. Ser. IV, XV (1962), 153–8.

CP, LXII (1967), 47–50, review of *Prolegomena*.

Index of passages cited

INDEX 2   MANUSCRIPTS AND TEXT

INDEX 3   LEXICAL, GRAMMATICAL, METRICAL

LEXICAL

Lexical, grammatical, and metrical index

conscriptus (unique usage), 341
consiliari, 257
conspirare, 397
corona, 294–5, 380
coturnus, see Index 2
crassus, 377
crepare, 293
(?) culillus, see Index 2
cupressus, 351 f.
cura peculi, 351
curae, 171
cursus, 397
custos, 235

dare (with inf.), 348
— iura, 389
debemus–debemur, see Index 2, -mur
deberi (usage), 150
decessere, 378
deciens, 323, 372
declinare, 144
deduco (with abl.), 291
defendere, 255
dehinc (spatial?), 219
delitigare (ἅπαξ λεγ., probably Horatian coinage), 178
demittere, 245
denatare (probably Horatian coinage), 178
denique, 103
deproeliari (probably Horatian coinage), 178
derisor, 410
desaeuire, 178
descendere in aures, 383
descriptas...uices, 172–3
desperare (rare in poetry), 222–3
detorqueo, 144
deus immortalis, 427
dicax, 280–1
dictum, 309
dies (fem.), 322
differre (with dat.), 286
difficilis, 240
dignus, 252, 316
dilator (ἅπαξ λεγ., probably Horatian coinage), 239
dinoscere, 405
diota, 143
discere (absolute), 399

discrepare, construction of, 224
ditare (archaic), 145
diui puerique deorum, 170
diuinus, 391
diurnus, 268
— (with gen.), 273
doceri (with acc. poetic and Silver usage), 155
dominantia (nomina) (not again recorded before Late Latin, probably Horatian coinage), 140, 285–6
dormitabo, 187
duces, 164
dumtaxat (prosaic), 104

effutire, 283
egere 'wish for', 230
elleborosus 'mad', 332
eloquium (poetic and Silver), 272
emungere (colloquial), 287
enim (elliptic), 331
eniti (with inf. archaic), 286
eo quod (prosaic), 279
equites, 357
eripere, 404
error, 422
et 'and indeed', 141; ? displaced, 232–3; explanatory, 303, 305, 351, 374, 393, 422
et fortasse (colloquial), 100
etiam (in first place of clause), 408
eu (colloquial), 350
ex animo, 410
exacuere, 392
exemplar, 306
exemplaria Graeca, 305–6
exigui elegi, 167
exire (meaning), 103
exlex, 280
exodia, 275–6
exprimere, 119
exsors, 335
extendere (poetic), 267
extimesco, 399
extrahere (with abl.), 356

ἦσθ' ἄρα, 99

facta, 164; (nuance of), 319; (poetic), 155–6

541

Lexical, grammatical, and metrical index

GRAMMATICAL

Lexical, grammatical, and metrical index

Prepositions, avoidance of, 255–6
Proper names, adjectival, 117

Rhyme, initial, 144
Rivers and mountains, names of, used
adjectivally, 97–8

Simple verb: and compound combined,
120, 251; for compound, 124, 319, 331,
352, 357, 384, 403, 429; preceded by
compound of same derivation, 120
Subjunctive, 426; prevalent in rhet. *an*
cl., 351

Tenses: future gnomic, 156, 416; future
in injunctions, 281; future of precept,
353; future part. in poetry and
Silver prose, 231; future prospective,
404; 'imperf. of neglected duty', 350;
perf. 'empirical', 92, 376; perf. inf.
aoristic in Latin verse, 181, 238, 361,
399, 411, 423; primary and secondary
combined, 207; *tempus (locus) erat*,
99
Tenses and Moods, Imperf. subjun. in
si cl., imp. ind. in apodosis, 413,
414

Verse ending, two main verbs, 424

Word-order, 86; interwoven, 138,
380

Zeugma, double, 292; variation of,
179–80

METRICAL

alterĭus always in Horace, 396
Aphaeresis at end of line in Horace's
hexameters, 400

Caesura, clearly marked middle, absent, 181, 302–3, 378
Change of stress in repeated words,
426

Dactylic lines, 97

Elisions: rare types of, 153; sequence of,
in Horace's hexameters, 415

Fourth-foot break after weak middle
caesura omitted, 200

Monosyllabic endings in Greek and
Latin hexameters, 215–16

neniae in troch. sept., 400
nequeo ignoroque, 173
nullius, prosody of, 345, 349

Prosody of final syllable in *cedro (et)*,
352

Spondees: in Horace, 319, 402; sequence of four, 301–2; spondaic
rhythm, 181; *uersus spondiacus*, 428

Tmesis, 321; between two lines,
404–5

547

INDEX 4 LITERARY THEORY

GREEK TERMS

ἀγρυπνίη, 307
ἀδρόν, 111
αἰσχρολογία, 317
αἴσθησις (in Aristotle's moral theory),
  116
ἀλληλουχία, 396–7
ἀμφίβολον, 419
ἀπλοῦς, 104
ἀρετή, 337–8, 359–61
ἁρμόττον, 143

βάρος, 346

δέσις, 252
διαλύειν, 208
διδάσκειν, 320–1

εἰκός, 355
ἔλεγος (derivation of), 165
ἐμφερόμενα, 89
ἐνάργεια, 246
ἐνδιάθετος λόγος, 188–9
ἔργον, 336
εὐπάρυφος (of style), 96
εὐφαντασίωτος, 189
εὐφυής (in Aristotle), 185, 189

ἡδύ, 355
ἠθοποιΐα, 232
ἡρωικὸν μέτρον, 163–4

ἴδια, 205–7, 209–10, 441–2
ἱστορία, 197–8, 354
ἰσχνόν, 111

καιρός, 99
κεφαλαιωδῶς, 221
κοινά, 205–7, 209–10, 441–2
κόσμος, 285
κυκλικός, κύκλιος, 213–14
κυκλικῶς, 210
κύριον, 285
—εἰωθός, 139

λεῖος, 109–10
λήκυθοι, 180
λῆμμα, 89
λόγος ἐνδιάθετος, προφορικός, 188–9

μανικός, 185, 189
μετέωρα, 283
μέτρα, 160
μέτριον, 142–3
μιμητής, 343
μῦθος, 197–8, 354

ὅλον, 117
ὄμματα: πρὸ ὀμμάτων τιθέναι, 246
ὀνόματα, 203

παιδομαθία, 398
πεποιημένα, 143
πλάσμα, 197–8, 354
ποικιλία, 95, 104
πρέπον, 233, 337–8
προνοούμενα, 340
προφορικὸς λόγος, 188–9

σαφήνεια, 418–19
σημεῖα, 141
σιωπώμενον, 221
σύμβολα, 141
συμπέρασμα, 221
συνήθεια, 159
συνομοπαθεῖν, 182

τάξις (ordo), a rhetorical concept,
  128
τέλος, 359–61

ὑποτύπωσις, 246
ὕστερον πρότερον Ὁμηρικῶς, 222

φιλάνθρωπον, 186
φύσις and τέχνη, 394–5

χαρακτηρισμός, 232
χρεία, 141
χρησιμολογεῖν, 353

548

VARIA

Advice offered to the novice a literary convention, 383
Aeschylus' grandeur of style and décor, according to literary theory, 315
Agrippa on Virgil's *cacozelia*, 288–9
Alexandrian: *ars critica* applied to the poet's work, 412–21; research on εἴδη, 'genres', 161–2, 163–74; theories on Satyric drama, 274; theories on Homeric narrative, 221; theories on origins and history of Greek drama, 310; views on Homeric *oeconomia*, 128
Allegory of myths, 387–8
Amateurism rejected in athletics but commonly condoned in poetry, 379–81
Amphion, myth of, allegorized, 388
Antonius, M., on difference between *disertus* and *eloquens*, 375
Apollonius, ὁ εἰδογράφος, 161
Appropriateness, *see* Horace, (vii)
Approval, aesthetic, vocabulary of, 406–7
Archaisms, verbal, in literary theory and Horace, 133–4, 157
Aristarchus, 419
Aristotle: analyses the 'arts', 373; analyses types of wit, 308–9; on appropriate style, 174–94; on characteristics of iambics, 169; compares poetry and the fine arts, 369; on consistency in plot-construction, 198; on Euripides, 288–9; on

Index of literary theory

Aristotle (*cont.*)

    Homer, 217; on Homeric *oeconomia*, 128; lacks metaphor of brilliance in *Poetics*, 223; on new subjects in poetry, 198; on οἶα ἂν γένοιτο and τὰ γενόμενα, 197–8; perhaps drawn on in Horace's account of appropriate characterization (*A.P.* 316), 342; Peripatetic theories on diction, 132–3; on τὸ σατυρικόν as origin of tragedy, 273; on style and ethos, 190–2; on theatrical audiences, 269, 270; his theory of Unity, 78–85; his typology of the young: Horace adds hunting and athletics, 235

Aristotle and Alexandrians on 'invention' of hexameter, 165

Aristotelian–Alexandrian principles applied in the Horatian Scholia, 130–1

ars and *natura*: in debates of the Schools, 394–400, 511–13; in prefaces to *Artes*, 76

Artes: introductory portions of, 75–6; *partitio*, 76

Arts, fine: examples of, in Aristotle, Cicero, Horace, 377; related to increase in wealth, 267

Arts, liberal and useful distinguished, 372–8

Athletics as a 'useless' art, 379

Bodily movement: and musical ethos, 270; and poetic ethos, 408

'Brevity', in literary theory, 108–9; precepts, 103, 353

Callimachean and neoteric aesthetics neglected, 346

Catullus probably referred to in Horace's advice to Piso's elder son, 383

Censoriousness absent from Aristotle's and Theophrastus' descriptions of moral character, 232

Characters of style, 109

Choerilus in Hellenistic and later literary criticism, 365–6

Chorus in drama, 254–60

Cicero: compares painting and poetry, 369; (*Am.* 88 ff.) concerned with the moral aspects of flattery in friendship, 412; and Horace on feigned emotion, 186; on *perfectus orator*, 372–3; on privilege of new coinages, 144, 146; as source for Horace, 79–80; his analysis of types of wit compared with Aristotle's and Horace's, 308–9; his use of *lex* metaphorical, 212; his view of jurisprudence and rhetoric differs from Horace's, 375

Cinna's *Zmyrna* model of neoteric elaboration, 383

Comedy, old, legal provisions against its free speech, 316–17

Consistency of character, 203

Criticism, literary and textual merged, 419

Democritus on inspiration in poetry, 329

'Dénouement', derivation of, 253

'Deviation' or 'neighbouring fault' in literary theory, 106–7

Didymus, similarity to Horace in account of elegy, 165–6

Diomedes criticizes Horace for use of terms *praetexta* and *togata*, 320

Dionysius of Hal., rhythm and composition in *De Compositione*, 161

Drama, discussion of, occupies a whole section of Horace's *Ars*, 224–7

Elaboration, ideal of, 321

Euripides: his pointed use of ordinary words, 289; his prologues, criticism of, 219

553

Horace (*cont.*)

384–94, 510–11; allegorizes myths in his account of primitive poetry, 387–8; contrasts Greeks and Romans, 296, 497–8, 502, 518

(xiii) style: joins *res* and *uerba*, 132–6, 339–40, 475; and Aristotle on style and dramatic circumstance, 174–5; and Aristotle on style and ethos, 190–4; and Aristotle on style and emotion, 182–90; and Cicero on feigned emotion, 186; his psychology of style, 188–90; on *pulchrum* and *dulce*, 183–4; on *psychagogia*, 183; on 'virtues of style', 105–113, 472–3; unlike Pseudo-Longinus, regards *grandia* (the Sublime) as a kind of style, 111; on how to use words in poetry, 133–4; ties together 'composition' and 'choice of words', 137; his *callida iunctura*, 139–40; does not discuss metaphors, 133, 139; on archaisms in language, 157; polemic in discussion of neologisms, 478; new coinages, when permitted?, 140–1; Greek precedence for new coinages in Roman poetry?, 140–1; applies simile of leaves to life of words, 146–50; common stock of changing language and poetry, 480

(xiv) *ordo*: in *A.P.*, 126, 128–31, 476–7; rhetorical theories on *ordo*, 127–9; his precepts on *ordo* exemplified from Virgil in the Scholia, 130–1

See also Index 5, Horace

Imagery, archaic for instruction, 353
Impossibilities, 93, 114
Incongruity in poetry, 88–90
Inspection, repeated, in poetry and painting, 368–72
Inspiration, in literary theory, 329
Isagogic writings, 75 n. 2
Isocrates on *uirtutes narrationis*, 216

Jurisprudence and rhetoric, Horace's anti-Ciceronian view of, 375

Language, its mutability, in grammatical theory, 147
Lightning and thunder in literary theory, 113
Literary criticism, doctrine of Unity in the tradition of, 77–85
Lucretius on new Latin words, 141, 145

Mediocrity and excellence in the arts, 372–8
Melancholia, 333–4
Metaphor, of 'coinage' for neologisms, 146; of untrodden path, 319
Metre, discussions of, by metrists and literary critics to be distinguished, 295
Midnight oil, 307
Music in drama, 260–73

Narrative: poetry and descriptive writing, 95, 96–7; swiftness of Homer's, 221–3
Neologisms, Latin: Horace, Quintilian, and Apuleius on Roman borrowings from Greek, 143
Neoptolemic hypothesis: how can it be proved?, xi–xiii; rebuttals of, xiii–xvii
Neoptolemus of Parium, 75, 77, 95; in what sense Horace's 'source'?, xviii–xx; on ψυχαγωγία and ὠφελεῖν, 352; his teachings in last part of Horace's *A.P.*, 325; was Horace's account of Society and Poetry derived from ?, 385

Index of literary theory

Theophrastus on σικελίζειν, 270; (?) Theophrastus on tragedy, 176
Three Actors, rule of, 253–4
Tragedy, happy endings in, 260
'Truth' and 'fiction' in literary theory, 197–8, 218, 223–4, 355
Tyrtaeus and Homer as poets of war, 392

'Unity' in literary theory, 77–85
usus presides over the change of words, 146; often animate in literary theory, 158

Varro, on *uates*, 391; on vocabulary, 133; his and Cicero's nomenclature concerning *togata*, 320; (?) his use of term *iunctura*, 139; the archaism of his poetic theory, xix
Virgil: ancient critics note his Homeric economy of narrative, 221
'Virtues of style' and 'Types of style', 105–16

'Weight' not a recommended quality in Callimachean and neoteric poetics, 345–6
Wit, theories of, 280–1
Words, impermanence of, 146–60; ordinary, in pointed context, 289–90

INDEX 5   GENERAL

General index

description, a poetic device, 85
Diana and Luna, 422–3
Diomede's Return, 220

Empedocles' leap into Aetna, 426–8
Engineering enterprises: Agrippa, 152, 155; Augustus, 151–2, 155; Caesar, 151
Ennius and Cato as creators of language, 145
Epic cycle, 210
ethologia, style of, 200
exodium, 494

Fable, 411
Fairy tales, 356
Fantastic subjects, Hellenistic and Roman interest in, 218–19
Faunus and Pan, 291
Fractions, computation of, 349
Friendship, 237, 400–1, 513–15

Goethe, 468 (Epigraph); and Schubert, 493
Graves, violation of, 429
Greek names, Latin verses consisting of, 219
Grotesques in decorative painting of the Italian Renaissance, 469
Groves in descriptions, 97

ἅμαξα (τὰ ἐκ τῶν ἁμαξῶν), 312
Harbours, construction of, 152–3
Helicon, 330
Hellebore, medicinal use of, 331–2
Homer not identified by name, 217; *Od.* I. 1–3, paraphrased by Horace, 217–18
Honey, Sardinian, 377
Horace
(i) *His persona*: Persius' paradox concerning him, 449; R. A. Brower's paradox concerning his seriousness, 449; seriousness and humour in his poetry, 448–9; fantasies at beginning and end of *A.P.*, importance attached to, 469, 516–17; sincerity in poetry demanded in *A.P.*, 482; use of first person and references to himself in *A.P.*, 107, 187, 308, *et al.*; use of first person plural, 92, 106, 107, 308, 351, 361; varying poetic *personae*, 518; his integrity, 449; personal involvement in sketch of mad poet, 516; self-criticism, 334; self-belittling, 145; critic, part of the poet's *ego* (Ep. II. 2. 110), or his friend, 400–1; personal emphasis, 144–5; addresses in *A.P.*, 90, 138, 227–8, 286, 374, 381, 393, 406; H.'s personality and personal motifs in *A.P.*, 107, 466–7, 477–8; private and public motifs in two Horatian lyrics, *C.* III. 4 and IV. 5, 460–1
(ii) *Poetic practice and literary theory*: *A.P.* as poem and theory, vii–viii, xx–xxi; overlays conventional pattern of an *ars poetica* with less conventional patterns, xii, xviii–xix, 484, 517–18; *A.P.*, does it succeed as literary theory and as a poem?, 518–22; *A.P.*, its symbolic nature, viii, 517; tradition and personal *ingenium* in *A.P.*, 521–2; position of *A.P.* in poetry and criticism of the West, 522–3; Aristotelian ideal of πρέπον in *A.P.* turned into a technical problem, 481; in what respects in agreement and disagreement with Aristotelianism, 520–1; use of Callimachean language, 208–9; and Cicero, 132; latinizes an unknown cyclic proem,

559

General index

Horace (*cont.*)

214; does he refer to the *Cypria*?, 220–1; and Homeric technique, 490; and Juvenal on old age, 229; echoes archaic verse (?), 181; Lucilius: influence of, in *A.P.* (419 ff.), 401–2, 405–6, 408–10; recast in *A.P.* (431–2), 408–10; and Cicero, debt to, in the sections on criticism and friendship, 513–14; Lucretian vein, 141–2; Simonidean reminiscence marks climax of passage of *A.P.*, 479; and Peripatetic typology, 229; *C.* I. 12 and its Pindaric model, 327; own poetic procedure discussed or hinted at, 476, 477, 488, 500, 517–18, 521

(iii) *Poetry and philosophy*: philosophical argument and truism in his poetry, 448–9; as a 'thinker' in his poetry, 448–9; oblique manner in argument, 365; his world not simple and static, 475; dialectical manner, 83–5, 393–4, 448–50, 468, 473, 474–5, 475–6, 477, 485–6, 500; abstract and concrete in the *A.P.*, 486; procedure of capping concrete detail by abstract term at end, 98; solves poetic puzzles at end of a section, 113–14; abstractions and doctrines, how related to whole Horatian poems, 448 with n. 1; rigid abstractions avoided in *A.P.*, 485–6; avoids prosaic ordering of topics, 327–8; conceptual structure of *A.P.* not rigid, 452–3; logical coherence, lack of, in *A.P.*, 521; avoids technicalities, 108–9; avoids spelling out tedious logical detail, 115–16; vagueness, alleged, of his terminology, 132; unequivocal critical notions absent from *A.P.*, 463; poetic coherence of *A.P.*, 521; 'tables of contents' in *A.P.*, 123–4, 459–60; imaginative ordering of topics concerning drama in *A.P.*, 226–7; unity and variety of subjects in his poems, 461; unity and variability in *A.P.*, 519

(iv) *Poetic procedure and modes of reading*: apt readers of his poetry, 449–50, 467; two interdependent modes of reading proposed, 105, 296, 468, 473, 483–6, 501–4; unity of his poems, how to apprehend, 467; progression of thought in his poems, 450 ff.; complexity of his poems, 460 ff., 485, 490–1, 517–19; *Odes* and hexameter poems compared, 450–67; varies own assessment of hexameter poems from 'poetic' to 'unpoetic', 445–6; structural characteristics of hexameter poems in the small compass of the lyrics, 450–67; structure of *C.* I. 1, 450–1; unilinear progression rare in his poems, 450–1, 484; 'ring composition': in his poems, 453–5, in *A.P.*, 453, in *C.* II. 10, 453–4, in his love poems, 454, in *C.* III. 26, 454, 456; 'open-ended' poems, 453; tripartition of *C.* I. 12 only apparently precise, 451–2; tripartite division and unity in *C.* I. 17, 461–2; *in medias res*: his own procedure, 80, 469, 490, 496, Homer's procedure according to *A.P.*, 490; *audi*, how used to introduce new topic, 227; combination of connectedness and abruptness in his poems, 460; disjointedness in first and last sections of *A.P.* only apparent, 456–9; simple juxtaposition, few, in *A.P.*, 457–8; paragraphing of hexameter poems, x–xi, 457; abruptness and transitions: in *Odes* and hexameter poems, 455–67, transitions in *A.P.*, 457, his abruptness, 81–5, 93–4, 105, 113–14, 117, 162–3, 174–5, 183, 195–7, 208–9, 225–7, 245, 262, 296, 311, 352, 359–61, 368, 379, 386, 394, 401, 421–2, 455, 456, 457–9, 470, 474, 480, 486, 490, 496, 498, 501–4, 504–5, 505–13, his 'gliding transitions', 124, 127–30, 131–2, 181, 190, 195–7, 209, 327–9, 450, 452, 455, 459, 461, 476–7, 480, 482, 486, 504, 505–6, apparent hiatus in his thought, 347–8, uses concealed *partitio* in last part of *A.P.*, 329, 335, combines abrupt and gliding transition, 195, transitions not superficial, 129–30; motifs and structure in the *A.P.*, 462–7; *ars* and *decorum* as motifs in the *A.P.*, 462–5, 475, 477, 481, 483–5, 487, 492, 497, 498, 518

(v) *Mores and other motifs: mores*: importance attached to by him, 226; character a major motif in *A.P.*, 192, 228, 465–6; characters as pen-portraits, 228–9,

560

General index

Horace (*cont.*)
230–44; on the four ages of man, 228–9; his perceptive eye for typical human features, 226; the national themes (Roman and Greek) as motifs in the *A.P.*, 466–7; death in the lyrics, *Satires* and *Epistles*, 479–80; friendship motif in hexameter poems, 400–1, 513–15

(vi) *Content, style and tone*: experience of the subjects discussed in the *A.P.*, how conveyed, 130, 145, 283, 285–6, 287, 292, 330, 361, 473, 476, 477, 480, 482, 485, 517, 521; variability and complexity of content, style and tone in *A.P.*, 446–9, 518; 'mixed' style of his hexameter poems, 446; levels of style in hexameter poems, 446; 'middle' style in hexameter poems, 446, 479–80; lyric note in *A.P.*, 478; sudden rise of poetic tone, 147; humorously employs style of lecture or treatise, 163, 296–7, 335, 496, 500; combines language of Roman law with literary theory, 209–10; his manner of dealing with remote past, 312; his compressed narrative, 356; comparison incomplete, 361; comparison irregular, 376

(vii) *Words and imagery*: on impermanence of human enterprises, 151–6; talks of words as if they were humans, 479; literal and metaphorical in his imagination, 448, 481–2; imagery: Horace's, 193, concreteness of, 155, of pruning, how applied, 416–19, of wax, 235, of years rising and falling, 241, mixture of, 430; unique character of simile of leaves, 147; and Virgil humanize nature, 154–5; animates words in *uerborum uetus...aetas*, etc., 150; colloquialisms, occasional, in hexameter poems, 445–6; vocabulary of hexameter poems largely drawn from the genres of Latin poetry, 445; sensitive to iteration, 230; polyptoton of verbs, 157; change of gender, 382; repeats last word of line at beginning of next, 129; his verbal imagination, 178; coinages, probable or possible, in *A.P.*, 139, 142 (50 n.), 145 (56 n.), 166, 178, 180, 214, 239, 255, 267, 292, 302, 319, 340; ἅπαξ λεγόμενα among Horatian verbs largely compounds, 178; rhymes in *A.P.*, 184, 187, 190, 241, 242–3, 289, 398; periodic structure, 151, 280, 423, *et al.*

See also Index 4, Horace
Horses celebrated in *epinicia*, 171
Humanistic theory of painting, 370–1

Iambus, personification of, 497
Ino, 201–2
Interest, monetary, computed in percentages, 349
Interlude, musical, as act-divisions, 255
Io, 202
io ciues, traditional cry for help, 425
Ixion, 202

Juvenal and Horace on old age, 229

Knights, Roman: ancestry of, 294; literary interests of, 293–4; status of, 293–4

Lamia, 356
Latium, 321
Lessing on *ut pictura poesis*, 371
liber legally defined, 380–1
'*Lucilius tragoediographus*', 287
Lucretius and Catullus contrasted with Horace, 449; Lucretius' type of phrase *terrai...abdita* in, 142

561

General index

Maecius Tarpa, Sp., 382–3
Masks, 313
Materialism, Roman, satirized, 347, 349–52
Medea's tears, 201
Meleager's Death, 220
Menander: Δὶς ἐξαπατῶν, 250; Χοροῦ in papyri of, 249
Messala Corvinus, M. Valerius, 375
Mourners, hired, 408–10
Mozart's *Magic Flute*, 494
Mytilene mosaics, 249

Naevius' *praetexta* and *togata*, 320
Nature as craftsman in Greek philosophy and Horace, 189
neniae used as illustrations by Horace, 400
Nero secures audience in theatre, 230

Orestes, 202
Ostia: is its harbour referred to in *A.P.?*, 152

Pan and Faunus, 291
Paragraphs in text of Horace, x–xi, xx–xxi
Peleus, 179–80
Persius' sensitive use of Horatian language, 186
Philemon: possible act-divisions in his comedies, 249
Piso's elder son an exemplary *persona* in the context of poetry and society, 374,
    381–4, 393–4, 509–10, 511
Pisones 88, 90, 286; fanciful genealogy of, 322
Pomptine Marshes, draining of, 153
Pope, Alexander, 521, 523
Poppy seeds, 377
Potters in ancient technology, 102
Pound, Ezra, *Mauberley*, 523
praeficae, 409
Pratinas, 277
Proverbs, 90–1, 99–100, 123, 201, 215, 218, 264, 278, 291, 323–5, 344, 364, 382,
    384, 400, 415, 431
Public as literary critics in Horace, 109, 356
pudor malus and ignorance, 174

Ramnes, 357
Rapael, 469
reditus Diomedis, 442
Romanticism, European, 523

quiritare, 425

Satyric drama at Athens, Alexandria, and (?) Rome, 273–7
Scanning with finger and foot, 309
Schubert, 493
Seating in theatre, 269–70

562